P9-CFS-428

# THE DAY
# WALL STREET
# EXPLODED

# THE DAY
# WALL STREET
# EXPLODED

....

A Story of America
in Its First Age
of Terror

BEVERLY GAGE

OXFORD
UNIVERSITY PRESS

# OXFORD

UNIVERSITY PRESS

Oxford University Press, Inc., publishes works that further
Oxford University's objective of excellence
in research, scholarship, and education.

Oxford    New York

Auckland    Cape Town    Dar es Salaam    Hong Kong    Karachi
Kuala Lumpur    Madrid    Melbourne    Mexico City    Nairobi
New Delhi    Shanghai    Taipei    Toronto

With offices in

Argentina    Austria    Brazil    Chile    Czech Republic    France    Greece
Guatemala    Hungary    Italy    Japan    Poland    Portugal    Singapore
South Korea    Switzerland    Thailand    Turkey    Ukraine    Vietnam

Copyright © 2009 by Beverly Gage

Published by Oxford University Press, Inc.
198 Madison Avenue, New York, NY 10016

www.oup.com

First issued as an Oxford University Press paperback, 2010

Oxford is a registered trademark of Oxford University Press

All rights reserved. No part of this publication may be reproduced,
stored in a retrieval system, or transmitted, in any form or by any means,
electronic, mechanical, photocopying, recording, or otherwise,
without the prior permission of Oxford University Press.

Library of Congress Cataloging-in-Publication Data
Gage, Beverly.
The day Wall Street exploded : a story of America
in its first age of terror / Beverly Gage.
      p.    cm.
Includes bibliographical references and index.
ISBN 978-0-19-975928-6 (pbk.)
1. Terrorism—New York (State)—New York—History.
2. Terrorism—United States—History.
3. Domestic terrorism—United States.    I. Title.
HV6432.44.N7G34 2009
974.7'1—dc22
2008022074

1  3  5  7  9  8  6  4  2

Printed in the United States of America
on acid-free paper

*To Dan and Nicholas, for their patience and love*

# CONTENTS

· · · ·

156–209
210–228
242–258
277–200
324–316

# CONTENTS

# THE DAY
# WALL STREET
# EXPLODED

# INTRODUCTION

AT THE CORNER OF WALL AND BROAD STREETS in lower Manhattan, there is a memorial to the victims of terrorism. It is easy to miss—just a dozen or so pockmarks along the north face of the old Morgan bank. The building has no plaque, no statue, no list of names. Only a tourist sign around the corner, set off from the bank's ornate front entrance, gives any mention of the terrorist attack that occurred here on a cloudy day almost nine decades ago. On September 16, 1920, as the bells of Trinity Church chimed the noon hour, a bomb planted on a horse-drawn wagon exploded into the lunchtime crowd at Wall and Broad, shattering windows throughout the financial district, killing thirty-eight people and wounding hundreds more. Until the Oklahoma City bombing in 1995, it was the worst act of terrorism in American history.

Erupting at the heart of financial capitalism, the Wall Street explosion inspired thousands of pages of anguished press coverage, much of it speculating about who had done what, and why. The official investigation emerged as a three-year global epic, involving no less than a dozen government agencies and extending into Russia, Italy, and Poland. The Wall Street case ultimately shaped some of the key political trials of the 1920s, including the prosecution of Italian anarchists Nicola Sacco and

Bartolomeo Vanzetti. It reached as well into the lives of some of the most controversial figures in American politics: the embattled attorney general, A. Mitchell Palmer, architect of the Palmer Raids; J. Edgar Hoover, the youthful head of the Justice Department's new Radical Division; the legendary bankers of J. P. Morgan and Company, the nation's most influential financial institution. Most of all, it cast a national spotlight on the hundreds of communists, anarchists, socialists, and militant unionists who had endured World War I and the postwar Red Scare only to find themselves accused once again of plotting violence and treason. "How many such persons this makes we are unable to say offhand," the *Evening Post* remarked as the investigation drew to a close at mid-decade, "but at the present rate they will be numerous enough to justify a special section of the census of 1930."[1]

The Wall Street explosion struck at a moment when millions of people around the globe believed that capitalism was on the verge of collapse, or at least of profound transformation. The immediate impetus for this belief was the Bolshevik Revolution, which had emerged from World War I as a shocking example of how easily the old order could be replaced by the new. Even within the United States, where, as Lenin himself admitted, revolution would "probably not come soon," the conditions spawned by industrial capitalism—and by Wall Street itself—had long been the subject of conflict and debate.[2]

The decades before the explosion witnessed the development of the great industrial corporation, the creation of vast new capital fortunes, the invention of the telephone and the electric light—and, not least, the rise of Wall Street as a financial and political power. They were nonetheless years of profound discontent, in which many Americans began to decry the economic system as a perversion of justice, run for the benefit of the few. Out of this clash came some of the great reform movements of American history, including the Populist insurgency of the 1890s and the Progressive drive of the 1900s and 1910s. These years saw the rise of smaller but far more militant groups as well: socialists, anarchists, and other revolutionaries dedicated not to the reform of capitalism but to its abolition. Finally, they yielded a series of violent conflicts between employers and a growing union movement— what many described as a "civil war" between capital and labor. It was in this context that Americans first came face-to-face with the specter of revolutionary terrorism.

Throughout the late nineteenth and early twentieth centuries, newspapers were filled with reports of violent attacks on the symbols of American government and business: bombs mailed to mayors and governors, assassination attempts on presidents and capitalists, dynamite found beneath railroad tracks or outside the factory door. In the years before the Wall Street explosion, such violence was a central preoccupation of American politics and culture, the stuff of blaring headlines and fierce editorials, of congressional debate and soapbox oratory. Then as now, the word *terrorism* conjured up images of clandestine plots, revolutionary zealots, and bombs planted to achieve the maximum psychological and political effect. Those images, in turn, helped to inspire a dizzying array of new laws aimed at containing radical and labor movements, from local ordinances against revolutionary speech to more sweeping federal restrictions on immigration and political dissent. This crackdown came to a peak in the Red Scare of 1919 and early 1920, when the federal government, led by Attorney General Palmer, deported hundreds of immigrant radicals on suspicion of advocating "force and violence" against the American government. Nine months after the final round of deportation raids, the Wall Street explosion erupted.

Americans recognized the explosion as a shocking event—"an act of diabolism unparalleled in the annals of terrorism," in the words of the *St. Louis Post-Dispatch*. At the same time, they saw the bombing as something predictable, even inevitable. "It is not surprising that the bomb massacre was accomplished in New York," noted the *Washington Post*. "Rather it would have been surprising if this festering sore had not come to its horrid head." To the *Post* and many others, the explosion seemed to be the culmination of a half century's worth of bitter political conflicts over the growing power of Wall Street, the rights of political radicals in the United States, the problems of political violence and terrorism, and the nature of industrial capitalism itself. In an instant, the explosion seemed to capture all of these disputes and send them hurling forth in a hail of metal and flesh and fire. It took the popular political metaphor of an "attack on capitalism" and made it real.[3]

I BEGAN RESEARCHING the Wall Street explosion in the late 1990s as a graduate student living in New York City. What attracted me to the subject then was the strangeness of the society it seemed to evoke. Nothing in my experience gave me an immediate understanding of why Americans would have been so accustomed to this sort of violence in 1920. It also seemed incredible that an event of such proportions—with dozens killed and hundreds injured at the hub of New York's financial district—had earned no more than a sentence, or occasionally a few pages, in the vast literature on American history. I set out to write a book that would describe a distant world in which terrorism could be considered "not surprising." Then came September 11.[4]

Even now, with the war on terror at the forefront of national politics, this remains a book about the past, not the present. And yet to dwell on the differences between the two is to avoid the obvious. What makes the Wall Street explosion such an intriguing event is at least in part the way in which it reflects our own experience. There are the coincidences of time and place: here is another attack in downtown New York in mid-September. And there are other resonances to be drawn out as well. Terrorism is not a form of violence restricted to one time or place. It has a history.

As an abstract concept, terrorism has never been easy to define. Its basic elements are clear: terrorism is a form of political violence designed to induce fear and thus destabilize the social order. But the task of coming up with more specific boundaries and limits has befuddled social scientists for decades. Historians have had little better luck in reaching a consensus about when terrorism first entered the world stage. Walter Laqueur has traced the idea as far back as the Zealots of the ancient world, who hid swords beneath their cloaks in order to commit clandestine political attacks. The word itself seems to date from the reaction against the French Revolution, when Edmund Burke, among others, denounced the Jacobins as "hell hounds called terrorists." In the United States, *terrorism* appears to enter common usage as a political epithet sometime in the first half of the nineteenth century, applied variously to the actions of slaveholders, abolitionists, labor unions, employers, and all stripes of politician.[5]

Arriving at a definitive conclusion about either the origins or definition of terrorism is beyond the scope of this book. What does seem clear is that terrorism as both a theory and a practice underwent a profound change beginning in the late nineteenth century. The invention of dynamite in 1866 transformed an individual's ability to create mass destruction and wreak havoc from afar. In tandem with this breakthrough came the spread of new ideologies calling for the overthrow of industrial capitalism and its replacement by a more egalitarian utopian order. As the two came together in theories of clandestine political violence, *terrorism* began to lose some of its more general connotations, emerging by the early twentieth century as a tactic associated primarily, though not exclusively, with the revolutionary left.

The European anarchist movement issued some of the first explicit calls for theatrical acts of violence to combat the power of capital. In the United States, trade unions and revolutionary groups debated the merits of such tactics in newspapers and open-air rallies as well as during strikes and sensational public trials. Throughout the late nineteenth and early twentieth centuries, the iconic figures of the American left—anarchists Emma Goldman and Alexander Berkman, labor leader "Big Bill" Haywood and Socialist champion Eugene Debs—argued frankly over the usefulness of violence and terrorism. They rarely came to a consensus on the matter. Nonetheless, they agreed, in ways shocking to twenty-first-century ears, that its merits were well worth discussing. In an age when some thirty-five thousand American workers died each year in industrial accidents, in which policemen and soldiers routinely fired on strikers and picketers, it was not unusual to hear the use of dynamite praised as a justifiable reaction to capitalist tyranny and a weapon of working-class self-defense.

And that talk did, at least on occasion, translate into action. By 1920, most Americans hearing of the Wall Street explosion could recall a long list of bloody incidents, from the Haymarket Affair of 1886 to the nationwide dynamite attacks of June 2, 1919, in which opponents of capitalism, or at least of the Wall Street "Money Trust," stood accused of employing bombing and assassination to achieve their ends. Some of the most dramatic incidents were targeted attacks on "plutocrats" or political leaders, rather than acts of mass-casualty terror. Often, the details of who had done what remained murky. All, however, contributed to the widespread impression that dynamite and assassination were a vital part of American class relations, as much a part of the new industrial age as electricity, financial trusts, and skyscrapers of steel.

This is not to suggest that the American left or the labor movement as a whole supported terrorism—or, for that matter, violence of any sort—during these years. If anything, talk became deed with remarkable infrequency, and even the talk itself was rarely as bloodthirsty or vitriolic as critics liked to suggest. One of the tricky aspects of writing about bombings and assassination is that they tend to reinforce stereotypes— of wild-eyed anarchist bomb throwers, of brutal labor thugs—that were themselves the products of controversy and manipulation in their day. Accusations about terrorism and bomb throwing served a variety of political agendas. Employers hoping to win public sympathy accused striking workers of fomenting violence and terror. Politicians used the specter of mass terrorism to whip up support for causes ranging from immigration restriction to their own political careers.

The absurdity of some of these accusations in turn led to a culture of conspiracy on the left, in which the first response of those sympathetic to labor and radical movements was to deny any possibility of individual guilt. The truth, however, is more nuanced than that. There were bombs and those who believed in bombs, and there were also scapegoating, stereotyping, and false accusation. The question, in 1920 as today, is how to distinguish between the two.

AS THE HISTORIAN RICHARD HOFSTADTER noted in 1970, Americans have a "remarkable lack of memory" when it comes to violence. When he wrote those words, Hofstadter was responding to a generation of American historians for whom the notion of "consensus," of a bounded and inescapable liberalism, seemed to be the defining feature of American politics. In the years since, historians have by and large rejected this romantic view, emphasizing the depth of conflict and real ideological dispute that went into crafting the American political tradition. But there remains a tendency to think of violence as an anomaly, something outside the American experience, rather than as one of the many ways that Americans have long carried out their political disputes. Few things testify to this phenomenon more eloquently than the declarations since 2001 that terrorism is something utterly new in the American experience, a horror without a past.[6]

There are many reasons for this kind of historical forgetting. As Hofstadter pointed out, there is something inherently difficult about assessing the role of violence in history. "It is committed by isolated individuals, by small groups, and by large mobs; it is directed against individuals and crowds alike; it is undertaken for a variety of purposes...and in a variety of ways." Certainly this is true of the labor and radical violence that is the subject of this book. In its range of forms and motives, its parades of charge and countercharge, it seems almost to resist analysis, to be a string of individual acts with little in common other than the possibility of bloodshed and death. And yet our comforting amnesia on this subject is also relatively recent. As late as the early 1930s, the significance of "class violence" in shaping the nation's economic and political development seemed self-evident to many observers. "To me," the social critic Louis Adamic wrote in his 1931 book, *Dynamite*, "it appears to be an inevitable result of the chaotic, brutalizing conditions in American industry, a phase of the dynamic drive of economic evolution in the United States."[7]

Adamic's book was the first major work to survey the use of violence, and especially terrorism, by the "have-nots against the haves." It was also the last. Within a few years, as federal legislation reduced the level of violence in labor conflicts, the issue of bombings and assassinations began to lose some of its currency. By the 1950s, it had become politically dangerous, a brush with which to tar an increasingly beleaguered American left. Horrified at the excesses of McCarthyism, many liberal historians—Hofstadter included—went out of their way during the postwar years to minimize past controversies over violence, terrorism, and class conflict. They tended to depict the first Red Scare as an anomalous episode, the result of paranoid delusions, not genuine social conflict. In this context, the great bomb cases of earlier decades began to be understood as cautionary tales about McCarthyism, more important for the "hysteria" and repression they produced than for the tensions they revealed.[8]

In the late 1960s, historians of anarchism began to rediscover the world of militant, revolutionary violence. For the most part, however, the issue has remained marginal, a matter of concern primarily for those interested in the factional disputes of the American left. While recent years have seen a handful of histories exploring some of the era's great bombing and assassination trials, broader questions about the impact of such violence on American society have received little attention. Many of the social historians who transformed the study of American radicalism and labor in the 1960s understood their task as a redemptive one, an effort to move beyond tired images of bomb throwers and dangerous subversives. They emphasized the unequal nature of class violence, in which strikers and protesters were often no match for policemen, soldiers, and guards. And they were admirably sensitive to the ability of those in power to channel public fear into campaigns of repression. In the process, however, they robbed at least a few revolutionaries of their militancy—of the idea that when they spoke of dynamite and armed resistance, they sometimes meant what they said.[9]

One goal of this book is to rediscover the genuine drama of class conflict in the United States—a story in which violence ran in at least two directions. From our current vantage point, it can be tempting to view the early years of the twentieth century as a time of gradual progress, in which Americans, shocked by the inequities and indignities of their new industrial society, set out to find better ways to ensure basic democratic and economic rights, History is less kind than that. Far from being an era of placid reform, the turn of the century was a moment in which the entire structure of American institutions—from the government to the economy—seemed to be up for grabs, poised to be reshaped by new movements and ideas.

To the degree that terrorism stoked this sense of disorder, providing a dramatic example of destruction and class vengeance, it was a remarkably effective political tool. Indeed, for the handful of men and women who undertook the task of setting bombs and planning attacks, this was precisely the goal: to illustrate the depravity of American industrial conditions and to put the society's leaders on notice that they, too, would suffer. Whatever the judgments of history, there can be no question that many Americans at the time took this threat seriously, believing that the nation was poised on the brink of chaos and revolution.

This sense of crisis may help to explain why the history of revolutionary and labor terrorism has so effectively disappeared from national memory. Despite our recent financial turmoil, the institutions that were so bitterly contested in the Gilded Age and Progressive Era—banks, corporations, factories, trusts—remain such an accepted part of the American landscape that it can be hard to imagine a time in which they were subject to revolutionary denunciation and to frequent, violent attack. This is particularly true of the post–Cold War world, when those who fought the tide of capitalism, who threw bombs and organized strikes, can sometimes seem like hopeless offshoots, deluded in their dreams of reversing the course of history.

Americans in 1920 did not have this benefit of hindsight. On September 16, as they gazed into the rubble on Wall Street, as they read in the papers of an enormous and mysterious explosion at the hub of American capitalism, they did not yet know what lay ahead.

# PART I

....

## SEPTEMBER 16, 1920

# 1

$\cdots$

# THE MIDDLE
# OF THINGS

JUNIUS SPENCER MORGAN never seemed quite at home on Wall Street. He wanted to be a marine architect; he was happiest on the water, racing yachts. But he was the eldest son of J. P. Morgan, grandson of the legendary J. Pierpont Morgan, namesake to Pierpont's father, the great gentleman banker Junius Spencer Morgan. So each day he went to work at the family bank. Thursday, September 16, 1920, was no exception. The morning dawned cool and damp. New York papers were predicting rain.[1]

Junius' destination, on that morning as on so many others, was an elegant little building on the southeast corner of Wall and Broad streets. There was no sign at the building's entrance; everyone who conducted business in the financial district knew about 23 Wall. It was the headquarters of J. P. Morgan and Company, the nation's most powerful bank and, to Junius, the family business. From an early age, Junius had been schooled in the commercial and personal values appropriate to a Morgan banking heir. He had learned that business was best conducted among a small and trustworthy elite, that a letter of credit from the proper source was worth more than cash. A banker was expected to be a man of great respectability: well bred, well spoken, decidedly Protestant. Earnings were not to be flaunted and spent; rather, they were to be harvested and tended, like saplings destined to become great trees. The bank's headquarters reflected this Morgan blend of understatement and confidence. In contrast to the showy skyscrapers that had sprung up around the neighborhood in recent years, the bank stood just four stories tall. Those four stories were made from the finest materials, however, including marble from a Tennessee quarry purchased in its entirety.[2]

Within the cloistered world of New York banking, Junius was known as a likable fellow. He was shy, handsome, even something of a "democrat." Mostly, he had done the expected thing: private school at Groton, then Harvard, then marriage to a suitable girl and a post with the bank. Along the way, in keeping with his family's philanthropic tradition, he offered symbolic gestures of humility. At Harvard, he avoided the hangouts of the rich boys, choosing to live among the working students on a modest budget. After graduating in 1914, he volunteered at a French military hospital; when he left, he donated two motorcars and artificial limbs. Now a newly minted partner in the world's most prominent bank, he was noted for his unassuming ways. Traveling to Wall Street from Long Island, he sometimes took one of the Morgan yachts. At other times, though, he rode the train, and to the delight of the society reporters, he often sat in the day coach.[3]

No matter how Junius arrived on Wall Street, once there he found it impossible to avoid at least a moment's contact with the city's workaday elements. The streets of the financial district swarmed with messenger boys, curb brokers, pushcart vendors—men for whom finance capitalism was a physical ordeal. Their running and shouting and aggressive elbowing had no place inside the House of Morgan, where business was conducted in hushed tones amidst brass and warm, dark wood. But given the bank's location in the geographic heart of American capitalism, given its awesome financial reputation, there was no way for a Morgan partner to entirely escape from the outside world. As Junius' father had recently boasted to a French colleague, the Morgan bank "stands, as it always has stood, in the middle of things."[4]

When he wrote those words, J. P. (or "Jack") Morgan was celebrating the bank's success in the Great War, a cataclysm that at first had looked as if it might bring the financial world to ruin. From its founding in the 1870s, J. P. Morgan and Company—or, as it was more imperiously known, the House of Morgan—was a matchless force in American economic life, a leading symbol, in the admiring words of the *New York Sun*, of "the heroic age in American industrial history." By the turn of the century, it had moved from engineering loose financial trusts to creating corporate behemoths—International Harvester, U.S. Steel—whose size and heft reshaped the industrial world. Along the way, the Morgan bank found itself on the winning side of countless national and international dramas: the railroad wars of the Gilded Age; William McKinley's campaign to defeat William Jennings Bryan and preserve the gold standard; the Panic of 1907, when the bank rallied Wall Street financiers to save the country from financial disaster. The Great War was only the latest crisis to be weathered and exploited, and there, too, the firm triumphed. The House of Morgan entered the war a mere cousin to the great London banks. It left as the undisputed leader of global finance. On September 16, Junius was walking into the most significant institution of its kind in the world.[5]

This story—of inexorable upward ascendancy, of vast power handled in gentlemanly fashion—was only part of the legacy that had been bequeathed to him, however. The rise of industrial capitalism and of banks such as Morgan, National City, and Kuhn, Loeb was not a seamless democratic process, inspired by the precepts of John Locke and Adam Smith. It had been a bitter contest, sometimes literally a war, fought with bombs, guns, and blockades. Beyond Wall Street's confines, the bank evoked ferocious criticism: from populists and progressives; from union men and small entrepreneurs; from anarchists, socialists, and communists; from isolationists, pacifists, and farmers. Some of it came in the form of threats and, on occasion, violence.

The Morgan men bore these challenges without panic, seeking interest and profit in an elite world where opposition was taken for granted. But the bank's great achievements, its many enemies, and even the possibility that capitalism might be a transient affair shaped what it meant to be a Morgan on September 16—what it meant to live "in the middle of things."

THE BANK THAT JUNIUS ENTERED that morning was dominated by a single man: not his father Jack but his grandfather Pierpont, the original J. P. Morgan. Pierpont had died in 1913, yet his influence endured at Wall and Broad, tangible in the bank's Italian design (he had been a great aficionado of all things Roman), its all-male social order (he had disliked female secretaries), even in the walls themselves (the bank's cornerstone held, among other items, a copy of his last will and testament). It was there, especially, in the memory of those who recalled what it had been like to work with the "financial Moses of the New World." Pierpont was no self-made man; his father, the first Junius Spencer, had been a prominent banker in his own right. Pierpont nevertheless earned a grudging respect even among his detractors for his accomplishments and the sheer force of his will. "I know that I came to feel, myself, what others on Wall Street felt," the muckraker and onetime Wall Street reporter Lincoln Steffens recalled, "a vague awe of the man."[6]

In 1920, the House of Morgan still occupied the site Pierpont had selected almost half a century earlier. Convinced that the United States would prove itself "the richest country in the world in natural resources," he and his partner Anthony Drexel had spent a million dollars for the lot at Wall and Broad in the early 1870s, the highest price ever paid per square foot for a bit of American real estate. The original headquarters—a six-story marble building with mansard roof, dormer windows, and an impressive internal elevator—opened in early 1873. Later that year, the post–Civil War rail boom collapsed, shuttering hundreds of brokerage firms, forcing the stock exchange to close for weeks, and ushering in the country's first major depression.[7]

Pierpont was one of the few on Wall Street to emerge unscathed. In 1873, Drexel, Morgan earned a million dollars, a hint of the uncanny acumen that would characterize Pierpont's later career. But the panic was a lesson for him as surely as it had been for the thousands of depositors who mobbed the district's muddy streets that autumn, hoping to extract cash before plunging railroad stocks destroyed their modest fortunes. He saw in the crash a sign of the dangerous volatility of the American economy, how unfettered competition doomed it to extremes of enthusiasm and despair. He was certain that he could find a better approach, some way for industrialists and financiers to profit while coordinating such matters as prices and rates. For the next fifty years, he acted as Wall Street's chief apostle of "organization," or, as it would come to be known, "Morganization": the idea that consolidation, not competition, held the key to a prosperous future.[8]

This faith in the power of bigness, in the rationality of the large corporation, soon emerged not only as Pierpont's personal doctrine but also as the organizing principle for a swift restructuring of the American economy. When Pierpont settled at Wall and Broad, the United States was still a provincial nation, a land of small farms and factories, dependent upon Europe for credit, imports, and capital. By his death in 1913, it was nothing less than an industrial monolith, producing a third of the world's goods and services, more than Great Britain, France, and Germany put together. None of this was Pierpont's work alone. But far more than industrial magnates such as Andrew Carnegie and John D. Rockefeller, Pierpont symbolized the new world of finance capitalism, in which a single banker's decisions mattered more than anything that happened in the mines or on the factory floor. Indeed, to most Americans, Pierpont Morgan *was* Wall Street. Over the course of his career, cartoonists had established his fat moustache, satisfied paunch, and omnipresent top hat as the essence of the banker: prosperous, cunning, and far removed from the muscular work of the men and women who created his paper fortune.[9]

By the time Junius joined the bank in 1915, the stories of his grandfather's triumphs were Wall Street lore. There was the 1879 sale of the New York Central, when Pierpont helped William Vanderbilt sell off the largest block of stock ever issued in the United States, then walked away with control of the railroad's board of directors. There was his famous emergency meeting during the Panic of 1907, when he gathered Wall Street's top financiers in his library on Thirty-sixth Street and insisted that they prevent a full-blown depression. And, inevitably, there were the stories of the vast riches that had resulted from these efforts. A devout Episcopalian, Pierpont always disapproved of the gilded indulgence so much the rage in New York society. But he was not above spending lavishly. The growing power of the Morgan empire could be measured by the size of Pierpont's yachts. His *Corsair*, built in 1882, was 165 feet. Less than a decade later, *Corsair II* expanded to 241 feet, making it the largest recreational vessel in the world. *Corsair III*, built just after the turn of the century, came in at a staggering 300 feet and required a seventy-person crew. In his affection for a fine boat, Junius was nothing if not his grandfather's heir.[10]

Of all Pierpont's achievements, none better captured his essence than the 1901 creation of U.S. Steel. The very idea was audacious. Rather than rely on the loose trusts that, more often than not, broke apart amidst squabbling and government opposition, Pierpont bought up some 228 of the nation's most promising steel-related entities, specializing in everything from ore extraction to shipping, and combined them into a single, massive company under centralized control. Capitalized at $1.4 billion—an amount equal to one-sixth of the value of all American manufacturing—U.S. Steel was the world's largest corporation at its moment of birth. It was also Pierpont's most celebrated accomplishment, a gargantuan effort that yielded not only profit but also something utterly new in the annals of industry. The *Wall Street Journal* affirmed this in February 1901, declaring the invention of U.S. Steel "a turning point in the market: The high tide of industrial capitalism." For his son, and now for his grandson, it was an imposing legacy.[11]

Wall Street marked Pierpont's death in 1913 as a quasi-royal event. "We have lost our foremost financial magnate," mourned Andrew Carnegie. Elbert H. Gary, Pierpont's longtime ally at U.S. Steel, declared him "the greatest man of the age." Behind all of the praise and hyperbole, however, was a note of uncertainty about what would come next, a skepticism about whether another man—presumably another Morgan—could or even should attempt to take Pierpont's place. "There will be no other king," National City Bank president Frank Vanderlip commented to a colleague. "Mr. Morgan was typical of the time in which he lived and can have no successor, for we are facing other days."[12]

At the time, Junius was still at Harvard, not yet expected to worry about assuming his grandfather's mantle. For his father, the pressure was immediate. Jack did his best to replicate his father's persona, acquiring the same top hats, the same suits, even the same fat cigars that had made Pierpont into an icon of finance. He changed his public name as well, dismissing the "Jr." and becoming, like his father, simply "J. P. Morgan." Still, everyone wondered if he might be too weak, too cautious, to measure up to his father's achievements. "Of course my greatest desire is to keep together the structure which Father reared," he assured his fellow bankers in 1913. As it turned out, history stepped in to smooth the transition. In June 1914, Serbian nationalists assassinated Archduke Franz Ferdinand in Sarajevo, setting in motion not only the Great War but also one of the greatest transfers of financial power in global history.[13]

Jack was wrong about the war, at least at first. "You will see how perfectly absurd all this talk of conducting the trade of the world in New York must be," he wrote to British partner Teddy Grenfell in September 1914. Like Pierpont, he maintained a deep faith in the superiority of all things English, from the London financial markets to the Anglican

Church, and he raised his sons to believe the same. Junius spent his early childhood in England, earning subpar grades in boarding school and studying cricket with a private coach. When war broke out, in 1914, his mother and sisters were still there, watching with alarm as the British authorities commandeered their horses and milk. Even as Jack attempted to secure their passage back across the Atlantic, he found it hard to believe that crass, disorderly New York, with its "clumsy and very individualistic banking system," would ever replace aristocratic London as the center of world finance. Still, he recognized that the United States would likely profit from Europe's poor decisions. "The war, by cutting down the trade of other countries, should be a tremendous opportunity for America," he wrote President Woodrow Wilson.[14]

Three months later, he made good on this prediction, taking advantage of his British contacts to secure the bank an appointment as the official British purchasing agent in the United States. By the time the United States entered the war, more than two years later, the Morgans had spent some $3 billion in British money, trading more in a single month than the world's GNP a half century earlier. What this meant for Jack and the bank were fees beyond anything Pierpont had ever imagined: $30 million for the purchasing work alone. And this was only a small part of the firm's wartime business. Jack's most famous act was the organization of a Wall Street syndicate involving sixty-one underwriters and 1,570 banks and financial firms to deliver the gigantic Anglo-French loan of September 1915. At $500 million, it was the largest foreign loan in Wall Street's history. Calculated for interest, it brought a hefty return.[15]

To Jack, this was not just good business. It affirmed, by war's end, that he had fulfilled his fondest hope: "to take Father's place in the community and help out in many ways." For others on Wall Street, the rewards of such work were more pragmatic in nature. By 1920, the war had produced forty-two thousand new millionaires in the United States, most of them in and around New York. Corporate profits tripled between the beginning and end of hostilities. Stock prices boomed, too: between 1914 and 1916, Bethlehem Steel, a Morgan interest, went from $33 per share to $600. But the most important effect of the war, from a banking perspective, was what it did to the stature of American finance. For the first time in its history, the United States was lending out more than it was borrowing from Europe. It became, almost overnight, a creditor nation. And within the United States, most of those payments flowed straight through New York Harbor into the vaults and counting books of Wall Street.[16]

AS JUNIUS APPROACHED the Morgan bank on the morning of September 16, nearly two years after the armistice, he could see the signs of this new prosperity all around him. Due to government building restrictions, financial firms had been severely pressed for space during the war. Now, with the return to peace, Wall Street seemed to be one great construction site. Blasting and hammering echoed through the district's canyons, and shipments of marble, wood, and machinery blocked the already congested streets. This was excellent news for the real estate market. "Sales and re-sales of property in the Wall Street district are greater than ever before," reported the *Wall Street Journal*. It was rather less welcome inside the established firms, where the constant din tended to distract from the work of sums and transactions.[17]

This was a particular problem for the Morgan employees, who faced on September 16 yet another morning of pounding and shouting courtesy of the New York Stock Exchange. Despite their mutual interests, relations between the two great engines of capitalism—the banks and the markets—were never entirely cordial; Jack rarely set foot in the exchange, viewing it as a loathsome symbol of chaos. Yet the Stock Exchange, with its famous Corinthian columns and elaborate marble frieze, was less than a minute's walk from the House of Morgan, just across Broad Street and a few dozen feet to the south. In September 1920, it was slowly inching closer. Capitalizing on the wartime boom, the exchange had decided to add a twenty-two-story annex at Wall and Broad, directly across from the Morgan bank's main entrance. Commissioned at a price of $3 million, the building was slated to be both a practical addition and a monument to Wall Street's new global power. That morning, though, it was little more than scaffolding. Work had begun weeks earlier, and the Morgan men had since learned to tolerate the persistent banging. "The expansion of...business," the *New York Times* explained, "...has been so extraordinary that more room has been urgently needed for some time."[18]

Along the Broad Street sidewalks, the men of the outdoor Curb Market, a lesser cousin to the New York exchange, found themselves similarly squeezed, both by postwar business and by the crowds it seemed to bring. Months earlier, they had appealed for space in the new annex, arguing that they, more than anyone on Wall Street, could show an urgent need. They made a good case: for more than a century, the Curb Market had operated outside in rain, sleet, snow, and sun, trading the junkier stocks and bonds scorned by the bigger markets. The Board of Governors, however, rejected their appeal, so the curb men had decided to construct a building of their own. It was going up not on Wall Street itself but a few blocks away, behind Trinity Church, in an area known as "Wall Street's backyard."[19]

Business on the other corners of Wall and Broad that morning was more stable and, at any rate, more subject to Morgan influence. On the northwest corner stood the great tower of Bankers Trust, thirty-five stories from base to roof, capped at the top by an incongruous seven-story Egyptian pyramid. All of it—the building as well as the business—was Pierpont's doing. Along with a syndicate of other bankers, he had spun off the company in 1903 to perform the trust work that President Theodore Roosevelt, among others, had begun to denounce. To give Bankers Trust a permanent home, Pierpont personally commissioned the tower as well as the pyramid, a symbol of his fascination with Egyptian antiquity (second only to his interest in Rome). He was pleased enough with the final product, completed in 1912, to invite the same firm to design the new Morgan bank on the corner's southeast lot. They constructed the design according to his specifications, though Pierpont died months before the new building was finished.[20]

The final site at Wall and Broad, the northeast corner, was both the most historic and, by 1920, the most symbolic of the district's recent largesse. A century and a half earlier, the site had hosted Americans' first successful attempts at a national government. There, on Wall and Broad's northeast lot, George Washington took his oath of office, the U.S. Congress met for the first time, and the Bill of Rights became law—all before the seat of federal power began its slide south to Washington. The building where those events took place had been demolished a few decades later to make way for a new customs house, its modest two stories replaced by a grand run of stone steps leading to a pillared Greek Revival landmark. In 1889, on the centennial of Washington's inauguration, city fathers added a bronze statue of the first president out front, a gesture toward the past in a neighborhood now obsessed with the future. By 1920, Washington still stood proudly, but the building itself had become a U.S. Sub-Treasury, devoted to collecting federal taxes.[21]

Like the rest of Wall Street, the Sub-Treasury was a great beneficiary of the war. And like their friends at the stock exchange, Treasury officials had decided to expand their reach. In July 1919, Treasury Secretary William McAdoo dedicated an ornate new assay office next door to the Sub-Treasury, just across Wall Street from the Morgan bank's northern face. "Every patriotic citizen takes a pride in this greatest metropolis of the world," he pronounced at the dedication, "and anything that affects the interests of New York should not fail to enlist the sympathy and the pride of American citizens everywhere." The new structure featured an ornate brass door—"one of the most ornamental ever constructed in a government office building," according to the *Sun and New York Herald*. It also boasted the largest vaults in the world. On the morning of September 16, government workers were busy transferring a billion dollars in gold coin and bullion along a wooden chute between the assay office and the Sub-Treasury. One newspaper estimated that it was "probably the greatest accumulation of this precious metal anywhere in the world to-day." And the new vaults, in anticipation of further interest due the United States, had been constructed to hold twice as much.[22]

This sense of opportunity, of boundless expansion, was not limited to Wall Street. By 1920 it was part of the fabric of New York itself. The city's economic picture was not entirely rosy. The cost of living, driven by wartime inflation, was spiraling out of control; the housing crisis (another wartime product) seemed all but insoluble; even the stock market had taken a turn for the worse in recent months. None of this had dampened the sense, particularly at the upper reaches of government and finance, that New York was the city of the future— that all things were possible, in the words of one recent telephone ad campaign, thanks to the "Bigness of New York." New York was home to the country's tallest buildings, its busiest port and longest subway, its most productive factories, its most crowded neighborhoods, its finest poets and artists and writers. New York's 5.6 million residents far surpassed Chicago's 2.7 million. Its 2 million foreign-born residents alone could populate a city the size of Philadelphia. The fact that these millions chose to settle in New York was a testament to the city's status as an international crossroads. Above all, New York was a place of motion and flow and change, the cosmopolitan capital of an emerging world power.[23]

In the first half of September alone, more than twenty-six thousand new U.S. residents had arrived at New York's Ellis Island, nestled off Manhattan's southernmost tip. Within the United States, migrants from small towns and cities, from regions to the north and south and west, made their way to New York as well, settling in neighborhoods such as "bohemian" Greenwich Village, a previously unassuming little district transformed in the prewar years into an avant-garde mecca. Then there were the newer groups of migrants, the 1.6 million men who found themselves marching through the city on their way to battle in Europe.[24]

New York had been the central city of the country's war effort—"the pivot," in the words of New York police commissioner Richard E. Enright, "on which all the war activities...revolved." The successful transport of more than a million troops demanded some 4.5 million tons of supplies: artillery, food, blankets, instruction manuals, uniforms. Much of it came direct from New York factories. The necessity of production, in turn, had attracted thousands of black southerners, eager, like immigrants from abroad, for decent wages and a little breathing room. Later, this northward movement would be labeled, with biblical aplomb, the Great Migration. In New York during the war years, though, it was just one migration of many.[25]

Even before the war, this flow in and, to a lesser degree, out—of money, of people, of cultures and prejudices and ideologies—had begun to transform New York into America's first world-class city, the sort of place where, as reformer Herbert Croly predicted in 1903, "something considerable may happen." By 1920, flush with victory, boosters could declare with passable truth, in Enright's words, that "this city stands today at the zenith of its development magnificence—beyond reach of competition."[26]

And yet predictions of "something considerable" occurring in New York also contained ominous overtones. As it grew, New York had become not a melting pot but a city of extremes: the capital of capitalism and of radicalism, of wealth and poverty, of high-minded reform and pragmatic enterprise, of the war effort and the antiwar crusade. Its very success as a magnet for the rich as well as the poor, for left as well as right, made it a city of frequent discord, a place where the conflicts of the rest of the nation—indeed, of much of the world—were compressed into a few square miles. With military mobilization came thousands of soldiers, accompanied by "all the other transformations bound to follow in the train of such a state of affairs," in Enright's words. With munitions manufacturing and shipping came the threats of sabotage and attack. With industrial life came strikes and union organizing. And with the concentration of national wealth on Wall Street came direct challenges that men such as Junius Morgan found themselves powerless to avoid.[27]

JUNIUS HAD MISSED the assassination attempt on his father, but not by much. On June 15, 1915, Junius married Louise Converse, a twenty-year-old artist and a member of "the Boston social elect," in what papers described as a "very simple" ceremony in a little white church in the Boston suburb of Dedham, Massachusetts. His parents were pleased to see him make such an appropriate match. "I think he is absolutely the most satisfied and contented person I ever saw," Jack wrote to a cousin in early 1915. To welcome Louise to the family, the elder Morgans planned a small honeymoon party, just thirteen guests, at Matinecock Point, their 250-acre estate on Long Island. Junius and Louise expected to stop by for a few refreshments and well-wishes before departing for Panama. Instead, when they pulled up to the Matinecock Point bridge late on the afternoon of July 3, they found their way blocked by armed guards and detectives. "Nobody," the *New York Times* reported, "wanted to be first to tell the truth to the young couple."[28]

As near as the police were able to determine, a clean, well-kept man bearing a card in the name of "Thos. C. Lester," of the "Summer Society Directory," had appeared at the manor house a few hours earlier, demanding to see "Mr. J. P. Morgan." When Henry Physick, the butler, refused to let him in, the man barreled his way through the front entrance armed with two guns and several sticks of dynamite. Jack encountered him on the stairs and tried to wrestle him to the ground, but one of the guns went off. Moments later, Physick (along with British ambassador Cecil Spring-Rice, a breakfast guest) managed to tackle and bind the intruder. Jack sustained two bullet wounds: one in the hip, another in the abdomen. By the time Junius and Louise arrived, he was settled in bed, under the care of family doctors. Physick took care of canceling the honeymoon party and sending the guests away on one of the Morgan yachts.[29]

Under police questioning, the gunman gave his name not as Thomas Lester but as Frank Holt. Later, he confessed that he was actually Erich Muenter, a onetime German instructor at Harvard who was wanted in another state for poisoning his wife. His aim, he explained to the police, was not to harm Jack but to hold his wife and children hostage while the Morgan leadership went about calling off the war. As evidence of this plan, Muenter shared a list in his pocket bearing the names of the Morgan children and of Jack's wife, Jane Norton Grew. He also confessed to planting a bomb beneath the switchboard of a public telephone at the U.S. Capitol before boarding the train for Long Island. All of it, he said, was meant to express his fellow Americans' despair over the war and over what the Morgans were doing to escalate it. "There are thousands of other persons in the United States who think as I do about the necessity of bringing this terrible world conflict to an end," Muenter explained to police, "but who lack the courage to take any decisive action." The bomb at the Capitol went off just before midnight on July 2, largely destroying the Senate reception room but causing no injuries.[30]

As Jack languished in bed, Junius assumed the role of family spokesman, patiently answering reporters' questions about his father's condition. The wounds were not terribly serious—one bullet passed straight through, and surgeons extracted the second from Jack's hip—and the family decided that a show of calm was the proper response. On July 4, the day after the shooting, Junius attended church with Louise. The following day, he took his father's modest fifty-foot yacht, the *Grayling*, for a spin in a local race. Finally, on July 6, as if to ensure the continuity of the family legacy, he arrived for his first day of work at Wall and Broad. Jack was quick to explain to friends that Junius was not signing on indefinitely but was merely "coming into the office to see if he is fit to go into the firm later on." But for Junius there was no going back. When he returned from his honeymoon later that year, he went to work at the bank full-time.[31]

Despite this public bravado, Junius and the family were shaken by what had happened—not just by Muenter's act but also by how it reflected the darker strains of the Morgan legacy. As long as Junius could remember, the Morgan men—indeed, all of Wall Street—had been denounced as a source of shame and evil; they were the "Money Power," the "Money Trust," "plutocrats," "monopolists," "capitalist Caesars." The reasons for the hostility were not hard to see. Walk a mile in any direction from the Morgan family's well-appointed Thirty-fifth Street townhouse and the evidence was there in all of its daily misery. "I saw the midnight bread lines," wrote Louis Duchez, a socialist who toured the city in 1910. "The thousands of homeless sleeping in the parks, upon the sidewalks and in the doorways of large shaded buildings in the off-streets. I saw them perched on the fire-escapes for eight and ten stories upwards, in order to get a breath of air that might possibly sweep through the long, narrow streets." Of all the American cities, New York best embodied the stark inequalities of the new industrial capitalism, in which the top 2 percent of the nation held 60 percent of the wealth and one in four poor children died before reaching adulthood. Duchez, like thousands of others, saw the roots of revolution in such conditions. "If there is one place in America where the workers have reason to revolt against capitalism and this thing called 'civilization' and to overthrow it," he concluded, "it is New York City."[32]

As a young boy, Junius could only have been dimly aware of this "other half," or of the political challenges to the industrial and financial order that his family was doing so much to create. By the time he reached adulthood, though, he could hardly read a newspaper without learning of the ills that his grandfather had foisted upon the country. To the populists, Pierpont was a brazen, selfish financier, a man whose hunger for profit, and especially for gold, had destroyed a virtuous freeholder republic. To labor unions, he was a plutocratic tyrant, despised for his claim that the nonunion shop was the cornerstone of American virtue, as well as for the brutal twelve-hour days and seven-day weeks at companies such as U.S. Steel. Socialists, anarchists, and other political radicals attacked him as the embodiment of a corrupt, capitalist system (which, Pierpont or no, was destined to fail, they believed), while progressives such as Theodore Roosevelt blamed him in turn for providing such groups with a plausible case for revolt.

Jack, for his part, remained convinced of Pierpont's righteousness, the ultimate virtue of a world where intelligent, well-bred men earned significant rewards for their business risks and acumen. "Of course we know there are *wrongs* in the world, and one man has a better chance than another, with much less work," he wrote to one of Junius' Harvard instructors in 1913, "nevertheless I think that even the socialistically inclined perhaps realise that with those good things comes to most people a sense of responsibility." But he proved no more capable than Pierpont at dispelling public criticism. In 1916, for instance, in an attack typical of Jack's early years at the bank's helm, South Dakota farmer advocate H. L. Loucks published *The Great Conspiracy of the House of Morgan Exposed and How to Defeat It*, described as "an expose of the greatest conspiracy ever conceived by the brain of men to control all the commerce and industry of a great nation, through a private monopoly of money, the life blood of commerce, by a group of avaricious, conscienceless financiers, whom for brevity I shall name The House of Morgan."[33]

Profitable though it proved to be, the war only increased this hostility, adding to the list of Morgan "crimes" the fact that the firm was, unmistakably, making millions off a catastrophic global conflict. This was Muenter's complaint. "Mr. Morgan...has more influence in this country about the war than anybody, because he is financing the war," he explained to police. "If he would say that shipping ammunition was to be stopped it would stop." If Muenter's actions were extreme, his views were not. By 1916, millions of Americans—isolationists, socialists, pacifists, even moderate progressives—shared his point of view, condemning the Morgans and the rest of Wall Street for profiting from the bloodshed in Europe. Some brought their protests to the corner of Wall and Broad, staging rallies to expose the bank's role in the European slaughter. Others made their views known from Washington. "What do Morgan and Schwab care for world peace," Senator Robert La Follette demanded, "when there are big profits in world war?" At least a few seized upon Muenter's attack as a model of righteous vengeance. "Holt only tried to kill one man," an anonymous correspondent wrote to Jack, using Muenter's pseudonym. "You are helping kill millions and for money you do not need and will never want."[34]

By the time the United States actually entered the war in the spring of 1917, Jack was living a near-fugitive existence, trailed by bodyguards, traveling under a false name, ever suspicious of contact with strangers. Junius, by contrast, fled the whole mess in April 1917, joining the navy within days of the United States' declaration of war. He started as an ensign on his family yacht, donated to help the war effort. By the end of hostilities, he was a junior officer on a destroyer, charged with escorting American supply and troop ships safely into European ports. At home, the newspapers applauded these actions as worthy of the Morgan name. Junius, the *New York American* noted, was "one of the first of Wall Street financiers' sons to get into the war." For Junius, though, there remained a measure of guilt. "I feel almost ungrateful being over here," he wrote in his diary in early December 1917 from his officer's cabin, "but know that he [Jack] would be far more worried if I was holding down my desk in JPM And CO at this time instead of serving the U.S. in some way."[35]

In the long months that followed, as he settled into the destroyer's rhythm of boredom interspersed with moments of high danger, he found abroad, as at home, that it was almost impossible to shake a growing sense of doom. Between official duties, he spent much of his time holed up in his bed, worried and ill. "I must confess that there have been many times during the past 24 hours when I have been afraid," he wrote on October 31. "However, it is all part of the game and I hope to get accustomed to it in time."[36]

He returned from the war a year later shattered and nervous, a shadow of the "satisfied and contented" boy his father had remarked upon in 1915. Nonetheless, he took up where he left off. By early 1919, he was back to work at Wall and Broad.

POSTWAR LIFE BROUGHT a curious blend of disruption and routine. In March 1919, Junius accepted an appointment to the board of Liberty National Bank—a sign, in the words of the *Atlanta Constitution*, that "he appears to be following in the footsteps of his forebears." At the House of Morgan, too, he buckled down to prepare for partnership, an honor that would be delivered by the end of the year. All of this was just as it should be, a resumption of expectations temporarily interrupted by war.[37]

Outside the bank's confines, though, the situation proved to be at least as unstable as when he left. The United States lost more than one hundred thousand soldiers during the war—a far cry from the millions sacrificed by European nations, but still the worst military toll in half a century. On the home front, an influenza epidemic killed six times that number in just a few months. These experiences might have brought the nation together in shared sacrifice. Instead, by 1919 it looked as if American society was tearing itself apart. During the summer, Chicago, Washington, and Detroit erupted in murderous "race riots," in which rumors of rape and criminal marauding became pretexts for vicious assaults on black homes and communities. From Versailles, President Wilson struggled— and failed—to convince Republican legislators to support the League of Nations. He argued (with Morgan support) that the League was the world's last, best hope for avoiding another catastrophic war. Moreover, he suggested, it might help contain the great threat of the postwar age. In November 1917, the Bolshevik Party had seized power in Russia. By early 1919, Lenin was calling for a global revolution.

Wilson had left thousands of troops in Russia after the armistice— ostensibly to guard war supplies and repatriate Czech prisoners, but effectively to battle the Bolsheviks. The presence of American soldiers, however, had no measurable effect on the Bolsheviks' power or on their influence around the world. From Mexico to Munich, the Russian example continued to inspire strikes, political agitation, even attempted coups. Within the United States, too, there was evidence of brewing discontent. In 1919, almost four million men and women, nearly one in five U.S. workers, joined the picket line, numbers far in excess of anything Pierpont had ever witnessed. They were not calling for revolution, but their demands showed a new scope and scale. The locomotive men, championing the "Plumb Plan," sought government ownership of the rails. The coal unions urged a federal takeover of the mines. In Seattle, what began as a walkout in the shipyards ballooned into a five-day general strike, soon followed by a similar but far longer uprising in Winnipeg, Canada.[38]

Accompanying all of this was a dramatic uptick in the sort of personal violence that the Morgans had come to fear in the wake of the Muenter assault. In late April, the New York post office uncovered a mail bomb addressed to "J. P. Morgan"—one of thirty similar bombs sent to prominent financiers, industrialists, and politicians as a May Day "gift." Thanks to insufficient postage, most of the bombs never reached their targets (the sole casualty was Ethel Williams, a maid to Georgia senator Thomas Hardwick, who lost both hands after opening a package on April 29). A month later, however, a new attack hit with more force.

On June 2, 1919, bombs lit up the midnight sky in seven eastern cities—a coordinated effort raising the specter of a widespread conspiracy. In Washington, the explosion sheared off the front of Attorney General A. Mitchell Palmer's house. In New York, a bomb at the home of Judge Charles Nott killed a night watchman, the only victim of the attack. Left behind at each bomb site was a handful of pink flyers warning all men of power that they might be next. "There will have to be bloodshed; we will kill because it is necessary," the flyers explained, in a warning that would soon come back to haunt the bank. "We will do anything and everything to suppres [*sic*] the capitalist class."[39]

The May Day and June 2 plots, combined with the world situation, put the Morgan bank on high alert; over the following year, Jack hired new detectives to investigate the Bolshevik movement and assess any possible threats. Their efforts did little, however, to stop the string of attacks. On April 18, 1920, a deranged gunman shot and killed Dr. James Markoe, a dear friend of the Morgan family, during the collection at St. George's Church, apparently believing Markoe to be the long-dead J. Pierpont

Morgan. After Markoe's funeral, everyone did his best, in the words of the *New York Times*, "to obliterate every hint of the tragedy which so shocked the whole community"—an expression of the same determined calm that had followed Jack's shooting. Nonetheless, the church was crawling with policemen, for fear that "some irresponsible crank might be moved to emulate the assassin's deed."[40]

If anything, the spirit of hostility toward the bank and its interests appeared to be on the rise as the immediate concerns of warfare gave way to larger, more intractable battles over the postwar relationship between capital and labor. September 1919 saw the eruption of a round of strikes stretching from the Pennsylvania coalfields to the streets of Boston, where the walkout of more than a thousand policemen threw the city into chaos. U.S. Steel itself, Pierpont's defining creation, was rocked by a shutdown in which some 365,000 steelworkers walked off the job nationwide, the largest revolt in the industry's history. Their agenda wasn't hard to fathom: steelmen worked twelve hours a day, seven days a week, often for wages "below the level set by government experts as the minimum of subsistence," by one commission's measure. But the strike was anathema at the House of Morgan, an assault on the entire idea that employers, not workers, should control the conditions of labor. In response to the strikers' demand for a single, industrywide union, Jack vowed to fight the rebellion tooth and nail. "Heartiest congratulations on your stand for the open shop, with which I am, as you know, absolutely in accord," he cabled to U.S. Steel president Elbert Gary, charged with suppressing the strike. "I believe American principles of liberty deeply involved and must win if we all stand firm."[41]

As so many times in the past, these efforts had, in the main, succeeded. By early 1920, the steelworkers' committee was defunct, the strikers convinced, in one investigator's view, that "it is useless to strike or fight the big companies." The wave of revolutionary ambition, too, seemed to be breaking down. In the wake of the June 2, 1919, bombings, Palmer had vowed to rid the United States of agitators who "seek to terrorize the country and thus stay the hand of the government." Beginning in November, he had followed through with a dramatic deportation campaign—the so-called Palmer Raids—that rounded up thousands of foreign-born anarchists and communists. In New York, state and local officials took action as well. In early January 1920, less than week after the final Palmer Raid, the state legislature expelled five Socialist assemblymen recently elected from some of the city's most radical districts—Harlem, the South Bronx, the immigrant neighborhoods of the Lower East Side—on the grounds that advocating socialism was tantamount to treason.[42]

None of this put the postwar turmoil entirely to rest. In the late summer of 1920, for instance, more than a hundred thousand miners struck in the Pennsylvania coalfields, defying their employers, their union leaders, and even President Wilson, who had attempted to mediate a compromise earlier in the year. In New York, too, a defiant labor movement chugged steadily along. The police department's list of the year's "important strikes" read like an occupational tally for the U.S. census: "glaziers, helpers and handlers of plate glass and sheet glass; lumber handlers; merchant truckmen; elevator operators; barbers; warehousemen; furriers; film producers; furniture handlers, chauffeurs, drivers and helpers; moving-van chauffeurs, drivers and helpers; bathing suit and sweater operators; outlaw railroad strike." Even the Socialist Party had managed to regroup and continue its struggle, in the words of ousted assemblyman Louis Waldman, "for the abolition of the special interests which exploit and deprive the people of life's happiness." In late August, New York governor Al Smith called the state assembly into "emergency" session to address the postwar housing crisis. To fill the Socialists' empty seats, he called for a special election, giving the former assemblymen a chance to regain their posts. The election was scheduled for September 16.[43]

JACK WAS NOT AT THE BANK that morning. He had left for Scotland in August, signing off with the warning to partner Harry Davison that "the recession in business is becoming more and more, and more and more am I certain that we are going to see rather bad times for the next few months." Junius stayed behind as his father's representative. Among the most urgent matters to contend with was the situation in the Pennsylvania coalfields. To discuss the matter, Junius had planned to have a meeting that day with John Markle, proprietor of one of the country's largest independent anthracite mining operations and an old family friend. Markle had been fighting unions since the big anthracite strike of 1902, when he famously informed his workforce that "I would rather fight than eat." This had earned him a reputation in labor circles for "fiendish cruelty," in the words of lawyer Clarence Darrow, surpassing "all the cruelty and violence committed in the anthracite region." At the House of Morgan, though, it won him respect. In 1913, after Markle had moved to New York, Jack sponsored him for membership in the elite Piping Rock Cub.[44]

Markle arrived sometime before noon, accompanied by his engineering assistant, A. B. Jessup. Despite its elegant furnishings, the interior of the Morgan bank was dark and slightly gloomy, brightened only by the colored glass dome over the main trading floor. The building featured large windows along both the Broad and Wall street sides, running almost to the lofty ceiling, but they were blocked by heavy curtains, and thick wire screens between the windows and curtains absorbed what little light remained. Upstairs, away from the din of the trading floor, each partner maintained an oak-lined office, within easy reach of the dining room and the barbershop supplied for Jack's comfort. Each partner had a rolltop desk downstairs as well. Beyond the partners' fireplaces and brass spittoons, the first-floor trading area was measured chaos: clerks scribbling away at their desks, tellers counting change in their "cages"—some five hundred men all told.[45]

On the morning of September 16, four of the partners—Dwight Morrow, Thomas Lamont, George Whitney, and Elliott Bacon—were upstairs, conducting their daily conference. For his meeting with Markle, Junius stayed in his first-floor office, separated by a stone railing and glass partition from the workaday crowd. At noon, seated at his desk, Junius faced directly onto the bank's Wall Street side. Markle sat across from him, his back to the street. In addition to Markle, Jessup, and Junius, the meeting included Thomas Joyce, head of the Morgan gold department and a loyal employee of the firm for more than thirty years.[46]

Markle later told the papers that he was chatting amiably with Joyce, preparing to leave the bank, when "[w]ithout warning . . . [t]here came the sound of a tremendous explosion."[47]

From the outside, a taxi chauffeur standing just a few feet from the bank's entrance, recalled the scene differently. "I was preparing to crank up," he told the *Tribune* later that afternoon, "when it seemed like the end of the world."[48]

# 2
. . . .

## THE END OF THE WORLD

THE BLAST CAME SYNCOPATED: a flash, a roar, a pause thick with dread. Fire-packed air smashed against buildings, burned through the lunch crowd, knocked buyers and sellers off their feet. One man recalled a sinking in the knees as the first alert of "something unusual." Another said it was as if a giant hook had swooped down from the sky, plucking him into flight. Skyscrapers three blocks north trembled from the impact.[1]

"I was working in the paying teller's cage at the time," recalled Andrew Dunn, a veteran Morgan clerk. "That was the loudest noise I ever heard in my life. It was enough to knock you out by itself."

"I was lifted completely off the ground," a fifteen-year-old messenger boy informed detectives, "and at the same instance a terrible explosion occurred to my right, the terrific force of concussion blowing my hat off my head."

"I was at the southeast corner of Wall and William Streets, walking east, when the terrible roar caused me to turn," exporter Elwood M. Louer remembered. "I saw two sheets of flame that seemed to envelop the whole width of Wall Street and seemed to reach as high as the tenth story of the tall buildings."

"I was sitting at my desk right under the glass dome," said Walter Dickinson, head of the Morgan credit department, "when I heard an explosion just like the sound of a gatling gun."[2]

Then, calm. Later, witnesses who found it hard to recall the color of the smoke or the order of events remembered that odd moment of silence— the last instant before terror became a conscious thing. Wall Street seemed to freeze in a tableau vivant. Runners lay flattened "like tenpins." There was just time to register smells of acid, blood, and dust before the district's windows shattered and plunged into the street.[3]

"It was a crash out of a blue sky," wrote an Associated Press reporter, "—an unexpected, death-dealing bolt which in a twinkling turned into a shamble the busiest corner of America's financial center and sent scurrying to places of shelter hundreds of wounded, dumbstricken, white faced men and women, fleeing from an unknown danger." On the telephone from Washington, a Treasury official heard something like "the closing of a large book" before the line went dead. One man thought the roar of the glass sounded like Niagara.[4]

George Lacina, an employee at the Equitable Life Assurance Society, was hurled down the steps of Fred Eberlin's New Street restaurant. His face hit one of the steps, and the world melted into a soft red. The spiked rail snagged his shoulder and one of his lapels, but he managed to hold on to a crumpled $5 bill—"payment of a little debt." He later noticed that his coat buttons had popped off and his watch was ten minutes slow. "I picked myself up somehow," he told the *World*, "and said to a fellow who was also at the bottom of the steps: 'What the hell has hit New York?'"[5]

"I ran to the window," remembered Walter Marvin, working on the fifteenth floor of the Equitable Building. "Wall Street was covered with dust, flying pieces of curtains and splinters. In the street near the Morgan office was some kind of vehicle burning."[6]

"When I collected my senses," said J. J. Blommer, visiting from the Milwaukee Association of Commerce, "I found a boy, evidently a messenger, standing alongside of me, his face covered with blood. I escaped without a scratch."

"What impressed me was the great blast of air, with all the paper and dust and debris and broken glass being whirled about as the explosive expended its force," said Captain Jean Parmentier, waiting in the Morgan lobby for a meeting with partner Harry Davison.

"I was at work on the eighth floor of No. 32 Wall Street and when the blow up came was struck all over the head and face and shoulders by plaster and broken pieces of lath," broker Alexander Cumings told the *World*. "I never knew what it was all about until long afterward."[6]

Inside the Morgan bank, Markle recalled a shudder followed by a blizzard of white. Desks skittered across the trading floor. Papers burst from their files. Overhead, the big glass dome creaked, threatening to erupt into a second storm. Thomas Joyce was thrown to the ground, unconscious. "When I came to myself the whole first floor seemed to be filled with smoke and dust, and was strewn deeply with glass," he remembered. Markle grabbed his felt hat and jammed it on his head, an instinctive gesture for an old mining hand accustomed to explosives. "It is hard to say what did happen after that," he recalled, "but it was pandemonium."[7]

Markle saw blood pouring from Joyce's scalp. Jessup was bleeding, too, and "many other persons who seemed to be badly cut" lay nearby. One young man stumbled along with a broken leg. "It had been smashed, I believe, by the concussion," Markle said. He offered to help the injured boy, but other employees rushed in to take his place, so he made his way to the entrance at Wall and Broad. "When we came out of the doors," he later told the *New York Times*, "we could see the havoc that had been wrought."[8]

Crowds ran from Wall and Broad in waves: north on Nassau, west on Broadway, east toward the river, south to Battery Park. Some later said that the force of the stampede bore them along. Men on fire dropped to the ground: "Save me! Save me! Put me out!" Customers fled barbershops with cream on their faces, aprons streaming behind in white streaks. "Oh, God! What has happened? What has happened?" an old man with a gray goatee screamed on the Sub-Treasury steps. Above him, the bronze statue of George Washington held up his hand as if in protest.[9]

John Mutch, a chimney repairman, woke to the sensation of hundreds of men and women "running over me, crying and shouting hysterically." An insurance solicitor named Leon Canning stopped to help a man whose leg was blown off, but they were both plowed under by the force of the crowd. Canning dislocated his shoulder. Another man broke his arm when he tripped, and the crowd continued over him. "Never in its history," one news report concluded, "has lower Manhattan witnessed such excitement."[10]

Warnings of a second blast pulsed through the crowd. "Go back! For God's sake, go back!" cried a man near Broadway. "There's another explosion coming!" Others shouted first impressions: "The Stock Exchange has been blown up!" "The Morgan bank has been blown up!" At Trinity Church, at the base of Wall Street, passengers fleeing a derailed streetcar filled the cemetery. They were mostly silent—immersed, one witness said, in "a feeling of awe and horror." Within a few minutes, as fears of another explosion subsided, they turned back to see what they had left behind.[11]

"Everything was like a dream," recalled J. M. Murphy, a rigger from Brooklyn. "I saw a horse on his back with three legs sticking up in the air, an automobile on fire and dead people spread out on the street."

"Almost in front of the steps leading up to the Morgan bank was the mutilated body of a man," wrote reporter George Weston. "Other bodies, most of them silent in death, lay nearby. As I gazed horror stricken at the site, one of these forms, half naked and seared with burns, started to rise. It struggled, then toppled and fell lifeless into the gutter."

"Under one of the high windows of Morgan's banking house, about ten feet from the burning automobile, a man lying in the midst of bleeding bodies seemed to have just recovered consciousness," salesman E. G. Fegert remembered. "He lifted his head a few inches and looked about him dazed. Then his head dropped to the cement sidewalk. The other bodies were motionless."

"A man had his left leg blown off, not far from me," an anonymous witness told detectives. "I do not know his name."[12]

Great War veterans said the devastation reminded them of a battlefield. Thick on the ground were dozens of bodies, some still flopping. Moans and screams punctuated the crowd's hum. Bits of flesh, horse and human, mingled with fragments of brick and stone. Near Wall and Broad, a large crater belched smoke and dust. Splotches of red stained the Morgan bank's pale walls, and rivulets of blood trickled through the gutters.[13]

An unscathed derby hat perched next to an overturned touring car, snapping and sizzling beneath a tower of flame. The fumes from the car lent a sharp chemical tang to odors of blood and burning flesh. Gray clouds billowed forth from empty window frames—"like a moving picture show of an explosion," one witness thought. "Am I alive?" asked a girl on Wall Street. "Tell my boss to send another boy to relieve me," instructed a messenger boy, dying. A hand hung from the tasteful cornice above the door to the Morgan bank.[14]

At the bottom of the Sub-Treasury steps, a young woman with a gash from ear to shoulder strained to lift her head out of the gutter. Two horse hoofs lay near her face. What appeared to be the arm of a messenger boy lay nearby, accompanied by cap and call book. A chauffeur parked on the north side of Wall had caught a slice of glass in the back of the neck, and it severed his head. A woman's shoe rested on a window ledge at Bankers Trust, her foot and ankle still inside.[15]

The first rescues were spontaneous: a tourniquet made from a suit coat, a dash for aid in a makeshift taxi. One woman, disemboweled by a hit to the stomach, died as two men tried to lift her. A gray-haired watchman had just crawled from under a steel door when he saw two young women burning from head to foot. Dazed, he grabbed the nearest object and ran after them, attempting to beat out the flames with "seared hands" and a "foolish book." In the front door of a cigar shop, a clerk sliced at three men with his knife, trying to cut away burning clothes. Workers leaned out of a jagged hole that had once been a seventh-story window to rescue a clerk dangling by his left foot. At the assay office, several men hurried to assist a screaming woman who had been hurled against the door. They stopped short because she had no arms.[16]

> "I ran into Wall Street to see what I could do," said Lawrence Driggs, former president of the Aviation Club of America, "and found a number of persons lying dead or disabled both on the sidewalks

and in the middle of the street. I helped lay about fifteen or twenty of the dead and dying in a long line on the pavement."

"I saw an old gentleman turn the corner of Nassau Street. I remember that he looked like a deacon," a surgeon recalled. "He carried an umbrella, a large one. He saw a man lying in the street. Even as I watched he tore off his neck tie, stooped down and tied the tie tightly around the man's leg above the cut. Then he inserted his umbrella under the tie bandage and made a tourniquet."[17]

Former soldiers, well versed in the mechanics of horror, merged into a few loose teams. One group tossed victims into private cabs and autos, separating the panicked from the injured and the injured from the dead. Another set locked arms and tried to form a dike against the rising tide of curious onlookers. Later, ambulances and cars took on priests as well as patients. The clergy delivered last rites in transit.[18]

The few doctors on site got to work on triage. One Dr. Goodfellow treated his first patient on the sidewalk in front of the Morgan bank. The man's leg was nearly severed, so Goodfellow amputated it on the spot. Outside of 10 Wall Street, Dr. Leroy Silvey found a man with no scalp. He wrapped a handkerchief around the man's head and knotted it under the chin.[19]

Inside the Morgan bank, Dr. A. J. Barker Savage drifted from punctured lung to broken arm to concussion to torn flesh. "There was so much confusion...," he said, "that I did not know where to turn, there were so many things to be done." On the banking floor, brown stains marred a white base of paper and glass. Fire had charred the pinkish marble walls an uneven black. In a small room off to the right of the entrance, detectives found two out of three stock tickers smashed and silent. Only the Dow Jones ticker had survived, and it continued to churn out reports of the day's events.[20]

The big news was an explosion on Wall Street.

SOON THERE WOULD BE OTHER NEWS as well, names and anguished stories to attach to the bodies of the dead. All too quickly, though, such human tales were pushed aside by more sensational, politicized questions: Was it an accident or a bomb? Who would do such a thing, and why? Even as police extracted the last victims from their offices, the financial district buzzed with dark rumors that it had been deliberately attacked. "The explosion is too much of a coincidence to be accepted as an accident," assistant district attorney Alfred J. Talley told the *New York Times*. "The factors that lead me to this belief are that the time of the explosion was at 12:01, when probably the greatest damage could have been done, and the location of the explosion was midway between the Morgan offices and the federal treasury." Talley, like thousands of others, felt he knew who had both the motive and the requisite passion to commit such an act: precisely those agitators—"Bolshevists," "anarchists," "communists," "socialists"—who had for so long targeted men such as Jack and Junius Morgan.[21]

The swiftness with which opinion coalesced around the bomb theory gave the afternoon a mobbish, thoughtless quality, an undertone of vigilante threat. Months later, many radicals would point to the hot words and quick judgments of that first day as evidence that nobody had ever much cared about justice, that the authorities—indeed, the American people—were far more interested in finding a scapegoat and crushing dissent than in maintaining the presumption of innocence.

But if prejudice and opportunism, even deep, irrational fear, each played a role that afternoon, the idea of a bomb plot was not pure fantasy. Since the earliest days of Pierpont's reign, a small core of revolutionaries had talked of just such a cataclysm, of the moment when the working class would rise—perhaps with dynamite—to strike a spectacular blow against American capital. Among their ranks were some of the most famous dissidents in American history: the anarchists Johann Most, Emma Goldman, and Alexander Berkman; the militant labor leader "Big Bill" Haywood; even, by certain measures, the socialist icon Eugene Debs. No less than Pierpont, they had created a vision of what it meant to fight and survive in the new industrial age. With little definitive evidence yet culled from the explosion site, investigators turned to that vision, crafted over forty years of "class warfare," to explain why they were so immediately certain that some "radical" had set off a bomb. When they looked into the rubble on Wall Street on the afternoon of September 16, eager to arrest a suspect in "the most serious outrage ever perpetrated by the radicals in New York," they saw what the past had prepared them to see.[22]

# PART II

....

# THE STORY OF DYNAMITE

# 3

....

# THE FIRST
# TERRORIST ACT IN
# AMERICA

JOHANN MOST was a bedraggled little man, barely five feet tall, with a misshapen left jaw covered by an unkempt, sandy beard. When he arrived in New York on the morning of December 18, 1882, after two weeks at sea, he was even less imposing than usual—"not," in the judgment of the *New York Times*, an "attractive" man. Still, it was said that when he was in the throes of political passion his words alone had the "impact of...bombs and dynamite." Among his other attributes, Most was a well-known anarchist disciple of "propaganda by deed," the theory that individual acts of terrorism, from bomb plots to assassination attempts, offered a vital way for the working class to liberate itself from the tyranny of capital. His arrival, the social critic Louis Adamic would conclude half a century later, launched "the story of dynamite—the actual 'stuff'—in the United States, as a weapon of the have-nots in their warfare against the haves."[1]

Johann Most did not bring "the actual 'stuff'" that day in 1882. In a lifetime of advocating "Nitroglycerine, Dynamite, Gun-Cotton, Fulminating Mercury, Bombs, Arsons, Poisons, etc.," he was never once caught with the "stuff" on hand. He brought something far more important: the idea that such weapons could be used to strike fatal blows against

41

capitalism and the state. Within a year of his arrival, Most emerged as the leading spirit of a small but vocal revolutionary anarchist movement, unyielding in its hatred of capital, government, the church, and all other forms of despotism. In the process, he helped to transform the neutral substance of dynamite into a great political symbol, shorthand for the vengeance of an aggrieved immigrant working class. Just as they adopted Pierpont Morgan as the embodiment of the new industrial and financial order, cartoonists used Most as a model for one of that order's fiercest adversaries: the bearded, foreign, bomb-throwing revolutionary anarchist.[2]

By the late 1880s, the image of the anarchist bomb thrower could be found not just in cartoons but also on the front pages of big-city newspapers, in lurid descriptions of bomb plots hatched in the sort of poor, dark, immigrant neighborhood that Chicagoans referred to as the "terror district." It appeared in the cheapest popular fiction and in high literature as well; Henry James, for one, found the pull of the assassination plot irresistible. Perhaps most important, the "anarchist menace" reached into halls of governance from the humblest municipality to the nation's capital, where the men whom Most referred to as the "capitalist exploiters" fumed for decades against the "evil-disposed persons" and "wild beasts" attempting to slip into the United States from their breeding grounds in Europe.[3]

This specter—of filthy and brooding foreigners, of a widespread proletarian menace—was far more powerful than the anarchist movement itself. For lack of well-tended lists, the number of the faithful was always unclear; even at the movement's height in the mid-1880s, the International Working People's Association, the nation's leading anarchist organization, attracted no more than five thousand to six thousand members, the majority of them German immigrants. Within this tight-knit subculture, only a militant few subscribed unreservedly to Most's brand of scorching vengeance; despite his influence, anarchism always attracted far more pacific, or "philosophical," anarchists, who rejected violence in all its forms. Fewer still were willing to carry out the sort of acts that Most described—for instance, placing dynamite "under the table at a high society banquet."[4]

From Most's arrival until his death in 1906, only three major acts of violence in the United States were attributed to anarchists: the Haymarket bombing of 1886, the shooting of industrialist Henry Clay Frick in 1892, and the assassination of President William McKinley in 1901. This was in an age when hundreds, if not thousands, of striking workers died at the hands of policemen and armed guards, and in which almost a hundred were killed each day in industrial accidents. While acts of anarchist terrorism were exceptional, however, they played a vital role in how Americans imagined the new world of industrial capitalism, providing early hints that the rise of Morganization would not come without violent resistance from below. Along with his early pupils Emma Goldman and Alexander Berkman, Most introduced Americans to the idea that dynamite could be a potent political threat, whether on the piers of New York in 1882 or some four decades later on Wall Street.

AS AN ADULT, Most liked to say that his birth was illegal. Born in 1846 to an unmarried German governess, he endured the sort of childhood that might have made even a gentler soul rage against the injustices of fate. His mother died while Most was a young boy. Next, at the age of thirteen, he underwent surgery for a mysterious illness in his jaw. The operation left him disfigured, a target of pity and outright hostility. It was a relief when he came of age and could hide his shame with a beard.

Socialism, he later wrote, gave him his first glimmer of human understanding, a hint of the liberation provided by dedication to a cause. In Europe in the 1860s, this hardly made him unique. Karl Marx and Friedrich Engels wrote the Communist Manifesto two years after Most's birth, in the revolutionary moment of 1848. Throughout Most's childhood, Europe remained haunted by the "specter of communism," an uneasy awareness that revolution might be less a distant dream than an immediate prospect. In 1871, the Paris Commune shocked the world both with the strength of the uprising—rebels held Paris for nearly two months—and the brutality of its repression, in which French troops killed thousands of Communards in the climactic *semaine sanglante*, or "bloody week." Most was in Austria during the Commune, but he had already felt the chill of the antisocialist backlash. In 1870, he earned a five-year jail sentence for advocating manhood suffrage. The following year, Austria banished him altogether, the beginning of a lifetime in exile.

For the next several years, Most found himself in constant motion, attempting to stay one step ahead of jail. In 1874, he won election to the German Reichstag on the Socialist ticket but also received a two-year prison sentence for his praise of the Commune. Four years later, he earned a second Reichstag seat, only to find himself once again in the wrong place at the wrong time. His election happened to coincide with an epidemic of revolutionary assassination attempts against European heads of state, including two failed plots directed at Germany's Wilhelm I. The German government responded with a raft of antisocialist laws, banning all revolutionary meetings, shutting down dozens of left-wing newspapers, and outlawing the formation of trade unions, among other measures. Driven from Germany, Most fled to London, joining a large and ever-shifting community of high-profile socialists cast out from their nations of birth. There he began to move away from electoral politics toward the tactics of revolutionary anarchism that he ultimately brought to the United States.[5]

For Most, as for thousands of others, the shift from socialism to anarchism was a response to repression, to the repeated arrests, crackdowns, and raids that accompanied more temperate efforts at reform. Among the first to make the break was the Russian revolutionary Mikhail Bakunin, who was expelled from Marx's International Working Men's Association in 1872 after Marx endorsed electoral politics and refused to sanction the tactic of small-scale armed revolt. By the late 1870s, Most was thoroughly in Bakunin's camp, convinced that mere education and agitation would never produce genuine social change. Like Bakunin, Most had come to view state power as an evil in itself, incapable of yielding justice whether socialists or monarchists were in charge. True Marxists sought a dictatorship of the proletariat, a powerful central government controlled by workers. Anarchists, by contrast, dreamed of a stateless world, where no man would exercise power over any other. Beginning in the 1870s, they also set out in search of a tactic that would allow the working class to strike a blow against capitalism without bringing down the heavy hand of the state.[6]

To outsiders, the talk of bombing and assassination that suddenly pulsed through revolutionary circles in the late 1870s sounded like little more than an indiscriminate call to violence. To Most and others within the anarchist movement, by contrast, the idea of propaganda by deed, or the *attentat* (attack), had a very specific logic. Among anarchism's founding premises was the idea that capitalist society was a place of constant violence: every law, every church, every paycheck was based on force. In such a world, to do nothing, to stand idly by while millions suffered, was itself to commit an act of violence. The question was not whether violence per se might be justified, but exactly *how* violence might be maximally effective for, in Most's words, annihilating the "beast of property" that "makes mankind miserable, and gains in cruelty and voracity with the progress of our so called *civilization*."[7]

To the anarchists who flocked to London in the late 1870s, the answer seemed to lie in the miraculous new substance of dynamite, created by the Swedish scientist Alfred Nobel in 1866. When Most arrived in London, anarchist circles were awash with praise for dynamite as a transformative revolutionary tool. As a weapon, it required little skill or effort; dynamite was cheap, available, and easy to use. Like a gun or a knife, it could be easily hidden, carried around for deployment at strategic moments. Dynamite gave its owner the ability to act anonymously; bombs could be planted on an enemy's doorstep or tossed from afar. Most of all, it provided the working class with firepower to match the armies of the state and to counter the sort of repression that had greeted the Paris Commune.[8]

What this amounted to, in the view of many London revolutionaries, was a near-perfect weapon for striking back against power, an ideal tool of the weak against the strong. They quickly found examples of how this might work in practice. Beginning in the late 1870s, the Russian insurgents of Narodnaya Volya (the People's Will) turned to dynamite in a desperate attempt to topple the autocratic czarist regime. In 1881, after numerous attempts, they succeeded in killing Czar Alexander II by planting dynamite beneath his carriage. Most, like many anarchists, cheered their act as a model for revolutionaries throughout the world. " 'The throw was good,' and we hope that it was not the last," he wrote. "May the bold deed . . . inspire revolutionists far and wide with fresh courage." For those words, he received sixteen months in a London jail. Upon his release, he left for New York.[9]

AT FIRST GLANCE, New York was not a terribly hospitable place for a revolutionary such as Most. In 1874, city police had descended, clubs drawn, on a rally organized by socialists "in sympathy with the suffering poor"—minor echoes of the crackdown that had followed the Paris Commune. Three years later, as a nationwide rail strike swept the country—the first in American history—local leaders had armed once again, anticipating a battle with "bullets and bayonets, canister and grape," in the words of one newspaper, if "the club of the policeman" did not suffice. New York escaped the worst of the troubles that year, though other American cities saw gun battles and serious casualties, including dozens of strikers killed by armed guards and police. City leaders nonetheless set out to ensure that leftover rumblings of discontent would never escalate into a full-blown uprising. In the months after the Great Strike, the city began construction on a long-debated armory to defend against its "dangerous classes," a term coined by New York reformer Charles Loring Brace in 1872. The first Junius Spencer Morgan, father of the young Pierpont Morgan, donated $500 to the effort—"a sure guarantee," he wrote, "for the future."[10]

Far from bringing a peaceable future, though, the building of the armory proved to be only the beginning of an era in which the city's great divides—between rich and poor, boss and worker, immigrant and native-born—seemed to be constantly on the verge of open warfare. "We are told every day that great social problems stand before us and demand a solution, and we are assailed by oracles, threats, and warnings in reference to those problems," Yale professor William Graham Sumner complained in 1883. Sumner concluded that no solution was necessary, that an unfettered economy would work itself out in good time. Many workingmen, however, sought more immediate action.[11]

In the wake of the rail strike, they began to flock to the Knights of Labor, whose vision of an artisans' republic, free of Wall Street tyranny, made it the fastest-growing labor organization of the age. Others, particularly German socialists, turned to more militant action, parading under the auspices of the Lehr-und-Wehr Verein (Education and Defense Society) with rifles acquired in the name of self-defense. Beginning in 1882, a new Central Labor Union (CLU) in New York sought to bring these divided wings together toward common ends. As one of its initial endeavors, the CLU staged the nation's first Labor Day parade on September 5, 1882, marching twenty thousand workers past city hall carrying placards calling for a return to the "Labor Republic" and the end of the "Money Monopoly."[12]

Arriving in this atmosphere of class tension, Most received less than a hero's welcome from the daily press. "His voice is pitched in a high key," the *Times* smirked, reviewing his first New York speech, "there are no modulations in its tones, and when he wishes to emphasize any particular sentiment he simply screeches and grows red in the face.... [He] reminds one of the boasting braggart who stands at a safe distance and calls other people hard names."[13]

Still, in New York, Most *could* speak—a fact of no small value to a man accustomed to jail cells and police harassment as the price of advocating revolution. Despite its stirrings of class conflict, New York in the 1880s was a place of relative tolerance, free of the speech laws and political policing that were increasingly the norm in Europe. Partly as a result, it contained a flourishing revolutionary community. New York was one of the few American cities where reform-minded socialists could battle with revolutionary anarchists, who in turn could struggle against devoted Marxists. Like Most, many of these men and women had arrived as political refugees, fleeing certain jail time, even death sentences, awaiting them in Europe. They found, if not a vigorous embrace, at least a grudging sort of home. When Most arrived in 1882, revolutionaries throughout the world viewed New York as a sanctuary, the kind of city where agitation would be protected against the worst forms of European despotism.

Among the left-wing sects that took root in the city during these years was the tiny but militant Social Revolutionary Club, founded in 1880 and modeled on the anarchists of Europe. Before Most's arrival, the club was ill-defined and diffuse, composed mainly of German immigrants scattered throughout the major American cities. Its greatest achievement had been attending a national congress of social revolutionary groups held in Chicago in October 1881, where twenty-one delegates affirmed their commitment to ending the tyranny of private property through a direct, revolutionary confrontation with the "Money Kings." They also endorsed assassination and "armed organizations of workingmen who stand ready to resist, gun in hand, any encroachments upon their rights." It was this group that invited Most to join them in New York.[14]

Settling first on the Bowery, then in an East Side rooming house, Most wasted little time in attempting to make U.S. rulers feel as threatened as the kings and queens of Europe. "Yes, tremble, ye canaille, ye bloodsuckers, ye ravishers of maidens, ye murderers and hangmen," he warned.

The day of reckoning and revenge is near. The fight has begun along the picket line. A girdle of dynamite encircles the world, not only the *old* but the *new*. The bloody band of tyrants are dancing on the surface of a volcano. There is dynamite in England, France, Germany, Russia, Italy, Spain, New York, and Canada.

Even as he linked the European and American struggles, though, Most made a sincere effort to tailor his message to his new American audience. After a rousing tour of U.S. cities, he returned to New York and reestablished *Die Freiheit*, the fire-breathing German-language paper that had gotten him into so much trouble abroad. In its pages, he described his hopes for an end to racial discrimination and hierarchy, for a society of communal ownership and cooperation. He also advocated the abolition of the wage system, the great "social monster" that kept mankind yoked to a cycle of starvation and overwork. He had little faith, though, that such a world could come about through reform of the existing system. "This monster cannot be tamed, nor be made harmless or useful to man;" he insisted to his new American readers. "[T]here is but one means of safety: unrelenting, pitiless, thorough war of extermination!"[15]

Most ran *Die Freiheit* out of a ramshackle office on William Street, just a few blocks removed from the financial district. While he maintained no great affection for the policemen and government officials who had hounded him in Europe, his new Wall Street neighbors came in for his greatest wrath in his adopted home. Most viewed the American plutocracy, with its massive fortunes and lack of accountability, as a far more dangerous class than European royalty. "In America the place of the monarchs is filled by monopolists," he wrote. "The *sovereignty of the people* falls prostrate into the dust before the influence of these money kings, railroad magnates, coal barons and factory lords."[16]

He offered a ready solution for this problem: propaganda by deed. Most's brand of terrorism was not a prescription for mass murder. Rather, he called for targeted attacks on the representatives of capitalism and government, to be undertaken at moments of repression or conflict when public opinion might be sympathetic. Properly carried out, he believed, such acts would inspire others to follow suit, creating a cascade of small revolts that might culminate in revolution. For Most the message accompanying the *attentat* was at least as significant as the deed itself. "We have said a hundred times or more that when modern revolutionaries carry out actions, what is important is not solely these actions themselves but also the propagandistic effect they are able to achieve," *Die Freiheit* instructed its German-speaking readers. "Hence, we preach not only action in and for itself, but also action as propaganda."[17]

All in all, it was a dark, brooding vision of class conflict as a literal war to the death. It was also a vision that resonated with thousands of committed revolutionaries, mostly German immigrants, schooled in the day-to-day experience of low wages and state brutality. As early as 1883, Most secured a central role within the American anarchist movement by helping to compose the Pittsburgh Manifesto (officially titled "To the Workingmen of America"), the founding document of the new International Working People's Association, successor to the social revolutionary clubs. The following year, he took a job under a false name at an explosives factory in Jersey City. Based on this new expertise, he issued a pamphlet with the unwieldy title *Science of Revolutionary Warfare: A Handbook of Instruction Regarding the Use and Manufacture of Nitroglycerine, Dynamite, Gun-Cotton, Fulminating Mercury, Bombs, Arsons, Poisons, Etc.* As the title suggested, the booklet offered technical advice for acquiring and detonating explosives (Most recommended theft rather than amateur manufacture). It also presented detailed suggestions for matching particular weapons to specific acts. Blowing up "small-to-medium structures," for instance, required about ten pounds of dynamite. Destroying "larger and more massive structures (such as palaces, churches, permanent military structures, law courts, etc.)" demanded forty to fifty pounds, strategically placed.[18]

As in Europe, this open advocacy of violence soon attracted the attention of state authorities. "[I]t should be remembered that destructive explosives are easily made," Secretary of War Philip Sheridan warned Congress as early as 1884, "and that banks, United States subtreasuries, public buildings, and large mercantile houses can be readily demolished and the commerce of entire cities destroyed by infuriated people with means carried with perfect safety to themselves in the pockets of their clothing." For Most's first few years in New York, however, little effort was made to rein him in. In 1886, that began to change. On April 23, Most led a rally at Germania Gardens in New York, calling on hundreds of cheering workers to transform an impending national strike called by the Knights of Labor into a violent revolution. "Buy these," he shouted, brandishing a rifle, "steal revolvers, make bombs, and when you have enough, rise and seize what is yours."

This was not dramatically different from anything he had been saying in *Die Freiheit*. Coming on the eve of the strike (scheduled for May 1), however, it brought Most a grand jury indictment. Rather than submit quietly, Most decided to hide from the police. As a result, he was nowhere to be found on May 4, when the "actual stuff" entered American politics in earnest.[19]

THE HAYMARKET AFFAIR began with a series of confrontations rather than a single bloody event. On May 1, heeding the Knights' call for a walkout in favor of the eight-hour day, some 350,000 workers left their jobs nationwide. In Chicago, where concerns about "distrust, dissatisfaction, discontent" had haunted employers for years, the numbers were somewhere between 40,000 and 60,000—enough to cause the city's leaders to expect, in the words of police inspector John Bonfield, "a great deal of trouble." There, too, the May Day events happened to coincide with a long-standing strike at the famed McCormick Harvester works, where Cyrus McCormick Jr., heir to his father's industrial fortune, had recently locked out his workforce rather than agree to hire only union men. On May 3, frustrated after months of stalemate, two hundred locked-out workers descended on strikebreakers leaving the McCormick works. Chicago policemen, their nerves on edge due to the demonstrations sweeping the city, followed to beat back the offending strikers. They carried pistols as well and began to fire, killing six workers and wounding many more.

The following evening, a small crowd of anarchists and strikers gathered in the Haymarket at Randolph and Desplaines streets, usually the site of fruit stands and peddlers' carts, to protest the deaths and affirm their support for the eight-hour goal. The meeting had begun to disperse—it was rainy, chilly, and dark—when protesters observed a column of blue-coated policemen moving toward the square. "I command you in the name of the people of the state of Illinois to immediately and peaceably disperse," Inspector Bonfield instructed. What happened after that was never entirely clear. Anarchist Samuel Fielden, according to his own account, cried from his perch on a hay wagon in front of the crowd, "But we are peaceable." Later, some patrolmen claimed they heard, "Here come the bloodhounds. You do your duty and I'll do mine." Next, all agreed, came the bomb—a hiss and an orange blur—tossed from some never-determined distance.

As the bomb detonated, sending metal bursting through their ranks, the policemen began to shoot into the crowd. Some of the protesters, aware of the events at McCormick and well armed in self-defense, fired back. At least three demonstrators died in the crossfire, with about three dozen others shot and injured. The toll for the police was far heavier. By the next morning, seven policemen lay dead, with approximately sixty injured, some by the bomb, some by friendly fire, some by the protesters' guns. Their deaths, not those of the strikers or demonstrators, became the focus of the ensuing investigation.[20]

From the beginning, Americans viewed the events at Haymarket as the inevitable product of Most's agitation. "The villainous teachings of the Anarchists bore bloody fruit in Chicago tonight," the *New York Times* wrote on May 5, "and before daylight at least a dozen [*sic*] stalwart policemen will have laid down their lives as a tribute to the doctrine of Herr Johann Most." While the bombing seemed easy to categorize, however, it also posed urgent new questions about how such an act ought to be addressed. In Europe, bombings and assassinations often provoked swift repression; the German antisocialist laws were only the most extreme examples of a more general trend. Within the United States, this sort of broad, draconian assault had frequently been condemned as a symptom of European tyranny, a trampling of free speech utterly at odds with the American republican tradition. In May 1886, however, faced for the first time with a major instance of "dynamite" on their own soil, many Americans turned to the European example with new interest and sympathy. Within two days of the Haymarket bombing, Chicago police raided more than fifty meeting places associated with anarchism and labor: publication offices, lecture halls, schools, even private homes. Where strikers gathered, the police moved in with clubs and revolvers as well. ("The police enjoy the situation," cheered the *Times*. "They feel that the public is on their side and handle their clubs with a vim they lacked a week ago.") The effect on the tenor of the city was dramatic. In contrast to the demonstrations, parades, protests, and marches of early May, silence suddenly reigned. By the end of the week, the Knights' nationwide walkout, declared in its earliest days to be a ringing triumph for labor, collapsed in a spasm of recrimination and fear.[21]

All of this, however, merely set the stage for the justice meted out in court, the crux of the Haymarket Affair. On May 27, three weeks after the bombing, an Illinois grand jury issued indictments against ten of the city's anarchist and socialist leaders. By the end of the following month, eight of them—August Spies, Michael Schwab, Louis Lingg, Albert Parsons, Oscar Neebe, George Engel, Adolph Fischer, and Samuel Fielden— were on trial for murder.

None of the men was ever accused of throwing the May 4 bomb. The state's attorney, Julius Sprague Grinnell, put them on trial for what they said and believed—for their desire, in his words, "to strike terror to the hearts of the capitalists and their minions" through talk of dynamite and revolution. These accusations, as far as they went, were true, and not difficult to prove. With perhaps two exceptions, the defendants subscribed openly, often in writing, to Most's scorching view of anarchist vengeance. What made their trial so controversial—what gave it dramatic and lasting influence far beyond its moment—was the question of whether, and to what degree, they should be punished for that fact.[22]

Courtroom proceedings began on June 21, less than six weeks after the bombing and just two weeks since the grand jury's report that "the attack on the police of May 4 was the result of a deliberate conspiracy." All sides acknowledged that only two of the defendants were at Haymarket Square when the explosion took place. Indeed, the bomb thrower himself remained (and remains) unknown. According to Grinnell, however, such material questions were of little consequence to the matter at hand. "It is not necessary in this kind of case . . . that the individual who commits the particular offense—for instance, the man who threw the bomb—to be in court at all," he explained. "He need not even be indicted. The question for you to determine is, having ascertained that a murder was committed, not only who did it, but who is responsible for it, who abetted it, assisted it, or encouraged it?" In mid-August, after a two-month trial, the jury delivered its answer. Seven defendants would hang for their words, while Oscar Neebe would serve fifteen years in jail.[23]

In accepting the sentences, Judge Joseph E. Gary went out of his way to identify the verdict as an expression of Americans' natural resistance to the ideas of a man such as Johann Most. "The people of this country love their institutions. They love their homes. They love their property," he proclaimed. "They will never consent that by violence and murder their institutions shall be broken down, their homes despoiled and their property destroyed." Alongside this robust confidence, however, was a nagging concern that American traditions of free speech and open immigration made the country uniquely vulnerable to acts of revolutionary terror. Grinnell suggested as much to the jury in his closing statement. "[I]n this country, above all countries in the world, is Anarchy possible," he warned. "In those strong European governments, where there is monarchical or strongly centralized government, they strangle Anarchy or ship it here."[24]

If anarchy had a future in America, though, it came as little comfort to the defendants, who began to prepare in the fall of 1886 to meet their deaths as martyrs. Schooled in Most's dictum that propaganda was as important as action, they endeavored to shape the meaning of their executions, to live up to the role that had been thrust upon them. Albert Parsons, a former abolitionist and the only American-born defendant, emerged as the most outspoken of the condemned men. While he remained unapologetic about his commitment to revolution and the *attentat*, Parsons insisted that the verdict was a tragedy for the country of his birth, a reversal of the very revolutionary traditions that had once distinguished the United States from Europe. "[Y]our Honor," he informed Gary in a phrase that would resonate with generations of admirers to follow, "I hold that our execution, as the matter stands now, would be judicial murder."

The state was unmoved. On November 10, 1887, Illinois governor Richard Oglesby commuted the sentences of Fielden and Schwab, who renounced violence and pleaded for their lives in passionate appeals. The other defendants he ordered to hang as planned the following day. Louis Lingg, the youngest and most militant, managed to deny Illinois its desire; he set off a dynamite cap in his mouth and bled to death in jail. On November 11, the remaining four men made their way down the corridors of Cook County Jail to the gallows. Clad in white muslin shrouds, the uniform of execution, they looked like ghosts, men already gone. Indeed, their last words had already been said. Standing on the high wooden scaffold, a noose around his neck, a white hood and mask shielding spectators from his pain, Parsons began to deliver a muffled message. "O, men of America!" he began. "May I be allowed the privilege of speech even at the last moment? Harken to the voice of the people." Then the floor disappeared beneath his feet and the rope went taut.[25]

LATER, MANY AMERICANS looked back on the Haymarket Affair as "one of the strangest frenzies of fear that ever distracted a whole community," in the words of reformer and novelist Brand Whitlock, a temporary burst of insanity that lumped the guilty in with the innocent, defying logic and constitutional law. In the end, though, the strategies and principles forged in that moment proved to have enormous staying power, not only for Chicago but also for the nation as a whole. Over the next few decades, as the sort of violence first displayed at Haymarket evolved into a familiar fact of American life, the responses pioneered in 1886—raids, speech laws, immigration restriction, police crackdowns—gained new currency. While Haymarket spawned a cycle of reaction, it also gave birth to another interpretation thoroughly at odds with Judge Gary's triumphal declarations. For the generation of anarchists, socialists, and labor militants who came of age over the next few decades, Haymarket stood as the darkest example of an essentially reactionary American state, consumed by its own fears and prejudices. Among them was the woman who soon replaced both Most and Parsons as the figurehead of American anarchism, and whose example would loom large over the events of 1920: a young Russian immigrant named Emma Goldman.[26]

At the moment of the Chicago executions, Goldman was just eighteen years old, a factory girl living and toiling in Rochester, New York. Her family had arrived in the United States some two years earlier, part of the great wave of Jewish immigrants fleeing pogroms and stunted lives in the Russian Pale. Goldman recalled her childhood as a time of frustration and confinement, marred by an abusive father as well as by the expectations assigned a bourgeois Orthodox girl. Even in Russia, though, she had found herself intrigued by the sort of open, violent rebellion that would later define her American image. The Goldman family moved to St. Petersburg in late 1881, just months after Narodnaya Volya assassinated the czar. And though her mother denounced the assassins as "[c]old-blooded murderers" who ought to be "exterminated," the teenage Goldman was drawn to their example. Five years later, when the family made its way to the United States, she was primed to see her new home through the lens of a Russian revolutionary.

Like many immigrants, Goldman found day-to-day life in America rather more tedious than her family's talk "of hope, of freedom, of opportunity" had led her to expect. There was the grind of stitching clothes all day; compared to Russia, Rochester factories were clean and bright, but "the work here was harder, and the day...seemed endless." More importantly, there were the events unfolding in Judge Gary's Chicago courtroom, her first real impression of what justice looked like in America. Reading of the Haymarket bomb and trial in the Rochester papers, Goldman was struck by "[t]he violence of the press, the bitter denunciation of the accused, the attacks on all foreigners." As the execution approached, she grew yet more outraged, seeking out socialist meetings to mourn and fight with likeminded critics. On the night after the hangings, she over-heard a woman in her father's house praising the executioners. In response, Goldman tossed a pitcher of ice-cold water into the woman's face—"Out, out, or I will kill you!" she screamed. Then she collapsed to the ground, racked with sobs and howls.

"The next morning," she later wrote,

> I woke as from a long illness, but free from the numbness and the depression of those harrowing weeks of waiting, ending with the final shock. I had a distinct sensation that something new and won-derful had been born in my soul. A great ideal, a burning faith, a determination to dedicate myself to the memory of my martyred comrades, to make their cause my own, to make known to the world their beautiful lives and heroic deaths.

In that moment, she later claimed, she decided to leave her husband, her parents, and her sisters to begin life anew as a revolutionary anarchist. "My mind was made up," she wrote in her autobiography. "I would go to New York, to Johann Most."[27]

When Goldman arrived in New York on the stifling late-summer afternoon of August 15, 1889, the city before her was far more hostile than the one Most had encountered some seven years earlier. In New York, as in Chicago, Haymarket had brought a wave of repression against anarchists and revolutionaries of all stripes. Immigrant neighborhoods in Jersey City Heights and Newark, New Jersey, as well as on Manhattan's Lower East Side, had been raided and upended. The reformer Henry George, running for mayor in 1886 on a single-tax platform, found him-self denounced as a communist and dynamiter—tainted, by virtue of his observation that "the association of poverty with progress is the great enigma of our times," with too much sympathy for the likes of Johann Most. Most himself had served almost a year in prison for his speech at Germania Gardens. After the Haymarket executions, he had been arrested yet again. On November 11, 1887, a date soon enshrined in anarchist lore, he vowed publicly to retaliate for the martyrs' deaths with an *attentat* against their executioner. For his trouble, he earned another year at the New York City prison on Blackwell's Island.[28]

The trade union movement, too, found itself reeling in the months after Haymarket. Before 1886, New York labor circles had been fluid, hardly circles at all. "In the early days," recalled future union leader Samuel Gompers, then a cigar roller on the Lower East Side, "the cause of labor was a free forum in which all participated who had a thought to contribute." In the wake of the Chicago bombing—a "catastrophe," in Gompers' view, that "halted our eight-hour program"—many union leaders began to argue that labor could no longer afford its revolutionaries, that it would have to draw a clear line between conservative union men and agitators such as Most and Parsons. Within months of the bombing, Gompers helped to found the tiny American Federation of Labor (AFL), which outlined a "pure and simple" path for labor by rejecting socialism, anarchism, and revolution in all its forms. By 1889, when Goldman arrived in New York, he had emerged as one of labor's few national spokesmen, urging scattered craft unions to join forces for common gain. Even as he called for unity, though, he built divides that would last for decades: between reform and revolution, between craft and industrial unions, between "American" visionaries such as the men of the AFL and foreign revolutionaries such as Johann Most.[29]

To Goldman, arriving alone and penniless in New York at the age of twenty, none of this was a deterrent, at least at first. The city seemed to vibrate with energy and possibility—a "new world..., strange and terrifying." On Goldman's first day in town, her sole anarchist acquaintance escorted her to Sachs' café on the Lower East Side's Suffolk Street, a famous gathering spot for the city's revolutionaries. There she found anarchists and socialists, poets and intellectuals ("Everybody forgathers here," her friend explained). She was struck by the sheer volume of the Yiddish and Russian conversations under way in the café's two packed rooms. Loudest of all was a thin young man who, in a boorish display of gluttony, hollered above the crowd for an "extra-large steak! Extra cup of coffee!"

His name, she learned, was Alexander Berkman. Eventually he would be her lover and greatest political ally, as well as one of the most notorious self-proclaimed terrorists in the United States. That August, though, he was "no more than a boy," just twenty-one years old, like Goldman a recent Jewish immigrant from Russia. Later that night, in their first joint act, Goldman and Berkman attended a lecture by Most, who delivered "a passionate tirade against those responsible for the Haymarket tragedy" as well as "a scorching denunciation of American conditions." The following day, Goldman appeared at the offices of *Die Freiheit* to petition for Most's wisdom and guidance.[30]

She made an unlikely revolutionary: "[a] little bit of a girl, just 5 feet high, including her bootheels, not showing her 120 pounds," in the description of journalist Nellie Bly, "with a saucy, turned-up nose and very expressive blue-gray eyes that gazed inquiringly at me through shell-rimmed glasses." Under Most's tutelage, she soon developed into one of the nation's leading anarchists, an impassioned orator and provocateur. During that first critical year in New York, Most taught her the principles of anarchism, pushing her to speak in public and to act as his disciple. Like Berkman, he became her lover as well. "I could have denied him nothing," Goldman recalled.

She soon grew disillusioned. Like many revolutionaries, Goldman found herself caught up in factional disputes, opposed to Most on issues ranging from the eight-hour day to the proper methods of anarchist agitation. As a woman, she expanded her views of liberation to include birth control, sexual freedom, and defiance of the restrictions of marriage. But in those first learning days, she was Most's faithful pupil, studying and absorbing his ideas about everything from opera and high art to the necessity of the *attentat*. Indeed, she arrived on his doorstep already persuaded that dynamite held the key to a revolutionary future.

On her first evening in New York, leaving Sachs' to seek a cool breeze and some relief from the August heat, she and Berkman strolled south through Manhattan to the Battery. There, she later recalled, while gazing out over the placid blue harbor and its new Statue of Liberty, they traded stories of their childhoods in Russia, their journeys to America, and especially their deep admiration for the Chicago martyrs.

"Lingg was right when he said: 'If you attack us with cannon, we will reply with dynamite,'" Berkman told her, quoting the Haymarket anarchist Louis Lingg. "Some day I will avenge our dead."

"'I too! I too!'" Goldman replied, according to her autobiography; "their death gave me life."

From there, they plunged together into the world of militant anarchism, awaiting an opportunity to fulfill Lingg's mandate. That chance came less than three years later, in July 1892, when they read of a great labor conflict stirring in the Pennsylvania steel town of Homestead.[31]

GOLDMAN AND BERKMAN were busy running a little ice cream parlor in Worcester, Massachusetts, when the Homestead strike erupted. While the trappings of their life were laughably conventional, its purpose was not.

Observing a new round of czarist atrocities in Russia, they had concluded that their true revolutionary calling lay in the land of their youth. They hoped to use the shop to raise money for passage overseas. Business was slow in the chillier months, when hankerings for ice cream were more subdued, but by the summer the little parlor was turning a profit. Then came the news from Homestead.

Goldman later described the headlines of July 1892—"Strikers Evicted from Company Housing," "Woman in Confinement Carried to Street"— as a tangible, physical blow. They "inflamed my mind," she wrote. "Indignation swept my whole being." Three years earlier, the Amalgamated Association of Iron and Steel Workers had won a hard-fought contract improving wages and hours at the Carnegie Steel Company's plant in Homestead, Pennsylvania. In the spring of 1892, with the contract poised to expire, the company announced it would no longer bargain with the union, offering a take-it-or-leave-it 18-percent wage cut. Then, in a coup de grace on July 2, Henry Clay Frick, manager of the steel works (and later a close ally of Pierpont Morgan's), abruptly fired all remaining union men, locking them out until they agreed to return under conditions to be determined by company fiat.[32]

By the time Goldman and Berkman began to pay attention, Homestead was a fortress city, its roads under military blockade, its railroad depot heavily guarded, the steel plant itself barricaded behind a twelve-foot-high fence. Despite this, the entire workforce, union members and not, amassed for battle. To Goldman and Berkman, this picture of solidarity appeared unprecedented. "This is, at last, what I have always hoped for from the American workingman," Berkman later wrote, recalling the thrill of those first moments: "once aroused, he will brook no interference; he will fight all obstacles, and conquer even more than his original demands." They made immediate plans to abandon the ice cream parlor and join the revolution in Pennsylvania.[33]

After a furious night of scooping and cleaning, cooking and serving, they handed off the shop keys to their landlord ("He replied that we were mad," Goldman recalled) and boarded a southbound train for New York. Initially, they planned to spend a few days in the city composing, then translating, a German-language manifesto urging the strikers to "throw off the yoke of capitalism." Events, however, interfered. On July 6, Frick dispatched three hundred Pinkerton guards on a barge up the Monongahela River to crush the strikers' resistance.

When the Pinkertons arrived at Homestead, the steelworkers fought them off with guns and explosives, hurling dynamite, cannonballs, and fireworks toward the trapped ship. By the following morning, nine strikers and seven Pinkertons lay dead. Reading the news from New York, Berkman and Goldman concluded that the "time for speech was past." They saw in the rising conflict at Homestead the perfect setting for the sort of dramatic act Most had so long prescribed as the spark for revolution—"the psychological moment," in Goldman's words, "for an *Attentat*."[34]

The details of what followed—who acquired the weapons, who provided shelter and money and information—were never made public. Though Berkman played the starring role, many others, Goldman included, helped to plan his act. Berkman later recalled that he was prepared, even eager, for martyrdom. "I am simply a revolutionist, a terrorist by conviction," he wrote in his memoir, published twenty years later, "an instrument for furthering the cause of humanity." His first weapon, a small dynamite bomb built according to Most's handbook, sputtered and died when tested on a secluded Staten Island beach. Next, Berkman selected a revolver, adding a poisoned dagger as support. He took the train to Pittsburgh alone, assured that Goldman remained in New York to proselytize his deed.

Arriving in mid-July, Berkman found his rage at the capitalist system enhanced by the dismal landscape before him. "In the distance, giant furnaces vomit pillars of fire, the lurid flashes accentuating lines of frame structures, dilapidated and miserable," he later wrote. "They are the homes of the workers who have created the industrial glory of Pittsburgh, reared its millionaires, its Carnegies and Fricks." Against this backdrop of a capitalist hell, he took the final steps to carry out his mission. On the afternoon of July 22, he entered Frick's office, pushed his way past the "colored attendant," and raised his gun. Before shooting, he began to call Frick's name, but stopped short at the "look of terror" on the victim's face.

The first bullet hit Frick, the second went astray, and the third round failed to fire. "Something heavy" struck Berkman on the back of the head. Finally, Berkman made a lunge to stab Frick in the thigh before a struggle with the office staff ensued. When the police finally arrived to take him to jail, Berkman admitted that he had set out to kill the "tyrant" of Homestead.[35]

In his memoir, Berkman proudly labeled his *attentat* "the first terrorist act in America." This was meant as no slight against the Haymarket
anarchists. But precisely because they had protested their innocence, precisely because they had been railroaded to their deaths, the whole affair, in
Berkman's view, "lacked the element of voluntary Anarchist self-sacrifice"
so crucial to an effective act of propaganda by deed. Only if an *attentat*
was claimed forthrightly, openly announced as a vital blow against an
oppressor, could it have its desired effects: illustrating the evils of capitalism, inspiring others, and putting the rich on notice that they, too, were
vulnerable.[36]

He envisioned his act as a test of sorts, a measure of how the American
public would respond to this sort of "European" class violence, undertaken in full deliberation, with no attempt to apologize or deceive.
Things did not go as planned. As a practical matter, Berkman was pain-
fully ill-equipped to shape his act's meaning before an American court.
He did not speak English, he was not a citizen, and aside from a few
anarchist acquaintances, he did not know a soul in Pennsylvania. Nor
did the strikers of Homestead rush to his support. Far from embrac-
ing him as a martyr, the labor movement scrambled to distance itself.
Even Most rejected his deed as so much misguided violence, destined
to revive the prejudices of Haymarket. He wrote in the late summer of 1892, "Americans have never heard anything good about the
Anarchists—now suddenly all the nonsense was revived which their
press had been funneling into their indecently long ears—especially
since 1886."[37]

To Goldman, these claims smacked of hypocrisy. "Most is a most contemptible coward, a liar, a dissimulator and at the same time a washrag,"
she responded in *Der Anarchist* in July. Later that year, as Most spoke
before a crowd of well-wishers, she strode onto the platform, brandished
a horsewhip, and lashed him across the face and neck, the definitive break
from a man she had once viewed as an "idol" and teacher. Outside of
anarchist circles, though, Goldman found herself powerless to shape the
meaning of Berkman's act. As planned, she kept the larger scope of the
plot secret, and her few, scattered speeches and essays supporting the deed
had little effect. Like Berkman, she watched helplessly as their grand revolutionary plan collapsed.[38]

In late July, the Homestead strikers—now tainted, like the eight-
hour movement, with the tag of anarchy—petitioned to return to work

on Carnegie Steel's terms. Berkman's trial two months later was an even greater disappointment. He refused to hire a lawyer ("an extraordinary phenomenon like an *Attentat* cannot be measured by the narrow standards of legality," he explained). Instead, he attempted through a court-appointed translator to redeem the Haymarket legacy, to deliver the glorious tirade against capital for which he had sacrificed so much. "The injustice of the ruling classes is to blame for this," he told the court. "I belong to those who were murdered at Chicago."[39]

The judge cut him off after an hour. In even less time, the jury declared him guilty of felonious assault, unlawfully carrying concealed weapons, and feloniously entering the Carnegie offices. The sentence was twenty-two years: one in a workhouse and twenty-one in the penitentiary. This, however, was not the worst indignity. Weeks earlier, Berkman learned that Henry Frick had survived his wounds, not much the worse for wear. By September, Frick was back in charge of Carnegie Steel.[40]

OVER THE NEXT SEVERAL YEARS, there were no further *attentat*s in the United States: no bombings or assassinations, no poisoned daggers aimed at the minions of capital. But something curious happened. Rather than disappearing from the national consciousness, the "anarchist threat" emerged in the 1890s as a dull, insistent problem, a constant reminder of the fragility of the modern world. As Berkman moldered in jail, composing anxious letters to "the Girl" (his jailhouse name for Goldman), Congress took up the first serious attempts to bar anarchists from entering the country and to make attacks on government property and representatives into federal crimes.[41]

What precipitated this alarm was in part the news from Europe. Far from being an isolated act, from a global perspective Berkman's attack on Frick had been one of the first ripples in a wave of bombings and assassinations "seldom equaled," as one U.S. magazine exclaimed, "in the history of modern civilization." In 1892 and 1893, Spain alone witnessed three major terrorist attacks, including a bomb tossed callously into a crowded Madrid theater, killing twenty and wounding hundreds. France, too, saw rising violence, with eleven major bombings at cafés, theaters, and even the national legislature between 1892 and 1894. There, the attacks fed on each other in a dismal cycle of state repression and revolutionary revenge. When the Italian anarchist Sante Caserio shot and killed French president Sadi Carnot in June 1894, for instance, he explained that Carnot was killed in retaliation for the execution of Auguste Vaillant, who had thrown a bomb into the Chamber of Deputies the previous year.[42]

As a model of a brutally successful *attentat*, the Carnot assassination struck a chord with American legislators. On the day after the assassination, Congress announced a day of rest in the French president's honor. In the weeks that followed, newspapers across the country appealed for more deliberate action. "Society must protect itself against the malignants," warned the *Chicago Tribune*, "or no one will be safe." By far their greatest worry was not what should be done about anarchists already on U.S. soil but how the United States might prevent such people from arriving in the first place. With repressive policies once again flaring up across Europe, federal officials warned of a new influx of terrorist refugees. "[N]early all the principal European countries are now legislating against this class of people," explained New York senator David Hill, "and if they are not excluded from the United States this country will soon be the dumping ground of the anarchists of the world." In August 1894, for the first time since Haymarket, Congress took up serious consideration of a ban on immigration by anarchists, self-proclaimed or otherwise.[43]

The debate over the ban revealed a persistent, grandiose image of anarchism as a powerful "menace to our institutions and danger to our people," in the words of Treasury Secretary John G. Carlisle. But it also showed a genuine hesitation among many legislators over the prospect of stepping away from American traditions of open immigration and free speech. "I do not like the idea of a conviction based upon mere abstract beliefs when there is no overt act," explained Illinois senator John Palmer. "I suggest, therefore, that this measure is in the spirit of our fears rather than in the exercise of wise political judgment."[44]

This skepticism extended to Chicago, where the Haymarket executions remained a pressing source of controversy well into the 1890s. On June 25, 1893, the anarchist-run Pioneer Aid and Support Association unveiled a grand bronze monument in Chicago's Waldheim Cemetery to honor the men executed for the Haymarket bomb. The following morning, after months of hesitation, Illinois governor John P. Altgeld announced that he would pardon the remaining three Haymarket defendants. In his written explanation, Altgeld insisted, "The soil of America is not adopted to the growth of Anarchy." He concluded, nonetheless, that whoever threw the bomb on May 4 had been provoked by police aggression. "Capt. Bonfield," he wrote, "is the man who is really responsible for the deaths of the police officers."[45]

Many anarchists (Goldman included) seized upon his words as a beacon of hope, official acknowledgment that the Haymarket defendants, and by extension all revolutionaries, were something more than a gang of cutthroat murderers. Despite the rise in antianarchist sentiment among legislators, many revolutionaries saw reasons for optimism as the 1890s wore on. In the spring of 1893, a new banking crash had plunged the United States into yet another depression. Out of this crisis arose dramatic new political movements—most notably the populist insurgency in the West—offering their own criticism of Wall Street as a bastion of greed, inequality, and autocracy.[46]

In the cities of the East, the depression crisis led to a similar surge in popular protest, as 20 percent unemployment translated into daily misery and insecurity. The numbers told a grim story in New York: 70,000 men and women out of work, 607 infants dead in city tenements in a single sweltering July week. In this desperate context, Goldman found that the notoriety she had achieved after Berkman's *attentat* (the papers described her as Berkman's "wife," their home as "an abiding place of bloodthirsty dynamiters") was suddenly a great political asset. In the turmoil of the early 1890s she offered a potent symbol of rage against groups such as the patronizing Committee of Prominent and Wealthy Citizens, organized by Pierpont Morgan to dole out alms to the poor. When Goldman proffered her own response to the crisis, helping to plan a rally at Union Square in late August, more than five thousand city residents turned out to show their support. "Demonstrate before the palaces of the rich; demand work," she urged in German. "If they do not give you work, demand bread. If they deny you both, take bread. It is your sacred right."[47]

That speech earned Goldman her first jail sentence; like Most in the days before Haymarket, she was charged with inciting to riot. The arrest also helped to make her a martyr for the cause of free speech. When she went to trial, she was represented by former New York mayor Oakey Hall, who objected to her politics but admired her bravery. Upon her release a year later, three thousand supporters greeted her with "vives," "vivas," "hochs," "bravas," and "bravos."[48]

All of this provoked alarm in the city's social and financial elites, who discovered that they could not ignore the anarchist movement, despite its small numbers. In 1897, for instance, when New York heiress Cornelia Martin planned a grand ball, re-creating Louis XIV's Versailles in the Waldorf Hotel, she hired detectives to stand watch for fear that "thieves or men of socialistic tendencies" might be inclined to disrupt the proceedings with bombs. In Europe itself, where royalty was no game, the drumbeat of assassination continued through the late 1890s: in 1897, Spanish premier Antonio Cánovas del Castillo; in 1898, Empress Elizabeth of Austria; in 1900, King Umberto of Italy. This last act caused a minor panic within the United States. The man who killed Umberto, a young anarchist named Gaetano Bresci, had lived in Paterson, New Jersey, for six years; he bought his revolver in Paterson and conducted target practice in Weehawken, New Jersey, before traveling to London, then Paris, and finally Italy to carry out his deed. What, many wondered, would have transpired if he had decided to remain in the United States? "The question has been many times asked since Humbert's assassination whether our own Government is in danger," journalist Francis Nichols wrote in August 1901, "and whether the President of the United States is regarded...as belonging to the same category with the rulers of Europe."[49]

The answer was not long in coming. On September 6, 1901, a self-proclaimed anarchist named Leon Czolgosz shot President William McKinley—once in the stomach, once in the chest—during a handshake session at the Pan-American Exposition in Buffalo, New York. When asked why he had done the deed, Czolgosz explained, "I shot the President because I thought it would help the working people, and for the sake of the common people." His inspiration, he added, came from a lecture he had attended in May. The speaker was Emma Goldman.[50]

IF MOST'S ARRIVAL launched concerns about "dynamite" in American politics, the McKinley assassination made them permanent. McKinley was not just the national figurehead. He was the great political champion of the financial and industrial system that had been built up since the Civil War—"a supple and highly paid agent," in Henry Adams' sneering words, "of the crudest capitalism." McKinley had come to office by defeating populist William Jennings Bryan, champion of free silver and the beleaguered farmer/worker coalition of the West. Pierpont Morgan himself had entertained McKinley on board the *Corsair II*, pledging a quarter of a million dollars to his campaign and outfitting 23 Wall with McKinley banners. With the gunshots of September 6, as Goldman commented, not only McKinley but also this entire ethos seemed to be under assault. "Never before in the history of governments," she wrote, "has the sound of a pistol shot so startled, terrorized, and horrified the self-satisfied, indifferent, contented, and indolent public, as has the one fired by Leon Czolgosz when he struck down William McKinley, president of the money kings and trust magnates of this country."[51]

As in 1892, this sentiment won her no shortage of enemies. In contrast to the Homestead strike, however, when her support for Berkman appeared hopelessly out of touch, in 1901 Goldman's analysis offered a fair description of events. As the first lethal *attentat* since 1886, the assassination suggested that Haymarket was not an aberration, that the problems highlighted in that earlier moment—class conflict, anarchy, labor violence—had become ongoing features of American politics. In that sense, Czolgosz did what Berkman failed to do: commit an *attentat* that changed, at least for a moment, how Americans thought about the history and fate of their ruling class.

Goldman vaguely remembered meeting Czolgosz at her May lecture in Cleveland. He struck her as a nice enough boy, a "young man" with a "girlish face." She had been speaking on Gaetano Bresci and other anarchist *attentateurs*, lauding them as men of great courage and sensitivity. She had not directly urged others to rush out and commit their own acts of vengeance. Instead, she championed Bresci and the others in more passive ways, as the regrettable but inevitable product of an unjust social order and of what she would later describe as "the psychology of political violence."

Friends begged her to disappear. "It will be the same as with Albert Parsons," they warned. "You must let us get you over to Canada." Goldman, flirting with martyrdom, refused to go. Instead, as if deliberately evoking the memory of Haymarket, she made her way to Chicago, where several anarchists were already being held. Police found her posing as a maid at a friend's house. Eventually, after a lengthy grilling, they transferred her to the Cook County Jail, where Parson, Spies, Engel, and Fischer had been hanged some fifteen years earlier. For Goldman, the effect was both terrifying and affirming. "Strange, indeed, the complex forces that had bound me to those martyrs through all my socially conscious years!" she later wrote. "And now events were bringing me nearer and nearer—perhaps to a similar end?"[52]

As it turned out, she was not held for long. Chicago officials, perhaps fearing another Haymarket themselves, refused to extradite her to New York without evidence beyond a few provocative speeches. Still, the McKinley assassination lent a new urgency to the calls for drastic action against what appeared to be a growing terrorist threat. In New York, Most was arrested and sent to jail yet again. Throughout the city, there were calls for more violent action as well. "In most places mad dogs are killed," Jack Morgan wrote to a friend after the assassination, "& I don't see why anarchists should not be suppressed when they create rabies in the feeble minded who listen to them." On this matter at least, the new president, Theodore Roosevelt, unintentionally the chief beneficiary of Czolgosz's act, agreed wholeheartedly. "The harm done is so great as to excite our gravest apprehensions," he announced to Congress in his first annual message, "and to demand our wisest and most resolute action."[53]

Roosevelt's proposals for restraining anarchism reflected ideas that had been circulating since Haymarket. He argued, first, for the importance of restricting words as a way of preventing further deeds. "Anarchistic speeches, writings, and meetings are essentially seditious and treasonable," he declared. As acts of high national "treason," Roosevelt argued, they should be addressed by the federal government itself. This meant, in part, passing the immigration ban so long under discussion. "They and those like them should be kept out of this country," Roosevelt insisted. "No matter calls more urgently for the wisest thought of the Congress."[54]

He went further as well—into what the *Chicago Tribune* labeled an international "War on Anarchists." From the high position of moral authority granted him in the months after McKinley's death, he called for an international treaty to define anarchism as a global threat, one that could be extinguished only when the Old World agreed to stop sending its worst offenders overseas to the New. As after Haymarket, the call for such action was based at least in part on the idea that anarchists were, in Roosevelt's words, "not 'the product of social conditions'"—that there was nothing so problematic within the United States that such a deed could be justified. They were also an acknowledgment, at least implicitly, of the potency of the anarchist threat: of the idea that without concerted action, more men might be tempted to follow the lead of Leon Czolgosz.[55]

About Czolgosz himself, there was little question of what to do. After a lifetime of petty jobs, unemployment, and isolation, he played the martyr tolerably well. "McKinley was going around the country shouting about prosperity when there was no prosperity for the poor man," he told one physician who was examining him for proof of sanity. "I am not afraid to die." In late October, after a brief trial, the Buffalo authorities carried out his death sentence by electric chair, then dissolved his body in acid to prevent further inquiry.[56]

Czolgosz's trial was only a small part of the "resolute action," in Roosevelt's words, undertaken after the assassination attempt. Over the next few years, the restrictions born with Haymarket and debated throughout the 1890s began to make their way into law. In 1902, the New York state legislature passed a pioneering "criminal anarchy" statute, outlawing all expression, in either speech or writing, of the idea "that organized government should be overthrown by force or violence, or by assassination." The following year, acting on Roosevelt's advice, Congress passed an immigration law banning the entry of any "person who disbelieves in or who is opposed to all organized government...or who advocates or teaches the duty, necessity, or propriety of the unlawful assaulting or killing of any officer...of the Government of the United States" (prostitutes, paupers, and the mentally ill were also excluded). The law reflected an impression formed in the days after Johann Most's arrival: that anarchism was a foreign infection whose spread could be prevented by keeping immigrants from U.S. shores. But it also showed just how much had changed over the course of those two decades. For the first time in national history, the U.S. government declared that a particular ideology was by law un-American.[57]

To Goldman, the arrival of such laws seemed to signal a fundamental shift in American identity—a blow to the country's already battered reputation as a haven for the politically oppressed. "What other conclusion can be reached, or inference drawn, than that America is fast being Russianized," she wrote to Chicago friends in November 1902, "and that unless the American people awake from the pleasant dream into which they have been lulled by the strains of 'My Country 'tis of Thee,' etc., we shall soon be obliged to meet in cellars, or in darkened back rooms with closed doors, and speak in whispers lest our next door neighbors should hear that free-born American citizens dare not speak in the open?"[58]

Her suspicions were more right than she knew. By the time the Wall Street explosion erupted two decades later, both she and Berkman had been expelled from U.S. shores, condemned as bomb throwers and subversives. First, though, the "story of dynamite" took a dramatic turn. As the McKinley assassination faded into public memory, the nation's attention began to shift from the exotic world of foreign-born anarchists onto a thoroughly American miner and cowboy named "Big Bill" Haywood.

# 4

· · · ·

# AMERICAN ROUGHNECK

LIKE JOHANN MOST, Bill Haywood bore the marks of a hard early life. At the age of nine, while whittling a slingshot, he sent a knife through his right eye, leaving a murky, sightless hole. Like Most, too, he projected a magnetism far beyond his physical frame. Barely six feet tall, Haywood was routinely described, by friends and detractors alike, as a "giant," "with the physical strength of an ox."

There the similarities ended. Most was a European refugee; his radicalism was, at least in popular depiction, the province of the bearded, foreign-tongued city immigrant. Haywood was a son of Utah, Idaho, and Nevada, a proud "roughneck" and miner, rarely seen without his black Stetson hat and his cowboy swagger. By some accounts, this marked him as a true frontier legend, a rugged gunslinger along the lines of Wild Bill Hickok or Calamity Jane. But Haywood's tale of the West, as he informed countless audiences, was less an adventurer's romp than a catalogue of injustice. His was not the West of the homestead but that of brute-force industrial capitalism, in which mine owners and workers fought for control with guns, armies, and in some cases dynamite.

Haywood was never an open advocate of propaganda by deed. He did not write long essays extolling the virtues of dynamite, nor did he call for the assassination of the nation's leaders. What he brought to the fight against men like Pierpont Morgan was a much more straightforward class militancy, an assurance that when he and his followers talked of revolution they might well mean what they said. Haywood used many names to describe this brand of class warfare; he was a union man, a socialist, a syndicalist, and above all a "Wobbly," the nickname for those who joined the Industrial Workers of the World (IWW) and embraced its dream of "One Big Union." But like the anarchists to whom he was often compared, Haywood believed that the conditions spawned by American capitalism— the maimings and starvation in the mines, the unrelenting misery of factory life, and especially the brutality of policemen, soldiers, and guards—gave American workers the right, even the obligation, to arm themselves and fight back. Out of his early experiences in the hand-to-mouth world of western mining had come a commitment to the overthrow of the entire wretched system and the use of all necessary means to achieve it.

Haywood came of age at a time when Americans were ready to entertain the idea that they bore some responsibility for this state of affairs. To the members of the progressive movement that rose to power in the new century, the rise of the labor-dynamite problem seemed less a foreign importation than the symptom of a national sickness. Much to Haywood's benefit, they proposed to cure it not only through repression but also through a stiff dose of national soul-searching and industrial reform.

Haywood, in short, was a thoroughly "American" radical—or so his supporters, eager to dispel the Mostian stereotype, liked to say. Haywood played along. "I'm a two-gun man from the West, you know," he often told audiences, slipping his two "guns" from their pocket holsters. One was the red card of the Socialist Party, which was growing like "prairie fire," as the slogan went, in the early years of the new century. The second was the similarly crimson card of the IWW, which Haywood helped to found in 1905. Beginning with his arrest the following year, this mix of western bluster and industrial militancy thrust Haywood into the nation's most serious conflicts over the sort of violence—assassination, bombings—once seen as the sole province of genuine anarchists. In the process, he came to serve as the symbol of an increasingly radical, growing, and decidedly American labor movement whose fate was tied, more and more, to the national debate over the problem of "dynamite."

By 1920, when the greatest bomb attack of the age stunned his countrymen, he had earned himself the dubious honor that Most once held.

"[H]e was seen as the leader of the forces of disintegration," the *New York Times* later wrote, "the most hated and feared figure in America." Just the sort of man, many papers speculated, who might set out to bomb Wall Street.[1]

HAYWOOD WAS BORN in Salt Lake City to a family "so American," he would later recall with sneering pride, "that if traced back it would probably run to the Puritan bigots or the cavalier pirates." The Haywoods arrived in North America well before the Revolution. Like the nation itself, each generation moved further west. His mother's family made the journey from South Africa in 1850, following the gold rush. By 1869, the year of Bill's birth, the get-rich-quick promise of that decade had faded. He spent his childhood in a string of grim mining towns, where schooling was both stern and brief. By the time Haywood was nine, he had taken his first job underground. By the age of fifteen, mining had become his principal occupation.

Years later, Haywood wrote in disgust of the brutalities he witnessed during his early life in the mines: the long and filthy days all too often punctuated by reports of some poor fellow crushed beneath a slab of rock, or killed in a blasting accident when dynamite, that trade tool of all miners, misfired as it burst through solid earth. Aboveground, conditions were not much better. "The people of this mining camp breathed copper, ate copper, wore copper, and were thoroughly saturated with copper," he wrote of Butte, Montana, in the 1890s. "The smoke, fumes and dust penetrated everywhere and settled on everything. Many of the miners were suffering from rankling copper sores, caused by the poisonous water. . . . Human life was the cheapest by-product of this great copper camp."

As a young man, Haywood spent little time considering how any of this might be changed. Still, it was impossible to live in the West during those years without absorbing some sense of discontent. His coming-of-age years saw the rise of the Populist movement, with its aggressive stance toward the East Coast's capitalists and bankers. Haywood remembered running into Coxey's Army, a ragtag band of "tramps" on their way to Washington to demand jobs and bread under the leadership of populist Jacob Coxey. Most of all, he remembered hearing of the events of 1886 and 1887 in far-off Chicago, ending with the deaths of the anarchist martyrs. Like Goldman, he later identified the Haymarket executions as a moment of political awakening, "a turning point in my life."[2]

If Haywood shared Goldman's memory of Haymarket, his formal plunge into revolutionary politics was rather slower in the making. A true itinerant, he devoted his energies over the next decade to acquiring the trappings of western manhood: finding a wife, experimenting with drink, becoming a father, homesteading, cowboying, and, most of all, finding steady work in the mines. Then, on July 19, 1896, he caught his hand between an ore car and the mine shaft, nearly severing his fingers and making him, at least temporarily, unfit to work. While languishing in Silver City, Idaho, waiting for his hand to heal, he decided to attend a speech by Ed Boyce, president of a militant new union called the Western Federation of Miners.

Boyce was a tall, thin veteran miner whose most obvious feature was a set of protruding teeth, the result of disease contracted while working with quicksilver in a quartz mill. He was also a longtime union man, a survivor of, among other struggles, Idaho's Coeur d'Alene labor wars of 1892. While in prison as a result of the Coeur d'Alene battle, Boyce explained to the packed Silver City hall, he and several other miners decided "that all of the miners of the West should come together in one organization" to oppose the rule of distant capitalists and claim the mines for the men who worked them. They came up with the Western Federation of Miners (WFM).[3]

The federation's vision was not terribly different from that of any other union. Members wanted the eight-hour day, regular work, better wages, and an end to conditions that left men such as Haywood nursing bum hands. But for the leadership of the WFM these fights were only part of a greater struggle. From its inception, the WFM distinguished itself as a fighting revolutionary union. "They not only want socialism," progressive Ray Stannard Baker concluded in 1904, after the WFM had split with the conservative AFL, "but they want it this morning." The WFM was distinguished as well by its tactics. In echoes of calls heard in the streets of Chicago and New York a decade earlier, WFM leaders urged their members to arm in self-defense, to engage, if necessary, in a literal war against capital.

This was not just a theoretical stance. Violence in the western mining camps was a fact of everyday life. As a boy, Haywood witnessed two gunshot deaths, a dynamiting, and a near-lynching—all before his teenage years. Later, there was the violence of the mines themselves. Haywood never forgot what it was like to see a miner with "his entire face blown off," the victim of an underground blasting accident. Nor did he take well to the violence committed by the authorities, to the hundreds of armed guards and troops inevitably called in to quell discontent among miners in places such as Coeur d'Alene. In this environment, the WFM believed it was foolhardy *not* to take up the weapons at hand. As an alarmed Idaho editor commented in 1899, the early members of the WFM were "men who have received the training of a lifetime in the handling of dynamite."[4]

HAYWOOD'S WORK WITH THE WFM began with a decidedly unglamorous stint on the Local 66 finance committee. Within a few years, though, he had a chance to see the WFM's tactics and principles play out in far more dramatic fashion. The setting, once more, was the craggy, isolated mining district of Coeur d'Alene. By 1899, only one employer, Bunker Hill and Sullivan, had refused to recognize the WFM and to pay its standard wage of $3.50 per day. That year, it also introduced new power drills, making mining jobs both more dangerous and less plentiful. "It could be summed up as less food, less clothes, less house-room, less schooling for the children, less amusements, less everything that made life worth living," Haywood later wrote.[5]

In response, the federation launched a new campaign to force Bunker Hill and Sullivan to mend its ways. At first the miners found success: wages went to $3.50 almost immediately. But the company refused to recognize the union, firing seventeen federation men in a single day and summoning all others to the office for similar treatment. The WFM, recognizing a provocation, decided to raise the stakes. On April 29, some 250 federation members descended on a Northern Pacific freight train near Wardner, Idaho, overpowered the engineer and conductor, loaded the boxcars with some four thousand pounds of dynamite, and set off to get Bunker Hill and Sullivan's attention. Along the way, the train—eventually known as the "Dynamite Express"—gathered almost a thousand other men, many of them masked, almost all of them armed, each wearing a bit of white muslin around his right arm or in his buttonhole. At the town of Kellogg, they disembarked and piled the dynamite in a five-foot-high pyramid in the street. A few hours later, they transferred the load a final half mile to their target, placing sixty boxes beneath Bunker Hill and Sullivan's concentrator, a massive machine vital for grinding and washing raw metal ore. At 2:35, after clearing the premises, they lit the fuse, blowing the concentrator (estimated value: $250,000) into thousands of fragments.[6]

Hearing of the events from his hospital bed, where he was suffering from a case of the grippe, Idaho governor Frank Steunenberg issued an immediate appeal for federal troops. Within a few weeks, the soldiers had rounded up about a thousand miners—selected more for proximity than for evidence of guilt—and placed them in a makeshift "bull-pen," a crude ring of one-story wooden buildings. There they stayed, without lawyers and without charges, some for several months. From inside, they hung banners painted on sheets naming their jail the "American Bastille." Outside, all men not under arrest found themselves required to obtain a sheriff's permit before they would be allowed into the mine, creating in intent as well as effect an official blacklist.[7]

Haywood witnessed all of this from afar. He was living in Silver City at the time, working his way up to president of the WFM local. But no less than Haymarket, news of the backlash in Coeur d'Alene came to him with the force of revelation. "They were men of my own kin," he gushed. "They were fighting my fight." Among the most painful ironies was the fact that the WFM had supported Steunenberg, a well-known Populist, in his initial run for governor. Haywood concluded that the ballot was of limited use in labor's cause, a conviction that he held for the rest of his life. In June 1900, he joined five other state WFM leaders in a manifesto denouncing Steunenberg as an enemy of the working class. "Resolved...that we condemn such arbitrary action of the said governor of Idaho as a usurpation worthy of the tyrants of the Middle Ages," read the declaration, "and that such a man is unworthy of the respect and support of all liberty-loving people."[8]

Haywood left Idaho the following year, heading south to Denver, Colorado, to take up a post as the WFM's secretary-treasurer. There he threw himself into literal warfare on behalf of labor, helping to maintain the struggling WFM through bloody strikes in Telluride, Cripple Creek, and Colorado Springs. He also led the founding meeting of the militant new Industrial Workers of the World, opening its first convention in 1905 with the rousing declaration that "this is the Continental Congress of the Working Class." He was not, however, quite done with Idaho. On December 30, 1905, a bomb blew off Steunenberg's legs as he opened the front gate to his home, leaving the former governor bleeding to death in the snow. Two months later, Haywood found himself under arrest for the crime—accused of being the new American apostle of dynamite.[9]

74

HAYWOOD WAS at a Denver "rooming house" (detectives said it was really a brothel) when the deputy sheriff came for him on February 17, 1906. He remembered a knock, then a voice. "I want to see you, Bill," came the muffled sound. When he opened the door, just enough for a glance outside, he saw the deputy waiting, armed and patient, in the hallway. The man admitted he didn't have a warrant. But Haywood, well acquainted with the methods of the Denver police, knew better than to court a beating by resisting arrest. Arriving at the jail, which the locals had nicknamed the "Hotel Kalamath," he found WFM president Charles Moyer and former Coeur d'Alene striker George Pettibone behind bars. He also discovered the reason for all of their arrests. "They're going to take you to Idaho," a sympathetic sheriff informed him. "They've got you mixed up in the Steunenberg murder."

At five o'clock the next morning, after a brief carriage ride through the quiet, drowsy city, the Denver authorities deposited Haywood, Moyer, and Pettibone at the railroad depot. A straight shot to Idaho was impossible; between fuel, water, and crew changes, the train would have to stop no fewer than twenty-four times along the way. Thanks to the advance planning of the authorities, though, they made the trip in just twenty-seven hours and fifteen minutes. The three men arrived in the Boise jail's "death cells" by midday on February 19. "Here we were in murderers' row, in the penitentiary, arrested without warrant, extradited without warrant, and under the death watch!" Haywood later wrote. It would be another two days before he talked to his lawyer, and more than a year before he became one of the most celebrated defendants in American labor history. Already, though, the three men's arrest and extradition had acquired national infamy as the Haywood-Moyer-Pettibone kidnapping.[10]

The arrest of the WFM leadership signaled the arrival of dynamite as a potent factor in the struggle for union power and recognition. The mere fact of violence in labor battles was nothing new; the WFM record attested to that. Since the 1870s, American workers had frequently used dynamite to attack employers' property, planting explosives beneath rails during streetcar strikes or, like the WFM, blowing up key pieces of equipment during particularly fractious strikes. As Homestead suggested, workers often engaged in armed warfare with Pinkertons or state militiamen, usually but not exclusively when fired upon. Some unions experienced episodes of internal violence as well, brutality that came with enforcing member payments, dissuading "scabs," or holding on to what little power there was to go around.[11]

The accusations that burst forth against Haywood that February were different, however, less like the open warfare of the picket line than like the calculated assassination plots long associated with revolutionary anarchists. Perhaps the best precedent for this sort of clandestine labor violence was the Molly Maguires' campaign of the 1870s, when a group of Irish miners in western Pennsylvania had used "organized terrorism"— murder, sabotage, arson—against the Pennsylvania mine bosses before being infiltrated by the Pinkertons and, in 1877, hanged by the state. In all, the Mollys dynamited dozens of work sites, doled out numerous beatings, and killed sixteen men, mostly mine officials. For these crimes, twenty men went to their deaths by state execution.[12]

The detective who engineered Haywood's 1906 "kidnapping" was the same man who had infiltrated and exposed the Mollys three decades earlier, a Pinkerton operative named James McParland. He eagerly made the connection between the two campaigns, denouncing Haywood and the WFM as the Mollys reborn. Even McParland, though, saw something different, more dramatic, in the latest accusations. "[L]et me tell you that the most fiendish work carried on by the Maguires was but child's play compared to the plots hatched by the officers of the Western Federation of Miners," he informed the press in February. He vowed that Haywood, Moyer, and Pettibone would meet the same fate as the Mollys' leaders. "They will never leave the state of Idaho alive," McParland promised.[13]

This was the cry of the daily newspapers: Haywood, Moyer, and Pettibone were the Mollys reincarnated, only in more vicious and anarchistic form. In the radical and labor press, by contrast, a different historical example held sway. For the thousands of socialists, unionists, and reformers who rallied to the defense of Haywood, Moyer, and Pettibone, the great specter from the past was not the Molly Maguire trials but the Haymarket Affair. Here, once again, were the arrests of labor radicals, men who had made no secret of their militancy. Once again, they had been arrested for a crime in which not only their individual fates but also the reputation of organized labor seemed to hang in the balance. Once again, they were accused not of having directly committed the crime but of having aided and abetted it from afar. Not even McParland suggested that Haywood, Moyer, and Pettibone had been anywhere near Idaho in

December 1905. Nonetheless, like the Haymarket men, they would face the gallows if convicted.

The parallel was not exact. At Haymarket, the bomb thrower remained unknown to the end. In this case, a WFM member known as Harry Orchard (his real name was Albert Horsley) had already confessed not only to the Steunenberg murder but also to a gruesome string of dynamitings and assassinations carried out at the WFM's behest. And there was another important difference, too. In the two decades since Haymarket, both the moderate and revolutionary strains of the labor movement had become far more organized and influential than they were two decades earlier. This time, acutely aware of the lessons of Haymarket, they were determined not to see a repeat of 1886. "There have been twenty years of revolutionary education, agitation and organization since the Haymarket tragedy," Socialist Party leader Eugene Debs declared in March 1906, just days after Haywood's arrest, "and if an attempt is made to repeat it, there will be a revolution and I will do all in my power to precipitate it."[14]

Like Haywood, Debs was a member of the new American-born generation of radicals, converted to revolutionary politics not through European texts but through his direct experience battling American capitalists. He did not, however, point to the Haymarket Affair as the searing experience that had awakened him to socialism. For Debs, that moment had come in 1894, when he led the American Railway Union in a historic strike against the Pullman Car Company. After Pullman refused to negotiate with the strikers, Debs had called for a nationwide boycott against the company, informing the railroads that they should disconnect their Pullman cars or risk a strike. The boycott provided an excuse for federal troops to put down the strike; according to President Grover Cleveland, a nationwide walkout threatened the orderly distribution of the U.S. mail. It also earned Debs a jail sentence of six months on charges of conspiracy and contempt of court. The violence directed at the rail workers during the Pullman battle, he later wrote, made him a revolutionary: "in the gleam of every bayonet and in the flash of every rifle *the class struggle was revealed*."[15]

Debs exaggerated the suddenness of this conversion. He did not simply walk away from the life he had led before. Nonetheless, in the years after the Pullman strike, Debs emerged as one of the country's most outspoken socialist leaders: a vigorous, charismatic man whom his followers likened to everyone from John Brown to Christ. ("Lincoln was great;

Debs is greater," wrote one typical admirer. "Lincoln proclaimed that the black man should be free. Debs proclaims that all men shall be free.") Debs' bald pate, thin frame, and fondness for bow ties gave him the air of an affable Indiana gentleman. When he spoke before a crowd, though, every vein and fiber alive with righteous anger, there was no mistaking him for anything other than the revolutionary he was.[16]

In 1901, Debs had been a driving force behind the creation of the Socialist Party of America, organized to join the country's fractured left into a single mass movement. Four years later, he signed on as a founding member of the IWW, one of a handful of socialist leaders to attend Haywood's "Continental Congress." By 1906, both organizations were still small. Debs polled 420,000 votes in the 1904 presidential election, but Socialist Party membership was just 20,000, and the IWW was far smaller. In the same year as Haywood's arrest, the German sociologist Werner Sombart wrote an essay puzzling over the weak state of American socialism, particularly in electoral politics ("Why Is There No Socialism in the United States?" was the title). His conclusion—that Americans were simply too individualistic, too covetous of their roast beef and apple pie—echoed Judge Gary's tribute to the country's love of property at Chicago some twenty years earlier. But by 1906 there were signs that this vision of socialism as the refuge of "broken-down Germans without any following," in Sombart's words, was beginning to change.[17]

Faced with a growing disjuncture between rich and poor, between workers and the Money Trust, thousands of reformers, loosely joined in the new progressive movement, had begun to reject the "standpattism" of the nineteenth century in favor of child labor laws, antitrust regulation, and the eight-hour day. The labor movement had begun to make stunning gains as well, with the American Federation of Labor ballooning from 250,000 members in 1897 to some 2 million by 1904. Neither movement adopted the label "socialist." Progressives, in particular, hoped to restore social order by strengthening government at all levels and providing outlets for discontent; they did not seek to foment revolution. Nonetheless, there was an unmistakable sense, among western populists as well as eastern reformers, among both the American- and foreign-born, that the old solutions were no longer sufficient to solve capitalism's growing social divides.[18]

As Debs surveyed the events of recent years, from the founding of the Socialist Party and the Wobblies to the call for progressive reform, he saw a nation ripe for transformation. The Haywood trial seemed like precisely the incident to join these disparate forces of unrest into a single, powerful socialist movement. "The crisis has come and we have got to meet it," he wrote in March 1906, just weeks after Haywood's arrest. "Upon the issue involved the whole body of organized labor can unite and every enemy of plutocracy will join us."

Debs' words came from an essay called "Arouse, Ye Slaves!" penned and published in a burst of indignation in the Socialist Party's newspaper *Appeal to Reason*. They set an uncompromising tone for the months ahead. To Debs, the accusations against the WFM leaders looked like nothing so much as a conspiracy of capital, a plot by the "gory-beaked vultures" of the Mine Owners' Association and their "pals in Wall Street, New York" to destroy the West's fighting unions. What made the essay significant, though, was less its analysis of events than its vision of the fate to be delivered upon such men if they dared to convict Haywood, Moyer, and Pettibone. Responding to McParland's prediction that the three men "shall never leave Idaho alive," Debs warned without hesitation that "if they don't the governors of Idaho and Colorado and their masters from Wall Street, New York, to the Rocky Mountains had better prepare to follow them."[19]

Accused of advocating assassination, Debs insisted that this was merely a metaphor and that the violence of a state poised to execute innocent men was the greater crime. ("We are not favoring violence, but resisting it," he wrote. "We are seeking, not to commit, but to prevent murder.") It was unlikely, at any rate, that Debs could have delivered on his promise to provide "a million revolutionists with guns" in the event of a conviction. But as a source of agitation, this talk, combined with parades, demonstrations, and endless, anxious coverage in the newspapers, succeeded in framing the Haywood trial as a referendum on the capitalist system, a showdown in the long-standing battle of "the Workers versus the Plutocracy." Even President Roosevelt took notice of the agitation. In January 1907, he published a letter in which he condemned Debs, as well as Moyer and Haywood, as the quintessence of an "undesirable…citizen."[20]

By the spring of 1907, the phrase "undesirable citizen" had become the rallying cry for a national movement to save the Idaho men from the Haymarket anarchists' fate. On May 4, for instance, New York socialists joined with the Central Federated Union for two simultaneous parades, complete with trumpets and cymbals, one heading up from the immigrant Lower East Side, the other heading south from the more placid uptown neighborhoods. The parade converged with a flourish on Lexington Avenue's Grand Central Palace, where socialist editor Joseph Wanhope, fresh from a trip to Idaho, led the course of denunciation. "Let us serve notice upon the capitalists, upon Wall Street, from which Idaho is governed," he urged a cheering crowd, "that we are going to watch this trial, and that if in the course of it our suspicions are justified, we are going to take the necessary steps to do away forever with an industrial system that depends upon murder for its continuance."[21]

THE HAYWOOD TRIAL began in late May with an acute consciousness on all sides that "[t]he eyes of the civilized world" were upon the frontier city of Boise, in the words of the *Idaho Statesman*. The socialist papers were there, of course. So was nearly every newspaper with a readership of even a few thousand. The Associated Press alone sent three correspondents. "Every movement was being scrutinized by more interested people," recalled Fremont Wood, the presiding judge, "than had ever before followed the trial of an individual case in the history of the country."[22]

Nobody attracted more attention than Clarence Darrow, the lead attorney for the defense. A lanky, sardonic midwesterner, Darrow was one of the country's most prolific crusading lawyers, famed for his courtroom theatrics on behalf of labor organizers, socialists, anarchists, and other dissenters against the capitalist status quo. He had defended Debs himself during the Pullman battle. (In a burst of affection, Darrow declared Debs "the bravest man I ever knew," wondering if "a kindlier, gentler, more generous man" had ever walked the earth.) Less than a decade later, he championed the anthracite miners in their 1902 strike against the Morgan-led coal trust. Darrow was not always successful; his effort to have Haywood's "kidnapping" tossed out by the Supreme Court failed in January 1907. But he was known to be a man who liked to put American society on trial along with his individual clients. As he explained to United Mine Workers official John Mitchell in the run-up to the Haywood trial, "Public sentiment is very necessary in a great case of this kind."[23]

Darrow's chief obstacle was the unavoidable fact of Harry Orchard, the man who had confessed more than a year earlier to murdering Steunenberg along with other WFM foes. Over several days of testimony, and later in the pages of *McClure's* magazine and a popular autobiography,

Orchard laid out an incredible tale of his six-year career as a dynamiter and assassin in the employ of the Western Federation of Miners. From 1899 to 1905, he claimed, he had traveled the West committing stealth attacks on the union's enemies: planting dynamite beneath a rail station at Independence, Missouri, an attack that killed fourteen nonunion men; sneaking explosives under the sidewalk outside Colorado governor James Peabody's mansion, only to grow nervous at the last minute; bombing the door of former Bunker Hill and Sullivan manager Fred Bradley's San Francisco apartment, an event falsely attributed to a gas explosion; and, of course, attaching the bomb to Steunenberg's gate in late December 1905.

There was little talk of socialist theory or revolution, of the nobility of labor's cause. As Orchard described them, the twenty-plus murders were acts of cold-blooded revenge by a small group of union leaders committed to the maintenance of their own power. This "inner circle"—Haywood, Moyer, Pettibone, and a few others—met with him repeatedly to plan the attacks, offer instruction in explosives, and, most importantly, to pay him $250 per job. The confession corroborated claims that the Mine Owners' Association had been making for years: "[t]hat a large number of criminals and lawless men have been welcomed, supported and sheltered by the Western Federation of Miners." It also supported the prosecution's claim that the WFM leaders were far worse than ordinary murderers. When he looked at the bloodstained snow in front of his friend Frank Steunenberg's house, prosecutor William E. Borah told the jury, "I saw murder—no, not murder—a thousand times worse than murder; I saw anarchy displaying its first bloody triumph in Idaho."[24]

The mention of "anarchy" was deliberate, an appeal to the dark and malevolent imagery so long associated with the anarchist movement. In contrast to Haymarket, however, where the defense had pleaded with the jury to focus on the question of criminal culpability, Darrow pushed the jurors to examine the social significance of the case. "I need not tell you how important this case is," he began. "How important to Society. How important to a great movement which represents the hopes and the wishes and the aspiration of all men who labor to sustain their daily life."

What followed was perhaps the best-known courtroom oration of its day, an eleven-hour summation that seemed to encapsulate the issues at stake in the nation's developing class war. Darrow urged the jury to see that Haywood had been placed on trial because he had fought too long and hard, with too much devotion, for the principle that "eight hours was as long as a man ought to twist his muscles and twist his bones in a smelter." He pleaded with the jurors to side not with the "spiders of Wall Street" but with the men who "toil with their hands…through our mills and factories, and down deep underneath the earth." If Steunenberg had met with a single horrible attack, he argued, these "toilers" were the victims of violence every day of their lives, at the hands of precisely those men—the mine owners and East Coast capitalists—who now accused them of fomenting war.[25]

Darrow took his argument one step further, into what the *Chicago Tribune* denounced as "the mad brawling of an anarchist." As he closed his summation, he urged the jury to acquit *even if* they believed Haywood, and union leaders like him, were guilty of the crimes at hand (as they quite possibly were). "I am here to say that in a great cause these labor organizations…have stood for the poor, they have stood for the weak, they have stood for every humane law that was ever placed upon the statute books," he declared. "I don't care how many wrongs they have committed— I don't care how many crimes…how many brutalities they are guilty of. I know their cause is just."[26]

As the *Tribune* suggested, this echoed just what Albert Parsons had said years earlier in his own defense, and what Goldman had argued about Czolgosz: that the conditions spawned by industrial capitalism made violence perfectly justifiable. This time, though, after more than twenty years of wrangling over dynamite, after a year of agitation on Haywood's behalf, the arguments fell on more receptive ears. On July 28, in a decision hailed by the WFM's *Miners' Magazine* as "a sparkling gem in the crown of organized labor," the Boise jurors returned a verdict of not guilty.[27]

AS DEBS HOPED, the Haywood trial emerged as the great counterexample to Haymarket, a testament to all that "twenty years of revolutionary education, agitation and organization" could accomplish. To Haywood's supporters, it seemed to confirm the country's new receptivity to socialist ideas, its willingness to entertain class war as a legitimate response to the Money Trust. "After all of the machinations of the trusts they did not reckon on the people," Debs crowed of his Wall Street adversaries. "They owned the courts, but not the people." To others, the apparent influence of socialist agitation on the trial was a rather less welcome development. "There has been a gross miscarriage of justice to my mind out in Idaho at the acquittal of Haywood," Theodore Roosevelt announced. "I suppose the jury was terrorized but it is not a pleasant matter from any standpoint."[28]

For Haywood himself, the verdict's meaning could be summed up in a single word: freedom. After more than a year in jail, he walked down the back steps of the courtroom, retrieved the books he had been reading in jail, and rushed to the Boise hospital to visit his mother, a "happy crowd" following him all the way. Already, he had decided to return to Colorado and reenter the union fight. "My intention," he informed the papers, "is to go back to Denver and take up my work where I left it off when I was placed under arrest."[29]

For a few days, as he made his way south by train, steaming through Idaho's vast ranchlands, through Wyoming's peaks and valleys, and on into the splendor of the Rockies, this did seem possible, as if time itself were being reversed. Whatever illusions he may have harbored in those first, relieved hours, when Haywood arrived in Denver he discovered just how much had changed as a result of his trial. Greeting him at the depot were thousands of cheering spectators—evidence, reflected *Miners' Magazine*, of a new "fraternity among the laboring people that will one day crystallize into a strength that will sweep the present murderous system from the face of the earth." At the WFM office, he found piles of telegrams. One came from Daniel De Leon, the leading voice of the Socialist Labor Party (a passionate, if tiny, rival to Debs' Socialist Party) and, that year, of the IWW as well. Later, De Leon would emerge as one of Haywood's fiercest critics. In 1907, though, De Leon—like almost everyone else within socialist and labor circles—had nothing but praise for Haywood. "Thanks to your own antecedents, your celebrated case, the unanimity of the Working Class in your behalf, and your triumphant vindication," De Leon wrote, "the capitalist class has itself hatched out the needed leader."[30]

Haywood embraced the role. Many friends urged him to be "quiet" and "humble," thankful for the acquittal. But he was in no mood for retreat. As invitations poured into the WFM office, Haywood took to the road, delivering dozens of lectures and speeches, repeating in each new city the story of how he had "whipped" the plutocrats in a plot of their own devising. Only once, he later reflected, did he break down and really consider how close he had come to losing his life. While in Chicago to deliver a lecture for forty-five thousand admirers, he ventured to Waldheim Cemetery, where the Haymarket anarchists lay beneath their grand new monument. "When I realized that I was standing at the foot of the monument to the workers who had been hanged twenty years before, I burst into tears," he later wrote. "The remembrance of these men had grown closer to me than a blood relationship, since the time when, as a boy, I had followed the details of their trial and execution."[31]

Over the next several years, Haywood's identification with the Chicago martyrs only continued to grow. The acquittal saved his life. He soon discovered, however, that it had done little to change the opinions of millions who had always seen him as an "anarchist" and "undesirable citizen." Far from erasing Haywood's association with violence, Orchard's gory revelations at the trial, combined with the publication of his confession in book form later that year, made Haywood the most obvious symbol of labor's "nitroglycerin and gas-pipe habit," in the words of one later critic.[32]

Just how significant this habit actually was remained a matter of considerable debate. Between 1881 and 1905, the year of Steunenberg's assassination, there had been more than thirty-seven thousand strikes in the United States. Of these, only a few hundred resulted in serious violence, much less the use of dynamite. But those eruptions of violence—and Haywood's trial in particular—shaped the public's imagination in ways that few peaceable strikes could muster. As Haywood began his new life beyond Idaho, headlines continued to feature reports of explosions and assassinations on labor's behalf. In 1908 alone, Americans could read of streetcars blown up during strikes in Cleveland and in Chester and Elgin, Pennsylvania; of bridges and dams bombed in Buffalo, in Oakland, and on Blackwell's Island in New York. "West's Labor War Renewed by Bomb," read one ominous headline in the *Chicago Tribune* in March 1908. "Attempted Assassination...Reopens Reign of Riot."[33]

At certain points in his new life as "the living incarnation of the Social Revolution," Haywood embraced this reputation for violence and all it brought with it, announcing forthrightly his intent "to overthrow the capitalist system by forcible means if necessary." At other points, he was more circumspect. "I, for one," he told a reporter in 1912, "have turned my back on violence. It wins nothing. When we strike now, we strike with our hands in our pockets." In either case, the association with violence established at his trial remained the essential feature of his public reputation for the next decade, as he struggled to find a home within an ever-factionalizing American left. The WFM's new leadership, battered by trial expenses, fearful of being associated with violence, no longer wanted him on their payroll. A small announcement printed in *Miner's Magazine* in early 1908 read, "The Executive Board...has decided to terminate the services of William D. Haywood as a representative in the field."[34]

Debs' Socialist Party took him in, but within a few years they, too, concluded that Haywood's views were more than they could bear. "We do not want any of it. None of it!" one Socialist delegate would declare in 1912. "We don't want the touch of it on us. We do not want the hint of it connected with us. We repudiate it in every fibre of us." "It" was the doctrine of sabotage and "direct action," which finally reunited Haywood with the Industrial Workers of the World and ultimately put them in direct confrontation with Wall Street.[35]

THE WOBBLIES BEGAN TO RUMBLE about "direct action" in 1908, when a group of Portland lumber workers tramped their way to the IWW's annual Chicago convention determined to revive the organization as the great refuge of the militant workingman. This was the vision that had animated Haywood three years earlier, when he led the group's founding convention. By the time he left prison, though, he was no longer an IWW member. As described in its preamble, the IWW had been created as an instrument of class struggle, free from the political infighting and conservatism of the AFL. While Haywood languished in prison, the promise of this early vision had collapsed into warring factions: one a cadre eager to run for office, the other dedicated to taking the fight directly to the employer and the picket line—the essence of "direct action."[36]

The Portland men supported the latter camp. Known as the "Overalls Brigade," they brought to the IWW a brash new proletarian style, one that was sympathetic with Haywood's gruff western identity. They bellowed out revolutionary songs, scorned the niceties of "bushwa" (bourgeois) society, and made a point of dressing in the workingman's garb that eventually became the Wobblies' trademark uniform: "black overalls and jumpers, black shirts and red ties,...an I.W.W. book in his pocket and an I.W.W. button on his coat." During the 1908 meeting, they also pushed through a vote eliminating all mention of "political action" from the Wobblies' preamble, establishing the vague term "direct action" as the preferred alternative. What this meant, in an immediate sense, was a rejection of voting and political party work in favor of strikes, slowdowns, and direct confrontation with employers—actions undertaken, in

Wobbly parlance, "at the point of production." But what it came to mean to many Americans, as the Wobblies grew from an isolated sect into a national political force, was what De Leon suggested as he grudgingly withdrew his support in 1908: that the Wobblies had become a bunch of "bums, anarchists, and physical force destroyers."[37]

Haywood, busy stumping for the Socialists, wary of the Wobblies' internal disputes, missed the crucial 1908 meeting where "direct action" became the official IWW platform. He also missed some of the first major ventures to thrust the Wobblies onto the national agenda: the 1909 strike in McKees Rocks, Pennsylvania, in which thousands of immigrant workers joined with the IWW in a brutal battle with strikebreakers, and the Spokane free-speech fight, in which some four hundred Wobblies spent months in jail (as well as paying visits to area emergency rooms) after protesting a city ordinance banning them from speaking in the streets. Haywood spent much of his time in Europe during those years as a hard-drinking, unvarnished, and wildly popular ambassador of American socialism ("the pent-up passion and excitement of the audience overleaped all bounds," reported one British admirer), a remarkable circumstance for a man who prior to 1907 had never traveled east of the Mississippi River.[38]

In Europe he found audiences aflame with talk of the aborted 1905 Russian Revolution, where self-proclaimed "terrorists" had proudly used bombings and assassinations to ward off repression by the czarist state. He also encountered the ideas of the syndicalist and French social critic Georges Sorel, whose 1908 *Reflections on Violence* declared that force was an unavoidable part of the class war. Sorel's syndicalism was a complicated blend of Marxist, anarchist, and trade union theories, all aimed at the creation of a single industrial union (essentially the Wobblies' "One Big Union"). On the ground, it was more straightforward. While in France in 1910, Haywood watched as a few thousand rail workers brought the nation's economic system to a halt simply by laying down their tools. Ordered to return to work, they slyly forgot how to do their jobs. "This is the way it worked.... namely, by making the capitalist suffer," he cheered. "There is only one way to do that; that is, to strike him in the place where he carries his heart and soul, his center of feeling—the pocketbook." He returned to the United States to rejoin the Wobblies and bring these tactics home.[39]

As Haywood often pointed out, there was nothing inherently violent in the idea of "direct action." "Shall I tell you what direct action really means?" one Wobbly pamphlet asked. "The workers on the job shall tell the boss when and where he shall work, how long, and for what wages and under what conditions." Chief among the tactics prescribed to achieve this end was the general strike, in which workers would rise en masse to assume the power of the state. Opponents derided the general strike as little more than a violent, anarchic uprising, but Haywood saw the potential for a peaceful transition. When all workers had reached "an understanding of the class struggle" and learned to recognize their common interests, he wrote in a 1911 pamphlet, *Industrial Socialism*, all strikes, by definition, would be general.[40]

Even "sabotage," perhaps the most controversial form of direct action, could mean something as placid as working a bit more slowly or pretending not to understand instructions—just what the French railmen had done. "Sabotage is the destruction of profits to gain a definite, revolutionary, economic end," explained Wobbly pamphleteer Walker Smith. "It has many forms." Louis Levine, a social scientist who studied the issue in 1912, came to a similar conclusion. "Direct Action may, but must not necessarily, assume violent forms," he wrote, "nor would all violence be Direct Action."[41]

Or so the theory went. But if there was one thing that united most Wobblies in the years after 1908, it was their rejection of theory in favor of action on the ground. What attracted the men and women who joined the IWW—the proud "bums" of America—was not its careful adherence to limits or its parsing of European concepts but its image of sheer, unbridled rebellion. Often this came from the organizers' willingness to take extreme physical risks: in strike after strike, they endured beatings, lynchings, and jailhouse tortures. Many Wobbly leaders wore their pariah status as a badge of honor. "That the Industrial Workers of the World are in a class by themselves," wrote Haywood in 1912, "is indicated by the uniformity of condemnation this organization receives from the many diversified sources and representatives of apparently conflicting interests."[42]

The ability to tolerate violence, though, was only part of their public image. As early as June 1907, in the midst of Haywood's trial, the *Los Angeles Times* reported suspected IWW involvement in placing dynamite beneath a building outside the radical mining camp of Goldfield, Nevada. Within a decade, the specter of "crime and terrorism" carried out by an "I.W.W. Menace" had solidified the Wobbly reputation as "those bomb-throwing I Won't Works." Haywood scoffed at accusations of bomb plots and assassination—and, as the National Civil Liberties Bureau pointed out, few, if any, Wobblies were ever convicted for acts of violence. But Wobblies also took a certain pride, in Haywood's words, in making "the capitalist class shudder and cringe in fear." "You are doomed," organizer James Thompson informed American businessmen. "The best thing you can do is to look for a soft place to fall."[43]

Some of the greatest Wobbly heroes were men who blended the imagery of violence with the suggestion that they might follow through on their words. Songwriter and accused murderer Joe Hill, whose execution by a Utah firing squad in 1915 was later memorialized by generations of left-wing bards, was perhaps the wittiest example. Writing in the *Industrial Worker* in 1911, he warned that workers would do best to avoid voting machines and instead adopt the "machine . . . which the capitalists use on us when we ask for more bread for ourselves and our families. *The one that works with a trigger.*" Haywood, with his one-eyed stare and thunderous voice, flung out a similar defiance of "bushwa" norms. "I despise the law, and I am not a law-abiding citizen," he assured an overflow crowd at Cooper Union in New York on December 21, 1911, "and more than that, no socialist can be a law-abiding citizen."[44]

Coming from a man who had been on trial for murder just four years before, this did little to persuade most Americans of the essentially peaceful nature of Haywood's intent. In the particular month of December 1911, it carried an extra dose of controversy as well. Three weeks earlier, brothers John and James McNamara had confessed their role in the greatest labor dynamite scandal since Haywood's trial in Idaho. To many people's surprise, they came not from the ranks of the IWW but from the International Association of Bridge and Structural Iron Workers, a pure and simple union in good standing with Samuel Gompers' AFL.

"TO REVIEW THE KIDNAPING of John J. McNamara and his associates is like reading a brief chapter of my own life," Haywood wrote in June 1911, soon after his return from Europe. First, there was the sensational crime: in this case, a fireball that ripped through the *Los Angeles Times* building in the early hours of October 1, 1910, smashing the main floor into the ceiling and lighting up the jumbled buildings of downtown L.A. Twenty-one men died, most from burns and suffocation, a few from missing the firemen's nets when they attempted to jump to safety. Later that day, investigators found two more time bombs: one at "the Bivouac," the Wilshire Boulevard mansion of *Times* publisher Harrison Gray Otis, the other—fifteen sticks of dynamite—nestled beneath a window at the home of Felix Zeehandelaar, secretary of the local Merchants and Manufacturers' Association. Like Steunenberg, Otis and Zeehandelaar were well-known foes of labor. Now, they surmised, they had come close to meeting Steunenberg's fate. "Must Blame the Unions," read an outraged headline in the *Los Angeles Times*.[45]

The next step was the arrests of midlevel union men: in this case, the McNamara brothers, John J. (also known as J.J.) and his younger sibling James. "Like" myself," Haywood wrote, John was "secretary-treasurer of a militant labor organization." James, or Jim, was more of an itinerant, an odd-jobber in the sometime employ of his brother. Jim was arrested in Detroit on April 12, 1911, carrying a valise full of dynamite. John's arrest came ten days later during a steelworkers' executive board meeting in Indianapolis. As if in a deliberate affront to Haywood, detectives whisked John away to California without a warrant or extradition papers. "The abduction of our brothers was so nearly like that of Pettibone, Moyer...and myself," Haywood wrote, "as to almost furnish a parallel case."[46]

From there, the McNamara Affair became almost a reenactment of the Steunenberg drama. The McNamaras encountered their version of Harry Orchard, a dodgy union member named Ortie McManigal who confessed to setting off dozens of bombs at the association's behest. They confronted their own McParland as well, a swashbuckling private detective and former Secret Service man named William J. Burns, whose reputation as a foe of dynamiters would bring lucrative contracts for years to come. Once again, Clarence Darrow took up the cause, rushing off to Los Angeles with a vow to save labor from such callow lies. Debs jumped in as well, composing a call to arms that was nothing if not an echo of "Arouse, Ye Slaves!" "We are again face to face with a crisis," he wrote. "There is no time to lose. The workers must be stirred and the nation aroused."[47]

And once again the "workers" answered his call, organizing meetings, parades, and rallies that quickly surpassed anything undertaken on Haywood's behalf. Millions of socialists and union members across the nation pinned on defiant "McNamara buttons" and stamped their letters with "McNamara stamps." The AFL itself turned Labor Day into "McNamara Day" in 1911, "a day of protest against the outrage," as pamphlets described it, "and as an evidence of our confidence in the innocence of our men." By the time jury selection began a few months later, all of the elements were in place to make the McNamara case a repeat of the Haywood triumph: the vast publicity, the star defense team, an aroused working class prepared to fight for its innocent men. On December 1, however, things took an unanticipated turn. "The McNamara drama, staged in the court of Los Angeles, held the entire country in tense anticipation and then came to a sudden farcical end," Emma Goldman later wrote. "The McNamaras confessed!"[48]

The McNamara case did for labor what the McKinley assassination had done for anarchism: confirm, in no uncertain terms, that the rumors of recent years—of bloodshed and murder, of secret plots and elaborate conspiracies—were more or less true. If anything, the McNamaras' pleas were far more damaging than Czolgosz's admission of guilt, both in the scope of the revelations and in their potential for political harm. In this case, it was not a single man but a significant portion of the union's leadership that had colluded in a dynamite campaign. What's more, by maintaining their innocence, the McNamaras had allowed thousands of other labor and radical leaders to put their own reputations at stake. "To the man familiar with the work and methods of trade unions," New York Socialist leader Morris Hillquit had written in June 1911 for a speech at Carnegie Hall, "the charge that a high official of a national organization was systematically engaged in organizing dynamite plots as a sort of routine of business, and paying for it from the treasury of the organization, is so absurd as to provoke uncontrollable laughter."[49]

This, nonetheless, was what the confessions revealed. Standing before Judge Walter Bordwell, nervously chewing gum and glancing at Darrow for guidance, Jim McNamara pleaded guilty to murder, effectively admitting that he had planted the dynamite that destroyed the *Times* building and killed twenty-one workingmen. His brother J.J., the "high official" of the two, confessed to ordering the Christmas Day bombing of the anti-union Llewellyn Iron Works, which took no lives but cost the company $25,000. In return, the court spared their lives. Jim received a life sentence, while J.J. ended up with fifteen years in jail.[50]

As further details emerged, the story grew even more damning and even closer to what Hillquit had mockingly described. According to one government report, between 1906 and 1911 the International Association of Bridge and Structural Iron Workers carried out no fewer than one hundred dynamite attacks on nonunion work sites: bridges, viaducts, even an opera house and a hotel. Only the *Times* bombing cost lives, and the McNamaras admitted their horror at the mistake. But the fact of a widespread intimidation campaign was undeniable: the union stored the dynamite at its Indianapolis headquarters and paid both McManigal and Jim McNamara directly from the union treasury. Many union members continued to support the leaders who had undertaken the campaign; the president, Frank Ryan, convicted of participating in the conspiracy, was reelected while in prison. For those who claimed to believe the McNamaras' claims of innocence, however, the evidence was devastating. Samuel Gompers, on his way from Washington to New York aboard the Congressional Limited, supposedly began to weep when a young Associated Press reporter informed him of the pleas. "If this is all true, my credulity has been imposed upon," he exclaimed, much to the skepticism of his critics. "I am astonished at this news."[5]

What ultimately proved most astonishing about the McNamara case, though, was how little it actually seemed to hurt labor's cause. In California, unions endured a painful crackdown as cities rushed to pass new antipicketing laws and speech restrictions. So did the Socialist Party, which in late November had been poised to win the Los Angeles mayoral election for the first time. The Socialists had modeled their campaign on Haywood's Idaho defense, championing the McNamaras, in Debs' words, as the victims of a "conspiracy...hatched in Wall Street" by "the brute" J. P. Morgan. "Of course we knew that we had no chance of election as soon as the plea of guilty was entered," mayoral candidate Job Harriman wrote to Hillquit later that month, "but, we would have been elected had this not happened."[52]

Outside California, by contrast, the McNamara pleas only seemed to fuel public desire for some sort of class rapprochement, an end to the cycle of violence that kept labor and capital at each other's throats. Lincoln Steffens, the New York muckraker famed for his exposés of urban corruption and Money Trust excess, had attempted to deliver just that in the early stages of the McNamara case, urging the brothers to plead guilty in return for light sentences and other gestures of goodwill from the local business community. The businessmen's promises had vanished after the guilty pleas (according to Steffens, they agreed to the deal, then promptly reneged), so Steffens took the proposition to the American public as a whole. "What are we Americans going to do," Steffens demanded in early

December 1911, "about conditions which are bringing up healthy, good-tempered boys like these McNamara boys to really believe, as they most sincerely do—they and a growing group of labor—that the only recourse they have for improving the conditions of the wage-earner is to use dynamite against property and life?"[53]

At home in New York, Steffens' fellow reformers rushed to propose answers. In December, *Survey* magazine, a bellwether of progressive sentiment, devoted an entire issue to ferreting out the "Larger Bearings of the McNamara Case." Identifying the source of the growing rift between capital and labor, *Survey* writers pointed to a vast array of structural problems in American society: a lack of legal protection for unions, employers' shameless hiring of strikebreakers and company spies, and, most of all, the domination of the economy by a handful of large corporations. "Is there not a causal connection between the development of these huge, indomitable trusts and the horrible crimes now under investigation?" asked attorney and future Supreme Court justice Louis Brandeis, one of the Morgan bank's great critics. To address these problems, the magazine proposed a solution not unlike what Steffens had suggested months earlier, appealing to President William Howard Taft to create a "Commission on Industrial Relations" to study the problem through the lens of social science.[54]

To Haywood, schooled firsthand in the violence of so-called industrial relations, this sort of talk seemed naive. He had called for a general strike on the first day of the McNamara trial, and even after the pleas he continued to support the brothers. "You can't see the class struggle through the stained-glass windows of a cathedral," he told the Wobblies. He discovered nonetheless that he benefited from the progressives' temperate response to the McNamaras' pleas. In January 1912, with his embrace of the McNamaras as backdrop, he set out on one of the most challenging fights of his career, rushing up to Lawrence, Massachusetts, where some ten thousand textile workers had suddenly walked out to protest a recent pay cut. By the middle of the year, the Wobblies had won their first major fight in the industrial East, bringing together a dizzying variety of immigrant workers—Lithuanians, Sicilians, Russian, Poles—in common cause. Even a new bomb plot failed to derail their efforts. On January 20, less than two months after the McNamaras' pleas, police uncovered three packages of dynamite in Lawrence. When police traced the dynamite to its source, however, they concluded that the whole affair had been staged by William Wood, owner of the American Woolen

Company and one of the town's leading industrialists, to stir up hostility to the strike.[55]

Other left-wing and labor groups found similar good luck in 1912. Despite lingering concerns from California, Debs won more than a million votes in the presidential election, more than twice his previous total. Indeed, every presidential candidate—including the victorious Democrat, Woodrow Wilson—ran on a platform reflecting labor's deepest concerns: that the American system was rigged in favor of the wealthy, that the workingman was not getting his just deserts, that something at last had to be done. The American Federation of Labor itself, home of the McNamaras, gained members in 1912. "It is now thirty-seven years since I became active in the labor movement," Debs noted. "[A]t last the labors of all these years are coming to fruition."[56]

In December, President Taft provided a final gesture of encouragement, signing into law the progressives' hoped-for Commission on Industrial Relations—the first time that "terrorism in America," as journalist Walter Woehlke described the dynamite campaign, had provoked anything of the sort. Looking back from the vantage point of 1918, historian and commission member John R. Commons would see the event as a turning point for labor. "What a difference," he wrote, "between the attitude of the public toward this case of extreme and premeditated violence and its attitude towards the suspected Chicago anarchists!"[57]

TESTIMONY BEFORE the Commission on Industrial Relations began in 1913, the year of Pierpont Morgan's death. Over the course of the next two years, the commission called forth hundreds of witnesses, from all sides of American industrial life, to air their views about how, and why, the United States had descended to such a state of chaos and violence. Among the witnesses were many veterans of the McNamara Affair: Otis, Darrow, Gompers, Steffens. There were survivors of other battles as well: workers from New York's Triangle Shirtwaist Factory, where a fire in 1911 killed 141 women trapped behind locked doors; miners from Ludlow, Colorado, where Rockefeller-hired guards used machine guns on a crowd of strikers before setting fire to their tent colony, killing fourteen women and children cowering in an underground pit.[58]

The commission's greatest coup was its summoning of the "plutocrats" of American industry to answer questions before the public. John D. Rockefeller testified in New York, informing the commissioners that even in retrospect "I would have taken no action" to prevent the guards from descending on strikers at Ludlow. Jack Morgan put in an appearance as well. Asked whether he thought steelworkers could survive on $10 per week, he responded honestly that that they ought to take what they could get.[59]

To commission chairman Frank Walsh, a former child factory worker turned labor attorney, what stood out were not these platitudes but the workers' own stories of how they had survived the sweatshops and mines and machinery of American industry. He particularly recalled two witnesses whose stories of rebellion and defeat, of violence and counterattack, moved him deeply. One was a grizzled Wobbly organizer named George Speed. The other was Big Bill Haywood.[60]

The Haywood who took the stand on May 12, 1915, was more subdued than the one who three years earlier had thundered into Lawrence, Massachusetts, to denounce the capitalist class. He was, for one thing, smaller and weaker. Years of heavy drinking, a poor diet, and an exhausting itinerant schedule had caught up with him, producing a stomach ulcer and the loss of some eighty pounds. He was also estranged from the Socialist Party, once his strongest source of support. In the spring of 1912, still reeling from the McNamara pleas, the party had passed a resolution expelling "any member of the Party who opposes political action or advocates crime, sabotage, or other methods of violence as a weapon of the working class"—a category that included Haywood himself. He had recovered from the blow in time to lead a blistering but unsuccessful textile strike in Paterson, New Jersey, in 1913; though the Wobblies garnered publicity from a benefit "pageant" at Madison Square Garden, they won few material improvements. The following year, seeking a bit of respite from the turmoil, he accepted the position of IWW secretary-treasurer in Chicago, his first desk job since his 1906 arrest.[61]

On the stand, Haywood summoned a bit of his old roughneck self, describing the United States as a land plagued by inequality and graft, dominated by callous plutocrats. From his early life in the mines, he conjured up images of poverty and despair. From his WFM years, he recalled how the miners had tried to bargain and strike, only to be turned back at the point of a gun. "It was a dramatic story that 'Big Bill' told," the socialist *Call* reflected, "a story of strike after strike, hundreds thrown into jail, workers charged upon by soldiers, men and women beaten, court orders binding the workers and constant revolt against exploitation."[62]

Even more dramatic was the report the commission issued a few months later. For an official government document, it was a stinging indictment of American society, affirming much of what Haywood had said on the stand. According to the report, the United States was no longer a democracy but a nation ruled by "a small number of wealthy and powerful financiers" in what amounted to "industrial feudalism." The report described what this meant in numerical terms: up to half of all factory workers and miners lived below "a comfortable and decent condition," and one out of every twelve people who died in New York was buried in a pauper's grave. But the commissioners did not restrict themselves to numbers. "The crux of the question," they declared, "...is, Have the workers received their share of the enormous increase in wealth which has taken place in this country...? The answer is emphatically—no!" The commission came perilously close to affirming what Goldman had been saying since the days of Homestead: that acts of violence arose in response to intolerable conditions. "Throughout history where a people or a group have been arbitrarily denied rights which they conceived to be theirs, reaction has been inevitable," the report announced. "Violence is a natural form of protest against injustice."

Walsh himself delivered a personal endorsement of this view. In a moving, if rather flowery, personal addendum, he pleaded with the American public to heed to the commission's words. "[W]e call upon our citizenship, regardless of politics or economic conditions, to use every means of agitation, all avenues of education, and every department and function of the government, to eliminate the injustices exposed by the commission, to the end that each other may 'secure the whole product of his labor,'" he wrote in the report's final draft.[63]

By the time the report came out in late 1915, though, Americans were beginning to turn their attention to other matters. The previous year, Europe had erupted in war. That development, and the upheaval that followed, did far more than the commission's words to shape how the nation would respond when dynamite exploded in the streets of New York.

# 5

. . . .

# THE WAR AT HOME

IN NEW YORK, as in Europe, the war opened with a bang. On June 28, 1914, Serbian nationalists assassinated Archduke Franz Ferdinand in Sarajevo. Less than a week later, on the morning of July 4, a townhouse exploded on Lexington Avenue in New York. City police found one corpse dangling from a fire escape. They pieced together a second body from a torso and leg gathered nearby. Both men were anarchists, as was a third man noted as "missing" in the initial reports. According to official accounts, all three were intimate friends of Alexander Berkman, co-conspirators in a dynamite plot aimed at John D. Rockefeller Jr.[1]

At first, these two events—a successful assassination in Sarajevo and a botched one in New York—seemed entirely unrelated. Franz Ferdinand was heir to the Austro-Hungarian throne; his murder was a nationalist blow against occupation. Rockefeller had been targeted for his action (or rather, inaction) in response to the Ludlow Massacre in distant Colorado. Over the next several years, however, the war between nation-states in Europe and the class war in the United States became increasingly intertwined. As the tentacles of war spread through Europe and entangled the United States, the spirit of progressivism that had led to the Commission on Industrial Relations and forced millions of Americans to question the

96

justice of their industrial order gave way to a darker, less tolerant outlook. Well before suspicions of a "radical plot" against Wall Street began
to emerge in September 1920, dissidents such as Goldman, Berkman,
Haywood, and Debs found themselves again marginalized and reviled—
wondering, in Goldman's words, if "we have not lived in vain during the
last thirty years."[2]

To any radical living in New York in July 1914, this prospect would
have seemed absurd, a relic of outmoded nineteenth-century thought.
Recent years had not brought unblemished victory, but they had brought
*progress*, that favored term of reformers. Progress, by its nature, did not go
backward. Once accomplished, it could not be undone. The growth of the
Wobblies, the new enthusiasm for socialism, the progressive questioning
of Morganized capital—all of these were signs of a golden revolutionary
age ahead. This, at any rate, was what Goldman and Berkman assumed as
they sought to transform the Lexington Avenue explosion into a moment
of triumphant martyrdom in the summer of 1914.

Goldman had come of age as an American icon in the progressive renais-
sance. Within New York, she still had her cadre of militant, foreign-born
admirers: Italian anarchists, French syndicalists, and, especially, Russian
revolutionaries who had fled to New York after the failed 1905 revolution. As the political climate had grown more receptive to talk of capitalist crimes, however, she began to broaden her activities, throwing herself
into causes as diverse as the birth control movement, the battle against
child labor, and the struggle for Wobbly free speech. She expanded her
social contacts as well, moving from the tight-knit anarchist circles of
her youth into the free-for-all of modernist Greenwich Village, where the
movement to examine the "larger bearings" of the McNamara case had
first taken hold. Among the new friends encountered in the downtown
swirl of salons and protest meetings was Haywood himself—"dear tender
Bill," as she called him—with whom she debated points of doctrine and
exchanged Christmas presents.[3]

Theirs was a natural affinity, born of a common faith in the implacable
nature of class warfare and a mutual contempt for those who believed
in piecemeal change. Much of Goldman's new Village circle was of a
decidedly more philosophical orientation. Mabel Dodge, the doyenne of
a famous Fifth Avenue salon, was an heiress with literary pretensions.
Hutchins Hapgood, a daily newspaper columnist, made his name translating the "queer and repulsive" life of Lower East Side Jews into literary

sketches for an American audience. Lincoln Steffens, bard of the Golden Rule, was perhaps the typical Village figure, sympathetic to radical views but himself basically "bushwa." Like Goldman and Berkman, these men and women shared a desire to tear down the existing order. "Whether in literature, plastic art, [or] the labor movement...," Hapgood wrote, "we find an instinct to loosen up the old forms and traditions, to dynamite the baked and hardened earth so that fresh flowers can grow." They did not, however, take their dynamite literally.[4]

The friendship of such men and women, with their public influence and deep pockets, had become a requisite part of Goldman's more progressive, Americanized identity. But it also posed certain delicate challenges, especially when it came to the subject of violence. Goldman never abandoned her faith in the essential justice of Most's vision or the nobility of the *attentat*. She had learned through bitter experience, however, that militancy on the subject often came at the price of alienating allies who otherwise shared her dislike of capitalism. Like Haywood, she found herself trapped by competing impulses, thrilled to find a place of influence within her adopted country but unwilling to jettison her revolutionary roots. She was also subject to intensive federal scrutiny, including a failed effort to deport her under the new antianarchist laws.

Driven by ambition as well as fear, she had learned to present more than one face to the world. To her fellow revolutionaries, she was the militant she had always been, a fiery spokesperson for propaganda by deed. "During revolutionary periods, such as the present one in Russia, for instance," she wrote in a resolution presented to fellow anarchists in Amsterdam in 1907, "terrorism...serves a twofold purpose: it undermines the very foundation of tyranny, and kindles in the timid the divine fire of revolt." To her growing audience of American socialists and reformers, her views tended to be more temperate. In a 1908 essay, "What I Believe," for example, she argued that she had never applauded violence, especially in the American context. "Who says that I do? Have you heard me, has any one heard me?" she demanded. This stance was convincing enough to persuade at least one publisher that she had been misjudged in the crucial days after Homestead and the McKinley assassination. "In fact and in truth Miss Goldman is a mild mannered little woman who would not kill a fly or a spider," publisher J. C. Hart wrote in an introduction to one of her pamphlets. "On the contrary she teaches peace, harmony and brotherly love among all men regardless of race, creed or color."[5]

Berkman, by contrast, never saw much point in catering to the new progressive creed. During his time in prison, he had learned to speak and write in English. After his release in 1906, he used these new skills to hone his message for an American audience, settling in New York and signing on as an editor at *Mother Earth*. He remained far more inclined than Goldman to embrace violence as an essential part of class revolution. In 1912, for instance, he published his autobiography, *Prison Memoirs of an Anarchist*, part of a minor literary boom on the subject of dynamite. In its pages, he recalled in affectionate detail how he had carried out his attack on Henry Clay Frick, emphasizing the pleasure of attempting such a pure, self-sacrificing deed. "The removal of a tyrant is not merely justifiable," he concluded; "it is the highest duty of every true revolutionist."[6]

This was precisely the kind of direct advocacy that Goldman sought to avoid (mercifully, Berkman left out any hint of her role in the attack). Perhaps to her surprise, though, her progressive and pacifist allies tolerated Berkman's views. As with the McNamaras, they urged the American people to look upon his story as a symptom of capitalism's corrupting, degrading effect on the human psyche. "Why not try to understand an honest man even if he feels called on to kill?" Hapgood asked in the book's introduction. "Do not read to agree, of course, but read to see."[7]

As a model of this sort of open, tolerant inquiry, they took up the question themselves. On a memorable night in 1912, Mabel Dodge invited Goldman, Berkman, and Haywood to debate the issue of "Direct Action" at one of her famous evening-dress salons. The night was an oratorical disaster, she remembered; Haywood, especially, "talked as though he were wading blindfolded in sand." Nonetheless, Dodge admitted a certain thrill at being so close to genuinely "Dangerous Characters." "Their obvious activity seemed to be publishing the anarchist magazine, *Mother Earth*," she later wrote, "but beneath this there was a great busy humming complex of Planning; and many times they referred to the day when blood would flow in the streets of New York."[8]

Despite all the talk, there was little evidence prior to July 1914 that anyone intended to follow these words with action. Even Berkman had been relatively pacific. He was arrested once, in 1908, for conspiring to dynamite a police cordon in Union Square, but the courts dismissed the charges for lack of evidence. (The bomb killed the young anarchist who threw it, shearing off his face, though it failed to reach its intended target.) Since then, he had limited himself to the standard run of protests and propaganda. Beginning in the depression winter of 1913, he threw his support behind a burgeoning unemployment movement in New York, staging rallies in public squares and descending on churches to demand bread and work. On March 21, 1914, he helped to lead hundreds of unemployed men in a grand parade up Fifth Avenue past the mansions of the city's gilded elite—"a march of the disinherited," as he described it, "whose very appearance was a challenge to the guilty conscience of the exploiters and well-fed idlers."[9]

For the first time, he found himself swept up in something approaching a mass movement, fighting side by side with socialists and progressives, with Wobblies and genuine proletarians. Even Mayor John Mitchel seemed to be on their side. On April 4, police raided one of Berkman's rallies in Union Square, sweeping in on horseback and beating the demonstrators with clubs. Four days later, Mitchel fired the police commissioner who approved the assault and replaced him with a patrician administrator named Arthur Woods. A Harvard graduate and former Groton schoolmaster, Woods had entered police work in 1907 as a deputy commissioner charged with reforming the detective bureau. One of his earliest acts had been to oversee Berkman's arrest in the 1908 bombing at Union Square. Since then, he had made a name for himself as a progressive champion of free speech, one of the few in police circles. Woods argued that the protection of dissent, combined with highly professionalized undercover crime detection, was the best means of assuaging the city's class conflicts. By 1914, he had concluded that this meant respecting the rights of a man such as Alexander Berkman to say his piece.[10]

What followed was a sort of idyll for Berkman, a purging of the rejection he had suffered two decades earlier when the miners rebuffed his generosity at Homestead. Goldman was far from New York that spring, raising money for *Mother Earth* on a western lecture tour. So Berkman fell back on his own propaganda skills. Each Saturday he stood in Union Square to affirm "the necessity for fighting the capitalist monster with all the weapons at the workers' disposal," and hundreds of people listened and applauded.[11]

This acceptance seemed to hold even after attention shifted from the city's unemployment crisis to the Ludlow Massacre. Throughout the spring, Berkman cooperated with socialist muckraker Upton Sinclair to orchestrate a "silent protest" campaign against Rockefeller, a model of peaceful, if provocative, dissent. Perhaps this is why nobody paid much attention in May when Berkman hinted that he was also thinking about a different sort of action. "This is no time for theorizing, for fine-spun argument and phrases," he declared in *Mother Earth*. "With machine guns trained upon the strikers, the best answer is—*dynamite*."[12]

When police questioned him on the morning of July 4, hours after the explosion on Lexington Avenue, Berkman denied any role in the bombing. He knew that his situation was precarious. All three dead bombers—Arthur Caron, Carl Hanson, and Charles Berg—had fought by his side during the Rockefeller protests, dutifully enduring their share of beatings and police assaults. Indeed, he had been with them just the night before, first in a political meeting, then in a hushed late-night session at an uptown café, allegedly to discuss Caron's recent arrest for protesting at Rockefeller's Tarrytown estate. Faced with the likelihood of another indictment and perhaps another long bout in prison, Berkman determined, like Albert Parsons before him, to go out in a blaze of revolutionary defiance. By the evening of July 4, he had begun to make plans for a grand public funeral in Union Square to honor his comrades' sacrifice for the revolutionary cause.[13]

This prospect horrified most city residents. "To permit any group of citizens publicly to treat these victims of their own murder conspiracy as martyrs seems like an expression of sympathy with the allies of the terrorist," wrote the *New York Tribune*. This was precisely Berkman's point. The Union Square rally, he announced, would be a test of the city's devotion to the promise of free speech and assembly. It would also be a measure of whether American attitudes had, in fact, changed since the Haymarket years: whether the glimmer of tolerance evident in the wake of the McNamara Affair would hold up in the face of yet another *attentat*.[14]

Supporters began to trickle into Union Square just after noon on July 11, arriving in clusters of two and three. The men wore red roses in their lapels. Women tied jaunty red ribbons in their hair or around their necks, symbols of their affection for revolution. Around two o'clock, a brass band struck up "La Marseillaise," the official start of the festivities, then fell silent as the speakers began.

Berkman set the tone. "If society has forced our friends to resist oppression with violence," he thundered, "then capitalist society is guilty of creating the spirit which can find expression only in violent methods." The speeches that followed reinforced themes that had echoed through revolutionary circles since Most's arrival: that violence was the product of industrial conditions, that the tyranny of the masters would beget the resistance of the slaves, that dynamite was the best possible retort. Rebecca Edelsohn, Berkman's recent love interest, affirmed these views in the most explicit terms: "I want to say that it's about time the working class came out frankly and openly and said, 'Yes, we believe in violence. We will use violence whenever it is necessary to use it.' "[15]

To Berkman, hearing such words spoken openly fulfilled a dream nurtured since his earliest days in New York. "Do you still ask me what the Anarchists have accomplished in a quarter of a century?" he wrote a few weeks later in *Mother Earth*. "Just this: They have taught the people that violence is justified, aye, necessary in the defensive and offensive struggle of labor against capital." He took pride in what did not happen as well. Under Woods' instructions, some eight hundred policemen watched the rally, but they made no move to silence the speakers.[16]

Berkman interpreted the policemen's hesitation as a sign that Americans had finally repudiated the legacy of 1886, that the shift in "public sentiment" after the Haywood and McNamara affairs had become a lasting part of American life. "The Haymarket bomb was followed by a terrible wave of the mob spirit: no Anarchist was safe from the blind fury of the murderous law-and-order hordes, in and out of uniform," he wrote. "What a difference after the Lexington Avenue explosion! . . . Times have indeed changed!"[17]

His confidence was misplaced. Within a few years, the "mob spirit" was back. Though it seemed hard to imagine in 1914, Berkman and Goldman were already spending their last years on American soil.

DESPITE ITS LEGENDARY RADICALISM, New York had seen surprisingly few acts of terrorism before the Lexington Avenue blast in 1914. The city had its minor sensations: a dynamite attack on industrialist Russell Sage in 1891 ("The Wall Street Bomb-Throwing," as the *Chicago Tribune* described it); a subway explosion in 1902 (though the blast killed six people, it turned out to be an accident); a rash of criminal and labor-related dynamitings, often in Italian neighborhoods; the 1908 debacle in Union Square. But the big affairs came mostly from rough-and-tumble western outposts such as Chicago, Idaho, and California. Even the McKinley assassination, New York's closest claim to a major national plot, occurred hundreds of miles away, in Buffalo.[18]

That changed quickly after the Lexington Avenue explosion. In August, police commissioner Woods announced the creation of an undercover bomb squad to infiltrate the anarchist movement and the IWW. Within a few months, the new squad found itself in the midst of the city's first full-blown dynamite epidemic.

In creating the bomb squad, Woods envisioned it as a genuinely progressive reform, a professionalization of the department's traditional ad hoc, reactive police work. Its only local precedent was the short-lived Italian Squad, which had been formed in 1906 to conduct undercover investigations in the Italian immigrant community and which became all but defunct after 1909, when its lead detective was gunned down in Italy. The bomb squad revived and reshaped these strategies, dispatching undercover men to populate radical meetings and cafés. Its goal, Woods later explained, was "not in trying to bottle up the preachers of any particular doctrine, but simply in finding out who were the plotters of violent deeds and bringing them to justice." He presented the squad as a desirable alternative to the old tactic of smashing up entire neighborhoods or movements. From her vantage point on the western lecture circuit, though, Goldman recognized all the makings of a tragedy.[19]

Goldman thought the plot had been carried out stupidly and recklessly, though she did not deplore its intent. "Comrades, idealists, manufacturing a bomb in a congested tenement-house!" she later wrote. "I was aghast at such irresponsibility." She worried especially about what it all might mean for *Mother Earth*. In July, Berkman dedicated the magazine's entire issue to the martyrdom of Caron, Hanson, and Berg, reprinting the speeches from Union Square and reminding labor to "knock the last master off the back of the last slave...by tempering oppression with dynamite." In that single essay, Goldman feared, Berkman undid her years of careful balancing on the dynamite issue, putting the magazine on record in favor of violence at just the moment when the police were preparing their next big assault on anarchism. "I had tried always to keep our magazine free from such language," she recalled, "and now the whole number was filled with prattle about force and dynamite. I was so furious that I wanted the entire issue thrown into the fire."[20]

But it was not until the fall that she realized how poor his timing actually was. Goldman returned to New York in September 1914 (the city "will always lure me back as the place of stress and sorrow, struggle and pain, work and hope," she assured the readers of *Mother Earth*). Within a month, bombs began to explode throughout the city: on October 12, at St. Patrick's Cathedral; on October 13, at St. Alphonsus Church; a week later, at St. Alphonsus again; on November 11, at the Bronx Court House; on November 14, at the Tombs police court.[21]

Nobody died or suffered much by way of injury. The worst damage was inflicted on property—shattered windows, blown-out doors, and the like. In the final episode the bomb even failed to detonate; Magistrate John A. Campbell found it sputtering beneath his chair as he went to sit down. Combined, however, the rash of bombings convinced the new police squad of an urgent need to rein in the city's anarchist movement, and began the end of Woods' policy of toleration. "The situation was disturbing," bomb squad chief Thomas J. Tunney later wrote. "We had to put a stop to bombing before the anarchists grew bolder and began to kill someone beside themselves." Under the circumstances, Berkman decided not to wait around to see how things turned out. In November, with Goldman's forceful encouragement, he headed west on a lecture tour of his own.[22]

As after Homestead, Goldman stayed behind to pick up the pieces. In her absence, Berkman had run up huge printing and grocery bills. "Money was owed to every store-keeper in the neighborhood," she complained. *Mother Earth* itself was all but bankrupt, and the Lexington Avenue bombing had thoroughly alienated any financial angels such as Mabel Dodge who might have come to the rescue. Though she continued to fight alongside reformers and socialists around issues such as birth control, Goldman quickly discovered that the arrival of genuine, literal dynamite had rather dampened the free-for-all spirit once so much a part of her Village life. "It is interesting to see the philosophers and sentimentalists and free speech advocates rushing to cover," the *Tribune* commented. "They cannot afford to have their names associated with bomb throwing."[23]

Even radical allies, Goldman found, could no longer be trusted. In early 1915, in the last great gasp of the McNamara Affair, California detectives arrested anarchists David Caplan and Matthew Schmidt on charges that they had supplied the explosives for the *Los Angeles Times* bomb. To her horror, Goldman learned that they had been turned in by one Donald Vose, who was the son of her friend Gertie Vose and who lived at *Mother Earth* throughout the summer and fall of 1914. Apparently Vose had been working for William J. Burns, the private detective who had "kidnapped" the McNamaras, while Goldman and other friends had been helping to harbor Schmidt and protect him from the law. "It was the most terrible blow of my public life of twenty-five years," Goldman confessed in *Mother Earth*.[24]

There was more terrible news to come. In February, the New York papers announced that the bomb squad had caught two Italian anarchists, Frank Abarno and Carmine Carbone, in the act of planting a bomb at St. Patrick's Cathedral. Both were members of the Harlem-based Bresci Group, an Italian anarchist organization named for Gaetano Bresci, who had left Paterson to assassinate King Humbert in 1900. The impressive nab, the trial revealed, was the work of Amedeo Polignani, a recent bomb squad recruit. In the wake of the October bombings, Polignani had gone undercover in anarchist circles as "Frank Baldo" to befriend the Bresci men, attending basement meetings and listening to "reams of oratory," in the description of one police official, "against the ruling classes, law, order and the churches." In late February, as uptown radicals were reeling from the news of the Caplan-Schmidt arrests, "Baldo" supplied Carbone and Abarno with antimony and chlorate of potash, then helped them figure out how to build a bomb. At their trial the following month, the setup earned them each six to twelve years in prison.[25]

To Goldman, the whole affair reeked of the provocateur tactics favored by the Russian secret service. "It is the most flagrant police conspiracy that has ever taken place in New York City," she wrote to a friend in early April. But a few months later she acknowledged with a glimmer of satisfaction that not all of the city's bomb plots were of police devising. On May 3, almost twenty-nine years to the day after the Haymarket bombing, a blast wrecked the southeast corner of Bronx Borough Hall, not far from where the fall's dynamite campaign had almost destroyed the Bronx Court House. "So busy are its detectives manufacturing crime . . . , planning pretty disguises, and entrapping victims, that they have time for nothing else," Goldman wrote with a bit of satisfaction. "Under their very noses the Borough Hall and Bronx Court House have been blown up." Indeed, the police soon got a taste of dynamite for themselves. On July 5, a year and a day after the Lexington blast, a bomb exploded at police headquarters on Centre Street, blowing off the front doors.[26]

That bomb proved to be the finale of the great "Anarchist Scare" of 1914–15. Over the next few months, police noted "a sharp decrease in bomb-throwing in New York." Still, for a city where dynamite had been largely unknown a year earlier, it was an astounding rash of violence: ten distinct acts of alleged anarchist terrorism in just twelve months. This did not include the many bomb plots that sputtered, then died, on the front pages of newspapers. Nor did it include the various assassinations and bombings related to the escalating war in Europe. By 1915, the United States was still firmly isolationist, but the violence of the war had already begun to spill across the sea into New York. On July 3, for instance, less than forty-eight hours before the police headquarters bombing, Erich Muenter had planted his dynamite at the U.S. Capitol, then rushed to New York to carry out his assassination attempt on Jack Morgan. "It was a troubled hour," recalled bomb squad chief Thomas Tunney, who himself hurried to Long Island to interview Jack, "and one in which it behooved us of the Police Department to keep our heads cool and our eyes open."[27]

As New York's role in war shipments increased over the following year, the bomb squad's attention began to shift from anarchists to "Huns," especially to acts of sabotage against the city's growing munitions machine. In their scale and potential, these quickly dwarfed the amateur efforts of the anarchist scare. Sabotage at the Black Tom munitions depot, located on an island just a few feet from the Statue of Liberty, nearly destroyed lower Manhattan. On July 30, 1916, when the explosions began, some two million pounds of ammunition were on site, awaiting shipment to the Allies. The blast killed at least four people, injured hundreds, and blew out windows as far north as Forty-second Street.[28]

All of this put the city on edge. But despite the attention garnered by the New York sabotage plots, the most significant dynamite case of the early war years came once again out of the American West. On July 22, 1916, a bomb exploded in a crowd of spectators at a "Preparedness" Day" parade in San Francisco, killing ten and sending forty-four others to the hospital. By the following week, city authorities had arrested five local anarchists and socialists. Among them was the man whose fate soon became a symbol of the war's darkening effects on American radicalism, a self-proclaimed "militant worker"—and a good friend of Berkman's—named Thomas J. Mooney.[29]

BERKMAN ENDED UP in San Francisco by process of elimination. He began his 1914 lecture tour in high spirits, thrilled to escape the chaos and recriminations of New York. "I *am* indeed glad I started!" he wrote. "[L]iving many years in New York one is apt to regard the Metropolis as a criterion of the whole country, in point of general conditions and revolutionary activity—which is far from correct." Just how incorrect it was, though, came as something of a shock. In Homestead, where he had hoped for a triumphal return, only a handful of supporters showed up. He found equally deflating receptions in Cleveland and Elyria, Ohio, and in Detroit."[T]he poor boy seems to have absolutely no luck with lectures," Goldman wrote to a friend in late 1915. "I wonder why. He is terribly discouraged, which I can readily understand."[30]

The one bright spot was California, where the Caplan and Schmidt arrests had put the tang of dynamite in the air once again. Berkman arrived in Los Angeles in the early spring, prepared to meet his scheduled lecture dates and move on. Within a few weeks, though, he began to flirt with the idea of staying. He hoped to transform the Caplan-Schmidt case into the next great rallying point for labor. "Think of Moyer, Haywood and Pettibone," he wrote in *Mother Earth*. "Not guilt nor innocence is the deciding factor. *The attitude of labor alone* weighs in the balance of capitalistic justice." Caplan and Schmidt's lawyers had a different strategy. They asked Berkman to leave, for fear that his presence would damage their clients' case. He decided to try his luck in San Francisco.[31]

Arriving in the fall of 1915, he found a city brimming with the same social conflicts he had left months earlier in New York: labor protests, a burgeoning "law and order" campaign, even the lingering memory of dynamite (towers at the antiunion Pacific Gas and Electric Company had been bombed in 1913). Already, however, these familiar battles were starting to acquire a new cast. As the war in Europe grew bloodier and more intractable, with almost four hundred thousand soldiers killed that spring alone, Americans had begun to consider more seriously what it would mean to join the fight. Did submarine attacks on civilian liners such as the *Lusitania* call for a military response? Would a German victory spell doom for American finance? Were vital American strategic interests at stake? In particular, they debated what philosopher John Dewey identified as "the social possibilities of war" and what Berkman described, somewhat more crudely, as "the war at home": the prospect that the European war could be used to reshape political and class relations within the United States.[32]

For Dewey, the growing drumbeat for war seemed to present a glorious opportunity: mobilization, he predicted, would shake up the status quo, expand state power, and give progressives the chance to mold society anew.

Berkman, like most radicals, was highly skeptical of such claims, wondering aloud if it would be quite so easy to control a war that seemed to have a momentum of its own. "The revolutionary movement of the world is now in great danger of being swept away in the general conflagration," he had written in *Mother Earth* in 1914. "Let us foresee this danger."[33]

By the time he arrived in San Francisco a year later, he had plenty of evidence to prove his case. In Europe, nearly every socialist party had collapsed under nationalist pressure, tossing off their loyalties to the world's workers in favor of homeland protection. Within the United States, the balance of power was already shifting in the direction of men such as Jack Morgan, busy coordinating multimillion-dollar loans for the Allies. To most progressives and revolutionaries, Wall Street's involvement in the war looked like a toxic brew of profit and bloodshed. "Out of international carnage they have made billions; out of the misery of the people and the agony of women and children the American financiers and industrial magnates have coined huge fortunes," Goldman wrote in *Mother Earth*. "[O]ld Pierpont Morgan would be astounded could he see the dazzling profits gathered in by his son through war speculations."[34]

They evinced particular disgust for the so-called preparedness campaign taking shape in coastal cities such as San Francisco and New York, where war-related commerce was on the rise. On its face, "preparedness" was just what it suggested: a mass movement to prepare the United States for battle by expanding the army and navy, manufacturing armaments, and planning for a draft. Its chief backers, however, came from the top ranks of business and finance, men such as Jack Morgan and Henry Frick, bound to profit handsomely. In San Francisco, employers openly advertised their desire to use the war effort, in the words of the Chamber of Commerce's new Law and Order Committee, to end the "long period of tolerance of lawlessness and intimidation" that characterized the progressive approach to labor—in other words, to remake San Francisco, long a haven for labor, into a stronghold of the "open shop." President Wilson himself had vowed in his 1915 preparedness speech to stamp out "creatures of passion, disloyalty, and anarchy," especially among the foreign-born. To Berkman, arriving in San Francisco in the midst of the preparedness buildup, this looked like the issue of the moment. In January 1916, he founded a fiery new "revolutionary labor weekly" intended to "prepare" workers for a final revolt against the capitalist war machine. He called it the *Blast*.[35]

The title was a deliberate provocation. Berkman envisioned his magazine a merciless champion of revolution in its most literal sense—a call to arms for the American worker. Unlike *Mother Earth*, with its digressions on art and literature, the *Blast* focused primarily on class struggle and the war. If Goldman took this as a challenge to *Mother Earth's* more temperate sensibility, she did not voice her concerns publicly. When she arrived in San Francisco for a visit in July, exhausted after serving a short jail sentence in New York for advocating birth control, she, too, flirted with the idea of staying. "It is all so wonderful," she wrote to friends back home. "I do not know just when I will be through with San Francisco, but I mean to stay as long as I possibly can."[36]

She soon changed her mind. According to Goldman, she was lunching with Berkman and his companion, Eleanor "Fitzie" Fitzgerald, on July 22 when the telephone rang. "Berkman went to the 'phone," she recalled breathlessly for her *Mother Earth* readership,

and we continued our conversation, but suddenly we realized in the replies of our friend that something serious had happened. We learned the truth only too soon. A bomb had been exploded during the Preparedness parade, a number of people killed and many wounded. Involuntarily, I exclaimed, "I hope we anarchists will not again be held responsible," but my hope was in vain. The very first extras which greeted me on the way to my apartment contained the usual glaring headlines, "Anarchist Bomb! All Anarchists must be driven out of town, etc., etc."[37]

Goldman presented the bombing as a complete surprise—yet another incident in which anarchists were unjustly suspected. The police, by contrast, believed that Berkman, if not Goldman, had had an active hand in its execution. The first arrests targeted five local labor activists—most notably, *Blast* contributor Tom Mooney and his friend Warren Billings, who had served time in prison for the Pacific Gas and Electric bombings a few years earlier. Berkman felt sure he was next. As in July 1914, though, he determined to press ahead, to create the same sort of grand, symbolic protest he had fashioned to such success in Union Square. "Now is the time to demonstrate, once for all," he wrote in the *Blast*, "that we of the awakened social consciousness will not tolerate a repetition of the hellish crime of the 11th of November, 1887."[38]

This time, however, with the war as a backdrop and patriotic appeals for a stiff sentence, few beyond a tiny band of supporters showed any interest in heeding the call. Nor did the jury show much inclination to extend the "period of tolerance" that had inspired the Commission on Industrial Relations and allowed Berkman to speak in 1914 in Union Square. The central fact of the Preparedness Day case was that the bomb was *not* aimed at a Frank Steunenberg or a John D. Rockefeller, or even an advancing cordon of police. It struck innocent bystanders attending a patriotic parade. "Here, gentlemen, was the offense," the prosecutor explained. "This American flag—this American flag was what they desired to offend. They offended that by killing the women and men that worshipped it." Faced with such accusations in the midst of rising calls for the United States to join the war, the jury delivered a swift blow. In January 1917, the California court sentenced Mooney to death, the first time since Haymarket that a labor radical was scheduled to die for using dynamite.[39]

The outcome was not a surprise to Goldman, but it worried her. "I am terribly discouraged," she wrote to a friend. "The situation is altogether awful....I really dare not think of it all." As talk of preparedness gave way to a more concerted mobilization, she found added cause for concern. On February 5, 1917, pleading wartime necessity, Congress passed a new immigration law ordering the deportation of anyone "found advocating or teaching the unlawful destruction of property, or...the assassination of public officials," an expansion of the 1903 antianarchist ban, which had merely sought to prevent them from coming in the first place. The following month, the state of Idaho approved a "criminal syndicalism" law, recommending lengthy sentences for advocates of "sabotage, violence or unlawful methods of terrorism as a means of accomplishing industrial or political reform"—the first in a wave of state laws reviving the speech restrictions that had followed McKinley's death.[40]

Finally, on April 2, 1917, after almost three years of hesitation, President Wilson asked Congress for a declaration of war. It was a radical break with U.S. tradition, the first time that the country intervened in a European conflict. As millions of observers predicted, it also intensified the war at home. Before 1917, the federal government had mostly left the problem of labor violence and revolutionary dissent to states, cities, and private employers (immigration law was the one great exception). Entry into the war licensed a far more active federal role. Within three months, Goldman and Berkman found themselves back in prison, this time in the custody of the U.S. government. Hundreds of their friends and sympathizers soon followed.

IN MAKING HIS APPEAL to Congress, Wilson warned that "disloyalty will be dealt with with the firm hand of stern suppression." Despite the advance notice, the swiftness of the crackdown caught Goldman and Berkman by surprise. In May, they helped to found the No Conscription League, devoted to resisting the impending military draft "by every means in our power," in the words of its manifesto. A month later, on June 15, U.S. marshal Thomas D. McCarthy appeared with a warrant for their arrest.[41]

They were, conveniently, together in New York, working a floor apart at the new offices of *Mother Earth* and the *Blast*. When the police arrived, Goldman requested a few minutes to change her clothes and select a book to read in jail. Berkman, leaning heavily on crutches thanks to torn ligaments in his foot, hobbled down from the *Blast* to join her. The charge, they learned, was "conspiracy to induce persons not to register," a violation of the Selective Service Act. Ironically, after years of being accused of subversion through violence, it was opposition to the draft—to "murder at the behest of the war profiteers," as they described it—that finally landed them in the custody of the federal government.[42]

When their trial began two weeks later, the U.S. attorney, Harold Content, had little trouble proving that they had spoken out against conscription. But he was not satisfied with limiting himself to such recent evidence. Eager to prove that the defendants were not merely pacific opponents of a brutal war, Content recalled for the jury some of the most notorious incidents of their shared past: how Goldman had supposedly inspired Czolgosz to murder President McKinley, how *Mother Earth* had cheered for "dynamite" in July 1914, and, of course, how in 1892 Berkman had taken it upon himself to transform word into deed. "You think this woman before you is the real Emma Goldman, this well-bred lady, courteous, and with a pleasant smile on her face?" he demanded. "No! The real Emma Goldman can be seen only on the platform. There she is in her true element, sweeping all caution to the winds! There she inflames the young and drives them to violent deeds."[43]

As in San Francisco, this blend of accusations—disloyalty and radicalism, dynamite and war resistance—met with a receptive audience. On July 9, in just thirty-nine minutes, the jury returned a guilty verdict. Later that afternoon, almost three years to the day since Berkman's triumphal appearance at Union Square, Judge Julius Mayer imposed the maximum sentence: two years in jail, with a $10,000 fine, to be followed by deportation to Russia.

Given the many "portents" of recent years, Goldman later reflected, they should have expected no less. As time went on they even began to count themselves lucky. The following month, the California authorities indicted Berkman in the Mooney case; his draft law conviction, fortuitously, put the federal authorities on his side in preventing extradition to San Francisco. Their early wartime sentences saved them from other, more dire consequences as well. On June 15, the same day that Marshal McCarthy paid his visit to *Mother Earth,* President Wilson announced the passage of the Espionage Act, outlawing any speech or political activity tending to encourage resistance to the draft or to U.S. military operations. Unlike the draft law, the Espionage Act carried a sentence of up to twenty years in prison.[44]

The passage of the Espionage Act brought an escalation of the federal campaign against war dissenters, an unprecedented venture into regulating and punishing political opinion. Over the next fifteen months, more than a thousand men and women went to jail for speaking out against the government, the war effort, and the role of American capitalists in fostering one or the other. Some of the new defendants were German-born aliens, swept up in the same wave of hostility that banned the German language in public schools, turned sauerkraut into "liberty cabbage," and, more ominously, led to vigilante assaults. Others were men such as the Montana rancher Ves Hall, unwise enough to complain that "the United States was only fighting for Wall Street millionaires." Hall was tried and ultimately found innocent; the court ruled that the mere expression of discontent with Wall Street did not tangibly disrupt the war effort. But some who made similar comments ended up in jail. In New Hampshire, a man who complained that "this was a Morgan war and not a war of the people" received three years in federal prison for his troubles.[45]

To Goldman, this wave of arrests showed how right men such as Hall actually were: politicians were now so subservient to Wall Street that they arrested anyone who criticized its shenanigans. Wilson himself had suggested that this would happen, warning Navy Secretary Josephus Daniels as late as 1917 that "[t]he people we have unhorsed will inevitably come into control of the country for we shall be dependent upon the steel, ore and financial magnates. They will run the nation." In fact, if not in intent, the Espionage Act furthered this shift, transforming grumbling about plutocratic tyranny from a common point of interest into a federal crime.[46]

The wartime postal regulations only reinforced this point. Postmaster Albert Burleson, empowered to suspend the mailing privileges of "seditious" publications, explicitly targeted any magazine treasonous enough to suggest "that the government is controlled by Wall Street or munitions manufacturers, or any other special interests," or to express support for the Wobblies. (Among his first targets were *Mother Earth* and the *Blast*.) As the war proceeded, Congress expanded these speech restrictions still further, passing the Trading with the Enemy Act, which required all foreign-language publications to provide a translation of articles critical of the U.S. government; the Sabotage Act, which designated a thirty-year sentence for acts of violence or work slowdowns aimed at war industries; and, finally, the sweeping Sedition Act of May 1918, which trumped them all by simply outlawing "disloyal, profane, scurrilous or abusive language about the form of government of the U.S. or the constitution of the U.S."[47]

As the Supreme Court later noted, all of these laws were based upon a claim of war necessity—the idea that, in the words of Justice Oliver Wendell Holmes, "when a nation is at war, things that might be said in time of peace are such a hindrance to its effort that their utterance will not be endured." But they also drew heavily on the strategies honed through years of domestic battles over labor, dynamite and terrorism. At the core of the new restrictions was the same idea expressed thirty years earlier in Chicago, when Haymarket prosecutor Julius Grinnell argued that words, rather than deeds, were the true danger to the republic. And despite the occasional exception, the law's chief targets were drawn from precisely those ranks—Wobblies, socialists, anarchists—who had long been accused of subversive speech.[48]

This was, in part, because these groups *did* oppose the war, and even after April 2 they made little effort to disguise the fact. Of the major national organizations that once opposed U.S. involvement, from the American Federation of Labor to the progressive American Union Against Militarism, only the Socialist Party, and to some degree the IWW, maintained their stance once hostilities began. In return, they found themselves accused not only of subversion and violence—the old standards—but also of treason itself. Many of the most aggressive attacks came from one-time progressive allies, determined to prove their patriotism and support Wilson's effort to craft a democratic "peace without victory." As the head of Wilson's new propaganda agency, the Committee on Public Information, former socialist sympathizer and progressive champion George Creel took the lead in encouraging newspaper readers to report any friend or neighbor "who spreads pessimistic stories…, cries for peace, or belittles our efforts to win the war." Those who remained in the Socialist Party found themselves subject not only to calumny but also to arrest and purging from political office. Among their ranks were dozens of moderate Socialists such as Milwaukee congressman Victor Berger, who had long denounced both Wobblies and anarchists as misguided terrorists wedded to "murder as a means of propaganda."[49]

As one of the first dissenters arrested, Goldman joked that her old reformist adversaries were perhaps getting what they deserved. "Now the American Huns no longer discriminated between one radical group and another: liberals, I.W.W.'s, socialists, preachers, and college professors were being made to pay for their former short-sightedness." Actually seeing old friends and allies suffer the gauntlet was much harder to take. On September 5, 1917, with President Wilson's personal approval, federal agents raided Wobbly headquarters in Chicago, arresting 166 alleged conspirators against the war. Among those seized was her old Village comrade, now secretary-treasurer of the IWW, Big Bill Haywood.[50]

Haywood knew his arrest was coming. What he did not expect was the scale of the operation, which dwarfed anything directed at either the anarchists or the socialists. On the same day that federal agents raided the Chicago office, teams swooped down on Wobbly headquarters in Sacramento, Wichita, and many other cities—the largest political raid in federal history. They accused the Wobblies not only of opposing the war but also of orchestrating a campaign of sabotage and strikes against critical war industries. In Chicago alone, the indictment charged the defendants with 17,022 separate crimes—a ridiculous number, in Haywood's view. Indeed, most were not even crimes in the standard sense. Of the 17,022 crimes alleged, there was not a single bomb or act of violence. Nor was there any evidence the Wobblies had persuaded anyone not to register for the draft. The only "overt acts" were those of publication: the Wobbly preamble declaring "the working class and the employing class have nothing in common"; Émile Pouget's *Sabotage*, reprinted in English by the IWW; an issue of *Solidarity* bearing the damning quote "We are absolutely and irrevocably dissatisfied with the present system of society. We consider it a useless system, and we mean to destroy it."[51]

As in Idaho a decade earlier, Haywood turned to Debs for help. "Anything you may be able to do in the way of organizing a Nonpartisan Defense League will be greatly appreciated," he wrote. Debs was happy to do what he could. "Wall Street mortally fears the I.W.W. and its growing menace to capitalist autocracy and misrule," he wrote in February 1918, rallying his socialist readers in support of the Wobblies at their upcoming trial. "The very name of the I.W.W. strikes terror to Wall Street's craven soul."[52]

Debs' influence barely made a dent. As at Goldman and Berkman's trial, the Chicago jury took less than an hour to deliver convictions for everyone involved. Haywood himself received the harshest sentence: twenty years in prison, to begin immediately.

The first leg of his incarceration brought Haywood back to the Cook County Jail, where he and the other Wobblies had been imprisoned since their arrest in September. It was the same jail where Goldman had stayed in the anxious days after the McKinley assassination and where the Haymarket martyrs, in 1887, had met their deaths. During the long months of confinement before trial, Haywood thought often about the Haymarket legacy. "From my cell, No. 275, I could look down into the end of the corridor, and could picture the scaffold that had been built there when it was the death scene of Parsons, Spies, Engel and Fisher [*sic*]," he later wrote. "Their words seemed to reverberate throughout the prison. Their silence spoke an undying tongue."

A few days later, as he sat in the downtown marshal's office filing an appeal to be released on bail, he learned that the legacy of Haymarket lived on in other ways as well. As he began to dictate notes to a stenographer, he felt the federal building rumble and heard glass crashing onto the street. Minutes later, he learned that a bomb had gone off in the first-floor post office, killing one woman and three men and injuring dozens of others. "Enough to say," he later wrote, "no bonds were granted for any of us."[53]

GOLDMAN FOUND HERSELF thinking often of Haymarket as she watched the war noose tighten. "Things even the most pessimistic of us never thought possible have become a fact," she wrote in the fall of 1917. "The persecution and prosecution of labor surpasses anything the world has ever known." She was particularly disturbed by reports of wartime justice meted out not by the government but by "the people" themselves. In Butte, Montana, a posse dragged crippled Wobbly organizer Frank Little from his bed, castrated him, and hanged him from a railroad trestle. In Bisbee, Arizona, mine bosses loaded some twelve hundred Wobblies and their families into rail cars and shipped them out to wither in the desert. In Tulsa, a bomb at the home of a Standard Oil official inspired a group of local businessmen and oil executives to drag sixteen Wobblies from jail, drive them at gunpoint to a ravine, then whip, tar, and feather them in what a local paper described as "a real American party."[54]

To Goldman, it appeared that the nation had gone crazy with hatred, much as it had in Chicago in 1886. "Through the length and breadth of the country," she later wrote, "stalked the madness of jingoism." Even Debs, sixty-three years old, the elder statesman of American socialism, did not escape. In May 1918, he delivered an antiwar speech in Canton, Ohio, championing the Wobblies as victims of government persecution. "Don't take the word of Wall Street and its press as final," he urged his audience. "The I.W.W. in all its career never committed as much violence against the ruling class as the ruling class has committed against the I.W.W." The U.S. attorney, reviewing these words, ordered his arrest under the new, revised Espionage Act.[55]

It was Debs' arrest, far more than the arrests of Wobblies and anarchists, that captured for many radicals how profoundly the war had changed the political landscape. Just six years earlier, Debs had been a viable, if not triumphant, candidate for the presidency. Now he was poised to go to prison—and, with a ten-year sentence, potentially to die there—for what was essentially an unchanged position. The government's logic confirmed the worst fears about the war's blanket effect on political dissent. "While, of course, [Debs] refrains from using the words, 'Government of the United States,' and substitutes therefore 'capitalism,' 'Wall Street,' etc., it is the present order of things that he is attacking," the U.S. attorney explained in recommending his prosecution. "This, of course, is the kind of criticism of the government of the United States which I believe Congress intended to forbid."[56]

To Goldman, this looked like nothing so much as the Haymarket prosecution enshrined in national policy—the abandonment of free speech. This conviction only increased in October 1918, when Congress passed yet another antianarchist law, declaring that mere membership in a revolutionary organization could be considered grounds for deportation. Locked away at the women's penitentiary in Jefferson City, Missouri, forbidden more than one letter per week, there was little she could do. When the thirty-first anniversary of Haymarket arrived on November 11, 1918, she made plans to protest by striking at the prison textile shop, where she worked. To her befuddlement, the prison authorities seemed to support her action. At ten o'clock in the morning, they shut down the machines, turned off the power, and granted all prisoners a day off. Goldman mingled with other women in the recreation yard, thinking quietly of "the days of 1887" and wondering if the dawn would ever come anew. Not until evening did she learn that the actual reason for the holiday was the Allied victory in Europe.[57]

Beyond prison walls, the armistice set in motion what was politely called "reconstruction" but what amounted to official chaos, as the federal government cancelled billions in wartime contracts, shipped hundreds of thousands of soldiers home, and summarily dismantled what had been, even at its best, a patchwork concatenation of wartime agencies. For the hundreds of radicals behind bars, it made little difference, at least at first. Restricted from most outside contact, worn down by months of defeat, they could barely participate in their own amnesty campaigns, much less help the hundreds of others in jails across the land. But they did find one cause for hope. In November 1917, to everyone's amazement, Bolshevik militants had seized power in Russia and declared the world's first socialist state. As the war drew to a close, the American left began to dream that they might soon follow that revolutionary example.

It is hard to overestimate the eagerness—even desperation—with which American radicals seized upon the Russian example. "From New York to San Francisco," recalled future communist leader Benjamin Gitlow,

> from Duluth to New Orleans, in mines and mills, on the corners
> of skid rows, in hobo jungles, beer halls, labor temples, at union
> meetings, among the denizens of Greenwich Village and Chicago's
> Dill Pickle Club, in squalid tenements and sumptuous apartments,
> socialists, anarchists, wobblies, liberals, intellectuals of the left,
> workers, aristocrats and bohunks of every shade and color, from
> light pink and yellow to deepest red, huddled together and in

heated discussions weighed the significance of what came from the lips of the Russians' red messiah.

The most committed went on to form two American communist parties in September 1919. But even those who never joined either party supported the Bolsheviks' cause in those early months. Goldman was struck by how little the old differences of opinion seemed to matter in the post-war world. "The Russian Revolution is indeed a miracle," she concluded. "It demonstrates every day how insignificant all theories are in comparison with the actuality of the revolutionary awakening of the people."[58]

Lenin himself had more modest ambitions for American workers—victims, as he saw it, of a reactionary, predatory state. "We know that help from you will probably not come soon, comrade American workers," he wrote, "for the revolution is developing in different countries in different forms and at different tempos." In those first few months, however, the American movement seemed poised to surprise him. On January 21, 1919, thirty-five thousand shipyard workers, many of them members of the IWW, struck in Seattle. Within two weeks, their walkout expanded into the first general strike in American history—a show of revolutionary ambition that rivaled anything the Wobblies or anarchists had accomplished before the war. To the hundreds of radicals watching anxiously from behind bars, this looked like good news at last, the opening shot in the postwar revolt.

Rather than expanding into a working-class revolt, however, it became the first major defeat of the postwar years. Summoned by Seattle mayor Ole Hanson, federal troops marched in and crushed the rebellion just five days after it began.[59]

What mattered about Seattle in retrospect was not its revolutionary promise but the proof, in Haywood's wry words, that "the Armistice did not settle the war in the United States." If anything, the public response ("NO COMPROMISE! No Compromise Now—or Ever!") was even less sympathetic to Wobblies and labor radicals than it had been during the war. To most Americans, the new pro-Bolshevik rhetoric on display in Seattle only confirmed the suspicion, hatched in the days of Johann Most, that those who spoke out against capitalism—who called for dynamite and revolution—were traitors to the nation.[60]

Over the next few months, as hundreds of thousands of soldiers returned home and Wilson pressed his Fourteen Points at Versailles, talk began in earnest about how to purge the nation of the men and women so long associated with the specter of revolution. Many of the ideas were old ones: enacting a ban on immigrants from countries such as Russia and Italy, where agitators were prone to breed; passing a federal sedition law that would outlaw violent, revolutionary speech. Others, such as loyalty oaths for teachers or the ban New York enacted on displaying the red flag, had a postwar tinge. In either case, they quickly deflated Goldman's postwar optimism. "I wonder how many times more I will have to serve [in prison] for remaining true to my ideal?" she wrote a friend in 1919. "Until the end, I suppose."[61]

That came sooner than expected. Less than three months after the Seattle strike, the May Day mail bomb conspiracy—the plot that had targeted Jack Morgan and dozens of other businessmen and politicians—thrust the issue of dynamite once again onto the front page. The June 2 plot, erupting a month later in seven different cities, raised public alarm to a fever pitch, marking the start of the postwar Red Scare and all but ensuring that wartime strategy of federal suppression would extend into peace. The logic of the federal response as it emerged over the next few months drew heavily on the language of war: The bombings were a revolutionary conspiracy, an attempted coup d'etat, a threat to the nation itself. Indeed, the coordinated nature of bombings, with their nationwide scope and multiple actors, seemed to grant a new urgency to the terrorism problem; there was no mistaking them for the work of a lone radical or a single deranged man. Safely locked behind bars, neither Goldman nor Berkman, much less Haywood or Debs, could be accused of taking part in the plots. But no less than the wartime crackdown, the 1919 bomb conspiracies helped to seal their fates. On June 3, Attorney General Palmer announced his new campaign to purge the country of its "anarchist element." By the time Goldman and Berkman left prison a few months later, he had settled on a policy of deportation.[62]

GOLDMAN'S DEPARTURE FROM PRISON on September 28, 1919, was a major public event. Photographers and supporters swarmed to Jefferson City, eager to hear her reflections on all that had happened since she disappeared behind bars. For once, worn down by loneliness, uncertain about the future, she had little to say. She simply wanted to get home to New York, "[b]ack to life and work again." She left Missouri at once, stopping only to deliver the $15,000 bail required of her by the Immigration Bureau. Berkman, released a few days later, did the same. Though they had completed their time in jail, both were slated for deportation to Russia.[63]

The prospect of returning to their homeland at this late date was not entirely unwelcome. They had discussed the possibility as early as March 1917, when the threat of prosecution in the Preparedness Day bombing had been hanging over Berkman's head. Even then, they had known that leaving for Russia might well mean a permanent separation from friends and family. "The irony of it is that we may now go to Russia and may not come back to America," Goldman wrote. "Verily, Democracy is an illusion and a snare." At the time, it had seemed like a desirable option, the fruition of the plan hatched decades ago in the little ice cream parlor in Worcester. Being forced to go to Russia by the attorney general was another matter.[64]

Reunited in New York, Goldman and Berkman plunged into one last public battle, pleading with supporters for money and energy to mount an appeal. They were entwined in a variety of legal struggles stemming from their wartime convictions, the Preparedness Day bombing, and the impending order of deportation. "This is the most crucial period in our lives," they wrote in a joint letter in late 1919. "We appeal to you, dear friend, most probably for the last time." Their hopes were not particularly high. Even as they put on a public show of outrage, they quietly began to prepare for departure. After the chaos of the war years, they no longer had much to get in order. "We had nothing left, neither literature, money, nor even a home," Goldman later reflected. "The war tornado had swept the field clean, and we had to begin everything anew."[65]

There was no fresh start, however, at least not in America. On November 7, the second anniversary of the Bolshevik Revolution, Attorney General Palmer initiated the first of his major deportation raids, arresting more than a thousand members of the little-known Union of Russian Workers, an anarchist organization composed mainly of Russian immigrants. He justified the arrests as an antiterrorist measure—a response to the May Day and June 2 plots, and a model for future action to contain the dynamite threat. Berkman saw the writing on the wall. "The U.S. government . . . has up to recently had no definite policy toward its social protestants," he wrote to his lawyer, Harry Weinberger, on November 11. "But the time has come when even the political bats in Washington have realized that a certain clear-cut and more or less consistent attitude is necessary toward rebels."[66]

From there, things moved quickly. On November 17, Palmer appeared before Congress to describe his plans for controlling radical aliens who "advised the defiance of law and authority." Chief among his exhibits was an account of Goldman and Berkman's shared history, from the Frick assassination attempt through the Lexington Avenue explosion and the No Conscription League. The report was something of a backhanded tribute to their influence. Of its 187 pages, 110 were devoted to evidence against them.[67]

Their fame did little to stall their departure. In a final burst of energy, Goldman and Berkman undertook a joint lecture tour in late November—a defiant hurrah and an excuse to say good-bye to scattered American comrades. During a farewell dinner in Chicago on December 2, a reporter burst into the room with the startling news that Frick had died. The press suspected the dinner had been planned to celebrate the fact, but Berkman disabused him of the notion. Unlike himself, Berkman retorted, Frick was "deported by God."[68]

The dinner in Chicago offered Goldman and Berkman's last moment of genuine freedom in the United States. From Chicago, they boarded a train to New York and turned themselves in to federal authorities, who promptly transported them to Ellis Island. Mingling with the other deportees, Goldman was struck by how little conditions had changed since she had first arrived in New York in 1885. "Their quarters were congested, the food was abominable, and they were treated like felons," she later wrote. She was struck, too, by the irony of such an inglorious end. After more than three decades in the United States, after willfully remaking themselves as an Americans, both she and Berkman were being deported as if they had never belonged at all.[69]

To many of their admirers, this denial of their Americanness was the final insult. "They were born in Russia, but they did their thirty years' work of enlightenment in this, our America," wrote the radical cartoonist Robert Minor, a former *Mother Earth* contributor. "I think they are therefore Americans, in the best sense, and the best of Americans." The immigration authorities did not agree. On the evening of December 20, federal agents hustled Goldman and Berkman out of Ellis Island and onto a tug waiting in New York Harbor.[70]

With them were 247 other deportees: 196 members of the Union of Russian Workers and another 51 unaffiliated anarchists and other undesirables. They were scheduled to depart on the *Buford*, an old warship refitted for the occasion, destined to be known as the "Soviet Ark." Altogether, they constituted the first mass political deportation in American history—a refutation, as Goldman described it, of the "spirit of asylum" that had once attracted so many revolutionaries to American shores.[71]

The *Buford* chugged out of New York Harbor just before dawn on December 21. Gazing out of her porthole, Goldman bid farewell to the land that had made her an anarchist—especially to New York, the city that had for so long nurtured her dreams. "I could see the great city receding into the distance, its sky-line of buildings traceable by their rearing heads," she later wrote. "It was my beloved city, the metropolis of the New World." She hoped to return someday, once things settled down, perhaps with Berkman at her side. "We'll be back," Berkman promised as he walked toward the ship, "and this time we'll fix you."[72]

His comments were aimed at all of those who had been his adversaries over the years: capitalism, government, even the liberals who had failed to save him in the end. But he had a more specific object as well. Standing on the pier that day, absorbing Berkman's scorn, was a paunchy, middle-aged detective named William J. Flynn. As head of the federal government's Bureau of Investigation, Flynn had helped to coordinate the deportation effort, vowing to rid the country of "the brains of the ultra-radical movement." Ten months later, with Goldman and Berkman long gone from U.S. shores, he would lead the investigation into the Wall Street explosion.[73]

# PART III

....

# A NATIONAL CRIME

# 6

....

# THE GREAT DETECTIVES

WILLIAM J. FLYNN entered the Raleigh Hotel in downtown Washington just before noon on September 16, prepared to enjoy a pleasant lunch with friends. At two hundred pounds, with a close-cropped moustache and thick shock of reddish hair, Flynn was one of Washington's most recognizable officials, a stoop-shouldered Catholic Irishman in a town of fine-postured Protestants. Before entering the dining room, he stopped at the hotel clerk's desk and put in a special request to be paged in case of a long-distance call from New York. Just as his quartet was being seated, the clerk recalled, a messenger rushed into the hotel lobby. Flynn excused himself to speak with the boy, then returned a few minutes later with terrible news. "What we have expected has happened," he announced to his luncheon party. "New York has been blown up."[1]

That, at least, was the story told by the *Washington Post*, eager to assure its readers that the federal government was well prepared for "an outrage such as this." If Flynn had any advance knowledge of the explosion, though, he had little to show for it in those first few minutes. The call from New York offered only sketchy details: "4 bodies are on the sidewalk in front of Morgan's office," Bureau superintendent Charles Lamb reported, with "6 bodies across the street. A number of bodies have been

125

removed from the wreck." Lamb described the damage at the Morgan bank—"office wrecked inside"—and the fact that "quite a number of persons have been injured by flying glass." He also managed to relay, with some uncertainty, what appeared to be the only good evidence about the source of the blast. "The explosion probably came from a wagon drawn by one horse," he explained. "The wagon has disappeared."[2]

None of this gave any clear picture of what had happened: whether it was an accident or a bomb, much less who might be responsible. But Flynn, like the *Post*, knew that the country would be looking to him for answers. A New York native, Flynn had come of age in the great urban battles over "law and order," first as a keeper at the Ludlow Street Jail, then as head of the New York branch of the Secret Service. He had put in time at the New York police department as well, taking up an appointment as second deputy commissioner in 1910 with a promise to transform the city's "big feet and thick neck detectives" into sleuths on par with those at Scotland Yard. That episode had proved disappointing: rather than backing his call for efficiency, his superiors dispatched him to bust up city gambling rings. But like his subsequent appointment as head of the Secret Service, where he made a wartime name hunting German spies, his years with the New York police had helped Flynn develop a reputation as a scourge of corruption, terror, and violence. "William J. Flynn . . . What boy has read that name and not had a thrill race up his spine as his fertile imagination weaved fancied adventures in the United States secret service?" asked the *Los Angeles Times* in 1918. "Thousands of boys hold William J. Flynn as the hero of their air-castle adventures."[3]

What made Flynn the obvious man on September 16, though, was a more recent set of events. On June 2, 1919, the nationwide bomb conspiracy had erupted on a grand scale. The following day, seeking to reassure a jittery public, and still shaken by the attack on his home, Attorney General Palmer had announced Flynn's appointment as the head of the Bureau of Investigation. The two men had been quietly discussing the job for weeks, part of a postwar reshuffling of the Justice Department bureaucracy. In the wake of the bomb attacks, however, Palmer portrayed Flynn as a last-minute savior, "the great anarchist expert in the United States," the one man capable of tackling "the biggest job in the business of crime detection today." The daily press followed Palmer's lead. Within a day of his appointment, Flynn was known throughout the country as the

"U.S. Official Who Will Lead Fight Against Terrorists," in the words of the *Chicago Tribune*.[4]

Flynn was not terribly fond of the limelight. He insisted that effective detection was a matter of teamwork and proper organization, not newspaper antics or flashes of Sherlock Holmes–style brilliance. For every article describing him as an intrepid adventurer, another identified him as "big-bodied," "slow-spoken," "unhurried," "phlegmatic." "I'm not much on the talk," he explained. "I'd rather do a thing first and talk about it afterward." Still, he had done his best to live up to the nation's high expectations in the wake of the June bombings, instructing his agents to conduct "a vigorous and comprehensive investigation of anarchistic and similar classes."[5]

In truth, he was not sure that the Bureau was up to the task. The agency had been founded in 1908 with a modest mission: Justice Department officials were tired of borrowing agents from the Treasury Department's Secret Service when they wanted to conduct investigations. The Bureau had spent most of its first decade drifting between interstate prostitution ("white slavery") cases, antitrust work, and a grab bag of other federal scandals. When the war came along, then-chief A. Bruce Bielaski had seized upon the opportunity for expansion, moving his agents into antiradical and "slacker" work (rounding up draft resisters and enforcing draft registration) and nearly doubling the Bureau's size. Most notably, he had created the American Protective League (APL), a volunteer detective force of some two hundred thousand untrained citizens, armed with badges and an overweening sense of righteousness, who aided the Bureau by spying on their neighbors and providing the manpower for mass raids. Like so much wartime work, the APL proved to be a temporary, hodgepodge effort, unsupported by any particular authority or central vision; it disbanded in 1918. But the question of what to do with the Bureau itself, whether to scale it back or preserve its new powers, had lingered for months after the war. One of Flynn's first goals after his appointment in June 1919 had been to secure the Bureau a peacetime place as the nation's preeminent federal detective force, especially when it came to matters of radicalism, terrorism, and revolutionary dissent.[6]

This had required some effort. Traditionally, jurisdiction over bomb cases, even important ones such as Haymarket or Preparedness Day, fell to local or state officials. Where those authorities lacked manpower, they often shopped out the work to private detective firms (the Pinkertons had investigated the Haywood case; the Burns agency had arrested the McNamaras). The June 2 bombings, by contrast, seemed to cry out for some sort of federal response. No local authority could handle an investigation covering seven cities in seven states. Moreover, the bombers' pamphlets, like some of the bombs themselves, had directly targeted the federal government. "The powers that be make no secret of their will to stop, here in America, the world-wide spread of revolution," read the bombers' "Plain Words." "The powers that must be . . . will have to accept the fight they have provoked."

Such language had serious implications for national security; just three months earlier, Lenin himself had called for a worldwide revolution to sweep capitalism from the earth. As Flynn realized, this new context also offered a strong argument for why a powerful and proactive federal police force might now be necessary, even if the country had managed to hobble along without it in the past. On June 17, 1919, he gathered with Palmer and other top Justice officials to devise a plan for converting the bomb emergency into a broader campaign against revolutionary organizations. Less than two months later, they unveiled the Justice Department's new Radical Division, a research wing designed, in Palmer's words, "with the purpose in view of collecting evidence and data upon the revolutionary and ultraradical movements."[7]

As a department created to keep tabs on political dissent, the Radical Division was controversial from the start—precisely the kind of federal spying that deportees such as Goldman and Berkman had denounced as a step toward czaristic tyranny. From Flynn's perspective, though, the new system worked beautifully, amassing more than two hundred thousand files on left-wing agitators in its first year of operation. This record was due in no small part to the diligence and zeal of its young chief, a recent law school graduate and onetime Library of Congress cataloguer named J. Edgar Hoover. Flynn and Hoover had their personal differences: Flynn was a father of six, and Hoover was twenty-four years old and a bachelor; Flynn loved few things more than a good cigar, while Hoover, a devout Christian, frowned on such habits. Professionally, though, they had managed to forge an effective relationship, with Flynn and his Bureau agents acting as the hands-on investigators while Hoover conducted legal strategy and paper research behind the scenes.[8]

This had been their approach to the deportation raids. When Bureau agents rounded up some thousands of alleged members of the Communist and Communist Labor parties on January 2 in the grandest and most controversial of the Palmer Raids, Hoover had served as point man and chief coordinator in Washington. Indeed, while Palmer was the figurehead for the raids, it was Hoover who had come up with the legal strategy and written the briefs describing why membership in a communist party ought to be a deportable offense. He had been responsible for orchestrating Goldman's and Berkman's deportations as well, compiling the evidence against them while Bureau agents carried out the actual detective work. "Emma Goldman and Alexander Berkman are, beyond doubt, two of the most dangerous anarchists in this country," he had written to Bureau officials, "and if permitted to return to the community will result in undue harm." While this system had worked tolerably well when it came to deportations and other mass actions against revolutionary groups, it had fallen far short of the mark in the investigation of the June 2 bombings, where the Bureau had failed to bring a single suspect to trial.[9]

With the news of September 16, Flynn saw a chance to make good on that failing. After instructing Hoover to send all clues and updates through the New York office, he commandeered a special train and headed north.

Despite his formidable reputation, Flynn knew he would face a challenge to his authority once he arrived. Technically, the explosion at Wall and Broad was a local case. Whether the cause of the disaster turned out to be an accident or a bomb, the New York police were the most obvious authority to lead the investigation. The Bureau's only legal claim for launching an inquiry rested on the damage to the Sub-Treasury and assay office; twisted grillwork and shattered windows constituted destruction of federal property. Even that charge might just as well fall under the purview of the Treasury Department's Secret Service, or even Military Intelligence, both of which had already dispatched agents to report back from the explosion scene.

This lack of formal power had been one of the Bureau's greatest frustrations in recent years. However much Flynn or Hoover might desire a broad-based campaign against revolutionaries, they operated under a limited mandate to investigate only federal crimes. The deportation raids themselves been conducted on the shakiest legal authority, with the immigration bureau issuing the warrants and local police making many of the arrests. Both Flynn and Hoover had supported the passage of a peacetime sedition law that would grant the Justice Department formal jurisdiction over citizen radicals, a federal version of the state criminal anarchy laws. And while they had been forced to backtrack thanks to the objections of civil liberties groups and newspaper publishers, they still held out hope that some emergency or new threat would show Congress the error of its ways. With its high-profile victims and intimations of a revolutionary plot, the explosion on Wall Street promised to be the event they were seeking—a fact making it all the more imperative that Flynn arrive in New York as soon as possible. If the Bureau was going to play a major role in the investigation, it was crucial that the public understand what had happened as an assault not upon the Morgan bank or the city of New York but upon the nation itself.

Proving this would be no easy matter. Thousands of pieces of evidence lay strewn throughout the financial district. Each would have to be gathered, sorted, interpreted, and preserved. Hundreds of eyewitnesses would have to be rounded up and questioned. The dead would have to be inspected, their friends and relatives interrogated. Dozens of leads would have to be followed. And all of it would have to happen in an atmosphere of bureaucratic chaos and official rivalry.

Despite his fame as the nation's premier "anarchist chaser," Flynn was not the only prominent detective hoping to make good on the explosion case. As he sped north on the afternoon of September 16, some of his greatest rivals were already on Wall Street, preparing to play the hero themselves.

JUNIUS WAS SAFE. That much Arthur Woods knew as he surveyed the wreckage inside the Morgan bank. The windows should have hit Junius directly as they exploded inward toward his first-floor office. As it happened, wire screens prevented much of the glass from reaching its natural target, a bit of good news that the papers later described as a triumph for "bomb-proof netting." By the time Woods made his way to Wall Street, "rush[ing] among the dead bodies and up the front steps of the Morgan office," Junius was busy tending to men worse off. Only after the ambulances had been loaded did Junius seek treatment for his own injuries: a few minor gashes on the hand and another, rumor had it, on the buttocks. Then, his wounds bound in crisp white bandages, he went to lunch. According to the *Globe*, he appeared "calm and collected" as he left the bank, a credit to the Morgan tradition of pressure under fire.[10]

Woods tried to show similar composure as he began to pick over the firm's battered interior. As police commissioner, he had investigated Muenter's assassination attempt on Jack Morgan, taking personal charge of the interrogation ("The man appears to be mentally unbalanced," he informed the papers before the prisoner hanged himself in the Mineola jail). Now he had an even more direct stake in the disaster. In 1916, he had married into the Morgan dynasty; his wife was Jack's niece and Junius' cousin. As a Morgan man, Woods understood the need for family leadership in a moment of crisis. Like Flynn, he was also aware that his public resume—New York police commissioner, founder of the city bomb squad, hunter of anarchists and saboteurs—gave his actions that afternoon a certain public weight.[11]

Flynn and Woods knew each other well from New York police circles (Flynn's name frequently came up as a candidate for commissioner). Woods was aware of being treated with skepticism by earthier, more experienced detectives as he dabbled in civil-service reform and boasted to the Commission on Industrial Relations that "in New York, we not merely permit free speech and free assemblage and picketing, but we protect it." Perhaps as a result, when the war arrived he had put many of his policies aside, assisting the federal authorities in arresting Goldman, Berkman, and other local radicals. After leaving the commissioner's post in late 1917, he kept an active hand in law enforcement, both as an army colonel and as a lecturer on police reform. Despite his support for the Espionage Act and other wartime speech restrictions, Woods still spoke proudly of his stand for free speech in the spring and summer of 1914, when he had protected anarchist meetings and allowed Berkman to speak in Union Square. Well into 1920, he continued to insist that undercover work and careful investigation—not mass raids and suppression of speech—remained the best hope for the peacetime social order. Like Flynn, he hoped to drive this point home by solving the mystery on Wall Street.[12]

Woods was not part of any official investigative body (since resigning his post as colonel, he had worked chiefly on coordinating federal hearings on the plight of unemployed veterans). His main concern, at least in those first few minutes, was for the security and safety of the family bank. All of the partners, he noted thankfully, had escaped the worst. Those in the conference room upstairs, well above the force of the blast, had been left shaken but untouched. Downstairs, the clerks and secretaries had not been so lucky. Thomas Joyce, who had been meeting with Junius just before the explosion, had been knocked unconscious and sustained a deep wound to the head, the result of a glass partition that shattered nearby. His son William, twenty-four years old and a Morgan clerk, had suffered a more serious blow. Some large object—a piece of furniture, or a plate of glass—had crushed the boy's skull. He had died instantly, pinned to a cage near the coupon department like a butterfly captured for display.[13]

Woods saw the dead boy in the office, but he didn't linger. Stepping onto the bank's front steps, he breathed in the familiar scents of disaster: acrid fumes from a burning automobile, the metallic tang of blood, the dusty flatness of pulverized stone. He also noted a new menace in the offing. No longer fearing a second explosion, thousands of survivors had begun to flow back into the district, clogging the streets and alleyways as they attempted to "jam their way" back to work. Curiosity seekers followed, drawn by the promise of photos and souvenirs, and professional cameramen and reporters added to the mix. The uniformed policemen were doing their best to manage the situation. But the sheer numbers overwhelmed them, as did the necessity of protecting and transporting the dozens of injured still being discovered in odd, narrow alleyways, or blown prostrate under their desks.[14]

Woods had spent enough time in police ranks to understand how easily this sort of situation, with its jittery, undisciplined crowds and air of panic, could erupt into a full-blown riot. As police commissioner, he had spent hours preparing for such an eventuality, sketching out elaborate plans to maintain public safety in the event of German bomb attacks, earthquakes, revolutionary uprisings, and other variations of disaster. Now he jumped in to remind the police of their duties, encouraging them to keep firm to their lines. When two battalions of the U.S. Army showed up around one o'clock (the Sub-Treasury had called them to protect the government gold), he hurried over to offer instructions. One group formed a tight line of khaki around the Sub-Treasury and assay office. Another began to clear the district of unnecessary nuisances. Glass crunched beneath their boots as they passed banks and stores, ordering customers out and instructing shopkeepers to close and lock their doors.[15]

By midafternoon, the district was stable enough to rescind the call for federal troops, a fact that the *Tribune* ascribed to Woods' foresight. "This general mobilization is an assembly of police conceived by former Commissioner Arthur Woods," noted the next day's paper. "Yesterday it had its first test and it worked without disappointing the officials." Woods knew, however, that some of the greatest challenges lay ahead, as the rescue efforts gave way to a broader public debate about what to do next. Since leaving the police department, he had watched in dismay as the progressive ideals he once championed—respect for free speech, careful investigation of the evidence—had given way to hysteria and fear. Much to his chagrin, his once-proud bomb squad had been among the worst offenders. Now it was they, not he, who would have jurisdiction over the explosion investigation.[16]

WOODS' SUCCESSOR as police commissioner, Richard E. Enright, appeared at Wall and Broad just before one o'clock on the arm of Mayor John Hylan—the same way, more or less, that he had arrived in office. Thanks to a split in the reform vote between the prowar Republicans and the antiwar Socialists, the Democrats had reclaimed city hall in 1917, installing Hylan in the mayor's seat. Hylan, in turn, had set out to restaff the police department, ousting Woods in favor of Enright. In thanks, Enright added Hylan's brother-in-law to the police payroll and offered a policemen's brass band to trumpet the mayor's virtue at public functions.[17]

Woods' shadow continued to darken Enright's office. When the first newspaper reports emerged on September 16, some lauded Woods, not Enright, for uncovering "the first real story of the explosion." Woods received credit as well for the afternoon's crowd management success, though it was Enright who ordered the nearly two thousand police officers to Wall Street and assigned them to their stations. (Enright was also the one who sent the federal troops away; "apparently," the *World* reported, he "did not think the call for the troops was necessary.") The *Wall Street Journal* was particularly harsh, accusing the "flabby and vacillating city government" of failing "to police the financial district in the way it should have been policed long ago, in the way it was policed during the administration of Mayor Mitchel and Commissioner Woods." Enright was not easily cowed, however, especially when an investigation of such a scope was at stake. "I have just had a conference with Mr. Lamont and Mr. Bacon and Mr. Junius Morgan of the firm J. P. Morgan & Co.," he announced around one o'clock, "and they say the cause of the explosion was most assuredly dynamite in the street."[18]

On matters of social background, career trajectory, and class loyalties, Enright could hardly have been more out of place at an institution such as the Morgan bank. The son of a middling family from upstate New York, he had arrived in the city as a young man brimming with ambition, prepared to buckle down as a Tammany ward heeler, responsible for rounding up the Democratic vote, as well as an officer of the law. Through a patient twenty-five-year campaign of letter writing, glad-handing, and fierce loyalty, he had worked his way up, during Democratic administrations, from patrolman to lieutenant. But he was less known for his detective prowess than for politicking and, it was alleged, graft. One of Woods' predecessors had transferred him out of the contract-heavy Bureau of Supplies and Repairs for fear that "if I left Enright there long enough he'd own the department." Enright had promptly taken up a desk job, whiling away most of his hours on the affairs of the Lieutenants' Benevolent Association. When Hylan came into office in 1917, Enright made history by leaping ranks from lieutenant to commissioner, skipping over captain and inspector in between. He had also jumped ahead of Flynn, whose name had been floated in 1917 as the most likely man for the police commissioner's job. Enright took great pride in being the first commissioner ever appointed from the uniformed ranks. The men referred to him as "Smooth Dick."[19]

Woods had stepped aside immediately, explaining that any commissioner needed "the whole-souled understanding and cooperation of the Mayor" and that under Hylan he seemed unlikely to get either. On one front, however, he refused to relinquish control. Woods had never liked Enright. During his time as commissioner, he had gone out of his way to deny Enright's requests, refusing his pleas to lead the new bomb squad and instead dispatching him to a backwater post at the Flatbush station house. When Hylan appointed Enright as commissioner, Woods could not bear to admit defeat and turn over the bomb squad, so he held on to the unit, arguing that any force fighting Germans and draft dodgers should be part of the federal government. Twenty-four of the bomb squad's thirty-four members followed him out of the police into the Military Intelligence Division, serving out the war under military auspices. Only when hostilities ended did Enright truly gain control over the bomb squad of his own police department.[20]

From Enright's perspective, Woods' high-minded attempts to hold on to power looked like little more than political gamesmanship. When he entered office, Enright determined to return the favor, appointing a raft of Tammany faithful to the department's most public positions. For head of the detective division he selected Capt. William J. Lahey, a Tammany man demoted by Woods on the grounds of general unfitness for the job. To lead the bomb squad, he selected James J. Gegan, a veteran of the early battles against Berkman and the unemployed movement and, just as important, a Tammany loyalist. To round out the squad's ranks, he fired all of Woods' men and appointed a raft of new detectives, including the mayor's brother-in-law.[21]

Under Tammany leadership, the bomb squad had quickly taken on a new, more aggressive tone, jettisoning whatever remained of Woods' Union Square tolerance. Just two weeks after the end of the war, Mayor Hylan ordered the police to arrest anyone flying the red flag of Soviet communism. "The display of the red flag in our thoroughfares seems to be emblematic of unbridled license and an insignia for law hating and anarchy," he announced, "like the black flag [of anarchy] represents everything that is repulsive to ideals of civilization and the principles upon which our Government is founded." He also commanded them to break up any "unauthorized assemblages," a category understood to apply to socialists as well as anarchists and communists. In both cases, he acknowledged that this was an unusual intrusion into the right of free speech. He justified the campaign on the grounds that the Bolshevik Revolution, combined with the bombings and strike waves at home, made the postwar months a unique moment of emergency. "No matter what may have been the practice in ordinary times," Hylan explained, "no unauthorized gatherings or meetings should be allowed in the public streets and thoroughfares of our city."[22]

In the months since, the bomb squad had played a crucial supporting role in nearly every major antiradical campaign, from the state's Lusk Committee hearings on "revolutionary radicalism" to the June 2 bombing investigation and the federally led deportation raids. In many cases, the bomb squad had even been ahead of Flynn and the federal authorities in targeting revolutionary groups for raids and arrests. In March 1919, for instance, the police raided the Union of Russian Workers under the state's criminal anarchy statute—a full seven months before the Justice Department swept through and dispatched the group's members back to Russia on the Soviet Ark. For their efforts, the Tammany men earned the enmity of the city's radicals. When postal officials uncovered the May Day mail bombs, they found packages addressed to both Hylan and Enright.[23]

The threat of personal attack, along with the spectacle of the June 2 bomb conspiracy, had only added new urgency to their plans. On July 4, 1919, responding to rumors of a general strike in support of Tom Mooney, recently convicted in the San Francisco Preparedness Day bombing, Enright had called out some eleven thousand policemen to guard the Stock Exchange, the Morgan bank, and other prominent buildings in anticipation of "Plans for Widespread Violence and Murder," in the words of one headline. Though the day passed without so much as a parade ("What does the credulous public think now?" Goldman had wondered from jail), Enright, like Flynn, began to craft long-term plans for a permanent espionage and surveillance force. In late July 1919, he announced plans for a volunteer "secret service" based on Wall Street. "The squad is not going to capture murderers," explained the *World*; "it is not going to go sleuthing for burglars, but it is going to make things hot for the Bolsheviki and the Anarchists." Six months later, he expanded his efforts to include a "riot regiment," complete with machine gunners and sharp-shooters "equipped and prepared at all times for riot duty and to combat revolutionary agitators."[24]

At their inception, the plans had met with resounding public approval. As 1920 wore on, though, Enright's efforts had stalled under an onslaught of criticism, much of it from Woods' progressive allies, who accused him of corruption and ineptitude in battling a postwar crime wave. Rather than worry about new regiments, in recent months Enright had undertaken a thorough review of the entire department, hoping to ward off a demotion. In early September, he announced a major reorganization of the police department, promising to return it to its former glory. Now, less than two weeks later, he had a golden chance to show what his new department could do. First, though, he would have to edge out his competitors, something rather easier said than done. By one o'clock, that meant contending not only with Flynn and Woods but also with the "Great Detective" William J. Burns, who had made his name bringing the McNamara brothers to justice in Los Angeles.[25]

BURNS HAD NEITHER TIME nor patience for the methods of the New York police. He often said investigative work was merely a matter of "common sense." He also liked to say that most detectives were sorely lacking in that essential quality. "I have always insisted that every criminal leaves a track—that many times Providence interferes to uncover the footprints left by the criminal," he instructed. Within police circles, his bragga-docio had earned him a reputation as a "brass band" detective, a private operator likely to bring a bugle corps or its verbal equivalent to trumpet his success in any available forum. Much to his critics' chagrin, however, Providence did seem to have a soft spot for Burns.[26]

In 1910, he had happened to be on his way to Los Angeles on the very night that an explosion ripped through the headquarters of the *Los Angeles Times*. ("This is certainly a stroke of fortune, you being right in the city at a time like this," the mayor had told him, agreeing to foot the bill for a Burns agency investigation.) He was also coincidentally under contract with the McClintic-Marshall construction company, investigating a string of dynamite blasts that had destroyed bridges, plants, and other nonunion construction projects in states from Illinois to California. The detective work took a few months, but Burns managed to combine both investiga-tions into a single, spectacular success. By the end of 1911, Burns had managed to "kidnap" the McNamara brothers, force their guilty plea, and win a reward of $50,000.[27]

The McNamara Affair had made Burns' reputation as a bomb hunter and labor investigator—Flynn's only true rival on a national scale. "William J. Burns," the *New York Times* had declared, "[is] the greatest detective certainly, and perhaps the only really great detective, the only detective of genius, whom this country has produced." So it seemed obvious that he, too, would have a hand in the explosion investigation unfolding at the corner of Wall and Broad. The Burns International Detective Agency operated out of the Woolworth Building (the "world's tallest commercial structure," as its financier, F. W. Woolworth, liked to proclaim), just a few blocks north of the financial district. When the explosion hit, all the Great Detective had to do was don his hat and follow the throngs stream-ing south.[28]

Like the Bureau, Burns had only the most tenuous justification for launching his own inquiry. When reporters asked him why he was there, he answered vaguely that he was working at the behest of the Morgan bank. This was not entirely implausible, though the Morgan bank refused to confirm his claim. The Burns agency held the security contract for the American Bankers Association, with eleven thousand member banks. He had also worked for the House of Morgan directly, investigating wartime espionage. Whether or not he was employed by the bank on the after-noon of September 16 was anybody's guess. At any rate, he didn't need an employer to sanction his effort. As a private detective, he could work where he liked. And as the man who had solved the McNamara case, he could be certain of gaining a public hearing.[29]

Burns cut a peculiar figure in the crowd at Wall and Broad, striding through the wreckage in search of such clues as Providence might care to present. Physically, he was a Teddy Roosevelt type: broad belly, thick moustache, large jowls. His face tended toward a pinkish hue, his hair was a bright shock of red, and he favored natty suits and derby hats. One reporter had described him, in not unkind mockery, as a "stage police-man," sporting the proper costume and manner. His moustache especially, the reporter hinted, showed signs of frequent and conscientious care. All in all, many observers concluded, he looked a lot like that other detective who shared his first name and middle initial, William J. Flynn.[30]

The resemblance was more than physical. As young men, the two had worked side by side in the Treasury Department's Secret Service, running down counterfeiters and exposing government corruption. Like Flynn, Burns advertised himself as a law enforcement crusader, his life's work the discipline and organization of otherwise unruly detectives. There were, however, some important temperamental differences. Where Flynn often shunned the limelight, Burns embraced it, eagerly providing newspapers with stories and quotations intended to mimic the great fictional detective Sherlock Holmes. Most reporters were happy to return the favor. "Some people," ran a typical newspaper comment, "say that William J. Burns is a greater detective than Sherlock Holmes was ever represented to be and that he has worked out more mystifying cases."[31]

Among the most oft-repeated legends were tales of Burns' early tri-umphs as a Secret Service operative: his foiling of a top-notch counterfeit ring, his exposure of senatorial land frauds in Oregon, his breaking up of a San Francisco bribery ring. As stories of a single public servant outwitting the wealthy and powerful, they appealed to popular sympathies as well as to the sensibilities of many progressives, who during these early years had celebrated the young Secret Service man as a bona fide reformer. During the San Francisco graft trials in 1906 and 1907, for instance, Lincoln Steffens had wired back glowing reports of Burns' focused and incorrupt-ible attacks on the city's ossifying political machine.[32]

His fame as an anticorruption crusader had given Burns the chance to escape from the $7-a-day drudgery of the Secret Service and found his own detective agency in 1909. But the mere act of entering the private detective industry had also threatened to undermine the reputation for integrity on which his hopes of profit depended. By the time Burns entered the profession, private detectives enjoyed a respectability roughly akin to that of slave traders a century earlier: at best, they were seen as a necessary evil; at worst, as parasites feeding on the body politic. The Pinkertons had launched the profession during the Civil War, hiring out agents to conduct Union espionage. In the years since, it had become associated with the more sordid aspects of detective work: adultery investigations, industrial espionage, and above all strikebreaking. Thomas Beet of Scotland Yard, a prominent police reformer, described private agencies as "veritable hot-beds of corruption, trafficking upon the honor and sacred confidences of their patrons." This might have been the only area in which he agreed with Bill Haywood, who, like nearly every labor sympathizer in the country, had ceased to view detectives as functioning members of the human race. "That you may know how small a detective is," Haywood wrote in 1911, "you can take a hair and punch the pith out of it and in the hollow hair you can put the hearts and souls of 40,000 detectives and they will still rattle. You can pour them out on the surface of your thumb and the skin of a gnat will make an umbrella of them."[33]

The omnipresence of detectives working as strikebreakers and industrial spies was a feature of labor relations unique to the United States. In Europe, where policemen and armies handily stepped in to suppress labor rebellion, businessmen more rarely saw the need for extra expenditures on spies and strikebreakers. In the United States, with its decentralized system and its underfunded, ill-coordinated legions of local police, the private detective industry had come to flourish in the void between business intention and government manpower. While private detectives often behaved like public police, they had no legal powers of detention or arrest. And while they often acted like a military force, swooping in armed and en masse as at Homestead, they were excluded from the government's monopoly on legitimate violence. In many cases, local authorities inclined to support the detectives' activities solved these problems by deputizing the private agents as temporary members of the public police. Indeed, private detectives had at least one advantage over their public counterparts: as private employees, they were not bound by the legal codes that restricted the public authorities, at least in name, to investigating actual violations of law.

Burns was well aware of his profession's reputation. "The average private detective," he often declared, "is one of the most diabolical evils with which we have to contend." To distinguish himself, he had initially set out to form a wholly new, hybrid institution: the world's first progressive detective agency. Almost alone among his colleagues, he considered himself a reformer—"the nemesis of certain kinds of social and political malaise, an avenger of wrongs, a restorative force for the 'good society' which sensible people longed for," as one biographer would later describe him. He supported woman suffrage and civil service testing. He had exposed the shady dealings of notorious bribery rings and political machines. And he had made a name for himself, among other attributes, as the scourge of his own profession—one honest man in an industry of thieves. To illustrate his commitment to the modern reform consciousness, Burns declared that his agency would accept only "legitimate Detective work," a category that did not include either divorce or strikebreaking cases.[34]

This high-minded stance paid off almost immediately, as the American Bankers Association and the National Retail Dry Goods Association switched their massive contracts over to his fledgling agency. "William J. Burns had proved himself to the men he called sons of bitches, so that when he organized a national detective bureau they joined it as subscribers," Steffens concluded. After the McNamara case, however, Steffens had reconsidered his view, denouncing Burns as a man who talked reform even as he strung up the people fighting for it. Burns professed contempt for his critics, dismissing them as compliant tools in the anarchists' "masked war" against society. But he also soon broke his pledge to refuse strikebreaking work. "Ever since the McNamara case we have made a close study of labor difficulties and have perfected our industrial organization," read one of his subsequent ads. "In pursuing this character of work we have organized the department in such a way that we are in a position to anticipate these difficulties."[35]

The years that followed brought new, swaggering ventures into nearly every area of detective work. "My name is William J. Burns," he wrote in his lengthy tome on the McNamara case,

and my address is New York, London, Paris, Montreal, Chicago, San Francisco, Los Angeles, Seattle, New Orleans, Boston, Philadelphia, Cleveland, and wherever else a law-abiding citizen may find need of men who know how to go quietly about throwing out of ambush a hidden assassin or drawing from cover criminals who prey upon those who walk straight.

In terms of pure public relations, his greatest victory had come in 1914, when he served as unofficial New York escort for Arthur Conan Doyle, the British author who had created Sherlock Holmes. Over four days, they attended a Yankees game, visited the fantasylands of Coney Island, and looked in on the Tombs jail (Doyle thought it "just the place for suffragettes"). Doyle referred to Burns throughout as the "Sherlock Holmes of America."[36]

Doyle's imprimatur implied that Burns had been a model for Holmes, but the influence clearly ran the other way as well. Burns' public self—the "Great Detective"—was no less a conscious creation than Doyle's fictional character. He discovered, however, that living up to such expectations was not always easy. Despite a steady stream of work, Burns had never quite replicated his McNamara success. In 1914, he had vowed to prove the innocence of Leo Frank, a Jewish factory manager in Atlanta accused of murdering a teenage girl in his employ. Instead, Burns had been run out of Georgia, losing his state detective license, and Frank himself had been lynched, the first major act of a revived Ku Klux Klan. That same year, Burns nearly lost his New York license as well. At the behest of the Morgan bank, he had planted a detectaphone—a sort of crude microphone—in the office of the law firm of Seymour and Seymour, suspected by the Morgan men of stealing confidential information about munitions contracts. Unfortunately for Burns, Morgan, and the whole operation, the lawyers had discovered the surveillance and reported it to the New York papers.[37]

The agency had continued to thrive throughout. But encomiums to Burns' genius, to "his honesty as well as ability,...courage as well as intelligence," were noticeably less frequent in 1920 than they had been in 1911. An early look at the Wall Street evidence, a take-charge attitude, and a touch of "brass band" publicity might position him well to change that situation.[38]

OF THE FOUR major detectives—Flynn, Woods, Enright, Burns—none stood out as the obvious man to lead the Wall Street investigation. Nor were they the only ones who descended on the financial district that afternoon eager to compete for the honor. By one o'clock, the city fire department had dispatched men to trace the explosives. The Buildings Department showed up to inspect for structural damage, and ran into the Secret Service poring over the assay office and Sub-Treasury. Travelers Indemnity, the Morgan insurer, launched its own investigation to determine possible liability. The September grand jury soon purged itself of other crimes in order to devote its time to tracking the Wall Street culprit—if, indeed, such a culprit existed. The medical examiner's office assigned its full staff to establish the victims' causes of death. Given Wall Street's strategic importance, Military Intelligence felt it, too, should get involved. And all of this was in addition to the hundreds of low-level agents and detectives dispatched from the Bureau, the Burns agency, and the New York police.[39]

Within the tons of glass, clothing, stone, and scrap clogging the financial district, three material clues immediately caught the investigators' attention. The first was the smoldering remains of a touring car that had been parked near the corner of Wall and Broad. The car had been thrown onto its side, and its chassis was pocked and chipped. The fact that it had caught fire indicated that the car had to have been somewhere near the center of the blast. A few feet away, the police uncovered a New Jersey auto license plate, N.J. 24246.[40]

The second clue consisted of the ruins of some sort of wooden wagon near the corner of Wall and Broad. The wagon, like the car, had been more thoroughly demolished than any other object in the area, leading detectives to assume that it must have been precariously near the blast. They had found one rim of what appeared to be a wagon wheel leaning against Wall Street's south curb, and splinters of wood, faintly red and yellow, mingled nearby with more readily identifiable debris. Parts of the horse thought to have drawn the wagon lay scattered about the neighborhood. Unlucky agents had been detailed to wade through the wreckage in search of horseflesh and bits of harness that might someday be reconstructed into a whole. The police made a special point of gathering the hooves and shoes, hoping that a local farrier might recognize his handiwork. The head and forelegs were in fine condition—distinctly part of what once had been an animal—but the rear had burst into thousands of damp bits.[41]

The final items of interest in the initial catalogue were hundreds of small, curved pieces of metal that investigators began to collect from the street, from office towers, and from victims' bodies. With the detonation of the explosion, the metal slugs had apparently flown every which way, rocketing as high as the thirty-eighth floor of the Equitable Building and as far north as John Street, five blocks away. One man reported that a thick piece of metal fell from the sky and bounced off his neck. When he tried to pick it up, it was too hot to touch. As near as the police could tell, the metal bits appeared to be fragments of window weights, covered with plaster, dust, blood, and flesh. These were common enough items, but their preponderance in the financial district presented a genuine mystery.[42]

The simplest formula linking the slugs to the car and wagon was that the auto's driver, short on skills, had crashed into a delivery wagon loaded with explosives and metal junk. It was common knowledge that explosives suppliers—especially E. I. du Pont de Nemours and Company—regularly ran dynamite to construction sites on Wall Street. On the morning of September 16, there were at least three construction projects under way in the neighborhood, including the stock exchange annex going up at Wall and Broad.[43]

This was the theory favored by the fire department, the military, and even certain members of the police. "Latest rumor," an army captain wrote to his superiors just before one o'clock, "to the effect that a wagon loaded with TNT was struck by a taxi causing the explosion." The fire department informed the Morgan partners that incompetence rather than malice had caused the disaster. "Fire marshal advances theory that automobile carrying dynamite exploded in street," the bank wrote in a memo to the Federal Reserve. "This seems probable and explosion may have been accidental."[44]

It was the premise advanced as well by the afternoon papers, their feature articles preempted by top-to-bottom "extra" explosion coverage. "The police theory is that the explosion was caused by an automobile colliding with a dynamite wagon . . . which was transporting explosives to the Stock Exchange Annex, now in the course of construction," reported the *Globe and Commercial Advertiser*, under a headline declaring, "Dynamite Blows Up in Street; Morgan Firm's Building Is Wrecked." "They do not put any credence in the report that a bomb was thrown at the Morgan office."[45]

The first test of this theory, undertaken Thursday afternoon, was a check on the licensed explosive companies that, according to witness reports, had been transporting dynamite through the crowds at a regular clip for many weeks past. If these companies had followed the regulations, a disaster such as the one on Wall Street should have been impossible. It was illegal to deliver explosives anywhere in New York between sunrise and sunset. Only two firms, DuPont and the Carl

Dittmars powder company, held permits to move explosives. According to city records, DuPont was bonded for one light truck (with a backup wagon for emergencies) and Dittmars used two horse-drawn wagons. The police, along with the Bureau of Combustibles, the Bureau of Investigation, and sundry other agencies, dispatched men to view the records on the assumption that the companies would be sore pressed to hide a wagon's absence.[46]

Unfortunately, all of the investigators thought of this plan more or less at once, and DuPont suddenly found itself deluged with visits and phone calls. The police scrutinized DuPont; so did the Bureau of Investigation and the fire department. The police collected slugs; so did the men from the Burns agency, the Bureau of Mines, the Bureau of Investigation, and the Secret Service. The Bureau of Investigation and the police surveyed stables for missing wagons and construction sites for missing dynamite. The police assembled witness lists; so did the Bureau of Investigation and the Burns agency.

At least one object of this investigative zeal found the repeat visits more than he could bear in silence. At the Carl Dittmars company, a weary manager snapped at a Bureau agent who arrived to check his permits late Thursday afternoon, complaining that he had already dealt with both the police and the fire department's Bureau of Combustibles. In a write-up of the encounter, the agent reported that the Dittmars man saw the explosion as "purely a city matter, adding that he did not see where the U.S. Department of Justice came in on this matter."[47]

In addition to their collective storming of the explosives companies' offices, a full army of detectives fanned out across the city in search of witnesses who might be able to confirm or deny by sight the presence of a wagonload of explosives. A few businessmen had squeezed past police lines and were wandering through the wreckage, trying to save their stock certificates from rain, neglect, and possible looters. Most employees in the district had already disappeared for home. Those who remained at work were often those least injured—precisely the men and women who had been snug inside at the moment of detonation and, as investigators discovered, had seen nothing of value.

The dispersion of witnesses, combined with the poor information relayed from the available men, led the police to issue a citywide call late Thursday afternoon for help. "All persons," read the plea, "in the vicinity of the scene of the explosion who can give any information, no matter how slight, regarding any of the details, especially regarding vehicles in the street, which might have caused the explosion, or the presence of any suspicious persons at the time of the explosion should communicate such information to the police at once." This was a routine request, but like nearly everything that happened that afternoon, it was also a bid for control of the investigation.[48]

The police got more than they anticipated. As witnesses began to hand-deliver or phone in their reports, detectives learned that the smoke from the explosion was black, yellow, blue, and brown. The force of the blast came from above and from below. The streets were particularly crowded, particularly deserted, and just as one might expect at noon on a business day. A few passersby remembered suspicious-looking men in the area. Employees of a law firm said they saw an auto packed with excited workmen speeding away from Wall Street. A stenographer in that office said the passengers looked "like thugs" and that one wore a bloodstained shirt. One of her colleagues recalled that the men were "poorly clad" and "emaciated-looking" and "appeared to be foreigners." A third man said that the moment he saw the car, he told a friend "that he saw the gang that did it." Detectives among both police and Bureau ranks doubted the foreigners' significance, assuming that the fleeing men, foreigners or no, were just hurt and scared like everyone else.[49]

Investigators had little more luck with those who, by virtue of their injuries, could be determined to have stood somewhere within a few dozen feet of the wagon. Unlike the able-bodied eyewitnesses, these men and women were easily located in area hospitals: at Broad Street, Downtown, St. Vincent's, and Gouverneur. Thanks to the nature of their injuries, however, many were less easily identified.

As the detectives surveyed each floor, the patients who were able to speak strained to be helpful, recounting in quiet tones how their world had suddenly slid from normal to grotesque. Mostly they could recall only a flash, a boom, or a sudden flood of air. One Brooklyn man, hospitalized for cuts and burns around his scalp and hands, told a Bureau agent that he had been chatting with a friend in front of 35 Wall Street just before noon. "All he knew," read the agent's final report, "was that he was thrown to the street." Another man said he was "so pained by being hit with glass that he could not think." A few victims fixed on odd minutiae. "The thing that most impressed him," one agent wrote, "was the fact that there were a great number of empty taxi-cabs on Wall Street at the time." In many cases, doctors forbade any sort of interview.[50]

A precise count of the victims would not, it was thought, be available for several days. Mrs. Helen J. Timko, a Red Cross volunteer, took charge of coordinating available information on the missing, injured, and dead. She had worked on a similar project in 1912, when the *Titanic* sank in the mid-Atlantic. This time, conventional wisdom suggested that the burn victims would be the hardest to identify, since fire melted distinguishing features. Mrs. Timko convinced the police department to post a man outside the Morgan bank with an updated list of victims, and the Red Cross set up an information bureau at its Twenty-third Street office.[51]

Acting on instructions from law enforcement, the hospitals had saved any possessions—watches, jewelry, clothing—that might aid in identification, and the small bundles of clues accompanied bodies shipped from hospital to morgue. The first six bodies had arrived for the medical examiner around one o'clock. Three more had appeared at three o'clock, four at six. The homicide squad insisted that the medical examiner be the first to inspect the corpses as they arrived, delaying the process of family identification. Police were called in from Bellevue to maintain order and prevent thrill seekers from imposing their curiosity on legitimate mourners. They watched as the same callers who had been making the rounds of the hospitals began, reluctantly, to stop in at the morgue. The coroner and his assistants received copies of the official hospital lists and, when they could, directed relatives to alternative sites. Once the medical examiner finished his preview, the visitors were ushered in to view the bodies. An occasional retching sound testified to the deformities under the sheets.[52]

The earliest identifications produced sorrow but, from a law enforcement standpoint, little useful information. Charles Dickinson identified his sister Caroline. She had been waiting for a friend at the corner of Wall and Broad when the blast struck. The friend was late. Caroline had died when a metal slug blew open the side of her neck. She was a stenographer from Long Island. Her death occasioned "particular sadness," said one newspaper, because her father and a brother had also died recently.[53]

Daniel Hanrahan collapsed at the morgue after identifying his son's body. The boy, Charles, had been a messenger for a Broad Street brokerage house. The explosion tore off his clothes and punctured his chest with dozens of small holes. His father said it was Charles' seventeenth birthday.[54]

Mrs. Sarah Mayer, too, was reported to be in "serious condition" as a result of the death of her son, Alfred. She identified him through the cards and letters found in his pocket. Alfred was twenty-three, a broker. He lived with his mother and two brothers on 138th Street. At noon, he had been delivering a corrected invoice to a Wall Street customer. The explosion opened up fifteen wounds in his chest.[55]

Despite their proprietary maneuvering, by the end of the day the police, the Burns agency, and the Bureau had all settled on the same limited set of facts. The hundreds of interviews, the tedious gathering of debris, and the visits to hospital and morgue yielded precisely two definitive clues. The first was the identification of Dunham Beldon, a Newark druggist who owned the smoking auto found near the blast site. Asked about the possibility of a collision, he assured detectives that at noon his car had been securely parked on Wall Street. Investigators had tracked him down in his accountant's office on Wall Street, where he was conferring about pharmaceutical pricing.[56]

Under repeated questioning by a parade of detectives, the DuPont and Dittmars companies also denied any possibility that their vehicles had been involved. DuPont's books showed that its explosives truck had never ventured below Sixteenth Street on Thursday, and the Dittmars men said their two horse-drawn wagons had stayed above Forty-fifth. By the end of the day, three of the vehicles were said to be snug in their home garages, while the DuPont truck was found to be under repair at the Commonwealth Truck Company on West Forty-sixth.[57]

And that was it. By the end of the afternoon, no culprits had confessed, no wagon owners had reported their vehicles missing, no manifestos had been released. What was known with some measure of certainty was the following: that an explosion had occurred at 12:01, that it had come from a horse-drawn wagon loaded with metal slugs, that the blast had killed dozens and wounded hundred, and that, according to company records, DuPont and Dittmars appeared to be uninvolved. As the basis from which to develop a comprehensive theory of the blast's origins and intent, it was not much to go on. This did not, however, stop investigators from trying. Pressed by reporters to declare whether the explosion had been a bomb or an accident, the police, the Bureau, and the Burns agency each issued statements that reflected not only the shared facts but also their rivalries, investigative styles, and bureaucratic interests.

BURNS WAS THE FIRST to declare in favor of a terrorist plot. "There is not the slightest doubt that it was a bomb which caused the explosion," he announced in time for the evening papers. "It might be closer to the truth to say that it was a wagon load of bombs. From my investigation I am certain that the bomb was in the wagon which was destroyed. There is no other reasonable theory."[58]

After only a two-hour examination of the bomb site, he offered a scenario remarkable in its precision and detail. "My theory," he explained to a writer from the *New York Tribune*, "is that the man assigned to carry the plot into effect drove up with the wagon loaded with explosives and then disappeared, leaving the horse, wagon and bomb to their fate." While he could not immediately identify the form of explosive used, he felt sure that "a mechanism, probably an alarm clock," had triggered the detonation. Based on the abundance of mysterious metal slugs "heavy enough to do the destruction of small cannon balls," Burns concluded that someone had loaded the bomb so that the metal bits "would be shot up and around like a spray, thus killing the greatest possible number of people."[59]

It was hardly a challenge to figure out who that someone might have been. "He said it was quite an easy plan for the radicals to carry out," reported the *Sun and New York Herald*, "and that it would be shown this was what had happened." Indeed, Burns claimed that he had sent out warnings of just such a calamity to his eastern clients at the end of August. Burns thought it likely that the bombing had been carried out by the same people who had engineered the May Day and June 2 conspiracies.[60]

Enright, for his part, was not so sure. Of all of the leading detectives, he was under the least pressure to declare in favor of a bomb; the police would have an investigation on their hands either way. Perhaps as a result, he continued as late as Thursday night to entertain the possibility that some sort of dynamite accident had occurred. Adjusting their theory to account for DuPont's official denials, the police proposed that a bomber had stolen the wagon and "possibly camouflaged [it] to look like the truck of some munitions concern" in order to deflect suspicion from any nefarious intent. Mostly, though, both Enright and fire commissioner Thomas Drennan acknowledged that the information thus far gathered brought more complication than clarification. "We are utterly unable to make any concrete conclusions, except of a negative nature," Drennan explained to the press Thursday evening, summarizing a report that his department planned to submit to the mayor. "We know what happened, and we know certain things that show it could not have happened if the law had been observed. In other words, whatever was the cause of the explosion, it was a cause due to some unlawful act by somebody. But we cannot tell why the explosion occurred, what exploded or how, nor are we in a position to determine what was the nature of the explosive. We simply know that something blew up on a horse-drawn truck at one minute after noon today in Wall Street, between the Sub-Treasury Building and the office of J. P. Morgan & Co. That 'something' had no lawful business there."[61]

Enright was even more circumspect, refusing to declare much more than the openness of his mind and options. "I do not wish it to be understood that I am convinced entirely that this explosion is the result of dynamite loaded in a wagon," he announced. "I have never said that it was and I do not wish it understood that the police are working exclusively on any one theory."[62]

Publicly, Flynn agreed with Enright's flexible stance. Arriving in New York just after ten o'clock, he sequestered himself with several of his top New York agents and informed an insistent press that "as yet I'm not well enough informed to discuss this matter." Privately, though, in wires and phone calls and whispers exchanged Thursday afternoon and evening, the Bureau had already abandoned the accident theory. "It looks like that the explosion occurred from a bomb," an agent in the New York office wrote at 7:15 P.M., citing the pervasiveness of metal shrapnel. Flynn himself acknowledged over the telephone just before ten-thirty that "[t]he fact that iron slugs were found at the point of explosion and in the vicinity would indicate that it is a bomb." He promised that he would know by 2:00 P.M. the next day "the exact nature of the explosion." In the meantime, he planned to head down to Wall Street to see the disaster for himself.[63]

# 7

. . . .

# BUSINESS AS USUAL

GREAT ELECTRIC ORBS lit Wall Street on the night of September 16. Reporters said the giant searchlights turned darkness to noon, but the point was less to prolong the recent day than to erase it. In an effort to cleanse the district, banks and exchanges imported a full "battalion" of sweepers, repairmen, street cleaners, stonemasons, and mechanics to work through the night, spreading as far south as Bowling Green and all the way east to the river. Bathed in the unnatural glow of arc lights, gangs of men scooped glass, stone, and plaster into the metal carts that circled the neighborhood, pausing like omnibuses to collect each load. The fire department hosed down the streets, washing dust and gore underground, while laborers tackled stubborn bloodstains with bleach. Inside the office buildings, scrubwomen worked in teams, righting furniture, sweeping up rubble, and setting aside scraps of cloth and flesh. A mournful banging accompanied their work as glaziers pounded windows into empty frames. Repairmen chalked numbers in doorways and windows, instructions to their coworkers. Camera flashes periodically blanked out the scene.[1]

When employees emerged from the subways the next day, clad in neat skirts and suits, they encountered an eloquently sanitized scene.

New York police officers restrain anxious onlookers near the steps of the U.S. Sub-Treasury on September 16, 1920. On the ground are bodies of explosion victims, covered in white sheets. New York Daily News / dailynewspix.com.

The Treasury Department summoned a U.S. Army battalion to protect almost a billion dollars in gold being transferred to the assay office next door on September 16. New York Daily News / dailynewspix.com.

*23 Wall St. After the bomb outrage - 17th Sept. 1920 -*

*Note the masses of broken glass on the floor -*

Inside the Morgan bank on September 16, 1920. The windows face onto Wall Street. Scrapbook of Jane Norton Grew; courtesy of the Morgan Library and Museum.

Twenty-four hours after the explosion, tens of thousands of spectators descended on Wall and Broad for a patriotic Constitution Day rally. New York World-Telegram and Sun Collection / Library of Congress.

A "bird's-eye view" of the bombing site. The explosion occurred on Wall Street between the Morgan bank (front left) and the federal assay office (front right). Next to the assay office is the federal Sub-Treasury building, followed by the Bankers Trust skyscraper. Across Broad Street from the Morgan bank is the New York Stock Exchange annex, under construction on September 16; the Stock Exchange itself, further down Broad Street to the left, is not pictured. The tall, dark building at the end of Wall Street is Trinity Church. *The World*, September 17, 1920

Detectives recovered hundreds of jagged metal slugs flung throughout the financial district as shrapnel. Underwood & Underwood / Library of Congress.

Rimember We will not tolerate any longer Free the political prisoner or it will be sure death is all of you American Anarchist fighters

THREAT MAILED JUST before The EXPLOSION...

A postal worker uncovered five copies of this flyer, printed by hand with rubber stamps, in a mailbox near the explosion at Wall and Broad. *The World*, September 19, 1920.

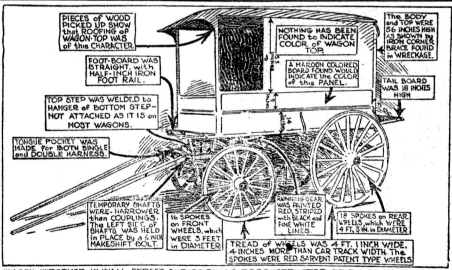

BOMB WAGON AS RECONSTRUCTED FROM RECOVERED FRAGMENTS

After careful reconstruction work, police determined that the explosives arrived on Wall Street in a rickety wooden "butter-and-egg" delivery wagon. The illustration is from *The World*, September 19, 1920.

Chemists at the City Laboratories examine metal fragments from the Wall Street explosion. New York World-Telegram and Sun Collection / Library of Congress.

The Bureau's composite portrait of the bomb-wagon driver, created in early 1921. A commercial artist drew the picture based on photographs of likely anarchist suspects. The drawing led to several arrests, but no definitive identifications. New York Daily News/dailynewspix.com.

Italian-born anarchist Tito Ligi, arrested in April, 1921, as the alleged wagon driver in the Wall Street explosion. New York Daily News / Dailynewspix.com.

William Linde (alias Wolfe Lindenfeld), the "consummate faker" and undercover spy who helped to sink the Bureau's Wall Street investigation. New York Daily News / Dailynewspix.com.

Junius Spencer Morgan, son of
J.P. ("Jack") Morgan, grandson
of J. Pierpont Morgan, bore the
weight of an imposing family legacy.
Pictured here in 1915. Bain News
Service / Library of Congress.

Thomas W. Lamont, one
of the wealthiest and most
cosmopolitan of the Morgan
partners, pictured aboard
the S.S. *Diulio* in 1925.
Underwood and Underwood
/ Library of Congress.

J.P. ("Jack") Morgan, father of Junius and son of
the original J.P. Morgan, arriving on Wall Street
via boat circa 1914. Library of Congress.

23 Wall Street, the headquarters of J.P. Morgan and Company, pictured soon after its construction in 1914. Irving Underhill / Library of Congress.

The floor of the New York Stock Exchange after a day of trading, circa 1920. Library of Congress.

The German-born anarchist Johann Most inspired the stereotype of the bearded, foreign-born, bomb-throwing anarchist. Pictured here in a speech at New York's Cooper Union, 1887. Frank Leslie's Illustrated Weekly / Library of Congress.

TYPICAL ANARCHIST.

This "typical anarchist" illustration is from *The World*, May 30, 1886. New York World Telegram and Sun Collection / Library of Congress.

A *Harper's Weekly* illustration of the Haymarket bombing in Chicago on May 4, 1886. Library of Congress.

Emma Goldman and Alexander Berkman, the most famous anarchists in America. Pictured here in 1917, on the eve of their wartime conviction for draft obstruction. Berkman's crutches are the result of torn ligaments in his foot. Bettmann/Corbis.

Leon Czolgosz shot President William McKinley on September 6, 1901. Pictured here on the cover of *Leslie's Weekly*, September 9, 1901. Library of Congress.

Thousands of supporters flooded Union Square on July 11, 1914, for a rally in honor of three anarchists killed while building a bomb intended for John D. Rockefeller. Alexander Berkman, who organized the rally, viewed it as the high point of anarchist influence in New York. George Grantham Bain Collection / Library of Congress.

The refurbished U.S. transport *Buford*, also known as the "Soviet Ark." On December 21, 1919, the *Buford* carried 249 deportees (including Goldman and Berkman) out of Ellis Island, bound for Russia, in the first mass deportation of political prisoners in American history. George Grantham Bain Collection / Library of Congress.

Wobbly leader "Big Bill" Haywood in exile in Moscow, 1924. Bettmann/Corbis.

Socialist Party leader Eugene Debs leaving the Atlanta Penitentiary on Christmas Day, 1921. Underwood and Underwood / Library of Congress.

California labor activist Tom Mooney, pictured at the moment of his release from San Quentin in 1939. Mooney was convicted of murder for a bombing that killed ten spectators at a 1916 Preparedness Day parade in San Francisco. New York World-Telegram and Sun Collection / Library of Congress.

Nicola Sacco (center right) and Bartolomeo Vanzetti (center left, with moustache), pictured manacled together, leading a crowd to the Dedham, Massachusetts, courthouse in 1927. New York World-Telegram and Sun Collection / Library of Congress.

The "Great Detective" William J. Burns (right), pictured with a reporter on the front steps of the Morgan bank on September 16. New York World-Telegram and Sun Collection / Library of Congress.

William J. Flynn, chief of the
federal Bureau of Investigation
and the lead detective on the
Wall Street case, circa 1920.
Copyright American Press
Association / Library of Congress.

Attorney General A. Mitchell
Palmer, architect of the Palmer
Raids. Copyright Clinedinst,
Washington / Library of Congress.

Twenty-nine-year-
old J. Edgar Hoover,
pictured months after
his appointment as
head of the Bureau
of Investigation in
1924. National Photo
Company Collection /
Library of Congress.

Former New York police commissioner Arthur Woods, posing with a troop of Boy Scouts in 1917. New York World-Telegram and Sun Collection / Library of Congress.

New York police commissioner and Tammany Hall loyalist Richard E. Enright, accompanied by supporters (undated). Bain News Service / Library of Congress.

"Everything was clean as a pin," wrote one observer, marveling at the absence of the "broken glass, crushed straw hats, fragments of clothing, [and] scraps of iron" that had so recently covered every inch of Wall and Broad. At buildings such as the Morgan bank and the stock exchange, muslin curtains and fitted boards covered the windows. Outer walls had been scrubbed clean of soot, even of the usual dust and grime, and the pockmarks seemed already less severe. Brilliant September sunshine highlighted the hand-lettered signs in the district's doorways advertising "Business as Usual."[2]

But despite the best efforts of the cleaning crews, all was not—could not be—"as usual." Policemen and guards, uniformed variously in blue and gray, wrapped around every important building, trying to distinguish between the curious and the legitimately employed. The tone of the crowd was too quiet, as acquaintances congratulated each other on close escapes and shared hopes for reprisal. There was none of the usual laughter. Where-were-you-when tales stood in for business haggling.[3]

Least usual of all was what was not said or seen. Even as the stock exchange's opening gong issued a restive peal and the market began, tentatively, to rise, the silence of dozens of missing men and women threatened to drown out the clatter of business.

The decision to reopen the financial district so quickly caught almost everyone off guard, even the men who had made it. The stock exchange had shut down immediately after the explosion, when president William Remick rang the bell to stem what he could of the panic. By twelve-thirty on Thursday afternoon, less than half an hour after the explosion, the New York Stock Exchange's governing committee had convened in a special meeting to decide the fate of the day's interrupted trades. Without much discussion, they ruled out the possibility of resuming business on Thursday afternoon. But they declined to state when the market might, in fact, be prepared to reopen. In a terse and unsentimental announcement delivered just before one o'clock, Remick suspended the delivery of securities until Monday, with payments of interest similarly delayed. The committee agreed to reconvene three hours later to consider the matter further.[4]

Newspapers interpreted this as a sign that the markets would be closed at least through the weekend, perhaps longer. "This practically foreshadowed the closing of the exchange for the balance of the week in order to repair the damage in the Exchange building resulting from the explosion," the *Evening Mail* concluded. By one o'clock, the cessation of business was already a moot point. Faced with the prospect of operating without either the stock exchange or the Morgan bank, nearly every major trading house voluntarily shut down on Thursday afternoon the Curb Exchange at 12:10, the Consolidated Exchange at 12:20, the foreign exchange market just before 1:00. The few businesses that continued to function—the cotton and produce exchanges, for instance—performed little useful business. "Gloom completely overshadowed a feeling of cheerfulness," the *Evening Mail* wrote of Wall Street's mood. "There was no activity conducted in the financial district this afternoon, every man, woman and child lending aid to relieve the heart-breaking suffering of those caught in the explosion."

In other financial districts across the country, sentiment was no more positive. Receiving news of the tragedy, exchanges suspended business throughout the country, retreating behind cover of armed guards from Boston to San Francisco. To the Wall Street leadership, charged with finding a course of action to relieve some of this pressure, the wave of panic appeared ominously similar to the disaster of July 1914, when markets throughout the world shut down after news of the war's outbreak in Europe. Then it took five months for the New York exchange to reopen, and full trading didn't resume until spring. The explosion on Wall Street hardly posed the prospect of such an extended closure, but it came with its own unsettling questions. Chief among them was the problem of what would happen to the markets when the exchange finally reopened.[6]

Until noon, September 16 had been a bull day—one of the few in recent months—with particular strength, the financial pages noted, in oil and rails. Remick's precipitous ringing of the gong less than a minute after the explosion managed, according to the *World*, to prevent a "serious demoralization" of the market. But it did little to forestall fears of a bottoming-out to come. As a temporary matter, the threat of a market crash might be solved in coming days by deliberately flooding the market with cash, an offer the Morgan men and the other major houses quickly extended to the exchange. The explosion's long-term impact, however, was harder to gauge. "If the bomb theory is found to be correct, it was argued that sentiment would be adversely affected," mused the *New York Tribune*. "But, on the other hand, financial folk are likely to exert themselves, it was held in some quarters, to reveal a strong, confident attitude."[7]

As the *Tribune* noted, early concerns about the explosion's financial consequences were intimately tied to the assumption, slowly being confirmed by investigators, that the attack had been deliberate, a blow at Wall Street's political and financial power. "For the first time in our history," summed up the *Commercial and Financial Chronicle*, "the New York Stock Exchange was closed as the result of a dastardly act by men who seem beyond question to have been 'Red' murderers." In a district that traded in confidence and optimism about the future, this was an alarming sign of vulnerability, proof that a horse-drawn wagonload of explosives could halt the nation's capitalist machine.[8]

Still, there was reason to believe, even in the chaos of those first few hours, that the explosion might ultimately redound to Wall Street's benefit. In its earliest comments on the explosion, the *New York Commercial* noted that recent market depressions had been due, in part, to a sense of foreboding, a general suspicion that the country was due for some sort of radical uprising. Now that the attack had apparently come and gone, the future could at last be greeted with "a sigh of relief." The *Evening Mail* reported a consensus around the leading banking houses that the explosion might eventually "prove of great constructive value, as it undoubtedly will so focus public sentiment militantly against radical activities as to mean a rapid end to all such movements in this country." In truth, it was too soon to say which way the latest attack would go: whether it would be taken as a sign of capitalism's weakness or as a spur to national defiance. But as the district leadership contemplated a course of action on Thursday afternoon, at least one imperative was already clear. If the blast was intended, as the *St. Louis Post-Dispatch* suspected, "to terrorize Wall Street," its success or failure would be measured in part by how financial leaders responded.[9]

Among the men acutely aware of this fact was Thomas Lamont, a one-time newspaper reporter who had migrated in middle age to the world of finance, first as an employee at Bankers Trust and now as a Morgan partner. Lamont was an unusual creature for the Morgan ranks: a friend of Democrats in a firm of Republicans, a progressive in a profoundly conservative environment, a newspaper owner (he had recently purchased the *New York Evening Post*) in a bank where publicity was all but anathema. Despite this outwardly odd fit, he had emerged by 1920 as one of the bank's most powerful partners; his duties included serving as its chief liaison with the Wilson administration and the peace talks at Versailles. Indeed, the very qualities that set him apart from the other Morgan men—particularly his comfort in the volatile spheres of politics and publishing—gave him a favored status among the partners. He was the man to be relied upon when, at moments of crisis, the Morgan bank needed to talk to the world. Now, with Jack out of the country and Junius too young and inexperienced to serve as spokesman, he was the obvious one to craft the bank's response to the explosion.[10]

Since his earliest years with the firm, Lamont had relied on a strategy of open engagement with Morgan critics. In 1913, he had invited Louis Brandeis to join him at the University Club to discuss why Brandeis' new book, *Other People's Money*, presented such a negative view of Morgan power. It was an awkward encounter, more of a debate than a conversation. But like other direct encounters with the bank's enemies, it had given Lamont a unique feel for how the Morgan image played out in the public mind. Now, as he faced a catastrophe destined to revive discussion of anti-Morgan sentiment, he seemed to embrace the challenge of shaping an effective message in response. It was his job, for at least the next few days, to make sure that the public did not end up concluding that bombs and murder were what the Morgan bank deserved.[11]

He had two models available for accomplishing this goal. The first was to launch an aggressive public crusade against groups suspected of involvement in the bombing—something along the lines of what had happened in Chicago in 1886, or what Otis attempted to do in Los Angeles in 1911. Many in the financial world supported this course of action. "In Chicago many years ago six [*sic*] of this sort were hanged in a row, and thereafter that city for many a long year was rid of agitators," wrote the *Commercial and Financial Chronicle*. "It is plain enough now that some such lesson should be meted out here in New York." This sort of overt anger, however, had never been the Morgan style. The bank preferred a more subdued, insulated approach, one that would keep the Morgan name out of the headlines.[12]

This strategy had worked well in earlier moments of crisis: the assassination attempt on Jack in 1915, Markoe's murder early in 1920. And while neither of those events matched the scale of this new disaster, Lamont and the other partners saw little reason to believe that a similar approach would not succeed here as well. By downplaying the significance of the crime, by simply proceeding with business, they calculated, the Morgan bank could project an image of strength and stability.

This was the line adopted by Lamont's *Post*. "Whatever may be discovered to be the nature of the catastrophe, it is plain what the proper attitude of the public mind should be at the present moment," the paper instructed. "And that is a firm resolve to go on with the business of the city and of the country while waiting for the facts upon which the law must proceed." In those first few hours, though, such lofty goals were more easily proposed than accomplished.[13]

As the demands of first aid gave way to rumor and speculation on Thursday afternoon, leading businessmen began to trickle into the Morgan bank: Seward Prosser from Bankers Trust, H. D. Underwood from the Erie Railroad, Remick himself from across the street at the exchange. They brought with them deflating reports of damage to the neighborhood buildings. At the stock exchange, every one of the grand front windows had been shattered. To the north, across Wall Street, the assay office "appeared to have been under bombardment by light artillery, so badly was it chipped and pitted," in the description of one observer. The Morgan bank itself was little more than a wreck. "That building—glorious temple to finance that once it was—stood devastated as ever ruins in Flanders stood," an Associated Press reporter commented of the situation on Thursday afternoon. "They told me that all the wires were down and the floors inside were piled with wood and glass. I imagined a sportive giant seizing window bars and twisting them as a child twists taffy candy; they were spiraled and jerked from each other that way."[14]

When the superintendent of buildings showed up to inspect the damage, he gave a far less dire assessment. Contrary to alarmist predictions, he informed the Morgan partners, the bank had sustained only cosmetic damage: broken windows, singed marble, and the like. The same held true at the stock exchange and the assay office, where the necessary repairs were already well under way. This report, so unexpected earlier in the afternoon, raised the prospect that the explosion's symbolic damage— to the financial markets, to Wall Street's image—might be minimized as well. When the stock exchange governors reconvened at three-thirty, Remick informed them that after conferring with "outside interests" he saw "no reason why the banks, and other financial institutions would not be in shape to take up business on the morning of September 17, 1920."[15]

Lamont had reached a similar conclusion. He sent a reassuring telegram to his wife, vacationing in North Haven, Maine. "You must not be concerned about exaggerated reports of street explosion," he cabled, "we are quite all right and shall do business as usual tomorrow." Then, well before the normal closure of the business day, he made the news public. After expressing his sympathy for the family of young William Joyce, the "valued employee" who had been killed in the explosion and whose father, Thomas, had been injured, he informed the press that the bank stood more or less unfazed.[16]

"None of the partners was in any way injured save that Mr. Junius Morgan had a slight cut on the hand," he explained. "Our building is not seriously damaged, but all the large windows on the first, and some on the second floor, were blown in. Our offices will be open for business as usual tomorrow morning."[17]

BY MOST APPEARANCES, the men and women who returned to Wall Street on Friday morning were not so different from the buildings they entered: functional, if rather battered. But there were moments—the backfiring of a car, the peal of Trinity's noon chimes—when even their hard-won composure gave way to shudders. Like dreamers awakening from a nightmare, they found their world more or less as they remembered it, but slightly off, not quite right.

Pure happenstance dictated the memories that accompanied them: how quickly someone happened to duck, how far a woman happened to run, where a man happened to spot this leg or that arm or a messenger boy crying for help. Arthur Anderson, head of the Morgan bond department, showed off a slice of glass embedded half an inch into the chair where he had been sitting. Thirty-two-year-old Joseph Kennedy, father of the future president, found himself thrown to the ground near Wall and Broad. The near miss experienced by Bankers Trust president Seward Prosser—"perhaps the most miraculous escape from serious injury and possible death"—grew in drama and portent with each new telling. "Through one of the windows," reported the *New York Times*,

> a bar of metal half an inch thick and some three inches long was hurled. This passed close to the President of the Trust Company, went on through a bookcase and landed against the marble on the far side of the room. Owing to the sound of the explosion the fact that this piece of metal had been cast into the Bankers Trust building was not discovered until some minutes later. So great was the

concussion that glass from the window was driven clear through a desk and a mass of papers, cutting them to ribbons.[18]

The repetition of such stories had an element of ritual, as if good-luck tales might turn the whole dismal event into a moment of triumph. For all of the gratitude and wonder at their continued existence, though, what haunted many of the men and women returning to work on Friday was what they had encountered once the smoke dissipated: the moans for help, the stumps where limbs had been. "Right opposite me were two fine touring cars," recalled Jacob Shar, who kept a newsstand at Nassau and Wall. "One was built so the chauffeur sat outside. The other was a sedan. The chauffeur was sitting in the first one and a piece of glass struck him back of the head and nearly cut his head off. I was told he was dead when the doctors took his body from the automobile."[19]

A few blocks south of the explosion, tiny Broad Street Hospital had emerged as the primary repository for the seriously injured, dying, and dead. The hospital was only three years old, with eighty-five beds, nineteen nurses, and less than a dozen doctors—in short, ill-equipped to handle an emergency on this scale. As battered refugees had arrived by car and on foot the previous afternoon, the meager medical staff enlisted chefs, janitors, and telephone girls to bind up wounds and hand out lemonade. One self-proclaimed "hardened surgeon" described to the *New York American* what they had seen. "Most of the faces could not be recognized as human," he recalled, "except for the discolored eyeballs, so badly cut were they with glass, brick and flying fragments and splotched with powder marks. Most of the injured were badly burned, and there were many ugly cuts. There were numerous cases of fractured arms and legs." The worst-injured sustained severe burns that turned their skin a crisp black. Some were singed on the soles of their feet and the palms of their hands. In several cases, the blast had blown off the victim's ears or nose. Fingernails were often burned down to the quick.[20]

That survivors harbored considerable unspoken guilt over having witnessed but escaped this sort of fate was evident in their response to Broad Street Hospital's fund-raising efforts. Even in the midst of the postexplosion frenzy, someone at the hospital had seen fit to write up an advertisement for the morning papers. Addressed to "You Men of Wall Street," the notice demanded to know if their empathy for the victims extended as far as their pocketbooks.

When you saw Broad Street hospital Thursday so pitifully handicapped by limited facilities in handling and succoring the wounded—when you saw them, lying there, even dying there, waiting for ambulances to take them to distant hospitals—

You said to yourself and to your neighbor, "Wall Street and lower New York needs, and can and should support, an adequately equipped hospital; it should not rely on the charity of other sections of the city."

Were your words empty words? Some few have contributed. Are you going to permit yourself to sink back into the same unprepared, unprotected condition?

The hospital dispatched a team of nurses, crisp white hats literally in hand, to make the rounds of the Curb Market in an appeal for funds. The response, in the estimation of the *New York Times*, "was probably the most remarkable and spontaneous ever had in the financial district." Brokers and traders emptied their pockets, and where cash was lacking made out lavish checks. By the end of the month, the hospital announced that it would launch a major program of expansion.[21]

Despite the mammoth cleanup effort, reminders of the explosion still marked the district's buildings. In the structures closest to the epicenter—the Sub-Treasury, the stock exchange, the assay office, the Morgan bank—hardly a slab of plate glass survived. About a block away, the odds were somewhat better. The quake from the explosion had reached as far north as city hall and the Municipal Building, but few windows there had shattered. At the Equitable Building, glass fell from as high as the thirty-second story. On Thursday afternoon and into the night, shouts of "Look out below!" had been a common refrain.[22]

Early reports placed the property damage throughout the district as high as $2.5 million to $3 million. The Morgan bank alone was said to need up to $600,000 in repairs. (The entire edifice had cost $4 million to build.) Insurance underwriters estimated they would be paying at least $200,000 just to replace the district's plate glass—not to mention the medical expenses incurred. Later, these estimates would be scaled back. Indeed, from an insurance perspective, the explosion was ultimately as much a boon as a tragedy, a chance to remind the public of the fragility of modern life. "That Was a Terrible Explosion Yesterday!" read an ad tucked into the back pages of the *New York Times* the morning after the explosion. "But Accidents Are Ever at Hand and They Come without Warning; Don't Wait until You Are Disabled!"[23]

News of the blast dominated the front page of nearly every American paper, pushing the League of Nations, the civil war in Russia, and the presidential election to forsaken territory near the sports and ladies' sections. The *Times* alone dedicated seventeen full pages to the catastrophe, including several lengthy pieces detailing the ins and outs of evidence and official speculation. Throughout the city, local dailies scurried to offer the most detailed photographs, the fastest updates, the most sensational headlines. By late Friday, the *Evening Mail* was already bragging that it had "beat every other paper" by a full twenty minutes, thrusting papers into the hands of unsuspecting citizens "even before the police found time to establish their lines or bring a semblance of order."[24]

Despite their efforts, the newspapers found it difficult to deliver accurate news about the explosion's death toll. On Thursday night, the *Globe and Commercial Advertiser* ran the headline "20 Dead, Over 200 Hurt." The *Milwaukee Journal*, the same evening, estimated "30 or more people" killed and "more than 300" injured. By morning, the variation remained, with the *Wall Street Journal* announcing "more than 15 persons" killed, and the *Washington Post* declaring in a headline "31 Dead, 200 Injured." The names of the known victims, ticked off in neat columns on the papers' front pages, provided little clarification. One murdered man, a twenty-nine-year-old clerk, was listed variously as Joseph Aubebury, Joseph Aresberg, Joseph Cranberry, Joseph Aaronberry, Joseph Kresberg, Joseph Aurebury, Joseph Arambarry, and C. H. Barnes.[25]

Reports from individual offices were similarly confused. Three people from National City Bank were reported missing in the newspapers, for instance, but when employees showed up they discovered, happily, that the number of dead was only two. Rumors that the stock exchange had taken great casualties proved unfounded: not a single person had been killed there. At the Morgan bank, according to one news report, no fewer than seven people were dead from the blast. Lamont corrected that claim early on Friday, when he announced that two Morgan employees were now dead. The first was William Joyce. The second, John Donohue, an accountant in the export department, had been somewhere near Wall and Broad when the blast went off, and was thrown into the fire.[26]

According to the city's chief medical examiner, Charles Norris, the vast majority of the victims were felled by "punctures or penetrating wounds" rather than burns or, as rumor would have it, heart attacks induced by shock. Other fatalities were the result of broken bones and hemorrhaging, Dr. Norris concluded, even when they did not hit "a vital spot." On the victims' death certificates, "compound fracture of skull" would eventually rank first as the most common immediate cause of death. Among other causes were "evisceration of brain," "fracture of spine," "laceration of liver," and "missile wound of lung and heart." The examiner noted the secondary cause of death as some variation of "explosion of bomb—Wall and Broad St."[27]

Even with the disjointed information yet available, it was evident by the time the opening gong sounded on Friday morning that most of the men and women killed were decidedly not of the capitalist class. They were messengers, stenographers, clerks, salesmen, drivers—part of the vast army of workers behind each trade. For them, Wall Street was not a grand symbol of American capitalism—or, at least, it was not only that. It was a place to make a modest living by selling milk, driving a car, typing reports, recording sales. Nineteen-year-old Bartholomew Flannery ran errands for the Commercial Cable Company. Mildred Xylander, twenty-seven, took dictation at a law office. Alexander Leith, sixty-four, was an office assistant, an immigrant from Scotland. Franklin Miller, twenty-one, sold adding machines.[28]

On the whole, the victims were remarkably young, the vast majority under the age of forty. Two sixteen-year-olds—Benjamin Soloway and Robert Westbay—matched each other for the honor of youngest victim. Soloway was an immigrant from Russia. Westbay had been born in New York and raised by his aunt and uncle, who identified him at the morgue.[29]

Perhaps the closest the explosion had come to felling a true aristocrat was Col. Charles Neville, scion of a top Savannah family, who headed an accounting firm with offices in Washington and New York. The explosion punctured his skin and lung. He lived for a few hours after the blast but, as one paper commented, "the odds against him were hopeless from the beginning."[30]

The attention devoted to Neville was noticeably lacking in the accounts of less esteemed victims. About John Johnson, a porter for the Bank of America, the papers provided only the barest of facts: "Johnson, John, 55 years; employee of the Bank of America and living at 160 West Eighty-fourth Street; identified by wife." Another victim was listed simply as

"Weir, John W., 460 West Fifty-seventh Street, died yesterday in Broad Street Hospital." But even such fragments of information, published in newspapers' victim lists and articles, reveal a universe of grief, a disruption of shared expectations. "The girls just went to work," cried one mother whose daughters lay covered with burns at Broad Street Hospital, "and here they are at the point of death."[31]

The final count, when it emerged months later, totaled the victims at 38 dead, 143 seriously wounded. Two-thirds were under the age of thirty. Four were teenagers. Five were women. Six had served in the expeditionary forces overseas.

EVEN WITHOUT A DEFINITIVE TALLY, editorial columns on Friday morning pulsed with grief and shock over the scale of the attack. They described the explosion in grandiose terms, as if seeking to surpass their competitors in outrage as well as sheer word count. The blast was a "ghastly exhibition of malice," a "dreadful deed," "a crime the calculated and wanton fiendishness of which passes description." The *Evening Mail* predicted that the "concussion that shook Wall Street yesterday, with its terrible toll of innocent lives, will find a response in every American heart and conscience." According to the *Sun and New York Herald*, the whole affair was "unprecedented in horror."[32]

In part, this claim for "unprecedented" suffering was only an expression of sympathy, the sort of hyperbole that the relentless lists of injuries— "arm broken," "scalp wounds," "wrenched back," "laceration of head and neck," "laceration and contusion of body," "suffering from shock," "left arm and right eye injured," "cut in head by flying glass"—seemed to demand. By one measure, though, it also contained an objective truth. If the explosion turned out to be an accident, the loss of life was regrettable but hardly unprecedented; more than a thousand people had died when  the steamer *General Slocum* sank in the East River in 1904, for instance, casualties of a boiler explosion, poor steering, and a set of crumbling life jackets. But if it was a deliberate attack, as investigators suspected, the Wall Street blast already ranked as the most deadly act in the nation's long history of dynamite terrorism.[33]

Without a definitive account of what had happened, the press was left to speculate about how this latest tragedy might ultimately fit into the long history of what one paper labeled "Bomb Outrages Laid to Reds." Beginning on Thursday night, newspapers began to complement reports on the explosion with lists of earlier violent episodes: Haymarket, Frick, McKinley, Steunenberg, Los Angeles, and so on to 1920. Even as they recounted this long, familiar history, though, many editors noted that the explosion, with its high number of casualties and its almost indiscriminate design, might well prove to be distinctly different from what had come before. "The United States has long been familiar with terrorist outrages of that kind," reported the *World*, "but hitherto they have been directed toward a definite object."[34]

As examples of this earlier, more targeted form of terrorism, the paper cited Haymarket (the consequence "of clashes between Anarchists and public authorities"), the Los Angeles dynamiting ("the product of bitter labor quarrels"), even the Preparedness Day bombing ("a method of protesting against militarism")—all of them the result, in the *World*'s view, of an identifiable local conflict. The explosion on Wall Street, by contrast, seemed altogether vague and ineffective: "No capitalist was injured. None of the Wall Street class so hated by radicals suffered." Even more frightening was fact that the high death toll seemed to be the *point* of the attack. As best as anyone could tell, this was no botched assassination or, as with the McNamara Affair, a case where the mass casualties were unintended. Instead, the bomb appeared to be designed to kill as many people as possible, raising new questions about whether even larger attacks lay ahead. "This was the most serious outrage ever perpetrated by the radicals in New York," the editors of the *Sun and New York Herald* concluded by Friday morning, already confident that they knew enough to declare the explosion's importance. "In many respects it is the most serious in the history of the country."[35]

Many business papers, by contrast, hesitated to incorporate the explosion into a broader tale of political or class conflict. The blast "killed an uncertain number of absolutely innocent and uninterested people," read the coverage in the *Wall Street Journal*. "It sent a sufficient number of injured to the neighboring hospitals to make a total record of casualties about equaling a raid in France in No Man's Land during the late war. And that is all it did." This uneasiness was particularly pronounced in the financial pages, where writers tried awkwardly to treat the blast as just another business event. "Terrific explosion, causing the loss of many lives, results in closing of Exchange for the day," reported the *Journal*. "Market had been strong, with the oils and dividend paying rails the leaders—Reading at new high for the year."[36]

The effect was incongruous, almost callous, as if the *Journal* refused to acknowledge that Wall Street was a flesh-and-blood community as well as a financial market. But it was no less calculated than the *Sun and New York Herald*'s call to arms. By treating the explosion as just another business event, the *Wall Street Journal*, like the House of Morgan, aimed to show the world all was "business as usual."

THOMAS COCHRAN WAS THE FIRST senior Morgan partner to arrive on Friday morning. The explosion had found him in the Adirondacks, enjoying the last few days of summer warmth. As if in penance, he had driven through the night to be at the office when business resumed.[37]

With him came several junior partners: Elliott Bacon, George Whitney, and Junius Morgan. Since the explosion, Junius had attempted to maintain a reassuring pose to friends and family, especially to his worried parents overseas. "Am in greatest anxiety," Jack had cabled to 23 Wall, "please wire instantly all information you have about explosion particularly as to any injury to Junius." The partners kept Jack's precise whereabouts secret from the press, a precaution undertaken after Muenter's assassination attempt. Privately, they did their best to keep him up to date. Among Junius' first tasks on Friday morning was to cable a note of reassurance to his father through the Morgan, Grenfell office in London. "Almost entire office force on hand this morning and except for lack of glass and some scaffolding under dome building looks normal," he wrote. "Hope everything going all right with you and that you will not consider returning on account things here."[38]

Lamont had tried to be similarly comforting the previous day. "Office looks rather bad now but will soon be cleaned up," he wrote in his first cable to London. With his prediction all but fulfilled by Friday morning, he prepared to assume Jack's role as the bank's public face. He arrived at the office just before eleven o'clock, a time that showed a studied lack of alarm over the bank's ability to function. Indeed, by then nearly every able-bodied Morgan employee was already at his post. This fact proved a pleasant surprise to partner Henry Davison, who appeared around the same time as Lamont. "The men were simply fine and while many of them were going around with bandaged heads there was not a sign of nervousness or fear, but rather one of loyalty and courage," he wrote to Jack. "Of course we would expect this from our partners but to find it without exception throughout the force is a fact of which we should take note."[39]

Outside, the corner of Wall and Broad was still roped off, protected by a phalanx of guards and police charged with keeping away unwanted visitors. They had relaxed their lines during the morning rush, allowing employees to squeeze past between the hours of eight and nine. But by midmorning they were back to scrutinizing every passerby. They found plenty of work. In addition to the returning employees, thousands of sightseers had ventured down to Wall Street, hoping to catch a glimpse of the financial district at its moment of cowed imperfection. "Downtown New York today is one mob," a Morgan man groused to colleagues in London. "There seems to be millions of people out on the street trying to get a sight." The fact that there wasn't actually much to see—some muslin curtains, a few pockmarks on the marble façade—did not deter them. The knowledge that men and women had died on that corner less than twenty-four hours earlier gave even the most mundane detail new interest and weight. "Wall Street is no longer Wall Street, as it was one day ago," Lamont's *Post* reflected. "Today it is a show-place, as much to be questioned with the eyes as are the battlefields of Northern France or any of the natural wonders of the world."[40]

As if in concession to this fact, Lamont extended a rare invitation to the press to enter the Morgan bank and observe its inner workings. "It was a novel sight," the *Times* man wrote, "to enter one of the biggest financial institutions in the world and see dignified executives at work with heads bandaged, to see clerks operating typewriters and adding machines with one disabled hand... and to feel at the same time the calm yet steady impulse of a great business organization running with unimpaired smoothness." Members of the grand jury came, too, having cast off their other responsibilities to concentrate on examining the explosion evidence. As the *Times* report suggested, the consensus of the visitors was that the bank, as well as the rest of the district, had recovered amazingly well. "Like a strong man who sticks to the line after binding up his wounds and sewing on his wound stripes," the *Sun and New York Herald* concluded, "Wall Street, from its lowly office boy to its most stately financier, went to work yesterday morning with head up and teeth set, determined to show the world that business will proceed as usual."[41]

In his quiet way, Lamont played into this image of the financier as embattled warrior, holding the line against chaos and fear. His public remarks singled out Junius for special note, describing how his "coolness" in all likelihood had prevented a panic among the Morgan ranks.

The *Wall Street Journal* went even further, comparing Junius to Henry Clay Frick as he faced down Alexander Berkman in 1892 and to Jack himself as he wrestled with Muenter in 1915. "[H]e stepped naturally into the leader's position, when a blast of shrapnel swept his office and killed at least one employee," the *Journal* wrote in late September. "This seems to be characteristic of big businessmen."[42]

Even as Lamont demonstrated that the Morgan men had borne up well under attack, he went out of his way to deny any suggestion that they had indeed been targeted. In his few public statements, he stressed that the explosion was most likely aimed neither at the Morgan bank nor at capitalism per se, but at the public in a more general sense. When asked by reporters if he intended to hire a private detective to perform an independent investigation, he dismissed the possibility. "The whole problem is one of public importance," he insisted. "It is the work for the regularly constituted police authorities and not for any private individual or firm. . . . This is wholly a public matter and it would be manifestly wrong for us to attempt to usurp the powers of the police."[43]

This did not turn out to be true; whatever their intentions on Friday, in the months to come the Morgan bank spent a good deal of money trying to hunt down the bomb plotters. But the significance of Lamont's point on Friday was less practical than ideological. As a symbolic measure, the decision not to hire a private investigator served the purpose of diverting attention from the Morgan bank as a particular target of hatred, allying the bank with the rest of Wall Street, and joining Wall Street with the nation as a whole. Though the other Morgan partners refused to speak for attribution, they seemed to agree with Lamont's approach. "It was clear that they did not regard the attack as directed at their company in particular," the *Tribune* reported, "but against American institutions in general."[44]

Many newspapers offered similar interpretations in their morning editions. "This is not a local but a national crime," the *Sun and New York Herald* declared, "a blow at the economic order of this country, a mystery which concerns the government itself." The business press, in particular, presented the blast as an attack on all Americans, an assault not only upon the symbols of finance capitalism but upon the nation itself. The *Journal of Commerce* declared the crime to be of "national significance" and called for all classes to join forces against the perpetrators. Walter Brown, the editor of the *New York Commercial*, the "National Business Newspaper,"

concluded, "If the blow was aimed at American institutions and principles it was aimed at something intangible, that exists not alone in Wall
Street, but throughout the country—something that cannot be reached
by bombs."[45]

This early rush of support must have come as a relief to Lamont and
the other Morgan partners, a hint that the bank would not have to stand
alone as a target of hatred and fear. For further proof they needed to look
no further than what was happening outside their front door. By chance,
September 17 was Constitution Day, a holiday created in 1919 to celebrate "the vital principles of our Government" and "furnish a specific
antidote to Bolshevism and kindred reactionary political heresies," in the
words of one supporter. As the noon hour approached, the Sons of the
American Revolution began to assemble for a ceremony on the site they
had selected weeks earlier: the corner of Wall and Broad.[46]

THE SONS INTENDED to follow through on their plans, bomb or no bomb.
This they explained to a policeman who, upon discovering their ceremony,
politely requested a deferral. The Sons claimed a long American lineage:
members were supposed to trace their family roots to a veteran of the
Revolutionary War. They argued that the rally would show that modern
Americans retained the defiant spirit of their forebears—and, anyway, it
was too late to stop. The fifer and drummer were already costumed and
the troops were ready to march. Commissioner Enright, called in to arbi-
trate, sided with the marchers. So, at the very moment on the very site
where the explosion had erupted twenty-four hours earlier, Wall Street
paused "business as usual" for a pageant marking the 133rd anniversary
of the signing of the U.S. Constitution.[47]

The crowd amassing that Friday at Wall and Broad was all out of pro-
portion to the Sons' typical audience. The *Daily News* said "thousands"
came, the *Sun and New York Herald* estimated "tens of thousands," the
*Tribune* saw "more than 100,000," and the *Globe* simply called it "a crowd
that will be remembered for its size in a city of famous crowds." The
willingness of so many to stop and watch was itself a show of bravado:
what better place for another "outrage" than a close-packed crowd of
patriots?[48]

To the *Washington Post*, the explosion further proved the need for holidays such as Constitution Day. "Anarchy knocks today on the gate of
America and seeks to destroy the edifice within. Mob violence and class

rule is proposed as a substitute for the supreme people's will as exemplified by the Constitution." The Sons' preplanned display of patriotism was just a coincidence, but to the *Post* it seemed like serendipity.[49]

A trumpeter on Broadway took the last of Trinity's midday chimes as his cue to sound the procession's start. A file of mounted policemen assumed the lead, using the advantages of height and weight to forge a path down the center of Wall Street. Next came the fifer and drummer, two young men dressed as the figures from the painting "Spirit of '76." They played "Yankee Doodle" and a few spectators joined in. Finally, the Sons themselves appeared, about two hundred altogether. They wore the uniforms of their Revolutionary ancestors. Most were far past soldiering age, and a few limped as if wounded in battle. They assembled on the Sub-Treasury steps beneath the statue of Washington.[50]

The Sub-Treasury's front pillars were dusted with soot, save for a few white spots where the stone was pitted and torn. Flanked by these reminders of violence, the Sons' president delivered the welcoming words, then turned the ceremony over to a soloist. The singer, a veteran of the Great War, led the audience in a bracing rendition of "America." When the last strains of "sea to shining sea" sputtered out, the appointed chaplain stepped forth to deliver a prayer for the nation's safety.

The day's featured speaker was Brig. Gen. William J. Nicholson, a gray-haired former army man. Judging by his speech that noon, his time in the military had taught him that enemies of America should be conquered without mercy. And the men who planned the Wall Street explosion, he told the vaguely nervous crowd, were enemies of the worst sort. "Any person who would commit such a crime or connive in its commission should be put to death!" Nicholson bellowed from his vantage point high above the crowd. "He has no right to live in a civilized community. Such persons should be killed whenever they rear their heads, just as you would kill a snake!"[51]

He put himself forward as a model of, even a martyr to, the duties of citizenship. "I am old and gray. My years are spent. But I would be proud to die in the work of hunting down and punishing such men and driving them from the land which we have dedicated to freedom under the Constitution." Then the trumpet, fife, and drum struck up "The Star-Spangled Banner," and the crowd united for a final roaring rendition. All in all, wrote the *Evening Mail*, the pageant had provided a splendid display of the national attributes that had so lately come under attack at Wall and Broad.[52]

AS THE SONS BEGAN TO REMOVE the trappings of their simulated colonial moment, they left behind the statue of George Washington, standing proud on the Sub-Treasury steps. A few feet away, the bronze bas-relief of Washington kneeling in prayer had been wrenched off the front of the Sub-Treasury, and the statue's marble base had been pitted and scraped in parts. But the statue itself was untouched—a sure sign, many observers thought, that Wall Street itself would pass through this trial uncowed.[53]

Whether or not Washington deserved credit, by the end of the day it began to seem that Wall Street had, financially speaking, pulled off something miraculous. From the first moment of awkward trading, the stock market had entered a protracted climb. Steel and oil gained in the morning, with railroads and tobacco succumbing in the afternoon to the apparently "irresistible impulse to rise." Mexican Petroleum did especially well, rising ten points. General Asphalt and American Writing Paper made small gains as well. As if in some sort of self-deprecating joke, investors also gave a boost to Aetna Explosives, bumping the stock up over eleven for the first time in several weeks.[54]

There were suggestions that at least some of this progress was due to the behind-the-scenes maneuvers of private bankers who, according to the *Tribune*, bore a "marked indisposition to permit traders operating for the decline to make capital out of the grewsome [*sic*] event." Others ascribed the day's progress to emerging hints that this explosion, like earlier bomb plots, would "result in country wide demands for the repression of terrorism." Whatever the reason, the consensus in the financial press was that there was real optimism across the board—"not alone in the stock exchange but in the entire financial district."[55]

By the closing gong on Friday, stocks were up more than they had been since August 9—a sign, all agreed, of better times ahead.

# 8

. . . .

## USUAL SUSPECTS

BILL HAYWOOD LEARNED that he was a suspect while boarding the train
to New York on September 17. He had been speaking in Philadelphia at
the Labor Assembly Hall, part of an ever-expanding tour launched after
his release from Leavenworth in July 1919. After more than a year as
prisoner 13106, he was happy to rejoin the political circuit and revive
the itinerant life of his youth. Despite outward appearances, though, he
was not a free man. His twenty-year sentence under the wartime statutes
still stood. Barring a reprieve from the Circuit Court of Appeals, he could
be recalled to Leavenworth at any moment. While out of jail, he had also
acquired two new indictments: one in Illinois on charges of "criminal
syndicalism" (a potential sentence of ten years) and another at the federal
level for "conspiracy to overthrow the government" (twenty years). At the
age of fifty-one, he acknowledged in a letter to his secretary, any one of
these sentences "practically means the rest of my natural life." With the
news of September 17, he faced the prospect of adding the Wall Street
bomb plot to this daunting list of legal entanglements. According to the
papers thrust into his hands as he left Philadelphia, the federal authorities were seeking to arrest him immediately "as a general precautionary
measure."[1]

Haywood wasn't sure he could survive another trial, much less another heavy sentence. His time in Leavenworth had aggravated all of his old infirmities: the ulcer induced by drinking, the rotting teeth from his impoverished youth. His diabetes had flared up as well; by the time he left jail, he could see only dimly out of his one good eye. Rather than provide rest and convalescence, his release had brought further bouts of debilitating stress. Still reeling from the wartime prosecutions, the Wobblies were all but "crippled," in Haywood's words, backed into a position of permanent defense. Even worse, many former comrades had turned their wrath not on the Justice Department but on Haywood himself, blaming him for diverting attention and funds from their own jailhouse struggles. Under these circumstances, Haywood had resumed his whiskey habit, convinced that any hope for revolutionary change in America now lay far in the future.[2]

Still, after years of tussling with the authorities, he knew better than to admit defeat. Faced with reports of his imminent arrest, Haywood adopted the same jocular, defiant pose that had served him so well in Idaho. "I was surprised to learn from the newspapers that the secret service was searching for me in connection with the Wall Street explosion," he told the press. "If they did not know that I made a speech in Philadelphia on Wednesday night . . . they certainly were remiss in their duty."[3]

Despite this, he had already concluded that he was in no position to withstand another battle in court. After a brief stop in New York, he departed for Chicago, throwing himself on the mercy of Otto Christensen, one of the Wobblies' indefatigable lawyers. Christensen helped him make his way to a summer resort where a Wobbly sympathizer served as caretaker at the home of a "Chicago capitalist." There, Haywood planned to do what he had done, with limited success, during the Palmer Raids in January: lie low and hope that the whole thing would blow over.[4]

There was some reason to believe that this might happen fairly soon. As Tom Mooney's brother Jack pointed out, the authorities seemed to be dragging their feet in making arrests. "I felt bad when I heard the news of the explosion on Wall Street the other day," Jack Mooney told supporters at New York's Yorkville Lyceum on the evening of September 17. "But I was immensely pleased that nobody has been framed up for the explosion, as happened to Tom Mooney in San Francisco four years ago." That same day, Haywood himself won a temporary reprieve from the Bureau of Investigation. Reading the articles predicting Haywood's imminent capture, Flynn assured the press that the Wobbly leader was safe, at least for the moment. "He is now out on bail," Flynn explained, "and any time that we want him we can call his bail in."[5]

Flynn's statement, with its implied promise of future arrest, did little to force Haywood to rethink his plans. Such assurances of safety and goodwill rang hollow in light of the Justice Department's other recent claims. On the afternoon of September 17, as Haywood began his flight to Chicago, Flynn announced that the Bureau, like the Burns detective agency, had ruled out the possibility of a dynamite accident. Hours later, Attorney General A. Mitchell Palmer dashed to New York to declare his intention to launch a new round of deportation raids.

THE FLYERS LOOKED CHILDISH, printed in red ink on cheap white paper. A postal carrier from the Hudson Terminal had discovered them just before noon on Thursday, dropped unwrapped and unaddressed into the box at Broadway and Cedar Street. He stuffed the flyers in his pockets, thinking someone official might want to look at them. Then he heard the boom from Wall and Broad. After running back to see what had happened, he hurried to the Hudson station and turned the documents over to his supervisor. By Friday morning, having traced a circuitous route through the postal bureaucracy, they were in Flynn's hands.

Whoever made the flyers had avoided a real printer, perhaps for fear that the source could be traced. The words were written with rubber stamps instead. With a different stamp for each letter, it didn't make for a great printing job. The words were lopsided and out of sync. They were misspelled, too. Four offered the word "rimember" instead of "remember" (the fifth used "rememer"); some had "prisoniers" rather than "prisoners." But the message was the same on all five sheets: "Remember, we will not tolerate any longer. Free the political prisoners, or it will be sure death for all of you." They were signed "American Anarchist Fighters."[6]

Flynn announced the discovery of the circulars on Friday morning, along with his conclusion that he had ruled out the accident theory. "A bomb—nothing else," he told the *New York Tribune*. "There is absolutely no doubt of it, and knowing this much, we can proceed toward the placing of the responsibility." The flyers themselves, however, offered only limited evidence about who had set the bomb or why. The first sentence suggested the explosion had been planned in retaliation for ongoing persecution, hardly a claim that much narrowed the field of suspects. The second phrase, with its reference to "political prisoners," seemed at first glance to offer more specifics. Several newspapers noted that Attorney General Palmer had met with Samuel Gompers on Wednesday morning to discuss the possibility of a mass amnesty for Wobblies, socialists, and other dissenters imprisoned during the war. That same afternoon, the Socialist Party had presented a lengthy petition calling for the release of Eugene Debs. Palmer turned down both requests, arguing that each case deserved an individual review and that the fortunate end of the war did not make treason less treasonous. "What officials regard as probable," the *Milwaukee Journal* reported, "is that some group of anarchists plotted the explosion to be one or two days after Palmer's refusal of the general amnesty."[7]

When questioned directly, Flynn offered little support for the theory. "I don't want it understood that I would mention his [Gompers'] name in connection with this terrible thing," he told the *New York Times*. He was more intrigued by the three words of signature at the bottom of the flyer: "American Anarchist Fighters." As Flynn pointed out to reporters, the architects of the June 2, 1919, bombs had used a nearly identical signature—"The Anarchist Fighters"—to identify their handiwork. And the flyers provided intriguing material clues as well. Someone had written them in a hurry and the inconsistency in misspellings indicated at least two sets of hands on the job. From the placement and timing of the circulars, Flynn speculated, the driver must have abandoned the horse on Wall Street—"having set the timing device a few minutes ahead"—and, not wanting to risk losing the circulars in the fire, walked to Cedar Street, about a four-minute trek, to drop them in the mailbox.[8]

As later events would show, Flynn already had his own ideas about who that might be. First, however, he needed proof. Convinced that "terrorists" had attacked Wall Street, he set out to gather the necessary evidence.

WITH JUST A HANDFUL OF AGENTS assigned to radical affairs, the Bureau's New York office could not handle the Wall Street case alone. So Flynn commandeered the members of a "flying squadron," a floating group of Bureau detectives who could be assigned to any task. Before the explosion, the squadron had been busy investigating profiteers and hoarders accused of conspiring to raise the ever-increasing cost of living.

On September 17, the explosion seemed like the more dire threat. Flynn gathered his men in the Bureau's office on Park Row to begin the formal phase of the investigation. In the process, he took pains to remind the public that the explosion was a national, not local, crime. "It was planted in the heart of America as a defiance against the American people and the American Government," he explained to the *Washington Post*. "That is my opinion."[9]

The connection between this view of the disaster and the Bureau's jurisdiction over the case was not lost on the press. "If it shall continue to appear that the crime was one aimed at government, let the government sift it to the bottom," wrote the *Sun and New York Herald*. "Whatever the weaknesses of the Department of Justice, it is the natural agent for this investigation." The New York police, however, were not willing to concede so easily. At an emergency meeting on September 17, while "business as usual" was being carried out a few blocks to the south, the city's Board of Estimate approved a reward of $10,500 for tips provided to the local authorities: $10,000 for a conviction, $500 for information about the horse and wagon.[10]

William J. Burns, the "Great Detective," advertised a reward as well. The Morgans continued to deny any plan to employ Burns or to offer their own reward. Burns managed nonetheless to gather $526 from a group of veterans who, like Flynn, viewed the explosion as an assault upon the nation. "They...pointed out that this outrage was apparently not aimed at any individual or group of individuals, but at organized government," Burns explained from his home on West Seventy-second Street, "and recalled that the Reds have frequently denounced our form of government and declared their intention of bringing about a revolution by terrorism." With that, he more or less disappeared from the investigation.[11]

Burns would later return in brass band fashion with his own theories about who had done what. So would Arthur Woods, who began to conduct his own, quiet investigation behind the scenes. In those initial days of uncertainty, though, the chief responsibility for sorting through the evidence fell to the public authorities—most notably, to the Bureau and the New York police. Flynn had already ordered his network of operatives to begin surveillance of radical organizations. "All under cover informants and the bomb squad of the Chicago Police Department were advised to endeavor to locate leading anarchist agitators and to check on their activities and recent movements," a Chicago agent later wrote, summarizing his branch's activities on September 16. The initial reports, however, had yielded little beyond the obvious. In Chicago, one spy noted that area Wobblies, like Haywood himself, seemed nervous about what the days ahead would bring. "The general sentiment seems to be that I.W.W. will be suspected and that arrests and raids will probably follow," he wrote on September 16.[12]

As the local investigating authority, the New York police retained custody of the explosion's physical evidence. As a result, they were able to claim credit for the first direct assessments of the horse-and-wagon debris. On Friday morning, detectives gathered the fragments at police headquarters. By evening, in what proved to be their most efficient work of the entire investigation, they were ready to offer a full description of the vehicle that had carried the bomb to Wall and Broad.

According to the police, the wagon was a run-down wooden "butter and egg" delivery wagon "of one or one and a half tons capacity, about 10 to 15 years old," with red running gear and wheel spokes striped black and white. The horse was even more ancient: twenty years old, fifteen and a half hands high, a dark bay, recently clipped. The report noted that the horse's hind shoes bore the letters *JHU*, the mark of the Journeymen Horseshoers' Union. More importantly, someone had shod the horse less than twenty-four hours before the explosion. On Saturday, two hundred police detectives began a canvass of livery stables, blacksmith shops, harness makers, and wagon manufacturers in search of the man who might recognize his handiwork.[13]

Progress was slower when it came to determining what type of explosive had caused the blast. The most likely substances were dynamite and TNT, though picric acid, black powder, nitroglycerine, and chlorate of potash all earned consideration. Each explosive produced a different color and smell (TNT produced black smoke, for instance, while the smoke from dynamite tended toward a yellow hue). But witnesses varied so wildly in their descriptions that experts called to the site found little to go on. Leland Summers, an occasional technical consultant for the House of Morgan, leaned toward TNT, a supposition supported on Friday by at least four fellow experts. By contrast, Hudson Maxim, a well-known inventor of high explosives, suspected dynamite, and at least the same number of observers agreed with him. "The action of good dynamite, say 60 per cent, would be very much the same as TNT," Maxim explained. "And in view of the fact that the results would be about the same, it would be a safer theory, because dynamite is not so hard to obtain." Everyone said that the question would require further study.[14]

This level of confusion was typical of the investigation's first few days. Even with the circulars and the description of the horse and wagon in hand, official thought about the origins and content of the explosion remained firmly planted in the realm of guesswork. Detectives could not agree, for instance, about what sort of device—a time clock or a burning fuse—might have detonated the bomb. Nor did they develop a single view of precisely where the wagon had been located or what direction it might have been facing.[15]

Well into the weekend, neither the Bureau nor the police could even say for sure whether the wagon driver himself was still alive. Initially they hoped that the body of a young blond man, lying unidentified at the morgue, might turn out to be the dead bomber. But this theory, like so many to follow, quickly disintegrated under the weight of the facts. On Monday, a Brooklyn woman identified the man as her twenty-one-year-old son, Elmer Kehrer. An "industrious lad" and sometime chauffeur, Kehrer had been looking for work on September 16, dressed in a brown suit and a checkered alpaca cap. His family assured detectives that Kehrer harbored no radical sympathies.[16]

The only intriguing new development of the first few days, other than the flyers and the description of the horse and wagon, came from Italy, a location that would soon figure prominently in the Bureau's suspicions. On September 17, hours after Flynn announced the Anarchist Fighters circulars, a dynamite explosion rocked the stock exchange in Genoa, raising fears that the Wall Street explosion might be part of an "international terrorist plot."[17]

Perhaps inspired by this speculation, on Sunday the *Chicago Tribune* reported that the Bureau was seeking Haywood's friend and wartime codefendant Carlo Tresca, along with four other Italian anarchists, as suspects in the Wall Street case. As with Haywood, Flynn swiftly quashed any rumors of imminent arrest. Lest men such as Tresca become too complacent, however, he offered a pointed reminder that he was still on watch. "We will seize any of these men," he assured the press, "anytime we are convinced that they can tell us something about the explosion."[18]

THE FIRST MAN actually "seized" by the authorities, a genial fellow by the name of Ed Fisher, fit nobody's picture of a bomb-throwing anarchist. A Wall Street gadfly, Fisher had once been employed at a prominent brokerage house and at the French High Commission. He had never been involved in revolutionary politics, other than harboring a general dislike for "all moneyed interests" and a certain admiration for Emma Goldman. The main group he seemed to belong to was the West Side Tennis Club, where his championship play—the Lawn Tennis Association ranked him number nine in the country in 1901—made him a popular partner.[19]

The one quality that set him apart from his fellow sports buffs was his gift for prescience, or what acquaintances uncharitably described as his "mental derangement." In the week before the explosion, Fisher had sent at least three notes to friends in the financial district alerting them, in a variety of phrasings, that a "Bolshevist professor" had instructed him to "[s]tay away from Wall Street this Wednesday afternoon." His warnings were off by a day, and his correspondents assured the Bureau that "no conspirators, after talking with Fischer [sic] for ten minutes, would consider letting him into a plot with them." Under the circumstances, though, both the police and the Bureau figured he was worth an interview. "Hold Edward Fisher," Chief Inspector Lahey cabled on Friday afternoon to the authorities in Canada, where Fisher had gone to attend a tennis tournament. "Our detective McCoy left for Hamilton this morning."[20]

Fisher had fallen on hard times during his stay in Canada. "At present I have 7 cents!" he wrote to his brother-in-law, who promptly requested that the "Lunacy Commission" detain him for his own good. By the time the Bureau agents arrived, Fisher was already in official custody and perfectly willing to chat. He was, however, a bit hard to follow. "He talked about many subjects very rapidly," Bureau agent W. L. Buchanan informed his superiors in New York. "[A]gent will only briefly quote subject matter which may be relevant." Among other tales, Fisher claimed:

> That he had received the information about the bomb explosion through God and the air
>
> That he had no real phychic [sic] power
>
> That he was against the Capitalists and money men; that to the workers should go the harvest
>
> That Morgan financed the war for England and the United States
>
> That money would be of no use in a very short time and Labor would be the medium for distribution of all things

Whether any of this constituted means and motive, Buchanan wasn't sure. He agreed, with the help of the city police, to transport Fisher to New York for further interviews.[21]

Fisher arrived rumpled in Grand Central Station with the Monday morning commuters. He wore a lopsided gray cap, a wrinkled gray suit, and a silk scarf around his waist. Later, he explained that the suit was the outermost of three full sets of clothes. Wearing multiple layers helped to keep him cool, he said, and meant he didn't have to carry baggage. Thanks to an advance tip, photographers were on hand to record his appearance when the train from Buffalo pulled in just after nine o'clock. They intercepted Fisher's entourage near the Lexington Avenue exit with whistles and hollers. After acquiring breakfast and a shave for their prisoner, the entire crew headed downtown for the interrogations.[22]

Neither the Bureau men nor the local police were terribly hopeful. "I feel fairly sure that Fisher had nothing to do with this," Bureau Superintendent Lamb told the *New York American*. The interviews soon confirmed this suspicion. According to Fisher, his premonition of the explosion came "from the air"; it made sense, since Wall Street was the "center of evil in the world." He also mentioned that he admired the nation of Canada, since "no country given a name with three A's could be bad." Based on these discoveries, the police decided not to present him to the grand jury. Instead, they sent him on to the psychiatric ward at Bellevue.[23]

In another context, the revelation that a "lunatic" had so nearly hit upon the theory favored by the authorities might have raised questions about the theory itself. In the tense atmosphere of mid-September 1920, however, it only seemed to underscore the obvious question: given how predictable the explosion had been and how ineffective current policy seemed to be, what should the government do to prevent such acts in the future?

ONE OF THE FIRST ANSWERS came from Attorney General A. Mitchell Palmer, Flynn's direct superior at the Department of Justice and the man whose name had become all but synonymous with the recent deportation campaign. Palmer arrived in New York on the evening of September 17 flanked by J. Edgar Hoover and Francis Garvan, his point men on radical affairs. A thick, jowly man with a bulbous nose and sardonic smile, Palmer had no trouble fitting in with the assembled detectives. Reporters hinted that he intended to take personal charge of the Wall Street investigation, but the attorney general denied it. He told the press he would stay the night in New York (the trip had been scheduled long before the explosion) before moving on to his hometown of Stroudsburg, Pennsylvania.[24]

While in New York, he reviewed the hundreds of tips and rumors already gushing in from across the country, then quickly threw his support behind Flynn's conclusions. "At present, I believe it to be the result of a criminal conspiracy," he told reporters on Friday night. "I hope that further developments may tend to prove the contrary—that it was an accident—but all the present indications are that it was a deliberate outrage." The following day, Palmer did depart for Stroudsburg. Before he left, he put the press on notice about what to expect in the days and weeks ahead. "If it is found that the explosion in Wall Street was beyond doubt a criminal act," he declared, "we may, with the support of public opinion, be able to take more drastic action with relation to the deportation of alien criminal anarchists—the only class we have been deporting."[25]

Famous for his bombast and opportunism, Palmer was well equipped to take advantage of the surge in public sympathy already being produced by the Wall Street explosion. Despite his reputation as an anti-radical militant, he was uncomfortable thinking of himself as much of a warrior. A Quaker and sometime pacifist, he had turned down President Wilson's offer to appoint him as secretary of war. Even now, faced with a very different battle, Palmer preferred to present himself as a reformer, or at most as the "Fighting Quaker," an intermediary charged with restraining extremists at both ends of the political spectrum. His appointment as attorney general simply happened to occur at a moment, in his view, when the greatest threat to stability and order came from the likes of Haywood, Goldman, Berkman, and Debs.

There was a time before the war when Palmer might well have counted himself on the radicals' side, at least where a reform-minded stance seemed likely to win votes. As a Democratic congressman from Pennsylvania and self-proclaimed progressive, he had earned high marks from the American Federation of Labor. Suffragettes, too, applauded him for his support of women's voting rights. In 1914, at the peak of his congressional career, he had delighted both constituencies by promoting a far-reaching child labor bill that banned interstate commerce in products made by children under fourteen. President Wilson refused to support the bill, but he and Palmer had continued to maintain a sympathy of interest on many policy

matters. Palmer won his appointments first as wartime alien property custodian and then as attorney general based not on his reputation as a hardline crusader but on his fealty to progressivism, bureaucratic efficiency,
and, above all, Wilson's Democratic Party.[26]

Like Wilson, Palmer had grown more conservative during the war,
less inclined to tolerate dissident speech. But it was not until the bombing of his home on June 2, 1919, that he had entered the limelight as the
nemesis of "Red Radicalism," in the words of one Justice Department
pamphlet. Thrust into the martyr's role, Palmer discovered that he rather
enjoyed it. "[T]he effect upon the country as reflected in the newspaper
editorial comments from one end of the country to the other was perfectly splendid," he recalled, boasting of the response to Flynn's hiring.
In the months that followed, he busied himself preparing for the deportation raids, flooding the country with flyers and statements decrying
Bolshevism as "the most brutal, the most corrupt, the most wickedly
fatuous insurrection of mob ignorance in all history."[27]

Central to this campaign had been a stream of warnings about the
threat of further terrorism. "On a certain day . . . , which we have been
advised of," he informed Congress in June 1919, "there will be another
serious and probably much larger effort of the same character which the
wild fellows of this movement describe as revolution, a proposition to rise
up and destroy the Government at one fell swoop." His chosen date, July
4, went off without a revolution (the Mooney supporters who had vowed
a general strike that day never followed through). Palmer was alarmed
to discover nonetheless that, as attorney general, he had little recourse
to constrain their efforts. Nothing in the peacetime federal statutes forbade the expression of revolutionary ideas. Nor, to Palmer's chagrin, did
the Justice Department have much power over acts of terrorism, even
when they targeted the federal government itself. "A man might walk
down Pennsylvania Avenue, in the city of Washington, with a bomb in
his hand," he complained to Congress, "intending and publicly threatening to blow up both Houses of Congress while in session, and be immune
from prosecution under any general Federal statute."[28]

Palmer's solution to this problem was a peacetime sedition law modeled on the wartime speech restrictions, combined with aggressive surveillance by the Radical Division and a program of mass deportation.
By October 1919, however, he had made so little progress on most of
these fronts that the Republican-controlled Senate issued a proclamation

(known as the Poindexter Resolution after its author, Republican senator Miles Poindexter) demanding that Palmer explain "whether or not the Department of Justice has taken legal proceedings, and if not, why not, and if so, to what extent, for the arrest and punishment of the various persons within the United States who... have attempted to bring about the forcible overthrow of the Government."[29]

November's raid on the Union of Russian Workers immediately put Palmer back in official favor. When the *Buford* steamed out of New York the following month with Goldman and Berkman aboard, the praise became even more rousing; at last, the country cheered, here was an attorney general free of misguided tolerance. After the much larger January 2 raid on communist parties, however, his popularity once again went into a precipitous decline. On January 12, 1920, in the first drop of the deluge of criticism to come, U.S. Attorney Francis Fisher Kane of Pennsylvania resigned from office, arguing that "the policy of raids against large numbers of individuals is generally unwise and very apt to result in injustice."[30]

Palmer was hurt and puzzled at being abandoned by onetime friends such as Kane. "In the security which a rigid enforcement of the laws has given them," he complained to the New York County Lawyers' Association in February, "some well-intentioned people now declare that the Government's action has been drastic; that there is no danger in the situation; and that attempts to legislate in the manner I have described will constitute an infringement upon the guaranties [*sic*] of the Bill of Rights." The following month, his troubles only increased. In early March, thanks to a series of health crises and resignations at the upper ranks of the Labor Department, a progressive editor and longtime free-speech advocate named Louis F. Post ascended to the position of acting secretary of labor. In the six months between his appointment and the Wall Street explosion, he also emerged as Palmer's most vocal critic.[31]

With his little Van Dyke beard and tousled mop of gray hair, Post looked every inch the radical. Before the war, he had worked side by side with both Goldman and Berkman on a variety of free-speech issues, battling against antianarchist laws and criminal syndicalism statutes. In 1913, he had joined the Labor Department as assistant secretary, one of hundreds of reformers who signed on to help Wilson create a new progressive age. Six years later, in a different atmosphere altogether, he had approved Goldman's and Berkman's deportation orders, an act that Goldman found beneath contempt. With his promotion to acting secretary of labor, Post determined to make up for such mistakes. For several crucial weeks, from mid-March through April 14, 1920, Post had taken it upon himself to nullify more than two thousand warrants for immediate deportation, arguing that they infringed on the principle of individual guilt. In his private journal, he went so far as to accuse Palmer of disloyalty to the traditions and laws of the United States. "There are signs of an overthrow of our Government as a free government," he wrote in early 1920. "It is going on under cover of a vigorous 'drive' against anarchists, an 'anarchist' being almost anybody who objects to government of the people by tories and for financial interests." On April 15, after he had been in office for just a month, the House of Representatives began proceedings to impeach him for his actions.[32]

Bureau agents had played a prominent role in Post's impeachment, leaking to favored House members tidbits about the assistant secretary's radical predilections, including his friendship with Goldman and Berkman. But what should have been Palmer's triumph—the impeachment of his greatest critic—turned out to be a devastating embarrassment. Rather than vindicating the Justice Department, the impeachment hearings allowed Post to explain, in great and public detail, his objections to Palmer's scare tactics and policies of guilt by membership. "A good deal was said in public and otherwise about the tremendous danger that we are confronting; these men with bombs were preparing to kill right and left," Post testified. "But in all these sweeping raids over the country, . . . there have been three pistols, I think it is, brought to our attention."[33]

Faced with this powerful indictment, Congress had absolved Post of wrongdoing and turned its critical eye instead toward Palmer, summoning him for a series of daylong hearings. Palmer put on a fiery show, reminding Congress that they, not he, had provided the money for the deportation campaign—indeed, that they had fairly insisted he take some sort of drastic action. He attacked Post personally as well, accusing him of "habitually tender solicitude for social revolutionists and perverted sympathy for the criminal anarchists of the country." As for the revolutionists themselves, he could only repeat what he had said so many times before: that Bolshevism was an imminent and violent threat to the national welfare.[34]

None of this went very far toward rescuing his reputation. The House drubbing had barely slowed to a thump when federal judge George W. Anderson issued his *Colyer* decision, accusing the Justice Department of employing lynch-law tactics—"hang first and try afterwards"—in its deportation raids around Boston. That same month, twelve prominent lawyers, including future Supreme Court justice Felix Frankfurter, issued *To the American People: A Report on the Illegal Practices of the United States Department of Justice.* The report condemned the "utterly illegal acts which have been committed by those charged with the highest duty of enforcing the laws–acts which have caused widespread suffering and unrest, have struck at the foundation of American free institutions, and have brought the name of our country into disrepute." The man at the top, they noted, was A. Mitchell Palmer.[35]

Palmer still had his supporters, many of them loyal Democrats. In July, with the House hearings behind him, he ventured to San Francisco to test whether their enthusiasm might take him over the top for the party's presidential nomination. Like his attempt to impeach Post, this effort brought a resounding rejection. Though he entered as one of the front-runners, Palmer left the California convention without receiving more than a handful of delegate votes.

By September, still smarting from the indignity, Palmer had thrown his support behind former Ohio governor James Cox, the party's chosen man against Republican Warren Harding. When the bomb exploded on Wall Street, however, he recognized a chance for redemption. "[L]et Washington take action," the *Sun and New York Herald* recommended on the morning of September 17, "and may Attorney-General Palmer atone for his shortcomings in other and less important instances. For so long as the man or group of men who did what was done in Wall Street yesterday are at liberty Washington itself is not safe."[36]

PALMER APPROACHED THE CHALLENGE of the Wall Street explosion with all the confidence of a vindicated man. If he lacked the authority of personal martyrdom that had so strongly figured into his experiences the previous year, he now had the grim advantage of being able to say, with a bit of selective distortion, "I told you so." After months of mockery for his supposedly alarmist stance concerning the threat of terrorism, he had no desire to hold back his contempt for his critics. Nor, in a presidential election year, did he intend to bypass an opportunity to embarrass the Republican Party. In Palmer's view, the explosion offered self-evident proof of the need to enact the reforms he had long advocated but which the Republican Congress had failed to deliver: a federal sedition law, a thorough deportation campaign, and an infusion of cash into the Justice Department's shrinking coffers.

Palmer's chief complaint was that Congress had emasculated the Justice Department's once potent and well-disciplined army of Red-hunters, a casualty of the springtime backlash against the deportation policy. The cut in Bureau funds, from a requested $2.5 million down to just $2 million, had resulted in a substantial loss of Justice Department manpower, including, according to Palmer, the decimation of Flynn's antiradical force. As a result, Palmer argued, the department had missed whatever warnings might have been available to predict the Wall Street attack.[37]

He suggested, further, that the proximity of these two events—the budget cuts and the bombing—was no mere coincidence, speculating that the bombers might have known about the cuts and therefore felt emboldened to attempt what before they would not have dared. "Acquiescing in the direction of the Republican-controlled Congress," Robert T. Scott, his private secretary, explained to the *New York Times*, "this department reduced its operating forces to meet the amount of money provided. Inevitably this cut became public. Three weeks after it became actually effective this outrage was perpetrated in New York City."

As a defense against blame, the logic of Palmer's argument worked out well. If things went right, the Justice Department could always claim credit. But if anything went wrong—bomb explosions, revolutionary uprisings—it was because Congress had not provided enough money for the work to be carried out properly.[38]

Despite their differences at the San Francisco nominating convention, neither Palmer nor his fellow Democrats were above using the explosion as a potential wedge in the presidential election season. On September 19, the national Democratic Party backed Palmer's outrage about the budget cuts, issuing a statement of support for a new campaign against radicalism. "Republican representatives in Congress...greatly reduced the appropriation to the Department of Justice that was designed to rid the country of Reds," the statement read. "It is significant that within a very few days after the Department was forced to reduce its force this awful outrage took place."[39]

The statement also accused the Republicans of cozying up to Bolshevists, appealing to "every radical element of discontent" to drum the Wilsonians out of office. This was a difficult argument to sustain, given that Cox had been running a campaign depicting Harding as "a creature of Wall Street." But Edmond H. Moore, the committeeman responsible for the Democrats' statement, made a go of it anyway. "The condition is unprecedented when big business has joined hands with bolshevism to secure the defeat of the Democratic candidate," he explained.[40]

The Republicans were reluctant to allow such accusations to stand. In a response issued by the Republican Publicity Association, the party attacked Wilson as a defender of dynamiters, citing his support for commuting Tom Mooney's death sentence. The statement also attacked Palmer's record as the supposed scourge of radicalism. "As a matter of fact," the Republicans pointed out, "the department has not distinguished itself by success in running down men guilty of violence." Calls for new raids began to emerge, though their purpose was not so much to urge the attorney general to take action as to give the Republicans a chance to claim credit. "It was only after denunciation in Congress," the Republican Publicity Association now reminded the faithful, "that the department got underway in its efforts to check Red activities."[41]

Another source of partisan rancor was the much-debated sedition bill, which Palmer now vowed to ram through a recalcitrant Congress. Had a sedition law been in place a few months earlier, he promised, the men who planted the bomb would have been in jail already. As it was, the country had a chance to listen to Palmer before the bombers struck again. A *Chicago Tribune* headline summarized his after-the-fact position on September 18: "'I Told You So,' Is Palmer's Plea for Drastic Law."[42]

IN HIS PLEA for "drastic" action, Palmer found wide support in the national press, especially in business publications that viewed the explosion as a direct threat. "The time has come," announced the *Commercial and Financial Chronicle*, "for concerted measures in this country to rid it of a dangerous element which should have been sternly dealt with long before this." The paper went on to compare the Wall Street perpetrators to the bombers at Haymarket. Hangings of dissenters, it suggested, would prove beneficial in the current instance, even if, as at Haymarket, those hung were not the men who set the bomb.[43]

Despite this support, and despite Palmer's own vocal pressures, other voices cautioned against a renewed antiradical campaign—not out of any sympathy for radicals, but out of a concern for what such measures would mean for the country at large. Among them were some of the most influential papers in New York: the conservative *New York Times* as well as the liberal *Evening Post*, Joseph Pulitzer's *World* as well as William Randolph Hearst's *New York American*. With the partial exception of the *World*, which would spend weeks trying to develop its own theories of the case, all of the publications accepted the idea that the explosion had come from a bomb set by radicals. But they viewed the matter of what to do as a far more complicated question than Palmer let on. The *Times* editorial on September 18, the day after Palmer's appearance in New York, was typical. "The most reasonable theory of the explosion is that it was intended as a terrorizing demonstration," the paper conceded. "It is not the first. It surely will not be the last. In what spirit and by what means are we to face and overcome the stealthy and lethal attempts to overthrow the established order by deeds of violence and horror?"[44]

The answers suggested by the *Times* bore the imprint of the criticism leveled at Palmer in recent months: There should be "no yielding to panic," nor should there be an effort to revise the law or rewrite the Constitution. The *Times* recommended, by contrast, that Palmer treat the explosion as an ordinary criminal case, with the plotters to be hunted, prosecuted, and sent to jail or execution while everyone else moved on with their usual business.[45]

Which of these views would ultimately hold sway depended, at least in part, on what happened in the investigation itself. If the Bureau and the police were able to track the explosion to a group of determined, committed revolutionaries, Palmer might well find the redemption he was seeking. If, on the other hand, the Wall Street explosion went the way of the 1919 investigations, petering out into an unsolved mystery, he would be vulnerable to the charge that he was simply fomenting "hysteria." The conduct of the investigation would matter, too: Did the Bureau and police seem to be acting with due caution, or did they seem to be swooping down on the first available man?

The first arrest of a bona fide radical offered no clear answer. On Saturday, September 18, the police bomb squad seized Alexander Brailovsky, a Russian-born communist, at his basement print shop on East Seventh Street, where he published the militant Russian-language weekly *Russky Golos*. According to witnesses, Brailovsky had been spotted laughing near Wall Street on Thursday afternoon, less than half an hour after the blast, a charge that seemed decidedly weak to Palmer's critics. In the days that followed, however, Brailovsky's story did not play out as these critics predicted. Brailovsky was not framed, beaten, deported, or held in jail; if anything, the Bureau proved to be his liberator. Unable to secure concrete evidence of his complicity, the bomb squad pleaded with the Bureau to take custody of the suspect as a possible deportee. Flynn, perhaps attempting to forestall criticism, perhaps acting on his own growing certainty about who had set the bomb, refused to act. "He was offered to us on Saturday night and twice Sunday, and each time I made it plain that I didn't want Brailovsky," he informed the papers, "that there was nothing I could want him for and that if there had been I would have sent out and got him before the police did."[46]

This tone of rivalry and mutual contempt did not bode well for the investigation. Indeed, by the following week, the press had already begun to ask whether "an unlucky star" might be rising over the Wall Street case. Like Flynn's initial release of Haywood, however, this came as small comfort to the city's radicals, who saw in Brailovsky's brush with the law a hint of their own possible fates. Despite Flynn's cautious approach, despite the calm words of publications such as the *World* and the *Times*, the talk of the Wall Street case as a "Red plot" seemed just as alarming on September 20 as it had on September 17, when Haywood fled to Chicago, sure that a frame-up was about to ensue. In response, the city's radicals did what they had always done in such situations: they began a propaganda campaign of their own.[47]

# 9
· · · ·

## A PERFECT ALIBI

ON SEPTEMBER 17, the day that the Bureau revealed the American Anarchist Fighters circulars, the *World* approached Elizabeth Gurley Flynn with a polite question. One of the few prominent women in the IWW, Gurley Flynn had long endured her share of misguided press inquiries about her views on violence and labor issues, and about her romantic ties to Carlo Tresca. That day, the *World* wanted to know whether she thought the Wall Street explosion "could not be linked, directly or indirectly," with the activities of some group of radicals. As a founder of the Workers' Defense Union, created to defend the victims of the Palmer Raids, Gurley Flynn must have felt obligated to answer. She refused, however, to accept the *World*'s frame of reference. "To discuss this question would be to admit the possibility that radicals were responsible for the gruesome disaster," she said. "There's no reason why every time such a tragedy happens radicals must rush in and shout the obvious—that they had nothing to do with it."[1]

The "obvious" had been an article of faith in left-wing circles once the first rumors of a Red plot began to appear on September 16. On the whodunit of the Wall Street blast, communists agreed with Wobblies, who agreed with trade unionists that, in the words of painters' strike leader Abe

Heilmann, "radicals are thinking more and bombing less than they ever did in their lives." From the IWW's New York Defense Committee came the affirmation that "[b]lowing up the innocent is not on the programme of the I.W.W., the aim of which is to educate people and not teach them to use dynamite." The socialist *New Yorker Volkszeitung* declared that "the bomb theory of the Palmerites has so far not the slightest basis." The communists, driven underground after the Palmer Raids, issued no immediate statements, but Frank Rosenfrag, an anarchist identified as "one of Emma Goldman's special writers for *Mother Earth*," took it upon himself to proclaim their innocence. "I don't know what's come of the Communist Party," he said, "and as for this stuff about bombing Morgan—well, the cops just have to talk about something."[2]

Weakened by the deportation raids and the wartime trials, these groups were ill positioned to exert much influence on public discussion. If they had drawn one lesson from four decades of contending with the problems of violence and terrorism, however, it was the importance of countering the government's official story. As Palmer clamored for new raids and sedition laws, the American left set out to show not only that such actions were unwarranted but also that the entire idea of a bomb plot was ridiculous.

At the forefront of this effort was the New York branch of the Socialist Party. Like the revolutionaries to their left, the Socialist leadership subscribed to the theory that the "bomb" was simply a misbegotten dynamite shipment, trumped up to look like a radical plot. "It would seem the Department of Justice is making good use of an accident," charged Algernon Lee, head of the party's Rand School of Social Science on East Fifteenth Street. "It is exploiting a tragedy for its own ends, its desire to show that dangerous radicals are extant, requiring its special attention." Unlike their more militant rivals, however, the Socialists were still functioning as an aboveground, legal party. Alone among the major institutions of the American left, the Socialist Party had managed to escape the full force of Palmer's deportation campaign. As a result, despite wartime jailings and crippling internal disputes, New York Socialists were uniquely positioned in September 1920 to mount the left's one serious challenge to the attorney general's point of view.[3]

THREE YEARS EARLIER, few local Socialists would have pictured themselves in such a defensive position. In the fall of 1917, less than six months after the national party declared "its unalterable opposition to the war," party leader Morris Hillquit, the Socialists' nearest approximation to a genuine "boss," surprised New York with an insurgent campaign for mayor. The Lower East Side had twice elected a Socialist congressman, Meyer London, during the run-up to war in 1914 and 1916. (Hillquit barely lost his own congressional bid in 1916, coming in a close second in a contested vote that reached as high as the U.S. Supreme Court.) In 1917, with thousands of soldiers shipping out to battle from New York Harbor, Hillquit had run a passionate antiwar campaign, presenting himself not only as a municipal reformer, dedicated to effective management of city resources, but also as the city's sole political champion of "life and happiness and peace." This platform did not win him the mayoralty; Hylan took the election easily, with some 313,000 votes. But it produced an electoral showing unlike anything the city's Socialists had ever seen. Hillquit won nearly 22 percent of the vote, almost half of Hylan's total and some five times the previous Socialist Party tally.[4]

Looking back, many Socialists remembered that autumn as a moment of unbridled intensity. "These were indeed exciting times, unforgettable and delirious nights," Socialist assemblyman August Claessens later wrote, describing street meetings that lasted as late as three o'clock in the morning. That sense had only increased on the day after the election, when the news arrived of the revolution in Russia. For the New York socialists, whose membership skewed heavily Russian and Jewish, the Bolshevik triumph was a personal as well as global event (Hillquit himself had been born Moishe Hillkowitz in Riga, Latvia). No less a personage than Leon Trotsky had been living in the city during the critical year of 1917, renting a Bronx apartment with his wife and two young sons. By day, Trotsky had worked downtown in a dingy basement on St. Mark's Place, where he helped to edit *Novy Mir*, a weekly Russian-language paper edited by his future comrade-in-arms Nikolai Bukharin. By night, he had thrown himself into Socialist Party activities.[5]

As a revolutionary, Trotsky never saw much point in electoral politics. "He loathed men like Hillquit...with a more intense hatred than he felt toward J. P. Morgan or the Czar," recalled Socialist assemblyman Louis Waldman. The antipathy was mutual; Hillquit saw Trotksy as a dangerous saboteur. But even Hillquit saw the Bolsheviks as ideal socialists in the early months of the revolution, when they seemed to stand "in the vanguard of democracy, in the vanguard of social progress." He soon found this revolutionary enthusiasm flattened by wartime repression at home. In addition to Debs' arrest in Canton, Ohio, dozens of local radicals went to jail in 1918 (the Socialist press joked that they might request their own local charter). Still, when the armistice arrived in November 1918, it looked as if the Socialist Party would surge forth into a triumphal future, with 109,000 active members nationwide, up from 80,000 in 1917. Within a year, however, membership had tumbled to just a third of that total, leaving the party at one of its lowest points since its creation almost two decades earlier.[6]

There were two reasons for this near collapse. The first was the ongoing hostility of the public and many local authorities, who seemed to blame the Socialists, in addition to Wobblies, communists, and anarchists, for the strikes and terrorist violence of 1919. On May Day, for instance, the staff of the *New York Call* had been celebrating the opening of their new offices when a posse of four hundred former soldiers and sailors muscled their way in, breaking furniture, clubbing the revelers, and sending seven *Call* employees to the hospital. Such vigilante attacks, as well as local raids on the Rand School and headquarters of the Socialist left wing in New York, played no small role in scaring off potential supporters. The greatest blow to Socialist strength, however, came from within the party itself.[7]

During its national convention in Chicago in September 1919, the party had split on questions of tactics: Would Socialists run for election or engage in direct action? Should the party affiliate with Russia or stand alone? The left wing—those who scorned electoral politics and advocated immediate revolution—broke off into not one but two communist parties, ideologically identical though divided on matters of organization and leadership. The first, the Communist Party, contained the so-called foreign-language federations; more than 90 percent of its mostly Russian membership was foreign-born. The second, the Communist Labor Party, offered an English-speaking leadership, including John Reed, though its membership, too, skewed heavily foreign-born. As a result of the split, Socialist Party membership fell dramatically, from the postwar peak of 109,000 down to just 36,000 by 1920.[8]

Many Socialists counted themselves lucky in the months following the break, as Palmer began to target communists for prosecution and deportation. While its members managed to escape such direct attacks, however, the Socialist Party was not without troubles of its own. In mid-January the New York state assembly had announced its incendiary plans to expel the five Socialist assemblymen—Louis Waldman, August Claessens, Samuel Orr, Samuel DeWitt, and Charles Solomon—recently reelected from East Harlem, the Bronx, Brooklyn, and the Lower East Side. The legislature charged them with nothing less than treason. "The Socialist Party of America is not a loyal organization, disgraced occasionally by the traitorous act of a member," accused Martin Conboy, one of the assembly prosecutors, "but a disloyal party of perpetual traitors." In response, Hillquit had rushed to Albany to defend the party as a temperate electoral force, all that stood between civilization and "the sluice gates of violent revolution." The legislators were unpersuaded. In April, they voted overwhelmingly to exclude the five Socialist assemblymen on the grounds that they were "little Lenins, little Trotskys in our midst."[9]

Such a naked assault on the democratic process had provoked cries of outrage from quarters far beyond the Socialist left. Supreme Court justice Charles Evans Hughes, a former Republican governor of New York and Wilson's rival for the presidency in 1916, viewed the expulsion as a "serious mistake." So did Al Smith, the state's current Democratic governor (and himself a future candidate for the presidency). Chief among their concerns was that denial of the voters' will might only encourage more aggressive tactics such as terrorism and sabotage. "Not all the anarchists from Herr Most's day down to this present hour ever did strike such a deadly blow at our system of free representative government," wrote the *New York Journal,* accusing the state legislature of fomenting insurrection. But it was not until mid-August, when Governor Smith called the assembly into emergency session, that any practical measure was taken to reverse course. Pointing out that the expulsion had left five New York districts without representation on a pivotal issue, Smith scheduled the special election for Thursday, September 16.[10]

From the first, the New York Socialists had understood the election as a chance to demonstrate that the party would last, perhaps even thrive, in the politics of the 1920s. "Come down to the headquarters of the Bronx county socialist party, and enroll—now," candidates Orr and DeWitt had pleaded, "or you may never get the opportunity again." On the night before the election, the five candidates delivered speeches at some fifty meetings—"the most strenuous pre-election day experienced by the Socialist party in recent years," according to the *Call.* The next morning, volunteers awoke at five o'clock to man the polls, commandeering bicycles and wagons for the young people's squads, checking and rechecking the voter lists.[11]

One of them, Alderman Abraham Beckerman, recalled that he was so busy that he somehow missed hearing the day's news. Around four o'clock, Beckerman entered an East Fourteenth Street polling place to investigate rumors that the Democrats and Republican were interfering with the Socialist vote. After sorting out the details, the chairman of the Board of Elections posed a question that gave Beckerman his first hint that something big was amiss. "What are you Socialists trying to do now," the chairman had asked, only half joking, "blow up Wall Street?"[12]

THE EDITOR of the *New York Call*, Charles W. Ervin, recognized as early as September 16 that his party might well be blamed, if only tangentially, for the Wall Street explosion. A longtime Socialist, an ally of both Hillquit and Debs, Ervin had guided the paper through many recent troubles: the wartime loss of its second-class mailing privileges, the May Day 1919 assault, and a mysterious spike in its printing bills designed to drive the paper out of business. Though it attracted a varied readership, the *Call* was essentially Hillquit's voice, a temperate, party-based organ devoted first to reform and only distantly to revolution. It was also one of the most influential Socialist publications in New York. In sheer circulation numbers, the Yiddish-language *Forverts* (Jewish Daily Forward) far outstripped the *Call*, attracting some ten times the *Call*'s readership of fifteen thousand. The *Call*, however, possessed one advantage that *Forverts* lacked: it was published in English, giving the party a direct way to deliver its message to those in power.[13]

The *Call*'s first editorial about the explosion, on September 17, established a blend of sympathy and denial calculated to deflect charges that Socialists were somehow responsible for the blast. "Its perpetrators must be sought and made to pay the penalty for their atrocious crime," it read. "Unfortunately, however, ... [w]hat we have done in the past is to punish those least responsible." Outside of the editorial pages, the *Call*'s coverage read like that of any other newspaper, at least initially. "Identification is extremely difficult because of the mutilated condition of the bodies," the lead article noted on September 17; "in almost the entire financial district there was scarcely a whole window to be found." But here, too, there were subtle hints of dissent. Alone among the English-language dailies, the

*Call* did not give the explosion top billing on September 17. That honor went to the news that all five Socialist assemblymen had been reelected by wide margins and would soon return to the state legislature.[14]

Whether or not these two events—the Wall Street bombing and the reelection of the Socialist assemblymen—would come to be linked in the public mind had not been immediately clear that first day, with Flynn, among others, refusing to commit to a single theory of what had caused the explosion. By the weekend, however, as the story of a bomb plot emerged as the de facto consensus, and as Palmer began his campaign to renew the deportation raids and sedition law, the *Call* adopted a more aggressive stance. "We could anticipate that before the cause of this awful disaster could possibly be known it would be used by the most reactionary journals to justify the suppression of free discussion and to damn any critical attitude that might be taken toward existing political and economic conditions," read an editorial on September 18.[15]

Despite the caustic tone, both editors and readers knew that talk of a Red plot did not bode well for the Socialists' chances of being seated in the state assembly. The *Washington Post* had already pointed to Eugene Debs as the man ultimately responsible for the explosion—the sort of agitator who inspired "weaker minds" to commit terrorist acts. Still, the *Call* vowed not to go down without a fight, and many reformers and progressives stepped forth to support its stance. Louis Post, Palmer's nemesis, came out swinging. "If the fire breathers and jingoes in this country had their way as regards the treatment of aliens," he predicted immediately after the attack, "we would make more new anarchists every day than we could deport in a week." Dudley Field Malone, gubernatorial candidate for the Farmer-Labor Party, sent a special letter to Mayor Hylan urging him "to exert your powerful influence to avoid and prevent the persecution of innocent men and women." Even the *New York Tribune*, which in other contexts wholeheartedly supported Palmer, jumped in to draw a distinction between "innocuous" socialists and the "murderously minded" terrorist who undoubtedly had attacked Wall Street.[16]

The distinction appeared to be lost on the state legislators who were preparing to sit in judgment on their reelected Socialist colleagues. An emergency session to address the housing crisis was scheduled to begin on Monday, September 20, just four days after the explosion. As the date approached, the assembly leadership boasted of new security measures, including "armed guards" and "special watchmen," dispatched to secure

Albany against Wall Street's fate. Additional reports suggested that wartime restrictions—closing the gallery to visitors, blocking the sweeping staircase entrance, requiring inspection of all people and packages moving in and out—might be necessary under the circumstances. Despite the Socialists' repeated assurances of their peaceful intentions, the *Sun and New York Herald* reported, the legislators who had led the springtime purge were suffering from "a bad case of fright."[17]

Stoking these fears was a rash of new bomb scares within New York City. On Saturday, police received an unsigned note telling of "a still bigger explosion...on Sunday: watch out for Sunday"—promptly translated in press headlines as "Sunday Set for Red Terror Day in U.S." A few days later, the Brooklyn post office received a request to "[c]lear the building at 12:15 Saturday for me" from someone using the pseudonym "TNT." Mark Prentiss, chairman of the United States Clearing House of Foreign Credits, became the subject of a bungled blackmail attempt. "We told you we were going to give your dirty bunch hell, eh!" read a message delivered September 18. "Now come on down with sterling, francs, or some of your bunch better look out for your damned skin."[18]

These rumors came to a head on Monday, September 20, as the reelected assemblymen arrived in Albany to take their seats. That afternoon, New York Custom House revenue collector William H. Edwards came across a note warning, "There is a plot to destroy the Custom House on Tuesday, September 21, 2:00." The police couldn't determine much from the material details: blue ink, a Grand Central postmark, an amateur job of handwriting disguise. Given the frayed nature of the district's nerves, revenue collector Byron Newton explained to his employees, it still made sense to view 2:00 P.M. on September 21 as a moment of potential peril. When the appointed hour arrived, police cleared the stone plaza in front of the Custom House. Less than a block up Broadway, flattened faces animated skyscraper windows, where local entrepreneurs had rented out space to spectators. Thousands who lacked the advantage of a window, or the wherewithal to pay for it, milled in the streets, cameras at the ready. At 2:01, when the Custom House failed to explode, a cheer swept through lower Broadway, but the district remained on edge. "This bomb business is like an epidemic," Newton complained as he once again prepared to resume the usual business.[19]

Albany, too, remained jittery. On the afternoon of September 21, as the Socialists' home districts celebrated the Custom House's close escape, the State assembly voted to expel the three most prominent Socialist candidates—Waldman, Claessens, and Solomon—on the grounds that their belief in socialism was incompatible with a vow of loyalty to the state of New York. By a similar margin, the assembly voted to admit the other two Socialists, DeWitt and Orr, a compromise measure designed to placate possible critics. Both men promptly resigned their posts and the five assemblymen departed together, but not before delivering a frustrated reproof. "The new era is coming. It is too late to stop it," Charles Solomon warned the assembly. "We refuse to go to the battlefield until we have fought it out at the ballot box, but if we ever do go to the bayonet the blame will be on your head."[20]

WITHIN HOURS OF THE EXPULSION, the *Call* announced the start of yet another assembly campaign, this one targeted at reelection in November. The editors also made plans to shape public debate in another way. Without definitive proof of the sort that had come forth in the McNamara case, neither the *Call* nor anyone else on the left was eager to concede that a radical could have been responsible for the Wall Street explosion. So, like Flynn, they began to gather evidence to make their case.

The most popular theory within socialist circles was the one first suggested by the police: that a wagon stocked with explosives had simply tipped over at the ill-fated hour of noon. This was the viewpoint championed by the *Call* as well as the communist *World Tomorrow*, the Yiddish-language *Forverts*, and the Hungarian-language *Elore*. Though it varied in the particulars, the gist of the theory was that the authorities had been perfectly correct in their early impressions of the situation and had been moving further from the truth ever since. "The explosion that broke all the windows in the dinky little stone structure housing Morgan & Company," wrote Robert Buck, editor of the Chicago-based *New Majority*, "...was an accidental explosion of dynamite on a truck that had no business taking dynamite into that part of New York at that time of day and with only one man on it. Everybody who knows anything about the explosion knows that this is the case."[21]

Among the most prominent exponents of this theory was Eugene Debs himself. Debs had entered prison in April 1919 with "my head erect, my spirit untamed and my soul unconquered," as he told his friends, convinced that the wartime "hysteria" was beginning to abate and that the government had already done its worst. Even in prison, though, he had felt the heat of Palmer's antiradical campaign. On June 13, in the uproar over the nationwide bomb conspiracy, Palmer had ordered Debs transferred from the prison in Moundsville, Ohio, to the maximum-security federal penitentiary in Atlanta. Despite the burdens of prison life, Debs had been relatively happy at Moundsville, where the warden granted him light work and extra reading privileges. Atlanta was a different sort of place. There the sixty-four-year-old Debs found himself "ill and depressed," wondering, like his old comrade Haywood, if all his years of struggle and provocation had been in vain.[22]

He nonetheless maintained his public optimism. In the spring of 1920, as supporters mounted an amnesty campaign on his behalf, Debs had accepted the Socialist Party's nomination as president—a first for a federal prisoner. In response, the Atlanta warden gave him the right to compose a weekly newspaper column. Debs used his column on September 25, 1920, to predict a frame-up in the Wall Street investigation, a repeat of the Haywood case, the Mooney affair, and "numerous other crimes and catastrophes." "Being in prison is not without its advantages," he wrote. "Had I made a speech in New York on the night before that Wall Street explosion there would have been a clear case against me. As it is, I have a perfect alibi."[23]

Despite its jovial tone, Debs' column contained a discouraging message: rather than call for a revolution, as he had done in Idaho after Haywood's arrest, he seemed to be simply waiting around to find who would be strung up for the crime. This was Haywood's stance as well. After his escape to Chicago on September 17, Haywood briefly came out of hiding to deliver a speech denouncing police tactics in the Wall Street case. His old enemies continued nonetheless to attack him as the guilty party. "[I]t is not surprising," the *Los Angeles Times* wrote on September 25, "that one who has preached direct action so broadly and so openly should be suspected of knowing something as to the identity of those who put that preaching into practice."[24]

Nor was it terribly surprising when, less than two weeks later, the circuit court denied Haywood's application for a new trial in his wartime conviction and ordered him back to prison. Haywood later blamed the explosion for destroying his chances before the court. "It is not difficult to imagine the influence that the Wall Street explosion had on the minds of the Judges," he wrote in his autobiography. With one conviction and two indictments hanging over his head, however, he was in no shape to mount a fight. Along with his fellow defendants, he filed an appeal to the Supreme Court, earning a temporary reprieve from jail. Then he went on waiting.[25]

At the offices of the *Call*, the editors engaged in a far more proactive campaign to rewrite the story of what had happened on September 16. The paper had long criticized Haywood and the Wobblies as anarchists and saboteurs. When it came to the Wall Street explosion, however, they recognized a common interest in preventing the explosion from erupting into the sort of frame-up that Haywood and Debs were predicting. Beginning in late September, the *Call* launched a series of articles poking holes in evidence assembled by the police and the Bureau as proof of a bomb plot. With limited resources, the *Call*'s reporters spent most of their time rehashing dubious assertions found elsewhere in the press, filtering the more outrageous claims of Palmer's supporters through the lens of socialist skepticism. They also began a careful sifting of the clues, especially the horse and wagon and the Anarchist Fighters flyers, that Flynn had advertised as the linchpins of his bomb plot inquiry.[26]

They came across some startling finds. First on the list was the inconsistent but provocative eyewitness testimony describing some sort of explosives wagon rolling through the financial district on the morning of September 16.

- A chauffeur named Hiram Davis had told detectives that he was driving east on Wall Street behind a "red explosives wagon" when he saw a flash and a concussion of air rip the roof from his car. He distinctly recalled that the wagon bore the name of the DuPont Powder Works. It also flew a red flag, he said, the required legal warning for dynamite.[27]
- A bond salesman named Robert Baker backed up Davis' claim, describing a red DuPont wagon on Wall Street just a few steps from the Morgan bank.[28]
- Gilbert Smith, a real estate dealer, reported that he had seen a truck rather than a wagon. Around eleven o'clock that morning, he swore in a statement to police, "a large red automobile truck with a red trailer and in large blue letters the name DuPont Powder Works" had passed him around Broadway and Vesey Street, several blocks north of Wall and Broad. This truck contained five hogsheads of what Smith could only assume was some sort of dangerous explosive.[29]

- An electrical engineer named Joseph Kindman claimed that he had seen a red wagon stuck in traffic on Broadway behind two quarreling drivers sometime before noon. "On the wagon was marked, DuPont Powder Company," he told the *Call*. "Right under this was inscribed the DuPont de Nemours Company, or some other words which I'm certain contained DuPont de Nemours. Then another marking was 'Danger' in white letters. A red flag was at the end of the wagon."[30]

- Kindman's description tallied plausibly well with the story offered by Rebecca Epstein, a stenographer at the Broadway brokerage house of Henderson and Loeb. She told police that she had seen a "reddish" wagon pull up alongside the Morgan bank just before the explosion. The wagon had side racks splattered with some sort of white plaster-like substance, and it flew a telltale red flag. The front of the wagon bore faded impressions of the three letters *D*, *N*, and *T*. The letters were separated by odd spaces, she said, as if they had once formed a word like "DuPont" or "Dynamite."[31]

Matched against each other, the stories were not entirely consistent. Was it a truck? A wagon? A DuPont cart? A generic explosives wagon? Was it on the curb near the Morgan bank? Or was it driving through the neighborhood? Where had the wagon been going? And where was it coming from? Nonetheless, the sheer number of sightings of something approximating a red horse-drawn wagon with some sort of explosives or DuPont label somewhere within a few blocks of Wall Street made a plausible case that the disaster had been, as police first suspected and as the *Call* now insisted, an explosives accident.

The police and the Bureau ruled out these reports as cases of mistaken identity. The DuPont truck that had been in the area, they explained, was carrying paint pigments, not explosives. The grand jury, assembled full-time to pore over the evidence, supported this view. In his instructions on September 17, presiding judge William H. Wadhams had asked the jury to "examine very carefully the question as to whether there is any attempt to conceal the true cause of this explosion and place the blame on anyone who was not responsible for it," inspiring flickering hopes at the *Call*. On September 24, however, after hearing "evidence secured from scores of witnesses," in the words of district attorney Alfred Talley, the grand jury dismissed the accident theory.[32]

The *Call* took greater heart in the rumors circulating among down-town contractors, who acknowledged that the daytime transport of dyna-mite was something of an open secret. More than one man in the financial district complained that "explosives were being carried through Wall Street with the reckless abandon of a load of watermelons in a village street" in the days before September 16. Based on this evidence, the *Call* pressed for a new inquiry into the DuPont company's activities on the afternoon of September 16. As the nation's chief munitions supplier, DuPont was second only to the Morgan bank in its reputation within socialist circles for greed indulged to the detriment of humanity. "In view of the fact known by thousands that the DuPont Corporation has been sending explosives through the streets during the most busy hours of the day," the *Call* declared, ". . . the manner in which the authorities have dealt with them in this investigation is a public scandal."[33]

There were other "public scandals" as well. Perhaps the most remarked upon was the discovery that the police had allowed the body of the horse—"their only tangible clue," in the *Call*'s formulation—to be sent off to Barren Island and ground into paste. "Are the authorities investigating the Wall Street explosion deliberately destroying evidence, or are they just stupid?" the paper demanded. The *Call* also attacked the investiga-tors for allowing street-cleaning crews, so eager to restore Wall Street's operating capacity, to flush several tons of potentially revealing debris into city drains.[34]

What physical evidence remained the paper took on directly, hiring an "expert wagoner" to sift through the debris on display at police head-quarters. He concluded that "the report given by the police . . . is at wide divergence from the actual facts of the vehicle's construction." Citing the fine make and condition of the wagon's axle nuts and other metal joints, he speculated that it had once been in the possession of some prosperous outfit or individual. "All in all, said he, the metal parts showed that the vehicle had been very well taken care of and had been kept by good stable men in a high-class stable"—perhaps one owned by DuPont?[35]

For all of the *Call*'s pestering and digging, the strongest evidence consistent with the accident theory came from none other than the Bureau itself. In late September, Chief Flynn had handpicked a chem-ist named Walter Scheele to determine the explosive's composition. Scheele was a strange choice for such a delicate task. A German citizen, he had been indicted during the war for participating in sabotage plots in and around New York. Regardless, his wealth of experience made him an expert on explosives. In mid-October, Scheele issued a report identifying fifty pounds of blasting gelatin—ninety-three parts nitroglycerin to seven parts nitrocellulose—as the agent of destruction on Wall Street.[36]

Left-wing editors were almost giddy at this revelation. "Again," crowed the *Seattle Union Record*, "the bomb theory advanced by agents of powder companies and the police…receives a serious blow." Blasting gelatin, a stabilized form of nitroglycerin, was commonly used for construction and excavation work, especially for tough jobs such as breaking through Manhattan bedrock. It was precisely the sort of material that any urban construction company could be expected to have on hand—or, more to the point, might need to have delivered. It was also one of the most widely manufactured explosives, churned out by both the DuPont and Dittmars companies. To the official investigators, this merely suggested the ease with which any determined bomber could probably acquire a load of the stuff. But to a skeptical left, Scheele's conclusion served definitively to undermine the government's case. "There is no particle of doubt in my mind," accused socialist writer Upton Sinclair, who threw his own voice into the debate beginning in mid-October, "…that the attribution of this Wall Street explosion to the radicals was a part of a deliberate plot of the authorities to discredit the radical movement."[37]

A SON OF NEW YORK CITY, short in stature but long on ambition, Sinclair was arguably the most talented and certainly the best-known of the Socialist Party's public intellectuals. Born in 1878, he was an early recruit to socialism; he joined the party in 1902, a year after its founding. Four years later, at the age of twenty-eight, he had burst into national consciousness with his novel *The Jungle*, which described how Chicago meatpackers exploited their immigrant workforce and deluded the American public by allowing rats, human body parts, and other niceties to be mixed with the nation's meat supply. Like all of Sinclair's novels, *The Jungle* blended melodrama, muckraking, and social realism, a combination that he subsequently applied to other national malefactors. His 1908 novel *The Moneychangers* featured a vicious, tyrannical banking mogul patterned on Pierpont Morgan. *The Brass Check*, which he published in 1920, excoriated the capitalist press as an unholy alliance of prostitutes out to destroy American socialism.

Despite a penchant for self-aggrandizement, Sinclair had managed remarkably well over the years to bridge the gaps between revolutionaries and reformers, between holders of high public office and those who preferred to achieve change in the streets. During Theodore Roosevelt's presidency, for instance, Sinclair had attended a White House dinner to celebrate the passage of the Food and Drug Act, inspired by *The Jungle*. Eight years later, during the protests against the Ludlow Massacre, he led parades along Fifth Avenue with Alexander Berkman at his side. Sinclair had always disagreed with Berkman's emphasis on violence as a method of social protest; direct action, to Sinclair, meant standing silently in front of the Standard Oil office with a black armband and a bitter gaze. After the Lexington Avenue tenement bombing, when Berkman was implicated in the Rockefeller bombing, Sinclair had promptly cut him off. Still, Sinclair continued to suffer for his association with the militant left. When he started his self-titled magazine *Upton Sinclair's* in April 1918, at the height of the war, the federal government nearly denied his second-class mailing privileges. The reason, according to the authorities, was his friendship with bomb-throwing anarchists.

What spared Sinclair in that case was his other set of acquaintances: the men who filled the nation's highest offices in Washington. In 1917, three months after the United States' entry into the war, Sinclair had resigned from the Socialist Party to throw his support behind the Wilson administration. He assured his socialist friends that he was not going "bag and baggage to the capitalist system." Indeed, when the Wilson administration began jailing his former allies and friends on the revolutionary left, Sinclair quickly withdrew his support for the president, gushing out his despair and sense of betrayal on the written page. In just six weeks in the summer of 1920, he dashed off a novel titled *100%: The Story of a Patriot* (a play on the term "100 percent Americanism"), which excoriated both the government and the press for its role in fomenting antisocialist hysteria. One critic summed up the novel as a "cumulative record of blackmail, espionage, intimidation, intrigue, unwarranted assaults, invasions, property destructions, paid witnesses, illegal jailings, horse-whipping, lynchings, frame-ups, 'patriotic' murder; an orgy of confiscation, Bolshevik-baiting, mad hysteria, mad fear, and a madder frenzy."[38]

This was what Sinclair saw when he looked at the early events of the Wall Street case. He opened his first column on the explosion, printed in the October 9 issue of *Appeal to Reason*, with a striking image: not of bodies strewn through the streets or businessmen nobly resuming their work, but of a truckman grinning before a newspaper pinned up on a city wall. The paper contained an announcement—erroneous, as it turned out— that the explosion had successfully destroyed the offices of J. P. Morgan and Company. "I wouldn't dare tell what happened," Sinclair joked; "I am sure that if I were to describe the grin that spread over the face of that truckman, I would have half a dozen of Attorney General Palmer's detectives out looking for me immediately."

Even without the description, Sinclair's message was perfectly clear: Jack Morgan should not misinterpret the public mourning over the bomb attack as a sign that his critics had any intention of backing down. Sinclair saw the explosion as a chance to go on the attack against the policemen, press agents, and explosives companies he had so often lambasted in his novels. Like the editors of the *Call*, he assumed that the explosion was an accident, puffed up into a bomb plot by newspaper editors, explosives companies, detectives, and capitalists who saw an opportunity for personal gain. He labeled this view an "economic interpretation" of the explosion, echoing historian Charles Beard's recent *An Economic Interpretation of the Constitution of the United States*, which accused the nation's founding fathers of acting not in the public good but in their own class interests. In the case of the explosion, Sinclair argued, the primary cause for all the drama and talk of "a bomb planted by some 'radicals'" was a similar kind of financial and class self-interest. With a bomb plot, he argued, editors sold more newspapers, capitalists gained more sympathy, and explosives companies protected themselves from liability.

Leading the list of self-interested liars were the very officials—Flynn, Enright, Burns, Palmer—charged with ferreting out the supposed truth. "Put yourself in the position of the head of a great detective agency," Sinclair suggested. "You are summoned to investigate, and you know that if a truckload of explosives has been set off by accident, the investigation will occupy only a few days, and you will be paid only a few thousand dollars; whereas, if there has been a bomb planted by some 'radicals,' you will have a free hand to investigate for years."[39]

This was not a flattering portrait of the nation's detective forces. But it was far more generous than some of the other scenarios circulating through the socialist press. Though the accident theory was by far the most popular, some observers entertained the possibility that a group of detectives—from either the Bureau, the police department, or the Burns agency—had actually planted the bomb themselves. "While I believe that the Wall Street horror was an accident," wrote Pennsylvania socialist James Maurer, "I also believe that, if it was a bomb plot, then it was accomplished by...bunglers, interested in holding their jobs as heresy-hunting sleuths, eager to serve the money-mad industrial kaisers of America, who are the only ones who could possibly hope to profit by bomb scares of any kind."[40]

As if to illustrate how such a conspiracy might work, in early October Enright came forward with a plea for $200,000 to form an undercover "secret service" within the police department to infiltrate and expose the radical left. He warned the Board of Estimate that this sort of appropriation was all that stood between the city of New York and a new outbreak of terrorist attacks. "The situation is one that threatens the very lives of the city and country. The pursuit and apprehension of criminals responsible for plots against society are essential to the safety of the community." Sinclair, like many socialists, scorned this appeal as yet more bald self-interest. "It took only $17,000 worth of rewards to cause the frame-up of Tom Mooney and four other people in San Francisco," he responded in *Appeal to Reason*. "At this rate the procedure of the New York authorities ought to result in the arrest of some thirty Reds for the Wall Street explosion."[41]

In New York itself, the *Call* went on the offensive against Enright, surveying dozens of public figures, both inside and outside Socialist circles, for their opinions on the appropriation. Unsurprisingly, given the selective nature of the effort, opinion was almost uniformly negative ("The prospects for wholesale hectoring of labor and radical leaders and organizations was [*sic*] never better," warned Elizabeth Gurley Flynn). Only Fiorello LaGuardia, president of the Board of Aldermen and future mayor of the city, suggested that it might be a good idea, assuring the *Call* that the police needed the money to hunt down violent criminals such as the ones who had attacked Wall Street "and for no other purpose."[42]

Indeed, for all the talk of frame-ups and railroads, of conspiracies and collective guilt, the actual hunt for the bomb plotters was the one area where the police and the Bureau seemed to be moving with remarkably little speed. Between September 19 and the beginning of October, neither the police nor the Bureau made a significant arrest. "Broadly speaking, they know about as much about the explosion today as they did two weeks ago and they are about as near to solving the mystery as they were then," the *New York Evening Post* summarized on October 2. When news broke two days later of a genuine arrest in Pittsburgh ("Wall Street Bomb Suspect Caught; Carries Dynamite, Fights Police," read the headline in the *Times*), it was no more conclusive than what had come before. The man arrested, Florian Zelenko, was a Polish immigrant and itinerant miner who had recently moved out of Brooklyn. When the Bureau searched his former residence, they found a trunk crammed with Russian literature of a "radical nature" and a pay stub for $46.55 from the Hercules Powder Company. But after grilling Zelenko—"Do you believe in the form of Government we have in this country?" "Have you ever heard any one talk about Anarchy, or Anarchists?" "Do you believe in the Soviet Form of Government under Levine [*sic*] and Trotsky now in Russia?"—they found little reason to move ahead with the case.[43]

The *Call* interpreted Zelenko's arrest as another attempted frame-up, staged to make the case for greater police appropriations. In truth, the explanation behind his quick dismissal was far more straightforward. The Bureau did not want Zelenko because Flynn already had his eye on another suspect.

# PART IV

. . . .

# FACCIA A FACCIA

# 10

. . . .

# THE ANARCHIST
# FIGHTERS

MOST AMERICANS HAD NEVER heard of Luigi Galleani. Around the
Justice Department, however, he was known as a force to be reckoned
with—"one of the most notorious anarchists in the United States,"
in Palmer's words. The son of a schoolteacher, Galleani had grown up
middle-class in the Piedmont region of Italy, seemingly destined for life
as a lawyer. Like so many young men who came of age in the wake of the
Paris Commune, he found his course in life disrupted by the lure of revolution. In a few short years in late adolescence, Galleani converted from
republicanism to socialism to anarchism. By the age of twenty-eight,
he had left Italy to join the workers' movement first in France, then in
Switzerland, from which he was expelled for organizing a commemora-
tion of the Haymarket executions. Within four years, he found himself in
jail in his native land, confined to the island penal colony of Pantelleria.
After escaping in 1900, reportedly by seducing his jailer's wife, he made
his way to Paterson, New Jersey, the former residence of King Umberto's
assassin, Gaetano Bresci. In the United States, he built up a devoted following among a small group of Italian immigrant anarchists, including
Nicola Sacco and Bartolomeo Vanzetti, whose Massachusetts murder case
would later be a cause celebre of the international left. Galleani's followers

had been Flynn's chief suspects in both the May Day and June 2 plots. Now, though Flynn was loath to share the details of the investigation with the press, they were also his main suspects in the Wall Street explosion.[1]

With his neatly trimmed beard and balding pate, Galleani looked less like the stereotype of the wild-eyed anarchist than like the lawyer he had once intended to be. Appearances were deceiving. Though less famous than Berkman, Goldman, and Haywood, Galleani surpassed them all in his espousal of violence as a means of vengeance and anticapitalist revolt. Where they hedged their bets on terrorism, he embraced it unapologetically, cheering almost every act of assassination and bombing that came to his attention. They shared neither a language nor a common set of historical experiences, but Galleani was Johann Most's true heir in America: a militant, charismatic devotee of revolutionary terror.

Had Galleani attempted to immigrate to the United States just a few years later, he might well have been barred from the country under the new antianarchist law. As it was, in 1901 his arrival was legal, but his welcome, like Most's some twenty years earlier, was not especially warm. In 1902, Galleani joined up with striking silk workers in Paterson, urging them to escalate their conflict into armed revolt. For his troubles, he was shot in the face by local police. He then fled the United States, crossing into Canada to escape charges related to the strike. After a brief stay in Canada, he sneaked back across the border and took up residence near the industrial town of Barre, Vermont, under the name Luigi Pimpino. In 1903, he began to publish *Cronaca Sovversiva* (Subversive Chronicle), an Italian-language "anarchist weekly of revolutionary propaganda." One Bureau agent later denounced it as "the most rabid, seditious and anarchistic sheet ever published in this country."[2]

In the pages of *Cronaca*, Galleani echoed Most's unyielding animosity both to the state and to amassers of private property. "Overthrow [the government], make the country free once [and] forever, with the triumph of true democracy—the one that is made by Americans, not by Wall Street," he instructed his readers. He also published articles in translation from other anarchist magazines, bringing the messages of Goldman and Berkman, among others, to his four thousand to five thousand Italian-speaking readers. Despite his association with prominent American radicals, he remained an obscure figure in the wider world of progressive politics, never forging the social ties with the American intelligentsia that Goldman struggled so hard to maintain. The vast majority of his followers were immigrant workingmen, manual laborers, and autodidacts who tended to congregate around industrial centers such as Paterson, Barre, New York, Boston, and Wrentham, Massachusetts, Galleani's final home on U.S. soil. In keeping with anarchist ideals, they acknowledged no bona fide leaders, hierarchies, or organizations. But their name—the Galleanisti—was a testament to Galleani's influence.[3]

Flynn was himself impressed with Galleani's eloquence, declaring the anarchist "[o]ne of the most difficult individuals the United States secret service has ever had to deal with, because he was the brainiest." It was what Galleani was saying, however—not merely how he was saying it—that attracted official scrutiny. From the moment of his arrival in the United States, Galleani openly espoused revolutionary warfare, calling for dyna- mite, nitroglycerin, knives, gunpowder, blasting gelatin, and pistols as the means to working-class liberation. In 1905 he published these ideas in a little red-covered book titled *La salute è in voi!* (Health Is Within You), essentially an update of Most's *Science of Revolutionary Warfare*. Though its prescriptions were not entirely reliable (one edition badly miscalculated the amount of nitric acid required for nitroglycerin), *La salute* proved to be essential reading for his followers, a step-by-step description of how to fight capitalists with the tools of their own making. Chapters included "Explosive Material," "Nitroglycerin," "Dynamite," "Fulminate of Mer- cury," "Preparation of Fuses," and "Capsule and Petard."[4]

*La salute* had captured the attention of the New York bomb squad during the dynamite scare of 1914 and 1915. "Mere possession of this wicked treatise," wrote bomb squad chief Thomas Tunney, "would sug- gest that the owner was up to no good." Official opinion was roughly similar concerning Galleani's *Faccia a faccia col nemico* (Face-to-Face with the Enemy), a compilation of essays published in 1914 by a group of admirers in East Boston. Like *La salute*, *Faccia a faccia* sported a bright red cover with gold embossing. Inside, it tended as much toward the inspira- tional as the practical. Each chapter featured a portrait of a lone anarchist who, in the words of one *Cronaca* advertisement, embodied "the ideals of justice, of courage, of victory, of vindication." Among their numbers were Gaetano Bresci, King Humbert's assassin; Sante Caserio, who had killed the French president in 1892; and Clément Duval, who made his name in 1886 by knifing a Parisian police officer "in the name of liberty." As one Bureau report noted, the book also illustrated "the minute construction of various bombs" used by such men to carry out their deeds.[5]

These examples proved inspiring to at least some of Galleani's admirers within the United States. While Goldman, Berkman, and Haywood were garnering headlines, the Galleanisti had emerged in the early war years as suspects in a series of scattered terrorist episodes, including the arsenic poisoning of some two hundred men and women attending an archbishop's banquet in Chicago in 1916. Once the United States formally declared hostilities in 1917, the pace of violence escalated, a tit-for-tat response to government jailings and deportation raids. Most of the wartime incidents were treated as local matters: the bomb left in the basement of an outspoken antiradical priest's church in Milwaukee (it exploded at the police station, killing ten detectives and a bystander); the three bombs packed with metal slugs that exploded overnight in Philadelphia in 1918, targeting the homes of a local judge, a police superintendent, and the president of the local Chamber of Commerce. Galleani himself managed to avoid implication in any of the crimes. As with Goldman and Berkman, what finally brought his freedom in the United States to an end, and what propelled him into direct confrontation with the federal authorities, was not his espousal of violence but his opposition to the war. Just after midnight on June 15, 1917, within hours of Goldman and Berkman's arrest, federal agents showed up at his door in Wrentham, Massachusetts, to seize him for obstructing the draft.[6]

The basis for this action was a column entitled "Matricolati!" printed in *Cronaca* on the eve of national draft registration. In it, Galleani argued that mandatory conscription infringed on the Thirteenth Amendment's protection against "involuntary servitude." He also warned against the possible induction of foreign citizens into the U.S. military, promising that aliens forced to enlist would fulfill the government's worst fears of domestic sabotage. In technical obedience to the new espionage law, he relied on suggestion rather than outright exhortation to instruct his readers in the fine points of draft avoidance. The Justice Department nonetheless recognized the message behind his words. Over the next year and a half, in an effort to build a stronger case against Galleani and his followers, federal agents raided *Cronaca* offices in nearly every major city between Chicago and Philadelphia. They also swept through Galleani's home, taking "letters, files, records, books, memorandum, etc." Based on this evidence, in January 1919 immigration authorities ordered Galleani deported from the United States as an anarchist and an undesirable.[7]

He did not take the insult lightly. As he prepared to leave the United States, Galleani urged his followers to seek revenge against the tyrannical and corrupt federal government. Almost immediately, they began to heed his call. In February 1919, a flyer titled "Go-Head!" announced the start of a new dynamite campaign against the federal authorities. "You have shown no pity to us! We will do likewise," read the flyer, found at various sites throughout New England. "And deport us! *We will dynamite you!*" The following month, their war began in earnest. Their opening shot was an accidental explosion of dynamite in Franklin, Massachusetts, where four anarchists, all killed in the blast, had been preparing a bomb for the American Woolen Company. In mid-April, Flynn believed, they had followed up this act with the May Day mail bombs, intended as a grand protest against Galleani's deportation. When the bombs failed to strike their targets, they had constructed the still greater conspiracy of June 2, 1919—and now the Wall Street explosion.[8]

THERE HAD NEVER BEEN much question around Bureau headquarters that *some* anarchist group had orchestrated the June 2 bomb plot. What Flynn and his men were less sure about, at least initially, was precisely which anarchists they were supposed to be seeking. According to a summary report prepared by Hoover, initial suspects came from four distinct communities: the Spanish anarchists of Pro Prensa, based in Philadelphia and New York; the L'Era Nuova group, composed mainly of Italian anarchists in Paterson, New Jersey; Berkman and Goldman's "individual followers," spread throughout the country; and "the Galliani [*sic*] group, with headquarters at Lynn and Boston, Mass., and Barre, Vt." Agents interviewed Galleani himself on June 23 at the Boston immigration depot, where he was awaiting deportation. Apparently, however, they were still unsure about his complicity. The next day, he was shipped off to Italy as scheduled.[9]

It was a decision Flynn soon came to regret. By midsummer the June 2 investigation had begun to focus almost exclusively on the Galleanisti. Indeed, the swiftness with which Flynn zeroed in on the Italian anarchists tended to contradict Palmer's far more public claims during those months about an ever-expanding radical menace. Even as the Justice Department called for a new sedition law and added appropriations, Flynn had begun to operate on the theory, in one agent's words, that "the bomb plots of June 2nd were conceived and directed by Luigi Galleani."[10]

The Bureau's theory stemmed in part from the bombers' choice of targets. Most of the bombs erupted in cities with powerful Italian anarchist movements: Boston, New York, Paterson. Within those cities, the would-be victims had frequently come into confrontation with the Galleanisti. Massachusetts state representative Leland Powers, who received a bomb at his home in the Boston suburbs, was the son of former congressman Samuel L. Powers, infamous in radical circles as counsel for the American Woolen Company. New York judge Charles Nott had sent anarchists Abarno and Carbone to prison in the failed 1915 attack on St. Patrick's Cathedral. Palmer himself, busy overseeing Galleani's deportation order, was one of the "'democratic' lords of the autocratic republic" denounced in the flyer "Plain Words."[11]

In addition to this circumstantial evidence, investigators had uncovered a wealth of material evidence pointing to the Galleanisti's complicity in the June 2 plot, much of it on Palmer's own front lawn in Washington, D.C. Scattered across the grass and in wet scraps throughout the neighborhood detectives had found the remains of a man, presumably the bomber, who had been standing remarkably near the explosion when it erupted. On the roof of a house on S Street, near some "spots that looked like brain," in the words of one police sergeant, they also came across "a small piece of scalp" sprouting a crop of black hair presumed, by the estimate of a local hairdresser, to belong to an Italian between twenty-six and twenty-eight years of age. Bureau agents traced the scalp to one Carlo Valdinoci, a dapper young Italian and, in his comrades' words, "un grande anarchico" who had worked by Galleani's side as the publisher of *Cronaca Sovversiva*.[12]

This identification, perhaps the most important discovery in the June 2 inquiry, ruled out rival anarchist groups as the plotters. It did not go terribly far, however, toward ruling in specific individuals—preferably living ones—who might be prosecuted. For that, the Bureau had relied upon its other major piece of material evidence, the "Plain Words" pamphlets found at the various June 2 bomb sites. As a guide to the bombers' motives, the "Plain Words" flyers fit perfectly with Galleani's message. "We have been dreaming of freedom, we have talked of liberty, we have aspired to a better world, and you jailed us, you clubbed us, you deported us, you murdered us whenever you could," the flyer accused. More importantly, "Plain Words" was printed on unusual pink paper, an aberration that led the Bureau to its second major break in the June 2 case.

During a February 1920 raid on the offices of *L'Era Nuova*, another Italian anarchist publication, agents happened upon a cache of pink paper that proved identical in stock to the sheets used for "Plain Words." During the course of that raid, they also arrested a prominent Italian anarchist named Ludovico Caminita. Though not a disciple of Galleani's, Caminita knew most of his followers. Moreover, he proved willing to talk.[13]

Under threat of deportation, Caminita had volunteered a torrent of detail linking the Galleanisti to the June 2 plot. ("He has a boy about ten years of age in whom he has centered his affection," noted Hoover, who personally conducted the investigation, "and it is through this boy by playing on Caminetta's [*sic*] emotions that much information has been obtained.") From memory, Caminita provided the names of nearly a dozen anarchists he considered to be the most likely perpetrators of the June 2 bombings, including a man named Nicola Recchi, a stonemason who had lost four fingers on his left hand in an earlier round of bomb making. At the Bureau's prompting, he also looked over a list of *Cronaca* subscribers, checking off the names of "dangerous individuals." Most remarkably, he informed the Bureau that Recchi had assembled the bombs at Galleani's house in Massachusetts. The "Plain Words" pamphlets, Caminita guessed, were printed at a Brooklyn shop by an Italian anarchist named Roberto Elia.[14]

Armed with this information, Flynn had moved to track down the various suspects. The easiest to locate was Elia, who was arrested at the Brooklyn shop on February 25 and charged with illegal possession of a gun. Two weeks later, the Bureau seized his coworker Andrea Salsedo, a Galleani disciple who had labored for years printing "various papers of the Italian Terrorist Type," in the words of one Bureau report. Rather than hold them in jail and risk letting the other Galleanisti know the Bureau's suspicions, Flynn secretly transported them to the Bureau's Park Row office. There, the two men were held in a small room together, sleeping on cots at night, playing cards with the agents by day, taking regular walks through the city for exercise, all without formal charges. At first, they refused to talk. "I do not know anything about the business of others," Elia insisted during his initial interrogation. Under the pressure of detention, however, they soon opened up. According to Bureau reports, both Elia and Salsedo confessed to Flynn that they had printed "Plain Words," that they knew Galleani and Recchi, and that they were certain that these men, along with a handful of others, had planned and carried out the June 2 plot.[15]

By April 1920, his case nearly complete, Flynn had made preparations to seize the Galleanisti in a round of triumphal arrests. Then, to his lasting distress, things went seriously wrong. At 4:20 A.M. on May 2, 1920, a policeman discovered Andrea Salsedo, clad only in his underwear, lying dead on the sidewalk in front of the Park Row office. According to the Bureau, Salsedo had become increasingly depressed while in detention; that night, without warning, he committed suicide.

To Salsedo's friends and family, this story rang false. They informed the press that Salsedo had been beaten by Bureau agents and possibly pushed to his death. Whatever the truth of the matter, the Salsedo incident destroyed months of painstaking work in the June 2 investigation, sending the Galleanisti scurrying for cover and exposing the Bureau to intensive criticism for its allegedly brutal methods. To Flynn's frustration, the Salsedo scandal robbed the Bureau of credit for its remarkable detective work in tracking the bombers, lending the impression that the June 2 investigation was a simple failure. With the Wall Street explosion, he intended to rewrite the story.[16]

FLYNN HAD BEGUN TO TRACK the Galleanisti within hours of the explosion on September 16. Even as the press focused on Haywood, Tresca, and other famous suspects, the Bureau had been busy establishing a program of surveillance at East Coast ports. Agents focused on vessels—the S.S. *Italia*, the S.S. *San Gennaro*—bound for Italy, and on passengers with Italian surnames. This was an effort to forestall what had happened after the June 2 bombings, when, as Flynn reminded the *Sun and New York Herald*, "many of those destructionists made their getaway by stowing away on transatlantic steamships." The Bureau's only catch, however, was twenty-eight-year-old Marazzo Domenico, found crouching in the hold of the S.S. *Cretic*. A onetime crew member of the ship, Domenico had apparently grown tired of his work as a longshoreman and a hat-factory hand and had returned to the *Cretic* to beg for his old job. When his offer was refused, Domenico decided to travel as a stowaway.[17]

Flynn had touted the arrest as a small triumph of Bureau surveillance. "We have kept watch this time and landed this young Italian," he told the papers. "However, there is no charge against him and we see no reason for holding him." He boasted as well that the Bureau was much better prepared than it had been a year earlier to meet the challenge ahead. On September 18, the day after discovering the flyers, he had publicly identified the Galleanisti as his top suspects. And while he admitted that there was as yet "no tangible evidence" pointing to their complicity, he assured the press that activity was humming behind the scenes. "In this case we have much more to work upon at the start," he explained to the *New York Tribune*, predicting a rash of new arrests. "The similarity of the circulars makes applicable all our knowledge of the gang who committed the outrages last year."[18]

This was not strictly true. Nationwide, the Bureau employed only three agents fluent in Italian. "I have been to some extent retarded in this investigation," Flynn later admitted to Palmer, "because of the lack of agents of Italian extraction capable of making criminal investigations amongst this element." At the General Intelligence Division, Hoover had compiled lists of nearly anyone who had ever received a copy of *Cronaca*, *L'Era Nuova*, or any of the other major Italian anarchist publications. With all of the misspellings, mistranslations, and phonetic guesswork in the files, however, agents had to assume that any given name was, at best, a creative approximation. Galleani, for instance, had been listed early on as "Louis Gallerini." Indeed, despite its importance to the ongoing bombing investigations, the Bureau had managed to misplace its entire file on the "Galliani group" earlier in the spring.[19]

Perhaps to make up for these technical shortfalls, Flynn set out in late September to reorganize the New York branch of the Bureau to facilitate the hunt for the Galleanisti. He established a special office on Nassau Street dedicated wholly to the Wall Street investigation. From Park Row he was joined by Charles Scully, head of the Bureau's New York radical division and a veteran of the June 2 case. In early October, Scully divided up the *Cronaca* subscription lists by city and sent them off to the northeastern offices—Providence, Buffalo, New York City, Boston, and others—for thorough checks on the subscribers' current whereabouts and activities. By October, he could boast that his quick thinking had resulted in a search for more than two thousand alleged Italian anarchists. Flynn admitted to Palmer, somewhat less enthusiastically, that not one of those Italians had been connected with the Wall Street explosion.[20]

Even this admission, however, understated the Bureau's discouraging record as the hunt for the Galleanisti got under way. Of fifty-nine *Cronaca* subscribers investigated in Buffalo, for instance, precisely eleven could be shown to have some sort of radical affiliation. Their numbers included five active Socialists, three anarchists, one former Socialist, one man convicted of espionage law violations, and one whose political affiliations leaned radical but were hard to quantify. The others fell into one of two categories. The greatest number of them, twenty-six, were simply missing, having moved or, perhaps, disappeared underground. The rest were ruled entirely free of radical sympathies.[21]

The June 2 precedent was little more effective in helping the Bureau to locate possible ringleaders. In his February statement, Caminita had named a raft of likely participants in the June 2 plot, including the stonemason Nicola Recchi; Galleani devotees Gemma Mello and Filippo Caci, who reportedly planted the bomb in Paterson; and Giuseppe Sberna, a New York anarchist and member of the Bresci Group who had allegedly helped to coordinate the entire plot. With the Wall Street explosion, the Bureau took pains to track them down once again. From Paterson, agents reported that Mello had shipped a package to a comrade in Stafford Springs, Connecticut, a town rumored to be "a rendezvous for terrorists." Sberna they sought under a variety of monikers, including Joe Sabana and Giuseppe Sabane. Reports described him as a dark-complexioned, dark-haired, medium-built Italian who tended to favor a checkered overcoat. When agents showed up at the door of his New York apartment posing as anarchist booksellers, however, they found no one matching that description. Sberna's wife, who answered the door, explained that her husband had left for Italy nine months earlier because he feared the police were after him.[22]

As for locating Recchi, the man said to have constructed the June 2 bombs, the Bureau pinned its hopes on the cooperation of the postmaster in Wrentham, Massachusetts, where Galleani had lived before his deportation. Galleani's wife and children were still in Wrentham, living in the same house where, according to Caminita, they had once sheltered Recchi. The Bureau apparently had no warrant to intercept the Galleani family's mail. Despite this, the postmaster generously agreed to look out for letters and return addresses "that looked suspicious in any way."[23]

Still smarting from the way Salsedo's death had exposed his efforts in the June 2 plot, Flynn did his best to keep the names of suspects out of the press in the early weeks of the investigation. He far preferred to be mocked for his ineptitude than to risk spooking his targets of interest. That included limiting what he had to say to the newspapers in early October, when the Bureau, assisted by the New York police, finally arrested an Italian anarchist.

IN THE EARLY MORNING HOURS of September 23, seven card players ambled into a poker hall posing loosely as a coffeehouse in Waterbury, Connecticut. One ordered coffee all around. Then they all drew their pistols and suggested that the patrons raise their hands on pain of being rendered "full of holes." First, they relieved the tables of their swollen pots. Next, they lined up the players and stripped them of diamonds, cuff links, excess cash, and other sundries. All told, one newspaper reported, the team made off with between $3,000 and $4,000 in loot, like "bandits from the wild and woolly West."[24]

Two weeks later, on the morning of October 6, the New York police swooped down on more than a dozen Italian men suspected of involvement in the heist. They grabbed a young man named Gaetano Caruso on an East Side elevated train platform around nine o'clock. Later that morning, they raided an East Fifteenth Street barbershop known to be frequented by Italians, loading the patrons into a waiting patrol wagon. At the station, police interviewed all fifteen men, but witnesses shipped down from Waterbury identified only a few as possible highway robbers. In addition to Caruso, they selected twenty-three-year-old Frank Ferro and Vincenzo Abato, a twenty-two-year-old stationery store clerk. The police also decided to hold Charles Fasulo, who owned the barbershop and therefore seemed to own the five pounds of black explosive powder uncovered on the premises. Caruso earned a gun charge; when arrested, he had been carrying a concealed and loaded .38 French automatic. The city held Ferro and Abato as "fugitives from justice."[25]

Nothing in the content of the charges suggested any connection to the Wall Street explosion. Newspapers were nonetheless quick to make a link. "Bomb Maker Held as Daring Robber," the *World* applauded in its front-page headline, identifying Caruso as the ringleader. The stories that followed described him as an anarchist, "a friend of Emma Goldman [and] Alexander Berkman," and most likely a member of the Galleani school. Flynn objected to any suggestion that Caruso was directly involved in the Wall Street case. "Suspect Is Not Bomb Plotter," read a chastened headline in the next day's *Sun and New York Herald*. He acknowledged, however, that he planned to interview Caruso on the matter. Indeed, the Bureau had been watching him for months as one of the likely participants in the June 2 plot.[26]

Caruso had first come to the Bureau's attention in April 1920, when he unwittingly shared plans for bombs "more powerful than the ones of

June 2" with an undercover informant. Their surveillance apparently trailed off two months later, in the wake of Andrea Salsedo's death. When the "more powerful" bomb erupted on Wall Street, they took up surveillance once again. They believed that Caruso was intimately acquainted with bomb throwers, whether or not he himself had engaged in such activity. Bomb squad detectives had described him as "a dangerous man associated with a bad crowd of Italians."[27]

This billing promised great drama for the Bureau agents assigned to track Caruso in mid-September. They discovered, however, that even a notorious bomb-plotting anarchist tended to lead a rather mundane existence from day to day. Caruso's routine began and ended at his home in Corona, Queens. In between, he made trips to his job (he worked as a steam presser) and to Fasulo's barbershop. Through round-the-clock surveillance, agents deduced that Caruso received his wages on Fridays (that was when men left the factory with pay envelopes) and that he seemed to enjoy playing with his infant child "in a family like manner." Rumors that he was hoarding nitroglycerin and blasting gelatin were never substantiated.[28]

The only criminal act that agents came close to witnessing was the robbery in Waterbury. On the afternoon of September 22, they had watched Caruso leave his house with a man of "swarthy complexion," and the two then made their way to Manhattan on the train. The Bureau men subsequently lost the duo—"they [the suspects] looked back once or twice and we allowed them too much headway"—but picked up their trail in time to board the train to Waterbury. Upon arrival, according to Bureau reports, Caruso and several friends met up with a handful of other Italians waiting on the platform and proceeded en masse down a street lined by factories and empty lots. In such an exposed environment, the Bureau men grew nervous of discovery, so they turned off the street, once again losing sight of their prey. The next morning, to their embarrassment, they heard that a group of out-of-town Italians had hijacked poker night at a coffeehouse.[29]

In custody two weeks later, Caruso refused to dignify the robbery accusation with more than a curt denial. He was slightly more voluble when it came to the bomb plots, laying out an offer, in Charles Scully's words, "to assist me on certain matters." Scully was eager to hear what he had to say. In a search of Caruso's house, undertaken while his wife lay in bed with a three-day-old child, agents had found a cache of anarchist literature, including copies of *Cronaca*, along with two letters that seemed to affirm their suspicions that Caruso might be a valuable inside man. The first, from a woman named Vera, passed along reports of her new cashier's job and an update from a mutual friend, Sberna—presumably Giuseppe Sberna, suspected in the June 2 plot. The second, signed by Roberto Elia, the man who had printed the "Plain Words" pamphlet, outlined costs of a possible printing job.[30]

This was enough to persuade Flynn to interview Caruso in person. On October 11, he arrived at the Tombs to meet with the prisoner. Caruso failed to name any names, but Flynn left the encounter optimistic. "I am of the opinion that he will soon consent to make a statement that will aid us materially," he wrote to Palmer. In the meantime, Flynn had a lead on two other Italian anarchists who might yield still better information. In contrast with many of their comrades, they were easy to locate. Nicola Sacco and Bartolomeo Vanzetti were already in jail in Massachusetts, awaiting trial for murder.[31]

IN THE FALL OF 1920, Sacco and Vanzetti were hardly household names— "just a couple of wops in a jam," as the *Call*'s city editor described them. Born in Italy, they had arrived (separately) in America in 1908, unnoticed newcomers in a peak immigration year that saw 130,000 Italians land on U.S. shores. They shared few physical characteristics beyond slight stature and dark coloring: Sacco was clean-shaven and square-jawed, whereas Vanzetti appeared more downcast, his face dominated by a bushy, drooping moustache. Their paths in America differed as well. Within a few years of arrival, Sacco had established himself as a skilled shoe worker in Massachusetts; he also married and became a father. Vanzetti was more of a loner, a self-taught intellectual who preferred to set his own hours by peddling fish or taking up odd jobs. Neither had anarchist leanings before coming to the United States. Once here, though, they quickly adopted Galleani's brand of militant anarchism. For Sacco, the turning point was the Lawrence strike, where he came face-to-face with the miserable conditions of America's unskilled workers. Vanzetti embraced anarchism around the same time, but for more personal reasons. Though he later established a nurturing community and found stable work in the Boston area, his early years in the United States had left him homeless and desperate.

Despite their later reputation as martyrs of American liberalism, both men espoused an unabashedly revolutionary form of anarchism.

"Both Nick and I are anarchists," Vanzetti explained, "the radical of the radical—the black cats, the terrors of many, of all the bigots, exploitators, charlatans, fakers and oppressors." They subscribed to *Cronaca*, and with it to Galleani's brand of class warfare and propaganda by deed. After the United States' entry into the war, both men had fled the United States for Monterrey, Mexico, joining a commune of Galleanisti hoping to escape conscription and plan for revolution in Italy. Though they had met briefly in Massachusetts, it was in Monterrey that they became friends. There, they also forged lasting bonds with many of the men ultimately suspected in the June 2 bomb plot, including Valdinoci, Elia, and Salsedo.

Sacco and Vanzetti were themselves likely involved in the June 2 conspiracy; Vanzetti, especially, was rumored to be the man who had made the bomb destined for Judge Hayden's house in Boston. Certainly they were active in the effort to shield their friends from the Bureau's suspicions. In late April 1920, Vanzetti had gone to New York to check up on Elia and Salsedo, then being held in federal detention. Though he never managed to contact his friends, he returned to Boston with ominous news of their predicament, instructing local allies to purge any incriminating evidence in anticipation of possible federal arrests. When Salsedo fell to his death a few days later, both Sacco and Vanzetti made plans to flee. Before they could depart, however, they found themselves under arrest.

Their alleged crime had little to do with revolutionary politics, at least on the surface. On April 15, just before Vanzetti's trip to New York, two unknown men had robbed and killed payroll guards Frederick Parmenter and Alessandro Berardelli in South Braintree, Massachusetts, making off with almost $16,000 in cash. Had Sacco and Vanzetti committed the deed, Galleani might well have approved; he believed in "expropriation" when necessary to fund revolutionary activity. As it was, the evidence against them was thin and contradictory. Nonetheless, the two Italian anarchists had found themselves enmeshed in the Massachusetts court system throughout the summer of 1920, all the while protesting their innocence. In early July, Vanzetti was convicted in an unrelated robbery case in South Bridgewater, Massachusetts. On September 11, 1920, five days before the Wall Street explosion, both Sacco and Vanzetti were indicted for the Braintree murders.[32]

It did not take long for their names to surface as possible conspirators in the Wall Street case. On September 16, while investigating anarchists in the midsized Italian stronghold of Milford, Massachusetts, Bureau agent

William Hill reported that Sacco had once lived in town, where he was "known as a rabid Anarchist." Four days later, the director of the Boston office noted that both Sacco and Vanzetti were starting to attract attention in Italian anarchist circles as victims of police misconduct. "[I]t is desired to advise that since the arrest of Bartolomeo Vanzetti and Nicola Sacco," he wrote to New York superintendent George Lamb, "...the Italian anarchists have been engaged in the circularization of anarchists throughout the United States for funds....This office," he concluded, "submits the above for whatever they may be worth."[33]

By the time the letter wound its way south from Boston, Flynn had begun to think that such information might be worth quite a bit. Unhappily ensconced in jail, Sacco and Vanzetti could not be considered actual suspects in the Wall Street case. As with Caruso, however, it seemed possible that they might know who had set the bomb and why. Considering the timing of their indictment, they might even be the "political prisoners" described in the American Anarchist Fighters pamphlets—men who would have to be freed on pain of "sure death for all of you." Given the unceasing newspaper coverage of the explosion and the long hours to be whiled away in jail, they might at least be privy to a name or a theory as yet unconsidered. In mid-October, Flynn decided to provide a willing audience on the off chance that they were forthcoming on this front. Still waiting for Caruso to break his silence in New York, the Boston office began making plans to put an undercover agent in Sacco's cell at the Dedham, Massachusetts, jail.[34]

Flynn was himself no stranger to the challenge of undercover work. As a young Secret Service agent, he had once tried to do the job himself, crafting an elaborate plan to infiltrate a meeting on Twenty-sixth Street in New York where Galleani was scheduled to speak. "I donned overalls, a bandana handkerchief, a queer looking hat of some sort or other and brogans," he later wrote, "which I took good care should be well coated with plaster and otherwise made to look like the boots of a laborer." When he arrived at the hall, he attempted to brush past a lookout standing in the door, but the man made him as a detective almost immediately, asking with some amusement which precinct Flynn belonged to. "Of course I got out," Flynn later wrote. He never went back.[35]

As head of the Bureau, he had nonetheless come to rely on undercover men (as well as informers such as Caminita) to penetrate radical networks off-limits to the average agent. Most undercover men were not full-blown Bureau employees but merely day-to-day contractors. In some cases, the Bureau simply borrowed them from private organizations— often business groups or wealthy individuals—who were willing to fund such activities. In 1919, for instance, a New York attorney named Alfred Becker had struck out on his own to hire an undercover man in the May Day and June 2 cases. His operative, an Italian immigrant named Eugenio Ravarini, managed to insinuate himself among the Galleanisti, providing Becker and, in turn, Flynn with a wealth of valuable clues. After a few trial months, Flynn formally hired Ravarini at the Bureau, where he helped to identify Elia, Salsedo, and Caminita. Like all under-cover men, Ravarini was known at the Bureau only by a code name. His was D-5.[36]

In the early weeks of the Wall Street investigation, Flynn had sought to replicate Ravarini's success, choosing two spies—N-122 and P-137—to infiltrate Italian anarchist circles in New York. Attempting anonym-ity, they loitered around coffeehouses, barbershops, and meeting halls. They also engaged in active political work, stamping envelopes and rais-ing defense funds at organizations such as the Italian Workers Defense League. Like their counterparts elsewhere in the Bureau, they were par-ticularly adept at gathering lists: membership lists, subscription lists, lists of contributors and supporters and would-be activists. Neither one, however, managed to uncover much about the bombing. Indeed, it was partly as a result of their failures that Flynn had turned his attention to Sacco's cell in Massachusetts.[37]

As Bureau agent William West would acknowledge six years later, the decision to spy on Sacco was in part an act of desperation. The man they selected, a local Italian immigrant named Domenico Carbone, was unfor-tunately not up to the task. Carbone appeared in the Dedham county jail on November 24 posing as an accused robber. He had been instructed that "he was, under no circumstances, to force himself upon Sacco but to let Sacco approach him," but he paid little attention. Placed in a cell adjacent to Sacco's, Carbone lost no time in asking his new friend about the best contacts for acquiring dynamite. He also bragged about his own vast criminal history, advertising a lifetime's worth of fictional exploits as mere precursors to the big blow-up to come.

The jail authorities helped him along by providing the two men with free run of the corridor and on occasion the yard, where they could stroll about and grow intimate. Sacco was more interested in professing his innocence in the Braintree murders than in arranging new dynamite plots. He described himself as a victim of cruel government oppression. "They have accused me of having committed a terrible crime," he protested in an Italian-language note slipped to Carbone, "simply because I have been the defender of the workers and also because I am an Italian. The Italians are despised by the Americans." According to Carbone's report, Sacco consistently maintained "that he was an anarchist, that he was against the capitalist, but that he had never killed any man." About the Wall Street explosion he had nothing to say. Carbone left the Dedham jail on December 3 after less than two weeks of confinement.

One reason for the quick extraction was the realization that his volubility concerning dynamite had raised Sacco's suspicions; "through his haste to secure information," a report later complained, "he had disclosed himself and rendered himself useless." Outside the jail, by contrast, the Bureau's surveillance continued unabated. To complement the work of his undercover operatives, in early November Flynn had quietly secured a warrant to read all correspondence delivered to the Boston office of a new organization known as the Sacco-Vanzetti Defense Committee.[38]

BUREAU AGENT WILLIAM WEST used the same procedure for each batch of mail: open, copy, reseal, resend. Once acquired, the letters were translated and assembled into a weekly report titled "Bomb Explosion, Wall St., New York City, September 16, 1920: Anarchist Activities." Though the correspondence concerned Sacco and Vanzetti's legal defense—a realm in which attorney-client privilege reasonably applied—the Bureau had managed to gain federal court approval for its actions. The warrant covered mail addressed not to Sacco and Vanzetti's lawyer but to Aldino Felicani, a friend and fellow anarchist who had undertaken the task of raising money and composing propaganda in preparation for their upcoming trial.[39]

As one of the few prominent Galleanisti living and working openly in the United States, Felicani was an obvious target of Bureau interest. As head of the fledgling Sacco-Vanzetti Defense Committee, he was also an invaluable repository of information. The committee had formed on May 9, four days after Sacco and Vanzetti's arrest for the Braintree murders. In the months since, it had been engaged in scattered fundraising and pamphleteering, operating out of two tiny rooms on Boston's North End. Its main achievement by the fall was hiring Fred Moore, a devoted if erratic defense lawyer who had helped to represent Haywood at his wartime trial. The Bureau had little interest in Moore, or in the details of the criminal case. With so many anarchists on the run, forced into exile, or biding their time underground, the committee stood out as one of the few places where the Galleanisti might still gather to organize and converse. From the Bureau's perspective, this made it one of the best available sources for tracking the sentiments and whereabouts of the bomb suspects who had so far escaped official scrutiny.[40]

Before taking up work on the Sacco-Vanzetti case, Felicani had been best known in anarchist circles as a prolific essayist, a self-taught radical thinker who subsidized his editorial work with factory wages. Unlike many Italian radicals, he was fluent in English, a skill that made him particularly well qualified to serve as a propagandist to the American public. According to Caminita, Felicani played a major role in the composition of "Plain Words" (he was "the type that does the thinking and the writing for those who do the dirty work," one agent noted). Not long after Elia and Salsedo's arrests, Bureau agents had called Felicani in for an interview in the June 2 case. They told him he was being interrogated for draft evasion (a ruse that undoubtedly seemed thin). For purposes of future identification, agents noted Felicani's "bushy blonde hair, thin on top brushed straight back," black velour hat, and blue serge suit. Then they released him in lieu of further developments.[41]

That "development" turned out to be the Wall Street explosion. In early October 1920, as the Caruso arrest was unfolding, New Jersey agent Frank Stone notified Flynn—based on information "from a very confidential and reliable source"—that Felicani seemed to be in touch with a wide range of Italian anarchists, including "such members of the Galliani Group who have not as yet left for Italy." He suggested that Felicani "be picked up" and "'tailed' (but not molested)" on the chance that he might lead the Bureau to some of his missing friends. His caution reflected Flynn's fear that any misstep could send the remaining Galleanisti scrambling for shelter underground. Indeed, though they continued to try to link him to the blast, Felicani was far more valuable to the Bureau as a free man than as a prisoner. By keeping him out of jail, the Bureau could wait and watch and hope that "a lead on the 'WALL STREET BOMB' may be developed."[42]

Felicani's mail appeared to be a godsend, a window into the tight-knit world of Italian anarchism. First, there were the names and addresses not only of defense committee organizers but of the hundreds of men and women who contributed a few pennies in response to one or another hometown canvass. Most were Italian anarchists and labor activists, poor men who often felt compelled to apologize for the small size of their donations. "[W]e are only a few," one Ohio supporter explained of his $35 collection, "and the majority of us are out of work." But they were not the only ones writing in. Though the Sacco-Vanzetti case had not yet emerged as a national scandal, it was beginning to attract the attention of small numbers of communists, socialists, reformers, and civil libertarians concerned that the men would be framed because of their Italian backgrounds and anarchist beliefs.[43]

Overall, the Sacco-Vanzetti supporters came across as a dispirited group, politically engaged but worn down by the challenge of survival in a hostile country. "We will do more in the future but it is very hard," promised Alfredo Zammarchi, writing from Haverhill, Massachusetts, "because we have generally been unemployed since eight months." Ironically, this sense of depression, of desperation, may well have heartened the Bureau translators who pored over the letters week after week. In contrast to their imagined portrait of militant anarchism, rife with encouragements toward violence and sabotage, they found a crowd of anxious men and women pessimistic about the prospect of victory. "Today my heart seems almost broken," wrote one Pennsylvania correspondent. "[N]ever did I ever dream my own land, my native land could...stoop to do to our own and of other nations the hellmark of these past three or four years."[44]

Calls for violence and uprisings were not totally absent. One Illinois radical sent a note denouncing the strategy of relying on lawyers to win an acquittal. "This is not our tactics, because it is a wrong action. *But who is ready for the direct action?*" To the Bureau's disappointment, however, most correspondents were far too savvy—or far too innocent—to reveal anything of an incriminating nature. Despite months of painstaking translation, despite weekly reports that expanded to fill dozens of pages, by the end of the year the Bureau found not a single mention of the Wall Street explosion.[45]

Elsewhere, the investigation seemed to be similarly stalled by late autumn, as the flurry of initial excitement gave way to the grind of waiting, watching, and reading. In October, with the help of police manpower, Bureau agents established that the stamps used to create the American Anarchist Fighters pamphlets belonged to the stock of the R. H. Smith

Company of Springfield, Massachusetts. They also managed to locate an Italian blacksmith named Gaetano DeGrazio, who said that he had shod the bomb wagon's horse on September 15 at his stable at 205 Elizabeth Street (a section of New York, Flynn noted, "notorious for its Italian criminals and for murders"). In neither case, however, had there been more concrete developments to date.[46]

None of these difficulties convinced Flynn to change his views about the Galleanisti. They did, however, make him increasingly wary of talking with the press. After Caruso's arrest in October, Flynn did not deliver a major statement about the investigation for another six months. As far as the public knew, the only development of note in the entire month of November was a *World* article claiming to prove that the bomb plotters were construction workers annoyed at being shut out of the stock exchange annex job by a Tammany-supported union. An unnamed Justice Department spokesman soon quashed the speculation. "We investigated this theory and other labor quarrel theories weeks ago," he informed the rival *Times*, "but found no connection between them and the explosion." Flynn himself had no comment.[47]

What could he have said? The Bureau's main activities, surveillance and undercover work, did not lend themselves to public scrutiny. Nor were there any grand new theories to report. If anything, the slow progress of the fall simply seemed to convince Flynn that more aggressive tactics would be necessary. In December, unbeknownst to all but a few hand-picked confidants, he quietly dispatched a man to Italy to find Luigi Galleani.

THE PLAN WAS SIMPLE BUT HIGH RISK. Sometime toward the end of the year, Flynn explained to State Department officials, an operative from the Bureau of Investigation would appear in Italy to find and infiltrate the circle of anarchists responsible for the Wall Street explosion. (Flynn "is fully convinced that the hand behind this and other bomb outrages is located in Italy," noted the State Department files.) The operative would arrive in Rome bearing a confidential card for identification. After confirming his bona fides, the American embassy would take charge of communicating his messages to the United States. The agent's life, one State Department official remarked, might well depend on keeping the cables secret. "If he is successful . . . [i]t will be a big plum in not only the eyes of the Department but of the whole country. If, however, the reverse is the case and the man is found out, I do not think we will even have to worry about shipping his body home."[48]

The man expected to assume this peril was Salvatore Clement, to be identified in communication only by the code name "Mull." Born in Italy, Clement was a rare breed, one of the few men in Flynn's employ capable of blending in with the Galleanisti. He had proven as much during his pre-war days in the Secret Service, when Flynn had assigned him to infiltrate Galleani's circle in Massachusetts and Vermont. Clement's skills of ingratiation were sophisticated enough that his double life had gone unexposed during the assignment and in the eight years since. It was hoped that his radical contacts from those days—many of them now in Italy—would lead him without subterfuge or suspicion to Galleani. He planned to pose as "a desperate anarchist" from Paterson.[49]

Clement departed New York on December 28 on the *Giuseppe Verdi*, bound for Naples. By way of identification, he carried only his U.S. passport and the special card provided to ensure his welcome at the embassy. The Bureau shipped ahead several photos of Italian anarchists, including one of Galleani, for Clement to pick up upon his arrival in Rome. After retrieving them, Clement journeyed to the home of an old acquaintance from his faux-radical days, a man named Antonio Mazzini, who kept an apartment in Milan. Staking out the flat from a nearby corner, he waited for his friend to return home from work, then popped in with greetings from abroad. Mazzini offered to cancel his dinner plans, but Clement said he'd much rather tag along with Mazzini and his friends. They went to a café, ordered dinner, and drank "a few bottles of wine." The magnanimous American visitor, Clement announced he would pay for everyone's meal. Only then, with his friend sated and thankful, did he broach the subject of Galleani.

Clement began with a cheerful jab at the Bureau's incompetence in the June 2 bombing investigations. "I said the job was done pretty slick," he wrote to Flynn, "and I was glad no one was caught." Mazzini agreed heartily—"He said everything was all right"—but mourned the loss of "poor Carlo Valdinucci [*sic*]." "This proves beyond doubt," Clement noted, "the identity of the man who was killed at the time of the bomb explosion at...Attorney General Palmer's home." On this particular tidbit, Mazzini's source was exemplary. In July, he claimed, he had shared confidences with none other than Galleani himself, apparently quite broken up over Valdinoci's death. "Galliani had tears in his eyes," Clement wrote,

paraphrasing Mazzini's account, "and as if talking to himself would say—
Poor boy, Poor boy." Mazzini also recalled that Recchi had been in and
around Galleani's circle in the past year but had recently disappeared.

As for Galleani himself, Mazzini knew only that he had fled the country, running this time from the Italian authorities rather than from the
Americans. After his deportation from the United States, Galleani had
resumed printing *Cronaca* on his old printing press, which had been dis-
assembled and shipped from Rhode Island to Italy. The Italian government, however, was no more hospitable than the Americans had been,
and in October they shut down the paper and issued a warrant for his
arrest. In response, Galleani had taken deportation into his own hands
and vanished.

Clement did manage to track down an apartment in Vercelli where a
sign over the door advertised the residence of one "Galliani" [*sic*]. A sweet
older woman who answered the bell informed him that Luigi, the man of
the house, was currently "out of town." She invited him to come back and
visit the lady of the house, Galleani's sister. When Clement stopped by
again, however, the sister was incredulous at his queries. "Don't you know
what happened?" she asked. "My brother had to leave the country."[50]

There was a certain irony to this outcome: had the United States not
deported Galleani in 1919, surely he would have been much easier for the
Bureau to find. If Flynn recognized this aspect of his predicament, however, he did not let on. By the time Clement returned to make his final
report in March, Flynn's critics had begun to wonder openly if the Wall
Street case would ever be solved. With a new Republican administration
coming into power in Washington, they were also beginning to speculate
that it might be time for a new Bureau director.

# 11

. . . .

## ILLEGAL PRACTICES

ATTORNEY GENERAL PALMER knew he was out when the Republican candidate, Warren Harding, won the 1920 presidential election. Harding's campaign, like the man himself, had been lackluster. But with President Wilson weakened by a stroke, with his proposed League of Nations floundering, the outcome of the vote was a foregone conclusion. An Ohio senator with few outstanding achievements, Harding had been plucked from obscurity by the Republican leadership only after the party's convention failed to settle on one of the top candidates. He spent the fall of 1920 campaigning from his front porch in Marion, Ohio, on a vague platform of reason and calm. "America's present need is not heroics but healing; not nostrums but normalcy," he maintained. His greatest quality, according to campaign manager Harry Daugherty, was that he looked the part: his six-foot frame and piercing dark eyes made him appear, in a word, presidential. When the totals were counted up in November, the nation agreed. Harding won more than 60 percent of the national vote. His Democratic rivals, James Cox and vice presidential candidate Franklin Delano Roosevelt, received 34 percent. Debs, running from prison, won just 3.5 percent—a disappointing showing, the *Call* conceded, that "fell far short of the general expectations."[1]

Palmer may have taken a certain amount of pleasure in Cox's defeat. Though the attorney general had dedicated his life to the Democratic Party, Cox rejected his offer of help in the campaign. He viewed Palmer as a dangerous force, an all-too-visible reminder of the Wilson administration's missteps in the transition from war to peace. Despite Palmer's initial hopes, the drama of the Wall Street explosion proved to be of little use in altering this reputation. "Cox stands for Palmer...," Forest Service founder Gifford Pinchot, an ardent progressive, had charged in early October, "who denied the rights of free speech and free assembly, imprisoned hundreds of people in defiance of the law he was sworn to enforce."[2]

Harding himself never offered a formal statement on the explosion. Nor did he talk much about the problems of terrorism and revolutionary agitation that had shaped so much of Palmer's recent career. This set him apart from his running mate, Massachusetts governor Calvin Coolidge, who had made a national name for himself by calling in federal troops to suppress the Boston police strike in 1919. "There is no right to strike against the public safety by anybody, anywhere, anytime," Coolidge had written to Samuel Gompers. Harding, by contrast, seemed to view labor conflict as a simple matter of miscommunication. "Not being imbued with the facts in the case," he explained during the campaign, "thousands of honest, well-meaning men become imbued with the idea that they are viciously oppressed; misunderstandings result, causing trouble that could be avoided by a simple exposition of the truth."[3]

He applied the same measured tone to the issue of revolutionary bombings and assassinations. "It is quite true that there are enemies of the Government within our borders," he explained. "However, I believe their number has been greatly magnified." Palmer found this not only insulting but positively dangerous. Despite Harding's victory, the attorney general continued throughout the late months of 1920 to prod the federal authorities into action against the terrorist threat. In his annual report for the year, released in December, Palmer pleaded with Congress to pass a peacetime sedition law. He also insisted upon claiming the deportation raids as a major success, citing the admission, allegedly uncovered by federal spies, that the "arrests made at the instance of the Department of Justice had resulted in the wrecking of the communist parties in this country." As a lame duck and discredited figure, however, he encountered little enthusiasm for the renewal of either campaign. When Palmer appeared before Congress in December to request extra funds for antiradical work, the committee saw fit to grant a $400,000 bonus, a subsidy to make up for the previous year's excess expenses. But it also pared down demands for a permanently enlarged antiradical budget. Palmer had asked for $2.65 million for the upcoming year; he got just $2 million.[4]

Behind this subtle rejection, many historians would later suggest, was a shift in national mood, an inability (or perhaps an unwillingness) to sustain the heightened levels of fear and anxiety necessary to enact Palmer's proposals. Whatever role such nebulous matters as mood and psychology may have played in preventing Palmer's revival, there were more concrete factors at work as well. Harding's lack of interest was a crucial element: when the incoming president felt that "too much has been said about Bolshevism in America," it was hard to stir up prolonged debate. Among Democrats, not only Cox but also key officials within several federal agencies, including the Labor Department, continued to shy away from cooperating with Palmer. Without their help, and without the support of Congress, there was little Palmer could do to translate his ideas into action.[5]

Nor, to be fair, did he try terribly hard. Despite his bold words after the Wall Street explosion, Palmer was not the crusader he had been a year earlier, when it appeared as if he might ride his martyrdom all the way to the presidency. The trials of managing the Justice Department, especially when it came to enforcing the new Prohibition law, had taken their toll on his health. So had the relentless criticism, with its caricature of him as a paranoid, vicious, and hysterical hunter of Reds. Palmer had attempted to counter this with a recommendation that President Wilson pardon Eugene Debs (Wilson rejected it out of hand). To most of the country, though, he remained the embodiment of the previous year's misbegotten raids. If anything, Flynn's policy of silence in the Wall Street case had only provided an opening for further attack, leaving a void that Palmer's critics were perfectly happy to fill. Throughout the late fall, as coverage of the investigation trailed off in the mainstream dailies, the socialist press stayed on the attorney general's case, mocking his "assertion," in the words of the New York Call, "that 'radical agitators' now in the United States are waiting for an opportunity to do many desperate things."[6]

This kind of contempt was to be expected from socialist quarters. More surprising, and ultimately more damaging, were the attacks coming from Congress itself. In early December 1920, a month after the presidential election, a Senate Judiciary Subcommittee announced hearings based on the springtime report that had accused the Justice Department of "illegal practices" and ruined Palmer's presidential aspirations. The twelve prominent lawyers who composed the report were not socialists, much less communists or anarchists. Nonetheless, they shared many of the assumptions being articulated in the left-wing press: that Palmer was a rogue agent, that he allowed Bureau agents to trample the rights of alien radicals, and that it was the Justice Department, not the anarchist or communist movement, that was "terrorizing" the nation.[7]

HAD THE SENATE WITNESSES been aware of what was happening behind the scenes in the Wall Street case, they might well have objected. The June report had listed many of Flynn's tactics, including the use of undercover operatives and the infiltration of radical groups, among its "illegal practices"—examples of government intrusions into the right of free speech and opinion. As it was, with the hunt for the Galleanisti safely out of the newspapers, the Wall Street explosion entered the Senate hearings only by inference, part of a tableau of Bureau incompetence and false accusation. Still, it is hard to imagine that the hearings would have gone the same way—or, indeed, that they would have been called at all—had the Bureau managed by January to come up with definitive proof of anarchist complicity in the Wall Street blast. With a solution to the Wall Street case in hand, Palmer might have approached the Senate's scrutiny from a position of strength, vindicated in his claim that radicals posed a significant threat to the national welfare. Instead, he found himself struggling to convince both the Senate subcommittee and the public that the United States had ever faced a bona fide terrorist emergency.

In a roundabout way, Emma Goldman bore a measure of responsibility for Palmer's predicament. Almost two decades earlier, in the aftermath of the McKinley assassination, she had joined with a group of like-minded New York libertarians to found the Free Speech League, the first formally organized civil liberties association in the United States. The league's agenda had reflected her concerns about the growing clamor for restrictions on speech, especially with the passage of the antianarchist law. Its earliest efforts focused on the case of John Turner, a British anarchist and friend of Goldman's who had the dubious honor of being the first man excluded from the United States under the new immigration law. While

Turner lost his appeal, the case set a precedent for the league's later activities as well as for the Wobblies' subsequent free-speech campaigns—and, now, for the activities of Palmer's critics.[8]

Dedicated in theory to the proposition of liberty for all, the Free Speech League had in practice mostly defended its own members: anarchists, birth control advocates, Wobblies, and other varieties of revolutionary. The civil libertarians who had emerged from the Great War and who had composed the June report on the Justice Department took a more distanced approach. Though passionately concerned with the rights of alien radicals, they were solid members of the establishment. Indeed, the twelve lawyers who signed their names to the June report had far more in common with Palmer than with Goldman. They taught law at places such as Harvard, Columbia, and Yale, and they tended to believe, in the words of signer Felix Frankfurter, that meritocratic institutions such as "the *Harvard Law Review*" in particular and the Harvard Law School in general" constituted "the most complete practices in democracy." Largely Democrats and Republicans, spiced with only the occasional Socialist, they entertained their own hopes of appointment to positions such as attorney general or justice of the Supreme Court. They did not stand on street corners with the Wobblies shouting, "Have you ever read the Constitution?" or "What is this, Czarist Russia, or Free America?" Instead, they appeared before the bench, issued reports, lent their good names, and testified in government hearings.[9]

A few of the report's signers were longtime champions of civil liberties and labor rights; Frank Walsh, who had led the prewar Commission on Industrial Relations, was the most notable. Others were relative newcomers to the cause. Frankfurter's own interest stemmed from his appointment as head of President Wilson's Mediation Commission, dispatched to the western states in 1917 to assess wartime labor unrest. Under the commission's auspices, he had traveled to Bisbee, Arizona, where twelve hundred Wobblies and strikers and their families had been "deported" to the desert without food or shelter. He also led the federal inquiry into the Mooney case; convinced that prosecutors had coerced witnesses and manufactured evidence, he urged Wilson to push for a new trial. Himself the son of immigrants, one of the few Jewish professors in the Ivy League, Frankfurter may have felt a natural sympathy for outsiders and underdogs. As a lawyer, he expressed this not by denouncing capitalism but by composing legal briefs and government reports.[10]

Frankfurter's Harvard colleague Zechariah Chafee, another of the report's signers, had arrived even later to the civil liberties cause. The son of a Boston industrialist, he attended Brown University and then Harvard Law School before joining the Harvard faculty in 1916. When the United States entered the war the following year, he grew concerned that the espionage and sedition acts were fatally undermining the country's democratic, libertarian traditions. Once converted, he took on the question wholeheartedly, publishing a pathbreaking 1920 book titled, appropriately, *Freedom of Speech*. In his book, Chafee acknowledged the genuine problem of revolutionary violence and terrorism. But he warned that a rush to restrict speech as a means of containing the crisis would ultimately endanger constitutional freedoms. As an example, he cited the injustice of Haymarket, suggesting that his countrymen, whatever their fears, might wish to avoid a repeat of the event. "If an emergency really exists," he argued, "it behooves us all to keep cool."[11]

Even for established lawyers such as Chafee and Frankfurter, speaking out on such questions proved to be a considerable risk. Chafee had nearly been fired from Harvard for expressing these sentiments (a measure suggesting that his employers had not actually read the title of his book). Others had lost friends, money, and social invitations. Nearly all had at one time or another been subjects of Bureau inquiry. Perhaps for these reasons, they went to considerable pains to forswear any sympathy or association with radicalism when they appeared before the Senate in 1921. "We who have signed this pamphlet did not go into the case because of the slightest sympathy with revolution," Chafee explained, "but as lawyers trained in the preservation of personal rights."[12]

Among those who accepted Chafee's distinction was Walter Nelles, another Harvard-trained lawyer who had found himself alarmed by Wilson's wartime suppression of dissent. After graduating from law school, Nelles had taken the standard path of joining a white-shoe law firm. In 1917, however, as preparedness gave way to war, he had abruptly abandoned his post to take up full-time work for the newly formed National Civil Liberties Bureau (NCLB), led by his Harvard classmate Roger Baldwin. Over the course of the war, the NCLB represented hundreds of imprisoned dissidents. By 1920, it had changed its name to the American Civil Liberties Union, or ACLU, but its mission remained the same. After the deportation raids, the ACLU provided legal counsel to scores of deportees, including several of the Galleanisti.

When the Wall Street explosion erupted on September 16, the ACLU's New York office promptly opened a clipping file in anticipation of prosecutions to come.[13]

Though not the first organization of its kind, the NCLB was by far the best-known and most influential of the civil liberties organizations to emerge during the war. Some of its founding members, such as Morris Hillquit and Elizabeth Gurley Flynn, were themselves socialists or communists. But many others, such as Nelles, were moderate lawyers, concerned less with their own right to speak than with far more abstract legal principles. "Civil liberty means this—that every one may think for himself upon every public question; that he may say what he thinks; and that he may do his utmost, and get his friend to do theirs, to bring what he thinks home to the minds and hearts of others," Nelles wrote in his pamphlet *Seeing Red*.[14]

Nelles spent hours each month compiling "Law and Freedom Bulletins" for the ACLU, outlining developments in the areas of "Due Process of Law," "Revocation of Second Class Mailing Privilege," and other civil liberties issues. Though operating on what Roger Baldwin characterized as "a bare living wage," he also took on the cases of dozens of anarchists, communists, and Wobblies. Among his clients in 1921 were the five ousted Socialist assemblymen in New York and the June 2 bomb plot suspects Roberto Elia and Andrea Salsedo. Just weeks after the Senate hearings began, Nelles filed suit against Palmer, Flynn, and New York Bureau chief Charles Scully on behalf of Marie Salsedo, Andrea's widow, accusing them of murder.[15]

Nelles did not actually sign his name to the June report on "illegal practices"; his partner, Swinburne Hale, helped to compose the report and signed it on behalf of their law firm, Hale, Nelles, and Schorr. Nonetheless, the stories of Nelles' clients, including the Galleanisti, played a major role in the report's indictment of Bureau practices. One of the most significant was the case of Gaspare Cannone, a Galleani follower who had been arrested in March 1920, allegedly for deportation but actually for suspicion of his involvement in the June 2 plots. According to an affidavit by Nelles, in the spring of 1920 Bureau agents had arrested Cannone without a warrant, beat and kicked him into submission, showered him with profanity, and forged his name on a confession that he longed for the government's violent destruction. Other cases in the June report told similar stories of police brutality, forgery, excessive bail, abysmal jail conditions, "compelling Persons to Be Witnesses Against Themselves," "Propaganda by the Department of Justice," and, most important, warrantless arrests.[16]

All of these accusations, and more, would come out once again during the Senate hearings.

PALMER ARRIVED at the hearings on January 19, 1921, accompanied by J. Edgar Hoover, who had slaved for weeks compiling exculpatory evidence for his superior's use. Throughout the Wall Street investigation, Hoover had been working behind the scenes, coordinating intelligence and initialing documents. In his annual report, Palmer had praised Hoover's General Intelligence Division for its fine work in such matters, pointing out that the division had compiled some two hundred thousand files on the country's radical agitators. "This card index makes it possible to determine and ascertain in a few moments the numerous ramifications of individuals connected with the ultraradical movement and their activities in the United States," he boasted (a claim belied by Flynn's experience with the Galleanisti). Hoover's role at the hearings was to provide information about how the Palmer Raids had been carried out. Other than a few points of reference and clarification—"No, sir, I do not"; "Yes; I have been advised of many cases where search warrants were obtained"— Hoover maintained a respectful silence. As attorney general, Palmer bore ultimate responsibility for what had taken place.[17]

The hearings unfolded around a long wooden conference table in one of the Capitol's corner suites, an intimate setting for an altogether personal confrontation. Three senators—Democrat Thomas Walsh (Montana), along with Republicans William Borah (Idaho) and Thomas Sterling (South Dakota)—sat in judgment, while witnesses trickled in and out. With only a few months left in office, with his political reputation at stake, Palmer had no intention of allowing the "so-called 'leading lawyers' of the country" to maneuver him into an admission of guilt. Seated before his senatorial inquisitors, he portrayed himself as an embattled Cassandra, a man who knew too well the doom that would soon descend upon his laughing, mocking liberal critics. "I apologize for nothing that the Department of Justice has done in this matter," he thundered. "I glory in it. I point with pride and enthusiasm to the result of that work; and if...some of my agents out in the field, or some of the agents of the Department of Labor, were a little rough and unkind, or short and curt, with these alien agitators whom they observed seeking to destroy their homes, their religion, and their country, I think it might well be overlooked in the general good to the country which has come from it. That is all I have to say."[18]

Thanks to Hoover's careful record keeping and bureaucratic zeal (the skills for which he had initially been hired), Palmer came well armed with affidavits, court decisions, editorials, and police records contradicting the lawyers' committee's published claims. His response to the charges concerning Cannone alone took up twenty-two pages of Senate transcript. In that case, as in many others, the issue came down to conflicting testimony. The lawyers' report said that Cannone had been provided with only five meals in four days of Bureau custody; Palmer said that he "was supplied with regular meals and was not limited to any specific amount." Cannone said he had been beaten and kicked by a "handsome agent in a blue-striped silk shirt" (later identified as New York agent Charles Scully, Flynn's right-hand man in the Wall Street case) and that agents had nearly drowned him in profanity. Scully himself claimed that no cursing or violence had occurred, and three colleagues backed him up. Similarly, they denied arresting Cannone without a warrant. Instead, they claimed that Cannone had "voluntarily" allowed them to interrogate him and to search his house. Any implications to the contrary, they asserted, were due to "the effort of Mr. Nelles to misstate the facts and to mislead the public."[19]

For all of this painstaking detail, Palmer's bid for redemption rested quite outside any factual corrections. In the first place, many of his claims were less than persuasive: was it really plausible, for instance, that Cannone would offer the agents carte blanche to search his home? In addition, the back-and-forth about who had signed what, when, and why failed to address the "fundamental legal principles" that lay at the heart of the deportation raids. "I should like to hear the Attorney General tell us by what authority of law an agent of the Department of Justice makes an arrest in deportation proceedings at all," demanded Walsh, who had organized the hearings with this question in mind. There Palmer was on exceedingly shaky legal ground. As Hoover had acknowledged in a February 1920 letter, the Justice Department's mandate for the deportation raids had been "supported by public opinion" rather than any actual statute. Unlike the allegations of brutality, profanity, and lack of blankets in the jail, this charge could not be met with an affidavit from an agent saying that he, for one, remembered that a statute had existed. In answer to these larger questions, Palmer turned away from a defense based on fact and toward one based on justification. If the Justice Department had exceeded its authority, if it had made a few mistakes (and Palmer wasn't saying that it had), wasn't it justified by the "emergency" the country had faced in 1919?[20]

Mustering his crusader's passion once again, Palmer argued the country had been engaged in a literal civil war in 1919 and 1920. In war, the normal rules, the restrictions of statutes and rights and procedure, did not always, or even often, have to apply. This was a view supported by several jurists, and Palmer did not hesitate to offer their decisions for the Senate record. Among them was the statement of Northwestern University Law School dean John H. Wigmore: "If some of the deportees were victims of their own ignorance or of subordinate officials' harshness—well, every soldier knows that such things will happen in war; and this was really war against an enemy. Mr. Palmer saved the country, in my opinion."[21]

In a final appeal, Palmer called upon his audience to remember the fear, deep and seemingly bottomless, that had gripped the country in the wake of the June 2 plots. "I remember, Mr. Chairman, the morning after my house was blown up, I stood in the middle of the wreckage of my library with Congressmen and Senators, and without a dissenting voice they called upon me in strong terms to exercise all the power that was possible to the Department of Justice to run to earth the criminals who were behind that kind of outrage." He also asked them to think about what sort of bombings or attempts at revolution might have disrupted the transition back to peace if the Justice Department had not swept in to clear out the muck at the bottom of society. His deportation strategy had been preventive, he maintained, designed to rid the country of its undesirables rather than "wait for the actual throwing of the bomb."[22]

Palmer stated this doctrine as if it were the simplest thing in the world, a matter of transparent common sense. What he was describing, however, was precisely the slippery slope down which civil libertarians feared to slide: if it was possible to arrest men in advance of any actual wrongdoing, who could not be deemed a danger to the national soul by one standard or another? At any rate, as a policy for preventing terrorism, Palmer's strategy had not worked terribly well. Though the hearings focused on earlier events, everyone present was perfectly aware of the stalled investigation into the Wall Street explosion.

PALMER WAS THE FIRST to testify. He was also the last, closing out the hearings with a letter defending his treatment of communist deportees. Among the witnesses who appeared in between were many signers of the report on illegal practices: Chafee (who testified by letter); Jackson Ralston, counsel for Louis Post and Samuel Gompers; Washington University Law School professor Tyrrell Williams; and former U.S. attorney Francis Fisher Kane, the first man to resign in protest of Palmer's policies. Other witnesses represented various civic reform groups. Helena Hill Weed journeyed from Norwalk, Connecticut, to recount the objections of the American Women's Committee, while manufacturing chemist Frederick F. Ingram came from Michigan to deliver a report from the Citizens of Detroit, a local businessmen's organization.[23]

Notably absent from the lineup was anyone—anarchist, communist, immigrant—who had experienced the Justice Department's "illegal practices" firsthand. Though Senator Walsh, a progressive Democrat, had initiated the hearings as a forum for criticizing Palmer's policies, the roster of witnesses was also a testament to how effectively those policies had foreshortened the range of permissible debate. Before the war, radicals had hardly been the architects of government policy, but they had at least been part of the conversation. Now they were thoroughly disinvited.

In an effort to negotiate the delicate imperatives of defending radical rights without seeming too sympathetic to the revolutionary cause, the critics who appeared throughout February and into March borrowed heavily from the same rhetorical arsenal that Palmer himself had deployed in his "war" on radicalism. They went out of their way to position themselves as the true guardians of American freedom against the influence of destructive forces. "We want...to look [like] patriots in everything we do," Nelles' friend Roger Baldwin, head of the ACLU, had instructed a colleague in a similar situation. "We want to get a good lot of flags, talk a good deal about the Constitution and what our forefathers wanted to make of this country, and to show that we are really the folks that really stand for the spirit of our institutions."[24]

By adopting and then redefining the language of superpatriotism, they hoped to use Palmer's own words against him. "There is no danger of revolution so great as that created by suppression, by ruthlessness, and by deliberate violation of the simple rules of American law and American decency," the lawyers warned in their June report. From the point of view of the Justice Department's critics, Palmer was the great danger to American institutions—the terrorist, the true revolutionary.[25]

It was ironic, therefore, that Palmer often took far more seriously than any of his critics the ideas and intentions of radicals and communists. By the logic of his own defense, Palmer was obligated to argue strenuously that Bolshevism was sweeping the world, that radical militants retained an unwavering and well-organized devotion to their cause, and that within the United States communists in particular wielded substantial power and persuasive ability. During an earlier round of hearings before the House of Representatives, for instance, he had nearly burst out singing "The Internationale." "All over the world," he had cried, "and in every major tongue, bands of workers, men and women, joined already in conscious and conspiring fraternization, are singing":

### The New International
*Stand up! Ye wretched ones who labor,*
*Stand up! Ye galley slaves of want.*
*Man's reason thunders from its crater,*
*'Tis the eruption none can daunt...*

Before the senators, he described a "great movement" afoot "for the overthrow of the Government of the United States, sponsored and adhered to by thousands of alien agitators, directed and engineered by the guiding hand of Lenin and Trotski."[26]

His critics, by contrast—the very men so often derided as "parlor pinks" and closet radicals—pooh-poohed the idea that radical movements had ever been either strong or serious enough to deserve government attention. After the trauma of war, they argued, when the country's collective mind was ripe for manipulation, ambitious politicians had stepped forward to channel the public's anxieties onto small groups of men and women with unpopular political views. "It is just because at this present time we had gotten into a frame of mind of hating somebody," attorney Charles Recht, who represented several prominent communists, told the Senate subcommittee, "and it was found to the advantage of some people to transfer a well-established hate to an object more nearly at hand, for reasons of their own."[27]

In his springtime testimony before the House, Palmer himself had offered an astute summary of his critics' main contentions: "First, that there has been no 'Red' menace in the country against which the Government ought to proceed; second, that the methods adopted by the Department of Justice have been high-handed and even unlawful and unconstitutional; and, third, that in the enforcement of this law and in its efforts to keep the peace in the country, the Department of Justice has attacked American labor." Palmer, it went without saying, thought such arguments "palpably false."[28]

And yet, without proof of who was behind the June 2 plots or the Wall Street explosion, the precise character or intent of that " 'Red' menace" remained thoroughly open to question. At the Bureau, Flynn would do his best to change that impression in coming months, conducting his first major arrests in the Wall Street case. For Palmer, though, the time was up. Along with an ill and limping President Wilson, he left office in early March, still awaiting vindication.[29]

# 12

····

# THE MARTYR
# WHO WASN'T

PALMER'S DEPARTURE should not have been a problem for Flynn. Though appointed under Wilson, a Democrat, Flynn had long been a dependable cog in the New York Republican machine. As a local party activist, he had helped to found the venerable Riverside Republican Club. Within New York, he had often defended Republican mayors against partisan attack. But given the failing state of the Wall Street investigation, suggested Palmer's replacement, Harding campaign manager Harry Daugherty, this record might not be enough to save his job. As he prepared to assume office in early March, Daugherty urged Flynn to reassure the country that the Bureau was indeed hard at work on the Wall Street investigation, and to come forward with "anything in connection with the bomb plot inquiry which might properly be made public."[1]

This Flynn refused to do, at least initially. He did, however, provide Daugherty with a confidential summary of a recent Bureau breakthrough. In a memo composed on April 4, Flynn reported that the Bureau had cobbled together a description of the driver who had abandoned the wagon at Wall and Broad and, as a result, had its eye on a new suspect. Over the next few months, this revelation would lead the Bureau agents back to where they had begun the previous fall: to the May Day bombs and the

June 2 plot, to Galleani and Sacco and Vanzetti. And while it would not ultimately yield a definitive solution to the bombing, it would have at least one lasting effect on the nation's politics. By keeping the threat of anarchist terrorism alive on the front pages of the press in the weeks leading up to their trial, the Wall Street case would help to secure Sacco and Vanzetti's conviction for the Braintree murders.[2]

Drawn from the distant recollections of a single witness, the description of the wagon driver was basically a matter of educated guesswork. Still, Flynn was confident in its essentials. In January, as Palmer prepared to begin his Senate testimony, Flynn had issued a flyer to all East Coast police chiefs featuring the wagon driver's vital details. The man described in the flyer was "apparently Italian." He was also

> 28 or 30 years old; 5 feet 6 inches; medium build; broad shoulders; dark hair; dark complexion; small dark moustache, which at the date of the explosion represented about two week's [sic] growth. He wore a golf cap, pulled down over his forehead, and a khaki shirt turned in at the neck.

To help investigators picture such a suspect, the Bureau contracted with a commercial artist to develop a composite sketch. That drawing, in turn, had led them to one Vincenzo Leggio, a member of the Galleani group who, according to a "reliable source," looked like the wagon driver.[3]

It was no accident that the description of the wagon driver seemed to fit so neatly with Flynn's long-standing suspicions of the Galleanisti. Intentionally or not, the Bureau had designed the search for the driver to produce precisely this outcome. In his memo to Daugherty, Flynn explained that he had invited the "only witness we have who can identify the driver"—apparently the blacksmith, Gaetano DeGrazio—to view "several hundred photographs of anarchists." Flynn did not offer the option of choosing men who were not anarchists; thus DeGrazio chose two suspects who conformed to Flynn's profile. Combining the selected photos, the artist made the composite drawing, which subsequently became the driver's official portrait. "Many replies to the circular [bearing the sketch] have been received," Flynn assured Daugherty, "all of which have been or are under investigation."[4]

One of those replies, presumably, identified Vincenzo Leggio. A barber and an immigrant from Palermo, Leggio fit nearly every aspect of Flynn's initial profile. He had once run a barbershop on East 106th Street in Manhattan, "which vicinity," one report noted, "is a 'hot-bed' of Anarchists." More importantly, he was a Galleani disciple, one of dozens who had been slated for deportation after the Bureau's 1918 raid on the *Cronaca* offices. Flynn considered him a prime suspect in the June 2 plot. The Bureau was also "positive that he knows something about the Wall Street explosion."[5]

The trick was actually finding Leggio. Reports from the Military Intelligence Division suggest that one Vincenzo De Lecce had been deported with Galleani in June 1919. If De Lecce was Leggio, however, the Bureau did not seem to be aware of the fact. Throughout February and March, agents searched for clues about Leggio's—or, as some documents called him, "Liggio's"—whereabouts, both inside and outside the United States. According to one report, Leggio was likely visiting friends in New England or upstate New York. Another suggested that he was traveling through Canada to collect funds for the Sacco-Vanzetti defense. In early April, agent Joseph Barbera reported that Leggio had actually left for Italy in the spring of 1920 "in company with a Jewess, with whom he had been living as man and wife." There were rumors that he planned to return to the United States, so the Bureau kept watch on all "incoming Italian ships...for the probable arrival of subject." They also searched Felicani's correspondence for any clues to Leggio's activities. Included in the search were any mentions of "Lefi," "Legu," and even "Lufi," names that had come up in past letters and which agents suspected might refer to Leggio.[6]

As Flynn admitted to Daugherty, the Bureau's efforts had not resulted in definitive information by the time the Harding administration took office in early March. Within weeks of that memo, however, the name Ligi brought the Bureau its first major arrest in months. On April 19, just in time to reassure Daugherty of the investigation's progress, police in Scranton, Pennsylvania, swooped down on an Italian anarchist named Tito Ligi, detaining him on charges of draft evasion. The Bureau suspected he was actually Vincenzo Leggio, the wagon driver in the Wall Street blast.

TO THE NEWSPAPERS, Flynn admitted that he couldn't be sure of Ligi's guilt. "While I am not wholly satisfied we have hit on a solution," he told the *New York American* on April 21, "I intend to probe the matter to the bottom. That is all I can say at this time." To his fellow Bureau men he expressed no such doubts. Despite the difference in name, Flynn was positive that Ligi was actually Leggio and that he would lead the Bureau to his fellow *Cronaca* subversives.[7]

Coming after months of inaction, the Ligi arrest immediately revived public hopes of a solution to the explosion mystery. "Federal Agents Think Wall Street Plot Cleared," read an encouraging headline in the *New York Sun*. It also emerged as a referendum on the Bureau's future, a chance to demonstrate to the public that the charges of incompetence and overzealousness paraded before the Senate had been vastly overblown. A resolution to the Wall Street case could not rewrite the past or even revive a new deportation campaign. It might, however, undermine the idea that the raids had been much ado about nothing.[8]

Starved after months of official silence, the papers relished the dramatic, spine-tingling details of Ligi's capture. At the suspect's soon-to-be-abandoned home, they reported, arresting policemen found two loaded Colt revolvers, along with a stash of radical literature. As with Caruso, they also found letters that, read with an incriminating eye, seemed to confirm Ligi's radical affiliations. One talked about "special work" or a "special job" to be carried out in the near future. Another scorned the European battlefield: "Sure, go to war and kill your brothers and get decorated with medals." According to news reports, Ligi claimed that he had moved around so much that he couldn't remember where he was between September 8 and September 16, 1920. Confidential Bureau documents suggested his memory was even worse. According to one, Ligi could account for himself only through the beginning of September 1920. "[W]hen questioned as to his whereabouts in September," Flynn informed Daugherty, "he, Ligi, immediately became ill and refused to talk further."[9]

When reporters and agents were indeed able to track his whereabouts and activities, the evidence didn't look much better. According to articles printed on the day after his arrest, Ligi had been living above an abandoned coal mine used for years as an anarchist hideout. ("Discover an Underground Passage Leading to a Subterranean Chamber," read one headline.) The lair featured a trap door and a passageway leading to several well-appointed rooms that were perfect, the papers speculated, for making bombs. Even more damning was a supply of sash weights "identical with the fragments of iron scattered through New York's financial center" discovered in a back room of the Scranton restaurant where Ligi had once worked. Scranton district attorney J. J. McCourt, ignorant of the Bureau's suspicions about Ligi's double identity, speculated that these sash weights alone might be sufficient to seal his fate. "They form the best evidence we have so far accumulated against the young Italian anarchist," he declared on April 21.[10]

Added to all of this was a development unprecedented in the Wall Street case: a live witness identification. On April 20, the day after the Scranton arrest, Flynn summoned two men to the Bureau's New York office to look at a photo of Ligi and judge whether he might have been the wagon driver. Wary of scrutiny, Flynn initially refused to reveal their names to the press. But two telegrams sent in code from New York to Scranton on the afternoon of April 20, 1921, leave little doubt about the witnesses' identities. "Pevvob states fir dimple demagogue exorbitances warble," read the first. "Fulmination also states dimple demagogue of habitant resembles bespice near pitfall dubbed to obscurant," read the second, arriving an hour or so later. Translated from Bureau code, the telegrams reported that a former New York fire lieutenant named Thomas Smith and a second explosion witness named James Nally thought the photo of Ligi looked like one of the men they had seen hanging around the bomb wagon on September 16.[11]

Two other witnesses failed to identify Ligi. Nonetheless, the Bureau pushed ahead with the identification, escorting several men, including Smith and Nally, to the Scranton jail on April 23. The results were not unanimous; at least one of the witnesses could not pick Ligi out of the crowd. Smith, however, was certain that he had seen Ligi on Wall Street, accompanied by a mustachioed friend and a clean-shaven one. "He walked right up to Ligi without hesitation and identified him as the man he saw standing with a shorter man," Bureau agent P. J. Ahern, Flynn's local point man on the Ligi case, reported.[12]

This wealth of evidence—eyewitnesses, sash weights, lack of alibi— immediately put Ligi in a category of his own: after months of effort, he was the first suspect to be arrested for something more tangible than having the wrong friends or laughing in the wrong place at the wrong time. The one problem was that he did not actually resemble the man described in the Bureau's recent circulars or in the composite photo. The circular had featured an alert for an Italian five feet six inches tall, with a "small, dark moustache." Ligi was tall and clean-shaven. Moreover, he was an itinerant worker: a sometime miner, sometime waiter, sometime pool-room owner—not, in short, a skilled barber from New York, as Bureau reports had described Vincenzo Leggio.[13]

In Flynn's view, these discrepancies apparently did not outweigh the other evidence, including what Ligi himself revealed to Bureau agents. Under interrogation, Ligi admitted that he had been born in Italy, that he was a devoted anarchist, and that he was "connected" with Galleani.[14]

THE APPEARANCE of Walter Nelles at Ligi's April 22 hearing on draft evasion offered the first public sign that an organized movement to dismantle the Bureau's case might be afoot. As the ACLU attorney whose clients had figured so prominently in the Senate hearings, Nelles was well known in both radical and Bureau circles as a capable legal warrior. Questioned by the press, he said he had been sent by "a sort of informal group" of political radicals from New York and Paterson, New Jersey—later identified as the Italian defense league, where the undercover agent code-named P137 had been quietly observing operations for some time. "The organization interested in Liggio [sic] thought he would be without counsel and sent me here to appear for him," Nelles explained to the World. He quickly learned that Ligi had also retained his own lawyer, Scranton attorney John Memolo.[15]

Neither man was able to do Ligi much good that day. After a brief hearing, the judge ordered Ligi held for trial on $10,000 bail. Compared to the litanies of abuse that had befallen other Nelles clients, however, this was a minor setback, and Ligi's supporters had no intention of backing down. On the evening of April 22, hours after Ligi's court appearance, Nelles summoned reporters to his New York office to release a letter from the Italian anarchist Carlo Tresca, himself an early suspect in the bombing, accusing Flynn and the Justice Department of attempting to railroad yet another Italian anarchist.[16]

Since his close call in September, when the press had issued his name as a likely culprit, Tresca had tried to steer clear of the Wall Street case. He had not been able to avoid it entirely. In late September, the Bureau had raided his New York office, absconding with literature and subscription lists. Undercover informant N122 kept watch on Tresca's quarters as well, though he complained that not much seemed to be happening. Throughout it all, Tresca had managed to keep his name out of the papers as either a suspect or an accomplice in the Wall Street plot. That respite came to an end with the Ligi arrest. News reports mentioned Tresca, along with Emma Goldman, as one of Ligi's acquaintances—an assertion clearly intended, in that context, as evidence of Ligi's guilt.[17]

Tresca's letter, addressed to Flynn himself, acknowledged the acquaintance and defended Ligi as "a man of the utmost moral integrity, whom it would be absurd to suspect of any connection whatever with such an outrage as the Wall Street bomb explosion." "I have suspected since the first sensational announcement of Ligi's arrest," Tresca wrote, "that there was nothing more in this story than in the many similar stories published in recent years by the Department of Justice in order to stampede the country into a wave of anti-radical hysteria." Ligi also appeared to be attracting support from Italians who had never so much as flirted with anarchism but who saw in his case evidence of American society's anti-Italian bias. Around Scranton, many of Ligi's neighbors refused to speak with reporters or even policemen, going so far as to "threaten" strangers seen lurking overlong in town. Nelles, by contrast, found an insider's welcome when he began his search for evidence that would contradict the government's case. "In the Italian colony of Scranton," he told the *New York Call*, "there was no doubt of Ligi's innocence. They seemed grateful to have found someone who was interested only in uncovering the facts of the case and not in making out a substantiation of assumed guilt."[18]

In Mocanaqua, Pennsylvania, where Ligi had once lived during his mining days, former neighbors denied that they had ever heard him utter so much as a criticism of the government. In a further gesture of support, they organized several community balls to help pay for his defense. Reflecting the deep suspicion with which they viewed the guardians of law and order, the immigrant miners vowed to carry guns with which to defend the festivities. ("[I]f the Pennsylvania State Police interfere with their meeting," noted one Bureau report, "there will be blood shed.") According to the press, a few of Ligi's acquaintances even promised to make their violence offensive rather than defensive. In early May, the *Times*, among other papers, featured the sensational news that members of the local "Black Hand"—a catchall term that vaguely encompassed both anarchism and organized crime—were plotting to murder John Cartusciello, the Scranton police detective who had helped to bring about Ligi's arrest.[19]

At the Rand School in New York, Socialist supporters scheduled a May Day protest meeting "for Salsedo and Ligi." Nelles and Tresca, among others, were slated to speak. Tresca also attended fund-raising dinners hosted by Ligi's friend Dante Antonucci, himself the subject of intense Bureau scrutiny. By mid-June a Bureau informant was reporting the dinner successful enough "that a lot of money has been collected to defend Ligi." That money, in turn, helped to support a detailed investigation of the evidence against Ligi—a repeat of the *Call*'s early dissection of the explosion evidence itself.[20]

As Nelles pointed out, the state of Pennsylvania had no law against gun ownership; the revolvers found in Ligi's home might have been uncovered in any of thousands of homes throughout the state, and they could hardly all have been involved in the Wall Street conspiracy. As he noted, too, the police would be hard-pressed to find anyone living in the anthracite region of northeastern Pennsylvania who did *not* live above an abandoned mine. "[T]he city [of Scranton] is built upon a thin crust of earth, supported by pillars of anthracite as slim as the law will permit the mining companies to leave them," Nelles wrote in an article titled "The Lynching Press," reprinted in both the reform-minded *Nation* magazine and in the socialist *Appeal to Reason*.[21]

As for Ligi's house, supposedly perched so suspiciously near an underground anarchist hideout, Nelles characterized it as "an ordinary Italian workmen's dwelling, occupied by three families, with no subterranean mysteries beyond that of an ordinary cellar." Even the window weights that the district attorney had felt were so valuable were, according to Nelles, utterly unremarkable. Indeed, they were not window weights at all. As Nelles noted, and as the Scranton police superintendent confirmed, the pieces of metal found in the restaurant where Ligi had worked were, in the words of the *New York Times*, "irregular blocks of iron and steel such as are used by Italians in the city playing a game somewhat like quoits." Nelles also boasted that Ligi, contrary to the government's dark hints about his September activities, could produce an airtight alibi. "I have convincing evidence that Ligi was not in New York City at the time of the Wall Street explosion," Nelles announced on April 24. The following day, he offered to produce no fewer than twelve witnesses willing to say that Ligi was in Scranton on September 16.[22]

By contrast, the positive identifications by the Bureau's witnesses began to fall apart as Ligi's case proceeded through the courts. Thomas Smith, who had selected Ligi's photograph and then identified him at the jail, continued to evince great certainty about his choice. But none of the other men brought in to view the suspect could offer supporting affirmation, a fact Ligi viewed with some delight. "[T]his time," Ligi wrote to Tresca, describing a jailhouse visit from Bureau agent P. J. Ahern and two of the witnesses, "he did not have crooked face Smith with him but two other poor idiots who...pointed to another man because the other man's hair had grown so long it was like my hair in my photograph." This weakening of the Bureau's case was serious enough, within a week of Ligi's arrest, to inspire a new skepticism even in the nonradical press. "What the police have done," the *Times* complained on April 24, "...is to show that Luigio [*sic*] belongs to the class of anarchists any member of which might have carried out a carefully planned explosion in Wall Street. Therein he is only like all the other members of that class, and the demonstration that he did it still remains to be made."[23]

In response, Nelles, along with Ligi's counsel John Memolo, attempted to deny that the Bureau had even proven that much. In an echo of the arguments that his fellow civil libertarians had offered in front of the Senate the previous month, Nelles contended that not only was Ligi innocent of blowing up Wall Street, but he was not even a true revolutionary. "[N]othing was proved," Nelles told the *Call*, "except that Ligi thinks the government today is not so good as it was in the time of Washington and Jefferson." Two days later, Memolo backed up Nelles' claim with an account of a recent conversation with Ligi. "He said he had a lot of literature, a lot of cheap books and pamphlets about anarchy, but he didn't really know much about the subject," Memolo explained. "I don't think he knows what anarchy really is."[24]

On this point, however, Ligi's true political views were better represented by the Bureau's accusations than by his own defense. Though he had told Memolo in conversation that "I do not believe in Anarchy nor in Russian Bolshevism," Ligi soon had second thoughts about this approach. In a letter to Tresca from jail, Ligi wrote in Italian that he had never wanted to deny his anarchist affiliations, that he was willing to accept deportation and even prison as the anarchist's badge of honor. He blamed the apparent obfuscation of his radical commitments on "my poor lawyer of mediocre height, but with brains more mediocre," who "urged me to deny everything that I had said in the beginning, but to what advantage? For the fear of a few months of prison perhaps?"[25]

Whatever its moral valence, the denial of his radicalism won him no permanent reprieve. Just over a week after Ligi's arrest, Flynn conceded publicly that "[w]e have no evidence implicating Ligi with the Wall street bomb explosion." This did not, however, mean that Flynn thought such evidence would never be found. In early May, the Pittsburgh federal court sentenced Ligi to a year in prison for draft evasion, a charge designed to keep him available in case of future developments. Prosecutors never mentioned the Wall Street explosion, but the Bureau, still convinced that Ligi was Leggio, set out to gather further evidence upon which to base an indictment.[26]

IN OTHER CIRCUMSTANCES, this might have been the end of the matter. Ligi's arrest could easily have faded from the papers, like those of Brailovsky, Zelenko, and Caruso. Two things worked against this. The first was the fact the Bureau was already watching an Italian immigrant named Giuseppe De Filippis, whose case seemed to parallel Ligi's. The second was that the Ligi arrest happened to come little more than a month before the trial of Sacco and Vanzetti.

Like Ligi, Giuseppe De Filippis may have come under suspicion due to coincidence: he happened to share a last name with one Salvatore De Filippis, a Galleani admirer who had joined Sacco, Vanzetti, and the others in Monterrey during the war. Certainly there was little in Giuseppe's background as a petty street fighter and manual laborer to suggest that he possessed either the motive or the skills to engineer the Wall Street plot. In 1913, Bayonne police had arrested him for fighting a man named Angelo Romano in City Park; neighbors had heard the gunshots, and by the time the police arrived Romano had slashed De Filippis across the left side of the face. A year later, De Filippis had spent three months in a Brooklyn jail for another, unrelated assault. The police had snapped him up again in 1917 for violating his parole. And in the summer of 1920, they had chastised though not jailed him after his truck sideswiped a child playing in the street.[27]

Nothing in his experience, however, prepared him for the news that he had killed thirty-eight people in a terrorist attack on Wall Street. When the Bayonne police came for him on May 18, De Filippis thought they were still upset about the child and the truck. The officers did not reveal their true purpose right away, saying only that De Filippis might be connected to "a matter in which the Government was interested."[28]

As in both Ligi's and Caruso's cases, the pretext for the arrest initially had no connection to the Wall Street explosion. Though the Bureau had asked for the arrest, it was the Bayonne police who seized De Filippis for violating an unspecified "city ordinance." Upon being transported to the Bayonne jail, De Filippis, like Ligi, was kept in "strict seclusion." Thomas Smith, once again, was the key eyewitness. "He made a positive identification of the subject," Scully reported, "claiming that de Fillipis [sic] was the man he had seen in conversation with TITO LIGI near the horse and wagon." Based upon Smith's word as well as identifications by two other witnesses, the Bureau had assigned undercover men to trace De Filippis for nearly a month before arresting him, just as they had with Ligi.[29]

There were, however, several important factors that set De Filippis' arrest apart from earlier ones, even from Ligi's. With at least three positive identifications, the case was somewhat stronger than the one against Ligi. It was strong enough, at any rate, for the Bureau to take a step unprecedented in its seven months of investigation. Seeking to defy newspaper complaints that "nothing seems to have been accomplished," the Bureau took its case to the local U.S. attorney, who promptly accepted jurisdiction and charged De Filippis with "exploding a bomb in the street and immediately in front of the United States Assay Office."[30]

As the *New York Herald* pointed out, De Filippis was an odd candidate to become the first man brought up on federal charges. "One of the peculiar facts in the case," the *Herald* wrote on May 20, "is that it is admitted that so far no evidence has been gathered by either the Bayonne police or by the Department of Justice which proves the prisoner was ever connected in any way with Italian anarchist groups, one of which, Chief William J. Flynn believes, was behind the outrage."[31]

De Filippis was sobbing and shaking when he arrived in court on May 20. According to newspaper accounts, he had neither slept nor eaten the night before due to excessive "moaning and crying." His wife, "a pretty little Italian woman of 20," according to the *Call,* was weeping in a chair near the courtroom's rear. Reporters heard De Filippis muttering to himself in Italian, and his lawyer volunteered to translate. "I know nothing of it," the lawyer said, paraphrasing De Filippis. "I never heard of the explosion. I don't know where Wall Street is." He would repeat this claim for the next several weeks, insisting that he had been selling grapes on September 16. When the judge ordered him returned to jail, De Filippis resumed trembling. "Apparently," the *Evening Post* reported drily, "he was unnerved."[32]

He was no more composed when he arrived in New York a few weeks later to face federal indictment for damaging a government building. He appeared at the Cortlandt Street ferry slip on May 28 with a U.S. marshal cuffed to his right wrist. As they strolled north to the Tombs jail, he complained once again that "I never seen Wall Street." "Well, take a look," his captor replied. "There it is, right across from the church. Now you can't say you never saw it."[33]

Three days later, on May 31, the papers reported that, due to an utter lack of evidence, the federal court had released De Filippis on $5,000 bail, though they held out the possibility of arraignment at a future date. That same day, in what proved to be the last major episode in Flynn's long hunt for the Galleanisti, Nicola Sacco and Bartolomeo Vanzetti went on trial in Massachusetts.[34]

VANZETTI HIMSELF LATER CLAIMED that the relentless and sensational press coverage of the Ligi and De Filippis arrests had damaged his chances in court. "It is evident that under this guise the federal police played a double game," he wrote in early 1922. "If they didn't manage to prove guilty some innocent [man], they managed beautifully, aided by the prostitute press, to stimulate more and more the political and racial hatred in the already so abnormal and excited mentality of the broad public, of which the future jury of our trial had to be composed."[35]

This ascribed perhaps too much intent to the Bureau's actions; Flynn's interest in the Sacco-Vanzetti case was always more peripheral than direct. But there can be no question that the image of the Italian anarchist bomb thrower, so recently revived by the Wall Street inquiry, helped to shape the atmosphere in which the Sacco-Vanzetti trial took place. Coming just weeks before the trial began, the Ligi and De Filippis arrests thrust back into public consciousness all of the old stereotypes of anarchism: guns, draft dodging, subterranean chambers. When the jurors entered the courtroom in late May, they found these threats confirmed by the armed guards and policemen standing watch in the courtroom. In the view of defense attorney William Thompson, who took over the case in 1924, this scene, combined with evidence about Sacco and Vanzetti's anarchist backgrounds, helped to prejudice the jurors against his clients. "These, they must have thought, are the men the police and the Federal Government have been after," he explained in a motion for appeal, "these are men considered capable of resorting to physical violence, otherwise a battalion of police would not be here to protect us."[36]

The trial itself proved to be a mammoth undertaking: six and a half weeks, 2,266 pages of transcript, 167 witnesses. Sacco and Vanzetti sat in a cage in the middle of the room, safely under watch, as teams of attorneys picked their way through evidence ranging from ballistics reports to discussions of anarchist philosophy. The courtroom itself had been secretly outfitted against the possibility of a bomb attack: what appeared to be wooden shutters on the windows were actually cast iron. The authorities had also installed sliding steel doors in the event that they needed to seal off the courtroom from the rest of the building. In the audience were several of the defense committee members the Bureau had been watching for the last six months, including Aldino Felicani.[37]

Flynn had cut off surveillance of Felicani's mail just before the trial; the last report surveyed June 1–6, the week that jury selection began. In its stead, he sent Joseph Barbera, one of his few Italian-speaking agents and the man who had worked the Ligi case, to observe the proceedings undercover. It was a risky move. Throughout the spring, the defense committee had begun to document federal involvement in the Sacco-Vanzetti case, publicizing, among other transgressions, Domenico Carbone's spying at the Dedham jail. The committee had also accused Flynn of attempting to frame Sacco and Vanzetti in retaliation for his failures in the June 2 and Wall Street inquiries. Committee member Art Shields, who had composed a report for the Workers Defense Union attacking Flynn's Wall Street evidence, suggested that the Bureau wanted to do to Sacco and Vanzetti what they had done to Andrea Salsedo. *Are They Doomed?* was the title of Shields' pamphlet; the cover depicted a tiny Salsedo tumbling from the fourteenth floor of the Park Row office.[38]

The Bureau did not, in fact, intend to meddle much in Sacco and Vanzetti's criminal case. Barbera had been sent, according to Bureau documents, strictly "for the purpose of observing any radical activities or demonstrations" that might occur. Barbera thought it wise nonetheless to keep his presence in Dedham quiet. He attended the trial as an ordinary Italian workingman.[39]

Barbera's assignment reflected the broader federal role in the Sacco-Vanzetti case. Like the Bureau as a whole, he was ever present, ever watchful, but rarely seen. His chief task was simply to observe who attended the trial, in the hope that he might spot someone who resembled a suspect in the June 2 or Wall Street conspiracies. It did not take long for him to conclude that his subjects were not quite so reckless. According to Barbera, anarchists in and around Massachusetts seemed to be holding back from any sort of demonstration—whether peaceful or violent—for fear of alienating the jury and encouraging a guilty verdict. They even seemed not to be attending the trial. Outside of Felicani and a few others, Barbera noted, the bulk of the supporters appeared to be "female parlor radicals."[40]

Barbera did manage to chat with Felicani and take his photo, an act that Felicani only "reluctantly agreed to." When not attending the trial, Barbera wandered Boston's Italian quarter, gathering opinions about Sacco and Vanzetti. (He learned that most Italians thought the two men were innocent.) He also loitered around the entrance to the Dedham jail, attempting to identify Sacco and Vanzetti's visitors. On one occasion, anonymous men bringing supplies to Sacco and Vanzetti stopped to talk long enough to tell Barbera, as he later phrased it in a Bureau report, that "this alleged frame up was instigated by the U.S. Government in reprisal for the strong interest subjects manifest in the dead anarchist, ANDREA SALSEDO."[41]

Despite Barbera's subterfuge, the Defense Committee began to suspect his government affiliation. Even worse, Barbera reported on June 10, defense counsel was threatening to expose the presence of Justice Department men in the courthouse "and make capital out of the same." His greatest obstacles, however, came from the very people who would have been most sympathetic had they known his true aims. The local police, noting a strange Italian laborer in their midst, encouraged him in no uncertain terms to leave town.[42]

Rather than have Barbera expose the Bureau's presence at a trial, Flynn recalled him to New York a few days later and replaced him with Dante DiLillo, another Italian-speaking agent, who quietly watched the trial as it reached its conclusion. Defense attorney Fred Moore did his best to present Sacco and Vanzetti as victims of government hostility and class persecution. As at Haywood's wartime trial, however, this claim fell on deaf ears. On July 14, as the Defense Committee had long predicted but also feared, the jury returned a guilty verdict, with the promise of a sentence of death.[43]

The committee responded to the decision with a horrified we-told-you-so, framing the outcome as proof that prejudice against Italians, and especially against anarchists, had sealed the defendants' fate well before the opening arguments. For sympathizers, this narrative would define the case for years to come. In his 1926 book, for instance, Felix Frankfurter blamed "the deepest prejudices of a Norfolk County jury, picked for its respectability and sitting in judgment upon two men of alien blood and abhorrent philosophy." Indeed, for Sacco and Vanzetti, the years of greatest fame and controversy lay ahead. For the Bureau, by contrast, the Sacco-Vanzetti connection proved to be yet another bust. Though agents continued to search for evidence implicating Ligi and De Filippis, the summer of 1921 came to a close without a solution to the Wall Street explosion.[44]

EXACTLY WHY these two cases had such different outcomes—why the state of Massachusetts successfully prosecuted two Italian anarchists while the Bureau failed so miserably in the Wall Street case—is difficult to say. The most obvious answer is that Ligi was innocent (as was De Filippis), while Sacco and Vanzetti were guilty. This may well have been true, but as decades of subsequent controversy would show, the evidence in the Sacco-Vanzetti case was hardly foolproof. Furthermore, many Bureau agents never accepted that Ligi and De Filippis were themselves actually innocent. In Pennsylvania, agent Ahern was so certain of their guilt that he spent the summer seeking out a third member of the conspiracy, "the short man who was with Ligi and De Fileppes [sic] at Wall and William Streets." Others thought it a futile effort "I think that LIGI was taken into custody because of the resemblence [sic] in the name of LIGI and LEGGIO," one agent later noted.[45]

A more persuasive explanation for the disparities in the cases may be found in the actions of the local police—specifically in whether they managed to cooperate with the federal authorities. Though the Bureau was not directly involved in the Sacco-Vanzetti prosecution, it nonetheless supported and affirmed the actions of local officials. In Ligi's case, by contrast, as in the entire Wall Street explosion investigation, the local police and the Bureau were at least as suspicious of each other as they were of the anarchists they were chasing. The Bureau had failed to alert the New York police about the plans to arrest Ligi and De Filippis. In retaliation, the police had publicly denounced the Bureau's evidence and methods, scorning witness Thomas Smith, for instance, as a notorious dissembler.[46]

Ligi himself credited his relative freedom to the actions of the Committee for Political Victims, along with other "prompt measures taken in my behalf" by fellow radicals—an assessment with which Tresca tended to agree. The mere fact of a defense committee, like the existence of prejudice, hardly set Ligi apart from Sacco and Vanzetti. Still, evidence suggests that the rush of attention may indeed have prevented the Bureau from moving forward too hastily. One lesson that the Bureau had learned in its surveillance of the Sacco-Vanzetti committee was that radical defendants could easily become celebrated victims. "There has been a noticeable effort upon the part of various so-called defense societies to propagate and carry on agitation in behalf of ultraradicals in the United States," the Justice Department's annual report noted in 1921. "Inconspicuous individuals in the ultraradical movement apprehended locally are martyred and propaganda started in their behalf, not only within the United States but throughout the entire world." At a moment of fierce attack and opprobrium from civil libertarians, Flynn may have decided that, lacking absolute proof of Ligi and De Filippis' guilt, it was simply too dangerous to risk turning them into martyrs.[47]

Certainly Flynn did not give up on the arrests because he was having doubts about his original theory of the Wall Street case. In late August, a month after Sacco and Vanzetti's conviction, a headline in the New York *Daily News* suddenly announced, "Wall Street Bomb Outrage Work of Boston Anarchists." The article that followed read like a Bureau press release: "Of course, this was not officially announced, but the DAILY NEWS is in a position to state that the most experienced Federal operatives and members of the police bomb squad worked almost entirely on the theory that members of the Galleani group set the gigantic infernal machine in Wall street." After the explosion, the article revealed, the Galleani anarchists had scattered; now they were regrouping under the auspices of the "terrorist society" known as the Sacco-Vanzetti Defense Committee.[48]

The paper identified the author of these charges only as "Investigator," but it didn't take much to guess that Flynn was the source. Indeed, a second article—this one printed in the *Boston Herald*—presented nearly identical claims six months later. "It was the Galleani Reds who conceived and carried out the Wall Street outrage," the article insisted. "Both Sacco and Vanzetti, the New England radicals, studied in the Galleani school." This time, the newspapers directly identified the author of the charges. "My Ten Biggest Man Hunts," read the headline, "Told by Chief W. J. Flynn."[49]

To members of the Defense Committee, immersed in trying to win a new trial for Sacco and Vanzetti, the articles seemed to be the final proof that Flynn had hoped to use the Wall Street case to blacken the anarchists' image. "These statements made by Federal officials just now tend to have the effective of prejudicing the public against them," one committee member complained after the "Investigator" series. Another author, responding to the later articles, denounced Flynn's work as a screed "inspired uniquely by the desire to harm us and to insult our principles." Like Flynn, this writer used a pseudonym of sorts, calling himself "Sacco-Vanzetti." But his identity, too, was obvious. The essay, handwritten in Italian, sent from a Massachusetts jail, was written by Bartolomeo Vanzetti.[50]

Vanzetti said that his purpose in responding to Flynn was not to prove his own innocence in the Wall Street blast, or even the innocence of his comrades. Rather, he wanted to drive home to his supporters the dangers of an overweening federal police. "[I]f our words achieved their end, that is, of demonstrating to the people in general, and to the comrades in particular, who their and our enemies are and what they are like, then neither you in reading us, nor we in writing, will have wasted time and effort," he concluded. It was a pointed warning, a summary of years spent *"faccia a faccia"* with his foes at the Bureau. By the time Vanzetti composed his essay, however, the tit-for-tat drama that had begun during the war was already drawing to a close. Flynn's articles were the nearest the Bureau would come to proving a link between the Galleanisti and the Wall Street explosion.[51]

# PART V

....

# THE RUSSIAN CONNECTION

# 13

· · · ·

## THE "GREAT DETECTIVE"
## RETURNS

FLYNN WAS VACATIONING in Saratoga on August 18, 1921, when a terse
little telegram from Attorney General Daugherty arrived on his New York
desk. In a few unceremonious phrases, the telegram informed him that the
U.S. government no longer required his services as director of the Bureau
of Investigation. Flynn refused all public comment; his dismay, however,
was already an open secret. Throughout the spring, as he struggled to
bring the Wall Street case to a close, Flynn had solicited letters from
Republican higher-ups testifying to his good character, investigative zeal,
and enormous popularity in New York. Unfortunately for him, Daugherty was best known for his political loyalty—or, in less elegant terms,
for doling out jobs to his friends. Before Flynn had time to respond to the
August 18 telegram, Daugherty announced that the new Bureau chief
would be Flynn's longtime competitor—and, not incidentally, Daugherty's good friend from Ohio politics—the "Great Detective," William
J. Burns.[1]

Since his initial flurry of publicity on September 16, Burns had maintained a low profile in the Wall Street case—so low, in fact, that he had
ceased to be in the public's consciousness. In the year since the explosion,
only two events of note had connected him with the investigation. The

first was his declaration in late September that communists allied with Lenin's Third International, not Italian anarchists, were responsible for the explosion. The second was his announcement two months later that the Burns agency would offer a $50,000 reward for any "facts that would materially aid" the identification of specific suspects. Many newspapers took this large sum as confirmation that Burns was working at the behest of "a group of financiers," presumably the Morgan bank, but Burns himself remained mum on the subject. The reward flyer suggested that evidentiary tips would be handled with "strict confidence."[2]

For a "brass band" detective, this relative lack of bombast seemed out of character, a reversal of the conventional wisdom that presented Burns as the showman, Flynn as the more taciturn and modest one. But as on earlier occasions their apparent differences in temperament and approach masked a few fundamental similarities. Like Flynn, Burns had advertised an early confidence in his ability to solve the bomb plot mystery. And despite his own run of setbacks and frustrations, nothing that had happened in the year since had convinced him of anything different. Even as Flynn's hunt for the Galleanisti collapsed in full public view, Burns had been quietly but doggedly pursuing his own investigation.

In announcing Burns' selection, Daugherty refrained from directing any overt insults at Flynn. Despite this outward diplomacy, his remarks seemed designed to denigrate Flynn's work. In a widely reprinted statement, Daugherty praised Burns as "an intelligent and courageous man and, at this time especially, is considered to be as high-class a man as could be secured to assume the important duties assigned him," implying that Flynn lacked such qualities. He described Burns' wish to "establish the most cordial relations with police officials and law enforcement officers throughout the entire country, and, in fact, throughout the entire world," a jab at Flynn's now notorious rivalry with the New York police. And he called for a thorough "housecleaning," citing the arrests of Ligi and De Filippis as the sort of sloppy police work that would from now on be anathema.[3]

With a chance to simultaneously please his new boss and embarrass his ancient rival, Burns was only too happy to reinforce this impression. "Strict orders are to be issued to all the branches of the bureau against arrests not justified by sufficient evidence," he promised in a lengthy interview with the *New York Sun*. "It will be the policy of the new administration to always, if possible, conduct an intelligent investigation to obtain proper evidence before a suspect is placed in jail. In this way we hope to eliminate many arrests which may subsequently prove to have been unjustified. We are dealing with human beings, and the Government agents should be ordered not to overstep themselves." He also planned to turn the Wall Street investigation in a new direction—not toward Italy, but toward Russia.[4]

FROM A PURELY IDEOLOGICAL STANDPOINT, Burns' suspicions of communist guilt did not fit neatly with the known facts of the Wall Street case. In Galleani and his disciples Flynn had identified a group of militants who openly applauded individual acts of assassination and terror. The communist stance on the subject of terrorism was far more nuanced and critical. Though self-proclaimed "terrorists" had used bombings and assassinations to great effect in the failed Russian uprising of 1905–6, in the years between that revolution and the Bolshevik success of 1917 such tactics had fallen into disrepute among many of the country's exiled socialist leaders. Leon Trotsky condemned individual acts of violence as little more than invitations for state repression. "The anarchist prophets of 'the propaganda of the deed' can argue all they want about the elevating and stimulating influence of terrorist acts on the masses," he declared in 1911. "Theoretical considerations and political experience prove otherwise." Lenin largely agreed, seeing individual terrorism as an ineffective substitute for coordinated mass action.[5]

Both Lenin and Trotsky remained fervent believers in violent rebellion, even assassination, as a catalyst to bring about the inevitable rise of the socialist state. But they distinguished between violence coordinated and carried out by an organized revolutionary vanguard and the sort of ad hoc assassinations and bombings that were the essence of propaganda by deed. After 1917, they also discovered a burgeoning tolerance for state terrorism imposed from above—the sort of revolutionary terror employed by the French Jacobins—arguing that repressive practices employed by a revolutionary socialist government were far different from those used by capitalists to crush challenges to their authority. "The terror of Tsarism was directed against the proletariat," Trotsky wrote in his 1920 work *Terrorism and Communism.* "Our Extraordinary Commissions shoot landlords, capitalists, and generals who are striving to restore the capitalist order. Do you grasp this...distinction? Yes? For us communists it is quite sufficient."[6]

In reality, the question of revolutionary violence and terror, by either those in power or those far from it, remained a source of tremendous contention within communist circles. This was true even within the United States, where the challenge of imposing a terror-induced socialist dictatorship was less pressing than the question of whether or not a tiny, ostracized group of militants had the obligation to support armed insurrection despite certain defeat. At their founding in September 1919, both the Communist and Communist Labor parties had openly applauded the prospect of a violent, revolutionary uprising through "mass action," a phrase that encompassed everything from the general strike to the armed overthrow of the state. After the Palmer Raids decimated their ranks four months later, at least a few members began to have second thoughts. In February 1920, just a month after the second round of Palmer Raids, the Central Executive Committee of the Communist Party (still an active rival to the even smaller Communist Labor Party) had engaged in a bitter dispute over whether to call for a violent rebellion by the nation's striking rail workers. While most committee members agreed, in the words of communist leader Charles Ruthenberg, that "the party must be ready to put into its program the definite statement that mass action culminates in open insurrection and armed conflict with the capitalist state," they split over the tactical desirability of calling for such rebellion in the here and now.[7]

Wracked by internal divisions, driven underground by the threat of deportation, the communist leadership never entirely resolved their differences on the question of armed revolt. They found far more common ground when it came to propaganda by deed. Like their Socialist Party rivals (and like Trotsky himself), most American communists viewed individual terrorism as an absurd and self-defeating venture—cathartic, perhaps, but fundamentally unsound. This was the accepted stance on the Wall Street explosion. Like the socialists of the *Call*, the few communists who had ventured a public opinion in the fall of 1920 agreed that the explosion was most likely the result of a dynamite accident or Bureau plot. For good measure, though, the United Communist Party (UCP), formed in the summer of 1920 as an uneasy alliance of the Communist and Communist Labor factions, also saw fit to issue a formal denial. "The Communists do not believe, and have never propagated, that the emancipation of the workers can be achieved by acts of individual terrorism, or by dynamiting capitalists or government officials," read the UCP's October 1920 statement. "No use to explain any further."[8]

As a man who had weathered months of similar denials by the McNamaras and their allies in 1910 and 1911, Burns put little stock in such ideological distinctions. In the Wall Street case, moreover, he believed that he had an ace in the hole. In the summer of 1920, as the UCP was being created, an informer named William Linde had approached Burns with the news that the communists were planning "something big" against the capitalist system, possibly in the next few months. Such warnings were fairly routine in the fraught environment of 1920; though he issued a routine warning to his banking clients, Burns paid little attention at the time. When the explosion erupted on September 16, however, Burns immediately thought back to what Linde had said. After assuring the press that "there is not the slightest doubt that it was a bomb," he sent agents to track the informer down and persuade him to go undercover within communist ranks.[9]

This was not a simple task. In the wake of the Palmer Raids, the communist movement had effectively gone to ground, operating in a quasi-legal universe of pseudonyms and secret codes. Gatherings were closely monitored for interlopers and government agents. "DON'T let any spies follow you to appointments or meetings," read item number 7 of the "Rules for Underground Party Work." The United Communist Party had been formed under these conditions, with thirty-two delegates meeting secretly in the woods near Bridgman, Michigan, in late May 1920 to lay the improbable groundwork for a proletarian dictatorship in America. The repressive atmosphere gave the communist underground a frisson of intrigue, an emotional connection to the clandestine operations that had preceded the Bolsheviks' coup. It did not, however, make a welcoming environment for William Linde.[10]

Born Wolfe Lindenfeld in Polish Russia, Linde had apparently begun his career as a Russian government spy, fleeing to the United States after his exposure in the years after the 1905 revolution. Since then, he had established himself as a minor fixture in New York's socialist and labor scenes, a cheerful busybody known to frequent local strikes and radical cafés. In 1918, for instance, he had attended the AFL's annual meeting in Atlantic City, drumming up an acquaintance with the radical journalist John Reed, recently returned from Russia and soon to complete his landmark book, *Ten Days That Shook the World*. The following year, Linde showed up at the Chicago convention where the two communist parties made their official split with the Socialists. Throughout it all, he had double-timed as an informant for both government and private agencies, providing tips and serving as the kind of stool pigeon that Bill Haywood had once denounced as the "lowest, meanest, most contemptible thing that either creeps or crawls."[11]

Burns viewed Linde, like most undercover operatives, with a certain skepticism. "We had to be careful of him and check up all the information he gave us," Burns later explained. Given the value of Linde's initial tip in the Wall Street case, however, he opted for benefit of the doubt. "We took him with us...because he convinced me and my two sons, Sherman and Raymond, that he was in a position to obtain valuable information about what was going on in the revolutionary movement," Burns recalled. "He was intelligent, well-educated, well-dressed, spoke several languages, and was a good-looking fellow with a good address."[12]

For the first few months after the explosion, Linde more than lived up to these expectations, fleshing out a detailed bombing conspiracy. According to Linde's reports, the Wall Street plot had been hatched during a July 1920 meeting of the United Communist Party's "technical committee," a subgroup reportedly devoted to agitation and violence. Some two months later, on September 8, the committee met once more on Madison Avenue in Chicago, where several prominent communists had recently been convicted under the state's sedition law. At the September meeting, according to Linde, they were joined by two couriers from the Third International, Bernard Wolf and a mysterious Russian chemist, who provided the money for the plot. There they also selected the lower-level operatives who would carry the plan into action: a man named Stevens, chairman of the technical committee, widely known as someone who "has no scruples over anything in the world, no conscience and no feeling," who helped to create the bomb; Steve Barber, a cobbler from Trenton and "technical committee" member who supposedly painted and repaired the wagon; and a mysterious Bohemian newspaper editor named Shetnuitis, Celunitius, Sheideneitus, or some variation thereof, allegedly the wagon driver who left the bomb at Wall and Broad.

Linde admitted he had little idea where they were or even whether they were using their real names. There was one important figure, however, who was readily available. According to Linde's theory, the money for the bombing had been funneled from the coffers of the Soviet Bureau, a semiofficial Russian diplomatic embassy with offices at 110 West Fortieth Street. In January 1921, as Flynn was opening his investigation of the Sacco-Vanzetti Defense Committee, Burns sent Linde to spy on the would-be ambassador at the Soviet Bureau's helm, Ludwig Christian Alexander Karl Martens.[13]

IF FELICANI SERVED as the de facto hub for the scattered Galleanisti, by 1920 Martens had come to play a similar role for the underground communists. Born in Russia to German parents, Martens had come of age as a socialist sympathizer, joining Lenin's League for the Liberation of the Working Class in 1895 before being thrown in jail the following year. After more than a decade of exile in Germany and England, he traveled to New York in 1916, quickly throwing himself into work on Trotsky's New York–based newspaper, *Novy Mir.* In 1919, as the armistice opened up new trading opportunities around the world, he received a request from Lenin to establish a Soviet diplomatic and commercial bureau in New York. Martens did as instructed, opening an office in the World Tower Building and hiring several prominent New York socialists, including Morris Hillquit, to join in its administration. With U.S. troops still stationed in Russia, the Wilson administration rebuffed Martens' overtures. When the May Day and June 2 bombings erupted a few months later, the New York state government joined the effort to deny Martens public legitimacy. On June 12, the state-sponsored Lusk Committee raided the Soviet Bureau's office, seizing thousands of pages of financial and propaganda material and hauling Martens to city hall for a four-hour public grilling. By early 1920, the Justice Department was calling for Martens' deportation.

At the center of this drama was the allegation that Martens was funneling money from Moscow to finance an American communist revolution, a charge that his lawyer Charles Recht, who later appeared as a witness against Palmer in the Senate hearings, denounced as "unnecessary and mainly for the purpose of spectacularism." Even the alleged means of delivery—uncut diamonds smuggled overseas in mysterious envelopes, secret couriers tramping through Finland—seemed to come straight from detective lore. In testimony before the Lusk Committee and then the Senate Judiciary Committee, Martens admitted receiving funds from Moscow but denied that they were being used to stir up discontent. Unsurprisingly, this did little to reassure his critics, who continued to call for his jailing and deportation. Internal Russian documents would later confirm their suspicions. Between July 1919 and January 1920, even as Martens was being grilled by the Lusk Committee and the Senate, Lenin managed to smuggle almost three million rubles to communist activists in the United States, much of it in the form of gold, jewels, and silver, and at least some of it through Martens' contacts.[14]

Burns, operating outside official circles, suspected Martens of all this and more. As early as January 1921, he had approached the Morgan bank with his conviction that Martens and his circle of contacts in the United Communist Party were to blame for the September attack. "Mr. Elliot Bacon of J. P. Morgan & Company believes that Ludwig C. A. Martens must have furnished the considerable sum of money necessary to pay for such an outrage," a Military Intelligence Division report noted in early 1921. "J. P. Morgan & Company have been employing the Burns Detective Agency."[15]

Proving this connection was William Linde's goal. In January 1921, with Burns' financial backing, Linde opened up his own office on the twelfth floor of the World Tower Building, just a few doors away from Martens' Soviet Bureau. According to Linde's business card, his quarters housed the International Slavic Press Bureau, where Linde served as chief news gatherer and editor. Unofficially, Linde spent most of his time chatting with his neighbors and trying to gather information about the bomb plot suspects. According to a Bureau agent who interviewed Burns in June 1921, Linde became fast friends with other labor sympathizers in the building (one man later lamented that he had given Linde a book listing every union member in the United States). Then, on January 22, the investigation hit a major glitch. Rather than wait around for the U.S. government to execute a deportation order against him, Martens abruptly gathered up his family and belongings and set sail for Russia in what the press dubbed "the second Soviet Ark."[16]

Loath to let his top contact escape quite so easily, Burns determined to follow Martens' trail overseas. In February 1921, as Palmer and Hoover squirmed before the Senate to justify their treatment of communists, Burns gave Linde nearly $3,000 and sent him off to find the Wall Street bomb plotters in Russia.[17]

FROM BURNS' PERSPECTIVE, what made Russia so alluring as a site for investigation was not only Martens himself but also the growing community of American refugees and exiles swirling around the new Bolshevik government. By early 1921, Moscow was home to hundreds of former

U.S. dissidents: anarchists, communists, and Wobblies who, by choice or deportation order, had decided to throw in their lot with the Soviet state. Among them were some of the very men and women who had long been at the center of American revolutionary politics and, more importantly, at the center of controversies over dynamite and propaganda by deed, including Emma Goldman and Alexander Berkman.

Goldman and Berkman had arrived the previous January after a miserable journey aboard the *Buford* (Berkman threatened to organize a mutiny) and an equally unpleasant armed escort through Finland's painful winter chill. Once there, they were amazed at the number of U.S. friends who turned up on Russian soil: John Reed, whose account of the revolution had thrilled Goldman in prison (Reed died of typhus in September 1920 and received a state burial in the Kremlin); Bill Shatoff, a former anarchist compatriot, now a Bolshevik official, who pelted them with questions about the Mooney case and the deportation raids; Robert Minor, who had helped to lead the Mooney defense as well as the last-ditch efforts to save Goldman and Berkman from deportation; and steel strike leader William Z. Foster, a recent convert to Leninist communism.[18]

By the spring of 1921, they had been joined as well by Bill Haywood, whose final months in the United States had offered a study in defeat and decline. After his near arrest in the Wall Street explosion and the upholding of his wartime sentence, Haywood had begun to consider the possibility that he might not bounce back from this latest round of government clashes. By early 1921, when Harding came into office without so much as whispering of a pardon, he gave his cause up for lost. Sick with diabetes, terrified of returning to prison, he accepted a year-old invitation from the Bolshevik government to join Lenin in Moscow as a labor advisor. In late March, he smuggled himself out of the United States via Hoboken, New Jersey, using a false Russian passport. "Good-by, you've had your back turned on me too long," he muttered as his ship passed the Statue of Liberty. "I am now going to the land of freedom."[19]

That was not what he found. When they arrived a year earlier, Goldman and Berkman had been shocked by the poverty and desperation of the supposedly liberated Russian people. Still, they had attempted to make the best of things, meeting with Lenin at the Kremlin ("Great stuff! Clear-cut analysis of the capitalist system, splendid propaganda!" Lenin cheered) and signing on for various semiofficial duties, including a whirlwind tour of the countryside seeking material for an anticipated Petrograd

Museum of the Revolution. By the time Haywood arrived, they had grown thoroughly disenchanted. As they journeyed through the country, Goldman and Berkman encountered dozens of tales of Bolshevik atrocities, including the jailing and assassinations of anarchist dissidents. Any remaining doubt about the tales' veracity was removed in March 1921 when sailors in the port town of Kronstadt rebelled in support of striking Petrograd workers. The Bolshevik government struck back with a force that made the coalfields of Colorado seem like a pacifist fantasy. After a ten-day battle, six hundred Kronstadt rebels lay dead, with another one thousand wounded and more than two thousand taken prisoner, casualties of the revolutionary government they had helped to put in power less than four years earlier.[20]

For Goldman and Berkman, this was the beginning of the end of the Russian dream; after Kronstadt, they began to make plans to leave for yet another country of exile. For Haywood, the process of disengagement was somewhat slower in the making. Like Goldman and Berkman, he met with Lenin in private session and won the Russian leader's effusive praise. A few months later, the two men signed a contract to establish an American workers' colony in the Kuznets region of Siberia, where Haywood hoped to rehabilitate aging steel plants and mines as working models of syndicalism in action. The so-called Kuzbas colony eventually ended in failure, a casualty of harsh winters, primitive conditions, and poor management. Along the way, though, Haywood's activities once again piqued the attention of the U.S. authorities. Based on information provided by Linde and other spies squirreled away in Russia, Kuzbas would soon earn its own chapter in Burns' Wall Street investigation.[21]

Linde later said that he had met Haywood in Moscow. (Goldman was apparently harder to find, as she was traveling around the country.) He also claimed to have spent a full six weeks meeting with high officials of the Third International, including Lenin and Trotsky, grilling them on the details of the Wall Street explosion. Linde had the good fortune to be circulating abroad at a moment when dozens of prominent radicals were on the move, attending conferences in Brussels, Amsterdam, and Moscow. Among the American exiles he happened to run across while making his way from Paris to Russia, he reported, were Ludwig Martens, who expressed interest in returning to America to foment revolution, and the mysterious Barber, the cobbler who supposedly prepped the bomb wagon.[22]

Burns did not have this information at hand when he assumed the leadership of the Bureau in August 1921; after leaving New York, Linde all but ceased communication. Despite this puzzling silence, Burns had reason to believe that his informer was on the up-and-up. In April, just after Flynn's arrest of Ligi, the Bureau and the New York bomb squad had orchestrated a raid on prominent members of the Communist Party's New York branch, absconding with membership lists and secret codes. Contained in those files, Burns claimed, was evidence that one "Linde" was in the confidence of the Third International. It was a mistake that would later cost the Bureau dearly.[23]

BURNS WAS LAID UP with a cold just after his appointment to the Bureau, the sort of minor illness that had become more than niggling as he passed age sixty. He decided to stay at his country home in Scarborough, New York, for at least a few days. To compensate for his temporary absence from Washington, he invited reporters to his house to discuss plans for reshaping the Bureau in the wake of Flynn's failures. Sniffles notwithstanding, he sounded like his old progressive self as he charted schemes for training, testing, and disciplining his agents into "the most effective secret service in the world." As a government post, the Bureau job promised to be the culmination both of his legendary career and of the growing fusion between federal and private police. Just as the federal government had recently begun to encroach on the traditional duties of local authorities, it had more and more come to assume the roles—strikebreaking, radical surveillance—long assigned to the private detective industry. As an entrepreneur returning to government service, Burns embodied both the past and future of law enforcement.[24]

To the financiers and industrialists who had long employed Burns men to investigate crimes and break strikes, this sounded like an ideal arrangement. "There is joy all along the [Pennsylvania] avenue," *Chicago Banker* magazine remarked, "on the report that President Harding is to make William J. Burns 'commander-in-chief' of all the detective and secret service departments of the government." There was joy along Wall Street, too. "[N]o man in his line in the United States," one bank vice president wrote to Washington, "has a stronger following among the bankers of the country than Wm. J. Burns."[25]

To those who viewed the consolidation of private and federal power with a bit more skepticism, the Burns appointment set off immediate alarms.

With the first hints that Burns might be on his way to Washington, trade unionists scrambled to compose protest letters, urging Harding to appoint someone "about whom no odium has ever been cast." Newspapers sympathetic to their cause joined the attack as well, dredging up accusations of jury rigging, corruption, and underhanded union-busting techniques. As *Chicago Banker* summed it up, the debate showed roughly that "Labor is 'ferninst' [against] Burns, but everybody not in the 'Union' is for him."[26]

In an effort to preempt criticisms that Burns would merely be a strikebreaker in government clothes, Daugherty assured the press that his old friend's private-detecting days were at an end. "Mr. Burns has severed his connection with the Burns Detective Agency and will come to Washington and devote his entire time to the service," he promised. Under a pact worked out in advance of Daugherty's announcement, Burns' eldest sons had agreed to take over the agency's day-to-day operations, with Raymond Burns assuming the title of president and his younger brother, Sherman, becoming secretary-treasurer. There had even been some talk that the agency might change its name to make clear the distinction between Burns the government man and Burns the private sleuth. In the end, the family decided to maintain the title of "William J. Burns International Detective Agency, Inc." Both Burns and his new corporate heirs swore nonetheless that the connection was, as Daugherty suggested, officially "severed."[27]

Though couched in the folksy language of his detective persona ("Let the crooks know their punishment will be swift and sure," he told the *Sun* reporter, "and they will think long and hard before they pull a job"), Burns' initial proposals for reshaping the Bureau focused primarily on bureaucratic matters. Never one to start small, Burns endorsed a merger of the entire federal detective apparatus—the Secret Service, the Post Office inspectors, perhaps even Military Intelligence—into a single agency under his personal direction. He also proposed the establishment of a national fingerprint index in the Bureau's Washington offices to replace the disparate and poorly organized resources currently in use. "It is a simple process requiring only the cooperation of the police departments in supplying duplicate identifications of criminals known to them," he explained. "The national identification system thus established will become a great help to the departments which have joined in creating it."[28]

On the question of what to do about the threat of radicalism, Burns' ambitions appeared to be more modest. Since coming to office Harding had maintained the same calm he showed during the presidential campaign, assuming rather than insisting that anti-Bolshevism was a basic part of American citizenship. Daugherty, too, had been reluctant to push the issue. On May Day 1921, he declined to issue a Palmer-style warning of impending revolutionary disturbance. "I believe it is best not to agitate the agitator," he explained. "I think we need less watching and more working in this country." With his appointment in August, Burns assured the public that he was fully in accord with these principles. His actions, however, suggested otherwise. On August 22, in one of his first official acts as Bureau director, Burns selected Palmer's young prodigy J. Edgar Hoover to be his second in command at the Bureau.[29]

SINCE APPEARING before the Senate with Palmer during the winter, Hoover had grown increasingly discontented with his weak position as head of the General Intelligence Division. His index file on radical activities continued to grow; the Justice Department's annual report advertised 450,000 cards by late 1921, up from just 150,000 in October 1920. Individual deportations (as opposed to mass raids) had been stepped up as well: between June 1920 and June 1921, the government deported 446 alien anarchists, compared with 314 the previous fiscal year. Hoover remained frustrated nonetheless by the Justice Department's lack of jurisdiction over native-born radicals. "The activities of the Federal Government are by law limited in so far as action against ultraradicalism is concerned to aliens," read the General Intelligence Division section of the Justice Department's annual report for 1921. "The Federal statutes unfortunately are not sufficiently broad enough to permit prosecution of American citizens engaged in activities tending for the overthrow of the Government of the United States by force and violence."[30]

Hoover seemed restless as well about the lack of progress in the Wall Street investigation. Throughout the spring, he had helped Flynn to coordinate his hunt for the Galleanisti (nearly every important document in the Bureau's case file bore the stamp "Read by J.E.H."). But he was never entirely convinced that the Bureau was on the right track. Like Burns, Hoover had long harbored suspicions that Flynn was taking an overly narrow view of the case—that communists, in addition to anarchists, might well be involved. When the Harding administration took office in the spring of 1921, he quietly began to correspond with Burns about assisting in the agency's private investigation. By June, he was one of the few government officials aware of what Burns was planning with William Linde. "I have been advised that Linde enjoyed the confidence of the leaders of the communist party in the United States," he explained to State Department officials in Warsaw. There is no evidence that Hoover informed Flynn of these activities; the correspondence remained entirely outside the official case file. Nor did he apparently come clean about his other interventions in the Wall Street case. Beginning in early 1921, Hoover had launched his own, secret effort to find the bombers in Russia.[31]

His partner in this investigation was none other than Arthur Woods, Junius Morgan's cousin by marriage and Flynn's onetime nemesis from his city detective days. Since the fall of 1920, Woods had settled back into his work at the American Legion, where he championed immigration restriction and aggressive cultural outreach to the foreign-born. He maintained his reputation as a squeaky-clean champion of civic virtue; rumor suggested he might be appointed as baseball commissioner to restore integrity in the wake of the "Black Sox" World Series scandal, or as an independent anticorruption candidate for mayor of New York. As far as the public knew, he played no role at all in the Wall Street investigation. Within the elite circles of high finance and the State Department, however, Woods' ongoing involvement in the case and in all manner of anti-Bolshevik intrigue was well known. By the time Hoover assumed his new post in August, Woods had personally toured nearly every major European capital in search of a solution to the bomb plot. With Hoover's help, he had also hired a Russian-born spy named Jacob Nosovitsky to carry the investigation on to Moscow.[32]

Woods had met Nosovitsky courtesy of Henry Marsh, a wealthy industrialist who had devoted his retirement and considerable resources to the cause of fighting Bolshevism. In the fall of 1920, just weeks after the bombing, Marsh brought Nosovitsky to Woods' office in the hope that he might be able to provide valuable intelligence about the communist situation—and, not incidentally, about the Wall Street bombing. Though Woods had access to the Morgan bank's contacts and resources (according to Nosovitsky, Woods was the one in charge of paying Burns), Marsh offered to foot the bill for Nosovitsky's service. He hoped that a solution to the bomb plot would provide a building block for his ultimate goal of creating an anti-Bolshevik intelligence bureau organized and run, in Nosovitsky's words, by "the important business interests."[33]

Nosovitsky came with a long string of pseudonyms: "Settlin" (a name he used to correspond with Hoover); "Joseph" and "James Anderson" (his undercover names with the British secret service); "the doctor" (adopted after the British secret service provided a false medical license); "Fox" (acquired in the fall of 1920); and most notably "N100," his Bureau designation. He also had extensive experience in negotiating the communist underground. In early 1919, while working for the British, he had secured a post as a courier for Martens' Soviet Bureau, shuttling gold and papers across the Atlantic. Later that year, the U.S. communist leadership selected him to escort delegate Louis Fraina to a gathering of Western communists in Amsterdam. Fraina, himself under (false) suspicion as a Bureau spy, abandoned Nosovitsky in Amsterdam. But Nosovitsky managed to send back valuable reports to the Bureau about what had taken place in the meetings. "All leaders of the communist and the communist labor party," he noted, "who are principally opposed to any terrorism, are afraid that such acts might give the government more reason to enact more drastic laws, and use more force in combating even the mildest revolutionary activities."[34]

When Woods and Marsh approached him about investigating the Wall Street plot, Nosovitsky drew on this history to shape his theory. As he explained to Woods, the communists did not "as a rule" support tactics of dynamiting or other "terroristic acts similar to the Wall Street explosion." Nosovitsky nonetheless believed that they had played a role in orchestrating the event. According to his theory, the Palmer raids and other bouts of repression had sparked a fury among Russian revolutionaries, who knew such tactics all too well from their homeland. "I will take the responsibility upon myself," Nosovitsky wrote, "to say that the Wall Street explosion was a direct and deliberate answer from those groups to the United States government."[35]

Apparently Hoover subscribed to this theory as well. "Hoover practically agreed that it probably was not an official Red act, but was strongly of the opinion that some criminally inclined individual communists might have committed the crime," Nosovitsky later claimed. As with Linde, Hoover was slated to play a crucial role as government point man for Nosovitsky, lending his good name and bureaucratic power to facilitate the spy's movements.[36]

Like Linde, Nosovitsky spent much of the fall of 1920 hanging around Martens' office, trying to glean information from his old communist contacts. After Martens' deportation in January, he proposed a trip to Moscow via Mexico, where he hoped to find communist friends who could secure his passage overseas. As it turned out, Nosovitsky only got as far as Mexico City before running into problems. He sent back a series of reports throughout March describing perilous revolutionary conditions in Mexico. By April, however, he was back in the United States, empty-handed.[37]

Given Nosovitsky's difficulties, Woods and Hoover decided to approach the case from another angle. In April 1921, relying on his longtime friendship with Harding's new secretary of state, Charles Evans Hughes (who had recently defended the New York Socialists' right to be seated in the state assembly), Woods gained a "confidential" appointment as a special assistant to the State Department, charged with establishing a "Central Bolshevist Bureau." Leaving Hoover in charge of Nosovitsky, Woods spent the spring of 1921 bouncing among various European cities, handing out terse questionnaires to diplomats on matter of vital national interest: "What methods government have found most useful in combating Red revolution?" "What deportation laws; under what conditions can aliens be deported and how are these laws administrated?" "Has the government any information which might be of value to us in fighting lawless revolutionaries at home?" And not least: "Have they any information regarding the Wall Street explosion?"[38]

The responses offered a wealth of recommendations for containing radicalism but little new information on the Wall Street plot. As Burns assumed office, however, Hoover and Woods remained confident enough in their theory of Russian involvement to mount one last joint effort. In August, they got back in touch with Nosovitsky and sent him off to Moscow.[39]

# 14

. . . .

# TRIPLE-CROSS

ON WALL STREET, the first anniversary of the explosion passed quietly. From police headquarters, Commissioner Richard Enright dispatched some eight hundred men to protect the Morgan bank, the stock exchange, and other likely targets. But as bomb squad chief James Gegan noted, there was no immediate threat at hand, no reason to believe that this particular day would be different from any other. As far as the newspapers could tell, neither the stock exchange nor the Morgan bank took any official notice of the day's significance. The major news on Wall Street included Standard Oil's decision to cut the price of gasoline to 21 cents a gallon and Guaranty Trust's reduction in its quarterly dividend—all in all, business as usual.

In the early weeks after the disaster, many district firms had taken measures to ensure their employees' physical safety; the stock exchange added wire screens to windows, eliminated the glass skylight over the board room, and hired an on-site nurse. These cosmetic reforms did little, however, to erase the memories of what had happened on September 16—a day "seared in the minds of those who passed through," in the words of the *Journal of Commerce*. Reminders of the bomb's human toll continued to crop up in city papers. During the winter, for instance, the local Red

277

Cross had issued a report outlining its ministrations to the victims' families. Of those killed, the Red Cross noted, nine had headed households with small children, while another ten had left behind widows. Among the injured, sixty-nine victims "presented acute problems" such as lost limbs or other serious wounds that would likely keep them from resuming their previous lives.[2]

Junius Morgan had kept a low profile in the year since the bombing, devoting himself to his family duties and to the occasional yacht race. He spent time as well on a committee to expand Broad Street Hospital, where the Bankers' Club estimated that one hundred additional beds might help to prevent the gridlock that had left so many victims waiting for treatment the previous year. Thomas Lamont, the Morgan partner who had done so much to restore business as usual on the day after the bombing, was far more active than Junius, traveling the world to coordinate loans with China, Mexico, and Japan, in addition to wrapping up his lingering work from the Versailles conference. With Jack Morgan still in Europe, Lamont had continued to operate as the bank's public face throughout the fall of 1920 (among other missives, he cabled to Jack that Junius was an asset in diplomatic work). Despite his close ties with Wilson, Lamont weathered the spring's change in presidential administrations with ease, meeting frequently with Harding to suggest appointments (he recommended Arthur Woods as assistant secretary of war) and discuss fiscal policy.[3]

One of the few sour notes of the year was the failure of the authorities, including Woods and Burns, to bring the September terrorists to justice. "If the crime had been committed in the middle of the Atlantic and the sea had closed over the wreckage," the *World* noted on the explosion's anniversary, "there could have been no more baffling lack of evidence." Even that seemed likely to change, however, with Burns' ascent as Bureau director. In one of his first official acts, he ordered the branch offices to hand over the entire contents of their yearlong bombing investigation, which he planned to sift for unnoticed clues.[4]

AS SEPARATE ENTITIES, the Bureau and the Burns agency had often been at cross-purposes, competing for glory rather than working toward a common end. Burns, the private investigator, possessed no formal right to view Bureau reports or examine physical evidence. (According to one employee, he nonetheless snatched a handful of metal slugs, which he displayed prominently on his desk.) Burns in turn had conducted his own inquiries under heavy secrecy, sharing no more with the federal authorities than absolutely necessary. As a result, his appointment to Bureau chief presented both an opportunity and a dilemma. In accepting his new post, Burns had promised to maintain a strict separation of his private and public duties. To do that in the Wall Street case, however, would be to forgo months of painstaking work. Burns chose the more efficient route. On September 8, hoping that the two investigations together might yield a solution, he instructed the New York office of the Bureau to lead a "detailed examination made of all of the reports . . . relating to the Wall Street Bomb Explosion."[5]

Perhaps aware of the explosion's importance to their new boss, Bureau agents responded almost immediately, flooding the New York branch with reports describing nearly every aspect of the case. Their summaries documented thousands of man-hours expended in pursuit of lost dynamite shipments, buyers of window weights, known and alleged anarchists, leads from concerned citizens, eyewitness testimony, and rubber stamps of the sort used in the American Anarchists' flyers. (Agents in the Buffalo district alone visited 522 stores that sold stamps.) They contained accounts of the leads that still poured in by phone and mail: accusations that someone had "made certain statements" or "inform[ed] two other Italians" about inside knowledge of the blast, or threats of further violence signed by "the crank I.W.W." There were elaborate charts of witness descriptions ("Horse looked old"; "Looked like builder's wagon") and accounts of all of the major suspects: Fisher, Brailovsky, Caruso, Zelenko, Ligi, De Filippis. In addition, the reports offered summaries on dozens, if not hundreds, of radicals whose names never made the newspapers and who never knew that they were under Bureau suspicion.[6]

As Hoover had noted in a July memorandum, the Bureau was still fairly sure about the status of the wagon. "The horse attached to the wagon was shod at . . . Elisabeth Street, New York City, by two Italian brothers named . . . De GRAICA [sic]," Hoover wrote. "The horse was shod on the day before the Wall Street Bomb explosion at about the hour of noon. It was brought to this address by a man speaking the Italian language but who resembled an Austrian or a North-Italian. He desired to have the shoes tightened on the hind hoofs of the horse, but was induced by the two blacksmiths to have new shoes put upon the horse, and in view of the load which was in the wagon, the shoes were made with extra calk."[7]

Bureau agents were by now also relatively certain about what had been inside the wagon. "Investigation has shown that the container of the bomb was probably an army box and that a German [blasting] cap was used [to detonate] the explosion," Hoover noted. On the matter of the explosives themselves, the Bureau largely accepted the October report prepared by Dr. Walter Scheele, which identified blasting gelatin as the culprit. In an effort to locate the source of the gelatin, agents had attempted to interview every explosives dealer, manufacturer, and customer in the Northeast—all to no avail. One office had spent several weeks documenting an explosives theft as far away as South Dakota, only to conclude that the thieves were trying to blow up a nearby dam. The outcome of the explosives inquiry was best summarized in the update from the Albany office. After interrogating every local company slated as a recent recipient of DuPont explosives, wrote agent in charge G. O. Holdridge, the local Bureau office had determined that

a more or less lax supervision exists over the use of the supplies of explosives; that almost any employee engaged in the work of blasting or similar work has such access to the explosives as to enable him to obtain small quantities; that the opportunities to obtain small quantities would be so very numerous as to make it entirely feasible for any such employee to accumulate considerable quantities of the explosive in a comparatively short time.

The final results of this "lead" produced no person or persons in the District who might be definitively classed as suspects.[8]

Such an outcome, Burns found, was all too typical. For all of the aching detail, the most significant sentences in the summaries were the ones that tended to close the paragraphs: "No information was secured"; "there were no leads in this district which would be of any use in the investigation"; "no developments of moment resulted." Indeed, the most viable hypothesis in the files was the one that Flynn had already made public. "It has always been my theory," wrote Newark supervisor Frank Stone, "that the 'CRONACA SOVERSIVA' [sic] outfit, if not the principal conspirators in the Wall Street explosion, they at least took an important part in it; . . . and that the operations were directed by its leader GALLEANI in Italy."[9]

Though he was pursuing a different line of inquiry, Burns did not entirely ignore that possibility. Beginning in November, he required daily reports on the Sacco-Vanzetti Defense Committee. He also later revived investigations of Tito Ligi and Vincenzo Leggio, apparently convinced that they were, indeed, two different men. Finally, he stayed in close touch with the State Department in Italy, where the search for Galleani, Recchi, and their comrades continued well into 1923. The Roman police reported back that "no proofs have been found of the complicity of the anarchists...in the outrage in question."[10]

Other than these tangents, Burns more or less kept going where he had left off. His informer William Linde was still somewhere in Europe, most likely in Warsaw, one of the easiest gateways to Bolshevik Russia. Unfortunately, Burns could not confirm this fact, as he had not heard from Linde in several months. Frustrated by this lack of communication, in August Burns turned to another undercover operative: a German-born ex-podiatrist named Paul Altendorf, who had made his name rooting out German saboteurs during the war. Altendorf had been to Russia and Poland in the spring of 1921 to investigate the explosion case, returning with the confident announcement that he had "solved [the] mystery of Wall Street bomb plot" and was ready to finger former Russian "ambassador" Ludwig Martens. Burns hoped now that Altendorf might find Linde and wrap up the whole story. After making his way to Poland, however, Altendorf, like Linde, disappeared.[11]

To sort out the mess, the Bureau decided to dispatch yet another agent, a former Burns agency employee named Sylvester Cosgrove. Arriving in Warsaw in October, Cosgrove managed to locate both Linde and Altendorf, but his initial reports on their situation were not encouraging. "Finally met him [Linde]...several interviews," he cabled to Burns in early November. "[I]f story true matter solved, doubt it." All of this echoed what Flynn had found in the Wall Street case: each tip seemed to set the investigation back rather than move it forward. As a matter of policy, the procession of operatives departing for Europe was also an obvious violation of Burns' promise to separate his public and private work. Technically, Cosgrove was working for the Justice Department, while Linde and Altendorf were still employed by the Burns agency. In practical terms, though, the distinction had little value.[12]

The line was similarly blurred in Hoover's relationship with his own privately employed spy, Jacob Nosovitsky. Before departing for Russia, Nosovitsky had offered two names as likely Wall Street suspects: Ivan Dudinsky, a former member of the Socialist Party and the Union of Russian Workers, and his cousin Jacob, known as "Korolenko." As Russian-born communists and former Newark residents, the Dudinskys were just the sort of men who easily fit Burns' theory. Despite this, Hoover made no effort to incorporate Nosovitsky's clues into the Bureau's official Wall Street file. This held true even after Nosovitsky contacted Arthur Woods from Warsaw in late October with the assurance that he was hot on Ivan's trail. "Allow me, my dear Colonel, to tell you that I consider it a matter of honor never to give up any case that I am working on, as a hopeless adventure," he wrote. "I say again I believe that the case will be solved and *must be solved*."[13]

In the end, the conflict between his private and public loyalties never proved of much consequence for Hoover. By December, Nosovitsky was back in New York, complaining to Hoover that Woods and Marsh had decided to defund the Dudinsky investigation for lack of progress. For Burns, though, what began as a tantalizing prospect—the possibility of combining his private and public inquiries about the Wall Street explosion—soon erupted into public scandal. On November 30, Cosgrove cabled to Burns that Linde had at last offered new details about the conspiracy behind the blast. "Can destroy Linde but fear perhaps enough truth to justify speculation on his return," he wrote. "[S]hall I use own judgment and return with Linde or go to Paris and mail my report and his statement and await your instructions."[14]

Before they could agree on a strategy, the Polish authorities placed Linde under arrest. The ensuing publicity exposed not only Burns' carelessness in combining his dual roles but also what appeared to be the patent absurdity of his entire explosion theory.

THE HEADLINES varied—"N. Y. Dynamiter Nabbed"; "Wall Street Bomb Plot Arrest Solves Mystery, Says Burns"; "Wall St. Bomb Arrest 'Right Story,' Burns of Secret Service Asserts"—but the essence of the articles was the same: Bureau of Investigation chief William J. Burns, with the aid of international agents Sylvester Cosgrove and Paul Bernardo Altendorf, "after a long chase covering more than a year" and "one of the most skillful pursuits of modern times," had at last arrived at the true solution to the Wall Street explosion.[15]

The story arrived in city newsrooms via Associated Press wire late on December 16, 1921. Datelined Warsaw, it outlined the arrest of one Wolfe Lindenfeld, also known as William Linde, a Polish-born radical who had been the target of a months-long Bureau hunt. Through the action-packed prose of a detective novel, the country learned over the next few days of Burns' long ordeal tracking Linde through far-off Europe: Altendorf, posing as a "confirmed Bolshevik," had ventured overseas to pick up Linde's trail. "When the time became ripe for action," Cosgrove had joined him, taking up the guise of "a prominent official of an American labor organization." The ruse was enough, according to the *New York Times*, to make Linde "wholly unsuspicious of pursuit." Just weeks before his arrest, he had disappeared from the detectives' surveillance, and they had been forced to chase him all the way to Lodz. "Fearing to lose his man again," the *Times* reported,

> Cosgrove went into a room alone with the powerfully built Bolshevik, carrying loaded revolvers and a dagger, and knocked him onto a bed. Gripping him by the throat, Cosgrove obtained the first admission of guilt from Lindenfeld, who then freed himself and rushed down the hotel corridor, followed by the detective. When the two reached the crowded lobby, Cosgrove twice hit Lindenfeld on the jaw, knocking the latter's head against a marble wall. Lindenfeld, nearly dazed, drew a knife from his hip pocket when Altendorf, who had waited in the lobby with three Polish secret agents, sprang upon him and clutched his arms and legs. Lindenfeld was then overpowered and taken to a waiting police wagon.

Only after several more hours of grilling and resistance, the article explained, did Linde deliver a confession that vindicated, after a year and a half, Burns' prediction that the bombers would be found by looking to Moscow.[16]

The details of the alleged confession bore a fair resemblance to what Linde had described in his reports to Burns: four or five communists, financed by Martens, had set out to assassinate J. P. Morgan and strike a blow against capital. There were a few additional items as well, such as the revelation that Martens had paid a whopping $30,000 for the plot. At least one crucial aspect of the story seemed to be missing, however. Caught up in the excitement of the suspect's capture, the initial news reports failed to mention that Linde worked for the Burns detective agency.[17]

Like many readers who awoke on December 17 to find the Russians accused in the Wall Street plot, Burns was taken aback at the news of

Linde's arrest. As he admitted to reporters after rushing from Washington to New York on the afternoon train, he had neither expected nor ordered nor been notified of what was under way in Warsaw. "It is a great surprise to me that it came out, and how it happened I don't know," he complained. Altogether, though, Burns wasn't entirely unhappy about this latest turn of events. "There is no question in the world that we have the proper solution of this mystery," he announced to the reporters mobbed near the entrance to the 6:10 train. "As a matter of fact," he added, ever the Holmesian, "we knew it all along."[18]

Standing on the platform at Grand Central Station, reaffirmed in his conviction that every criminal leaves a trail, Burns fairly trembled with satisfaction. "He made no effort," wrote the *New York American*, "to hide the intense triumph he felt at the promised solution of probably the most gigantic extremist conspiracy in the annals of the country." For the next several minutes, he was once again the Burns of the McNamara trials, the Burns of the graft hearings, the Great Detective who could succeed where others failed. He had said, standing in the rubble on Wall Street on September 16, that radicals were behind the plot. At last, the whole world would see that it was so. "The story that the confession of Lindenfeld, which is his right name, is about 10,000 words in length is true," he explained. "It is also true that it names the people who set and exploded the bomb."[19]

Burns did take issue with several items in the newspaper accounts. It seemed, he said, not quite right to call the man's statement a "confession," since Linde himself "was not implicated in the plot except that he knew about it." It was also not correct, he thought, to suggest that Linde was a violent radical, though he was, indeed, a secret representative of the Bolshevik government. Most importantly, Burns took offense at what he called the "ridiculous" charge that the bomb had been aimed at Jack Morgan, who had been happily ensconced in Britain on that particular September 16. "The bomb was not intended for J. P. Morgan," he explained. "The purpose...was to terrorize the entire community."[20]

Now, Burns promised, that purpose had been thwarted once and for all. He predicted that the plot's exposure would quash whatever vestiges of support the communists could still muster in the United States. "I expect to clean up the whole case in the end...in spite of all obstacles," he announced. "When this is done, it is my opinion that the backbone of the radical movement in this country will be broken forever."[21]

Many editorials offered similarly high hopes. The *Globe and Commercial Advertiser* heard the death knell of radicalism in the United States. Given the Bolsheviks' long-standing disavowal of terrorism, the paper added, the confession seemed poised to undermine the faith of even their most committed acolytes. "The assertion at once calls to mind the Los Angeles Times explosion, which was accurately traced to the door of ironworker unionists. That union certainly did not believe in the creed of violence, but a small band of leaders did practise destruction and killing."[22]

This was precisely the analogy that had guided Burns through the long months of uncertainty: Linde would be his Ortie McManigal, the Wall Street case another McNamara Affair. Ultimately, though, a different historical analogy came to seem more apt. At his Idaho trial in 1907, Bill Haywood had won his freedom because the jurors did not believe Harry Orchard, the man who claimed to have the inside scoop on the Western Federation of Miners plots. Within twenty-four hours of his front-page arrest, Linde had begun to show a similar vulnerability. As news of the Warsaw report spread through New York, it began to appear that Burns was the *only* one who had ever believed a word spoken by William Linde.

BURNS' DESCENT FROM HERO TO LAUGHINGSTOCK began with a push from the New York police. On December 17, the day that the Linde story broke in the city papers, bomb squad chief James Gegan informed the *Evening Post* that despite years of immersion in both city radicalism and the Wall Street investigation, he had never heard of anyone named Linde or Lindenfeld. Other police officials later pointed out that the AP story had identified Lindenfeld as a former Russian spy who had snitched on his countrymen during the 1905 revolution—hardly a recommendation for membership in an organization, the Third International, now run by those selfsame revolutionaries. And there were other unexplained oddities: Why was Altendorf, who had "caused considerable trouble for Government officials...during the war," involved in the investigation? Where was the text of the confession? Why hadn't Burns known of the arrest in advance? Most important, what was to be made of the rumors, printed on the morning of December 18, that Linde himself was not a genuine radical but rather a "spy," a "stool pigeon," a "fink" in the employ of none other than William J. Burns?[23]

"Oh, yes, we used Linde," Burns told the *World* when confronted with the accusation. "We used him as an informant on the affairs of radicals." His choice of words conveyed surprise, even indignation, that such details should matter. But among the socialists and labor activists who knew Linde all too well, it served to invalidate Burns' entire theory. "The consensus of opinion yesterday," the *Call* declared on December 18, "was that William Linde, small schemer, who had busied himself around the edge of the local movement, had put over one of the biggest hoaxes of the century, a canard to which William J. Burns, head of the United States Secret Service [*sic*], had fallen a victim."[24]

What initially struck the *Call*'s editors was the same thing noted by the *Globe*: the fact that communists usually argued with great vehemence against the tactic of individual terrorism. "The Third International has never supported the commission of such insane acts as the Wall Street explosion," the *Call* pointed out on December 18. The Bolshevik government itself eventually affirmed this position, notifying the Western press through Karl Radek, a prominent member of the Comintern's West European Secretariat and a close associate of Lenin's, that it disavowed all suggestions that it would provide money for such a plot. In the United States, the Communist Party watched the proceedings anxiously, compiling reports of each new revelation in the press.[25]

From Burns' perspective, the communists' denials were to be expected: did anyone think that Lenin and Trotsky would simply admit that they had been caught? Far more troubling were the rumors that Linde, far from being a respected member of the communist underground, was known as a "kibitzer," a fraud, and a fake.[26]

The *Call* waxed poetic in its metaphors: Linde was Baron Munchausen, he was Charles Ponzi. The personal testimony of Linde's socialist acquaintances backed up this view. "[H]e was a braggart, always talking 'big' about what he was going to do and what he was," Julius Gerber, executive secretary of the Socialist Party, reported in the *Call*. "He's a terrible bluff," added Alex Simon, a union delegate in the garment trade. "His statement is a fake. Linde, as we knew him best, was full of fake stories." Even Linde's wife, Dora, tracked down at the boardinghouse where she lived with her young son and crippled daughter, offered only well-wrought disdain. "I did not know that he ever worked for detective agencies or anything like that, but he was such a liar that he could easily be a loud mouthed revolutionist and a secret service agent at the same time," she recalled. "He lied about everything."[27]

With no further news coming in from Warsaw, finding local figures to denounce Linde became something of a pastime for the New York press. It was an easy task, as Linde seemed to know—or to be known to—nearly everybody who had ever been anybody in even the most pallid of left-wing circles. Over the course of the week following his arrest, acquaintances gleefully shared their most annoying, entertaining, and pathetic encounters. I. M. Sackin, who had served as Linde's lawyer in several petty disputes, recalled Linde as a dapper Beau Brummel type who wore his hair "wavy, in the artistic fashion" and always talked "big money." "He appeared to be very prosperous at times and on other occasions I found him almost penniless," Sackin said, adding that Linde had been jailed at least once for debt. At the Rand School, a Socialist Party member said that Linde liked to go around impersonating assemblyman Louis Waldman.[28]

Waldman himself recalled running into Linde at the Socialists' Chicago convention in September 1919, where activists caught Linde hanging around their train car—"he often crashed into places where he had not been invited," noted Socialist alderman Abraham Beckerman—and threw him out on suspicion of detective activities. "During the convention he came to us with so much information about spies in the other camp that our suspicions about him were confirmed," Waldman explained.[29]

Coming so relentlessly, one after another, the stories bore the markings of a coordinated effort. Still, they had the ring of truth. The same men and women who denounced Linde as a liar and a fake were the only ones able to say where exactly he had been on the afternoon of September 16. Late on the night before the explosion, Linde had joined Abraham Beckerman at the Broadway Central Hotel; the hotel registry confirmed Linde's presence. When they heard about the explosion the next day, Beckerman remembered, Linde seemed as surprised as anyone else.[30]

AFTER MORE THAN TWO DECADES in the detective profession, Burns knew better than to be intimidated by this sort of political warfare. "He said he was just as positive today as he was on the day of the explosion that the crime was the handiwork of the Third Internationale [*sic*]," the *San Francisco Chronicle* reported on December 19. To his confidants at the Justice Department, however, he was openly worried. Hours after the story had broken, Hoover wired his State contacts in Warsaw to complain that the Bureau was besieged with press inquiries and at a loss about how to respond. "The arrest of Linde," he wrote, "... is a complete surprise to us here."[31]

The Bureau wrote to Warsaw again two days later with a complaint that "we have had no official confirmation of the Linde arrest or the matters connected therewith." Three days later, Burns sent yet another cable, his tone by now frantic. "I have been waiting seven days to hear from you and not a line has been received," he wrote to Cosgrove. "Why don't you cable what the situation is? ... I asked American Minister seven days ago through State Department for statement of situation but no reply. Did you receive my messages? Answer at once." The silence from Warsaw continued for five more days.[32]

By then, the damage to Burns' reputation was irreversible. Instead of transcending the investigation's longtime curse, he had emerged as just another Flynn, the butt of jokes and gleeful jabs. "Radicals, ultra-radicals, Socialists, labor unions officials, the intelligentsia of Second avenue, Wall Street clerks, butchers, bakers and candlestick makers, City Hall, and even the police department were having a good laugh over the Warsaw reports," the *Call* jeered, without much exaggeration. Even the *Wall Street Journal*, hardly the *Call*'s ideological bedmate, jumped on board. On December 19, police had put Wall Street under special watch amid rumors that a new explosion would soon destroy the financial district. This false alarm, combined with the Linde fiasco, provoked the normally impassive *Journal* into an outburst of frustration. "It is difficult to speak with common patience of the Secret Service Department in its conception of suitable means to protect Wall Street from agitators who carry their own theories into practice," the paper declared the next day. "If a detective's head were merely solid bone from the ears up his reactions would be calculable."[33]

One of the most puzzling aspects of the Linde story was just how it had gotten to this point—how thousands of dollars and fifteen months of time could have been expended on what appeared to be such a bald-faced lie. In the ten days between Linde's appearance on the front page and his departure from public discussion, Burns was exposed as having abandoned nearly every tenet he had identified as crucial to the strength and integrity of his new Bureau. He had vowed a separation of public and private work; the revelations about Linde had exposed the two in joint humiliation. He had promised that only the "best men" would work for the Bureau; Linde and Altendorf, "braggarts" and "double-crossers" both, hardly qualified. He had repeated his claim that the one inviolate rule of sleuthing was absolute secrecy; the message had clearly failed to make much of an impression. He had said he would cooperate with the police, but the police had turned against him. And all of it—the blockbuster revelation, the promise of vindication, the discombobulating slide from Great Detective to shame-tainted fool—had happened in little more than a week. The question, by the time the holidays rolled around, was why what could have been a breakthrough had turned into such a complicated, well-publicized, international repetition of his predecessor Flynn's experiences.

Among the press, explanations for this mystery tended to fall into one of two categories. The more charitable view framed Burns as a victim, a decent and well-meaning investigator taken in by "one of the cleverest 'double-crossers' known to detective bureaus." If this view did not embrace Burns' indictment of the Third International, neither did it entirely blame him for Linde's betrayal of faith. Burns was naive, perhaps even overweening in his attempt to cover up his mistake in judgment. But whatever deliberate dishonesty might be occurring, by this account it was occurring overseas.[34]

The alternative interpretation, and the one favored by the *Call*, cast Burns himself as the instigator of the entire ordeal, foiled in his attempt to frame the Bolshevik government by public exposure of his prevarication. Here, the imagined purpose behind the plot varied. Charles Recht, Martens' former attorney, saw an attempt to disrupt U.S.-Russian trade. "My explanation of the whole Lindenfeld yarn is this: The story is a frame-up to cause distrust of the Soviet and its leaders among American businessmen who are on the verge of entering into important Russian contracts, and is done in the interest of the business rivals of these concerns." The Bolshevik government itself, in a wireless message intercepted by the Bureau, declared that the Linde case had been manufactured "to delay the recognition of Soviet Russia." "The Bourgeoisie can level a thousand reproaches at the Bolsheviks but not that of being accomplices in individual terrorism, which is opposed entirely to their doctrines and tendencies," read the statement. "If Lindenfeld took part in the outrages, it was not as a Communist, but as an 'agent provocateur' in the service of Burns' Detective Agency."[35]

A third theory suggested that Burns never believed any part of Linde's confession but promoted it nonetheless for political and financial gain—precisely the view that the socialist press, especially Upton Sinclair, had held for so many months. "It recalls the 10-year period following 1886," the *Call* concluded, "when the anarchist scare in Chicago enabled certain detectives to capitalize it by obtaining handsome contributions from merchants and bankers on the score of 'protecting' them from some impending calamity."[36]

The truth, once again, was likely far less complicated than these conspiracies would suggest. Whatever his hopes for gain and glory, Burns genuinely believed that Linde had uncovered a solution to the Wall Street explosion. And like Flynn, he continued to be loyal to his theory long after the rest of the world had dismissed it as a frame-up and hoax. Even Cosgrove's message, when it finally arrived on December 27, could not persuade Burns to change his mind. After ten days of silence, Cosgrove wrote that Linde had "[c]onfessed he never attempted to keep faith with you, admits false reports and larceny of the $2700." Rather than give up on Linde in the wake of this disappointment, Burns renewed his determination to prove the validity of his theory. As the Warsaw story faded from the headlines, he launched an effort that would eventually bring the explosion inquiry to a close, culminating in a historic raid on the Communist Party.[37]

# 15

. . . .

# THE WALL STREET CURSE

EUGENE DEBS' ADMIRERS often compared him to Christ: Debs the persecuted, Debs the pure of heart, Debs the savior of the downtrodden. So they must have appreciated the timing of President Harding's commutation. On December 23, 1921, as Burns retreated to Scarborough to nurse his bruised ego, Harding declared that Debs, along with twenty-three other political prisoners, would be freed from jail in time for Christmas. Two days later, at eleven-thirty on Christmas morning, the Socialist leader walked out the front gates of the Atlanta federal penitentiary, his first taste of freedom since the spring of 1919. In an admitted breach of protocol, the warden threw open cell doors throughout the prison, and a wave of cheers swept Debs through the waiting crowd of reporters into the awkward arms of friends. Debs turned to raise his hat and cane in solidarity with the men left behind. He cried a little, too.[1]

Debs looked smaller, more wizened, than he had during his presidential campaign, when he tossed off his bitter (and fairly accurate) prediction that "[t]he Wall Street explosion must be proved the result of a plot and fastened upon some red conspirators." Despite his failing health, until Harding's surprise announcement the amnesty campaign on Debs' behalf had offered little hope for an early release. Now, with liberty suddenly at hand, Debs wanted nothing more than to go home and rest. First, how-ever, he had official obligations to fulfill. The government had bought him a train ticket to Washington, since President Harding wanted to say hello. "I've heard so damned much about you, Mr. Debs," the president said when they were finally face-to-face, "that I am now very glad to meet you personally." Then it was on to Terre Haute, Debs' hometown, where some fifty thousand fans turned out for a parade. "It seems to me that I can hear your hearts throb and I would like to put my arms around each one of you," Debs told them. "I cannot make a speech tonight but I can love you, and I do thank you from the depths of my heart."[2]

The White House assured the public that Debs' release was meant as a "gracious act of mercy," not as an acknowledgment of injustice. "There is no question of his guilt," an executive summary issued Christmas Eve declared, "and that he actively and purposely obstructed the draft." But for many of Debs' supporters, it was tempting to interpret the rush of cheers and sobs as a sign that the hostility of recent years might be giving way to something resembling the uneasy tolerance that had existed before the war. Like Harding's claim that "too much has been said about Bolshe-vism," Debs' release seemed to mark the end of an era, a dissipation of the Red Scare energies that had polarized American politics in recent years.[3]

Such hopes were premature. Despite its façade of goodwill, the Hard-ing administration was not so much repudiating antiradical policy as adapting and refining it for the new conditions of 1922. In the revised crusade against Bolshevism, the Linde fiasco would play a crucial, if hidden, role.

THOUGH LINDE'S NAME DISAPPEARED from the front pages as the new year dawned, it did not disappear from the Bureau files or, more important, from Burns' mind. Despite the guffaws he would have endured had the fact been made public, Burns was still inclined toward the view that Linde was, even now, telling the truth about the Wall Street plot. He grew even more convinced in January after receiving a thirteen-page missive—the much-touted Warsaw "confession"—containing Linde's sheepish account of what he had been up to since disappearing the previous spring.

The document pulsed with self-justification. It also served, conve-niently, to reinforce Linde's original claim that a shadowy communist "technical committee" was behind the Wall Street conspiracy. Still, there was enough new information—names, dates, suggested targets of surveillance—to persuade Burns to give Linde yet another chance. "I arrived in Paris March 7, 1921," Linde wrote, "and registered at the Continental Hotel." From there, he claimed, he had done just what Burns instructed, joining up with communist acquaintances in the hope of finding passage to Moscow. After Paris, Linde allegedly traveled to Brussels, then on to Prague and Warsaw and finally to Moscow, where he managed to meet up with Martens and insinuate himself into the Third Congress of the Communist International. "My boss, Mr. William J. Burns told me by all means to attend all the meetings," he wrote. "I ascertained they are organizing armies and sending out agitators and planning all sorts of revolutions and riots."

About the Wall Street explosion Linde offered several tantalizing tidbits that served both to confirm his old theories and to provide fodder for a revived investigation. While in Paris and Brussels, Linde reportedly spent several days with Barber and his wife, Miriam, who admitted their involvement in the plot. They also offered up the name of one Stanley, an accomplice who had helped to build the bomb "on 4th Street, N.Y. in a shop." This contradicted Linde's account of a conversation in Russia with one "Reinsteinem"—presumably Boris Reinstein, a Russian-born communist with close ties to Martens' Bureau—who notified him that "Barber, Stevens and the rest are [now] in the United States." Linde assured Burns that the whole picture would come together if they proceeded with patience. "It was clearly stated as I have reported," he wrote, "and I would give my head as a guarantee." Apparently convinced of his sincerity, in January 1922 Burns launched a new investigation of 110 West Fortieth Street, now home not only to the ailing Soviet Bureau but also to the recruitment arm of Haywood's Kuzbas colony.[4]

With Martens himself out of the country, Burns concentrated his efforts on a disbarred lawyer named Henry Kuntz, one of several hangers-on around the Soviet Bureau. Beginning in January 1922, agents watched Kuntz on a near-daily basis, following him to and from work, listening in on his phone conversations, pumping undercover operatives for background information on alleged murder plots and document caches in and around the suspect's home. The elaborate legwork yielded little about any of the names in Linde's report. But it did give Burns an entrée into the lives of Kuntz's business partners and, not incidentally, Martens' chief business contacts in the United States, the father-son team of Julius and Armand Hammer.[5]

A doctor and a founding member of the Communist Labor Party (as well as a close friend of Boris Reinstein's), Julius had gained notoriety in the spring of 1920, when he was sentenced to jail for performing an illegal abortion that killed the wife of a Russian diplomat. Burns was far more interested, however, in the Hammers' role as Soviet couriers and financiers. With his son's help, in 1917 Julius had founded the Allied Drug and Chemical Company, an American corporation half owned by Martens and designed to funnel Russian funds back and forth from the United States. After his father's departure for prison, Armand Hammer had gone to Russia to serve as a conduit for the deported Martens, returning to New York in December 1921 to negotiate deals with American manufacturers. He also played an early role in getting Haywood's Kuzbas colony off the ground, pressing Lenin for extra funds.[6]

Presumably Burns suspected Allied Drug of helping to launder the money that, in Linde's theory, had paid for the Wall Street bomb. He also may have wondered if the Hammers had played a role in the premature exposé of Linde's activities. Both Julius and a shadowy newspaper publicist named William Edward Cope had been Linde's intimates at the World Tower Building (Cope had testified at Hammer's abortion trial; he had also sponsored Linde for membership in the New York Press Club). As early as November 1921, Burns had received warnings that Cope was trying to contact Linde in Warsaw. At least one agent eventually concluded that it was "COPE who hoaxed Burns" by persuading Linde to deliver a false confession, a fear that Burns may have shared. By the end of the year, in addition to watching Kuntz, Hammer, the Kuzbas recruiters, and the other denizens of 110 West Fortieth Street, Burns had launched a "personal and confidential" investigation of Cope himself.[7]

All of this activity took place at a moment when the "Red Scare" was supposed to be fading, when concerns about bombs and revolution and national strikes had allegedly been relegated to the wartime past. To Burns, though, the relative quiet that had overtaken the country merely suggested a need for increased vigilance. In an appearance before Congress in March 1922, he warned that, contrary to popular opinion, labor radicalism was on the increase, as violent and destructive as it had ever been. The following month, his prediction seemed to be borne out by the eruption of a national coal strike that brought open warfare from both sides of the picket line. After police forces killed two strikers in Herrin, Illinois, for instance, the miners commandeered an airplane and began dropping bombs on areas where strikebreakers gathered. More than a thousand miners also took up arms, launching an armed assault that killed nineteen strikebreakers and forced the rest to leave town. Burns presented this not as a response to economic desperation or police aggression but as the result of a communist conspiracy. "[T]he Third International sent a great many instructions to their representatives in this country," he later explained. "[T]hey were to do everything possible to arouse the striking miners to the point of armed insurrection."[8]

About his ongoing effort to link the Communist Party with the Wall Street explosion, Burns was much more secretive. Even as he revived the investigation, he resolutely kept his activities out of the press. He hid them as well from the majority of Bureau agents, instructing both the New York and Chicago offices to limit their inquiries to a few dependable men. This was especially true when it came to tracking down the mysterious suspects originally named by Linde as the key players in the explosion conspiracy. Making do with the scattered bits of information from Warsaw, in mid-January Burns assigned two handpicked agents to locate the various men and women—Celunitius, Barber, Stevens, Wolf—named as participants in the plot. He also sent men to interview Linde's wife, Dora, and his former secretary, Lena Spector, in the hope that they might reveal additional documents. After a few weeks' investigation, Chicago agent Jacob Spolansky reported no progress on any front.[9]

Bereft of other options, Burns decided to revisit the case with Linde himself. Thanks to an appeal to the Polish authorities by Attorney General Daugherty ("The information in the possession of this Department indicates quite clearly that Linde has intimate knowledge of the perpetrators of the Wall Street Bomb explosion"), Linde was still behind bars in Warsaw. Cables from the State Department warned, however, that he might be released at any moment. Hoping to prevent Linde from disappearing once again, Burns sent a new pair of agents to Warsaw with the aim of transporting him back to the United States.[10]

In terms of maintaining the firewall between private and public service, the new Linde team was no more scrupulous than the last. Allen O. Myers, the lead detective, was a Burns agency veteran, a pioneer in the world of privately funded antiradical activities. On the afternoon of the bombing, he had accompanied Burns to Wall Street, alerting the papers that "[t]he Communist Party is behind it all. They are planning to wreck buildings, murder and commit all kinds of atrocities." By 1922, though still employed by the Burns agency, he was traveling in a semiofficial capacity as a federal representative, identified at various times as a Bureau special agent, as a "representative of the Department of Justice," and as "the personal representative of Mr. Burns." His new partner, Clinton Wood, occupied a similar official limbo. One of Arthur Woods' protégés and a former head of the police "industrial squad," Wood had frequently visited Linde at the World Tower Building, trading tips about goings-on within the labor movement. Now he was merely on loan to the federal government until Linde could be lured back to New York.[11]

The new team left the city on May 10 after pledging a vow of silence to Burns. Arriving in Poland by early June, they split almost immediately on the question of Linde's veracity. "Subject damnedest liar ever lived," Myers cabled back to Washington after his first interview with Linde, "further efforts with him useless, waste of time and money." Wood, described by the wary men of the State Department as "a very quiet and gentle sort of soul" and a true standout "in all this welter of human cussedness," was less inclined toward a quick dismissal. Linde was such a poor liar, Wood argued, that it was easy to find the few morsels of truth within his half-baked fabrications. If there was still any possibility that Linde had an inside track on the bombing, he wondered, what did the Bureau have to lose by further inquiry?[12]

Perhaps it was Wood's logic that influenced Myers. Or perhaps it was Linde's apparent willingness, after being released from prison in early summer, to devote his free time to updating Myers on his activities. Whatever the inspiration, by mid-July Myers was frantically cabling Burns to declare, "The opinion I express in my cable message of June 10 has been changed." In contrast to the casual contempt with which he had first greeted Linde, Myers suddenly believed the situation to be of "such vital importance that I refuse to pass final judgment." By August, he had become so agitated over Linde that he defied Burns' orders to move on to Italy and instead hopped the first steamer from Paris to New York. "Information and data in my possession of such importance that I am taking full responsibility to disregard your instructions," he wired before leaving.[13]

There remains no official record of the conversation that transpired between the two when Myers arrived. Measured by future events, however, his "information and data" were sufficient to reinforce Burns' confidence. "Am satisfied Linde will play fair," Burns wrote to Wood, left behind to babysit Linde in Poland, "and am more convinced after talking with Myers." A week later, at Wood's prompting, Linde himself wrote a long, apologetic note to Burns, promising that "I never thought and do not think now to double-cross you."

Linde's words appealed to Burns' vanity and sense of historical mission. "I take this opportunity, for the good of our investigation,—not only for the investigation of the bomb plots, but greater and bigger investigations—that you may be able to choke the radical movement in the United States if you would take a trip for a couple of weeks and come over here," Linde wrote. Rejecting this offer, Burns decided to stake his claim at home. In mid-August, less than two weeks after receiving Linde's note, he ordered a raid on the Communist Party.[14]

AS JACOB SPOLANSKY remembered it, he was sitting at his desk in the Chicago branch office when the telegram from Burns arrived. "Secret convention of Communist Party now in progress somewhere in vicinity of St. Joseph, Michigan," the message read. This was the same location where the communists had gathered two years earlier for their first tentative "unity" meeting—the beginning of the conspiracy, according to Linde, that resulted in the Wall Street bomb. Accompanied by agent Edward Shanahan, Spolansky left for Michigan on August 19. At St. Joseph, the local sheriff directed them to the town of Bridgman, a pastoral little vacation spot where radicals seeking anonymity might be mistaken for tourists. The Bridgman postmaster said they might want to follow up on the "foreign-looking people" who had recently set out en masse for a Lake Michigan retreat. When Spolansky spotted a "drunk" staggering through the nearby woods, he figured he had happened on the right spot. The vagrant was carrying a flashlight, indicating to Spolansky that he was probably some sort of communist scout on the watch for law-enforcement interference.

Spolansky was well trained to recognize such subtleties. A Russian-born immigrant to the United States, he had spent the last three years immersed in anticommunist surveillance, first as an undercover operative and later as an agent in the Bureau's Chicago office. In September 1919 he had attended the Communist Party's founding convention in Chicago, taking detailed notes on various bouts of factional wrangling. Under Flynn, he had helped to conduct the deportation raids and to keep an eye on Martens' Soviet Bureau. With Burns' appointment, he had moved into the Wall Street case as well. It was Spolansky who had the misfortune earlier in 1922 to inform Burns that Linde's suspects were "absolutely unknown" within Chicago. He anticipated better news from Bridgman.[15]

Like the Bureau itself, the Communist Party had undergone a minor transformation since the early months of the Wall Street investigation, when it seemed as if federal repression, combined with an incessant cycle of factionalization, might doom the movement altogether. In the spring of 1921, as Palmer was leaving the attorney general's office, the fractured national communist leadership had met in secret to iron out old ideological disputes and reinforce unity within the party structure. The result was the new Communist Party of America (CPA), which professed to speak with a single voice for some ten thousand self-proclaimed communists within the United States. Like its predecessors, the CPA operated almost wholly underground, organizing clandestine gatherings where members used party names and communicated in written code. It also initially advocated violence as a necessary concomitant to revolution, at least in theory. "Mass action culminates in armed insurrection and civil war," affirmed the CPA's unity declaration in May 1921.

By the time Spolansky encountered them in the Michigan woods the following year, some of these revolutionary trappings had begun to fall away, casualties of the disappointing sense, in the words of one communist leader, that "[w]e have virtually disappeared from the public scene." In December 1921, the CPA formed the Workers Party, a legal political party that eschewed talk of "armed insurrection" and proposed candidates for political office. The Bridgman convention itself was part of this trend, an effort to abide by recent instructions from Russia to bring the party out of its underground limbo and into the political open. The chief item on the agenda on the day that Spolansky appeared was the resolution of a dispute between the "Liquidators," who hoped to eliminate the underground party, and the "Goose caucus," which maintained that the threat of repression was still serious enough to merit an underground apparatus.[16]

After catching sight of the scout, Spolansky and Shanahan returned to town to buy overalls, the standard Bureau disguise for radical surveillance. Dressed as humble workmen, they paid a visit to Mrs. Wulfskeel, a local matron who rented cottages to urbanites fleeing the summer heat. It was raining, and Mrs. Wulfskeel apologized for her lack of available shelter. A foreign "singing society," she explained, had rented every last cottage.

Two days later, Spolansky, now accompanied by five other Bureau agents and a small posse of local citizens and police officials, rumbled back across muddy but still passable roads to the Wulfskeel resort. Mrs. Wulfskeel had estimated the "singing society" at eighty-six men, but when the roundup squads arrived they found only seventeen remaining. All seventeen were arrested, including Workers Party secretary Charles Ruthenberg and William F. Dunne, labor editor of the *Worker*, a leading communist paper. Over the next few days, the Bureau captured several more men and women who had attended the meeting—most notably William Z. Foster, one of the chief architects of the 1919 steel strike, now the founder and head of the communist-affiliated Trade Union Educational League. Thanks to instructions from the undercover operative who had first alerted them to the meeting, the Bureau also discovered a promising cache of documents. Hastily hidden in potato barrels near the meeting site were seventy-three parchment envelopes stuffed with sensitive party materials: voting records, membership lists, convention minutes, and letters to the Third International.[17]

As the first mass raid against communists since the Palmer era, the Bridgman crackdown struck many observers as an unfortunate throwback, a return to the "lawless repressive tactics," in the words of the ACLU, that had seemed so impossible just nine months earlier, at the moment of Debs' release. This impression was only strengthened the following week when Daugherty went to court to obtain what Secretary of Commerce Herbert Hoover called "one of the most sweeping and drastic injunctions ever issued in the United States" against the nation's striking rail workers, who had walked off the job in July. With more than four hundred thousand shopmen on strike, the rail workers' action dwarfed the springtime coal wars. And it, too, attracted its share of violence, with casualties on both sides. Like Burns, Daugherty presented such conflict as part of an unfolding revolutionary plot—a "conspiracy worthy of Lenin and Zinoviev." Both the injunction and the Bridgman raid, coming within days of each other, fulfilled the implicit promise Daugherty had made at the time of Debs' release: that a renewed "national peril" might someday require drastic "powers and instrumentalities" to combat it.[18]

As with the Palmer Raids, it was not immediately clear that the Justice Department exercised any formal jurisdiction in the Bridgman cases. While the Bureau planned and directed the raid, the actual arrests occurred under Michigan's criminal syndicalism statute, which forbade advocacy of "crime, sabotage, violence or other unlawful methods of terrorism as a means of accomplishing industrial or political reform." As a federal agency, the Bureau had no particular reason to be involved in enforcing Michigan state law. Nor did it propose to offer one. When pressed on the question, Daugherty's office explained that the Bureau had been investigating a federal crime rather than enforcing a state sedition statute when it sent agents to Michigan. Burns himself later hinted at what crime that might be. "We got a lot of these Reds when they held their last meeting, and I want you to read the evidence at that trial," he explained in February 1923. "At a former meeting they planned the Wall Street explosion."[19]

As they began to pore through the files rescued from the potato barrels, Bureau agents encountered the names of several men who had already figured prominently in Linde's story. Boris Reinstein—Linde's "Reinsteinem" of Moscow fame—was there, sent from Russia as a representative of the Comintern charged with encouraging the Americans to come aboveground. So were Edward Lindgren and Abram Jakira, the New York communists whose captured files had already done so much to affirm Burns' faith in Linde as a party insider. And there were other circumstantial connections to Linde's account as well. In his initial New York statements, Linde had asserted the guilt of "Bernard Wolf, a courier from the Third International who, along with an unnamed Russian chemist, transferred both money and dictates from Russia." The Bridgman attendance rolls contained no Bernard Wolf, but they did show the presence of Bertram Wolfe, an American-born communist of German extraction. Similarly, the lists offered no mention of Steven Barber, though they did include the name of Max Bedacht, a German-born party leader from Detroit, who operated under the party name of "Barber."[20]

If Bureau agents made any significant connections on these matters, they had little to show for it in the days that followed. By the time the second anniversary of the bombing arrived on September 16, 1922, a dozen men, including Lindgren, Jakira, and Wolfe, had been indicted for advocating criminal syndicalism and terrorism on Michigan soil. But as Burns acknowledged in a cable to Linde a few days later, the Wall Street case was still in crisis. "[T]he investigation is at a complete stand still," he wrote to Linde in Warsaw on September 24, "and nothing can be done until I have a conference with you."[21]

LINDE'S VISIT to Ellis Island was supposed to be a secret. As in Warsaw, someone leaked the news anyway. His boat arrived around midday on December 1, 1922, and by the evening the *Post* was reporting that "Wolfe Lindenfeld...was taken to Ellis Island today from the steamship *Lithuania*." During the voyage, he had posed as Wood's Polish interpreter, but several passengers noted something odd about him. According to one woman, who happily shared her impressions with a *New York Times* reporter, Linde seemed to spend an awful lot of time chattering about the Bolsheviks. He declared Trotsky "the greatest man the world had ever known."[22]

As his note to Linde had suggested, Burns decided to handle the interrogation himself. According to the *World*, J. Edgar Hoover came, too, and spent several hours locked up with the two men. The papers correctly assumed that Linde's return was connected to the explosion investigation. Official comments, however, were kept to a minimum. Immigration authorities said they knew nothing. The New York police said no one had informed them of any arrest. The Burns agency directed all questions to the Justice Department, which confirmed Linde's arrival but offered no further details.

In their correspondence, Burns had spoken kindly to Linde. "I...believe," he had written, "you will be straightforward and sincere in your efforts to aid and assist me." Their encounter at Ellis Island was not so civil. Technically, Linde was being detained as a person likely to become a public charge. Practically, he was Burns' prisoner. He occupied Room 6 in the first-class ward, where Justice Department guards watched him twenty-four hours a day. He was not permitted to leave his room or to mix with other detainees, though he did win a reprieve to watch a charity concert from his balcony. According to witnesses, he "stood and gazed solemnly on the crowd" during the playing of "The Star-Spangled Banner."[23]

By some reports, Linde was not allowed even a moment of contact with the waiter who delivered his meals. For the first few days, this hardly mattered, since Linde went on an immediate hunger strike to protest his ongoing detention. On December 2, he returned a breakfast of eggs, bread, and butter. In lieu of subsequent meals, he subsisted on hard candy and cigarettes. On December 3, his resolve weakening, he requested an apple, which was promptly supplied.[24]

Burns had assured Linde full and unfettered freedom if he came willingly to the United States. Secretly, however, he also had promised the

Polish authorities that he would return Linde when he was done. On December 27, Linde was trundled back onto a transatlantic liner bound, in the words of one State Department official, for "his perfectly good steam heated room in the Warsaw jail."[25]

As to what went on during Linde's three and a half weeks at Ellis Island, the public record is blank. "What they did with him or got out of him while he was detained at Ellis Island," read correspondence from U.S. officials in Warsaw, "I cannot say and I do not think that I shall even ask." Linde must have confirmed some connection between the Bridgman delegates and the Wall Street plot, however, because in the months that followed Burns scrambled to bring the case full circle. In January, he sent Spolansky to conduct another search for Celunitius and Wolf (they are "absolutely unknown within the extreme radical circle of this City," Spolansky reminded him). In March, he followed up with an inquiry into one Joseph Zack, also known as "Stevens" (among other pseudonyms), a Bridgman delegate and a future ally of Foster's in the Communist Party's trade union division. "The fact that this man is a suspect is not publicly known as he has never been brought up for examination," one agent noted, "or in any way questioned by the Federal authorities on this particular matter."[26]

Burns may have hoped to use the pressure of the Michigan arrests to elicit inside information from Zack or other communist defendants, much as Flynn had done during his investigations of the Galleanisti. If so, the strategy backfired. The only revelations produced by the Bridgman raid came from one of Burns' own employees.

ACCORDING TO HIS AGENCY REPORT, Albert Bailin had been surprised to see the communist leader Lechovitsky in Milwaukee. The two men knew each other from Russia's prewar radical scene: Bailin had emigrated to the United States soon after the 1905 revolution, while Lechovitsky had stayed on to become a midlevel Bolshevik. Then in late September 1920, two weeks after the Wall Street explosion, they ran into each other in the lobby of the Stag Hotel. Bailin stopped to chat, since he was working at the time for both the Burns and Thiel detective agencies as an undercover man on the Wall Street case. Lechovitsky told Bailin that he had been sent to Milwaukee to help U.S. communists recover from factional malaise. He also said he had a bagful of rubles to distribute "for the purpose of planting bombs and assassinating high public officials."

Bailin reported that Lechovitsky had seemed terribly excited about two recent meetings he had attended in New York. The first had been relatively large, featuring ninety-four of the top communists in the United States. The second was more intimate but still drew some well-known men, including Martens and Haywood. Lindgren, Wolf, and a man named Barber were there as well. Both meetings were tactical affairs, convened to determine how best to move capitalism toward its historic destiny of collapse. According to Bailin, the communists ultimately concluded that terrorism was the best means available. "It was...decided that a bomb be thrown in the heart of Wall Street," he reported, "and see what effect it will have on the Chamber of Commerce, and what they will have to say."[27]

As a story of communist treachery, this account of the Wall Street plot was nearly indistinguishable from Linde's. Both versions featured the clandestine summer meetings, the revolutionary aspirations, the conspirators—Lindgren, Wolf, Barber, and others—humbly obeying the Third International. The only major difference between the two was that Linde claimed that his story was true. Bailin, on the other hand, readily admitted that his own reports were nothing but lies. He said he invented the whole tale at his employers' behest to destroy the Communist Party.

Bailin delivered this bombshell during a February 1923 deposition for *State of Michigan v. William Z. Foster*, the first of the Bridgman cases scheduled to come to trial. It was not the first time that he had issued such claims. A naturalized Russian immigrant and onetime union official, Bailin had initially come under public scrutiny in November 1920, when the New York police arrested him for sending a false bomb threat to the Woolworth Building under the misspelled signature "Nights of the Red Star, American Anarchist Fighters" ("We will not tolerate any longer unless you free all the political and industrial prisoners," the note read, echoing the Wall Street flyer). At the time, he insisted that he was following the instructions of his employers at the Burns agency, who wanted to scare up extra funds for their work. The only place where his claims had been noticed and taken seriously, however, was in the left-wing press, where his story played a minor role in the mounting evidence for the accident theory.[28]

In the months that followed, Bailin had abandoned the detective industry and re-created himself as an amateur muckraker, parceling out seamy tales of detective shenanigans and betrayals. In early 1921, he cooperated in an exposé for the *Seattle Union Record*, describing how he had been instructed to falsify reports, encourage bomb throwing and window breaking, write fake left-wing pamphlets, forge threatening letters, steal reports from other agencies, and spy on union meetings during his time in the detective industry. He claimed that Burns himself knew that his agents were fabricating reports accusing Haywood, Martens, and the others of planning the Wall Street bomb. As with his earlier allegations, though, nobody outside of the left-wing press had paid much attention. In 1923, with the high-profile Bridgman cases on their way to court, with Burns at the helm of the Bureau, and with the Linde debacle fresh in public memory, he found a different reception.[29]

Bailin's questioning in the Bridgman proceedings unfolded in the law office of William Cunnea, a socialist lawyer and former Chicago mayoral candidate who had donated his facilities for the occasion. The room was just big enough for a handful of reporters and photographers invited by the defense team to record the allegations. Over the course of his five-day grilling, Bailin testified to every imaginable detective sins—and even a few previously unimagined. He claimed, for instance, that Allen O. Myers, his onetime boss at the Burns agency, had ordered him to compose the threat on the Woolworth Building in order to "create newspaper publicity, so the bankers would raise a larger fund than they have already raised to investigate the Wall Street explosion." Though he had no proof, Bailin added that he wouldn't be surprised if the Burns Agency had actually planted the bomb on Wall Street.[30]

What he could prove was that the reports he had submitted to both the Thiel and Burns agencies in connection with the explosion were total fabrications, as were the reports he had submitted connecting William Z. Foster to the explosion case. According to Bailin, the Burns agency had instructed him to loiter around a well-known radical café to listen for mentions of Foster's name. The café was rumored to be frequented by the blacksmith who had shod the Wall Street horse, and Bailin was supposed to pay special attention to anything that might link Foster with the blast. In this assignment, as in so many others, the point was not so much to find out who had committed the crime as to drum up new business for Burns. "The steel corporations," Myers supposedly told Bailin, "would give us any amount of money if we could do away with Foster." As with so many other queries, nothing much had come of the Foster reports. According to the Bridgman defense team, though, this was only because the frame-up had taken another few years to complete. With Bailin's deposition as evidence, Foster's lawyers intended to show that the Bridgman prosecution was "part of a general conspiracy and plan" laid years earlier "to destroy Foster and other [communist party] members."[31]

The task of transforming Bailin's accusations into a legal defense fell to Goldman and Haywood's old Village acquaintance Frank Walsh, the former head of the prewar Commission on Industrial Relations. As a long-time defender of radical clients, Walsh knew that one of his greatest challenges at trial would be to prevent jurors from fixating on Foster's politics. One of the best ways to do that was to present a villain even more distasteful than the defendant himself. By focusing on the underhanded tactics of the Burns agency—and, by implication, of the Burns-led Bureau—Walsh hoped to transform Foster's trial, like Haywood's almost two decades earlier in Idaho, from a prosecution of radicals into a referendum on detective tactics.

Burns assembled a formidable propaganda machine to discredit his former employee. According to Burns' son Sherman, Bailin had indeed worked on the Wall Street investigation but had been fired "because his mind was so active and inventive that we could not place any confidence in him." Bailin had also worked for Henry Ford as a researcher on his notorious *Dearborn Independent* series "Jew Mania," in which he revived the canard of a global Jewish banking conspiracy behind nearly all of the world's sins. This—along with the fact that "you didn't marry a Jewish [*sic*] yourself, did you?"—was presented as a symptom of Bailin's inherent treachery not only to his coreligionists but to nearly everyone who had ever trusted him. "I challenge Mr. Walsh," Burns said, "to put this fellow on the witness stand."[32]

In the end, Walsh did not take him up on it. When Bailin finally closed his deposition on February 17, 1923, he was greeted by several Chicago police officers, who promptly arrested him for criminal libel. A week or so later, the Justice Department announced it would bring federal charges against him for mail fraud in the Woolworth bomb threat case. This convinced Walsh that Bailin was a less than ideal witness, but as with the Linde story, much of the damage to the Bureau's reputation had already been done. In an interview after Foster's trial, the sole female juror said that the jury had found it impossible, after so many years of scandal, to believe the claims of government witnesses. "The stage setting of the prosecution seemed overplayed with such a display of detectives and undercover men," she explained, "that it appeared more like trying to railroad Foster than like prosecuting him."

As a result, the jury split on Foster's guilt, an inauspicious beginning for the Michigan prosecutors who were facing months of similar trials. "The six on my side did not believe that the Communist Party advocated violence," the juror told the *Times*. "The other six believed that it did. That was all there was to it."[33]

THE COLLAPSE of the Foster case, far more than Debs' release, signaled the start of a new era for the Communist Party, bringing the cessation, at least until the 1930s, of overt federal suppression. After Foster, only one more defendant, Charles Ruthenberg, came to trial; due to a lengthy series of appeals, he died before serving a single day in prison. The Communist Party itself continued to move aboveground, tentatively but surely, abandoning the explicitly violent language of its youth in favor of more temperate calls for revolution. The Bureau, by contrast, turned increasingly to secrecy and subterfuge, continuing to watch and wait but increasingly reluctant to make arrests or take public action. This was its approach to the arrest of Noah Lerner, an alleged Soviet courier and recent transplant from Haywood's Kuzbas colony who emerged as the last major suspect in the Wall Street case.[34]

Outwardly, Lerner met Burns' loose definition of a Russian communist. A twenty-three-year-old electrician, he had ventured to Kuzbas in the spring of 1921 as part of a contingent of skilled workers eager to join "the first industrial colony in the world where engineers will find freedom to work out experiments they cannot attempt under the profit system," in the words of an early recruiting pamphlet. While there, he had come in contact with many of the men who had once figured prominently in the Wall Street case, including Haywood and Martens. He had also met the Doyle family, transplants from Baton Rouge who became disenchanted with the colony's paltry food supplies and internal squabbling. Upon their return to the United States, the Doyles had offered Lerner's name to the New York police as a possible suspect; he had allegedly bragged about driving a wagon on Wall Street on September 16. The Bureau was already watching him, attempting to prove his connection with other Kuzbas residents suspected of smuggling Bolshevik funds into the United States. When the New York bomb squad proposed to arrest Lerner, Burns put up no objection. In a sign of just how much had changed since the investigation's early days, however, the Bureau begged the police to keep the federal involvement secret from the press.[35]

It was a smart move. Despite the Bureau's confidence that Lerner, his wife, and several other acquaintances were transporting money for the Soviets, it proved only a matter of time before Lerner's story succumbed to the Wall Street curse. On May 13, the day after his arrest, the headlines had him all but convicted: "Arrest Russian Red as Wall St. Bomber," read the front page of the *Times*. By the following week, thanks to an airtight alibi, he was a free man. Like Linde, Lerner had passed the night before the bombing at the Broadway Central hotel. On September 16, 1920, he had spent all day campaigning on behalf of the ousted Socialist assemblymen.[36]

With the Lerner arrest, the Wall Street case completed its slide from ignominy into hopelessness. "One more person arrested as a 'suspect' in connection with the Wall Street explosion of 1920 has been discharged," the *Post* noted plaintively. "...In every instance the procedure has been the same." The *Call*, as usual, was even more passionate in its distress. "It is about time that Burns himself should be investigated and his actions sifted to the bottom," read an editorial in the May 25, 1923, issue.[37]

In official correspondence, Burns continued to claim that he had solved the Wall Street case. "We have information that the Third Internationale [*sic*] through Ludwig Martens, their Soviet Representative in the United States, was responsible for the explosion," he wrote to the American embassy in Germany in early 1924. "We knew at least six weeks in advance that it was going to take place, but we didn't know where. We also knew from positive proof we have that a number of people did know exactly where it was to take place and we have the documentary proof of this."[38]

Just why he would allow so much of his career and reputation to depend on the word of someone as dubious as Linde remains hard to fathom. Perhaps, as Bailin suggested, the idea of linking the explosion to the Bolsheviks was simply too tantalizing, and too profitable, to be left by the wayside. More likely, Burns simply made the sort of mistake that had destroyed Flynn's investigation of the Galleanisti. According to an internal investigation conducted by the Communist Party at the height of Linde's public exposure, there was indeed a Linde within the party ranks. He was not, however, the "consummate faker" employed by Burns.[39]

Linde himself denied to the end that he had ever attempted to deceive anyone. "I am going back to Poland," he declared before departing from Ellis Island, "and I will work with all my ability to show the American people that I was not a fourflusher and not a double crosser. I was working honestly, and I condemn the act that was taken by the Reds on Wall Street where forty-one people [*sic*] let loose their lives." When he arrived in Poland, he immediately stopped in at the American legation to set up a system for delivering new discoveries straight to the Bureau. Much to the relief of the State Department, it was the last they heard from William Linde.[40]

# 16

· · · ·

# THE ROAR
# OF THE TWENTIES

NOAH LERNER was not the last Wall Street suspect. In March 1924, a London convict named Ralph Thurber accused one "Girlie O'Day" of having planted the bomb on Wall Street; Bureau agents found that Miss O'Day did not exist and that Thurber was an "awful liar."[1]

⌈The following October, a New Yorker named Richard O'Hara stumbled into the police precinct on West Forty-seventh Street and confessed that he had been the wagon driver; the police sent him off to Bellevue to be treated for alcoholism.[2]⌋

In February 1925, San Quentin prisoner Herbert Wilson, a friend of Thurber's, testified in an unrelated case that he had sold thirty quarts of stolen nitroglycerin to the Wall Street bombers in 1920; Burns thought his claim was "bunk."[3]

Later that year, a southerner named Elmer Garel wrote to the Morgan bank offering his confession in return for cash to travel from Alabama to New York, stressing that "[t]his is not a crank letter or from one who is insane"; the Bureau managed to investigate Garel and dismiss him while keeping Morgan's name out of the papers.[4]

Noah Lerner was not the last suspect, in short, but his was the final serious arrest, the last time any investigator boasted that the case would soon be solved. As the story of the explosion began, so would it end: with a few scraps of evidence and a distinct absence of answers.

What came to a close with the Lerner arrest was not simply the Wall Street saga but the "story of dynamite" as it had been known to Americans for more than four decades, starting with Johann Most's arrival on U.S. shores. Though a few scattered bombs continued to explode in American cities throughout the 1920s, especially as the Sacco-Vanzetti case emerged as an international controversy, none caused either the physical devastation or the national alarm that the Wall Street plot had occasioned. After decades of escalating death tolls—seven victims at Haymarket, twenty-one at the *Los Angeles Times*, thirty-eight on Wall Street—the mid-1920s brought a sudden lull in bombings and assassinations, a pronounced decline in terrorism as a weapon of class warfare. Nor did such acts seriously revive in the 1930s, when workers and employers once again squared off over capitalism's relentless cycles of boom and bust. By the mid-1930s, as political scientist David Rapoport has noted, labor experts had declared terrorism and assassination all but defunct, predicting that "assassinations and acts of terror were declining so much that in the future the subjects would be interesting to historians or antiquarians only!" This assessment would hold for decades to come. The Wall Street explosion would not be surpassed until 1995, when Timothy McVeigh blew up the federal building in Oklahoma City, killing 168 people, a very different act of terrorism in a very different America.[5]

Why, after decades of escalation, after hundreds of anguished efforts at prevention, repression, and reform, did this form of violence disappear so suddenly—and at the very moment when so many anticipated that it would increase? Part of the answer can be found in the changing nature of revolutionary politics, both in the United States and around the world. By the mid-1920s, the Soviet-led communist movement came to dominate global revolutionary circles, consigning anarchists and syndicalists to the margins of power when it did not convert them or, in Russia itself, send them to their deaths. As a result, tactics such as sabotage and propaganda by deed—explicitly rejected by the communist leadership—fell into disrepute, hangovers from an era when socialism had been struggling to achieve its first existing state.

Within the United States, the lingering impact of the Red Scare only hastened this transition. Though A. Mitchell Palmer would ultimately be remembered as one of the great rogues of the Justice Department, his deportation policies in fact achieved many of their aims, driving hundreds, if not thousands, of revolutionaries either underground or out of the country altogether. For the fledgling communist movement, this proved to be a temporary setback; by the early 1930s, communists had rebuilt their movement with Soviet support (though they would endure their own federal battles—and ultimate defeat—some two decades later). For those unable to rely on the Soviet government, however, the Red Scare years proved to be a fatal blow. After the early 1920s, fractured and bereft of outside support, neither the anarchists nor the Wobblies ever successfully regrouped. In that sense, the Red Scare did eliminate those groups most often described as the nation's chief acolytes of "terrorism." Ironically, it also helped to secure the position of the Communist Party as the defining organizing of the revolutionary left.

The passage of immigration restriction played a role in these changing dynamics as well. By 1924, scattershot deportation policies had been replaced by permanent, far-reaching immigration quotas, the nation's first major cap on immigration and one of the most consequential pieces of legislation passed during the decade. Based on the U.S. population of 1890, the quotas reflected a nativist hierarchy. Immigration by Italians and eastern European Jews was heavily restricted (Asians were banned altogether), while "old-stock" immigrants from places such as Britain and France were welcomed in greater numbers. Combined with deportation policies aimed specifically at radicals, these quotas proved to be serious barriers for would-be emigrants from Europe, eliminating the easy back-and-forth that once brought advocates of terrorism such as Most and Galleani to U.S. shores. Indeed, limiting the influx of foreign-born radicals had been a key part of the law's intent. By design, the quotas restricted immigration primarily from those areas of Europe—Italy, Russia, Poland—suspected of harboring anarchists and communists. In that sense, they were not so much a break with the past as the fruition of the policies first proposed after Haymarket.[6]

While restriction and repression contributed to the decline in terrorism, reform also played its part. In the mid-1930s, appealing to a receptive federal government, the labor movement finally won many of the federal protections it had been demanding since the 1870s, solving, in the words of labor historian John Commons, its "paramount problem": "the right to exist." This was precisely what reformers such as Lincoln Steffens had prescribed in the aftermath of the McNamara Affair, predicting that labor reform would lead to a steep decline in terrorism and violence. Like Palmer, they turned out to be at least partially right. While the labor battles of the 1930s did not come without bloodshed, they were largely devoid of the bombings and assassinations that had played such a prominent role in earlier struggles at Homestead and Ludlow, in Los Angeles and Coeur d'Alene. The greatest dynamite case of the 1930s turned out to be a mere holdover from the prewar years. In 1939, after more than two decades of agitation on his behalf, Tom Mooney finally won a pardon and release from jail. With a formal federal body to mediate labor disputes, with a receptive New Deal government, the forms of violence that had once been at the heart of the western labor wars faded into history with him.[7]

Thus, within a decade of the Wall Street bombing investigation's collapse, "the story of dynamite," as Louis Adamic described it in 1931, proved to have a happy ending of sorts—one that suggested that the problems of labor terrorism and propaganda by deed, once so apparently intractable, might after all be solved. In the mid-1920s, however, as news of the failed Lerner arrest hit the front page, that reassuring conclusion lay in the future, as unimaginable as the idea that the soaring stock market would soon come crashing down. Without a grand trial and verdict to conclude the Wall Street explosion story, without any definitive resolution, the same factions that had for so long struggled over the contours of the investigation took up the challenge to shape its ultimate meaning. Like the thousands of men and women who had rushed to Wall and Broad on the afternoon of September 16, they were left to rely on history, imagination, self-interest, and ideology to make sense of what had happened.[8]

IN 1923, JUST AS the Wall Street investigation was winding down, Palmer's longtime critic Louis Post published a short memoir, *The Deportations Delirium of Nineteen-Twenty: A Personal Narrative of an Historic Official Experience*, which traced, among other events, the struggle between the Justice and Labor departments over the Palmer Raids. As the title suggested, Post claimed that the fear and repression of the immediate postwar years had been the product of a "delirium," a psychological malady to which American citizens "fell victims" just as they had more than three decades earlier during the Haymarket Affair. This mental frailty—a "popular hysteria," in Post's words, bred by the trials of war—had led Americans to misinterpret events such as the Wall Street explosion as revolutionary assaults, and to assign such events far more significance than they actually had. The truth, according to Post, was that terrorism and genuine revolutionary sentiment had never posed any real threat to the United States.[9]

In decades to come, his claims would be adopted by a generation of liberal historians and activists who came to condemn the postwar years as a time of "hysteria" and "poor reality testing"—in essence, a precursor to the McCarthy years. This view rested in part on the fact that the major bombings of the earlier period—May Day, June 2, and especially the Wall Street explosion—remained unsolved. The indeterminate nature of the investigations allowed critics of the antiradical effort to suggest that the whole series of events that had once seemed so threatening and divisive, so full of conflict—strikes, bombings, deportation raids—had been merely the products of an overactive national imagination. After all, Post argued, if the combined forces of the New York police, the Burns agency, and the federal government could not manage to identify and prosecute some poor radical for the bombing, "what inference is possible, in all reason, except that the crimes were not of 'ultra-radical' origin, or else that the detectives were grossly inefficient?" Without a definitive answer one way or another, he concluded, the best that the country could do was to put the whole thing behind it.[10]

By the mid-1920s, this impulse to erase and minimize the story of conflict, to put it firmly in the past, had already begun to shape how Americans came to terms with the explosion's legacy. As early as August 1925, on the eve of the bombing's five-year anniversary, a *Wall Street Journal* reporter noted a startling lack of memory about what had taken place. Even in the financial district, passing stenographers could not identify the pockmarks in the north face of the Morgan bank. "How quickly time effaces the memory of startling events," the paper mused.[11]

But it was not time alone that allowed the country to forget. The process of erasing the Wall Street explosion was deliberate as well as natural. By 1925, nobody—not investigators, not the suspects, not civil libertarians, not even the Morgan bank—had an interest in maintaining the memory of an event that had caused all of them so much embarrassment, fear, and grief. To the hundreds of detectives who had worked on the case, it lingered as a great symbol of failure, a towering example of all that had gone wrong in the antiradical campaign. To the radicals who had been the objects of attack, the bombing was equally painful, a reminder of their dread and powerlessness in the face of official whim and sanction.

Perhaps most importantly, the leaders of Wall Street—the men who might have organized memorials and moments of silence, whose slightest utterances earned widespread notice in the papers—made no move to preserve the memory of the occasion. Privately, they remembered. As late as 1963, Morgan partner George Whitney recalled the day as "[d]isagreeable... people were dead all around you." Outwardly, though, Wall Street emerged remarkably fit and confident in the 1920s. Faced with an act of terrible violence, and with a new communist foe, by the middle of the decade American finance capitalism had emerged more triumphant and profitable than ever. To the young stenographers in 1925 who wondered what had created the pitted walls of the Morgan bank, it must have seemed impossible that Wall Street had once been so vulnerable, and so much under attack.[12]

THROUGHOUT THE 1920S, the Russian economic experiment continued to attract the admiration of revolutionaries convinced, as Lincoln Steffens had declared in 1919, that "I have seen the future and it works." It was the American economy, however, that emerged as the envy of the world. By the mid-1920s, American factories produced as much as the combined countries of Europe. Americans themselves consumed far more per capita than anyone else on the planet. In the 1920s, an American bought, ate, and used twice as much as a French or German citizen, and 50 percent more than an Englishman. Much of what they consumed they had always consumed: grain, milk, oil, leather. But there were also thousands of new products and new salesmen to promote them; a rising generation of marketers hawked cars, films, appliances.[13]

This material boom would give the decade its moniker of the "Roaring Twenties"; writers, historians, and politicians recalled a time of frivolity and apolitical excess. "Americans had at last clearly demonstrated that they wished to be less concerned with weighty and compelling foreign and domestic problems," historian Robert Murray wrote in 1955, describing how interest in social conflict suddenly seemed to fade, "and more with radios, sports contests, Mah Jong and homemade gin recipes." But beneath the advertisers' sheen was the darker legacy of the "weighty and compelling" conflicts of the wartime and postwar years. If Americans were less inclined toward agitation than consumption, it was partly because the range of political opportunities had been drastically condensed, and because the cost of political involvement had grown so high. The galloping success of American capitalism in the 1920s rested to some extent on the successful repression of available alternatives that had taken place in the preceding years.[14]

Though the level of prosperity had changed, the fundamental distribution of power in the country looked much as it had before the war; indeed, wealth grew only more concentrated at the top as the decade wore on. By the end of the 1920s, the two hundred largest nonfinancial companies controlled almost a quarter of the country's wealth. With business in full merger mania there were fewer of those companies to go around. In autos, it was Chrysler, General Motors, and Ford; in electricity, Westinghouse and General Electric. The era's buzzword was democratization, with thousands of Americans investing in the stock market for the first time. Millions more, however, were left out altogether. Fully one-fifth of the nation still lived in poverty. On farms throughout the Midwest, falling prices and global competition presaged the depression to come. Among laborers, the story was much the same: prosperity was all around, but it remained in any real sense elusive.

Within industry and finance, by contrast, the New York Stock Exchange rose to rollicking new heights; the number of listed stocks grew four times over the course of the decade, and the Dow Jones average shot up just as fast. Nobody was in a better position to take advantage of the country's new economic supremacy than the one institution that had long symbolized American capital to the rest of the world: the House of Morgan. The boom that fueled car purchases for other Americans generated annual salaries for the Morgan partners of well over $1 million in the 1920s, a fact noted in the financial pages as proof that no more plum position could be found. Morgan wealth was nothing new. What set the 1920s apart from previous decades was the degree to which that financial power had become fused with the workings of American government. Before the war, the bank had sought, except when absolutely necessary, to avoid political involvement. Ten years later, its partners proudly identified themselves as businessmen-statesmen, and the bank operated openly as a financial and strategic center of American "dollar diplomacy."[15]

By the mid-1920s, not only Jack but all of the Morgan partners were bona fide celebrities, their travels and social gatherings—even their golf games—recorded in detail in the papers and newsreels. Junius emerged as a society column fixture, attending royal garden parties at Buckingham Palace or thwarting his opponents on the water. Within the financial world, he never quite lived up to the promise of his overdetermined youth. In 1922, he moved to London to observe the workings of Morgan, Grenfell—yet another of the "Millionaires' Sons Who Follow in Father's Footsteps," in the words of the *Christian Science Monitor*. Next came a string of directorships in some of the great behemoths of the twenties boom: General Motors in 1925, U.S. Steel four years later. Unlike his father and grandfather, though, Junius proved unable to translate the opportunities of his historical moment into either personal power or financial innovation. As befit a man of his position, he devoted considerable time to philanthropy; in 1927 he helped his explosion-day comrade in arms John Markle establish a foundation "to promote the general good of mankind" and thus defuse Markle's fearsome antilabor reputation. His proudest accomplishment was his election in 1932 as commodore of the New York Yacht Club, a position that reflected both family tradition and his own heart's desire. For the next thirty years, Junius bided his time on Wall Street as a prosperous though second-rank Morgan partner, amiable and well regarded but never one to inspire the Morgan awe.[16]

With Junius, like his younger brother, Harry, unable (or unwilling) to assume leadership, with Jack increasingly in retreat from a prying press, the task for charting the bank's new direction fell instead to the other Morgan partners, especially to Thomas Lamont. Now towering above the London banks as the world's highest financial authority, the House of Morgan needed someone who could move easily in global, cosmopolitan circles, who could sell the conservative Morgan ethos in the new age of advertising. Lamont's efforts toward this end earned him a fortune; aside from Jack, he was the richest of the Morgan partners, with his salary alone approaching some $5 million per year. He maintained a home on East Seventieth Street, an island off the coast of Maine, and a country estate in the Palisades. His social circle, filled with artists, luminaries, European royalty, and American plutocrats, epitomized the bank's new status as a global entity. As the premier bank in a shaky postwar world, the Morgan firm was called upon repeatedly to bail out governments as distant as Japan's and Austria's and as close at hand as Cuba's, largely without interference from the U.S. government. One of the hallmarks of the 1920s was the impunity with which the Morgan firm conducted its own foreign policy, restrained by little more than its bedrock conservatism.[17]

The 1924 presidential election offered perhaps the most dramatic example of the new Morgan intimacy with formal politics. Calvin

Coolidge, who rose to the presidency after Harding's fatal stroke the previous year, was the Republican candidate. He was also a former college roommate of Morgan partner Dwight Morrow, who ranked second only  to Lamont in his defining presence at the bank. While the Morgan men backed Coolidge, though, they hardly would have been devastated had the election gone the other way. The Democratic candidate, John Davis, was Jack's backgammon and cribbage partner, in addition to being the bank's chief counsel.[18]

As president, Coolidge became an icon of the "New Era" of corporate prosperity. But his rise to power also showed the degree to which the exuberant celebration of capitalism in the 1920s depended on the marginalization of capitalism's longtime critics. Coolidge's election and popularity marked the successful melding of "Americanism" and "capitalism" that had been so much promoted in the aftermath of the Wall Street explosion. "Never before," the *Wall Street Journal* applauded, "here or anywhere else, has a government been so completely fused with business."[19]

For Wall Street itself, a pliant federal government formed one of the foundations of the New Era boom. The language of "plutocrats," "capitalist Caesars," and the "Money Trust" all but disappeared from the national conversation. William Z. Foster, recovered from his Bridgman trial and running for president on the Communist ticket in 1924, continued to denounce both Davis and Coolidge as "agents of Wall Street." At the Democratic convention, William Jennings Bryan pleaded against nominating "a Wall Street man." Such voices had become exceptions, though, throwbacks to a different political era. More typical were the milquetoast sentiments of the *New Republic*, which noted meekly that the magazine "would rather not have these Morgan boys quite so much at home around the White House."[20]

Even as the financial world catapulted toward the disaster that would descend in October 1929 and ultimately inspire a revival of anti–Wall Street sentiment, it was easy to believe that both Wall Street and the Morgans had vanquished their critics once and for all.

AS WALL STREET'S LEADERS strode aggressively into the future, the radical left moved into a thoroughly defensive position. Under attack from the federal government, trade unionists, progressives, and other liberals, revolutionary groups began to slough off their militant identities as the decade wore on. Between 1920 and 1926, the Socialist rolls dropped from thirty-six thousand to fewer than nine thousand members. The Wobblies, already weakened by wartime repression, had just seven thousand to eight thousand members by the decade's end. Russian and Italian anarchists, always fragmented, were split between various countries or living underground. After Bridgman, the exact membership of the Communist Party became almost impossible to determine, but when the party emerged from underground in 1923, it had at most ten thousand members. Grigory Zinoviev judged from Russia, "Probably there are fewer than 5,000 Communists in America upon whom we can really depend."[21]

The American Federation of Labor found itself battered as well. With the help of a flourishing private detective industry (one estimate put the number of labor spies at two hundred thousand by 1928), industrialists succeeded in scaling back wartime union gains. Membership in the AFL decreased from 5 million in 1920 to 3.6 million by the end of the decade, and open-shop policies hampered new organizing. Employers used the new techniques of propaganda and advertising to sell policies of "welfare capitalism" and company-run unions to workers who had once demanded such high-minded principles as autonomy and democracy. In place of the union flyers that they might once have received at the factory gates, workers found pamphlets in their pay envelopes assuring them that "Bolshevism will vanish when every worker produces useful goods to the greatest extent of his ability."[22]

There were a few bright spots for the left and the labor movement. In 1925, union firebrand A. Philip Randolph led African-American sleeping-car porters in a successful rout of the Pullman company, triumphing where Debs had been defeated in 1894. Socialists, too, found small victories where they could. In 1922, New York voters returned August Claessens to the legislature, which agreed to seat him. It was even possible for a reform coalition to run a prominent national politician for president. In 1924, Progressive Party candidate Robert La Follette won 16 percent of the national vote, nearly half of Democrat John Davis' total, on a platform advocating public control of rails, mines, and utilities. As La Follette's campaign showed, however, any progressive, union man, or civil libertarian now had to contend with accusations of disloyalty and hidden allegiance with Bolshevism. Coolidge himself explained that the voters would have to decide "whether America will allow itself to be degraded into a communistic or socialistic state or whether it will remain American." In response, La Follette attacked Coolidge as a tool of business.

But he directed even more ire against the communists themselves as "mortal enemies" of all decent Americans.[23]

La Follette's denunciation of radicalism said far more than Coolidge's about the ways in which the trauma of the war and its aftermath had changed American political culture. Before the war, radicals and progressives had not necessarily cooperated, but neither had there been a clear line separating their camps. By the mid-1920s, opposition to radicalism of any sort had become a litmus test for entry into American politics. In many cases, the new antiradicalism, especially anticommunism, was more assumed than explained—something so deeply understood that it no longer needed to be articulated with the force expressed in a year such as 1919. Most progressives simply altered their language and their platforms to avoid seeming too "communistic." As one activist later explained, in the 1920s any do-gooder hoping to raise money from wealthy patrons "carefully avoided any identification with the phraseology of social reform."[24]

TO THE MEN AND WOMEN who had once devoted themselves to forging such links, who had sought to create a unified movement of reformers and revolutionaries, the 1920s were a period as bleak as any they had ever known. Eugene Debs, the preeminent spokesman for a unified, American-based vision of socialism, left prison in late 1921 only to find himself enmeshed in wearying partisan squabbles over the Bolshevik Revolution. With Lenin in power in Russia, with socialist numbers dwindling at home, he was forced to wonder if history itself had passed him by. Audiences at his speeches were small and restless. "Had the lecture been delivered by anyone other than Debs, many in the audience would have walked before the conclusion," a friend observed. His health was failing, too. Debs spent his postprison years in and out of sanitariums. On October 15, 1926, during one of those stays, he suffered a heart attack. He died five days later.[25]

In Russia, Bill Haywood faced the collapse of the Kuzbas colony as a final defeat. Unable to return to the United States, equipped with only pidgin Russian, he watched quietly as the promise of a workers' democracy gave way to the undeniable facts of starvation, unemployment, and permanent Soviet dictatorship. Like Debs, Haywood spent his final years "alone and disconsolate," in the words of the *Chicago Tribune's* Moscow reporter, "contemplating the ruin of his ideals, the frailty of human friendship and the burst bubble of his Utopian dream." On

May 18, 1928, two months after a crippling stroke, he died in exile in Moscow. Following a boisterous public funeral, the Bolshevik government had his body cremated, interring half of the ashes in the walls of the Kremlin and sending the other half, as Haywood requested, to be buried at Waldheim Cemetery in suburban Chicago, near the graves of the Haymarket martyrs.[26]

Emma Goldman would eventually join him there, finding a last resting place in the United States after her death in 1940. In Russia in the 1920s, however, their friendship proved short-lived. Goldman and Berkman fled the Soviet regime in late 1922, appalled at its mass executions, its violations of free speech, and especially its brutal suppression of the Kronstadt sailors' rebellion. For nearly two decades, they remained exiles, taking up residency in Riga, Stockholm, Berlin, Nice, London, St. Tropez, and many other European cities. For Goldman, that journey ended in Toronto, where she spent her final years agitating against fascism as the ultimate expression of capitalist greed and the tyrannical state. Berkman's wanderings came to a close in France, where he lived year to year, sometimes month to month, awaiting renewals of his visa. At the age of sixty-five, suffering from prostate cancer, he shot himself in the spine at his apartment in Nice. He died hours later.

Goldman herself managed to make one brief visit to the United States after her deportation, embarking on a whirlwind book tour to promote her new autobiography, *Living My Life*, in 1934. In the book, she recalled how the Haymarket executions had first transformed her into an anarchist and how she and Berkman had decided to follow their example in 1892, publicly admitting that she had helped to plan the attack on Frick. She also described the long history of tit-for-tat violence that had shaped her experiences as an American, from Czolgosz's attack on McKinley through the McNamara and Mooney affairs and on into the upheaval of 1919. When it came time to lecture, however, she found herself muzzled, forbidden by the terms of her visa to expound on political subjects. She hoped that adhering to the law might win her a reprieve—permission, at last, to resume living in America. As it turned out, she was not the only one who remembered the turmoil of those years. When she left for a lecture in Canada that May, the attorney general received a letter suggesting that she not be allowed to return. It was written by onetime Radical Division chief, now the director of the Bureau of Investigation (known as the FBI after 1935), J. Edgar Hoover.[27]

OF ALL THE MAJOR PLAYERS in the Wall Street bombing investigation, only Hoover emerged from the turmoil of the 1920s with his power enhanced and secured. In 1924, not long after the Bridgman trials, Burns and Daugherty undertook an investigation of yet another "Communist leader," in Daugherty's words, "no more a Democrat than Stalin, his comrade, in Moscow." This time, however, the Bureau's target was no ordinary radical. He was Burton K. Wheeler, the U.S. senator from Montana, who had called upon Congress to look into abuses within the Justice Department and thus earned Daugherty's wrath as a coddler of Reds. When Wheeler discovered that Daugherty had retaliated by rifling his office and putting agents on his trail, he called for hearings to examine the Bureau's confidential files. After Daugherty refused to hand them over, President Coolidge demanded his resignation. Without Daugherty's protection, Burns, too, became a casualty. In mid-May 1924, after admitting that he had dispatched Bureau agents to investigate a U.S. senator (among other illegal acts), he resigned his post as Bureau chief and handed the reins to Hoover.[28]

For Burns, the Wheeler scandal proved to be the end of a long downhill slide that landed him "out on the dung," in Haywood's words, "where he properly belonged." The Wobblies themselves had a hand in his disgrace, publishing a series of stolen Burns agency reports that showed Burns detectives and Bureau agents working openly with Arizona copper companies to suppress labor activism. Burns narrowly avoided a jail term as he left office; several associates earned convictions for jury tampering and assorted other crimes. Indeed, the Wheeler charges proved but a minor incident in the Harding administration scandals, including the Teapot Dome oil corruption scheme. Scorned by his onetime benefactors in both Ohio and New York, Burns moved with his wife to Sarasota, Florida, where he occupied himself composing rollicking stories of his former exploits and nursing a fledgling Hollywood career. But as the *Washington Star* commented in 1924, "The days of the 'Old Sleuth' are over." Burns died in 1932 after several heart attacks, leaving the detective agency to his sons.[29]

Flynn's final years were less scandalous, though no more successful. While he indicated a certain willingness to return to detective work (rumor suggested he might someday return to the Secret Service), Flynn spent his post-Bureau years limping along as the head of the tiny Flynn Detective Agency, never any competition for the powerhouses of

Pinkerton and Burns. He also took up editing *Flynn's Weekly*, a detective fiction magazine in which the hero always got his man. After a lifetime of pooh-poohing the Sherlock Holmes image, the plunge into the world of mythmaking was a major concession. Like his role at the Flynn agency, his editorship of the *Weekly* did not last long. Flynn died of heart disease in October 1928, his fictional triumphs belied by his failure to solve the last great case of his career.[30]

Eager to forge a different path, Hoover did his best to separate himself from his predecessors, explaining on the day of Burns' resignation that he had been forced to play an "unwilling part" in their misguided raids and botched investigations. These claims elided his critical role behind the scenes; despite his junior status, he had brought his full enthusiasm and skills to bear in the antiradical campaign. His clean-scrubbed image and lawyerly assurances nonetheless convinced Daugherty's replacement, former Columbia Law School dean Harlan Fiske Stone, that Hoover was a different sort of man—"a scholar, a gentleman, and a scientist," in the words of *Literary Digest*, in contrast to the "much-discussed Burns." Stone himself viewed the Bureau as a dangerous entity, capable of destroying vital liberties if not properly checked. One of his first actions as attorney general was to shut down Hoover's General Intelligence Division, banning further collection of information related to "political or other opinions of individuals." Despite pressure from his fellow civil libertarians, however, he declined to eliminate the Bureau itself, arguing that the Justice Department needed some sort of investigative force. Instead, he enlisted Hoover to help with the gargantuan task, in the words of *New Republic* essayist Sidney Howard, of "cleaning the Augean Stables which Messrs. Palmer, Daugherty, Flynn and Burns bequeathed to him."[31]

And for his first few years, Hoover did just that. Initially appointed as Burns' temporary replacement, Hoover vowed to fulfill both the letter and spirit of Stone's new directives, to prove himself the reformer that Burns and Flynn never were. "I could conceive of nothing more despicable nor demoralizing," he promised, "than to have public funds of this country used for the purpose of shadowing people who are engaged in legitimate practices in accordance with the constitution of this country and in accordance with the laws of the country." He threw himself instead into such areas as Prohibition enforcement and antitrust campaigns. With such activities to occupy him, he agreed to cease the active collection of antiradical intelligence. He also eliminated the use of undercover operatives to surveil and disrupt political activity.[32]

While Attorney General Stone and his supporters may have won the battle in 1924, over the course of the next several decades they slowly but inexorably lost the war. Despite his acknowledgment of certain legal limits on his power, Hoover remained convinced that a violent, subversive left-wing conspiracy threatened the stability of the United States. In response, he sought ways to evade Stone's directive, remaining true to the letter but not necessarily the spirit of the law. Even as he eliminated the Bureau's active intelligence gathering, Hoover kept up his correspondence with outside investigators such as Arthur Woods, who returned from Europe in 1925 with news of an "International Entente" being formed by global capitalists to combat "the insidious influences of Communism." Hoover accepted reports as well from other federal agencies and from local bomb squads in cities such as New York, where undercover investigations continued to flourish.[33]

Hoover continued to hope that the Bureau might one day reenter the antiradical field in a more forthright manner. "I would like to be able to find some theory of law and some statement of facts to fit it that would enable the federal authorities to deal vigorously with the ultra-radical elements," he wrote to a colleague in 1926. As he watched the Communist Party regroup in the turmoil of the early 1930s, Hoover began to press the new president, Franklin Delano Roosevelt, to allow the Bureau to resume its former activities. Roosevelt, in the midst of reviving hundreds of other government experiments from the Progressive Era, ultimately conceded, authorizing Hoover to investigate first fascists and then communists within the United States. In 1939, with the exigencies of war and domestic subversion once again at the forefront of the national agenda, Hoover revived the General Intelligence Division, including its famous card index. The following year, he finally won passage of the peacetime sedition act that had so long eluded him. Under the auspices of the 1940 Smith Act, federal law assigned a ten-year jail term and a $10,000 fine for anyone—citizen or alien—convicted of advocating, in print, in person, or by virtue of membership in an organization, "the duty, necessity, desirability, or propriety of overthrowing or destroying any government in the United States by force or violence."[34]

By the end of the 1940s, Hoover and the Justice Department would finally use the Smith Act to do what they had failed to do at Bridgman and in the Wall Street investigation: convict the leadership of the Communist Party of national treason. The political context of that moment was different from what Hoover had known some three decades earlier: concerns over espionage and Soviet nuclear arms, not over bombs and immigrants, dominated the anticommunist crusade. To Hoover, though, little had changed. Throughout his forty-eight years at the helm of the Bureau, he remained convinced that "force and violence" were at the heart of the domestic communist agenda. As he explained in testimony before the House Committee on Un-American Activities in 1947, "the American Communist, like the leopard, cannot change his spots."[35]

EVEN AS HE EMERGED as one of the nation's most formidable political figures, Hoover never entirely gave up on the Wall Street investigation, closing the file repeatedly only to reopen it when new information surfaced. Most of what came forth in the years after 1924 was useless, wild allegations mailed in by mental patients and amateur sleuths. In 1930, the Bureau corresponded with one Harry Brant, allegedly a former undercover operative eager to supply proof that the bomb had been staged by a private detective agency. A man named Stephen Doyle proffered a similar story four years later, charging that the bombing had been a conspiracy of Burns and Morgan, aided by Flynn, "to lead the gullible citizenry of the U.S.A. to believe that the Russian Soviet Republic was about to overthrow our government and murder all the rich people in this nation." Hoover declined to reengage this old canard, explaining curtly that the Bureau no longer sought jurisdiction over the Wall Street investigation. He showed slightly more interest in 1944, when an Erie Railroad employee wrote in with the novel suggestion that the tennis champion and would-be seer Ed Fisher had collaborated with a Japanese engineer to cover up their role in the plot. Like so many of the theories proffered over the years, this was an idea suited to its historical moment, grafting wartime concerns over Japanese subversion onto the now venerable mystery. And like so many of its predecessors, it turned out to be worthless, little more than a jumble of prejudice and political fantasy.[36]

The 1944 investigation marked the Bureau's last engagement with the Wall Street explosion as an active case. While that venture failed to yield any new information, it did produce one item of great significance. With almost a quarter century elapsed since the commission of the crime, the New York office felt obligated to provide a description of both the bombing and the ensuing investigation. Surprisingly, given the events of Burns' administration and the political atmosphere of 1944, the memo hardly mentions the possibility of communist involvement. Rather, it ends up roughly where Flynn left off in 1921. "An investigation was...made by the confidential employees in the various radical groups in this district such as the Union of Russian Workers, the I.W.W., Communist, etc.," read the summary, "and from the result of the investigations to date it would appear that none of the afore-mentioned organizations had any hand in the matter and that the explosion was the work of either Italian anarchists or Italian terrorists."[37]

Though the Bureau said little publicly, this remained the most popular theory among the few journalists and historians who tackled the issue in the years that followed. On September 11, 1960, on the eve of the bombing's fortieth anniversary, *Daily News* reporter Ruth Reynolds went in search of New York bomb squad members who might remember the case. She managed to locate Clinton Wood and former bomb squad leader James Gegan, who at the ages of ninety and eighty-six, respectively, were among the few living veterans of the investigation besides Hoover himself. Wood, who had spent so much time with Burns' informer William Linde, announced to Reynolds' disbelief that the whole affair had been "an accident—pure and simple," an illegal dynamite shipment gone awry. Gegan, by contrast, subscribed to the Bureau's view that "an anarchist—but not a Russian" had set the bomb, a conclusion Reynolds seemed inclined to accept. "Sacco and Vanzetti were indicted on September 11, 1920. The devastating bomb exploded at Broad and Wall Streets just five days later," she wrote. "Was this the first of many bomb attempts to focus world attention on the pair who were eventually executed for a crime they insisted they didn't commit?"[38]

More than thirty years later, the historian Paul Avrich answered this question with a powerful yes. In his 1991 book, *Sacco and Vanzetti: The Anarchist Background,* Avrich identified the Wall Street bomber as Mario Buda (also known as Mike Boda), a friend of Sacco and Vanzetti's and one of Galleani's disciples in the United States. According to Avrich, the Italian-born Buda had collaborated with Sacco and Vanzetti, along with dozens of other Galleanisti, to plan both the May Day and June 2 bomb conspiracies of 1919. He was suspected as well of involvement in the holdup at South Braintree in the spring of 1920 that resulted in his friends' famous arrests. While Sacco and Vanzetti waited in jail, according to Avrich, Buda went into hiding, first in East Boston, then in New Hampshire. When his friends were indicted on September 11, 1920, he felt called to leave his position of safety and take action. After selecting a target, he made his way to New York, where he assembled the horse, wagon, and bomb materials. After depositing his load on Wall Street, he left for Providence, acquired a passport, and fled to Naples.

Despite Flynn's intense hunt for the Galleanisti, Buda's name is nowhere to be found in the Bureau's case file. Indeed, Avrich admitted that the case likely would never be definitively closed. "That Buda was the Wall Street bomber cannot be proved," he wrote; "documentary evidence is lacking. But it fits what we know of him and his movements. I have it, moreover, from a reliable source and believe it to be true." That reliable source may have been Charles Poggi, an Italian-born New York waiter who knew many of the Galleanisti and who once told Avrich that Buda's nephew Frank Maffi openly boasted about "my uncle's bomb." Certainly there is little doubt that Buda was one of the architects of the 1919 bomb plots. As Flynn noted in 1920, the Wall Street explosion suggests a similar foreknowledge and pattern. The American Anarchist Fighters pamphlets, printed by hand stamp rather than printing press, may have reflected the bombers' awareness that Flynn had traced their identity through the *Plain Words* pamphlets of 1919. The name on the flyers, too, was an extension of the Galleanisti's political signature. Most importantly, the Galleanisti, including Sacco and Vanzetti themselves, believed in and preached the art of terrorism as a noble political act. Perhaps the best judgment we can make, so many decades after the Wall Street explosion, is to take them at their word.[39]

IN THE END, it was the Sacco-Vanzetti case, rather than the Wall Street bombing, that emerged as the great political controversy of the 1920s. As appeals to commute their death sentence began to fail by the middle of the decade, the tiny defense committee launched by Felicani in 1920 expanded into a global protest movement, joining communists, anarchists, and progressives in thousands of rallies seeking to save the anarchists' lives. Inside the United States, the case garnered the attention of hundreds of high-profile intellectuals and reformers, who pleaded with "the newspaper editors the old judges the small men with reputations the college presidents the wardheelers," in novelist John Dos Passos' words, not to show the nation to be "slimy and foul." Their efforts failed. On

August 23, 1927, more than seven years after their arrests, Sacco and Vanzetti died in the electric chair in Massachusetts.[40]

To many American supporters, the executions appeared to be the grim culmination of the antianarchist frenzy begun some four decades earlier, part of "a pattern of hate and fear toward radicals," in the words of one despairing protester, "set in 1887." It also seemed to mark the final hurrah of the "deportations delirium," a drama of bias and hysteria that took some seven years to play out. As Dos Passos noted in a letter to journalist Francis Russell, the entire affair, from arrest to execution, had been shaped by years of agitation "about such things as the Wall Street bombing, the rise of Bolshevik power in Russia—all the after war unrest."[41]

This had been the assumption as well of Upton Sinclair, who decided to write a book about Sacco and Vanzetti soon after their execution. Early in 1927, he had published his novel *Oil!*, in which he presented a final summary of his earlier writing on the Wall Street explosion, describing it as a blasting accident turned into a "Bolshevik plot" by the "sleuth-celebrity" Burns. Sinclair went into his next project planning to portray the Sacco-Vanzetti case in much the same way, hoping to demonstrate how two innocent Italian anarchists had been strung up for championing the working class. He emerged from his research somewhat chastened, still convinced that Sacco and Vanzetti had received an unjust trial but increasingly uneasy with what he had discovered about both their actions in the spring of 1920 and their broader political commitments. As Sinclair pointed out in his novel *Boston*, Sacco and Vanzetti were not merely pacific men caught up in the frenzy of their times. They were passionate revolutionaries whose lives had been defined by a militant vision of anarchism, "direct actionists" who "believed in and taught violence" as a means of class war.[42]

They maintained this commitment to the end. In 1926, as their execution came to seem more and more certain, the two prisoners began, elliptically, to urge their supporters to avenge their impending deaths. In June, in an insider's reference to Galleani's terrorist manual, the Defense Committee magazine *Protesta Umana* featured the headline "As the Day of Execution Approaches, the Prisoners Warn: LA SALUTE È IN VOI!" A few months later, Sacco wrote sadly that he could do no more to fight for justice, but begged his allies to retaliate for his murder. "We are proud for death and fall as the anarchists can fall. It is up to you now, brothers, comrades!" Vanzetti was even more explicit. "If we have to die for a crime

327

of which we are innocent," he wrote, "we ask for revenge, revenge in our names and in the names of our living and dead."[43]

They got what they asked for. Beginning in March 1927, bombs began exploding at American banks and embassies throughout the world: in Bulgaria, in France, and in Buenos Aires. Then, on August 5, with the impending execution all but certain, they struck home in the United States. Within twenty-four hours, bombs went off in three different cities, a final echo of the nationwide plot of June 2, 1919. In Philadelphia, a blast tore through the Emanuel Presbyterian Church. In Baltimore, an explosion hit the back porch and kitchen of the mayor's house, shattered the windows, and started a fire. In New York, two bombs went off between 11:17 and 11:37 at subway stations along Twenty-eighth Street, injuring eighteen people and rippling the sidewalks.[44]

The bombs of August 5 quickly disappeared from the headlines. For at least a moment, though, they forced New Yorkers to think about what might have been. The following day, the *New York Times* wrote, "[a]s the report of the subway explosion spread it immediately recalled to many New Yorkers the Wall Street bomb explosion of Sept. 16, 1920." In the seventeen days between the August explosions and the executions, the Bureau resumed its surveillance of Sacco-Vanzetti supporters; the prevention of attacks on federal buildings, Hoover argued, now justified such actions. In Washington, guards closed off most entrances to the Capitol and searched all visitors. In New York, police sent motorbike patrolmen to guard the major institutions of the financial district, where many employers were already adding private guards. Using its own resources, the Guaranty Trust Company hired fifteen watchmen. Standard Oil increased its security, too.

Spokesmen for the Morgan bank and the New York Stock Exchange said they were unconcerned and offered their support for the public police. But some observers thought they were feeling more nervous than they let on. According to the *Times*, a financial district rumor suggested that they planned to hire a few extra guards. Just in case.[45]

# APPENDIX

. . . .

## IN MEMORIAM

The following men and women died as a result of the Wall Street explosion:

Joseph Arambarry, 29, clerk
Margaret Helen Bishop, 21, secretary
Carolyn M. Dickinson, 43, stenographer
John A. Donohue, 38, accountant
Marguerite A. Drury, 29, stenographer
Reginald Elsworthy, 23, clerk
Worth Bagley Ellsworth, 20, student
Bartholomew Flannery, 19, messenger
Harold I. Gillis, 27, salesman
Charles A. Hanrahan, 17, messenger
Amelia Newton Huger, 23, clerk
William Fulton Hutchinson, 43, insurance clerk
John Johnson, 58, porter
William A. Joyce, 29, clerk
Elmer Kehrer, 21, chauffeur
Bernard J. Kennedy, 30, clerk
Alexander Leith, 64, office assistant
Charles A. Lindroth, 25, bookkeeper
Alfred G. Mayer, 23, clerk
Colin Barr McClure, 24, banker
Jerome H. McKean, 33, broker
Franklin G. Miller, 21, adding machine salesman
Charles Neville, 42, accountant
Thomas Montgomery Osprey, 24, clerk
Theodore Peck, 36, bond salesman

William Ernst Peterson, 29, clerk
Alfred G. Phipps, 28, broker
Ludolph F. Portong, 29, clerk
Joseph Schmitt, 30, clerk
Lewis K. Smith, 34, bond salesman
Benjamin Soloway, 16, messenger
Francis B. Stoba, 34, bank employee
Edwin Sweet, 67, banker (retired)
Irving Tannenwald, 38, grocery clerk
Mildred Xylander, 27, stenographer
John Weir, 27, salesman
Robert Westbay, 16, messenger
William West White, 63, promoter

# ACKNOWLEDGMENTS

. . . .

I owe large debts to many smart and talented people who helped to turn an early research idea into a book. Librarians and archivists at the Morgan Library & Museum, the Tamiment Library & Robert F. Wagner Archives at New York University, the Library of Congress (especially the Prints and Photographs Division), the National Archives at College Park, Maryland, the Municipal Archives of the City of New York, the New York Stock Exchange, the New York Public Library, the Boston Public Library, Harvard University's Baker and Lamont libraries, and the Columbia and Yale University library systems provided crucial guidance and assistance. Shawn O'Sullivan at DailyNewsPix.com located many hard-to-find images and prepped them for public consumption. I am especially grateful to the Freedom of Information Act officers at the Federal Bureau of Investigation, who responded to requests for files with good will and efficiency.

At Columbia University, where I conducted my graduate work, professors Alan Brinkley, Eric Foner, Kenneth Jackson, Elizabeth Blackmar, Simon Schama, and Casey Blake offered valuable comments, suggestions, and encouragement in the project's earliest stages. Many fellow graduate students at Columbia also took time away from their own work to provide criticism and support in workshops and other discussions; they are too numerous to name, but they know who they are. At Yale, my colleagues David Blight, Laura Engelstein, Paul Freedman, John Gaddis, Glenda Gilmore, Jennifer Klein, John Merriman, Joanne Meyerowitz, Stephen Pitti, Marci Shore, and Jay Winter intervened at later but equally critical moments with advice and support. I am especially indebted to the many fellow historians who volunteered their insights and professional scrutiny by reading all or part of the manuscript, including Alan Dawley, Candace Falk, Jennifer Fronc, David Huyssen, Jennifer Luff, Julia Ott, Barry Pateman, Nunzio Pernicone, Ellen Schrecker, and Moshik Temkin. Finally, there are many authors whom I have never met, but whose work profoundly influenced my own, most notably, Ron Chernow, the late Paul Avrich, and the late J. Anthony Lukas.

Like any research project, this one required material support. Columbia's history department, Institute for Social and Economic Research and Policy, and Graduate School of Arts and Sciences provided financial and institutional assistance during the dissertation stage, as did the Miller Center of Public Affairs at the University of Virginia. Yale University's Morse Fellowship fund granted me a year of sabbatical to complete the manuscript, and the Yale history department provided much-needed research funds. David Huyssen and Nicholas Webb stepped in to offer research assistance in early stages of revision; what I know of the lexicon of terrorism I learned from their painstaking work. I am particularly grateful to Todd Holmes, whose patience and keen eye for detail as a research assistant helped to polish the book in its final stages.

At Oxford, Tim Bartlett and Peter Ginna saw the promise of this book in its earliest form. Dayne Poshusta, Joellyn Ausanka, and Sue Warga ushered it through the final editorial and production process with great patience and professionalism. My agent, Sydelle Kramer, guided the book across many bumps in the road. I am particularly indebted to my editor, Timothy Bent, whose careful reading and many words of encouragement improved the manuscript immeasurably.

Countless friends and colleagues provided support in the form of last-minute child care, housing for research trips, and all manner of emotional sustenance; hopefully I have already expressed my gratitude for their help. A few bear special note. Kim Philips-Fein was a patient and peerless friend; I am lucky to have ended up in graduate school with her. Shari Motro, one of my oldest and dearest friends, offered near-daily support and read the manuscript in its entirety. My parents, Barbara and Martin Gage, watched proudly as I set off down the long road of becoming a historian, as did my sister Karen, who lent her ear and often her home to see the project to fruition. It is a great sorrow to me that my mother died before she could see this work in print.

Most of all, I thank my husband, Dan, and my son, Nicholas, who often put aside their own interests to help me with mine. Without their patience and love, I could not have completed this project. Though it is only a small hint of my gratitude, I dedicate this work to them.

# NOTE ON SOURCES

$\cdots$

The process of researching the Wall Street explosion investigation entailed both joy and frustration. The main Bureau of Investigation file on the explosion (BI 61-5) can be obtained from the FBI through the Freedom of Information Act. The file is a rich source of detail; like all sources, however, it has many flaws. First released in the 1980s, the file is still heavily redacted. Many names and details—sometimes entire paragraphs and pages—remain inaccessible to historians. In addition, the file bears the marks of the chaotic bureaucracy in which it was created. Numbering of individual reports and memos is inconsistent (the file actually combines two investigations under different numbering systems, BI 211205 and BI 61-5). The photocopied documents are sometimes difficult to decipher, especially where the original source had already faded. I have endeavored to provide enough information to allow fellow researchers to identify individual documents within this very large file, though the scope of the titles, authors, and other identifying details is necessarily inconsistent. For reports that cite both a date for the period covered in the report and a date when the report was submitted, I have cited only the date submitted.

Other Bureau files also contain valuable information about the Wall Street case. The bulk of the Bureau's early antiradical investigations (prior to 1921) can be found on microfilm at the National Archives in College Park, Maryland (Record Group 65, M1085). This collection contains many individual files, usually organized by name, on suspects in the Wall Street explosion as well as more general surveillance activities. (Footnote.com has recently made these files accessible in electronic form.) Inquiries after 1921 can be found in the Bureau's paper files at the National Archives, also RG 65, organized according to individual or event names, beginning with the prefix 61-, or through the Freedom of Information Act. A few of the more famous files from this period, including the Bureau file on the Sacco-Vanzetti case (61-126), are available online through the FBI's electronic reading room at fbi.gov.

Outside of the Bureau documents, the most valuable federal material on the Wall Street explosion can be found in the records of the State Department at the National Archives (both RG 59 and RG 84), which provide details on investigative activities in Italy, Poland, and other European countries. J. Edgar Hoover's Official and Confidential file, published on microfilm, contains a folder on Hoover's work with Jacob Nosovitsky and Arthur Woods. Scattered additional federal reports, focusing mainly on the immediate response to the explosion, can be found at the National Archives in the papers of the Justice Department (RG 60), the Bureau of Mines (RG 70), the Secret Service (RG 87), and the Military Intelligence Division (RG 165).

This narrative relies heavily on the story of the federal investigation partly because other rich sources of investigative detail have been lost to time. The New York Police Department's historical records are extremely limited; a Freedom of Information Act request, along with searches in city archives, produced no police documents of note. The present-day bomb squad discovered a few odds and ends in their files, which Sgt. Tony Biondolilo kindly shared with me in 2004. The Burns agency maintains no active historical archive and according to agency spokespeople holds no information about the Wall Street explosion. (Burns combined with the Pinkerton firm in 2001 to form Securitas Security Services USA Inc., which advertises itself as the largest private security firm in the world.) J. P. Morgan and Company (now JPMorganChase) maintains a tiny file on the explosion, consisting of a few newspaper clippings but no investigative detail. The papers of J. P. Morgan, Jr., at the Morgan Library and Museum, like the papers of Thomas Lamont at Harvard's Baker Library, offer insight into the bankers' personal responses but no information about the investigation. Arthur Woods' papers at the Library of Congress contain useful material about Woods' career but little about his investigation into the Wall Street explosion beyond a few newspaper clippings.

Undoubtedly future researchers will find other investigative documents squirreled away under odd classifications in both government and private files. I look forward to their discoveries.

# ABBREVIATIONS USED IN NOTES

. . . .

| | |
|---|---|
| *ABH* | William D Haywood, *The Autobiography of Big Bill Haywood* (New York: International Publishers, 1977) (Orig. pub. 1929) |
| *AC* | *The Constitution* (Atlanta) |
| ACLU | *American Civil Liberties Union Archives: 1912–1950* (Wilmington, DE: Scholarly Resources, 1995) |
| AFSV | Aldino Felicani Sacco-Vanzetti Collection, Boston Public Library, Boston, Massachusetts |
| AG | U.S. Department of Justice, *Annual Reports of the Attorney General of the United States* (Washington, DC) |
| *AR* | *Appeal to Reason* |
| AW | Arthur Woods Papers, Library of Congress, Washington, DC |
| *BA* | *Boston Advertiser* |
| *BG* | *The Boston Daily Globe* |
| *BH* | *Boston Herald* |
| BI | Records of the Federal Bureau of Investigation, RG 65, National Archives, College Park, Maryland |
| BI FOIA | Records of the Federal Bureau of Investigation, obtained through the Freedom of Information Act |
| BM | Records of the Bureau of Mines, RG 70, National Archives, College Park, Maryland |
| *CFC* | *The Commercial and Financial Chronicle* |
| COD | Certificate of Death, Municipal Archives of the City of New York |

| | |
|---|---|
| CPUSA | *Files of the Communist Party of the USA in the Comintern Archives* (New York: IDC, 1999–2000) |
| *CSM* | *The Christian Science Monitor* |
| *CT* | *Chicago Daily Tribune* |
| DJ | Records of the Department of Justice, RG 60, National Archives, College Park, Maryland |
| DS | Records of the Department of State, RG 59/84, National Archives, College Park, Maryland |
| EG | *The Emma Goldman Papers: A Microfilm Edition,* ed. Candace Falk, Ronald J. Zboray, Alice Hall, et al. (Alexandria, VA: Chadwyck-Healey, 1990–) |
| EHJP | Edward Holton James Papers, Harvard Law School Library, Cambridge, Massachusetts |
| EVD | *The Papers of Eugene V. Debs* (New York: Microfilming Corporation of America, 1982) |
| FW | Frank P. Walsh Papers, New York Public Library, New York, New York |
| *HC* | *The Hartford Courant* |
| HOC | *Federal Bureau of Investigation Confidential Files: The J. Edgar Hoover Official and Confidential Files,* ed. Athan Theoharis (Bethesda, MD: University Publications of America, 1990) |
| House | U.S. Congress, House, Committee on Rules, *Attorney General Palmer on Charges Made Against the Department of Justice by Louis F. Post and Others,* Hearings, 66th Cong., 2nd Sess., Parts 1–3 (Washington, DC: Government Printing Office, 1920) |
| HW | Harry Weinberger Papers, Manuscripts and Archives, Sterling Memorial Library, Yale University, New Haven, Connecticut |
| *ISR* | *International Socialist Review* |
| *JCCB* | *The Journal of Commerce and Commercial Bulletin* |
| JPM | J. P. Morgan Jr. Papers, Morgan Library and Museum, New York, New York |
| *LAT* | *Los Angeles Times* |
| *LML* | Emma Goldman, *Living My Life* (New York: Dover, 1970) (Orig. pub. 1931) |

| | |
|---|---|
| *ME* | *Mother Earth* |
| MH | *Morris Hillquit Papers*, ed. F. Gerald Ham (Madison: State Historical Society of Wisconsin, 1969) |
| MID | Records of the Military Intelligence Division, RG 165, National Archives, College Park, Maryland |
| MIR | *U.S. Military Intelligence Reports: Surveillance of Radicals in the United States, 1917–41* (Frederick, MD: University Publications of America, 1984) |
| *MJ* | *The Milwaukee Journal* |
| *MM* | *Miners' Magazine* |
| *NM* | *The New Majority* |
| NPGL | National Popular Government League, *To the American People: Report Upon the Illegal Practices of the Department of Justice* (New York: National Popular Government League, 1920) |
| *NYA* | *New York American* |
| *NYC* | *The New York Call* |
| *NYCM* | *New York Commercial* |
| *NYDN* | *The News* (New York) |
| *NYEM* | *The Evening Mail* (New York) |
| *NYEP* | *The Evening Post* (New York) |
| *NYET* | *The Evening Telegram* (New York) |
| *NYG* | *The Globe and Commercial Advertiser* (New York) |
| *NYH* | *The New York Herald* |
| *NYHT* | *New York Herald Tribune* |
| *NYJ* | *The Evening Journal* (New York) |
| NYPD | Annual Reports of the Police Department of the City of New York |
| *NYS* | *The Sun* (New York) |
| NYSE | Archives of the New York Stock Exchange, New York, New York |
| *NYT* | *The New York Times* |
| *NYTR* | *New York Tribune* |
| *NYW* | *The World* (New York) |

| | |
|---|---|
| *PMA* | Alexander Berkman, *Prison Memoirs of an Anarchist* (New York: Mother Earth, 1912) |
| Senate | U.S. Congress, Senate, Subcommittee of the Committee on the Judiciary, *Charges of Illegal Practices of the Department of Justice. Hearings on "Report upon the Illegal Practices of the United States Department of Justice," Made by a Committee of Lawyers on Behalf of the National Popular Government League, and a Memorandum Describing the Personnel of the Committee. Referred "for Such Action as the Committee on the Judiciary May Care to Take with Reference to the Same." January 19 to March 3, 1921*, 66th Cong., 3rd Sess. (Washington, DC: Government Printing Office, 1921) |
| *SFC* | *San Francisco Chronicle* |
| *SLPD* | *St. Louis Post-Dispatch* |
| *SNYH* | *The Sun and New York Herald* |
| SPA | *Socialist Party of America Papers, 1897–1963* (New York: Microfilming Corporation of America, 1975) |
| SS | Records of the Secret Service, RG 87, National Archives, College Park, Maryland |
| *SUR* | *Seattle Union Record* |
| TWL | Thomas W. Lamont Papers, Baker Library, Harvard University, Cambridge, Massachusetts |
| USCIR | *Final Report and Testimony Submitted to Congress by the U.S. Commission on Industrial Relations Created by the Act of August 23, 1912* (Washington, DC: Government Printing Office, 1916) |
| *WP* | *The Washington Post* |
| *WSJ* | *The Wall Street Journal* |

# NOTES

· · · ·

## INTRODUCTION

1. "Wall Street Explosion 'Suspects,'" *NYEP*, May 24, 1923.
2. Vladimir Lenin, "Letter to American Workers," 1918, in Lenin, *Lenin on the United States: Selections from the Writings of V. I. Lenin* (New York: International Publishers, 1970), 347.
3. "Accident or Design?" *SLPD*, Sep. 17, 1920; "Americanism Aroused," *WP*, Sep. 19, 1920.
4. When I began writing this book, the secondary literature on the Wall Street explosion was extremely limited. The most expansive treatments were Paul Avrich, *Sacco and Vanzetti: The Anarchist Background* (Princeton, NJ: Princeton University Press, 1991), which devoted three pages to identifying an anarchist suspect (205–7); Ron Chernow, *The House of Morgan: An American Banking Dynasty and the Rise of Modern Finance* (New York: Simon and Schuster, 1990), which described the reaction at the Morgan bank (212–14); and John Brooks, *Once in Golconda* (New York: Harper and Row, 1969), which used the bombing as the unlikely opening scene for Wall Street's boom decade in the 1920s (13–32). More recently, the explosion has received additional attention, most importantly: Charles McCormick, *Hopeless Cases: The Hunt for the Red Scare Terrorist Bombers* (Lanham, MD: University Press of America, 2005), which dissects the federal investigation into the bombing (64–145), and Mike Davis, *Buda's Wagon: A Brief History of the Car Bomb* (London: Verso, 2006), which identifies the Wall Street explosion as the world's first major car (or, rather, wagon) bomb (1–3).
5. The attempt to define terrorism has inspired a vast literature, though much of it has little application to the historical context of the late nineteenth and early twentieth centuries. For a comprehensive, if somewhat dated, primer on definitions, see Alex Schmid, *Political Terrorism: A Research Guide to Concepts, Theories, Data Bases and Literature* (New Brunswick, NJ: Transaction Books, 1984). For a briefer and more accessible discussion, see Bruce Hoffman, *Inside Terrorism* (New York: Columbia University Press, 1998), 13–44. On the origins of the word *terrorism*, see esp. Walter Laqueur, *A History of Terrorism* (New Brunswick, NJ: Transaction Publishers, 2002), 6–8; Hoffman, *Inside Terrorism*, 15–17. For general histories of terrorism before the mid-twentieth century, see esp. Martha Crenshaw, ed., *Terrorism in Context* (University Park: Pennsylvania State University Press, 2001); Matthew Carr, *The Infernal Machine: A History of Terrorism* (New York: New Press, 2006); Laqueur, *The Age of Terrorism* (Boston: Little, Brown, 1987); Gerard Chailand and Arnaud Blin, *The History of Terrorism from Antiquity to Al Qaeda* (Berkeley: University of California Press, 2007); Michael Burleigh, *Blood and Rage: A Cultural History of Terrorism* (London: HarperPress, 2008); Albert Parry, *Terrorism: From Robespierre to Arafat* (New York: Vanguard Press, 1976); Richard E. Rubenstein, *Alchemists of Revolution: Terrorism in the Modern World* (New York: Basic Books, 1987); James M. Lutz and Brenda J. Lutz, *Terrorism: Origins and Evolution* (New York: Palgrave Macmillan, 2005); Isaac Land, ed., *Enemies*

*of Humanity: The Nineteenth-Century War on Terrorism* (New York: Palgrave Macmillan, 2008). For a thoughtful comparison between past and present forms of terrorism, see Isabelle Duyvesteyn, "How New Is the New Terrorism?" *Studies in Conflict and Terrorism* 27 (2004): 439–54.

6. Richard Hofstadter, "Reflections on Violence in the United States," in Hofstadter and Mike Wallace, eds., *American Violence: A Documentary History* (New York: Knopf, 1970), 3.

7. Hofstadter, "Reflections," 4; Louis Adamic, "Author's Note," *Dynamite: The Story of Class Violence in America* (New York: Viking, 1931).

8. Adamic, *Dynamite*, 3. Robert Murray's *Red Scare: A Study in National Hysteria, 1919–1920* (New York: McGraw-Hill, 1955) is the classic account of the Red Scare as a moment of psychological hysteria. Later works on the Red Scare, most notably Murray Levin's *Political Hysteria in America* (New York: Basic Books, 1971), reflect this interpretation. Regin Schmidt recently revised this view, arguing that the Red Scare was imposed from the top down, in *Red Scare: FBI and the Origins of Anticommunism in the United States, 1919–1943* (Copenhagen: Museum Tusculanum Press, 2000). For Hofstadter, see "The Paranoid Style in American Politics," in *The Paranoid Style in American Politics and Other Essays* (Cambridge, MA: Harvard University Press, 1964), 3–40.

9. Paul Avrich, Candace Folk, and Barry Pateman have performed pioneering work on the history of American anarchism and violence. For Avrich, see esp. *Sacco and Vanzetti; The Russian Anarchists* (Princeton, NJ: Princeton University Press, 1967); *American Anarchist: The Life of Voltairine de Cleyre* (Princeton, NJ: Princeton University Press, 1988); *The Modern School Movement: Anarchism and Education in the United States* (Princeton, NJ: Princeton University Press, 1980); *The Haymarket Tragedy* (Princeton, NJ: Princeton University Press, 1984); *Anarchist Portraits* (Princeton, NJ: Princeton University Press, 1988); *Anarchist Voices: An Oral History of Anarchism in America* (Princeton, NJ: Princeton University Press, 1995). For Falk and Pateman, see esp. Candace Falk, Barry Pateman, and Jessica M. Moran, eds., *Emma Goldman: A Documentary History of the American Years* (Berkeley: University of California Press, 2005). For event histories, see esp. J. Anthony Lukas, *Big Trouble: A Murder in a Small Western Town Sets Off a Struggle for the Soul of America* (New York: Simon and Schuster, 1997); Geoffrey Cowan, *The People v. Clarence Darrow: The Bribery Trial of America's Greatest Lawyer* (New York: Times Books, 1993); Richard H. Frost, *The Mooney Case* (Stanford, CA: Stanford University Press, 1968); Curt Gentry, *Frame-up: The Incredible Case of Tom Mooney and Warren Billings* (New York: Norton, 1967).

Melvyn Dubofsky's *We Shall Be All*, still the classic account of the Industrial Workers of the World, is the most notable example of the effort to rewrite established images of bomb throwing and subversion as part of the social history turn. "Wobblies did not carry bombs, nor burn harvest fields, nor destroy timber, nor depend upon the machine that works with a trigger," he writes. "Instead they tried in their own ways to comprehend the nature and dynamics of capitalist society, and through increased knowledge, as well as through revolutionary activism, to develop a better system for the organization and functioning of the American economy." Dubofsky, *We Shall Be All: A History of the Industrial Workers of the World* (Chicago: Quadrangle Books, 1969), 147. Other pioneering works on the social history of radicalism and labor during this period perform similar work by focusing on questions of institutional change, working-class culture, and political philosophy. See esp. David Montgomery, *The Fall of the House of Labor: The Workplace, the State, and American Labor Activism, 1865–1925* (Cambridge: Cambridge University Press, 1977); Nick Salvatore, *Eugene V. Debs: Citizen and Socialist* (Urbana: University of Illinois Press, 1982); Herbert C. Gutman, *Work, Culture and Society in Industrializing America* (New York: Vintage Books, 1977). Other New Left historians prided themselves on the rediscovery of conflict and violence but focused mainly on general strikes and picket-line warfare. See esp. Jeremy Brecher, *Strike!* (New York: Two Continents/South End Press, 1977).

In the past decade, several historians have begun to reexamine questions of violence within labor and radical movements, and my own work builds upon their insights. James Green approaches the subject of anarchist bombings and assassinations in the 1880s from a broad social and narrative perspective. See Green, *Death in the Haymarket: A Story of Chicago, the First Labor Movement, and the Bombing That Divided Gilded Age America* (New York: Pantheon Books, 2006). Eric Rauchway's *Murdering McKinley: The Making of Theodore Roosevelt's America* (New York: Hill and Wang, 2003) explores the social and cultural politics of the McKinley assassination. Jeffory Clymer, *America's Culture of Terrorism: Violence, Capitalism and the Written Word* (Chapel Hill: University of North Carolina Press, 2003) discusses the era's terrorist plots from a literary perspective. In labor history, Kevin Kenny, Andrew Wender Cohen, and Scott Martelle, among others, have begun to offer fresh looks at the role of violence in union struggles. See Kenny, *Making Sense of the Molly Maguires* (New York: Oxford University Press, 1998); Cohen, *The Racketeer's Progress: Chicago and the Struggle for the Modern American Economy, 1900–1940* (Cambridge: Cambridge University Press, 2004); Martelle, *Blood Passion: The Ludlow Massacre and Class War in the American West* (New Brunswick, NJ: Rutgers University Press, 2007). Other scholars, most notably Tom Goyens, maintain the earlier tradition of "debunk[ing] the myth of the cloaked, bomb-carrying anarchist." See Goyens, *Beer and Revolution: The German Anarchist Movement in New York City, 1880–1914* (Urbana: University of Illinois Press, 2007), 4.

## CHAPTER 1

1. For Junius Morgan's ambitions and state of mind, see his wartime diary (Junius Spencer Morgan, "Diary—Autograph Manuscript," 1917–18, ARC1565, Morgan Library and Museum); Chernow, *House of Morgan*, 266. For descriptions of the weather on Sep. 16, see "The Weather," *NYT*, Sep. 16, 1920; "The Weather," *NYT*, Sep. 17, 1920.

2. For background on the Morgan bank's history, culture, and unique place in American history, see esp. Chernow, *The House of Morgan* and Jean Strouse, *Morgan: American Financier* (New York: Random House, 1999). Where not otherwise cited, well-established dates and events from the bank's history can be found in these two works. For a critical early view of the Morgans, see Lewis Corey, *The House of Morgan: A Social Biography of the Masters of Money* (New York: G. H. Watt, 1930). For other significant accounts of Pierpont Morgan's life and legacy, see Frederick Lewis Allen, *The Great Pierpont Morgan* (New York: Harper, 1949); Vincent P. Carosso with Rose Carosso, *The Morgans: Private International Bankers, 1854–1913* (Cambridge: Harvard University Press, 1987); Edwin Palmer Hoyt, *The House of Morgan* (New York: Dodd, Mead, 1966); Andrew Sinclair, *Corsair: The Life of J. Pierpont Morgan* (Boston: Little, Brown, 1981). On the rise of industrial capitalism in New York and the culture of Wall Street, see esp. Sven Beckert, *Monied Metropolis: New York City and the Consolidation of the American Bourgeoisie, 1850–1896* (New York: Cambridge University Press, 2001); Steve Fraser, *Every Man a Speculator: A History of Wall Street in American Life* (New York: HarperCollins, 2005); Thomas Kessner, *Capital City: New York City and the Men Behind America's Rise to Economic Dominance, 1860–1900* (New York: Simon and Schuster, 2003); Charles R. Geisst, *Wall Street: A History* (New York: Oxford University Press, 1999), chs. 3–5. For "Tennessee quarry," see Chernow, *House of Morgan*, 165.

3. "Marriage of Democratic Young Junius Morgan to Miss Louise Converse," *CT*, Jun. 20, 1915; "Blast Perils Life," *MJ*, Sep. 16, 1920; "Germany Prepared to Stop Printing All Paper Money," *CSM*, May 27, 1922. For descriptions of typical Morgan dress, see Chernow, *House of Morgan*, 21–22, 535.

4. J. P. Morgan to Herman Harjes, Sep. 20, 1914, Box 11, Letterpress Book 15, JPM.

5. Strouse, *Morgan*, 15. The firm began its life as the Drexel, Morgan Company. It became J. P. Morgan and Company in 1895.

6. Chernow, *House of Morgan*, 165–71; Strouse, *Morgan*, ix; Lincoln Steffens, *The Autobiography of Lincoln Steffens* (New York: Harcourt, Brace, 1931), 189.

7. Chernow, *House of Morgan*, 29.

8. Ibid., 37.

9. The one-third figure comes from Eric Foner, *Give Me Liberty!* (New York: Norton, 2005), 594. For influential general accounts of the United States' rise to industrial power, see esp. Martin J. Sklar, *The Corporate Reconstruction of American Capitalism, 1890–1916* (New York: Cambridge University Press, 1988); Nell Irvin Painter, *Standing at Armageddon* (New York: Norton, 1987); Robert Wiebe, *The Search for Order, 1877–1920* (New York: Farrar, Straus and Giroux, 1967); Stephen Skowronek, *Building a New American State: The Expansion of National Administrative Capacities, 1877–1920* (Cambridge: Cambridge University Press, 1982).

10. For *Corsair* measurements, see Chernow, *House of Morgan*, 53, 60, 80–81.

11. Strouse, *Morgan*, 406.

12. "Tributes to Morgan by Noted Financiers," *CT*, Apr. 1, 1913; Sklar, *Corporate Reconstruction*, 16.

13. Chernow, *House of Morgan*, 169; Morgan to Messrs. J. P. Morgan and Co., Apr. 24, 1913, Box 9, Letterpress Book 11, JPM; Morgan to James Stillman, May 13, 1913, Box 9, Letterpress Book 11, JPM.

14. Morgan to Edward Grenfell, Sep. 5, 1914, Box 11, Letterpress Book 15, JPM. For Junius' childhood activities, see Morgan to P. H. Morton, Aug. 3, 1904, Box 2, Letterpress Book 3:4, JPM; Morgan to Endicott Peabody, Nov. 17, 1904, Box 2, Letterpress Book 3:4, JPM; Morgan to A. Grace, Mar. 18, 1903, Box 2, Letterpress Book 2:3, JPM.

15. Chernow, *House of Morgan*, 183–204.

16. Morgan to Harjes, Sep. 20, 1914, Box 11, Letterpress Book 15, JPM; William Leuchtenberg, *The Perils of Prosperity 1914–1932* (Chicago: University of Chicago Press, 1993), 39; Fraser, *Every Man*, 347.

17. "Wall Street District Is Steadily Expanding," *WSJ*, Jul. 4, 1919.

18. Chernow, *House of Morgan*, 305; "22-Story Building for Stock Exchange," *NYT*, Feb. 13, 1920.

19. "Curb Moving Will Relieve Wall Street," *NYT*, Dec. 21, 1919.

20. Susan Aaronson, "Bankers Trust Company," *Encyclopedia of New York City*, ed. Kenneth T. Jackson (New Haven, CT: Yale University Press, 1995), 74.

21. Barbaralee Diamonstein, "Federal Hall National Memorial, 1834–42," *The Landmarks of New York III* (New York: Abrams, 1998), 76. For the early history of the Federal Hall site, see Edwin G. Burrows and Mike Wallace, *Gotham: A History of New York City to 1898* (New York: Oxford University Press, 1999), 296–306.

22. "Lay Cornerstone of Assay Office," *NYT*, Jul. 2, 1919; "Wall Street Loss Set at $2,500,000," *SNYH*, Sep. 17, 1920; "Billion in Gold Near Scene of the Explosion," *NYTR*, Sep. 17, 1920.

23. "The Bigness of New York," *SNYH*, Sep. 12, 1920; Matthew Drennan and Cathy Matson, "Economy," Norman Brouwer, "Port of New York," and Nathan Kantrowitz, "Population," in *The Encyclopedia of New York City*, 360–63, 926–29, 921; Nathan Miller, *New World Coming: The 1920s and the Making of Modern America* (New York: Scribner, 2003), 64.

24. "The Bigness of New York," *SNYH*, Sep. 12, 1920; Gerald Carson, "America's Junction: New York in the 1920s," *The Great Metropolis: Poverty and Progress in New York City*, ed. Kenneth T. Jackson (New York: American Heritage, 1993), 212.

25. NYPD 1918, 127; Carson, "America's Junction," 216.

26. Christine Stansell, *American Moderns* (New York: Metropolitan Books/Henry Holt, 2000), 64; NYPD 1920, 164–65.

27. NYPD 1920, 166.

28. "Arrive for Morgan-Converse Wedding," *BG*, Jun. 15, 1915; "Junius Morgan Weds," *WP*, Jun. 16, 1915; Morgan to James J. Goodwin, Feb. 18, 1915, Box 11, Letterpress Book 15, JPM; Chernow, *House of Morgan*, 262–63; "J. P. Morgan Shot by Man Who Set the Capitol Bomb," *NYT*, Jul. 4, 1915; "Morgan Estate an Armed Camp," *NYT*, Jul. 4, 1915.

29. Henry Physick, deposition, Jul. 3, 1915, Box 147, Folder 130, JPM; "Intruder Has Dynamite," *NYT*, Jul. 4, 1915; "Morgan Estate an Armed Camp," *NYT*, Jul. 4, 1915; Chernow, *House of Morgan*, 192–95.

30. "Notes of Examination of Frank Holt, the Assaulter of J. P. Morgan," Jul. 6, 1915, Box 147, Folder 130, JPM; Chernow, *House of Morgan*, 193; "J. P. Morgan Shot Twice by Peace Fanatic Who Set Off Bomb in Capitol," *NYW*, Jul. 4, 1915; "Holt Says He Planned to Hold Banker's Family as Hostages," *NYW*, Jul. 5, 1915 (the quote is New York police Captain Thomas Tunney's paraphrase of Holt's statement); "Wilson's Guards Reinforced After Bomb Explosion," *NYW*, Jul. 4, 1915.

31. "J. P. Morgan's Condition 'Favorable,'" *NYW*, Jul. 5, 1915; "Death of Mrs. Morgan and Children Part of Holt's Plan," *WP*, Jul. 5, 1915; "Vanderbilt Steers Vanitie to Victory," *NYT*, Jul. 6, 1915; "Young Morgan Goes to Work," *WP*, Jul. 7, 1915; Chernow, *House of Morgan*, 168.

32. USCIR, 28, 12; Louis Duchez, "New York City and the Revolution," *ISR*, Sep. 1910.

33. Morgan to Henry L. Higgson, Mar. 24, 1913, Box 9, Letterpress Book 11, JPM; H. L. Loucks, *The Great Conspiracy of the House of Morgan Exposed and How to Defeat It* (Watertown, SD: Loucks, 1916), 4.

34. "Notes of Examination of Frank Holt, the Assaulter of J. P. Morgan," Jul. 6, 1915, Box 147, Folder 130, JPM, 12; Chernow, *House of Morgan*, 191; Anonymous to Morgan, undated, Box 147, Folder 129, JPM.

35. "Morgan's Son an Ensign," *WP*, May 15, 1917; "Morgan, Bacon Two of Those Who Suffered," *NYA*, Sep. 17, 1920; J. S. Morgan, "Diary—Autograph Manuscript."

36. J. S. Morgan, "Diary—Autograph Manuscript."

37. "New Generation of Wall Street," *AC*, Mar. 23, 1919.
38. For overviews of the tumultuous year of 1919, see esp. Ann Hagedorn, *Savage Peace: Hope and Fear in America, 1919* (New York: Simon and Schuster, 2007); David Mitchell, *1919: Red Mirage* (New York: Macmillan, 1970); Burl Noggle, *Into the Twenties: The United States from Armistice to Normalcy* (Urbana: University of Illinois Press, 1974); Eliot Asinof, *1919: America's Loss of Innocence* (New York: Donald I. Fine, 1990).
39. "Plain Words," MID 10110-1279 (also reprinted in House, 165; Avrich, *Sacco and Vanzetti*, 81). For overviews of the May Day and Jun. 2 plots, see esp. Avrich, *Sacco and Vanzetti*, 165–95; McCormick, *Hopeless Cases*, 43–64.
40. "Lunatic Kills Dr. James W. Markoe," *NYT*, Apr. 19, 1920; "To Hurry Markoe's Slayer to Asylum," *NYT*, Apr. 20, 1920; Strouse, *Morgan*, 296–99, 332–34; "J. P. Morgan's Condition 'Favorable,'" *NYW*, Jul. 5, 1915; "Dr. Markoe Rites Held Under Guard," *NYT*, Apr. 22, 1920.
41. Interchurch World Movement, *Report on the Steel Strike of 1919* (New York: Harcourt, Brace and Howe, 1920), 85, 110–11.
42. "'Attempt to Terrorize Has Failed,' Says Palmer," *WP*, Jun. 4, 1919.
43. NYPD 1920, 100–101; "1,000 Socialists Cheer Waldman at Ratification," *NYC*, Sep. 2, 1920; "Limits Legislature to Housing Laws," *NYT*, Sep. 14, 1920.
44. Morgan to Harry Davison, Aug. 12, 1920, Box 17, Letterpress Book 28, JPM ; "Men Meet Tomorrow to Take Vote on Strike," *NYT*, Aug. 31, 1920; "Miners' Heads Fight to Prevent Strike," *NYT*, Sep. 1, 1920; "Mine Workers Quit, Defying Leaders," *NYT*, Sep. 2, 1920; "Incorporation of Markle Foundation Sought," *NYT*, Feb. 4, 1927; "Coal Commission Ends Its Hearings," *NYT*, Feb. 14, 1903; Morgan to Henry Warner, Jan. 27, 1913, Box 8, Letterpress Book 10, JPM.
45. "Havoc Wrought in Morgan Offices," *NYT*, Sep. 17, 1920; Chernow, *House of Morgan*, 165–66; "Red Plot Seen in Blast," *NYT*, Sep. 17, 1920; "Morgan Firm Received No Warning Says Lamont," *NYW*, Sep. 17, 1920.
46. "Cause Still Mystery as Dead Are Identified," *NYC*, Sep. 17, 1920; "Terrific Explosion Outside Morgan's Office," *WSJ*, Sep. 18, 1920.
47. "Havoc Wrought in Morgan Offices," *NYT*, Sep. 17, 1920.
48. "Street Strewn with Dead," *NYTR*, Sep. 17, 1920.

## CHAPTER 2

1. "Stock Exchange Trading Ends with a Shower of Glass," *NYCM*, Sep. 17, 1920; "Loss Due to Breakage of Glass Alone Estimated at $200,000," *NYCM*, Sep. 17, 1920; "Street Strewn with Dead," *NYTR*, Sep. 17, 1920. Where general descriptions are consistent across many news accounts, no specific articles have been cited.
2. "Statement of [name redacted]," Sep. 17, 1920, BI FOIA 61-5-85; "Morgan Firm Received No Warning Says Lamont," *NYW*, Sep. 17, 1920.
3. "Bomb Disaster in Wall St.," *NYET*, Sep. 17, 1920.
4. "Reporter Caught in Blast Tells Story," *SNYH*, Sep. 17, 1920; "29 Dead, Hundreds Injured," *JCCB*, Sep. 17, 1920; "Bomb Disaster in Wall Street," *NYEM*, Sep. 16, 1920.
5. "Eyewitnesses Tell of Shock and Panic," *NYW*, Sep. 17, 1920.
6. "Broad and Wall Like War's Havoc," *WP*, Sep. 17, 1920; "Trace I.W.W. Terrorist Plot to Milwaukee," *MJ*, Sep. 18, 1920; "Other Experts Agree Bomb Held Heavy Charge of Nitric Compound," *NYW*, Sep. 18, 1920; "List of Dead Stands at 28," *NYW*, Sep. 17, 1920.
7. "Havoc Wrought in Morgan Offices," *NYT*, Sep. 17, 1920; "Morgan Firm Received No Warning Says Lamont," *NYW*, Sep. 17, 1920.
8. "Morgan Firm Received No Warning Says Lamont," *NYW*, Sep. 17, 1920; "Havoc Wrought in Morgan Offices," *NYT*, Sep. 17, 1920.
9. "Eyewitnesses Tell of Shock and Panic," *NYW*, Sep. 17, 1920; "Financial District in a Panic," *NYA*, Sep. 19, 1920.
10. "Eyewitnesses Tell of Shock and Panic," *NYW*, Sep. 17, 1920; "Wall Street Explosion on Sep. 16th. [name redacted]." Sep. 20, 1920, BI FOIA 61-5-351; "Panic Reigns," *MJ*, Sep. 16, 1920.

11. "World's Richest Corner Buried in Wreckage," *NYC*, Sep. 17, 1920; "Eyewitnesses Tell of Shock and Panic," *NYW*, Sep. 17, 1920; "Reporter Caught in Blast Tells Story," *SNYH*, Sep. 17, 1920.

12. "Terror in Financial District," *WP*, Sep. 17, 1920; "Wall Street Explosions, Sep. 16, 1920," Sep. 21, 1920, BI FOIA 61-5-427.

13. "Wall Street Scene Is Compared to a Battlefield," *NYW*, Sep. 17, 1920; "Flame Cone Leaps Skyward," *MJ*, Sep. 16, 1920; "Men Trample Women Under Hell in Street in Safety Dash," *NYA*, Sep. 19, 1920.

14. "Financial District in a Panic," *NYA*, Sep. 17, 1920; "Wall Street Explosion on September 16th. [name redacted]," Sep. 21, 1920, BI FOIA 61-5-442; "Praise Injured Youth for Devotion to Duty," *NYW*, Sep. 18, 1920; "Explosion Warning—'Get Out of Wall Street,'" *SNYH*, Sep. 17, 1920.

15. "Eyewitnesses Tell of Shock and Panic," *NYW*, Sep. 17, 1920; "World's Richest Corner Buried in Wreckage," *NYC*, Sep. 17, 1920; "Financial District in a Panic," *NYA*, Sep. 17, 1920.

16. "World's Richest Corner Buried in Wreckage," *NYC*, Sep. 17, 1920; "Blinding Burst of Fire Leaps to Fifth Story," *SNYH*, Sep. 17, 1920; "Financial District in a Panic," *NYA*, Sep. 19, 1920; "Wagon Axle Hurled 38 Stories," *NYTR*, Sep. 17, 1920.

17. "Eyewitnesses Tell of Shock and Panic," *NYW*, Sep. 17, 1920; "Hospitals Rush Aid to Victims," *NYT*, Sep. 17, 1920.

18. "Ex-Service Men Aid in Handling Crowd," *NYT*, Sep. 17, 1920; "Scene in Hospital Like Field Station After Big Battle," *NYW*, Sep. 17, 1920.

19. "Scene in Hospital Like Field Station After Big Battle," *NYW*, Sep. 17, 1920.

20. Ibid.; "Terrific Explosion Outside Morgan's Office," *WSJ*, Sep. 17, 1920.

21. "Explosive Stores All Accounted For," *NYT*, Sep. 17, 1920.

22. "10 Years' Long List of Bomb Outrages," *SNYH*, Sep. 17, 1920.

# CHAPTER 3

1. "Arrival of Herr Most," *NYT*, Dec. 19, 1882; Avrich, *Haymarket Tragedy*, 65; Adamic, *Dynamite*, 48. Most was not the first anarchist in the United States to advocate dynamite. However, his fame and his ability to attract press attention helped to thrust the issue into the broader public consciousness.

2. The quote comes from the Desert Publications translation of Johann Most's *Revolutionäre Kreigswissenschaft: Ein Handbüchlein zur Anleitun betreffend Gebrauches und Herstellung von Nitro-Glycerin, Dynamite, Schiessbaumwolle, Knallquicksilber, Bomben, Brandsatzen, Giften u.s.w, u.s.w* (New York: Verlag des Internationalen zeeitungs-Vereins, 1885). Most, *Science of Revolutionary Warfare: A Handbook of Instruction Regarding the Use and Manufacture of Nitroglycerine, Dynamite, Gun-Cotton, Fulminating Mercury, Bombs, Arsons, Poisons, Etc.* (El Dorado, AZ: Desert Publications, 1978). Paul Avrich translates the title as *Revolutionary War Science: A Little Handbook of Instruction in the Use and Preparation of Nitroglycerin, Dynamite, Gun-Cotton, Fulminating Mercury, Bombs, Fuses, Poisons, Etc., Etc.* (Avrich, *Haymarket Tragedy*, 164). Avrich notes the cartoonists' adoption of Most in *Haymarket Tragedy*, 61.

3. The idea of a "terror district" can be found in Green, *Death in the Haymarket*, 165. Henry James' *The Princess Casamassima* (New York: Macmillan, 1886) revolves around a failed assassination plot against an English aristocrat, in which the would-be revolutionary Hyacinth Robinson commits suicide rather than carry out the deed. Joseph Conrad later took up the subject of anarchist terrorism in *The Secret Agent: A Simple Tale* (London: Methuen, 1907). For discussions of terrorism-inspired literature, see esp. Carr, *Infernal Machine*, 37–54; Clymer, *America's Culture of Terrorism*; Barbara Arnett Melchiori, *Terrorism in the Late Victorian Novel* (London: Croon Helm, 1985); Arthur F. Redding, *Raids on Human Consciousness: Writing, Anarchism, and Violence* (Columbia: University of South Carolina Press, 1998). For quotes, see Most, *Science*, 40; "An Anti-Anarchist Bill," *NYT*, Aug. 3, 1894; Henry Holt, "Punishment of Anarchists and Others," *Forum*, Aug. 1894.

4. Most, *Science*, 14. Avrich estimates IWPA membership at approximately 5,000 members in the mid-1880s. (Avrich, *Haymarket Tragedy*, 82–85). Green offers a slightly higher count, estimating that in 1885 the IWPA had "5,000 to 6,000 sympathizers," if not full-fledged members, in Chicago (Green, *Death in the Haymarket*, 126). Tom Goyens describes a "total membership of three thousand and an additional four thousand sympathizers" in early 1885. Goyens, *Beer and Revolution*, 108.

5. Most composed and published a four-volume autobiography, *Memoiren: Erlebtes, Erforschtes und Erdachtes* (New York: Johann Most, 1903). Unfortunately, there is no English translation of this text. The most useful English-language sources on Most are Frederic Trautmann, *The Voice of Terror: A Biography of Johann Most* (Westport, CT: Greenwood Press, 1980); Goyens, *Beer and Revolution*; Avrich, *Haymarket Tragedy*, esp. chs. 5–12; and Max Nomad, *Apostles of Revolution* (New York: Macmillan, 1932), 257–301. The "Directory of Individuals" in Falk et al., eds., *Emma Goldman: A Documentary History of the American Years, Made for America, 1890–1901*, vol. 1 (Berkeley: University of California Press, 2003), contains a concise biographical summary. Where not otherwise cited, redundant biographical information can be found in these texts. For more on socialism and anarchism in Germany during the volatile 1870s and 1880s, see Vernon L. Lidtke, *The Outlawed Party: Social Democracy in Germany, 1878–1890* (Princeton, NJ: Princeton University Press, 1966).

6. Two useful general histories of European anarchism during this period are James Joll, *The Anarchists* (Cambridge, MA: Harvard University Press, 1980) and George Woodcock, *Anarchism: A History of Libertarian Ideas and Movements* (New York: Penguin Books, 1986). For a recent biographical portrait of Bakunin, see James Mark Leier, *Bakunin: The Creative Passion* (New York: Thomas Dunne Books/St. Martin's Press, 2006).

7. Most, *The Beast of Property: Total Annihilation Proposed as the Only Infallible Remedy: The Curse of the World Which Defeats the People's Emancipation* (New Haven, CT: International Workingmen's Association, n.d.), 3.

8. In 1881, this vision of dynamite received the endorsement of the landmark International Social Revolutionary Congress, convened to establish an anarchist alternative to Marx's defunct International. Avrich, *Haymarket Tragedy*, 55–59.

9. *The "Freiheit" Prosecution: The Trial of Herr Johann Most, with Verbatim Report of the Address of Mr. A. M. Sullivan, M.P. for the Defence* (London: n.p., 1881), 12. For a concise account of Narodnaya Volna as "the world's first self-styled terrorist organization," see Carr, *Infernal Machine*, 13–36.

10. Burrows and Wallace, *Gotham*, 1025–27, 1036; Charles Loring Brace, *The Dangerous Classes of New York, and Twenty Years' Work Among Them* (Washington, DC: National Association of Social Workers, 1973 [orig. pub. 1872]); Beckert, *Monied Metropolis*, 233. For the role of violence in the 1877 rail strike, see especially Robert V. Bruce, *1877: Year of Violence* (Chicago: Ivan R. Dee, 1959).

11. William Graham Sumner, *What Social Classes Owe to Each Other* (New York: Harper and Brothers, 1883), 7.

12. Burrows and Wallace, *Gotham*, 1089–96. For the Knights of Labor, see especially Leon Fink, *Workingmen's Democracy: The Knights of Labor and American Politics* (Urbana: University of Illinois Press, 1983); Kim Voss, *The Making of American Exceptionalism: The Knights of Labor and Class Formation in the Nineteenth Century* (Ithaca, NY: Cornell University Press, 1993); Craig Phelan, *Grand Master Workman: Terence Powderly and the Knights of Labor* (Westport, CT: Greenwood Press, 2000).

13. "Arrival of Herr Most," *NYT*, Dec. 19, 1882.

14. Avrich, *Haymarket Tragedy*, 58–61.

15. Ibid., 163–64; Most, *Beast*, 15, 10. See also Most, *The Social Monster: A Paper on Communism and Anarchism* (New York: Bernard and Schenck, 1890).

16. Most, *Beast*, 9.

17. "Action as Propaganda," *Freiheit*, Jul. 25, 1885, reprinted in Walter Laqueur, *Voices of Terror: Manifestos, Writing and Manuals of Al Qaeda, Hamas, and Other Terrorists from Around the World and Throughout the Ages* (New York: Reed Press, 2004), 108–9.

18. Most, *Science*, 22, 47.

19. "Report of the Secretary of War," 48th Congress, 2nd Session, Pt. 2, Vol. 1, 49; Trautmann, *Voice of Terror*, 143, 250. One of the most daunting examples of terrorist tactics came from London, where Fenian dynamiters carried out an elaborate campaign of bombings in the mid-1880s. For a brief account of the Fenians' cultural impact in the United States, see Clymer, *America's Culture*, 69–71.

20. Haymarket has been the subject of numerous historical works. The most important are Green, *Death in the Haymarket*; Avrich, *Haymarket Tragedy*; Bruce Nelson, *Beyond the Martyrs: A Social History of Chicago's Anarchists, 1870–1900* (New Brunswick, NJ: Rutgers University Press, 1988); Henry David, *The History of the Haymarket Affair: A Study in American Social-Revolutionary and Labor Movements* (New York: Russell and Russell, 1958). For quotes, see Green, *Death in the Haymarket*, 86, 146, 158, 186, 188.

21. "Rioting and Bloodshed in the Streets of Chicago," *NYT*, May 5, 1886; Avrich, *Haymarket Tragedy*, 221; "The Anarchists Cowed," *NYT*, May 6, 1886.

22. Michael J. Schaack, *Anarchy and Anarchists* (Chicago: F. J. Schulte, 1889), 565.

23. Green, *Death in the Haymarket*, 210, 214. The debate over the identity of the bomb thrower continues to the present day. Police insisted that the bomb was thrown by anarchist Rudolph Schnaubelt, a theory widely though not universally accepted at the time. (Schnaubelt fled Chicago immediately after the bombing.) Novelist Frank Harris repeated this theory in *The Bomb* (London: John Long, 1908). Paul Avrich has suggested that the bomber was actually Chicago anarchist George Schwab (Avrich, *Haymarket Tragedy*, 437–45). Historian Timothy Messer-Kruse recently reopened the case by testing the surviving bomb fragments, preserved at Yale University's Beinecke Library. See Messer-Kruse, James O. Eckert Jr., Pannee Burkel, and Jeffrey Dunn, "The Haymarket Bomb: Reassessing the Evidence," *Labor* 2, 2 (2005): 39–52.

24. Schaack, *Anarchy and Anarchists*, 606, 560.

25. Green, *Death in the Haymarket*, 235–38, 268–70.

26. Ibid., 199.

27. Goldman remains one of the legendary figures of American radicalism. Her two-volume autobiography, *Living My Life* (*LML*), is a rich source of information and reflection, though like all autobiographies it presents Goldman only as she wished to be seen. For secondary accounts of her U.S. years, see esp. Richard Drinnon, *Rebel in Paradise* (Chicago: University of Chicago Press, 1971); Alice Wexler, *Emma Goldman in America* (Boston: Beacon Press, 1984); Marian J. Morton, *Emma Goldman and the American Left: "Nowhere at Home"* (New York: Twayne, 1992); Candace Falk, *Love, Anarchy, and Emma Goldman* (New York: Holt, Rinehart, and Winston, 1984); Avrich, *Anarchist Voices* (Princeton, NJ: Princeton University Press, 1995), Part 2. Of unsurpassed value for Goldman scholars are Falk's two edited collections of Goldman's papers: Falk et al., eds., *Emma Goldman*, and Falk et al., eds., *The Emma Goldman Papers: A Microfilm Edition*. For Berkman, see esp. Gene Fellner, ed., *Life of an Anarchist: The Alexander Berkman Reader* (New York: Four Walls Eight Windows, 1992); Linnea Goodwin Burwood, "Alexander Berkman: Russian-American Anarchist," Ph.D. dissertation, State University of New York at Binghamton, 2000; Avrich, *Anarchist Portraits*, 200–207. For quotes, see *LML*, 28, 11, 16, 7, 10.

28. Henry George, *Progress and Poverty* (New York: Robert Schalkenbach Foundation, 1940 [orig. pub. 1879]), 10. See also Burrows and Wallace, *Gotham*, 1092–110. For Most's arrest, see Trautmann, *Voice of Terror*, 143–66, 250. Blackwell's Island was renamed Welfare Island in 1921, a name it maintained until 1973 when it took on its present name, Roosevelt Island.

29. Samuel Gompers, *Seventy Years of Life and Labor* (New York: Dutton, 1925), 215, 174. On Gompers and the birth of the AFL, see especially Montgomery, *Fall of the House of Labor*; Julie Greene, *Pure and Simple Politics: The American Federation of Labor and Political Activism, 1881–1917* (New York: Cambridge University Press, 1998); Stuart Bruce Kaufman, *Samuel Gompers and the Origins of the American Federation of Labor* (Westport, CT: Greenwood Press, 1973); Harold C. Livesay, *Samuel Gompers and Organized Labor in America* (Boston: Little, Brown, 1978).

30. *LML*, 3–6, 31.

31. "Nellie Bly Again," *NYW*, Sep. 17, 1893, reprinted in Falk et al., eds., *Emma Goldman*, 155; *LML*, 48, 31, 85.

32. *LML*, 85. For Goldman's full account of Homestead, see 83–114. Berkman also offered a detailed autobiographical account in his 1912 *Prison Memoirs of an Anarchist* (*PMA*), 1–92. For the Homestead strike, see esp. Paul Krause, *The Battle for Homestead, 1880–1892: Politics, Culture, and Steel* (Pittsburgh: University of Pittsburgh Press, 1992); Leon Wolff, *Lockout: The Story of the Homestead Strike of 1892: A Study of Violence, Unionism, and the Carnegie Steel Empire* (New York: Harper and Row, 1965).

33. *PMA*, 6.

34. *LML*, 85–87; *PMA*, 5, 9–10.

35. *PMA*, 9–10, 22, 33–34, 7.

36. *PMA*, 59.

37. Falk et al., eds., *Emma Goldman*, 1:119 n. 1.

38. *Der Anarchist*, Jul. 30, 1892, in Falk et al., eds., *Emma Goldman*, 1:119–21; *LML*, 113.

39. *PMA*, 91; "Frick's Assailant Sentenced," *NYT*, Sep. 20, 1892.

40. Drinnon, *Rebel in Paradise*, 50–51.

41. "The Girl" appears throughout *Prison Memoirs* as Berkman's code name for Goldman. See, for instance, 1–2.

42. "Editor's Outlook," *Chautauquan*, Aug. 1894, 630. For an overview of European anarchist terrorism, see esp. Richard Bach Jensen, "Daggers, Rifles and Dynamite: Anarchist Terrorism in Nineteenth Century Europe," *Terrorism and Political Violence* 16, 1 (Spring 2004): 116–53; Martin Miller, "The Intellectual Origins of Modern Terrorism in Europe," in Crenshaw, ed., *Terrorism in Context*, 27–62; Joll, *The Anarchists*, 111–19. For anarchist terrorism in 1890s France, see John Merriman, *The Dynamite Club: The Bombing of the Café Terminus and the Origins of Modern Terrorism in Fin-de-Siècle Paris* (New York: Houghton Mifflin, 2009).

43. "Adjournment of Congress," *NYT*, Jun. 26, 1894; "The Climax of Anarchy," *CT*, Jun. 26, 1894; "Almost Became a Law," *WP*, Sep. 12, 1901.

44. "An Anti-Anarchist Bill," *WP*, Aug. 3, 1894; "Anti-Anarchist Bill," United States Senate, *Congressional Record* 8238, Aug. 6, 1894.

45. John P. Altgeld, *The Chicago Martyrs: The Famous Speeches of the Eight Anarchists in Judge Gary's Court, October 7, 8, 9, 1886, and Reasons for Pardoning Fielden, Neebe, and Schwab* (San Francisco: Free Society, 1899), 132, 153.

46. For the populist movement, see esp. Lawrence Goodwyn, *The Populist Moment: A Short History of the Agrarian Revolt in America* (New York: Oxford University Press, 1978); Charles Postel, *The Populist Vision* (New York: Oxford University Press, 2007).

47. Fraser, *Every Man*, 162; Burrows and Wallace, *Gotham*, 1186–88; Falk et al., eds., *Emma Goldman*, 1:27; *LML*, 123. For a discussion of the controversies over the exact wording and translation of Goldman's speech, see Falk et al., eds., *Emma Goldman*, 28–33.

48. "Hailed Emma Goldman," *NYW*, Aug. 20, 1894, reprinted in Falk et al., eds., *Emma Goldman*, 1:203.

49. Beckert, *Monied Metropolis*, 2; Francis H. Nichols, "The Anarchists in America," *Outlook*, Aug. 10, 1901.

50. Rauchway, *Murdering McKinley*, 53. See also A. Wesley Johns, *The Man Who Shot McKinley* (New York: Barnes, 1970); Sidney Fine, "Anarchism and the Assassination of McKinley," *American Historical Review* 60, no. 4 (Jul. 1955): 777–99.

51. Rauchway, *Murdering McKinley*, 171; Emma Goldman, "The Tragedy at Buffalo," *Free Society*, Oct. 6, 1901, reprinted in Falk et al., eds., *Emma Goldman*, 1:471.

52. Goldman, "Tragedy at Buffalo," reprinted in Falk et al., eds., *Emma Goldman*, 1:477; Goldman, *The Psychology of Political Violence* (New York: Mother Earth Publishing Association, 1911); *LML*, 298–304.

53. Fine, "Anarchism," 786–87; Morgan to [illegible], Sep. 10, 1901, Box 1, Letterpress Book 2:1, 2:2, JPM; Theodore Roosevelt, "First Annual Message," *State Papers as Governor and President, 1899–1909* (New York: Scribner's, 1926), 83.

54. Roosevelt, *State Papers*, 85.

55. "Plans for War on Anarchists," *CT*, Sep. 8, 1901; Roosevelt, *State Papers*, 85.

56. Rauchway, *Murdering McKinley*, 42.

57. For annotated reprints of the laws, see Nicholas Kittrie and Eldon Wedlock, eds., *Tree of Liberty: A Documentary History of Rebellion and Political Crime in America* (Baltimore: Johns Hopkins University Press, 1986), 263–65. New Jersey and Wisconsin passed similar criminal anarchy laws. Legislation that would have punished "incitement" to assassination with twenty-five years in prison failed at the federal level, largely due to a lack of consensus about the desirability of speech restrictions. See Fine, "Anarchism," 788–96. For a comparison of the U.S. and European responses, see Richard Bach Jensen, "The International Anti-Anarchist Conference of 1898 and the Origins of Interpol," *Journal of Contemporary History* 16, 2 (Apr. 1981): 323–47.

58. Goldman to *Lucifer*, Nov. 30, 1902, reel 1, EG.

## CHAPTER 4

1. Haywood is the subject of three significant biographies: Peter Carlson, *Roughneck: The Life and Times of Big Bill Haywood* (New York: Norton, 1983); Melvyn R. Dubofsky, *"Big Bill" Haywood* (Manchester: Manchester University Press, 1987); and Joseph R. Conlin, *Big Bill Haywood and the*

*Radical Union Movement* (Syracuse, NY: Syracuse University Press, 1969). Haywood also wrote a memoir, *The Autobiography of Big Bill Haywood* (*ABH*). Because Haywood left no collection of personal papers, his autobiography offers one of the few firsthand accounts of his personal life and political evolution. It is somewhat suspect as a source, however, since Haywood composed the book while in exile in the Soviet Union in the late 1920s, and Soviet officials took the liberty of completing the manuscript after his death. Like all autobiographies, it is most useful when viewed in conjunction with secondary research and the published primary source record. Where not otherwise cited, redundant biographical information can be found in these works. For quotes, see Adamic, *Dynamite*, 135; Carlson, *Roughneck*, 16; "'Big Bill' Haywood Dies in Moscow," *NYT*, May 19, 1928.

2. *ABH*, 7, 82–83, 53, 31.

3. *ABH*, 62, 63, 200.

4. Some of the best work on the Western Federation of Miners can be found in accounts of Haywood's 1907 murder trial as well as in the Haywood biographies (above). See esp. Lukas, *Big Trouble*; David H. Grover, *Debaters and Dynamiters: The Story of the Haywood Trial* (Corvallis: Oregon State University Press, 1964). For quotes, see Grover, *Debaters*, 43; *ABH*, 69; "Coeur D'Alene Labor Troubles Report," H.R. Rep. No. 1999, 56th Cong., 1st Sess. (1900), excerpted in Kittrie and Wedlock, *Tree of Liberty*, 1:262–63.

5. Carlson, *Roughneck*, 52; *ABH*, 80.

6. Lukas, *Big Trouble*, 111–15.

7. *ABH*, 86.

8. *MM*, Jun. 1900, 15.

9. Joyce Kornbluh, ed., *Rebel Voices: An IWW Anthology* (Chicago: Charles H. Kerr, 1988), 1.

10. The Haywood kidnapping and trial is the subject of two full-length books, Grover's *Debaters and Dynamiters* and Lukas' *Big Trouble*. Where not otherwise cited, redundant facts have been drawn from these two works. For quote, see *ABH*, 193–94. For Haywood's journey, see Lukas, *Big Trouble*, 248–87.

11. In 1899 alone, the year of the WFM's battle at Coeur d'Alene, the national press contained reports of dynamite controversies during streetcar strikes in Duluth, Cleveland, and Brooklyn. See, for instance, "Strikers Use Dynamite," *WP*, May 6, 1899; "Strikers Use Dynamite; Serious Phase to Brooklyn Car Line Trouble," *CT*, July 19, 1899; "Dynamite in Cleveland," *NYT*, July 22, 1899. I am grateful to Jennifer Luff for pointing out to me the many distinct varieties of labor violence during the Gilded Age and Progressive Era.

12. The best recent account of the Molly Maguires controversy is Kenny, *Making Sense of the Molly Maguires*. For quote, see Adamic, *Dynamite*, 19. For numbers of Molly murders, see Kenny, *Making Sense*, 3.

13. Lukas, *Big Trouble*, 272.

14. Eugene V. Debs, "Arouse, Ye Slaves!" *AR*, Mar. 10, 1906.

15. On Debs, see esp. Salvatore, *Eugene V. Debs*; Ray Ginger, *The Bending Cross: A Biography of Eugene Victor Debs* (New Brunswick, NJ: Rutgers University Press, 1949). On the Socialist Party, see esp. David A. Shannon, *The Socialist Party of America* (Chicago: Quadrangle Books, 1967); James Weinstein, *The Decline of American Socialism, 1912–1925* (New York: Monthly Review Press, 1967). For quote, see Salvatore, *Eugene V. Debs*, 150.

16. Walter Hurt, *Eugene V. Debs: An Introduction* (Williamsburg, OH: Progress, 1913), 15.

17. Werner Sombart, *Why Is There No Socialism in the United States?* trans. Patricia M. Hocking and C. T. Husbands (White Plains, NY: International Arts and Sciences Press, 1976 [orig. pub. 1906]), 15. For Socialist election numbers, see Shannon, *Socialist Party*, 5.

18. Painter, *Armageddon*, 212. AFL membership began to fall in 1905 and 1906 but maintained levels exceeding those of the nineteenth century, reaching three million by 1917.

19. Debs, "Arouse, Ye Slaves!" *AR*, Mar. 10, 1906.

20. Debs, "To the Rescue!" *AR*, Apr. 28, 1906; Debs, "Prepare for Action!" *The Socialist*, Mar. 3, 1906, reel 17, EVD; Lukas, *Big Trouble*, 394. Roosevelt's letter actually attacked a corrupt businessman, making the point that his venality made him "at least as undesirable a citizen as Debs, or Moyer, or Haywood."

21. Lukas, *Big Trouble*, 476.

22. Ibid., 521; Grover, *Debaters*, 93.

23. Lukas, *Big Trouble*, 311, 328. See also Clarence Darrow, *The Story of My Life* (New York: Grosset and Dunlap, 1932), esp. chs. 7–8, 12–14, 18, 21.

24. Harry Orchard, *The Confessions and Autobiography of Harry Orchard* (Waukesha, WI: Metropolitan Church Association, 1907), chs. 9–16. For quotes, see Colorado Mine Operators' Association, "Criminal Record of the Western Federation of Miners: Coeur d'Alene to Cripple Creek 1894–1904," reprinted in Abe C. Ravitz and James N. Primm, *The Haywood Case: Materials for Analysis* (San Francisco: Chandler, 1960), 27; William E. Borah, "The Awful Story," reprinted in Ravitz and Primm, *Haywood Case*, 168.

25. "A Governor Is Murdered," Arthur Weinberg, ed., *Attorney for the Damned* (New York: Simon and Schuster, 1957), 443–44, 487.

26. "Haywood Acquitted," *CT*, Jul. 29, 1907; "A Governor Is Murdered," in Weinberg, *Attorney*, 275.

27. "Haywood Not Guilty," *MM*, Aug. 1, 1907.

28. "Public Feeling Freed Haywood," *Terre Haute Tribune*, Aug. 12, 1907, reel 17, EVD; Carlson, *Roughneck*, 139.

29. *ABH*, 217; Carlson, *Roughneck*, 137.

30. "Haywood Home Again," *MM*, Aug. 8, 1907; *ABH*, 221.

31. Carlson, *Roughneck*, 142; *ABH*, 222–24.

32. Walter V. Woehlke, "Terrorism in America," *Outlook*, Feb. 17, 1912.

33. Falk et al., eds., *Emma Goldman*, 1:19; "Cleveland Cars Blown Up," *CT*, May 22, 1908; "Unionites Use Dynamite," *LAT*, Jun. 3, 1908; "Dynamite in Elgin Strike," *CT*, Jul. 30, 1908; " 'Open Shop' Bridge Blown Up," *CT*, Jul. 2, 1908; "Wrecked by Bomb," *LAT*, Apr. 23, 1908; "Dynamite Under New Bridge," *NYT*, Mar. 9, 1908; "West's Labor War Renewed by Bomb," *CT*, Mar. 29, 1908.

34. "The Haywood Meetings," *ISR*, Mar. 1911; Haywood, "Socialism the Hope of the Working Class," *ISR*, Feb. 1912; Dubofsky, *"Big Bill,"* 65, 50.

35. *Proceedings: National Convention of the Socialist Party*, 1912, reel 76, SPA, 123.

36. On the IWW, see Dubofsky, *We Shall*; Paul Brissenden, *The I.W.W.: A Study of American Syndicalism* (New York: Columbia University Press, 1920); Philip Foner, *The Industrial Workers of the World, 1905–1917* (New York: International Publishers, 1965); Fred Thompson and Patrick Murfin, *The IWW—Its First Seventy Years, 1905–1975* (Chicago: Industrial Workers of the World, 1976); Patrick Renshaw, *The Wobblies: The Story of Syndicalism in the United States* (Garden City, NY: Doubleday, 1967); Salvatore Salerno, *Red November Black November: Culture and Community in the Industrial Workers of the World* (Albany: State University of New York Press, 1989); Nigel Anthony Sellars, *Oil, Wheat and Wobblies: The Industrial Workers of the World in Oklahoma, 1905–1930* (Norman: University of Oklahoma Press, 1998); Peter Cole, *Wobblies on the Waterfront: Interracial Unionism in Progressive-Era Philadelphia* (Urbana: University of Illinois Press, 2007). For quote, see Preamble (1905), reprinted in Kornbluh, *Rebel Voices*, 12.

37. Dubofsky, *We Shall*, 137; Dubofsky, *"Big Bill,"* 64, 54.

38. "W. D. Haywood in London," *ISR*, Dec. 1910.

39. Georges Sorel, *Reflections on Violence*, trans. T. E. Hulme (New York: P. Smith, 1941). Haywood saw explicit analogies between the United States and France; Haywood, "The General Strike," *ISR*, May 1911. For accounts of terrorism and the 1905 revolution in Russia, see esp. Anna Geifman, *Thou Shalt Kill: Revolutionary Terrorism in Russia, 1895–1917* (Princeton, NJ: Princeton University Press, 1993).

40. Dubofsky, *We Shall*, 159; Haywood and Frank Bohn, *Industrial Socialism* (Chicago: C. H. Kerr, 1911), 57.

41. Walker C. Smith, *Sabotage: Its History, Philosophy and Function*, 1913, reprinted in Salvatore Salerno, ed., *Direct Action and Sabotage* (Chicago: Charles H. Kerr, 1997), 60; Louis Levine, "Direct Action," *Forum*, May 1912.

42. Haywood, "The Fighting I.W.W.," *ISR*, Sep. 1912.

43. "Find Dynamite Under Building," *LAT*, Jul. 13, 1907; "Fire and Terrorism Cited at I.W.W. Trial," *CT*, Jun. 2, 1918; "Authorities Here Prepare to Handle I.W.W. Menace," *LAT*, Jul. 17, 1917; National Civil Liberties Bureau, *The Truth About the I.W.W.* (New York: National Civil Liberties Bureau, 1918); Haywood, "News from Europe," *ISR*, Dec. 1910; Dubofsky, *We Shall*, 155.

44. Dubofsky, *We Shall*, 146; Haywood, "Socialism the Hope of the Working Class," *ISR*, Feb. 1912.

45. The best book-length account of the Los Angeles dynamiting is Cowan, *People v. Darrow*; where not otherwise cited, I have drawn background from this account. Sidney Fine's *"Without Blare of*

*Trumpets": Walter Drew, the National Erectors' Association, and the Open Shop Movement, 1903–57* (Ann Arbor: University of Michigan Press, 1995) places the bombing in the context of industrial labor relations. A brief popular account by Paul Greenstein, Nigey Lennon, and Lionel Rolfe, *Bread and Hyacinths: The Rise and Fall of Utopian Los Angeles* (Los Angeles: Classic Books, 1992) adds useful detail. For quotes see Haywood, "Get Ready," *ISR*, Jun. 1911; "Must Blame Unions," *LAT*, Oct. 2, 1910. For "firemen's nets," see "Fire Kills 19; Unions Accused," *NYT*, Oct. 2, 1910.

46. Haywood, "Get Ready," *ISR*, Jun. 1911.

47. Debs, "Another Kidnaping Plot!" *AR*, Apr. 29, 1911.

48. Cowan, *People v. Darrow*, 129, 167–68; *LML*, 486.

49. Morris Hillquit, "In Behalf of McNamara," Jun. 24, 1911, reel 5, MH. The speech in Hillquit's papers is in draft form.

50. For a description of the Llewellyn bombing, see Cowan, *People v. Darrow*, 99.

51. The number comes from Luke Grant, *The National Erectors' Association and the International Association of Bridge and Structural Ironworkers* (Washington, DC: United States Commission on Industrial Relations, 1915), 123. Subsequent secondary accounts differ in their estimate of the number of dynamitings. Clymer reports eighty-six jobs blown up (*America's Culture of Terrorism*, 173), for instance, while Cowan claims seventy (see *People v. Darrow*, 78). Details of particular plots can be found in William J. Burns, *The Masked War* (New York: George H. Doran, 1913), 33–39, a firsthand account of the detective's efforts to arrest the McNamaras. For Ryan and Gompers, see Cowan, *People v. Darrow*, 274, 261.

52. Debs, "Wanted—A Few Men Not Afraid to Die," *AR*, Sep. 2, 1911; Job Harriman to Hillquit, Dec. 19, 1911, reel 2, MH.

53. Paul U. Kellogg, "Conservation and Industrial War," *Survey*, Dec. 30, 1911. For Steffens' account of the attempted plea deal, see Steffens, *Autobiography*, 659–89.

54. Louis D. Brandeis, "Ascertain the Underlying Cause," *Survey*, Dec. 30, 1911. For a full account of the Industrial Commission, see Graham Adams, *The Age of Industrial Violence: 1910–1915* (New York: Columbia University Press, 1966).

55. Haywood, "Socialism the Hope of the Working Class," *ISR*, Feb. 1912. For a recent account of the Lawrence strike, with a detailed history of the dynamite plots, see Bruce Watson, *Bread and Roses: Mills, Migrants, and the Struggle for the American Dream* (New York: Viking, 2005).

56. Debs, "This Is Our Year," *ISR*, Jul. 1912, reel 7, EVD.

57. Woehlke, "Terrorism in America"; John R. Commons et al., *History of Labour in the United States* (New York: Macmillan, 1918), 2:528–29.

58. The proceedings of the Industrial Commission were published in several volumes (USCIR).For recent accounts of the Triangle fire and the Ludlow massacre, see David von Drehle, *Triangle: The Fire That Changed America* (New York: Grove Press, 2003); Martelle, *Blood Passions*.

59. Jack Morgan was highly discouraged by his testimony. "I do not think I did any good," he confessed to an acquaintance a few weeks after testifying, "because I had not at the time, and have not now, any remedy for the difficulties of the country." Morgan to Bruce R. Payne, Feb. 16, 1915, Box 109, Folder 407, JPM.

60. Carlson, *Roughneck*, 227; Francis M. Carroll, "Frank M. Walsh," in *American National Biography*, ed. John A. Garraty and Mark C. Carnes (New York: Oxford University Press, 1999).

61. Dubofsky, *"Big Bill,"* 59–60.

62. Carlson, *Roughneck*, 224–25. For Haywood's testimony, see USCIR, 10569–98.

63. USCIR, 116, 2, 10–12, 8, 139–40, 302. Perhaps unsurprisingly, the Commission was divided over these conclusions. The final report contained dissenting and more conservative statements by commissioners who found Walsh's approach too radical. See Adams, *Industrial Violence*, 204–26.

## CHAPTER 5

1. "Exploded in Apartment Occupied by Tarrytown Disturbers," *NYTR*, Jul. 5, 1914. A fourth person, a bystander named Marie Chavez, was also killed. For accounts of the bombing, see Stansell, *American Moderns*, 116–17; Paul Avrich, *Modern School Movement*, 183–215; Thai Jones, "The Best Answer

Is Dynamite," unpublished, Department of History, Columbia University, 2007. For a firsthand account, see Marie Ganz, *Rebels* (New York: Dodd, Mead, 1920).

2. Goldman, "Stray Thoughts," *ME*, Sep. 1916.

3. Goldman to Ben L. Reitman, Dec. 24, 1911, reel 5, EG. For accounts of Goldman's experiences during the Progressive Era, see especially Morton, *Emma Goldman*, 36–58; Wexler, *Goldman in America*, 115–225; Drinnon, *Rebel in Paradise*, 87–172. For a powerful discussion of Goldman's reconsideration of propaganda by deed, see Falk et al., eds., *Emma Goldman*, 2:9.

4. Stansell, *American Moderns*, 25, 2.

5. Goldman, "The International Anarchist Congress," *ME*, Oct. 1907; Goldman, *What I Believe* (New York: Mother Earth Publishing Association, 1908), 13, reel 47, EG; Goldman, *A Beautiful Ideal* (Chicago: J. C. Hart, 1908), reel 47, EG. In 1911, she attempted to reconcile these views in her classic essay "The Psychology of Political Violence." The essay urged Americans to view "the *Attentater*" as a desperate soul driven to madness by the "heartless, cruel efforts" of "the money power." At the same time, it praised men such as Czolgosz and Berkman for their bravery, placing them in a long line of patriots leading back to Thomas Jefferson. Goldman, *The Psychology of Political Violence*, esp. 11, 29.

6. *PMA*, 7. The years between 1908 and 1914 saw the publication of several works addressing the subject of dynamite from within the American left. Among the most significant are Frank Harris' *The Bomb*, a fictional account of the Haymarket Affair, and Socialist muckraker Robert Hunter's *Violence and the Labor Movement* (New York: Macmillan, 1914), which juxtaposes the history of anarchism and socialism with the rise of the private detective industry.

7. Hutchins Hapgood, introduction to *PMA*, n.p.

8. Mabel Dodge Luhan, *Movers and Shakers* (Albuquerque: University of New Mexico Press, 1985), 88–89, 58–59.

9. Berkman, "The Movement of Unemployed," *ME*, Apr. 1914, 36. The man who threw the Union Square bomb, Selig Silverstein, was a member of the New York Anarchist Federation, which Berkman and Goldman helped to found in early 1908. He brought the bomb to Union Square in an effort to retaliate against police advancing on a socialist demonstration, but the bomb went off prematurely. Coming just days after anarchist attempts to assassinate a priest in Denver and kill the police chief in Chicago, and less than a year after Haywood's acquittal, the Union Square bombing set off a minor "anarchist scare." See "Emma Goldman Blames Police," *CT*, Mar. 29, 1908, reprinted in Falk et al., eds., *Emma Goldman*, 2:297–99; *LML*, 413–23.

10. Arthur Woods, *Policeman and Public* (New Haven, CT: Yale University Press, 1919), 73–78; Avrich, *Modern School Movement*, 184–91; Thai Jones, " 'Eternally and Comprehensively Vigilant': Arthur Woods and the Progressive Origins of Political Surveillance," M.A. thesis, Columbia University, 2008.

11. "Observations and Comments," *ME*, Jun. 1914. The "Observations and Comments" section is unsigned, but since Berkman was editing *Mother Earth* at the time, it is safe to assume that these are his words.

12. "Observations and Comments," *ME*, May 1914. I am grateful to Thai Jones for alerting me to the significance of this quotation.

13. It is likely that Berkman actually did help to plan the plot against Rockefeller, perhaps during that meeting. Publicly, Berkman never admitted a direct role. But both the circumstances of the plot (including his close alliance with the dead men and his leading role in the Rockefeller protest) and his ideological commitments suggest that he was intimately involved. This is the conclusion of Paul Avrich, among others. See *Modern School Movement*, 196–202.

14. "Let the Anarchists Parade," *NYTR*, Jul. 9, 1914.

15. "5,000 at Memorial to Anarchist Dead," *NYT*, Jul. 12, 1914; "The Lexington Explosion," *ME*, Jul. 1914.

16. Berkman, "A Gauge of Change," *ME*, Jul. 1914; "5,000 at Memorial to Anarchist Dead," *NYT*, Jul. 12, 1914.

17. Berkman, "A Gauge of Change," *ME*, Jul. 1914.

18. "The Wall Street Bomb-Throwing," *CT*, Dec. 5, 1891; "Death in Tunnel," *NYT*, Jan. 28, 1902.

19. For accounts of the Italian Squad and the bomb squad's early years, see Jones, "Eternally and Comprehensively Vigilant," 12–15, 30–31; Richard Polenberg, *Fighting Faiths* (Ithaca, NY: Cornell University Press, 1987), 55–61; Jennifer Fronc, *New York Undercover* (Chicago: University of Chicago Press, 2009), ch. 5. For a critical perspective on the creation of urban bomb squads and red squads,

see Frank Donner, *Protectors of Privilege* (Berkeley: University of California Press, 1990). For quote, see Woods, introduction to Thomas J. Tunney, *Throttled!* (Boston: Small, Maynard, 1919), xi.

20. *LML*, 536; Berkman, "A Gauge of Change," 168; *LML*, 538.

21. Goldman, "A Review of Our New York Activities," *ME*, Apr. 1914, 55.

22. Tunney, *Throttled!* 44; Avrich, *Sacco and Vanzetti*, 97–102. The bombs' targets were opponents of the spring's unemployment protests. The dates, too, were significant. Oct. 13 marked the anniversary of the execution of Francisco Ferrer, the Spanish anarchist. Nov. 11 was the day of the Haymarket executions. Again, Berkman's actual role in the bombings, if any, is unclear. The most likely perpetrators were members of the Harlem-based Bresci Group, named for Gaetano Bresci, who had left Paterson to assassinate King Humbert in 1900.

23. *LML*, 540; "Blown Up," *NYTR*, Jul. 6, 1914.

24. Goldman, "Donald Vose: The Accursed," *ME*, Jan. 1916, 356. I am grateful to Candace Falk and Barry Pateman for pointing out Goldman's clandestine role in harboring Schmidt.

25. Tunney, *Throttled!* 49–59.

26. Goldman to Ellen Kennan, Apr. 2, 1915, reel 8, EG; "Dynamite Hall of Bronx Borough," *NYT*, May 4, 1915; "Observations and Comments," *ME*, Jul. 1915; "Bomb Rocks Police Headquarters," *NYT*, Jul. 6, 1916.

27. Tunney, *Throttled!* 68, 8.

28. For a full account of Black Tom and other acts of German sabotage, see Jules Witcover, *Sabotage at Black Tom: Imperial Germany's Secret War in America, 1914–1917* (Chapel Hill, NC: Algonquin, 1989).

29. The Mooney case has been the subject of four book-length treatments: Gentry, *Frame-up*; Frost, *The Mooney Case*; Estolv Ethan Ward, *The Gentle Dynamiter: A Biography of Tom Mooney* (Palo Alto, CA: Ramparts Press, 1983); Henry Thomas Hunt, *The Case of Thomas J. Mooney and Warren K. Billings* (New York: Da Capo Press, 1971). Where not otherwise cited, I have drawn redundant background material from these books. The phrase "militant worker" comes from Mooney's own newspaper, *Revolt: Voice of the Militant Worker*.

30. Berkman, "An Innocent Abroad," *ME*, Jan. 1915; Goldman to Kennan, Nov. 22, 1915, reel 9, EG.

31. Berkman, "Labor on Trial," *ME*, Jul. 1915. Caplan and Schmidt were eventually convicted of supplying the dynamite for the Ironworkers' campaign.

32. John Dewey, "The Social Possibilities of War," reprinted in Joseph Ratner, ed., *Characters and Events: Popular Essays in Social and Political Philosophy* (New York: Holt, 1929), 551–60; Berkman, "The War at Home," *ME*, Oct. 1915.

33. "War on War," *ME*, Aug. 1914.

34. Goldman, "The Promoters of the War Mania," *ME*, Mar. 1917. For overviews of World War I on the home front, see especially David Kennedy, *Over Here: The First World War and American Society* (New York: Oxford University Press, 1980): Robert H. Zeiger, *America's Great War* (Lanham, MD: Rowman and Littlefield, 2000); Alan Dawley, *Changing the World: American Progressives in War and Revolution* (Princeton, NJ: Princeton University Press, 2003); Christopher Capozzola, *Uncle Sam Wants You: World War I and the Making of the Modern American Citizen* (New York: Oxford University Press, 2008). For World War I and the labor movement, see esp. Joseph S. McCartin, *Labor's Great War: The Struggle for Industrial Democracy and the Origins of Modern American Labor Relations, 1912–1921* (Chapel Hill: University of North Carolina Press, 1997).

35. *Law and Order in San Francisco: A Beginning* (San Francisco: San Francisco Chamber of Commerce, 1916), Group 53, Series 1, Box 39, Folder 7, HW; Kennedy, *Over Here*, 67. The *Blast's* nearly two-year run has been assembled in a single useful volume: Barry Pateman, ed., *The Blast* (Oakland, CA: AK Press, 2005).

36. Goldman, "Stray Thoughts," *ME*, Aug. 1916.

37. Goldman, "Stray Thoughts," *ME*, Sep. 1916.

38. Berkman, "Planning Another 11th of November," *Blast*, Aug. 15, 1916, reprinted in Pateman, *Blast*, 141. Arrested with Mooney and Billings were labor activists Israel Weinberg and Edward D. Noland, as well as Mooney's wife, Rena. Their arrests came weeks after an unsuccessful attempt to organize a streetcar strike in San Francisco. For the broader context of the arrests, see esp. Gentry, *Frame-up*, 33–81; Frost, *Mooney Case*, 1–79. On labor organizing in San Francisco, see Michael Kazin, *Barons of Labor: The San Francisco Building Trades and Union Power in the Progressive Era* (Urbana: University

of Illinois Press, 1987). For Mooney as a *Blast* contributor, see Tom Mooney, "Will Organized Labor Help?" *Blast*, Apr. 1, 1916, reprinted in Pateman, *Blast*, 87.

39. Frost, *Mooney Case*, 138. The Mooney case remained famously contentious for decades after the initial trial. In 1917 and 1918, new evidence showed that several eyewitnesses had perjured themselves at the behest of prosecutor Charles Fickert. A federal commission convened by President Wilson to examine the evidence concluded that the San Francisco authorities had undertaken the case in order to suppress the local labor movement. This has been the conclusion of every major book on the Mooney-Billings case. Several historians have presented theories pointing to the culpability of other groups and individuals. Avrich suggests that the bombing was actually the work of the Galleanisti, a group of Italian anarchists subsequently suspected in a string of later dynamitings, including the Wall Street explosion. Avrich, *Sacco and Vanzetti*, 138. Richard Spence argues that the bombing may have been the work of German saboteurs. Spence, *Trust No One: The Secret World of Sidney Reilly* (Los Angeles: Feral House, 2002), 147; Spence, "K. A. Jahnke and the German Sabotage Campaign in the United States and Mexico, 1914–1918," *Historian* 59, 1 (1996): 89–112. There remains the likely possibility that Berkman was involved in planning the explosion. As with the Lexington Avenue bombing, the precise extent of his involvement, if any, remains unknown.

40. Goldman to Agnes Inglis, Feb. 13, 1917, reel 10, EG; William Preston, *Aliens and Dissenters: Federal Suppression of Radicals, 1903–1933* (New York: Harper Torchbooks, 1966), 60, 83; Eldridge Foster Dowell, *A History of Criminal Syndicalism Legislation in the United States* (Baltimore: Johns Hopkins University Press, 1936), 150.

41. *War Messages of President Woodrow Wilson*, 65th Cong., 1st Sess., 1917, no. 5, serial no. 7264, 3–8; Goldman and Berkman, "The No Conscription League," *ME*, Jun. 1917. For an overview of war resistance, see Gilbert C. Fite and H. C. Peterson, *Opponents of War, 1917–1918* (Madison: University of Wisconsin Press, 1957).

42. *LML*, 610–11; "No Conscription!" reprinted in Fellner, *Life of an Anarchist*, 155.

43. "The Trial and Imprisonment of Emma Goldman and Alexander Berkman," *ME*, Jul. 1917, 134; *LML*, 620.

44. Many historians have identified federal restrictions in World War I as a watershed in the history of U.S. civil liberties. See especially Polenberg, *Fighting Faiths*; Kennedy, *Over Here*, 43–92; Capozzola, *Uncle Sam*; David Rabban, *Free Speech in Its Forgotten Years* (Cambridge: Cambridge University Press, 1997), 248–341; Paul L. Murphy, *World War I and the Origin of Civil Liberties in the United States* (New York: Norton, 1979); Donald Johnson, *The Challenge to American Freedoms: World War I and the Rise of the American Civil Liberties Union* (Lexington: University of Kentucky Press, 1963). For a lively overview of free speech questions in wartime, see Geoffrey R. Stone, *Perilous Times: Free Speech in Wartime from the Sedition Act of 1798 to the War on Terrorism* (New York: Norton, 2004). For the Ves Hall case, see Arnon Gutfeld, "The Ves Hall Case, Judge Bourquin, and the Sedition Act of 1918," *Pacific Historical Review* 37, 2 (Mar. 1968): 163–78. For quotes, see Polenberg, *Fighting Faiths*, 27; Kennedy, *Over Here*, 59.

46. Alan Dawley, *Struggles*, 196.

47. Kennedy, *Over Here*, 76; Stone, *Perilous Times*, 186.

48. Kennedy, *Over Here*, 84.

49. James R. Mock and Cedric Larson, *Words That Won the War: The Story of the Committee on Public Information, 1917–1919* (Princeton, NJ: Princeton University Press, 1939), 65; SPA, 1912, reel 76, 130. For Creel's account of his work at the CPI, see Creel, *How We Advertised America* (New York: Arno Press, 1972 [orig. pub. 1920]).

50. *LML*, 641. For a full account of the Wobbly raids, see Preston, *Aliens and Dissenters*, 88–207. Kennedy mentions Wilson's approval of the raids, *Over Here*, 88.

51. The number, later scaled down in courtroom proceedings, comes from National Civil Liberties Bureau, *Truth About the I.W.W.*, 50; *ABH*, 316.

52. Haywood to Debs, Nov. 2, 1917, reel 2, EVD; Debs, "The I.W.W. Bogey," *ISR*, Feb. 1918, 396, reel 8, EVD.

53. *ABH*, 307–8, 326. Eventually the Wobbly defendants, including Haywood, were released pending appeal. But their release did not come until the spring of 1919, well after the war was over.

54. For quotes, see Goldman to Catherine Breshkovskaya, Oct. 4, 1917, reel 10, EG; Sellars, *Wobblies*, 3.

55. *LML*, 640; *Debs and the War: His Canton Speech and His Trial in the Federal Court at Cleveland, September, 1918* (Chicago: National Office, Socialist Party, 1918).

56. Eswertz to John Lord O'Brian, Jun. 17, 1918, DOJ 77175-A-19, reel 2, EVD.

57. For the antianarchist law, see Avrich, *Sacco and Vanzetti*, 130–34. For Goldman, see *LML*, 669.

58. Benjamin Gitlow, *The Whole of Their Lives* (New York: Scribner's, 1948), 3–4; Goldman, *The Truth About the Boylsheviki* (New York: Mother Earth Publishing Association, 1917), reel 10, EG, 4.

59. Lenin, "Letter," 347. For the Seattle strike, see Robert L. Friedheim, *The Seattle General Strike* (Seattle: University of Washington Press, 1964).

60. *ABH*, 352; Murray, *Red Scare*, 261.

61. Goldman to Stella Ballantine, Aug. 15, 1919, reel 10, EG.

62. Avrich, *Sacco and Vanzetti*, 165–66.

63. *LML*, 691.

64. Goldman to Inglis, Mar. 31, 1917, reel 10, EG.

65. Goldman and Berkman to "Friends," undated (ca. Oct. 1919), Group 53, Series 1, Box 27, Folder 18, HW; *LML*, 700–1.

66. Berkman to Harry Weinberger, Nov. 11, 1919, Group 53, Series 1, Box 27, Folder 18, HW. The exact number of URW members and alleged members has long been a matter of dispute. These numbers come from Schmidt, *Red Scare*, 268.

67. "Letter from Attorney General, A. Mitchell Palmer," Nov. 17, 1919, United States Congress, Senate, Committee on the Judiciary, *Investigation Activities of the Department of Justice*, 66th Cong., 1st Sess. (Washington, DC: Government Printing Office, 1919), 5. Goldman's sole claim to citizenship came through her former husband Jacob Kershner, who had become a naturalized citizen. Berkman never became a U.S. citizen. See Falk et al., eds., *Emma Goldman*, 2:66–69; Schmidt, *Red Scare*, 260–62.

68. *LML*, 709.

69. Ibid., 713.

70. Robert Minor, introduction, in Goldman and Berkman, *Deportation: Its Meaning and Menace, Last Message to the People of America* (New York: Fitzgerald, 1919), 3.

71. Schmidt, *Red Scare*, 27; Goldman to Weinberger, Jun. 29, 1919, Group 53, Series 1, Box 27, Folder 18, HW.

72. *LML*, 717; "249 Reds Sail, Exiled to Soviet Russia," *NYT*, Dec. 22, 1919.

73. Schmidt, *Red Scare*, 275.

## CHAPTER 6

1. "On Explosion Clews," *WP*, Sep. 17, 1920. For physical description, see "William J. Flynn, Long of Secret Service, Is Dead," *NYHT*, Oct. 15, 1928.

2. "On Explosion Clews," *WP*, Sep. 17, 1920; "Memorandum in Re: Explosion in J. P. Morgan's Office," Sep. 16, 1920, BI 386228.

3. Despite his fame and his importance to the history of the Red Scare, Flynn has yet to find his biographer. For biographical details, see Charles Willis Thompson, "Flynn Is to Give New York a Real Detective Force," *NYT*, Oct. 30, 1910; "Flynn Here, Bares Working of Vast German Spy Network," *LAT*, Apr. 7, 1918. For Flynn's disaffection with his gambling assignment, see "Flynn Has Quit His Police Job," *NYT*, Apr. 27, 1911. For an overview of Flynn's life, see "William J. Flynn, Long of Secret Service, Is Dead," *NYHT*, Oct. 15, 1928; "W. J. Flynn, Noted Detective, Dead," *NYT*, Oct. 15, 1928.

4. "Statements of Hon. A. Mitchell Palmer, the Attorney General, and Mr. Charles E. Stewart, Chief Clerk," Mar. 28, 1920, reprinted in Senate, 632; "U.S. Official Who Will Lead Fight Against Terrorists," *CT*, Jun. 4, 1919. Appointed along with Flynn to improve the Justice Department's antiradical capabilities were former New York assistant district attorney Francis P. Garvan, hired as assistant attorney general, and former Secret Service operative Frank Burke, who became Flynn's assistant director at the Bureau. Schmidt points out that while many historians have portrayed these actions as a "spontaneous response to the bombings," most of the appointments were under way well before Jun. 2. See Schmidt, *Red Scare*, 150–51.

5. "Flynn Is to Give New York a Real Detective Force," *NYT*, Oct. 30, 1910; Frank Donner, *The Age of Surveillance: The Aims and Methods of America's Political Intelligence System* (New York: Vintage Books, 1980), 34.

6. For the early history of the Bureau and its later role in the Red Scare, see especially Schmidt, *Red Scare*; Max Lowenthal, *The Federal Bureau of Investigation* (New York: Harcourt Brace Jovanovich, 1950); David J. Williams, "Without Understanding: The FBI and Political Surveillance, 1908–1941," Ph.D. dissertation, University of New Hampshire, 1981; David J. Williams, "The Bureau of Investigation and Its Critics, 1919–20: The Origins of Federal Political Surveillance," *Journal of American History* 68, 3 (1981); Rhodri Jeffreys-Jones, *The FBI: A History* (New Haven, CT: Yale University Press, 2007), chs. 3–4; Fred Cook, *The FBI Nobody Knows* (New York: Macmillan, 1964), chs. 2–3. Frank Donner's *Age of Surveillance* traces the Bureau's broader history as a political police force. For the American Protective League, see Joan M. Jensen, *The Price of Vigilance* (Chicago: Rand McNally, 1968).

7. "Plain Words," MID 10110-1279; AG 1920, 172–73. For an account of the Jun. 17 meeting, see Powers, *Secrecy and Power: The Life of J. Edgar Hoover* (New York: Free Press, 1987), 63.

8. Hoover has been the subject of numerous biographies. Kenneth Ackerman's *Young J. Edgar* (New York: Carroll and Graf, 2008) offers an account of Hoover's early life, focusing on his Red Scare activities. Other important biographies include Powers, *Secrecy and Power*; Athan Theoharis and John Stuart Cox, *The Boss: J. Edgar Hoover and the Great American Inquisition* (Philadelphia: Temple University Press, 1988); Curt Gentry, *J. Edgar Hoover: The Man and the Secrets* (New York: Penguin Group, 1992); Anthony Summers, *Official and Confidential: The Secret Life of J. Edgar Hoover* (New York: Putnam, 1993). For the figure 200,000, see AG 1920, 173.

9. Ackerman, *Young J. Edgar*, 91, 159–60; "Wall St. Explosion Kills 28; Injures 130," *NYW*, Sep. 17, 1920. Schmidt estimates that the two major Palmer Raids on Nov. 7, 1919, and Jan. 2, 1920, rounded up approximately 10,000 suspected radicals in total. Schmidt, *Red Scare*, 236.

10. Both the extent and precise location of Junius Morgan's injuries are difficult to ascertain. Nearly every newspaper cites cuts to his hand or hands, as does the official statement of the Morgan bank. The *Wall Street Journal* also mentions an injury to the head. See "Terrific Explosion Outside Morgan's Office," *WSJ*, Sep. 17, 1920. According to John Brooks, the Morgan partners long claimed that Junius sustained a cut on the buttocks and that the newspapers were simply too polite to mention it. Brooks, *Once in Golconda*, 6. For quotes, see "Terrific Explosion Outside Morgan's Office," *WSJ*, Sep. 17, 1920; "Ghastly Wreck Scene Meets Eyes of Curious," *NYEM*, Sep. 16, 1920; "Heard 2 Blasts," *NYG*, Sep. 16, 1920.

11. "Death of Mrs. Morgan and Children Part of Holt's Plot," *WP*, Jul. 5, 1915; "Gotham Police Head Engaged; To Wed Grand-Daughter of J. Pierpont Morgan," *LAT*, Mar. 18, 1916.

12. For a brief overview of Woods' police career, 1915–20, see Jones, "Vigilant," 32–40; "Arthur Woods, 72, Is Dead in Capital," *NYT*, May 13, 1942. For details, see "Friends Urge Flynn for Head of Police," *NYT*, Apr. 30, 1911; "Chief of Secret Service Resigns," *WP*, Dec. 23, 1917; "Rebelling Police Tell Woods They Dislike His Rule," *NYT*, Jan. 2, 1915; Woods, testimony, USCIR, 10550; "Government to End all Anarchy Here," *NYT*, Jun. 17, 1917. For Woods' lectures on police reform, see Woods, *Policeman and Public*.

13. Joyce's account is from "Morgan Firm Received No Warning Says Lamont," *NYW*, Sep. 17, 1920. For details of William's death, see especially "Morgan Firm Clerk Killed, Thirty Hurt," *SNYH*, Sep. 17, 1920. For Woods' account of his postwar work, see Arthur Woods, "Finds Soldiers Jobs," *WP*, May 4, 1919.

14. For quote, see "Ghastly Wreck Scene Meets Eyes of Curious," *NYEM*, Sep. 16, 1920. For accounts of police work, see NYPD 1920, 167–68; "Suspect Bomb Plot in Wall Street Blast," *MJ*, Sep. 16, 1920; "Red Plot Seen in Wall Street Blast," *NYT*, Sep. 17, 1920.

15. "New York Police Department Is on a War Footing," *NYT*, Feb. 11, 1917; "Wall St. Explosion Kill 28; Injures 130," *NYW*, Sep. 17, 1920; "Bomb in Wall Street Kills 29," *NYA*, Sep. 17, 1920; "Ghastly Wreck Scene Meets Eyes of Curious," *NYEM*, Sep. 16, 1920.

16. "1,700 Police Put on Guard Within Hour," *NYTR*, Sep. 17, 1920.

17. "Woods Must Go as Police Head, Hylan Decides," *NYT*, Nov. 9, 1917; Polenberg, *Fighting Faiths*, 59–60.

18. "30 Killed, 300 Hurt," *NYEM*, Sep. 16, 1920; "Wall St. Explosion Kills 38," *NYW*, Sep. 17, 1920; "Dynamite for Wall Street," *WSJ*, Sep. 17, 1920; Chernow, *House of Morgan*, 212.

19. "Enright Politician, Not a Policeman," *NYEP*, Dec. 20, 1920; "Chicago Asks Enright How to Check Robberies," *NYW*, Aug. 14, 1919; "Government Forces to Round Up Spies," *NYT*, Dec. 24, 1917; "Hylan Enlightens Enright on Ways to Defeat Crime," *NYW*, Jun. 20, 1919.

20. "Woods Will Quit When Mayor Does," *NYT*, Nov. 10, 1917; "City's Bomb Squad Goes to the Army," *NYT*, Dec. 13, 1917; Polenberg, *Fighting Faiths*, 60. For the broader context of the battles between reformers and police organizations during this period, see esp. Robert M. Fogelson, *Big-City Police* (Cambridge, MA: Harvard University Press, 1977), 74; Eric Monkkonen, *Police in Urban America, 1860–1920* (New York: Cambridge University Press, 1981).

21. "Enright's Cronies Rule Departments," *NYEP*, Dec. 23, 1920; "Tunney Assigned to New Job," *NYT*, Nov. 5, 1918; "Inspector Tunney Quits Police Duty," *NYW*, Aug. 14, 1919; "Attacks Hylan Promotions," *NYT*, Jun. 6, 1919. For Gegan's history, see "I.W.W. Invaders Seized in Church," *NYT*, Mar. 5, 1914; "I.W.W. Army Riots in Cooper Union," *NYT*, Mar. 20, 1914; "Says I.W.W. Leader Expected Violence," *NYT*, Mar. 25, 1914.

22. "Down the Red Flag, Hylan Tells Police," *NYT*, Nov. 19, 1918.

23. For an overview of New York politics during the Red Scare, see Julian Jaffe, *Crusade Against Radicalism: New York During the Red Scare, 1914–1924* (Port Washington, NY: Kennikat Press, 1972); Thomas E. Vadney, "The Politics of Repression: A Case Study of the Red Scare in New York," *New York History*, Jan. 1968, 56–75. For the Lusk Committee and state politics, see Todd J. Pfannestiel, *Rethinking the Red Scare: New York's Crusade Against Radicalism, 1919–1923* (London: Routledge, 2003); Lawrence Chamberlin, *Loyalty and Legislative Action: A Survey of Activity by the New York State Legislature, 1919–1914* (Ithaca, NY: Cornell University Press, 1951), 9–52; David R. Colburn, "Governor Alfred E. Smith and the Red Scare, 1919–1920," *Political Science Quarterly* 88 (1973).

24. Murray, *Red Scare*, 116; Goldman to unknown, Jun. 11, 1917, reel 10, EG; "Bureau of Investigation, Bulletin of Radical Activities, Jan. 25–31, 1920," in MIR, 25.

25. "Old Byrnes System Revived Under Enright," *NYT*, Sep. 5, 1920.

26. "William J. Burns Expounded the Detective's Art," *NYT*, May 2, 1909; Burns, *Masked War*, 23; Charles Schneider, "Detectives of the Old School," *NYT*, Apr. 12, 1914. The best biography of Burns is William R. Hunt, *Front-Page Detective: William J. Burns and the Detective Profession 1880–1930* (Bowling Green, OH: Bowling Green State University Press, 1990). For a biography sanctioned by the Burns firm, see Gene Caesar, *Incredible Detective: The Biography of William J. Burns* (Englewood Cliffs, NJ: Prentice-Hall, 1968). For a narrative account of Burns' major cases, see Alan Hynd, *In Pursuit: The Cases of William J. Burns* (Camden, NJ: Thomas Nelson, 1968).

27. Hunt, *Front-Page*, 55–57; Burns, *Masked War*, 20; Cowan, *People v. Darrow*, 99.

28. "Apologies Due to a Detective," *NYT*, Dec. 4, 1911; Frank Winfield Woolworth, *The Master Builders: A Record of the Construction of the World's Highest Commercial Structure* (New York, 1913).

29. "Explosion Spreads Ruin in Wall Street," *WP*, Sep. 17, 1920; "Wall St. Explosion Kills 28," Sep. 17, 1920; "Morgans Not Making Blast Investigation," *NYT*, Sep. 19, 1920; Hunt, *Front-Page*, 53; Caesar, *Incredible Detective*, 161.

30. "Burns, a Detective from Whom Lecoq Might Learn," *NYT*, Apr. 30, 1911; Hunt, *Front-Page*, 9.

31. Hunt, *Front-Page*, 19; "Be a Detective, Says Famous Sleuth," *NYT*, Jan. 19, 1913.

32. Hunt, *Front-Page*, 10–51.

33. Ibid., 283–84; Rhodri Jeffreys-Jones, *Violence and Reform in American History* (New York: New Viewpoints, 1978), 111; Haywood, "A Detective," *ISR*, Dec. 1911, 345. The problem of the rogue private detective profession was one of the most pressing issues in labor politics during the Progressive Era, taken up at length by the Industrial Commission and various reform organizations. For contemporary views from the left, see esp. Hunter, *Violence and the Labor Movement*, and Sidney Howard, *The Labor Spy* (New York: New Republic, 1924). Despite its importance to Progressive Era politics, the industry has received relatively little attention from historians. See Jeffreys-Jones, *Violence and Reform*, chs. 6 and 7; Stephen H. Norwood, *Strikebreaking and Intimidation: Mercenaries and Masculinity in Twentieth-Century America* (Chapel Hill: University of North Carolina Press, 2002); Howard R. Lamar, *Charlie Siringo's West: An Interpretive Biography* (Albuquerque: University of New Mexico Press, 2005). On the Pinkertons, see esp. Frank Morn, *"The Eye That Never Sleeps": A History of the Pinkerton Detective Agency* (Bloomington: Indiana University Press, 1982).

34. "Frank Case Easy, Burns Asserts," *NYT*, Mar. 20, 1914; Hunt, *Front-Page*, 85, 91.

35. Caesar, *Incredible Detective*, 161; Steffens, *Autobiography*, 570; Howard, *Labor Spy*, 25.

36. Burns, *Masked War*, 10; Hunt, *Front-Page*, 201–2.

37. Hunt, *Front-Page*, 104–18. For more on Burns' role in the Frank case, see Leonard Dinnerstein, *The Leo Frank Case* (Athens: University of Georgia Press, 1987), 100–105; Steve Oney, *And the Dead Shall Rise: The Murder of Mary Phagan and the Lynching of Leo Frank* (New York: Pantheon Books, 2003), 385–426.

38. Caesar, *Incredible Detective*, 188.

39. *Annual Report of New York City Fire Department*, 1920 (New York), 36; "Flynn Hurries Here by Palmer's Order," *NYT*, Sep. 17, 1920; "Daily Report of Agent, New York District," Sep. 16, 1920, SS T915; "Blast Brings Big Insurance Losses," *JCCB*, Sep. 17, 1920; "Grand Jury Begins Inquiry," *NYTR*, Sep. 18, 1920; "Morgue Besieged Until Midnight by Surging Crowd," *NYTR*, Sep. 17, 1920; George W. Bicknell, "Memorandum for the Director," Sep. 16, 1920, MID 10110-2065. For a rundown of the various agencies involved, see esp. "Officials Convinced Time Bomb Caused Explosion on Wall Street," *WP*, Sep. 18, 1920.

40. Photograph, *NYT*, Sep. 17, 1920; "20 Dead 200 Hurt, in Wall St. Explosion," *NYG*, Sep. 16, 1920.

41. "Broken Bits of Sash Weights Which Pitted Office Buildings May Have Been in Huge Bomb," *NYW*, Sep. 17, 1920; "Explosive Not for a Lawful Purpose, Asserts Drennan," *NYW*, Sep. 17, 1920.

42. "Explosion Hurls Iron Slugs over Tops of Office Buildings," *NYW*, Sep. 17, 1920; "Evidence of Bomb in Body of Victim," *NYT*, Sep. 17, 1920.

43. "Explosive Record Kept from Public," *NYEP*, Sep. 21, 1920; "Dynamite Blows Up in Street," *NYG*, Sep. 16, 1920; "Experts Differ on Cause of Disaster," *NYA*, Sep. 18, 1920.

44. Bicknell, "Memorandum for the Director," Sep. 16, 1920, MID 10110-2065; "Letter from Federal Reserve Board Assistant Secretary R. G. Emerson to Attorney General," Sep. 16, 1920, BI FOIA 61-5 211205-1.

45. "Dynamite Blows Up in Street," *NYG*, Sep. 16, 1920.

46. "Broken Bits of Sash Weights Which Pitted Office Buildings May Have Been in Huge Bomb," *NYW*, Sep. 17, 1920; "Drennan Infers It Was a Bomb," *NYG*, Sep. 17, 1920; "Memorandum," Sep. 16, 1920, BI FOIA 61-5-31; "Explosives Permits and Licenses Issued by New York Fire Department, Bureau of Combustibles," Sep. 17, 1920, BI FOIA 61-5-93; City of New York Fire Department, "Permit to Use Explosives Issued by Brooklyn Office," n.d., BI FOIA 61-5; "Explosive Not for a Lawful Purpose, Asserts Drennan," *NYW*, Sep. 17, 1920.

47. "Memorandum," Sep. 16, 1920, BI FOIA 61-5-32.

48. "$10,000 City Reward for Bomb Evidence," *NYT*, Sep. 17, 1920.

49. "Bits of Sash Weights Probably in Bomb," *NYW*, Sep. 17, 1920; "Statement of [name redacted], Residing at [address redacted], Business Address 25 Broad Str., c/o HAYDEN-STONE Co.," date illegible, BI FOIA 61-5-53; "Statement of [name redacted] of Westbury, L.I.," Sep. 16, 1920, BI FOIA 61-5-35.

50. G. J. Crystal, "Wall Street Bomb Explosion. [name redacted] (Injured) Monmouth, N.J.," Sep. 29, 1920, BI FOIA 61-5; "Statement Taken at New York Hospital of [name redacted] N.Y.," Sep. 17, 1920, BI FOIA 61-5-74; "Statement Taken at Volunteer Hospital of [name redacted]," Sep. 17, 1920, BI FOIA 61-5-59; Crystal, "Wall Street Bomb Explosion. [name redacted] (Injured). #1187 Bedford Ave., Brooklyn," Sep. 29, 1920, BI FOIA 61-5; "Hospitals Rush Aid to Victims," *NYT*, Sep. 17, 1920.

51. "Quick Response by Organized and Volunteer Workers in Relief Work," *NYT*, Sep. 17, 1920; "Red Cross Quick to Aid Injured," *NYW*, Sep. 17, 1920.

52. "Many at Morgue Seeking Friends," *SNYH*, Sep. 17, 1920; "Morgue Besieged Until Midnight by Surging Crowd," *NYTR*, Sep. 17, 1920; "Coroner's Doctor Finds Bomb Clues," *NYW*, Sep. 17, 1920; "Hundreds Crowd Morgue to View Bomb Victims," *NYA*, Sep. 17, 1920.

53. "Morgue Besieged Until Midnight by Surging Crowd," *NYTR*, Sep. 17, 1920; "List of Dead Stands at 28," *NYW*, Sep. 17, 1920; "Eight of the Dead Served with A.E.F.," *NYW*, Sep. 18, 1920; "Many at Morgue Seeking Friends," *SNYH*, Sep. 17, 1920; "53 Bomb Victims Still in Hospital," *NYT*, Sep. 18, 1920; "Complete List of the Dead," *NYG*, Sep. 17, 1920; "36 Now Dead by Explosion," *NYEM*, Sep. 17, 1920.

54. "List of Dead Stands at 28," *NYW*, Sep. 17, 1920; "Eight of the Dead Served with A.E.F.," *NYW*, Sep. 18, 1920; "Identified Dead and the Injured," *NYT*, Sep. 17, 1920; "Explosion Victims Number

33," *NYT*, Sep. 18, 1920; "Death List from Explosion Grows," *NYEP*, Sep. 17, 1920; "Dead, Missing and Injured," *SNYH*, Sep. 17, 1920; "Weird and Pitiful Tales Mark Wall Street Explosion," *NYDN*, Sep. 18, 1920.

55. "List of Dead Stands at 28," *NYW*, Sep. 17, 1920; "Col. Chas. Neville One of Bomb Dead," *NYT*, Sep. 17, 1920; COD 25631, Alfred G. Mayer. Mayer's age conflicts in various newspaper accounts, but his death certificate lists him as twenty-three years old.

56. "Suspect Bomb Plot in Wall Street Blast," *MJ*, Sep. 16, 1920.

57. "Summary, Wall Street Explosion of Sep. 16th in Re: Dittmer Powder Company Wagon," Sep. 20, 1920, BI FOIA 61-5-34; "Du Pont Nemours," Sep. 16, 1920, BI FOIA 61-5-38.

58. "Explosive Stores All Accounted For," *NYT*, Sep. 17, 1920.

59. "Two Warnings Were Issued," *NYTR*, Sep. 17, 1920.

60. "Red Plotters Use Powder Signs to Divert Suspicion," *SNYH*, Sep. 17, 1920.

61. "Bomb Plot, Not an Accident, Say Officials," *SNYH*, Sep. 17, 1920; "Explosive Not for a Lawful Purpose, Asserts Drennan," *NYW*, Sep. 17, 1920.

62. "Explosive Stores All Accounted For," *NYT*, Sep. 17, 1920.

63. "Wall St. Explosion Kill 28, Injures 130," *NYW*, Sep. 17, 1920; J. G. Tucker and Charles J. Scully, "Memorandum in Re: Explosion at J. P. Morgan's Office," Sep. 16, 1920, BI 386228; Greene, "Telephone Message from Mr. Flynn, 10:25 P.M.," Sep. 16, 1920, BI FOIA 61-5-303.

## CHAPTER 7

1. "Work All Night to Remove Debris," *SNYH*, Sep. 17, 1920; "Toil All Night to Repair Damage," *NYW*, Sep. 17, 1920; "Stock Exchange Closed by Blast," *NYW*, Sep. 17, 1920; "Blast Brings Big Insurance Losses," *JCCB*, Sep. 17, 1920; "Ghastly Wreck Scene Meets Eyes of Curious," *NYEM*, Sep. 16, 1920; "Wall Street Patches Up Damage and Resumes Its Business," *NYW*, Sep. 18, 1920; "Thousands Go to Work," *SFC*, Sep. 18, 1920; "Wall Street Night Turned into Day," *NYT*, Sep. 17, 1920; "Financial District in a Panic," *NYA*, Sep. 17, 1920.

2. "Wall St. Goes Back to Work," *NYG*, Sep. 17, 1920; G. E. Stouch to John Axten, Sep. 17, 1920, Box 110, Folder 424, JPM; "Clear Wreckage from Explosion," *NYEP*, Sep. 17, 1920; "Work All Night to Remove Debris," *SNYH*, Sep. 17, 1920; " 'Open House' at Broad and Wall," *JCCB*, Sep. 18, 1920; "Morgan Offices Like a Hospital; Business Resumed," *NYT*, Sep. 18, 1920; "Resume Business in Bomb Zone," *NYCM*, Sep. 18, 1920.

3. "Wall St. Goes Back to Work," *NYG*, Sep. 17, 1920; "Stock Exchange Closed by Blast, Reopens To-day," *NYW*, Sep. 17, 1920; " 'Open House' at Broad and Wall," *JCCB*, Sep. 18, 1920.

4. "Remick Nips Panic on Stock Exchange," *NYT*, Sep. 17, 1920; Minutes of the New York Stock Exchange Governing Committee, Sep. 16, 1920, NYSE.

5. "Ghastly Wreck Scene Meets Eyes of Curious," *NYEM*, Sep. 16, 1920; "Midday Explosion Halted Wall Street Activity," *WSJ*, Sep. 17, 1920; "To-day's Market," *NYEM*, Sep. 16, 1920.

6. "All Exchanges in U.S. Shut by Disaster," *NYTR*, Sep. 17, 1920; "Bank Centers Turned into Armed Camps," *MJ*, Sep. 17, 1920; "Seattle Financial Houses Are Guarded," *SFC*, Sep. 18, 1920. For World War I, see Chernow, *House of Morgan*, 184; Fraser, *Every Man*, 346–47; Geisst, *Wall Street*, 146–47.

7. "Blast Stops Big Advance," *MJ*, Sep. 16, 1920; "The Stock Market," *WSJ*, Sep. 17, 1920; "Blast Halts 'Bull' Raid on Rail Stocks," *NYW*, Sep. 17, 1920; "Market Tone Firm on Easier Money Before Explosion," *NYTR*, Sep. 17, 1920.

8. "The Financial Situation," *CFC*, Sep. 18, 1920.

9. "Stock Market Situation," *NYCM*, Sep. 18, 1920; "News of the Street," *NYEM*, Sep. 17, 1920; "Accident or Design?" *SLPD*, Sep. 17, 1920.

10. The fullest account of Lamont's life can be found in *Ambassador from Wall Street* (Lanham, MD: Madison Books, 1994), written by his grandson Edward Lamont. Lamont also composed two memoirs: *My Boyhood in a Parsonage* (New York: Madison Books, 1946), an account of his early life; and *Across World Frontiers* (New York: Private Printing, 1950). His biography of Morgan partner Henry Davison provides insight into the workings of the Morgan bank. See Lamont, *Henry P. Davison: The Record of a Useful Life* (New York: Harper, 1933).

11. Chernow, *House of Morgan*, 178–81.

12. "The Financial Situation," *CFC*, Sep. 18, 1920.

13. "Accident, Plot, or Lunacy?" *NYEP*, Sep. 17, 1920.

14. "Terrific Explosion Outside Morgan's Office," *WSJ*, Sep. 17, 1920; "Wall Street Loss Set at $2,500,000," *SNYH*, Sep. 17, 1920; "'Broad and Wall' Like War's Havoc," *WP*, Sep. 17, 1920.

15. "Havoc Wrought in Morgan Offices," *NYT*, Sep. 17, 1920; Minutes of the New York Stock Exchange Governing Committee, Sep. 16, 1920, 3:30 P.M., NYSE.

16. Lamont to Mrs. Thomas W. Lamont, Box 27, Folder 9, TWL; "Havoc Wrought in Morgan Offices," *NYT*, Sep. 17, 1920.

17. "Havoc Wrought in Morgan Offices," *NYT*, Sep. 17, 1920.

18. "Remick Nips Panic on Stock Exchange," *NYT*, Sep. 17, 1920; "Financial District in a Panic," *NYA*, Sep. 17, 1920; "Terrific Explosion Outside Morgan's Office," *WSJ*, Sep. 17, 1920.

19. "Morgan, Bacon Two of Those Who Suffered," *NYA*, Sep. 17, 1920.

20. "Broad Street Hospital Is Proof Dreams Come True," *NYET*, Sep. 24, 1920; "Scene in Hospital Like Field Station," *NYW*, Sep. 17, 1920; "Hard to Tell Injured Were Human, Declares Physician," *NYA*, Sep. 17, 1920; "Victims' Burns Show Blast's Upward Force," *SNYH*, Sep. 17, 1920; "Hospitals Rush Aid to Victims," *NYT*, Sep. 17, 1920.

21. "You Men of Wall Street," *NYTR*, Sep. 20, 1920; "Brokers Help Hospital," *NYT*, Sep. 18, 1920; "Curb Brokers Aid Hospital," *NYCM*, Sep. 18, 1920; "Curb Brokers Help Broad Street Hospital," *JCCB*, Sep. 18, 1920; "Broad Street Hospital Is Proof Dreams Come True," *NYET*, Sep. 24, 1920.

22. "Terrific Explosion Outside Morgan's Office," *WSJ*, Sep. 17, 1920; "Bomb Disaster in Wall St.," *NYET*, Sep. 16, 1920; "Blast Damage Estimated at $1,000,000," *NYTR*, Sep. 17, 1920; "Financial District in a Panic," *NYA*, Sep. 17, 1920.

23. "Explosion Shatters J. P. Morgan Office," *MJ*, Sep. 16, 1920; "Loss Caused by Blow-Up $3,000,000," *NYG*, Sep. 17, 1920; "Terrific Explosion Outside Morgan's Office," *WSJ*, Sep. 17, 1920; "Blast Damage Estimated at $1,000,000," *NYTR*, Sep. 17, 1920; "Morgan Bank and Subtreasury Annex Suffer Greatest Damage," *WP*, Sep. 17, 1920; "That Was a Terrible Explosion Yesterday," *NYT*, Sep. 17, 1920.

24. *NYT*, Sep. 17, 1920; "Evening Mail First with Explosion News," *NYEM*, Sep. 16, 1920.

25. "20 Dead, 200 Hurt," *NYG*, Sep. 16, 1920; "Suspect Bomb Plot in Wall Street Blast," *MJ*, Sep. 16, 1920; "Terrific Explosion Outside Morgan's Office," *WSJ*, Sep. 17, 1920; "Explosion Spreads Ruin in Wall Street," *WP*, Sep. 17, 1920; Aubeury, *NYT*, Sep. 17, 1920; Aresberg, *WP*, Sep. 18, 1920; Cranberry, *NYW*, Sep. 17, 1920; Aaronberry, ibid.; Kresberg, *NYEM*, Sep. 17, 1920; Aurebury, *SNYH*, Sep. 17, 1920; Arambarry, *NYTR*, Sep. 17, 1920; Barnes, *NYW*, Sep. 17, 1920.

26. "Many at Morgue Seeking Friends," *SNYH*, Sep. 17, 1920; "20 Dead, 200 Hurt in Wall Street Explosion," *NYG*, Sep. 16, 1920; "Morgan Offices Like a Hospital," *NYT*, Sep. 18, 1920; "Eight of the Dead Served with A.E.F.," *NYW*, Sep. 18, 1920; "Death List Reaches 33," *NYW*, Sep. 18, 1920; "Morgan and Co. Has No Theory in Blast Cause," *NYTR*, Sep. 18, 1920; "Resume Business in Bomb Zone," *NYCM*, Sep. 18, 1920.

27. "Piece of Bomb Casing Found in Body of Unidentified Youth," *NYW*, Sep. 19, 1920; COD 25693, Joseph Schmitt; COD 25696, Jerome H. McKean; COD 25614, John Johnson; COD 25683, William Fulton Hutchinson; COD 25745, Charles A. Hanrahan; COD 25677, Bartholomew Flannery; COD 25694, Franklin G. Miller; COD 25673, Bernard J. Kennedy; COD 205631, Alfred G. Mayer, *NYW*.

28. "Death List Reaches 33," *NYW*, Sep. 18, 1920; COD 25677, Bartholomew Flannery; COD 25643, Mildred Xylander; COD 25709, Alexander Leith; COD 25694, Franklin Miller.

29. COD 25621, Benjamin Soloway; COD 25634, Robert Westbay; "Only One Body of the 33 Dead Is in the Morgue Unidentified," *NYW*, Sep. 19, 1920.

30. "Col. Chas. Neville One of Bomb Dead," *NYT*, Sep. 17, 1920; "Eight of the Dead Served with A.E.F.," *NYW*, Sep. 18, 1920; "Savannah Mourning Death of Col. Neville," *AC*, Sep. 17, 1920; COD 25627, Charles Neville.

31. COD 25614, John Johnson; "Explosion Victims Number 33," *NYT*, Sep. 18, 1920; "Hospitals Rush Aid to Victims," *NYT*, Sep. 17, 1920.

32. "The Wall Street Outrage," *NYEM*, Sep. 17, 1920; "The Crime's Origins," *NYTR*, Sep. 17, 1920; "The Wall Street Explosion," *NYW*, Sep. 17, 1920; "10 Years' Long List of Bomb Outrages," *SNYH*, Sep. 17, 1920.

33. "Like Disasters Are Recalled by Explosion," *NYC*, Sep. 17, 1920.

34. "Bomb Outrages Laid to Reds," *MJ*, Sep. 16, 1920; "A Police Job of First Magnitude," *NYW*, Sep. 18, 1920.

35. "A Police Job of First Magnitude," *NYW*, Sep. 18, 1920; "Red Plotters Use Powder Signs to Divert Suspicion," *SNYH*, Sep. 17, 1920.

36. "Review and Outlook" and "The Stock Market," *WSJ*, Sep. 17, 1920.

37. "Morgan Offices Like a Hospital," *NYT*, Sep. 18, 1920.

38. "Morgan Jr. Wires to Family Relatives Here," *SFC*, Sep. 18, 1920; Changeless to 23 Wall, Sep. 17, 1920, Box 110, Folder 424, JPM (based on the memos and telegrams in this folder, "Changeless" seems to be Jack Morgan's code name—a poetic one at that); Junius Morgan to J. P. Morgan, Sep. 17, 1920, Box 110, Folder 424, JPM.

39. Lamont and Dwight Morrow to Morgan, Grenfell, Sep. 17, 1920, 10 A.M., Box 110, Folder 424, JPM (though the telegram is dated Sep. 17, its tone and information indicate that it was sent from New York the previous day); "Morgan Jr. Wires to Family Relatives Here," *SFC*, Sep. 18, 1920; unsigned to J. P. Morgan, Sep. 20, 1920, Box 110, Folder 424, JPM. Though this last letter is unsigned, we can surmise that Davison was the author due to his description of these activities on Sep. 16 (he was out of town on a hunting trip) as well as his complaints about headaches and dizziness—soon diagnosed as a brain tumor. For Davison's health problems, see Chernow, *House of Morgan*, 218–19.

40. "Wall Street Patches Up Damage and Resumes Its Business," *NYW*, Sep. 18, 1920; Stouch to Axten, Sep. 17, 1920, Box 110, Folder 424, JPM; "Wall Street Recovers Quickly," *NYEP*, Sep. 17, 1920.

41. "Morgan Offices Like a Hospital," *NYT*, Sep. 18, 1920; "Resume Business in Bomb Zone," *NYCM*, Sep. 18, 1920; "Back at Work in the Street," *SNYH*, Sep. 18, 1920.

42. "Morgan Firm Received No Warning Says Lamont," *NYW*, Sep. 17, 1920; "Public Sentiment as Read by the Betting," *WSJ*, Sep. 28, 1920.

43. "Resume Business in Bomb Zone," *NYCM*, Sep. 18, 1920.

44. "Morgan and Co. Has No Theory on Blast Cause," *NYTR*, Sep. 18, 1920.

45. "The Wall Street Horror," *SNYH*, Sep. 17, 1920; "Labor's Duty to Itself," *JCCB*, Sep. 20, 1920; "The Financial Situation and Business Outlook," *NYCM*, Sep. 20, 1920.

46. "Constitution Day to Stir Loyalty," *NYT*, Mar. 30, 1919.

47. "Crowd of Thousands Gives Prompt Answer to Plotters," *NYEM*, Sep. 17, 1920.

48. "Thousands Attend Celebration," *NYDN*, Sep. 18, 1920; "Big Crowds Flock to Disaster Scene," *SNYH*, Sep. 18, 1920; "100,000 Observe Constitution Day," *NYTR*, Sep. 18, 1920; "Punish Outrage, Officer Urges Noonday Crowd," *NYG*, Sep. 17, 1920.

49. "Constitution Day," *WP*, Sep. 17, 1920.

50. "Punish Outrage Officer Urges Noonday Crowd," *NYG*, Sep. 17, 1920; "Crowd of Thousands Gives Prompt Answer to Plotters," *NYEM*, Sep. 17, 1920.

51. "Wall Street Patches Up Damage and Resumes Its Business," *NYW*, Sep. 18, 1920.

52. "Crowd of Thousands Gives Prompt Answer to Plotters," *NYEM*, Sep. 17, 1920; "But the Constitution Is Unshaken," *NYEM*, Sep. 18, 1920.

53. "Red Plot Seen in Blast," *NYT*, Sep. 17, 1920; "The Crime's Origins," *NYTR*, Sep. 17, 1920.

54. "The Stock Market," *JCCB*, Sep. 18, 1920; "Bomb Scares Bears Almost into Panic," *NYA*, Sep. 18, 1920; "Curb Prices Move up Slightly with Improved Outlook," *NYTR*, Sep. 18, 1920.

55. "Stocks Advance in Month's Most Active Trading," *NYTR*, Sep. 18, 1920; "Stock Market Situation," *NYCM*, Sep. 18, 1920; "Exchange Reopens with Stock Advance," *NYT*, Sep. 18, 1920.

## CHAPTER 8

1. *ABH*, 343–44; Carlson, *Roughneck*, 286; "Haywood's Arrest Ordered," *NYT*, Sep. 17, 1920. For general background on Haywood's life and health during this period, see Carlson, *Roughneck*, 283–315; Dubofsky, *Big Bill Haywood*, 128–40. The exact chronology of Haywood's actions after the explosion is difficult to establish. The *Chicago Tribune* suggests that Haywood actually left Philadelphia on Wednesday night, departing for Chicago on Thursday, though most other records suggest a day's delay. "Bill Haywood Here," *CT*, Sep. 18, 1920.

2. Carlson, *Roughneck*, 297.

3. "Bill Haywood Here," *CT*, Sep. 18, 1920.

4. *ABH*, 344.

5. "Frameup Told by Jack Mooney," *NYC*, Sep. 18, 1920; "Flynn Refutes Newspaper Yarns of U.S. Order for 'Red Round Up,'" *NYC*, Sep. 18, 1920.

6. "'Anarchist Fighters' Warned of Bomb," *NYW*, Sep. 18, 1920; "Death Threat in Missives of Anarchists," *NYTR*, Sep. 18, 1920; "Fac Simile of 'Red' Threat in Mail Box Near Explosion," *NYW*, Sep. 19, 1920.

7. "Death Threat in Missives of Anarchists," *NYTR*, Sep. 18, 1920; "Circulars Clue to Plot," *NYT*, Sep. 18, 1920; "Palmer Views on 'Bomb' Explosion Infuriate A. F. of L.," *SUR*, Oct. 9, 1920; "To Push Anti-Red Law," *MJ*, Sep. 19, 1920.

8. "Circulars Clue to Plot," *NYT*, Sep. 18, 1920; "N.Y. Bomb Big Plot Against the Government," *CT*, Sep. 18, 1920; "'Anarchist Fighters' Warned of Bomb," *NYW*, Sep. 18, 1920; "Anarchist Death Threats," *WP*, Sep. 18, 1920; "Fac Simile of 'Red' Threat in Mail Box Near Explosion," *NYW*, Sep. 19, 1920; "Flynn Sure 'Reds' to Blame for Disaster," *NYEP*, Sep. 18, 1920.

9. "Death Threat in Missives of Anarchists," *NYTR*, Sep. 18, 1920; "Circulars Clue to Plot," *NYT*, Sep. 18, 1920; "Man Who Shod Horse Has Been Found," *NYA*, Sep. 18, 1920. For "flying squadron," see "Time Bomb Set Explosion, Flynn's Official Report," *NYEM*, Sep. 17, 1920. For quote, see "Anarchist Death Threats," *WP*, Sep. 18, 1920.

10. "The Wall Street Horror," *SNYH*, Sep. 17, 1920; "City Reward of $10,500 in Bomb Mystery," *NYTR*, Sep. 18, 1920. The police department advertised its reward a week later in a circular distributed throughout the New York area, describing the horse and wagon. "Police Offer Blast Reward," *NYET*, Sep. 25, 1920; "Police Distribute Notices of Reward for Bomb Arrests," *NYTR*, Sep. 26, 1920. For a full copy of the circular, see BI FOIA 61-5-159.

11. "$10,500 Rewards Offered by City," *NYW*, Sep. 18, 1920; "Ex-Service Men Organize to Seek Punishment of Reds," *NYT*, Sep. 18, 1920. The Preferred Accident Insurance Company offered a $10,000 reward as well, bringing the total to more than $20,000. "Rewards in Blast Case Now $20,500," *NYG*, Sep. 18, 1920.

12. Louis Loebl, "Wall Street Bomb Explosion, September 16, 1920—Resume," Oct. 1, 1921, BI FOIA 61-5; "Bomb Explosion in New York: Alleged I.W.W. Matter," Sep. 16, 1920, BI FOIA 61-5-87.

13. "Experts Sift Debris for Evidence of Infernal Machine," *NYTR*, Sep. 18, 1920; "Explosion Mystery Still Unsolved," *NYEP*, Sep. 18, 1920.

14. "TNT or Picric Acid Used, Two Experts Declare," *NYW*, Sep. 17, 1920; "'Anarchist Fighters' Warned of Bomb," *NYW*, Sep. 18, 1920; "Tag on the Horse That Drew Bomb Wagon New Clue," *NYW*, Sep. 23, 1920.

15. "Circulars Clue to Plot," *NYT*, Sep. 18, 1920.

16. "In re: Wall Street Explosion—September 16th, 1920, New York City Morgue," Sep. 20, 1920, BI FOIA 61-5-319; "Wall Street Explosion of September 16th—Elmer Wallace Kehrer," BI FOIA 61-5-425; "Bomb Explosion on Wall Street Setpember [*sic*] 16th," Sep. 20, 1920, BI FOIA 61-5-445; "Body May Be That of Wagon Driver," *NYW*, Sep. 19, 1920; "Unidentified Victim of the Explosion," *NYW*, Sep. 20, 1920; "Detectives Out to Find Clew to Unclaimed Body," *NYTR*, Sep. 20, 1920; "Who Is This Man?" *NYA*, Sep. 20, 1920; "Identifies Last Explosion Victim," *NYEP*, Sep. 20, 1920; "Widen Bomb Inquiry," *NYG*, Sep. 20, 1920; "Grand Jury Halts Bomb Inquiry," *NYW*, Sep. 21, 1920.

17. "Flynn Sure 'Reds' to Blame for Disaster," *NYEP*, Sep. 18, 1920; "Time Bomb Is Exploded at Stock Exchange in Genoa," *NYW*, Sep. 18, 1920; "Time Bomb Exploded in Genoa Stock Exchange," *NYCM*, Sep. 18, 1920; "Rake U.S. for Reds Who Had Parts in Wall Street Bomb Plot," *MJ*, Sep. 18, 1920; "Hold 18 for Genoa Blast," *MJ*, Sep. 19, 1920; "Genoa and New York Blasts Link in World Plot," *NYTR*, Sep. 19, 1920; "Genoa Police Find Two Bombs in Stables," *SNYH*, Sep. 20, 1920; "New Genoa Bombs Linked with Plot Reaching to U.S.," *NYA*, Sep. 20, 1920; "Fear World Plot," *MJ*, Sep. 21, 1920. For quote, see "Italian Bomb Plots May Extend to U.S.," *NYW*, Sep. 20, 1920.

18. "Five Anarchists Sought by Flynn," *NYT*, Sep. 19, 1920; "Flynn Evinces Interest," *NYTR*, Sep. 20, 1920; "Flynn Again Inflicts Setback on Press in Its 'Bomber' Hunt," *NYC*, Sep. 20, 1920; "Wall Street Bomb Being Traced," *SNYH*, Sep. 20, 1920; Nunzio Pernicone, *Carlo Tresca: Portrait of a Rebel* (New York: Palgrave Macmillan, 2005), 100.

19. Newspapers and Bureau documents offer both Fisher and Fischer as proper spellings. They also offer both Edwin and Edward as Fisher's first name. I have used the spelling most consistent with the Bureau files. For the Bureau's investigation, see esp. W. L. Buchanan, "In re: Wall Street Explosion—September 16, 1920. Edwin P. Fisher," Sep. 21, 1920, BI FOIA 61-5-434; "4:30 P.M. Memorandum of Telephone Information from Mr. Lamb, at New York, to Mr. Neale," Sep. 17, 1920, BI FOIA 61-5-300; F. S. Hoeckley, "In re: Wall Street Explosion—September 16th," Sep. 17, 1920, BI 61-84; "Phoned from Buffalo, 9 P.M.—9-17-20," BI 61-84. For his tennis ranking, see "Bomb Warner Taken Insane in Canada," *NYA*, Sep. 18, 1920; "Five Here Were Warned That Disaster Menaced Wall Street," *NYTR*, Sep. 18, 1920; "Fischer, Who Sent Warnings, Put in Insane Asylum," *NYW*, Sep. 18, 1920.

20. "Five Here Were Warned That Disaster Menaced Wall Street," *NYTR*, Sep. 18, 1920; "Fischer Called Insane," *NYT*, Sep. 18, 1920; "Bomb Plot Day Set in Warning," and "Held in Prison as Undesirable," *SNYH*, Sep. 18, 1920; "Former Attache of French Commission Held by Ontario Authorities," *NYC*, Sep. 19, 1920.

21. "Fischer Called Insane," *NYT*, Sep. 18, 1920; Buchanan, "In re: Wall Street Explosion—September 16, 1920. Edwin P. Fisher," Sep. 21, 1920, BI FOIA 61-5-434.

22. "Fischer Closely Questioned by Police," *NYEP*, Sep. 20, 1920; "Fischer Is Taken to Bellevue Ward," *NYW*, Sep. 21, 1920.

23. "Assassins May Try to Escape," *NYA*, Sep. 19, 1920; "Fischer Called Insane," *NYT*, Sep. 18, 1920; "Held in Prison as Undesirable," *SNYH*, Sep. 18, 1920; "Five Here Were Warned That Disaster Menaced Wall Street," *NYTR*, Sep. 20, 1920.

24. "'Anarchist Fighters' Warned of Bomb," *NYW*, Sep. 18, 1920; "Flynn Certain Bomb Caused Wall Street Catastrophe," *JCCB*, Sep. 18, 1920; "Alien Extremists Blamed for Wall Street Disaster by Department of Justice Officials," *NYCM*, Sep. 18, 1920; "Palmer Puts Entire Force on Red Hunt," *NYTR*, Sep. 18, 1920.

25. "Palmer Puts Entire Force on Red Hunt," *NYTR*, Sep. 18, 1920.

26. Stanley Coben's 1963 biography, *A. Mitchell Palmer: Politician* (New York: Columbia University Press, 1963) offers the most complete account of Palmer's life and character.

27. Schmidt, *Red Scare*, 297; "Statements of Hon. A. Mitchell Palmer, the Attorney General, and Mr. Charles E. Stewart, Chief Clerk," Mar. 28, 1920, reprinted in Senate, 632; House, 34.

28. Lowenthal, *Federal Bureau*, 76, 77; House, 29.

29. "Senate Resolution 213," reprinted in Senate, 580.

30. Francis Fisher Kane to Palmer, Jan. 12, 1920, reprinted in Senate, 347.

31. "Address of A. Mitchell Palmer, Attorney General of the United States," reprinted in Senate, 626.

32. For Post's account of his time in office, see Louis F. Post, *The Deportations Delirium of Nineteen-Twenty: A Personal Narrative of an Historic Official Experience* (Chicago: C. H. Kerr, 1923). Also see Dominic Candeloro, "Louis F. Post and the Red Scare of 1920," *Prologue* 11, 1 (1979). For quotes, see *LML*, 711; Post, *Deportations Delirium*, 90.

33. House, 4.

34. Avrich, *Sacco and Vanzetti*, 177.

35. Coben, *A. Mitchell Palmer*, 237–38; NPGL, 4.

36. "The Wall Street Horror," *SNYH*, Sep. 17, 1920. On Palmer, see "Palmer Will Win, M'Cormick Asserts," *NYT*, Jul. 1, 1920; "Palmer Big Factor in Beating M'Adoo, Cared More for That Result than for the Nomination," *NYT*, Jul. 7, 1920; Coben, *A. Mitchell Palmer*, 246–62.

37. Schmidt, *Red Scare*, 154–55; "Palmer Puts Entire Force on Red Hunt," *NYTR*, Sep. 18, 1920; "Palmer Comes Here to Direct Inquiry," *NYT*, Sep. 18, 1920. Based on Schmidt's calculations, Palmer somewhat exaggerated the extent of the cut, citing a cut of $750,000, or up to a third of the requested amount.

38. "Circulars Clue to Plot," *NYT*, Sep. 18, 1920.

39. "Says Republicans Appeal to Radicals," *NYT*, Sep. 19, 1920.

40. Ibid.; "The Crime's Origin," *NYTR*, Sep. 18, 1920.

41. "Palmer's Drive Against Reds Called Fizzle," *SFC*, Sep. 27, 1920.

42. "I Told You So, Is Palmer's Plea for Drastic Law," *CT*, Sep. 18, 1920.

43. "The Financial Situation," *CFC*, Sep. 18, 1920.

44. "To Put Down Terrorists," *NYT*, Sep. 18, 1920.

45. Ibid.; "Washington Fears Wall Street Explosion Another Attack by Reds on Prominent and Wealthy Men," *NYCM*, Sep. 17, 1920.

46. "Russian Anarchist Arrested," *NYW*, Sep. 19, 1920; "Held as Undesirable Alien," *NYT*, Sep. 19, 1920; "Russian Is Clutched as Probable Suspect in Wall St. Tragedy," *AC*, Sep. 19, 1920; "Police Free Editor Brailovsky," *NYW*, Sep. 21, 1920. Brailovsky had previously drawn the attention of the Bureau for his criticism of the war. See Feri F. Weiss, "In re: Alexander Brailovsky: European Neutrality Matter," Aug. 24, 1917, BI 49792.

47. "Chief Flynn Refuses to Take Russian Editor Brailovsky," *NYW*, Sep. 20, 1920.

## CHAPTER 9

1. "Radicals Join in Denying a Plot," *NYW*, Sep. 18, 1920.

2. "Radicals Resent Blame Suggestion," *NYW*, Sep. 17, 1920; "Bomb Views of Radicals," *NYT*, Oct. 3, 1920.

3. "Radicals Join in Denying a Plot," *NYW*, Sep. 18, 1920.

4. For the Hillquit campaign, see esp. Weinstein, *Decline of Socialism*, 149–54; Shannon, *Socialist Party*, 104–5; Norma Fain Pratt, *Morris Hillquit: A Political History of an American Jewish Socialist* (Westport, CT: Greenwood Press, 1979), 129–30; Frederick C. Giftin, "Morris Hillquit and the War Issue in the New York Mayoralty Campaign of 1917," *International Social Science Review* 74, 3–4 (1999): 115–28. For quotes, see "St. Louis Manifesto of the Socialist Party," reprinted in Albert Fried, ed., *Socialism in America from the Shakers to the Third International* (New York: Columbia University Press, 1992), 521; Weinstein, *Decline of Socialism*, 179.

5. August Claessens, *Didn't We Have Fun* (New York: Rand School Press, 1953), 89; Pratt, *Morris Hillquit*, 3; Leon Trotsky, *My Life* (New York: Pathfinder Press, 1970), 270–78.

6. Louis Waldman, *Labor Lawyer* (New York: Dutton, 1944), 65; Jaffe, *Crusade Against Radicalism*, 78–79; Weinstein, *Decline*, 178, 141, 232; Heale, *American Anticommunism*, 65.

7. Phillip Foner, *History of the Labor Movement in the United States: Postwar Struggles: 1918–1920* (New York: International Publishers, 1988), 8:23; Frederick Lewis Allen, *Only Yesterday: An Informal History of the 1920s* (New York: Harper and Brothers, 1931), 44.

8. Theodore Draper, *The Roots of American Communism* (New York: Viking, 1957), 190; Weinstein, *Decline*, 232.

9. Waldman, *Albany: The Crisis in Government* (New York: Boni and Liveright, 1920), 194–95, 76; Foster Rhea Dulles, *The Road to Teheran: The Story of Russia and America, 1781–1943* (Princeton, NJ: Princeton University Press, 1944), 164. For another firsthand account of the expulsion, see Charles Solomon, *The Albany "Trial"* (New York: Rand School of Social Science, 1920).

10. Waldman, *Albany*, 30–31, 40. For Smith's account, see Alfred E. Smith, *Up to Now: An Autobiography* (New York: Viking, 1929), 199–206.

11. "Hylan and Smith Urged to Enforce Voting Law," *NYC*, Sep. 15, 1920; "Passes Today on Socialist Plea," *NYC*, Sep. 14, 1920; "Socialist Candidates Confident of Victory," *NYC*, Sep. 16, 1920.

12. "No Soviet Funds Backed Wall St. Outrage—Radek," *NYC*, Dec. 22, 1921.

13. Charles W. Ervin, *Homegrown Liberal*, ed. Jean Gould (New York: Dodd, Mead, 1954), 67–69, 91–99; Shannon, *Socialist Party of America*, 110; Jaffe, *Crusade Against Radicalism*, 84, 14; "Our History," www.forward.com/about/history (accessed on Jul. 3, 2008). The *Forward's* Web site notes that circulation was as high as 275,000 in the early 1930s.

14. "The Explosion at Broad and Wall Streets," *NYC*, Sep. 17, 1920; "Cause Still Mystery as Dead Are Identified," *NYC*, Sep. 17, 1920.

15. "Press Opinion and the Disaster," *NYC*, Sep. 18, 1920.

16. "Fruit of Radicalism," *WP*, Sep. 18, 1920; "Washington Fears Wall Street Explosion Another Attack by Reds on Prominent and Wealthy Men," *NYCM*, Sep. 17, 1920; "Ask Mayor to Start Fund for Victims," *NYT*, Sep. 19, 1920; "No Wholesale Indictments," *NYTR*, Sep. 21, 1920.

17. "Armed Guards for N.Y. Capitol," *SNYH*, Sep. 19, 1920.

18. "Custom House Next, Card Warns," *NYEP*, Sep. 20, 1920; "Sunday Set for Red Terror Day," *MJ*, Sep. 19, 1920; "'Red Cart' Tales Cause Calling of Powder Men," *NYA*, Sep. 23, 1920; "Bases Bomb Hopes on Slender Clues," *NYT*, Sep. 25, 1920.

19. "Custom House Next, Card Warns," *NYEP*, Sep. 20, 1920; "Custom House Mark of Plot," *NYW*, Sep. 21, 1920; "Custom House Unharmed at 2 P.M.," *NYG*, Sep. 21, 1920; "Thousands Gather at Custom House," *NYT*, Sep. 22, 1920.

20. "Bad Time for Making Threats," *NYET*, Sep. 23, 1920.

21. "The Wall Street Tragedy and Its Lessons: From the World Tomorrow," *NYC*, Oct. 5, 1920; "Bomb Views of Radicals," *NYT*, Oct. 3, 1920; Robert M. Buck, "Bombs and Bombast," *NM*, Sep. 25, 1920.

22. Salvatore, *Eugene V. Debs*, 308–17; Ernest Freeberg, *Democracy's Prisoner: Eugene V. Debs, the Great War, and the Right to Dissent* (Cambridge, MA: Harvard University Press, 2008), 148–89.

23. "Debs Sees Plot to Involve Radicals," *NYC*, Sep. 25, 1920.

24. "'Big Bill' Haywood Speaks at Roxbury," *BG*, Oct. 1, 1920; "Haywood Recants," *LAT*, Sep. 25, 1920. In Boston, the National Theater initially refused to let Haywood speak. "Haywood Meeting Barred at Theatre," *BG*, Sep. 29, 1920.

25. *ABH*, 344.

26. The Workers' Defense Union, headed by Elizabeth Gurley Flynn, mounted a similar, though more limited, dissection of the evidence, producing a report reprinted in the *Call* in late September. See Elizabeth Gurley Flynn, *Rebel Girl* (New York: International Publishers, 1955), 308–9; "The Explosion Outside of J. P. Morgan," and "Du Pont Firm's Story on Blast Is Contradicted," *NYC*, Sep. 28, 1920.

27. "Ghastly Wreck Scene Meets Eyes of Curious," *NYEM*, Sep. 16, 1920.

28. "Disaster Witness Saw What Seemed to Be Du Pont Dray," *NYC*, Sep. 17, 1920; "Explosion Death List Mounts to 37 as Sleuths Seek Cause of Disaster," *NYC*, Sep. 18, 1920.

29. "Explosive Stores All Accounted For," *NYT*, Sep. 17, 1920.

30. "DuPont Wagon Near Explosion Scene," *NYC*, Sep. 20, 1920.

31. "Experts Sift Debris for Evidence of Infernal Machine," *NYTR*, Sep. 18, 1920.

32. "Grand Jurors Begin Inquiry," *NYTR*, Sep. 18, 1920; "All Explosion Inquiries Fail to Yield a Clue," *NYW*, Sep. 25, 1920; "Jury Decides Explosion Was No Accident," *NYTR*, Sep. 25, 1920.

33. "Justice Department Fails to Press Inquiry into Explosive Companies," *NYC*, Sep. 19, 1920; "A Question for the District Attorney," *NYC*, Sep. 20, 1920.

34. "Destroying Evidence," *NYC*, Sep. 22, 1920.

35. "N.Y. Grand Jury Inquires into Wall St. Disaster" and "Description of Blast Wagon by Police Denied," *NYC*, Sep. 21, 1920.

36. "Blasting Gelatine in Bomb That Killed 38," *NYW*, Oct. 16, 1920; "Blasting Gelatine Caused Disaster in Wall St., Expert Says," *NYC*, Oct. 16, 1920; "Gelatine Caused Wall St. Explosion," *NYTR*, Oct. 16, 1920. The seventy-page Scheele report is missing from the National Archives and the Bureau file, but Bureau reports confirm its contents. See especially William J. Flynn, "Memorandum for the Attorney General: In re: Wall Street Explosion: Progressive Report of Investigation," Oct. 29, 1920, BI FOIA 61-5 211205-175 1/2. Scheele's notebook was destroyed in January 1944. O. H. Patterson, "Memorandum for Mr. Nichols re: Wall Street Explosion of 1920," Dec. 17, 1943, BI FOIA 61-5-5528.

37. Upton Sinclair, "The 'Bomb' Again," *AR*, Nov. 13, 1920.

38. For background on Sinclair, see esp. Leon Harris, *Upton Sinclair: American Rebel* (New York: Thomas Y. Crowell, 1975); Anthony Arthur, *Radical Innocent: Upton Sinclair* (New York: Random House, 2006); Kevin Mattson, *Upton Sinclair and the Other American Century* (New York: Wiley, 2006). Also see Sinclair, *The Autobiography of Upton Sinclair* (New York: Harcourt, Brace and World, 1962). For quotes, see Arthur, *Radical Innocent*, 171, 182.

39. Sinclair, "The Wall Street 'Bomb!'" *AR*, Oct. 9, 1920; Charles Beard, *An Economic Interpretation of the Constitution of the United States* (New York: Macmillan, 1913).

40. James Maurer, "The Wall Street Explosion," *NYC*, Sep. 24, 1920.

41. "$200,000 Voted to Police to Hunt Down Reds and Wall Street Bomb Plotters," *NYTR*, Oct. 5, 1920; Sinclair, "The 'Bomb' Again," *AR*, Nov. 13, 1920.

42. "Misuse of Policy Spy Fund Feared," *NYC*, Oct. 6, 1920.

43. "Disaster Solution Is Still Far Away," *NYEP*, Oct. 2, 1920; "Wall Street Bomb Suspect Caught," *NYT*, Oct. 4, 1920; "N.Y. Won't Ask for Pittsburg's [*sic*] 'Bomb Suspect,'" *NYC*, Oct. 5, 1920; Thomas J. Callaghan, "Wall Street Explosion: Arrest of Florian Zelenko," Oct. 5, 1920, BI FOIA 61-5-8-52; H. J. Lenon, "Interrogation of Florian Zelenko," Oct. 4, 1920, BI FOIA 61-5-8-48. The initial *Times* article identified Zelenko as Florean Zelenska, though later articles use the names "Zelenko" and "Zalenska" ("Zelenko's Bail Is $2,000," *NYT*, Oct. 7, 1920; "4 Seized in Wall St. Bomb Investigation," *NYT*, Oct. 7, 1920). Other newspapers offer similar variation in nomenclature. I use Florian Zelenko because it seems most consistent with linguistic rules and appears most frequently in BI FOIA 61-5.

## CHAPTER 10

1. For English-language sources on Galleani, see esp. Avrich, *Sacco and Vanzetti*, 48–57; Rudolph J. Vecoli, "Luigi Galleani," in *American National Biography*, www.anb.org/articles/home.html; Nunzio Pernicone, "Luigi Galleani and Italian Anarchist Terrorism in the United States," *Studi Emigrazione/ Études Migrations* (Rome) 30, 111 (1993): 469–88; Robert D'Attilio, "La Salute è in Voi: The Anarchist Dimension," *Sacco-Vanzetti: Developments and Reconsiderations—1979, Conference Proceedings* (Boston: Boston Public Library, 1982), 75–89; David Wieck, "'What Need Be Said,'" *Sacco-Vanzetti: Developments and Reconsiderations*, 69–73; Max Sartin, "Introduction," in Luigi Galleani, *The End of Anarchism?* trans. Max Sartin and D'Attilio (Orkney: Cienfuegos Press, 1982). For the broader context of anarchism in Italy, see Nunzio Pernicone, *Italian Anarchism, 1864–1932* (Princeton, NJ: Princeton University Press, 1993). On Italian radicalism within the United States, see Philip V. Cannistraro and Gerald Meyer, eds., *The Lost World of Italian American Radicalism: Politics, Labor, and Culture* (Westport, CT: Praeger, 2003). For Palmer's quote, see House, 42.
2. Avrich, *Sacco and Vanzetti*, 49–50, 27; Weiss, "In re Cronaca Sovversiva (Luigi Galleani et al.)," Sep. 3, 1918, BI 20713.
3. Rayme W. Finch, "In Re Luigi Galleani, Rafael Schiavina, John Eramo and A. Bottonelli," Mar. 27, 1918, BI 20713. For an example of Goldman's writing in *Cronaca*, see Goldman, "Ernest Crosby," *Cronaca Sovversiva*, Mar. 11, 1907, reel 47, EG.
4. Flynn, "My Ten Biggest Man Hunts, Told by Chief W. J. Flynn," *BH*, Mar. 5, 1922; Avrich, *Sacco and Vanzetti*, 98–99; Pernicone, "Luigi Galleani," 482; D'Atillio, "La Salute è in Voi!" 81–82.
5. Tunney, *Throttled!* 53; Avrich, *Sacco and Vanzetti*, 97–98; D'Atillio, "La Salute è in Voi!" 82–83; Finch, "In re Luigi Galleani, Rafael Schiavina, John Eramo and A. Bottonelli," Mar. 27, 1918, BI 20713; Emmett T. Drew, "Summary Report in re Explosion of Bomb at Paterson N.J. on the Night of June 2, 1919," May 14, 1920, BI FOIA 61-5. After fleeing his Devil's Island prison, Duval lived out his days secretly ensconced among Galleani's followers.
6. For details of the terrorist plots, see Avrich, *Sacco and Vanzetti*, 93–136. For a description of Galleani's arrest, see Henry M. Bowen, "In re: Louis Gallerini and John Eramo: European Neutrality Matter," Jun. 18, 1917, BI 20713.
7. Finch, "In re: Cronaca Sovversiva, Anarchist Publication for Spreading of Propaganda," date illegible, BI 20713. For a translation of "Matricolati!" see "Translation of Article from Cronaca Sovversiva, Published at Lynn, Massachusetts, May 26, 1917," BI 20713. For background, see Avrich, *Sacco and Vanzetti*, 59, 135.
8. Avrich, *Sacco and Vanzetti*, 137–39; Drew, "Special Report. In re Cronaca Sovversiva, Weekly Anarchist Newspaper for Revolutionary Propaganda," Nov. 1, 1920, BI 20713.
9. "The Radical Division of the Department of Justice," reprinted in House, 159; Avrich, *Sacco and Vanzetti*, 168.
10. Drew, "Summary Report," May 14, 1920, BI FOIA 61-5.
11. Avrich, *Sacco and Vanzetti*, 149–53; "Plain Words," MID 10110-1279.
12. Sergeant Burlingame, untitled report, Jun. 21, 1919, MID 10110-1279; Avrich, *Anarchist Voices*, 92. The Bureau's summary of the May Day and June 2 investigations can be found in "The Radical Division of the Department of Justice," reprinted in House, 157–65. For other detailed accounts, see esp. Avrich, *Sacco and Vanzetti*, 165–95; McCormick, *Hopeless Cases*, 43–64.

13. "Plain Words," MID 10110-1279; Avrich, *Sacco and Vanzetti*, 180; "MEMO. to Mr. Flynn," Mar. 8, 1920, BI FOIA 61-5-484.

14. "MEMO. to Mr. Flynn," Mar. 8, 1920, BI FOIA 61-5-484; "MEMO. to Chief Flynn," Mar. 8, 1920, BI FOIA 61-5. Avrich identifies Hoover as the author of the March 8 memos. Avrich, *Sacco and Vanzetti*, 181.

15. Joseph A. Barbera, "Roberto Elia: Alleged Anarchist," Feb. 25, 1920, BI 61-260; Scully, "In re: Andrea Salsedo and Roberto Elia: Bomb Explosions of June 2d, 1919," May 22, 1920; "Memorandum Re Bomb Plot of June 2, 1919," May 3, 1920, BI 61-1003; "Statement of Roberto Elia," May 7, 1920, BI 61-260; "Statement of Roberto Elia at Raymond Street Jail, Brooklyn, New York," Feb. 28, 1920, BI 61-260; "Examination Made by W. J. Flynn," Mar. 11, 1920, BI 61-260; "Statement of Special Agent Frank B. Faulhaber," May 17, 1920, BI 61-260; "Radical Division," reprinted in House, 161–65. Elia was initially arrested on gun charges, an attempt to evade the Bureau's lack of a search warrant. Only after the local court dismissed the gun charges did he move to the Park Row offices. "Resume of Case Roberto Elia," May 26, 1920, BI 61-260.

16. Henry Dotzert, "In re: Special Report—Andrea Salsedo and Roberto Elia.—Bomb Explosions of June 2, 1919," May 24, 1920, BI 61-260; "Radical Division," reprinted in House, 163–65. The available evidence largely supports the Bureau's account of Salsedo's death as a suicide.

17. W. R. Palmera, "In re Search of Stowaways on S.S. Italia—Wall St. Explosion," Sep. 25, 1920, BI FOIA 61-5-7-17; Palmera, "In re: Wall Street Explosion Sept. 16, 1920 S.S. San Gennaro—Search for Stowaways," Sep. 25, 1920, BI FOIA 61-5-7-18; "New Bomb Plot Clues Are Obtained," *SNYH*, Sep. 19, 1920; Palmera, "In re: Marazzo Domenico—Stowaway on S.S. Cretic, Wall Street Explosion. September 16, 1920," Sep. 20, 1920, BI 218680.

18. "New Bomb Plot Clues Are Obtained," *SNYH*, Sep. 19, 1920; "Police Find Blacksmith Who Shod Horse," *NYW*, Sep. 19, 1920; "Flynn Still Links Tragedy with 1919," *NYTR*, Sep. 19, 1920.

19. Flynn, "Memorandum for the Attorney General," Oct. 29, 1920, BI FOIA 61-5 211205-175 1/2; Bowen, "In re: Louis Gallerini and John Eramo: European Neutrality Matter," BI 20713; J. Edgar Hoover to Flynn, Mar. 15 or 16, 1920, BI 20713; Hoover to Anthony Caminetti, Mar. 16, 1920, BI 20713.

20. For Nassau Street, see "Wall Street Bomb Mystery Solved by Arrest," *NYT*, Dec. 18, 1921. For Scully's work on the June 2 case, see Scully, "General Summarization of the Investigation Made of the Bomb Explosions of June 2d, 1919," May 13, 1920, BI FOIA 61-5-406. The Wall Street file contains many examples of Scully's directive. See, for instance, Joseph A. Killeen, "Wall Street Explosion, List of Names of Italian Anarchists Sent to This Office by Agent Scully, New York City," Oct. 27, 1920, BI FOIA 61-5 211205-17. For Scully and Flynn, see Scully, "Memorandum for Director W. J. Flynn in re: Wall Street Explosion," Oct. 18, 1920, BI FOIA 61-5-203; Flynn, "Memorandum for the Attorney General," Oct. 29, 1920, BI FOIA 61-5 211205-175 1/2.

21. See all reports by Killeen, Buchanan, J. D. Parrish, Vincent P. Creighton, and W. S. Bachman, titled "Wall Street Explosion, List of Names and Addresses of Alleged Anarchists Received by Agent in Charge Blackmon from Agent Scully of New York City" (or similar title), Oct. 27–Dec. 1920, in BI FOIA 61-5 211205. Of the three bona fide anarchists located in Buffalo, two were allegedly Galleanisti, vaguely suspected of tangential roles in the June 2 plot. Rather than arrest them immediately, the investigating agent decided to hold off until such time as the Bureau could "take these men into custody for a good thorough grilling." Buchanan, "Wall Street Explosion, List of Names and Addresses of Alleged Anarchists Received by Agent in Charge Blackmon from Agent Scully of New York City," Oct. 27, 1920, BI FOIA 61-5 211205-166.

22. For the June 2 confessions, see "MEMO. to Mr. Flynn," Mar. 8, 1920, BI FOIA 61-5-484; Drew, "Summary Report," May 14, 1920, BI FOIA 61-5; "Examination Made by W. J. Flynn," Mar. 11, 1920, BI 61-260. For Mello, see Frank R. Stone, "Special Report, in re: Cronaca Sovversiva (Galliani Group) Anarchists (Individualists—'Terrorists')," Oct. 18, 1920, BI FOIA 61-5-9-79. For Sberna, see George Lamb to Mortimer Davis, Mar. 15, 1920, BI 373874; Scully to Davis, Mar. 13, 1920, BI 373874; J. F. Loren, "In re Bomb Outrages of June 2d, 1919. (Sberna)," Nov. 29, 1920, BI FOIA 61-5 211205-304. For background on the suspects and their possible roles in the June 2 plot, see Avrich, *Sacco and Vanzetti*, 99–102, 157–58, 180–89, 197, 237.

23. William E. Hill, "Bomb Explosion of Sept. 16, Wall St., N.Y.C. All. Anarchist Activities. The Galleani Family, 85 West Street, Wrentham, Mass.," Nov. 1, 1920, BI FOIA 61-5-11-2.

24. "Bold Robbers Raid Coffee House, Holding Up Many Card Players in Wild and Woolly Fashion," unidentified news clipping, Sep. 23, 1920, BI FOIA 61-5.

25. Scully, "In re: Italian Anarchists. (Caruso)," Oct. 7, 1920, BI FOIA 61-5-9-16; H. C. Leslie, "In re: Italian Anarchists. (Caruso)," Oct. 8, 1920, BI 384519. Also see "4 Seized in Wall St. Bomb Investigation," *NYT*, Oct. 7, 1920; "Bomb Maker Held as Daring Robber," *NYW*, Oct. 7, 1920; "Police Seize 14 Italians in 'Bomb Plot,'" *NYC*, Oct. 8, 1920. Bureau records identify Caruso's first name variously as Giacomo, Giatano, and Gaetano.

26. "Bomb Maker Held as Daring Robber," *NYW*, Oct. 7, 1920; "4 Seized in Wall St. Bomb Investigation," *NYT*, Oct. 7, 1920; "Suspect Is Not Bomb Plotter," *NYS*, Oct. 8, 1920.

27. Flynn, "Memorandum for the Attorney General," Oct. 29, 1920, BI FOIA 61-5 211205-175 1/2; J. J. Haas, "In re Gaetano Caruso, Alleged Anarchist," Jun. 9, 1920, BI 384519. The earliest report in Caruso's file, BI 384519, cites surveillance beginning on April 10, 1920 (A. R. Reid, "In re: Caruso," Apr. 12, 1920, BI 384519); the last reported surveillance of the spring was June 9 (see Haas, cited above). In his memo to Palmer on October 29, Flynn suggested that the surveillance had been carried out for "six months," though apparently not continuously.

28. Reid, "In re: Caruso, Anarchistic Activities," Apr. 19, 1920, BI 384519; P131, "In re: Bomb Raids, Report of Special Confidential Employee P 131," May 7, 1920, BI 384519; Leslie, "In re: Caruso—Explosives at His Home," May 19, 1920, BI 384519.

29. Leslie, "In re: Italian Anarchists (Caruso)," Sep. [date illegible], 1920, BI 384519; Ed Anderson, "Caruso. Waterbury, Conn.," Sep. 30, 1920, BI 384519.

30. Scully, "In re: Italian Anarchists. (Caruso)," Oct. 7, 1920, BI FOIA 61-5-9-16; Leslie, "In re: Italian Anarchists, (Caruso)," Oct. 8, 1920; Barbera, "Translations of Letters Found in Effects of Caruso," Oct. 8, 1920.

31. Flynn, "Memorandum for the Attorney General," Oct. 29, 1920, BI FOIA 61-5 211205-175 1/2.

32. The Sacco-Vanzetti case is the subject of dozens of books, articles, films, and inquiries. Paul Avrich's *Sacco and Vanzetti* stands out as the most valuable source on the suspects' anarchist backgrounds. Other useful secondary accounts include Michael M. Topp, *The Sacco and Vanzetti Case: A Brief History with Documents* (New York: Bedford/St. Martin's, 2005); Bruce Watson, *Sacco and Vanzetti: The Men, the Murders, and the Judgment of Mankind* (New York: Viking, 2007); *Sacco-Vanzetti: Developments and Reconsiderations—1979* (Boston: Boston Public Library, 1982); Francis Russell, *Tragedy in Dedham: The Story of the Sacco-Vanzetti Case* (New York: McGraw-Hill, 1971); Russell, *Sacco and Vanzetti: The Case Resolved* (New York: Harper and Row, 1986); William Young and David E. Kaiser, *Postmortem: New Evidence in the Case of Sacco and Vanzetti* (Amherst: University of Massachusetts Press, 1985); Louis Joughin and Edmund M. Morgan, *The Legacy of Sacco and Vanzetti* (Chicago: Quadrangle Books, 1964); Lisa McGirr, "The Passion of Sacco and Vanzetti: A Global History," *Journal of American History* 93, 4 (2007): 1085–1115; Moshik Temkin, *The Sacco-Vanzetti Affair: America on Trial* (New Haven, CT: Yale University Press, 2009). For quotes, see Eugene Lyons, *Assignment in Utopia* (New York: Harcourt, Brace, 1932), 32; Watson, *Sacco and Vanzetti*, 56; Avrich, *Sacco and Vanzetti*, 45, 160. For their possible role in the June 2 plot, see esp. Avrich, *Sacco and Vanzetti*, 158–62; Watson, *Sacco and Vanzetti*, 15–17.

33. Hill, "Ferdinando Sacco: Dedham Jail, Dedham, Mass:—Alleged Murderer; Highway Robbery and Anarchistic Activities," Oct. 13, 1920, BI 360257; John Hanrahan to Lamb, Sep. 20, 1920, BI FOIA 61-5-344.

34. William J. West to Hoover, Aug. 15, 1927, BI 61–126; John A. Dowd to Hoover, Jul. 17, 1926, BI 61-126-706.

35. Flynn, "My Ten Biggest Man Hunts," *BH*, Mar. 5, 1922.

36. Avrich, *Sacco and Vanzetti*, 178–80.

37. For samples of undercover investigative work, see esp. BI 194561 and BI 384519. For examples of their activities in Caruso's circle, see esp. P137, "In re: Caruso, Bomb Outrages, June 2d, 1919," Sep. 22, 1920, BI 384519; P137, "In re Italian Anarchists. (Caruso)," Sep. 24, 1920, BI 384519; N122, "In re: Italian Anarchists (Caruso)," Sep. 25, 1920, BI 384519. N122 also spent time watching Carlo Tresca. See N122, "In re: Italian Anarchists. (Caruso)," BI 384519.

38. For quotes, see Dowd to Hoover, Jul. 8, 1926, BI 61-126-700; West to Hoover, Aug. 15, 1927, BI 61-126; "Memoranda re: Sacco-Vanzetti Matter," Mar. 10, 1951, BI 61-126-847. For background on Carbone, also see Dowd to Hoover, Jul. 17, 1926, BI 61-126-706; Russell, *Tragedy in Dedham*, 122;

Young and Kaiser, *Postmortem*, 128. The 1951 Bureau memorandum notes Carbone's first name as Domenico. Russell identifies Carbone as "Antony" rather than Domenico. Correspondence from Sacco and Vanzetti's lawyer, Fred Moore, refers to Dominick Carbonari. See Hanrahan to Lamb, Jan. 14, 1921, BI 202600-418; Fred Moore to Carlo Tresca, Mar. 11, 1921, MS 2030, 4A, AFSV. The Bureau also discussed planting an informant named John Ruzzamenti near Vanzetti's cell, but the effort was never completed. See Russell, *Tragedy in Dedham*, 121–22; Watson, *Sacco and Vanzetti*, 94.

39. West, "Bomb Explosion, Wall Street, New York City, Sept. 16, 1920 (Anarchist Activities)," Nov. 11, 1920, BI FOIA 61-5 211205-240.

40. Watson, *Sacco and Vanzetti*, 64–65, 85–88.

41. "MEMO. to Chief Flynn," Mar. 8, 1920, BI FOIA 61-5; Davis, "In re: Bomb Explosions of June 2nd: Felicani (or Feliciani)," Mar. 12, 1920, BI 383537; Davis, "Bomb Outrages of June 2, 1919," Mar. 26, 1920, BI 383537.

42. Stone, "Special Report," Oct. 2, 1920, BI FOIA 61-5-8-21. The Bureau briefly believed that it had tied Felicani to the Wall Street bomb when a Boston-area salesman recalled selling a set of rubber type to a man fitting Felicani's description. Agents arranged for the man to view Felicani, but he failed to link Felicani with the American Anarchist Fighters flyer. Hill, "Bomb Explosion of Sept. 16, 1920: J. P. Morgan and Co., Wall St., N.Y.C., Possible Anarchistic Activities," Oct. 15, 1920, BI FOIA 61-5-217; Hanrahan to Flynn, Oct. 16, 1920, BI FOIA 61-5-207; Hanrahan to Flynn, Oct. 22, 1920, BI FOIA 61-5-174; Hill, "Bomb Explosion, J. P. Morgan and Co., Wall St., N.Y.C. September 16th, 1920. (Anarchistic Activities) Rubber Stamp Used in Anarchist Circular," Oct. 23, 1920, BI FOIA 61-5 211205-144.

43. Dante DiLillo, "Bomb Explosion, Wall Street, New York City. September 16, 1921 [*sic*]: Anarchist Activities," Feb. 2, 1921, BI FOIA 61-5 211205 466.

44. DiLillo, "Bomb Explosion, Wall St., N.Y.C., Sept. 16, 1920: Anarchist Activities," Jan. 20, 1921, BI FOIA 61-5 211205-448; DiLillo, "Bomb Explosion, Wall Street, New York City. September 16, 1921: Anarchist Activities," Feb. 2, 1921, BI FOIA 61-5 211205-466.

45. Hill, "Bomb Explosion, Wall St., N.Y.C., Sept. 16th: Anarchist Activities," Dec. 7, 1920, BI FOIA 61-5 211205-345.

46. Flynn, "Memorandum for the Attorney General," Oct. 29, 1920, BI FOIA 61-5 211205-175 1/2; Scully, "Memorandum for Director W. J. Flynn in Re: Wall Street Explosion," Oct. 18, 1920, BI FOIA 61-5-203. File 61-5 contains voluminous information, including dozens of lists, documenting queries into individual stationery stores and stamp companies.

47. "Identify Man Who Drove Horse That Drew Bomb Wagon," *NYW*, Nov. 12, 1920; "Deny Union Men Set Wall St. Bomb," *NYT*, Nov. 12, 1920.

48. William Hurley to Frank Gunther, Oct. 21, 1920, DS U-H File, Classified Records, File 6.

49. American Consul, Turin, to American Embassy, Rome, Feb. 4, 1920, DS U-H- File, Classified Records, File 6; Hurley to Gunther, Oct. 21, 1920, DS U-H File, Classified Records, File 6; Hunt, *Incredible Detective*, 157; "Report of S. J. Clement, Covering Confidential Investigations in Italy for the Period of December 28, 1920, to March 25, 1921," BI 61-1003-6.

50. Hurley to Gunther, telegram, Dec. 22, 1920, DS U-H File, Classified Records, File 6; "Report of S. J. Clement," BI 61-1003-6. For background on Galleani's final years in Italy, see Avrich, *Sacco and Vanzetti*, 208–9. For the shipping of the *Cronaca* printing press, see Young and Kaiser, *Postmortem*, 128.

## CHAPTER 11

1. For quotes, see Murray, *Red Scare*, 261; Freeberg, *Democracy's Prisoner*, 255. On the Harding campaign and the 1920 election, see esp. Francis Russell, *The Shadow of Blooming Grove: Warren G. Harding in His Times* (New York: McGraw-Hill, 1968), 337–47, 395–418; Robert Murray, *The Harding Era* (Minneapolis: University of Minnesota Press, 1969), 43–70; Andrew Sinclair, *The Available Man: The Life Behind the Masks of Warren Gamaliel Harding* (New York: Macmillan, 1965), 101–77; Samuel Hopkins Adams, *Incredible Era: The Life and Times of Warren Gamaliel Harding* (Boston: Houghton Mifflin, 1939), 121–85; John W. Dean, *Warren G. Harding* (New York: Times Books, 2004);

David W. Pietrusza, *1920: The Year of the Six Presidents* (New York: Carroll and Graf, 2007), esp. 311–30, 408–12.

2. Coben, *A. Mitchell Palmer*, 262; "Pinchot Tells Readers Why He Is for Harding," *NYT*, Oct. 4, 1920.

3. Leuchtenberg, *Perils of Prosperity*, 73; Sherman Rogers, "Senator Harding on Labor," *Outlook*, Aug. 18, 1920.

4. Sherman Rogers, "Senator Harding on Labor," *Outlook*, Aug. 18, 1920; "Reds Card Indexed, Palmer Discloses," *NYT*, Dec. 11, 1920; AG 1920, 176; Schmidt, *Red Scare*, 156.

5. For examples of the mood shift thesis, see esp. Murray, *Red Scare*, 239–62; Coben, *A. Mitchell Palmer*, 265–67. For quote, see Rogers, "Senator Harding on Labor," *Outlook*, Aug. 18, 1920.

6. Coben, *A. Mitchell Palmer*, 263; Ackerman, *Young J. Edgar*, 351; "Palmer Plans New 'Red' Hunt," *NYC*, Nov. 29, 1920. Palmer went on to suffer a series of heart attacks beginning in 1922.

7. Ackerman, *Young J. Edgar*, 348–49; NPGL, 5–6, 30–31. For "terrorizing," see "Colyer et al. v. Skeffington, Com'r of Immigration," reprinted in Senate, 59.

8. Rabban, *Free Speech*, 23–76; Falk et al., eds., *Emma Goldman*, 2:20–24, 471–72; *LML*, 346–49.

9. Rabban, *Free Speech*, 315, 83–84. For the activities of civil libertarians during the Red Scare, see esp. W. Anthony Gengarelly, *Distinguished Dissenters and Opposition to the 1919–1920 Red Scare* (Lewiston, ME: Edwin Mellen Press, 1996); Polenberg, *Fighting Faiths*.

10. For Frankfurter, see esp. Liva Baker, *Felix Frankfurter* (New York: Coward-McCann, 1969), 13–100; Melvyn Urofsky, *Felix Frankfurter: Judicial Restraint and Civil Liberties* (Boston: Twayne, 1991); Helen Shirley Thomas, *Felix Frankfurter: Scholar on the Bench* (Baltimore: Johns Hopkins University Press, 1960); Ackerman, *Young J. Edgar*, 135–40, 147–52, 142–49.

11. Zechariah Chafee, *Freedom of Speech* (New York: Harcourt, Brace, 1920), 164. For Chafee, see esp. Rabban, *Free Speech in Its Forgotten Years*, 4–8, 316–35; Leonard Levy, *Legacy of Suppression: Freedom of Speech and Press in Early American History* (Cambridge, MA: Harvard University Press, 1960), 2, 198, 213–14; Donald L. Smith, *Zechariah Chafee, Jr., Defender of Liberty and Law* (Cambridge, MA: Harvard University Press, 1986); Jerold S. Auerbach, "The Patrician as Libertarian: Zechariah Chafee, Jr., and Freedom of Speech," *New England Quarterly* 42 (1969): 511–31. Chafee's book was an expanded version of an article, "Freedom of Speech in War Time," published in the *Harvard Law Review* in 1919.

12. Rabban, *Free Speech*, 315–16; Polenberg, *Fighting Faiths*, 272–84; Senate, 199.

13. There is no full-length biography of Nelles. One valuable source on Nelles is his biography of his friend and colleague Albert DeSilver, a founder of the ACLU, especially the introduction by Roger Baldwin. Walter Nelles, *A Liberal in Wartime: The Education of Albert DeSilver* (New York: Norton, 1940). For further background, see Avrich, *Sacco and Vanzetti*, 190; Robert C. Cottrell, *Roger Nash Baldwin and the American Civil Liberties Union* (New York: Columbia University Press, 2000), 57, 123. For the early years of the ACLU, see Cottrell, *Roger Nash Baldwin*, 121–50; Rabban, *Free Speech*, 304–15; Murphy, *World War I*, 133–78; Samuel Walker, *In Defense of American Liberties: A History of the ACLU* (Carbondale: Southern Illinois University Press, 1999), 11–50; Peggy Lamson, *Roger Baldwin: Founder of the American Civil Liberties Union* (Boston: Houghton Mifflin, 1976); Johnson, *Challenge to American Freedoms*. The clipping file, titled "Wall Street Bomb Explosion," can be found in the New York case section on reel 22, ACLU.

14. Walter Nelles, *Seeing Red: Civil Liberty and Law in the Period Following the War* (New York: ACLU, 1920), 3.

15. "Law and Freedom Bulletin," ed. Walter Nelles, Apr. 11, 1921, reel 22, ACLU; "Law and Freedom Bulletins," Jun. 24, 1921, reel 22, ACLU; Baldwin, "Introduction," in Nelles, *A Liberal in Wartime*, 14; Jaffe, *Crusade Against Radicalism*, 170; Cottrell, *Roger Nash Baldwin*, 57; "Brutality Charged to Palmer Agents," *NYT*, Feb. 26, 1921.

16. Senate, 134–35; NPGL, 31, 3–8. For a rundown of the various lawyers who participated in the crafting and signing of the report, see Gengarelly, *Distinguished Dissenters*, 328.

17. AG 1920, 173; Senate, 19–20. Hoover briefly addressed the senators directly at the end of February. Senate, 649.

18. Ackerman, *Young J. Edgar*, 349; Senate, 582.

19. Senate, 134–55; NPGL, 31. For quotes, see Senate, 136–39.

20. Senate, 634–35; Powers, *Secrecy and Power*, 112.

21. Avrich, *Sacco and Vanzetti*, 177.

22. Senate, 580, 573.
23. Senate, 755–88; 165–207; 247–94; 207–24; 294–350; 651–80; 725–43. Palmer delivered his testimony in several stages, resuming the stand in person in mid-February.
24. Cottrell, *Roger Nash Baldwin*, 58.
25. NPGL, 8.
26. House, 16; Senate, 573.
27. Senate, 384.
28. House, 7.
29. "Wilson's Exit Is Tragic," *NYT*, Mar. 5, 1921; "New Department Heads Take Reins," *WP*, Mar. 6, 1921.

## CHAPTER 12

1. "Flynn to Keep His Post," *NYT*, Mar. 2, 1921; "Burns Talked of to Succeed Flynn," *NYT*, Apr. 1, 1921.
2. Flynn to Harry Daugherty, Apr. 4, 1921, BI FOIA 61-5 211205-512. Flynn's letter to Daugherty complains that a correspondent leaked news of the composite photograph to the press.
3. Flynn to W. H. Newman, Jan. 31, 1921, BI FOIA 61-5; Flynn to Postmaster, Feb. 25, 1921, BI FOIA 61-5; Flynn to Daugherty, Apr. 4, 1921, BI FOIA 61-5 211205-512; Barbera, "In re: Vincenzo Liggio—Italian Anarchist. Wall Street Explosion," Apr. 6, 1921, BI FOIA 61-5-15-28.
4. Flynn to Daugherty, Apr. 4, 1921, BI FOIA 61-5 211205-512.
5. Barbera, "In re: Vincenzo Liggio," Apr. 6, 1921, BI FOIA 61-5-15-28.
6. Avrich, *Sacco and Vanzetti*, 135; Barbera, "In re: Vincenzo Liggio," Apr. 6, 1921, BI FOIA 61-5-15-28; Flynn to Postmaster, Feb. 25, 1921, BI FOIA 61-5; T. M. Reddy to M. F. Blackmon, Feb. 10, 1921, BI FOIA 61-5-14-23; Reddy to Hanrahan, Feb. 10, 1921, BI FOIA 61-5-14-1; DiLillo, "Bomb Explosion, Wall St., New York City: (Anarchist Activities) September 16, 1920," Feb. 28, 1921, BI FOIA 61-5 211205-489.
7. "Bomb Suspect Identified as Death Driver," *NYA*, Apr. 21, 1921; Scully, "Memorandum for W. J. Flynn, Director. Re: Wall Street Explosion (Scranton Investigation)," Apr. 22, 1921, BI FOIA 61-5-15-45; DiLillo, "Bomb Explosion, Wall St., New York City, (Anarchist Activities) September 16, 1920," May 5, 1921, BI FOIA 61-5 211205-541. Both the Bureau documents and the press coverage contain multiple variations of Ligi's name, including Ligio, Luigio, and Liggio. For purposes of consistency and brevity, I use Ligi as the preferred option. This was how the suspect signed his own name and it is also how his lawyers referred to him.
8. "Federal Agents Think Wall St. Plot Clears," *NYS*, Apr. 21, 1921.
9. P. J. Ahern, "Wall Street Bomb Explosion," Apr. 25, 1921, BI FOIA 61-5-15-47; "Identify Suspect in Wall St. Bomb Plot," *NYW*, Apr. 21, 1921; "Luigio Linked with Patterson Anarchists," *NYT*, Apr. 22, 1921; "Memorandum from Director W. J. Flynn, by Telephone from New York, N.Y.," Apr. 22, 1921, BI FOIA 61-5.
10. "Discover an Underground Passage Leading to a Subterranean Chamber," *NYS*, Apr. 20, 1921; "Several Identify Luigio, Says Flynn—Officials Here Silent," *NYEP*, Apr. 21, 1921; "Sash Weights Give a Strong Clue to Bomb," *NYS*, Apr. 22, 1921.
11. "3 Identify Picture of Luigio as That of Bomb Wagon Driver," *NYT*, Apr. 22, 1921; Reddy to Ahern, Apr. 20, 1921, BI FOIA 61-5-15-40; Reddy to Ahern, Apr. 20, 1921, BI FOIA 61-5-15-41; "Memorandum from Director W. J. Flynn, by Telephone from New York, N.Y.," Apr. 22, 1921, BI FOIA 61-5; "Makes Face to Face Identification of Explosion Suspect," *NYT*, Apr. 24, 1921. For earlier news coverage of Smith's claims, see "Bomb Plot Suspect Identified," *NYDN*, Sep. 21, 1920.
12. Anderson, "Memorandum. Wall Street Explosion. Mr. Meagher and Mr. Teograph—Witnesses," Apr. 23–25, 1921, BI FOIA 61-5 211205-526x; Ahern, "Wall Street Bomb Explosion," Apr. 25, 1921, BI FOIA 61-5-15-47; "Sash Weight Clew in Bomb Plot," *NYDN*, Apr. 22, 1921; Ahern, "Memorandum for Director Mr. Wm. J. Burns," Mar. 6, 1922, BI FOIA 61-5.
13. "Identify Suspect in Wall St. Bomb Plot," *NYW*, Apr. 21, 1921; Ahern, "Wall Street Bomb Explosion," Apr. 25, 1921, BI FOIA 61-5-15-47; Flynn to Postmaster, Feb. 25, 1921, BI FOIA 61-5.

14. "Memorandum from Director W. J. Flynn, by Telephone from New York, N.Y.," Apr. 22, 1921, BI FOIA 61-5-514.

15. "Hunt Sweetheart of Bomb Suspect," NYT, Apr. 23, 1921; J. T. Flourney, "Re: Tito Ligi, alias Augusto Vitaletti," Mar. 23, 1922, BI 61-1263; P137, "In re: Italian Anarchists," Oct. 5, 1920, BI 194561, BI FOIA 61-5-8-50; "Liggio Committed Under $10,000 Bond," NYW, Apr. 23, 1921.

16. Ahern, "Wall Street Bomb Explosion," Apr. 25, 1921, BI FOIA 61-5-15-47; "Liggio Committed Under $10,000 Bond," NYW, Apr. 23, 1921; "Fail to Recognize Luigio," NYT, Apr. 23, 1921.

17. Pernicone, Carlo Tresca, 100–101; N122, "In re: Italian Anarchists. (Caruso)," BI 384519; "Wall St. Suspect Goldman Disciple," NYW, Apr. 22, 1921.

18. "Tresca Refutes 'Bomb' Canard," NYC, Apr. 23, 1921; "Ligi Story Gives Police New Clews," NYDN, Apr. 25, 1921; "Ligi Absent During Wall St. Blast—Nelles," NYC, Apr. 24, 1921.

19. "Doubt Luigio Is Radical," NYT, Apr. 23, 1921; Arthur Ramsdell, "Re: Wall Street Explosion, at Shickshinny and Mocanaqua, Pa.," date illegible, BI FOIA 61-5-16-6; Ramsdell, "In re: Wall Street Bomb Explosion," Apr. 27, 1921, BI FOIA 61-5-211205-533; "Informer Is Killed for Blackhand Raid," NYT, May 4, 1921.

20. Barbera, "Memorandum—Wall Street Explosion," May 4, 1921, BI FOIA 61-5-16-55; Ahern, "Memorandum for Director W. J. Flynn," Jun. 15, 1921, BI FOIA 61-5-17-6.

21. "Ligi Charge False, Lawyer Asserts," NYEP, Apr. 25, 1921; Nelles, "The Lynching Press," AR, May 28, 1921.

22. "Ligi Absent During Wall St. Blast—Nelles," NYC, Apr. 24, 1921; "Hunt Sweetheart of Bomb Suspect," NYT, Apr. 23, 1921; "Lawyer Says Ligi Can Prove Alibi," NYW, Apr. 25, 1921; "Lackawanna Valley Searched for Clue in Bomb Explosion," NYT, Apr. 25, 1921. In Bureau interviews, Ligi said he had been working in mid-September as a laborer helping to build a country road but that a strike had disrupted the work. He also said that during his time in the United States he had rarely left the Pennsylvania anthracite region. See BI FOIA 61-5-15-47; BI FOIA 61-5-15-51.

23. Among the other witnesses sent to Scranton to see Ligi were James Nally; Ray Clark, a construction foreman at the stock exchange annex who said he had spoken with a man looking for his horse soon after the explosion; and the blacksmith DeGrazio. For more information about these witnesses, see news coverage in the New York Times and World, Apr. 23–24, 1921. Tito Ligi to Tresca (trans. by unnamed Bureau agent and Joseph Barbera), Jun. 23, 1921, BI FOIA 61-5; "Makes Face to Face Identification of Explosion Suspect," NYT, Apr. 24, 1921.

24. "Ligi Absent During Wall St. Blast—Nelles," NYC, Apr. 24, 1921; "Ligi Denies He Had Hand in Explosion," NYW, Apr. 26, 1921.

25. Ligi, "Statement Taken by John Memolo," Apr. 25, 1921, BI FOIA 61-5-15-51; Ligi to Tresca, Jun. 23, 1921, BI FOIA 61-5.

26. "Flynn's Bubble Bursts in Wall St. 'Bomb' Episode," NYC, Apr. 27, 1921; Ahern, "Memorandum for Director Mr. Wm. J. Burns," Mar. 6, 1922, BI FOIA 61-5; "Wall Street Bomb Suspect Gets Year as Draft Dodger," NYW, May 7, 1921.

27. Avrich, Sacco and Vanzetti, 66; "De Filipis First Man Accused of Wall St. Bomb," NYW, May 20, 1921; "Bayonne Man Held as Driver of Bomb Wagon to Wall St.," NYH, May 20, 1921; "Bayonne Prisoner Identified by 5 as Bomb Wagondriver," NYT, May 20, 1921. Newspapers also identify De Filippis as Giuseppi De Fillipos ("New Wall Street Suspect Held," NYT, May 19, 1921), Giuseppe De Filippo ("3 Identify Suspect as Wall-St Bomber," MJ, May 19, 1921), Giuseppe de Filips ("Prisoner Accused of Wall St. Bomb Plot," NYS, May 19, 1921), etc. Bureau documents contain similar variation. For purposes of consistency, I use the spelling De Filippis.

28. "New Wall Street Suspect Held," NYT, May 19, 1921.

29. Scully, "In re: Giusepi de Fillipis," May 21, 1921, BI FOIA 61-5 211205-55 (date partly illegible); "De Filipis First Man Accused of Wall St. Bomb," NYW, May 20, 1921; "In re: Wall Street Bomb Explosion (Di Filippo)," Apr. 25, 1921, BI FOIA 61-5 211205-528; "In re: Wall Street Bomb Explosion (Di Filippo)," May 2, 1921, BI FOIA 61-5 211205-536; "In re: Wall Street Explosion (De Filippo)," May 3, 1921, BI FOIA 61-5 211205-538; Scully, "Memorandum for Mr. Flynn," May 9, 1921, BI FOIA 61-5-16-60; "In re: Wall Street Explosion (De Filippo)," May 17, 1921, BI FOIA 61-5 211205-549; "In re: Wall Street Explosion (De Filippo)," May 23, 1921, BI FOIA 61-5 211205-555.

30. "Bayonne Man Held as Driver of Bomb Wagon to Wall St.," *NYH*, May 20, 1921; "Bayonne Prisoner Identified by 5 as Bomb Wagondriver," *NYT*, May 20, 1921; "Saw De Filippo at Blast Scene," *NYA*, May 21, 1921. A convicted murderer named Archie Patterson attempted to implicate De Filippis as well, apparently in an effort to secure a Bureau interview in New York and escape from jail. See BI 61-1300.

31. "Bayonne Man Held as Driver of Bomb Wagon to Wall St.," *NYH*, May 20, 1921.

32. "De Filipis in Court as Driver of Wall Street Bomb Wagon," *NYS*, May 20, 1921; "Police Fail in Indicting of Bomb Suspect," *NYC*, May 21, 1921; "Held Without Bail," *NYEP*, May 20, 1921; "Bomb Suspect Is Held Though Only One Identifies Him," *NYW*, May 21, 1921; "Delay Examination of Bomb Witness," *NYT*, May 22, 1921.

33. "Bomb Suspect Sees Wall Street," *NYEP*, May 28, 1921.

34. Scully, "In re: Giuseppe De Fillipis, Suspect—Wall Street Explosion," Jun. 1, 1921, BI FOIA 61-5 211205-570; "Bomb Suspect's Hearing Adjourned for Week," *NYEP*, May 31, 1921; "Filipis Freed on Bail in Wall St. Bomb Case," *NYS*, May 31, 1921.

35. Bartolomeo Vanzetti, "William J. Flynn..." (rest of title illegible), MS 2030, 1B, AFSV. The quoted passages are from an original translation by Benjamin Martin.

36. Avrich, *Sacco and Vanzetti*, 15; *The Sacco-Vanzetti Case: Transcript of the Record of the Trial of Nicola Sacco and Bartolomeo Vanzetti in the Courts of Massachusetts and Subsequent Proceedings, 1920–7* (New York: 1928–29), 5:5266.

37. Watson, *Sacco and Vanzetti*, 102–3; D'Atillio, "La Salute è in Voi," 87; Russell, *Tragedy in Dedham*, 138–39.

38. DiLillo, "Bomb Explosion, Wall Street, New York City: September 16, 1920," BI FOIA 61–5 211205-589; Gurley Flynn, *Rebel Girl*, 309; Art Shields, *Are They Doomed?* (New York, 1921), 10.

39. "Summary of Files of Bureau of Investigation, United States Department of Justice, Relating to Nicola Ferdinando Sacco and Bartolomeo Vanzetti," Aug. 8, 1927, BI 61-126-789. Other Bureau agents occasionally joined Barbera, as did two members of the New York bomb squad. See Barbera, "In re: Sacco and Vanzetti—Italian Anarchists," Jun. 6, 1921, BI 202600-418-38 and Dowd to Hoover, Jul. 8, 1926, BI 61-126-700, among other files. For a summary of the Bureau's role at the trial, see Kaiser and Young, *Postmortem*, 128–30.

40. "Summary of Files of Bureau of Investigation, United States Department of Justice, Relating to Nicola Ferdinando Sacco and Bartolomeo Vanzetti," Aug. 8, 1927, BI 61-126-789; Barbera, "In re: Sacco and Vanzetti," Jun. 3, 1921, BI 202600-418-36; Barbera, "In re: Sacco and Vanzetti," Jun. 10, 1921, BI 202600-418; Barbera, "In re: Sacco and Vanzetti," Jun. 11, 1921, BI 202600-418.

41. Barbera, "In re: Sacco and Vanzetti," Jun. 13, 1921, BI 20-2600-418; Barbera, "In re: Sacco and Vanzetti," Jun. 10, 1921, BI 202600-418; Barbera, "In re: Sacco and Vanzetti—Italian Anarchists," Jun. 6, 1921, BI 202600-418-38; "Summary of Files of Bureau of Investigation," Aug. 8, 1927, BI 61-126-789; Barbera, "In re: Sacco and Vanzetti," Jun. 6, 1921, BI 202600-418-39.

42. "Summary of Files of Bureau of Investigation," Aug. 8, 1927, BI 61-126-789; Barbera, "In re: Sacco and Vanzetti," Jun. 11, 1921, BI 202600-418; Barbera, "In re: Sacco and Vanzetti," Jun. 10, 1921, BI 202600-418.

43. "Summary of Files of Bureau of Investigation," Aug. 8, 1927, BI 61-126-789; Reddy to Flynn, Jun. 15, 1921, BI 202600-418-50. According to Kaiser and Young, the New York police also sent a member of the bomb squad, though no Bureau records detail his surveillance. Kaiser and Young, *Postmortem*, 127.

44. Felix Frankfurter, *The Case of Sacco and Vanzetti: A Critical Analysis for Lawyers and Laymen* (New York: Grosset and Dunlap, 1961), 40. The Bureau's surveillance of Ligi lasted sporadically into 1922. For these later developments, see esp. BI 61-1263. The Bureau took a statement from De Filippis on Jul. 18, 1921; after that, the investigation seems to have trailed off before De Filippis was officially cleared of charges in early August. See "Statement of Giuseppe de Filipos," Jul. 18, 1921, BI FOIA 61-5; "Bomb Suspect Freed After Three Months," *NYT*, Aug. 6, 1921.

45. Ahern, "Memorandum for Director W. J. Flynn," Jun. 15, 1921, BI FOIA 61-5-17-6; Ramsdell to Burns, "Attention of Mr. Hoover; Re: Wall Street Explosion," Sep. 11, 1921, BI FOIA 61-5-18-19.

46. "Seeks Sweetheart of Bomb Suspect," *NYW*, Apr. 25, 1921; Barbera, "Wall Street Explosion: Memorandum for N.Y. Office. (Tito Ligi)," Apr. 28, 1921, BI FOIA 61-5-16-17.

47. Ligi to Tresca, Jun. 23, 1921, BI FOIA 61–5; AG 1921, 130.
48. "Wall Street Bomb Outrage Work of Boston Anarchists," *NYDN*, Aug. 25, 1921. A nearly identical article appeared the next day in the *Boston Advertiser*. Follow-up articles appeared in both papers—and presumably in others—in subsequent days.
49. "Wall Street Bomb Outrage Work of Boston Anarchists," *NYDN*, Aug. 25, 1921; Flynn, "My Ten Biggest Manhunts," *BH*, Mar. 5, 1922. The *New York Herald*, and perhaps several other papers, also printed the article.
50. "'Unseen Hand' Attacks Sacco, Says Counsel," *BA*, Aug. 27, 1921; Vanzetti, "William J. Flynn...," MS 2030, 18, AFSV.
51. Vanzetti, "William J. Flynn...," MS 2030, 18, AFSV. The Sacco-Vanzetti trial was followed in 1921 by a wave of minor bombings and growing protests throughout the United States and Europe. See Temkin, *Sacco-Vanzetti Affair*, ch. 1; McGirr, "Passion of Sacco and Vanzetti," pars. 17–21; Russell, *Tragedy in Dedham*, 218–19; Watson, *Sacco and Vanzetti*, 178–89.

# CHAPTER 13

1. Don Whitehead, *The FBI Story: A Report to the People* (New York, 1956), 55–56; "Flynn to Keep His Post," *NYT*, Mar. 2, 1921; "William J. Burns Will Head Bureau of Investigation," *NYW*, Aug. 19, 1921; "W. J. Burns to Head Secret Service," *NYT*, Aug. 19, 1921; "Burns Succeeds Flynn as Chief of Investigation," *NYH*, Aug. 19, 1921.
2. "W. J. Burns Convinced Crime Will Be Fastened on Band of Reds," *SNYH*, Sep. 28, 1920; "Burns Blames 'Reds' for Bomb in Wall St.," *NYG*, Sep. 27, 1920; "Moscow Reds Blamed for Bomb Explosion," *LAT*, Sep. 28, 1920; "$50,000 Reward Offered in Wall Street Explosion," *NYTR*, Nov. 23, 1920; "Burns Adds $50,000 to Bomb Rewards," *NYT*, Nov. 23, 1920; "$50,000 for Bomb Evidence," *WP*, Nov. 23, 1920.
3. "W. J. Burns to Head Secret Service," *NYT*, Aug. 19, 1921; "Burns Succeeds Flynn as Bureau Chief," *NYEP*, Aug. 18, 1921.
4. "Burns Aims to Prevent Crime," *NYS*, Aug. 22, 1921.
5. Leon Trotsky, *Marxism and Terrorism* (New York: Pathfinder, 1995), 10. For Lenin's views on terrorism, see esp. Roland Gaucher, *The Terrorists: From Tsarist Russia to the O.A.S.* (London: Secker and Warburg, 1968), 71–100. Anna Geifman points out that this denunciation of terrorism was often more rhetorical than real. Russian revolutionaries of many stripes continued to employ terrorist tactics well into 1917. Geifman, *Thou Shalt Kill*, esp. 223–56.
6. Leon Trotsky, *Terrorism and Communism: A Reply to Karl Kautsky* (London: New Park Publications, 1975), 78–79.
7. Draper, *Roots*, 213–15. For discussions of the origins of "mass action," also see Draper, 89–90.
8. United Communist Party, "Dynamite and Bombs," reprinted in *General Intelligence Bulletin* 34 (Oct. 23, 1920), in MIR.
9. "U.S. Agents Work with Police," *NYJ*, Dec. 19, 1921; "Explosive Stores All Accounted For," *NYT*, Sep. 17, 1920. Burns offered several variations on the timing and exact outlines of his initial encounter with Linde. See esp. "Explanation of Explosion Due Soon, U.S. Chief Says," *NYC*, Dec. 18, 1921; "Detectives Guard Wall St. Against New Bomb Outrage," *NYT*, Dec. 19, 1921.
10. Executive Committee, Communist Party of America, "Rules for Underground Party Work," reel 2, delo 34, CPUSA. For more on the early underground period, see esp. Draper, *Roots*, 197–209; Bryan D. Palmer, *James P. Cannon and the Origins of the American Revolutionary Left, 1890–1928* (Urbana: University of Illinois Press, 2007), 113–34; Irving Howe and Lewis Coser, *The American Communist Party: A Critical History (1919–1957)* (Boston: Beacon Press, 1957), 41–96. For personal recollections of the period, see esp. James P. Cannon, *The First Ten Years of American Communism: Report of a Participant* (New York: Lyle Stuart, 1962); William Z. Foster, *History of the Communist Party of the United States* (New York: International Publishers, 1952); Benjamin Gitlow, *Whole of Their Lives; Gitlow, I Confess: The Truth About American Communism* (New York: Dutton, 1940).
11. The details of Linde's background are not entirely consistent in news reports or Bureau documents. For cited details, see "Wall Street Bomber Nabbed," *SFC*, Dec. 17, 1921; "Wall Street Bomb Suspect,

Caught in Poland, Confesses," *NYT*, Dec. 17, 1921; "Arrest in Warsaw Gives Sure Key to Bomb in Wall St., Burns Declares," *NYW*, Dec. 18, 1921; "Wall Street Bomb Mystery Solved by Arrest, Says Burns," *NYT*, Dec. 18, 1921; "Detectives Guard Wall St. Against New Bomb Outrage," *NYT*, Dec. 19, 1921. For Haywood quote, see Haywood, "A Detective," *ISR*, Dec. 1911.

12. "Detectives Guard Wall St. Against New Bomb Outrage," *NYT*, Dec. 19, 1921.

13. Unfortunately most of Linde's reports for the Burns agency are missing from the Bureau file. The remaining documents are heavily redacted, unlabeled, inconsistent, and difficult to decipher, making details a matter of educated guesswork. For the best outline of Linde's theory before Burns' arrival as Bureau chief, see "New York Investigator [illegible]," Jan. 14, 1921, BI FOIA 61-5-14-7 (this appears to be one of Linde's reports to the Burns agency); "Re Informants Reported by Investigator [redacted]," Aug. 2, 1921, BI FOIA 61-5-18-10. These reports do not cite Steve Barber directly as the "Barber" from Trenton, New Jersey, supposedly involved in the bomb plot, but a memorandum signed by Hoover in July 1921 identifies him more forthrightly. See Hoover, "Memorandum," Jul. 19, 1921, BI FOIA 61-5-17-25. Other names mentioned as possible conspirators and "technical committee" members include John Gallegan, T. M. Malloniu, D. D. Goody, Leo Spivac, J. Huton, Seddler, Garbaldo, Weintraub, Visinoff, Rose Smuk, and Marian Heyman. Shetnuitius allegedly operated under the party name of Reuben Kopsky.

14. Background on Martens is drawn from Pfannestiel, *Rethinking the Red Scare*, 37–74; Draper, *Roots*, 161–63. For quotes, see Pfannestiel, 67. For the Martens raid, see Jaffe, *Crusade Against Radicalism*, 123–24. Details of the courier system can be found in John Earl Haynes and Harvey Klehr, *The Secret World of American Communism* (New Haven: Yale University Press, 1999), 21–22.

15. Assistant Chief of Staff to Director, Jan. 15, 1921, MID 10110-2065-22.

16. "Card Used by William Linde—Original," DS 811.108 L641, Decimal File; Bannerman to Sharp, Jun. 30, 1921, DS 860c.72, U-H File.

17. Tucker, "In re: Wall Street Explosion," Apr. 4, 1921, BI FOIA 61-5-x20. The *Call* later suggested that Linde had himself traveled aboard the "second Soviet Ark" with Martens, but this seems unlikely. "Linde Well Known as Arch Swindler," *NYC*, Dec. 18, 1921.

18. Both Goldman and Berkman published extensive accounts of their time in Russia. See Berkman, *The Bolshevik Myth: (Diary 1910–1922) Including "The Anti-Climax"* (London: Pluto, 1989 [orig. pub. 1925]); *LML*, 718–927; Goldman, *The Crushing of the Russian Revolution* (London: Freedom Press, 1922); Goldman, *My Disillusionment in Russia* (Garden City, NY: Doubleday, Page, 1923); Goldman, *My Further Disillusionment in Russia* (Garden City, NY: Doubleday, Page, 1924). For a secondary summary of these years, see esp. Wexler, *Emma Goldman in Exile* (Boston: Beacon Press, 1989), 9–113.

19. Haywood's account of his time in Russia is heavily truncated in his memoir, either due to illness (as the text suggests) or to official censorship (as historians have speculated). Haywood, *Autobiography*, 344–45, 359–65. Also see Carlson, *Roughneck*, 313–18; Dubofsky, *Big Bill*, 132–36.

20. For quote, see *LML*, 765. For background, see esp. Wexler, *Emma Goldman in Exile*, 21–56. For Kronstadt, see Paul Avrich, *Kronstadt 1921* (Princeton, NJ: Princeton University Press, 1970), 211. According to Avrich, Kronstadt casualties on the government side numbered as high as ten thousand. Several hundred of the rebel prisoners were shot in retaliation for the rebellion.

21. For Kuzbas, see J. P. Morray, *Project Kuzbas: American Workers in Siberia, 1921–1926* (New York: International Publishers, 1983). For Haywood's view, see *ABH*, 362–65.

22. "Twenty Second for Hurley for Justice," Nov. 23, 1921, BI FOIA 61-5; document beginning "I arrived in Paris on May 7, 1921," undated, BI FOIA 61-5; "Lindenfeld Names Wall St. Bomb Maker," *NYT*, Dec. 19, 1921; "New Statements Made by Linde," *NYW*, Dec. 20, 1921.

23. The papers were seized from Edward Lindgren, along with Israel Amter and Abram Jakira, members of the Communist Party's executive committee. For a summary, see AG 1921, 246. Jakira later petitioned the federal authorities, apparently unsuccessfully, for the return of the documents. For details of the Lindgren seizure, see BI 202600-1775. For claims that Linde's name was in the Lindgren papers, see "Linde's Famous Bombing Story Fails to Arrive," *NYC*, Dec. 20, 1921; "Insists Lindenfeld was Trotzky Agent," *NYT*, Dec. 21, 1921; "Burns Here, Silent on Lindenfeld Case," *NYT*, Dec. 24, 1921.

24. "W. J. Burns to Head Secret Service," *NYT*, Aug. 19, 1921; "Burns to Specialize in Crime Prevention," *NYS*, Aug. 19, 1921. Regin Schmidt makes a similar point about Burns' significance. "This federalization," he writes, "was personified by William J. Burns, the head of the Burns Detective Agency,

famous for his sensational crime cases and notorious for his aggressive anti-union tactics." Schmidt, *Red Scare*, 54.

25. Whitehead, *FBI Story*, 55–56.
26. Ibid.
27. "Burns Succeeds Flynn as Bureau Chief," *NYEP*, Aug. 18, 1921; "William J. Burns Will Head Bureau of Investigation," *NYW*, Aug. 19, 1921; "W. J. Burns Succeeds Flynn as Secret Service Chief," *NYS*, Aug. 18, 1921.
28. "Burns Aims to Prevent Crime," *NYS*, Aug. 22, 1921; "William J. Burns Will Head Bureau of Investigation," *NYW*, Aug. 19, 1921.
29. "Daugherty Sees Turn to Normal Conditions," *NYT*, May 3, 1921.
30. Gentry, *J. Edgar Hoover*, 104; AG 1921, 129–31.
31. Hoover, "Memorandum for Mr. Grimes," Aug. 4, 1921, DJ 202600-2262.
32. "Gold Shipment from Russia to America Puzzles," *CT*, Oct. 5, 1920; "Ellis Islanders Discover Alien Is Human Being," *CT*, Oct. 7, 1920; "Offered Job as Head of Commission," *HC*, Nov. 2, 1920; "Independents Want Woods Next Mayor," *NYT*, Dec. 26, 1920.
33. "Spy Learns Capitalist Plans While Guest in Castle," *BA*, Nov. 1, 1925.
34. "Scotland House" report, Feb. 14, 1920, BI 349701. The name Settlin appears repeatedly in Hoover's "Official and Confidential" file. See, for instance, Settlin to Hoover, Dec. 15, 1920, HOC; Hoover to Settlin, Dec. 16, 1920. Nosovitsky used the name Joseph Anderson to cross the border at Mexico. "Declaration of Alien About to Depart for the United States," American Consul, Nuevo Laredo, Mexico, Mar. 26, 1921, HOC 120. A mention of his adoption of "James," "Fox," and "the doctor" can be found in unsigned to Lanier Winslow, Oct. 29, 1920, DS Classified Records, U-2 File, 195. For background on Nosovitsky, see Draper, *Roots*, 227–36; McCormick, *Hopeless Cases*, 117–24. McCormick first identified and dissected Hoover's "Official and Confidential" file on the Wall Street case.
35. Nosovitsky to Woods, Oct. 31, 1921, HOC 120.
36. "International Spy, Hired by Capitalists, Probes Wall St. Explosion," *BA*, Dec. 13, 1925.
37. Nosovitsky to Woods, Jan. [date illegible], 1921, HOC 120; "Mexico To-day," unsigned report, HOC 120. In a series of articles in 1925, Nosovitsky confessed that he had fabricated most of the reports in Mexico. "Super Spy Tells 'How I Faked the Constitution of the Red Army in Mexico to Scare the U.S.,'" BA, Sep. 27, 1925. For evidence of Hoover's involvement in the Mexico venture, see Anderson to Hoover, Mar. 28, 1921; Jack to Hoover, Mar. 27, 1921; Breniman to Baley, Mar. 29, 1921; Baley to Breniman, Mar. 29, 1921; Anderson to Hoover, Mar. 31, 1921, all HOC 120. An internal Bureau letter after Nosovitsky's reentry confirms that "he was acting for the Bureau in Mexico." E. T. Needham to Breniman, Apr. 2, 1921, HOC 120. Hoover's last intervention for Nosovitsky in the border crossing was the retrieval of Nosovitsky's Colt pistol. Breniman to Hoover, Apr. 4, 1921, HOC 120.
38. [Name illegible], Office of the Under Secretary, Department of State to Mr. Stewart, Apr. 7, 1921, DS 123W854, Decimal File; Winslow to Hurley, Apr. 12, 1921, DS 000–1690, U-H File.
39. Gunther to Hurley (with attachments), Jun. 18, 1921, DS 000-1774, U-H File; Nosovitsky to Woods, Oct. 31, 1921, HOC 120. According to Nosovitsky's letter, he left for Europe on Sep. 3, 1921.

## CHAPTER 14

1. For descriptions of police activity, see "800 Police Guard Wall Street District," *JCCB*, Sep. 17, 1921. For reports of market activity, see "The Stock Market," *WSJ*, Sep. 17, 1921.
2. Minutes of the New York Stock Exchange Construction Committee, Sep. 20, 1920–Mar. 28, 1921, NYSE; Minutes of the New York Stock Exchange Arrangements Committee, Sep. 17, Sep. 21, Oct. 26, 1920, NYSE; Minutes of the New York Stock Exchange Governing Committee, Feb. 23, 1921, NYSE; "800 Police Guard Wall Street District," *JCCB*, Sep. 17, 1921; "199 Families Affected by Wall St. Explosion," *NYW*, Jan. 2, 1921. For more details on Red Cross activities, see *The Newsletter*, Atlantic Division, American Red Cross, Sep. 27, 1920, and American Red Cross, *First Report of the Disaster Relief Committee for the Metropolitan Area*, New York, Dec. 1920.

3. "Yachts Creep in Under Light Airs," *NYT*, Jul. 5, 1921; "Bankers Aiding Hospital," *NYT*, Jul. 21, 1921; Lamont, *Ambassador*, 168–86. For Lamont's work, see also Chernow, *House of Morgan*, 206–9, 225–43.

4. "A Year Without a Clue," *NYW*, Sep. 16, 1921.

5. Burns to Brennan, Sep. 8, 1921, BI FOIA 61-5 211205-610.

6. Walter O. Lewis to Burns, Oct. 1, 1921, BI FOIA 61-5 211205-643; Blackmon, "Wall Street Explosion," Oct. 3, 1921, BI FOIA 61-5-18-16; Harold L. Scott, "Bomb Explosion Wall Street New York City, September 16, 1920—Anarchist Activities," Oct. 3, 1921, BI FOIA 61-5 211205-657; Claude P. Light, "Wall Street Explosion, Resume of Information," Oct. 1, 1921, BI FOIA 61-5 211205-638; G. O. Holdridge to Burns, "Re—Wall Street Bomb Explosion—Albany Office Operations," Sep. 30, 1921, BI FOIA 61-5 211205-637; Brennan to Burns, "Re: Wall Street Explosion," Oct. 4, 1921, BI FOIA 61-5 211205-653; R. B. Spencer, "Wall Street Explosion—New York City," Oct. 5, 1921, BI FOIA 61-5 211205-662; J. F. McDevitt, "Wall Street Explosion," Oct. 3, 1921, BI FOIA 61-5 211205-651; Stone to Brennan, Sep. 30, 1921, BI FOIA 61-5.

7. Hoover, "Memorandum," Jul. 19, 1921, BI FOIA 61-5-17-25.

8. Ibid.; Loebl, "Wall Street Bomb Explosion, September 16, 1920,—Resume," Oct. 1, 1921, BI FOIA 61-5 211205-644; Holdridge to Burns, "Re—Wall Street Bomb Explosion—Albany Office Operations," Sep. 30, 1921, BI FOIA 61-5 211205-637.

9. Loebl, "Wall Street Bomb Explosion, September 16, 1920,—Resume," Oct. 1, 1921, BI FOIA 61-5 211205-644; F. J. Roderer to Brennan, Oct. 1, 1921, BI FOIA 61-5-18-27; E. W. Byrn, "Wall Street Bomb Plot, New York City," Oct. 5, 1921, BI FOIA 61-5 211205-663; Stone to Brennan, Sep. 30, 1921, BI FOIA 61-5.

10. For Sacco and Vanzetti, see Kaiser and Young, *Postmortem*, 129. For Ligi, see Ramsdell to Burns, Sep. 10, 1921, BI FOIA 61-5-18-17; McDevitt, "Wall Street Explosion," Oct. 3, 1921, BI FOIA 61-5 211205-651; also BI 61-1263, BI 61-115, BI 61–2053. For Leggio (also listed as Liggio), see BI 61-1518; DS 865.0-158, U-H File; DS 865.0-165, U-H File. For Galleani et al., see esp. BI 61-1003; BI 61-260; DS 865.0-141, U-H File; DS 811.108, Decimal File; DS Classified Records, File 6, U-H File. For quote, see Norman Armour to Burns, Nov. 28, 1923, BI FOIA 61-5-493.

11. For background on Altendorf, see DS 812.0-683, U-H File; "Airs German Plot in Latin America," *NYT*, Aug. 24, 1919; "Would Execute Witsche," *NYT*, Dec. 30, 1919; "Burns Silent on Arrest," *NYT*, Dec. 17, 1921; Spence, "K. A. Jahnke," 89–112; "Kurt Jahnke," in Normal Polmar and Thomas B. Allen, eds., *Spy Book: The Encyclopedia of Espionage* (New York: Random House Reference, 2004), 333–34. For Altendorf's solution to the bomb plot, see Hugh Gibson to Hurley, May 13, 1921, DS 812.0-683, U-H File; Gibson to Hurley, May 12, 1921, DS 811.108 AI 72/2, Decimal File. For Altendorf's presence in Europe in August 1921, see Gibson, "Memorandum re Dr. Paul B. Altendorff," Aug. 13, 1921, DS 812.0-683. In addition to Martens, Altendorf had identified the socialist activist Agnes Smedley, who had worked in Martens' office and was heavily involved in the anticolonial movement in India, as one of his bombing suspects. For Altendorf's mention of Smedley, see Benjamin Thaw, "Memorandum," Aug. 31, 1921, DS 812.0-683, U-H File. For background on Smedley, see Janice R. MacKinnon and Stephen R. MacKinnon, *Agnes Smedley: The Life and Times of an American Radical* (Berkeley: University of California Press, 1988).

12. For background on Cosgrove, see "Lindenfeld Names Wall St. Bomb Maker," *NYT*, Dec. 17, 1921. For cable, see Hurley to Burns, Nov. 7, 1921, BI FOIA 61-5-418. For an example of confusion over affiliations, see Hoover to Hurley, Aug. 24, 1921, DS 812.0-683, U-H File.

13. Hoover to Hurley, Aug. 24, 1921, DS 812.0-683, U-H File; Nosovitsky to Woods, Oct. 31, 1921, HOC 120.

14. Nosovitsky to Hoover, Dec. 15, 1921, HOC 120; untitled cable, Secretary of State stamp, Nov. 23, 1921 (received at Dept. of Justice Nov. 30, 1921), BI FOIA 61-5. The cable transcription includes a handwritten note "from the Burns Confidential File."

15. "N.Y. Dynamiter Nabbed Abroad and Confesses," *SFC*, Dec. 17, 1921; "Wall Street Bomb Plot Arrest Solves Mystery, Says Burns," *NYEP*, Dec. 17, 1921; "Wall St. Bomb Arrest 'Right Story,'" *NYG*, Dec. 17, 1921; "Warsaw Police Nab Suspect in Wall Street Blast," *WP*, Dec. 17, 1921; "Wall Street Bomb Suspect Caught in Poland," *NYT*, Dec. 17, 1921.

16. "N.Y. Dynamiter Nabbed Abroad and Confesses," *SFC*, Dec. 17, 1921; "Lindenfeld Known as 'Double-Crosser,'" *NYT*, Dec. 22, 1921.

17. For a typical account of Linde's confession, see "N.Y. Dynamiter Nabbed Abroad and Confesses," *SFC*, Dec. 17, 1921.

18. "Burns, With List, Sets Net for Wall St. Bomb Plotters," *NYH*, Dec. 18, 1921; "Arrest in Warsaw Gives Sure Key to Bomb in Wall St., Burns Declares," *NYW*, Dec. 18, 1921.

19. "Great Mystery Cleared Up in 24 Hours More, Burns Predicts," *NYA*, Dec. 18, 1921.

20. "Wall Street Bomb Mystery Solved by Arrest, Says Burns," *NYT*, Dec. 18, 1921; "Linde Well Known as Arch Swindler," *NYC*, Dec. 18, 1921.

21. "Detectives Guard Wall St. Against New Bomb Outrage," *NYT*, Dec. 19, 1921.

22. "The Wall Street Bomb," *NYG*, Dec. 17, 1921.

23. "Wall Street Bomb Plot Arrest Solves Mystery, Says Burns," *NYEP*, Dec. 17, 1921; "Roundup of Wall St. Bomb Gang Near," *NYS*, Dec. 17, 1921; "Arrest in Warsaw Gives Sure Key to Bomb in Wall St., Burns Declares," *NYW*, Dec. 18, 1921; "Wall Street Bomb Mystery Solved by Arrest, Says Burns," *NYT*, Dec. 18, 1921; "Linde Well Known as Arch Swindler," *NYC*, Dec. 18, 1921; "Wall Street Bomb Yarn Bears Evidence of Fake," *Solidarity*, Dec. 24, 1921.

24. "Arrest in Warsaw Gives Sure Key to Bomb in Wall St., Burns Declares," *NYW*, Dec. 18, 1921; "Linde Well Known as Arch Swindler," *NYC*, Dec. 18, 1921.

25. "The Warsaw Version of the Wall Street Crime," *NYC*, Dec. 18, 1921; "No Soviet Funds Backed Wall St. Outrage—Radek," *NYC*, Dec. 23, 1921. The Communist Party's file on the Wall Street explosion, located in the party records held for decades in the Soviet archives, consisted mainly of verbatim summaries of news reports, interspersed with occasional sardonic commentary about Burns. Untitled, beginning with "New York Times, Sep. 17, 1920," reel 1, delo 18, CPUSA.

26. "Linde Well Known as Arch Swindler," *NYC*, Dec. 18, 1921.

27. Ibid.; "Lindenfeld's Wife Has Had Hard Struggle," *SFC*, Dec. 19, 1921.

28. "Wall Street Bomb Mystery Solved by Arrest, Says Burns," *NYT*, Dec. 18, 1921; "Arrest in Warsaw Gives Sure Key to Bomb in Wall St., Burns Declares," *NYW*, Dec. 18, 1921.

29. "Socialists Wreck Lindenfeld's Tale," *NYW*, Dec. 23, 1921; "Detectives Guard Wall St. Against New Bomb Outrage," *NYT*, Dec. 19, 1921.

30. "Socialists Wreck Lindenfeld's Tale," *NYW*, Dec. 23, 1921.

31. "Small Army to Guard Wall Street," *SFC*, Dec. 19, 1921; Hoover to Hurley, Dec. 17, 1921, DS 860c.72, U-H File.

32. Hoover to Hurley, Dec. 17, 1921, DS 860c.72, U-H File; Burns to Cosgrove, Dec. 22, 1921, BI FOIA 61-5-51x.

33. "'Windy's' Tale Still Myth, But Burns 'Sticks,'" *NYC*, Dec. 21, 1921; "Bombing Wall Street," *WSJ*, Dec. 20, 1921.

34. "Lindenfeld Known as 'Double-Crosser,'" *NYT*, Dec. 22, 1921.

35. "Linde's Famous Bombing Story Fails to Arrive," *NYC*, Dec. 20, 1921; Hoover, "Memorandum for Mr. Burns," Mar. 3, 1922, BI FOIA 61-5-238.

36. "The 'Great Detective,'" *NYC*, Dec. 20, 1921.

37. Thaw to Secretary of State, Dec. 21, 1921, DS 860c.72, U-H File. The Warsaw legation had actually sent the message via naval radio on December 21, though the document indicated that it was not received at the State Department in Washington until December 27.

## CHAPTER 15

1. "Debs Is Released," *NYT*, Dec. 26, 1921; Salvatore, *Eugene V. Debs*, 327–29; Freeberg, *Democracy's Prisoner*, 293–98.

2. "Debs Sees Plot to Involve Radicals," *NYC*, Sep. 25, 1920; Leuchtenburg, *Perils of Prosperity*, 91; "Throngs of 50,000 Welcome Debs Home," *NYT*, Dec. 29, 1921.

3. "Harding Frees Debs and 23 Others Held for War Violations," *NYT*, Dec. 24, 1921.

4. Document beginning "I arrived in Paris Mar. 7, 1921," undated, BI FOIA 61-5. Given the vagaries of the Bureau's filing system, it is unclear whether Cosgrove carried Linde's account to the United States or Linde sent it himself from abroad. Because the document is undated, it is also difficult to pinpoint exactly when it arrived. Both the account itself and Burns' subsequent burst of activity

suggest that the document arrived in early to mid-January. Linde's confession also included several other names, most notably: "Androshine," an American delegate to the Third International; "Aswry," a friend of Androshine's tangentially implicated in planning the explosion; and "Heller," a U.S. lawyer with access to the highest reaches of the Third International. "Androshine" and "Aswry" were presumably George Andreytchine and Charles Ashleigh, former Wobblies who had been convicted with Haywood at the Chicago trial and subsequently fled with him to Russia in the spring of 1921. "Heller" most likely referred to Abram A. Heller, a Russian-born U.S. communist with close ties to Martens' Soviet Bureau. For the location of the Kuzbas office, see Morray, *Project Kuzbas*, 81. For background on Andreytchine and Ashleigh, see *ABH*, 361; George Pirinsky, "Bulgarian Americans," and Joyce L. Kornbluh, "Industrial Workers of the World," in Mari Jo Buhle, Paul Buhle, and Dan Georgakas, eds., *Encyclopedia of the American Left* (New York: Garland, 1990), 114–15, 357; Conlin, *Big Bill Haywood*, 194. For Heller, see David W. McFadden, *Alternative Paths: Soviets and Americans, 1917–1920* (New York: Oxford University Press, 1993), 276–84; Draper, *Roots*, 162; Edward Jay Epstein, *Dossier: The Secret History of Armand Hammer* (New York: Random House, 1996), 40.

5. Kuntz's name first appears in the Wall Street file in early January 1922. Haas, "Re: Wall Street Explosion: [redacted]—Informant," Jan. 5, 1922, BI FOIA 61-5-44. The last document bearing his name appears in mid-May. George Starr, "Re: Henry Kuntz: Wall St., Explosion: (Tracings of Mail)," May 11, 1922, BI FOIA 61-5-386. The documents also refer to five other suspects identified by number rather than name, as #1, #2, etc. It is possible that these figures, not Kuntz himself, were the true targets of the investigation; #3 may have been Carlo Tresca. See Palmera, "In re: #3," Dec. 29, 1922, BI FOIA 61-5-87-993. Earlier Bureau files, classified separately from the Wall Street case, also document surveillance of Kuntz. See esp. BI 61-2272.

6. The names Hammer and "Armond" appear repeatedly in the Kuntz surveillance files. See, for instance, Samuel Gurevich, "Re: #5," BI FOIA 61-5; William E. Dunn, "Re: #5," BI FOIA 61-5-237; Dunn, "Re: #5," BI FOIA 61-5-247. For background on Hammer, see esp. Epstein, *Dossier*, 33–110. Also see Draper, *Roots*, 144–47, 422 n. 43; Pfannestiel, *Rethinking*, 41–44. Morray mentions Armand Hammer's desire to join the Kuzbas effort; *Project Kuzbas*, 65–66. Epstein notes that the Hammers were targets of Bureau surveillance as early as 1919 due to their political activities (49–52). According to John Earl Haynes and Harvey Klehr, documents in the Soviet archives confirm that the Hammers acted as Soviet couriers channeling money into the United States in the mid-1920s. See Haynes and Klehr, *Secret World*, 27. Armand Hammer also composed an autobiography: Armand Hammer with Neil Lyndon, *Hammer* (New York: Putnam, 1987).

7. Cope is one of those mysterious figures who appears to occupy a no-man's-land between his roles as a newspaper publicist specializing in antiradical affairs and as an undercover operative working for both private agencies and government firms. Correspondence with Hoover suggests that Cope played a role in seizing and publicizing correspondence between Emma Goldman and her niece Stella Ballantine. William Cope to Hoover, Jan. 27, 1920, BI 202600-33-28 2/3. Burns clearly had some preexisting relationship with Cope, whether friendly, unfriendly, or a combination of both. See H. A. Strauss to Marlborough Churchill, Jan. 16, 1920, MID 10560-335; Churchill to Strauss, Jan. 20, 1920, MID 10560-335. For more on Cope, see BI 61-74, which details Burns' confidential investigation; also see Epstein, *Dossier*, 42, 50–51. Quotes are from "Twenty Second for Hurley for Justice," Nov. 23, 1921 (received Nov. 30, 1921), BI FOIA 61-5; Higgins to Sharp, Jun. 5, 1924, DS 811.911/134, Decimal File. For public discussions of the connections among Hammer, Linde, and Cope, see "Lindenfeld Member of N.Y. Press Club," *NYT*, Dec. 22, 1921; "Lindenfeld Denies He Is Bomb Plotter," *NYH*, Dec. 22, 1921.

8. "Burns Says Red Plots Grow Here in Secret," *NYT*, Mar. 28, 1922; Schmidt, *Red Scare*, 156–57; Brecher, *Strike!* 155–56; Lowenthal, *Federal Bureau of Investigation*, 272–73.

9. See esp. Burns to Rooney, Jan. 14, 1922, BI FOIA 61-5-58; Burns to Rooney, Jan. 14, 1922, BI FOIA 61-5-59; Burns to Rooney, Jan. 14, 1922, BI FOIA 61-5-60; Burns to Brennan, Jan. 14, 1922, BI FOIA 61-5-60; Burns to Brennan, Jan. 19, 1922, BI FOIA 61-5-63; Brennan to Burns, Jan. 20, 1922, BI FOIA 61-5-65; Jacob Spolansky, "Joe Celunitius or Joe Shetnuidus or Joe Sediniders: Alleged Suspect in Wall Street Bomb Explosion," Feb. 11, 1922, BI FOIA 61-5-73; Spolansky, "Bernard Wolff: Alleged Suspect in Wall Street Bomb Explosion. Anarchist Matter," Feb. 11, 1922, BI FOIA 61-5-72.

10. Daugherty to Secretary of State, Feb. 17, 1922, BI FOIA 61-5-80.

11. "Get Out of Wall Street as Gong Strikes, Warned," *SNYH*, Sep. 17, 1920; Burns to Hurley, May 4, 1922, BI FOIA 61-5-380; Department of State to Department of Justice, Feb. 3, 1923, BI FOIA 61-5 211205-708; Hurley to Sheldon Whitehouse, May 5, 1922, DS 860c.72, U-H File; Tucker, "In re: Wall Street Explosion," Apr. 5, 1921, BI FOIA 61-5-x20.

12. Burns to Hurley, May 2, 1922, BI FOIA 61-5-381; Burns to Hurley, May 4, 1922, BI FOIA 61-5-380; Hurley to Burns, Jun. 3, 1922, BI FOIA 61-5-396; Gibson to Hurley, Jun. 17, 1922, BI FOIA 61-5-409.

13. Cable Message from American Legation at Warsaw, No. 76, Jul. 18, 1922, BI FOIA 61-5; "For Hurley for Justice for Burns," Jul. 18, 1922, DS 811.108 L641/21, Decimal File; "For Hurley for Justice for Burns from Myers," Jul. 21, 1922, BI FOIA 61-5-403.

14. Burns to Wood, Aug. 1, 1922, DS 811.108 L641/23a, Decimal File; Linde to Burns, Aug. 9, 1922, BI FOIA 61-5-428.

15. Spolansky, *The Communist Trail in America* (New York, 1951), 23–25. For background on Spolansky, see Spolansky, *Communist Trail*, 1–9, Draper, *Roots*, 182, 368–72; Hunt, *Front-Page*, 164.

16. For quotes, see Howe and Coser, *American Communist Party*, 72; Draper, *Roots*, 353. For background on the formation of the CPA and the Workers' Party, see esp. Draper, *Roots*, 341–62; Palmer, *James P. Cannon*, 128–65; Howe and Coser, *American Communist Party*, 72–104.

17. For the Bridgman arrests, see Spolansky, *Communist Trail*, 25–30; Draper, *Roots*, 369–75; Powers, *Secrecy and Power*, 138–39; Gitlow, *I Confess!* 143–46. Richard Whitney, a leading voice in the anti-Communist American Defense Society, later cooperated with the Bureau to turn the Bridgman documents into a popular book advertising the perils of Communist thought and organization, as well as the prowess of the Bureau of Investigation. Richard Merrill Whitney, *Reds in America: The Present Status of the Revolutionary Movement in the United States Based on Documents Seized by the Authorities in the Raid upon the Convention of the Communist Party at Bridgman, Michigan, Aug. 22, 1922, Together with Descriptions of Numerous Connections and Associations of the Communists Among the Radicals, Progressives and Pinks* (New York: Beckwith Press, 1924).

18. "Liberties Union Offers to Aid Wm. Z. Foster," *NYC*, Aug. 25, 1922; Powers, *Secrecy and Power*, 139; Colin J. Davis, *Power at Odds: The 1922 National Railroad Shopmen's Strike* (Urbana: University of Illinois Press, 1997), 89–90; "Daugherty's Report on Release of Debs," *NYT*, Dec. 31, 1921.

19. "Michigan Moves to Have Foster Brought to Trial," *NYW*, Aug. 25, 1922; Lowenthal, *Federal Bureau*, 278; John W. H. Crim to American Civil Liberties Union, Oct. 31, 1922, Folder: "Walsh, Frank P. 1864–1939; Legal Papers; 1922–26; Michigan Cases; Miscellaneous correspondence," Box 67, FW; "Burns Calls for Aid in Fighting Radicals," *NYT*, Feb. 8, 1923. Burns asserted as well that the Bridgman communists had been planning to "kill off prominent individuals one by one" at the 1922 meeting.

20. For the presence of Reinstein, Wolfe, Amter, Jakira, Lindgren, and Bedacht at Bridgman, see Harvey Klehr, "The Bridgman Delegates," *Survey* 22, 2 (Spring 1976): 87–95; Draper, *Roots*, 363–74; Spolansky, *Communist Trail*, 30. In his memoir, Wolfe claimed that the documents captured at Bridgman identified him only by his party name, Albright. Bertram D. Wolfe, *A Life in Two Centuries: An Autobiography* (New York: Stein and Day, 1981), 261–72. For Bedacht's pseudonym, see Jeffrey B. Perry, "Pseudonyms: A Reference Aid for Studying American Communist History," *American Communist History* 3, 1 (2004): 61. Perry's article also mentions a Bernard Wolfe who operated under the pseudonym of "Ben Hardee" (118), though he was not apparently present at the Bridgman conference. There is no evidence that Bedacht, Wolfe, or any of the other Bridgman delegates was involved in the Wall Street bombing, but the coincidence of names makes it possible that they were among Burns' suspects.

21. Burns to Linde, Sep. 24, 1922, BI FOIA 61-5-428.

22. "Lindenfeld, Sought in Wall St. Bomb Case, Brought Back," *NYEP*, Dec. 1, 1922; Baltic America Line to Department of Justice, Apr. 4, 1923, BI FOIA 61-5-463; "Lindenfeld Starts on a Hunger Strike," *NYT*, Dec. 3, 1922.

23. Burns to Linde, Aug. 15, 1922, DS 811.108 L641/24; Burns to Hurley, Aug. 14, 1922, BI FOIA 61-5-107; "Warsaw Captive in Wall St. Plot Here Under Guard," *NYW*, Dec. 2, 1922; "Lindenfeld, Sought in Bomb Case, Brought Back," *NYEP*, Dec. 1, 1922; "Bomb Prisoner Faces U.S. Grill,"

*NYT*, Dec. 2, 1922; "Secrecy Ordered About Lindenfeld at Ellis Island," *NYW*, Dec. 3, 1922; "Linde Eats Apple 4th Day of 'Fast,'" *NYW*, Dec. 4, 1922.

24. "Secrecy Ordered About Lindenfeld at Ellis Island," *NYW*, Dec. 3, 1922; "Warsaw Captive in Wall St. Plot Here Under Guard," *NYW*, Dec. 2, 1922; "Foodless Four Days, Lindenfeld Eats," *NYT*, Dec. 4, 1922; "Linde Eats Apple 4th Day of 'Fast,'" *NYW*, Dec. 4, 1922.

25. "Statement to Commissioner Landis from E. A. Linde," Dec. 27, 1922, BI FOIA 61-5.

26. For State Department, see unsigned to Gibson, Dec. 30, 1922, DS 860c.72, U-H File. For Spolansky's search, see Spolansky, "Joe Celunitius or Shetnuidus or Sediniders and Bernard Wolff: Anarchist Matter," Jan. 10, 1923, BI FOIA 61-5-450. For Zack, see O'Donnell to Leon Bone, Mar. 16, 1923, BI FOIA 61-5-460. For Zack's presence at Bridgman, see Klehr, "The Bridgman Delegates," 95; Spolansky, 26–27. For background on Zack, see Harvey Klehr, "Zack, Joseph," in Bernard K. Johnpoll and Klehr, eds., *Biographical Dictionary of the American Left* (New York: Greenwood Press, 1986), 433–4. Zack may be the "Ziatz" or "Zaitz" mentioned in early Linde reports. "Reports Investigator No. 4," Aug. 2, 1921, BI FOIA 61-5-18-10. He may also be the "Joe" whose name cropped up in Linde's longer confession. Document beginning "I arrived in Paris...," undated, BI FOIA 61-5.

27. "Deposition of Albert Bailin Alias Albert Balanow," Feb. 13–17, 1923, Box 67, 3–4, 420–42, FW; Untitled, undated statement, Box 67, Folder "Walsh, Frank P. 1864–1939; Legal Papers; 1922–27; Michigan Cases; Albert Balanow," 36, FW; "Gave False Scent on Wall St. Plot," *NYT*, Feb. 15, 1923. As Burns pointed out, the details of Bailin's account were not entirely consistent, though the gist of the accusations remained the same.

28. "Hold Man in Threat to Bomb Building," *NYT*, Nov. 2, 1920; "Collapse of 'Red' Hunt Seen in Bailin Case," *NYC*, Nov. 5, 1920; "Death Threat Here Laid to Burns Man in Spy Testimony," *NYT*, Feb. 14, 1923.

29. "Bailin Describes Spy Activities in Cigarmen's Union," and "Lying Reports Big Features of Sleuth Work in Chicago," *SUR*, Feb. 19, 1921; "Bomb Murders in East Charged to Greedy Detectives," *SUR*, Feb. 26, 1921.

30. "Explosion Halts Hearing on Radicals," *NYEP*, Feb. 13, 1923; "Deposition of Albert Bailin alias Albert Balanow," Feb. 13–17, 1923, Box 67, 247, FW. On Bailin's second day of testimony, one photographer lost control of his flash equipment, setting off an explosion that blew out all of the office windows and ripped the law books from their shelves. Ida Silverman, the court stenographer, sustained bad glass cuts on one side of her face. The bailiff lost an arm. The prosecution and defense agreed to postpone Bailin's deposition until the next morning, Feb. 14, 1923.

31. "Bailin Says Detective Agencies Sought U.S. Trade Body's Fall," *NYDN*, Feb. 15, 1923; "Gave False Scent on Wall St. Plot," *NYT*, Feb. 15, 1923; "Deposition of Albert Bailin Alias Albert Balanow," Feb. 13–17, 1923, Box 67, 262-3, 122, FW.

32. "Spy Said He'd Bomb Woolworth Tower," *NYH*, Feb. 14, 1923; "Bailin Tool for Ford, Hearst in Semitic Dispute," *NYH*, Feb. 17, 1923; "Deposition of Albert Bailin Alias Albert Balanow," Feb. 13–17, 1923, Box 67, 808, FW; "Death Threat Here Laid to Burns Man in Spy Testimony," *NYT*, Feb. 14, 1923.

33. "Criminal Libel Charge Placed Against Bailin," *NYC*, Feb. 18, 1923; "U.S. Will Try Bailin," *NYT*, Feb. 27, 1923; "Tells Why Her Vote Was to Free Foster," *NYT*, Apr. 7, 1923. For additional material on Burns' campaign against Bailin, see BI 61-2365. For Foster, see James Barrett, *William Z. Foster and the Tragedy of American Radicalism* (Urbana: University of Illinois Press, 1999), esp. 133–34.

34. Draper, *Roots*, 376–95; Palmer, *James P. Cannon*, 156–65.

35. "Arrest Russian Red as Wall St. Bomber," *NYT*, May 13, 1923; Morray, *Project Kuzbas*, 81; "Haywood Agent Held for Murder in Wall St. Blast Which Killed 34," *NYW*, May 13, 1923. Morray mentions Lerner as one of the first batch of skilled engineering recruits; *Project Kuzbas*, 86–87. He also offers an account of the Doyles' misadventures and those of other Kuzbas critics; *Project Kuzbas*, 126–28. The official Wall Street file (BI FOIA 61-5) contains little information about Lerner. However, Lerner was part of an extensive inquiry focusing on the Soviet courier system and its relationship with Kuzbas. In addition to Lerner, the Bureau was actively investigating Kuzbas participants Charlotte MacDonald, Anna Kipness (or Kipnis, apparently Lerner's wife, perhaps only for purposes of immigration), and several others both as couriers and as possible participants in the Wall Street bombing. Some of that information is still classified or otherwise off-limits to researchers. For the available files, see esp. BI 61-3762, 61-3827, 61-3842, 61-3275, 61-3818.

36. "Arrest Russian Red as Wall St. Bomber," *NYT*, May 13, 1923. The Bureau investigated and confirmed Lerner's alibi independently of the police. See esp. 61-3818-14.

37. "Wall Street Explosion 'Suspects,'" *NYEP*, May 24, 1923; "Another 'Suspect' Released," *NYC*, May 25, 1923.

38. Burns to American Embassy, Germany, Jan. 18, 1924, BI FOIA 61-5-494. Interestingly, this letter notes that Burns suspected the involvement of "two Italians" paid by Martens, an indication that he may have been seeking to blend the two dominant theories of the explosion.

39. Untitled, beginning with "New York Times, September 17, 1920," reel 1, delo 18, 42, CPUSA. Historian Tim Davenport has tentatively identified Linde as the party name of Samuel Agursky, a Russian Communist sent from Moscow to oversee proceedings at the 1920 Bridgman convention. See "Delegates to the 1920 Founding Convention of the United Communist Party," http://www.marxistsfr.org/history/usa/eam/cpa/cpa-ucp20delegates.html (accessed Jul. 25, 2008); "'Joint Unity Convention'—Bridgman, MI—May 26–31, 1920," http://www.marxists.org/history/usa/eam/cpa/communistparty.html (accessed Jul. 25, 2008). For a mention of Agursky's role at the conference, see United Communist Party of America, "Report to the Communist International on the Joint Convention of May 26–31, 1920," http://www.marxists.org/history/usa/parties/cpusa/1920/06/0600-ucp-reportonconv.pdf (accessed Jul. 25, 2008). The identification of Agursky fits with Burns' mistaken claim that Linde was an "accredited representative of the Third International." Ironically, Burns might have made this connection himself if he had been willing to put more stock in the word of his own informers. In Dec. 1921, as Linde was being exposed in the press, an informer reported that Edward Lindgren denied that the two Lindes were the same man. See "In re: Workers League: Communist Activities," Dec. 28, 1821, BI FOIA 61-5. Lindgren made this claim publicly as well. See "Lindenfeld Changes Story," *NYT*, Dec. 21, 1921.

40. "Statement to Commissioner Landis from E. A. Linde [*sic*]," Dec. 27, 1922, BI FOIA 61-5; Gibson to Hurley, May 8, 1923, DS 860c.72, U-H File.

## CHAPTER 16

1. "Police Say Thurber Was Not a Bomber," *NYT*, Mar. 6, 1924. Also see assorted reports, Mar. 3–17, 1924, BI FOIA 61-5.

2. "Says He Drove Bomb Cart," *NYT*, Oct. 31, 1924; Brennan to Burns, "In re: Wall Street Explosion (Richard O'Hara)," Oct. 31, 1924, BI FOIA 61-5-511; Starr, "Re: Michael Feeley alias Richard O'Hara: Wall Street Bomb Explosion Suspect," Nov. 7, 1924, BI FOIA 61-5-512.

3. "Wilson Says He Stole Nitroglycerine for Wall Street Blast," *NYT*, Feb. 19, 1925; Brennan to Burns, "In re: The Wall Street Explosion," Oct. 17, 1923, BI 61-4505-6. The Bureau had investigated and publicly dismissed Wilson's claims once before, in 1923. See "Discredit Confession on Wall Street Bomb," *NYT*, Apr. 1, 1923; "Burns Sees Convict on Wall St. Bomb," *NYT*, Apr. 19, 1923.

4. Starr, "In re: Wall Street Explosion," Nov. 6, 1925, BI FOIA 61-5-519; Starr, "In re: Wall Street Explosion," Dec. 11, 1925, BI FOIA 61-5-530. For the complete Bureau investigation of Garel, see BI FOIA 61-5-517 through BI FOIA 61-5-532.

5. David C. Rapoport, "Introduction," in David C. Rapoport and Yonah Alexander, eds., *The Morality of Terrorism: Religious and Secular Justifications* (New York: Columbia University Press, 1989), xi. This was Rapoport's assessment of articles on "Terrorism" and "Assassination" from the *Encyclopedia of the Social Sciences* (New York: Macmillan, 1933).

6. Antiradicalism was only one of many forces—including anti-Catholicism, concerns over war refugees, scientific racism, labor policy, partisan politics, and the Americanization movement, to name a few—driving immigration restrictions in the 1920s. The new laws placed no restrictions on immigration from Latin America—a concession to West Coast employers. See esp. John Higham, *Strangers in the Land: Patterns of American Nativism, 1860–1925* (New Brunswick, NJ: Rutgers University Press, 1998), 234–330; Mae Ngai, *Impossible Subjects* (Princeton, NJ: Princeton University Press, 2004), 57–81.

7. Warren Billings was freed along with Mooney in 1939, though he was not officially pardoned until 1961. For accounts of Mooney and Billings' final years, see esp. Frost, *Mooney Case*, 466–95; Gentry, *Frame-up*, 407–40. The quote is from Commons et al., *History of Labour in the United States*, 4:621.

For labor in the 1930s, see especially Irving Bernstein, *Turbulent Years* (Boston: Houghton Mifflin, 1969); David Brody, *Workers in Industrial America* (New York: Oxford University Press, 1991); Lizabeth Cohen, *Making a New Deal* (Cambridge: Cambridge University Press, 1992); Steve Fraser, *Labor Will Rule* (New York: Free Press, 1991); Robert Zieger, *The C.I.O.* (Chapel Hill: University of North Carolina Press, 1995).

8. Adamic, *Dynamite*, 48.

9. Post, *Deportations Delirium*, 307.

10. Post, *Deportations Delirium*, 46–47. This interpretation of the Red Scare as a product of America paranoia received its scholarly imprimatur in the 1950s and 1960s. See esp. Murray, *Red Scare;* Coben, *A. Mitchell Palmer;* Higham, *Strangers in the Land*, 222–33; Leuchtenberg, *Perils of Prosperity*, 66–83.

11. "The Forgotten Past," *WSJ*, Aug. 29, 1925. Unsurprisingly, *New York Times* reporter James Barron found few people who remembered the event when he canvassed the corner of Wall and Broad on the bombing's eighty-third anniversary in 2003. "No Memorials on Wall Street for Attack That Killed 30," *NYT*, Sep. 17, 2003.

12. Reminiscences of George Whitney (Jan. 1963) in the Columbia University Oral History Research Office Collection.

13. Dawley, *Changing the World*, 326, 308–9.

14. Murray, *Red Scare*, 261. The classic book that defined this view of the 1920s is Allen, *Only Yesterday*. For useful overviews of 1920s culture and politics, see esp. Dawley, *Changing the World*; David J. Goldberg, *Discontented America: The United States in the 1920s* (Baltimore: Johns Hopkins University Press, 1999); Geoffrey Perrett, *America in the Twenties: A History* (New York: Simon and Schuster, 1982); Ellis W. Hawley, *The Great War and the Search for a Modern Order: A History of the American People and Their Institutions, 1917–1933* (New York: St. Martin's, 1979); Joan Hoff, *The Twenties: The Critical Issues* (Boston: Little Brown, 1972); Leuchtenberg, *Perils of Prosperity;* Lynn Dumenil, *The Modern Temper* (New York: Hill and Wang, 1995); Arthur Schlesinger, *The Crisis of the Old Order, 1919–1933* (Cambridge, MA: Houghton Mifflin, 1957). Political repression of other sorts also shaped the political culture of the 1920s; for instance, the Ku Klux Klan surged in popularity between 1915 and 1924.

15. Dawley, *Struggles for Justice*, 298; Fraser, *Every Man a Speculator*, 384–87. For general background on the Morgan bank in the 1920s, esp. Thomas Lamont, see Chernow, *House of Morgan*, 254–301.

16. "King and Queen Give Garden Party," *NYT*, Jul. 7, 1923; "J. S. Morgan Back in Yacht Racing," *NYT*, Dec. 20, 1924; "Millionaires' Sons Who Follow in Fathers' Footsteps," *CSM*, Mar. 27, 1922; "Junius S. Morgan, Jr., on G.M. Board," *WSJ*, Oct. 1, 1925; "Young Morgan Follows Sires into U.S. Steel," *CT*, Dec. 19, 1928; "Incorporation of Markle Foundation Sought," *NYT*, Feb. 4, 1927; "Markle Foundation Ready to Operate," *NYT*, Apr. 30, 1927; "Junius S. Morgan Named Commodore," Dec. 16, 1932; Chernow, *House of Morgan*, 535.

17. Chernow, *House of Morgan*, 219–29, 260–64, 277–86; Lamont, *Ambassador from Wall Street*, 186–269. Lamont's son Corliss, perhaps influenced by the cosmopolitan environment of his upbringing, became a socialist in the 1930s. See Corliss Lamont, *Yes to Life: Memoirs of Corliss Lamont* (New York: Horizon Press, 1981).

18. Chernow, *House of Morgan*, 254–55.

19. Leuchtenberg, *Perils of Prosperity*, 103. For the 1924 campaign, see esp. David Greenberg, *Calvin Coolidge* (New York: Times Books, 2006), 91–107.

20. Louis Galambos, *The Public Image of Big Business in America, 1880–1940: A Quantitative Study in Social Change* (Baltimore: Johns Hopkins University Press, 1975), 216–17; "William Z. Foster Opens First Red Campaign," *NYT*, Aug. 18, 1924; Chernow, *House of Morgan*, 254–55.

21. For an overview of membership numbers, see Schmidt, *Red Scare*, 330. For 1920 Socialist membership, see Heale, *American Anticommunism*, 90. David Shannon cites the number of Socialist Party members in 1928 as 7,793, almost half of them members of the foreign-language federations. Dubofsky notes that the Wobblies claimed between 100,000 and 250,000 in the immediate prewar years, falling to 7,000–8,000 by the 1930s. Dubofsky, *We Shall*, 445, 474. For Communist membership in 1923, see Draper, *Roots*, 391. Schmidt notes that Communist membership may have fallen by as much as half, to 6,000, by the end of the decade. For Zinoviev, see Murray, *Red Scare*, 277.

22. Morn, *"Eye That Never Sleeps,"* 185; Schmidt, *Red Scare*, 34, 340; Norman Hapgood, *Professional Patriots* (New York: Albert and Charles Boni, 1927), 68. For the open-shop movement and welfare

capitalism, see esp. Montgomery, *Fall of the House of Labor*, 453–55; David Brody, "The Rise and Decline of Welfare Capitalism," in John Braeman, Robert H. Bremner, and David Brody, eds., *Change and Continuity in Twentieth-Century America: The 1920's* (Columbus: Ohio State University Press, 1968), 147–78; Allen M. Wakstein, "The Origins of the Open Shop Movement, 1919–1920," *Journal of American History* 51, 3 (Dec. 1964): 460–75; Cohen, *Making a New Deal*, 159–211; Fine, *"Without Blare of Trumpets,"* 210–71; Stuart D. Brandes, *American Welfare Capitalism, 1880–1940* (Chicago: University of Chicago Press, 1976); Nelson Lichtenstein, *State of the Union* (Princeton, NJ: Princeton University Press, 2002), 178–246.

23. "Fail to Oust Claessens," *NYT*, Mar. 2, 1922; Hapgood, *Professional Patriots*, 54; Heale, *American Anticommunism*, 91; Dawley, *Changing the World*, 329. On A. Phillip Randolph, see esp. William Harris, *Keeping the Faith: A. Philip Randolph, Milton P. Webster, and the Brotherhood of Sleeping Car Porters, 1925–1937* (Urbana: University of Illinois Press, 1977). On La Follette, see esp. David P. Thelen, *Robert La Follette and the Insurgent Spirit* (Boston: Little, Brown, 1976); Nancy Unger, *Fighting Bob La Follette: Righteous Reformer* (Chapel Hill: University of North Carolina Press, 2000). For the Socialist Party's role in the La Follette campaign, see Weinstein, *Decline of Socialism*, 290–323.

24. Heale, *American Anticommunism*, 90.

25. Salvatore, *Eugene V. Debs*, 329–42; Freeberg, *Democracy's Prisoner*, 295–318. For quote, see Salvatore, 338–39.

26. "Bill Haywood, Lonely, 'Broke,' Quits 'Utopia,'" *CT*, Jan. 4, 1923; *ABH*, 364–65; Carlson, *Roughneck*, 322–25; Dubofsky, *Big Bill*, 136–40.

27. *LML*, 993–94; Wexler, *Emma Goldman in Exile*, 92–245; Burwood, *Alexander Berkman*, 314–43; Drinnon, *Rebel in Paradise*, 231–314; Morton, *Emma Goldman*, 129–51. For the Hoover incident, see Drinnon, *Rebel in Paradise*, 278–79. For published letters between Goldman and Berkman during this period, see Fellner, ed., *Life of an Anarchist*, 264–70, 349–52. For a detailed account of Goldman's Canadian years, see Theresa Moritz and Albert Moritz, *The World's Most Dangerous Woman* (Vancouver: Subway Books, 2001).

28. For quote, see Lowenthal, *Federal Bureau of Investigation*, 293. For background on the Justice Department, the Wheeler scandal, and Burns' resignation, see esp. Cook, *FBI Nobody Knows*, 117–36; Gentry, *J. Edgar Hoover*, 117–27; Powers, *Secrecy and Power*, 65–74; Murray, *Harding Era*, 474–82; Hunt, *Front-Page*, 177–83. For Daugherty's account of events, see Daugherty, with Thomas Dixon, *The Inside Story of the Harding Tragedy* (New York: Churchill, 1932). Another highly partisan account depicting Daugherty's impeachment as a communist plot is Blair Coan, *The Red Web: An Underground Political History of the United States from 1918 to the Present Time Showing How Close the Government Is to Collapse and Told in an Understandable Way* (Chicago: Northwest, 1925). For an entertaining if highly embellished account from a former Burns agency operative, see Gaston B. Means as told to May Dixon Thacker, *The Strange Death of President Harding, from the Diaries of Gaston B. Means* (New York: Guild, 1930).

29. *ABH*, 359; Hunt, *Front-Page*, 167–68, 192; Gentry, *J. Edgar Hoover*, 134. For a recent account of Teapot Dome, see Laton McCartney, *The Teapot Dome Scandal: How Big Oil Bought the Harding White House and Tried to Steal the Country* (New York: Random House, 2008).

30. "W. J. Flynn, Noted Detective, Dead," *NYT*, Oct. 15, 1928; "William J. Flynn, Long of Secret Service, Is Dead," *NYHT*, Oct. 15, 1928.

31. Gentry, *J. Edgar Hoover*, 126, 139, 144; Schmidt, *Red Scare*, 325; Howard, *Labor Spy*, 120. Hoover denied that he had played a major role in the Palmer Raids for decades to come. "I deplored the manner in which the raids were executed then," he told the *New York Herald Tribune* in 1947, "and my position has remained unchanged." Lowenthal, *Federal Bureau of Investigation*, 304.

32. Schmidt, *Red Scare*, 325.

33. For Hoover's correspondence with Woods about the International Entente, see DS 861.0-2480, Classified Records, esp. Feb. 13–Mar. 17, 1925. Hoover sought a closer relationship with the New York bomb squad on the Wall Street case beginning in 1925. See Hoover to R. A. Darling, Nov. 18, 1925, BI FOIA 61-5/ 61-25-524.

34. Schmidt, *Red Scare*, 329; Preston, *Aliens and Dissenters*, 243; Lowenthal, *Federal Bureau of Investigation*, 300–304; "An Act to Prohibit Certain Subversive Activities (Smith Act)," reprinted in Kittrie and Wedlock, *Tree of Liberty*, 356.

35. Hoover, "Testimony Before HUAC, Mar. 26, 1947," reprinted in Ellen Schrecker, *The Age of McCarthyism: A Brief History with Documents* (New York: Bedford/St. Martin's, 2002), 128. Schrecker has traced many of the institutional continuities between the first and second Red Scares. See Schrecker, *Many Are the Crimes: McCarthyism in America* (Princeton, NJ: Princeton University Press, 1998), 42–85.

36. For Brant, see assorted correspondence, Nov. 14, 1930–Dec. 2, 1930, BI FOIA 61-5-539–61-541. For Doyle, see assorted correspondence, Oct. 13, 1933–Dec. 15, 1934, BI FOIA 61-5-543–61-5-545/DJ 211205. For the Japanese connection, see James T. Duke, "Unknown Subjects; Wall Street Explosion, Summer [redacted]; Informant; [redacted]," Apr. 21, 1944, BI FOIA 61-5-555.

37. SAC, New York, to Hoover, "Unknown Subjects, Wall Street Explosion, Summer of 1920," circa 1944, BI FOIA 61-5-556.

38. "Carnage in Wall Street," *NYDN*, Sep. 11, 1960. One additional theory has come to light in the years since the bombing. Richard Spence, a historian of espionage, has proposed that the bomb was set by "a ruthless, skillful and influential cabal of anti-Bolsheviks" who hoped to prolong the Red Scare and prevent recognition of the Soviet Union by planting the bomb. Spence argues that a German double agent named Kurt Jahnke, Altendorf's former espionage boss in Mexico, planted the bomb at the cabal's behest. According to Spence, Jahnke worked with military intelligence operative Boris Brasol and British spy Sidney Reilly to orchestrate the plan. As evidence for Jahnke's involvement in the Wall Street explosion, Spence notes that Altendorf carried Jahnke's picture to Poland with him. (See Huddle to Gibson, Mar. 23, 1921, DS 812.0-863, U-H-File.) He also suggests that Ed Fisher might have met the conspirators through his work for the French High Commission. Finally, Spence argues that the true conspirators used William Linde as a red herring to prevent detection. Though the theory is intriguing, more proof is required for a definitive case. See Spence, "Cui Bono? Reds, Anti-Reds and the Wall Street bombing of 1920," unpublished, Department of History, University of Idaho. Spence also mentions his theory of the Wall Street explosion in *Trust No One*, 304–6. Background details on Jahnke's activities are available in Spence, "K. A. Jahnke."

39. Avrich, *Sacco and Vanzetti*, 204–7; Avrich, *Anarchist Voices*, 133. The Bureau may have been seeking Buda in October 1920 when it launched a search for one "Mario Bovo," an alleged anarchist in Pennsylvania. See assorted reports, Oct. 11, 1920–Nov. 2, 1920, BI FOIA 61-5. The Bovo investigation also briefly resumed in July 1921. See Barbera, "Wall Street Explosion. Joseph Granata, Mario Bovo, Frank Brancazi, and Tony Babtello," Jul. 12, 1921, BI FOIA 61-5 211205-594. An interview with Buda from 1928 is available in the papers of Edward Holton James at the Harvard Law School Library; the interview focuses on the Sacco-Vanzetti case rather than the Wall Street bombing. See "The Story of Mario Buda Before the Jury of the World," Feb. 14–16, 1928, EHJP. In *Anarchist Voices*, Avrich corrects the claims of Spencer Sacco, the grandson of Nicola, who claimed that Giuseppe Valdinoci, brother of Palmer's front-lawn bomber Carlo Valdinoci, set the Wall Street bomb. According to Avrich, Carlo's brother's name was Ercole, and he had left for Italy long before the Wall Street bombing. Avrich, *Anarchist Voices*, 92.

40. Leuchtenberg, *Perils of Prosperity*, 82. For the international movement to save Sacco and Vanzetti, see esp. Temkin, *Sacco-Vanzetti Affair;* McGirr, "The Passion of Sacco and Vanzetti"; Watson, *Sacco and Vanzetti*, 310–50.

41. I am grateful to Moshik Temkin for alerting me to the John Dos Passos quote. See Dos Passos to Russell, Oct. 21, 1961, MS 2030, 7A, AFSV.

42. Upton Sinclair, *Oil!* (New York: Albert and Charles Boni, 1927), 274–75; Sinclair, *Autobiography*, 242; Avrich, *Sacco and Vanzetti*, 161. Sinclair's *Boston* mentions the Wall Street explosion as part of a dinner conversation between protagonist Cornelia Thornwell and her son Henry, who notes that "the Boston anarchists made no attempt to conceal their glee when they learned of that explosion." Sinclair, *Boston* (New York: Albert and Charles Boni, 1928), 284. *Boston* also discusses the presence of "direct actionists" within the Communist Party. For a discussion of Sinclair's evolution on the Sacco-Vanzetti case, see Arthur, *Radical Innocent*, 216–22; Mattson, *Upton Sinclair*, 142–46; Avrich, *Sacco and Vanzetti*, 160–62.

43. Avrich, *Sacco and Vanzetti*, 212.

44. "Bombs Explode in Two Subway Stations Here," *NYT*, Aug. 6, 1927; Avrich, *Sacco and Vanzetti*, 212–13; Watson, *Sacco and Vanzetti*, 324–25. For Bureau surveillance, see assorted reports, Aug. 8–Aug. 23, 1927, BI 61-126. The Baltimore bombing occurred on August 6, the night after

the New York and Philadelphia bombings, but was understood as part of this larger campaign. "Baltimore Mayor's Home Is Bombed," *NYT*, Aug. 7, 1927. The Sacco-Vanzetti case produced a rash of bombings in the fall of 1921, but the level of violence declined until 1927, as the executions approached. A minor bombing related to the Sacco-Vanzetti case occurred in 1926 at the Bridgewater, Massachusetts, home of Samuel Johnson, whose brother Simon had offered police an important tip in the Sacco-Vanzetti case. Massachusetts governor Alvin Fuller was also sent a mail bomb on May 10, 1927, but Boston police officials intercepted it. Other bombings related to the Sacco-Vanzetti case followed the August 5, 1927, bombings, including at the home of juror Lewis McHardy in East Milton, Massachusetts. After the executions, the homes of both the executioner, Robert G. Elliott, and Judge Webster Thayer were bombed. Avrich, *Sacco and Vanzetti*, 212–13; Watson, 334–35. Charles McCormick notes that there was a revived campaign of bombings against Italian government officials, presumably by Italian anarchists, in the early 1930s. McCormick, *Hopeless Cases*, 142–44.

45. "Wall St. Sets Up a Strong Guard," *NYT*, Aug. 7, 1927.

# INDEX

····